The Myths That Divide Us

How Lies Have Poisoned American Race Relations

JOHN PERAZZO

WORLD STUDIES BOOKS
Briarcliff Manor, New York

World Studies Books
1858 Pleasantville Road, Suite 131
Briarcliff Manor, New York 10510
TEL: (914) 747-7670
FAX: (914) 747-2910

Copyright © 1999 by John Perazzo
2nd Edition

ISBN: 0-9651268-1-1

Library of Congress Catalog Card Number: 99-73860

CONTENTS

PREFACE

Twenty-four centuries ago, when the Greek playwright Euripides wrote that "cleverness is not wisdom," he scarcely could have foreseen the lamentable degree to which the greater part of mankind would fail to grasp such a simple yet profound truth. Indeed, our contemporary society is filled with prevaricators who exalt cleverness far above wisdom, and for whom a lie told convincingly makes a satisfactory substitute for truth. Dazzling us with their verbal maneuvering, they waltz away from reality with carefully worded ambiguities and evasions. Effortlessly they twist their faces into pained and pious countenances, thereby giving the appearance of passion and sincerity. And when their orations have ended, media pundits and academics expertly analyze their "performance," as if to imply that deception is a skill which, when practiced artfully, is in itself worthy of admiration. Politicians traditionally have been the most visible of these deceivers. Less scrutinized have been the mainstays of the modern-day civil rights establishment who, under the guise of promoting brotherhood, have made an art form of fomenting interracial enmity.

This book does not tread lightly in its assessment of those individuals currently recognized as the foremost civil rights leaders in the United States. It exposes them, without apology or euphemism, as charlatans who choose to sermonize rather than educate; who deliver hollow platitudes rather than knowledge; and who substitute elaborate exhibitions of moral preening for reason. With incessant fervor, they mischaracterize our country as a racist wasteland wherein African Americans are doomed to misery and failure under the yoke of white bigotry. Upon these pages are their lies exposed. Herein is the sorrowful story of the millions whose lives they have ruined and whose souls they have corrupted. Ultimately, this book's purpose is to demonstrate that under the light of reason, the elaborate myths of these demagogues silently melt away like ice sculptures in the sun.

John Perazzo

ACKNOWLEDGMENTS

The information contained in this book was culled from a wide variety of sources. For granting me permission to reprint numerous quotations, I express my gratitude to HarperCollins Publishers, Random House, the Associated Press, Tribune Media Services, Georges Borchardt, *The New Republic*, *The New York Times*, United Media, Simon & Schuster, the Hoover Institution, *U.S. News & World Report*, Beacon Press, William Morrow & Company, *National Review*, New York's *Daily News*, *New Perspectives Quarterly*, Saint Martin's Press, and the *Washington Post* Writers Group. For his excellent proofreading and editing services I thank John Piazza, and for his invaluable technical assistance I am indebted to Claude Cartaginese.

Samuel Johnson once said, "The greatest part of a writer's time is spent in reading, in order to write; a man will turn over half a library in order to make one book." This indeed has been the case in assembling the information contained in this volume. Particularly important to my research were the insightful writings of Thomas Sowell, Walter E. Williams, Dinesh D'Souza, William Wilbanks, Shelby Steele, Jared Taylor, George Gilder, Michael Meyers, Stephan Thernstrom, and Abigail Thernstrom.

Chapter 1

The Myths That Divide Us

*Every man who attacks my belief diminishes in some degree
my confidence in it, and therefore makes me uneasy,
and I am angry with him who makes me uneasy.*
                                                    —Samuel Johnson[1]

The noble civil rights movement of the 1950s and 1960s has degenerated during the past three decades into a meaningless charade. Martin Luther King, Jr., who articulated a theme that our nation desperately needed to hear, has been replaced by a band of opportunistic liars whose message is both anachronistic and destructive. These prevaricators have poisoned American race relations and demoralized countless souls, relentlessly advancing the spurious notion that the black community is downtrodden in this "racist" land. Marching and remonstrating, they have carried their message to every corner of our society. Citing a selfless desire for justice as their sole motivation, they have gone largely unchallenged in spreading their fables. Under the protective banner of "civil rights," they have cultivated the bitter fruit of racial division. These are serious charges. This book demonstrates that the charges are true.

The civil rights movement's current moral decay began some three decades ago and continues to this day with ever-increasing momentum. Like the fragmentary ruins of a once-magnificent edifice, the movement's present condition is but a scant reminder of the moral splendor that attended its birth—a birth which was a natural and necessary outcome of America's growing intolerance of racial injustice.

That injustice was particularly abhorrent in the South, where, following the long epoch of slavery, Jim Crow laws mandating segregation treated blacks as less than fully human from the 1890s through the early 1960s. As recently as 1962, southern blacks were barred from sharing with whites such public facilities as bathrooms, drinking fountains, restaurants, lunch counters, theaters, hotels, boardinghouses, hospitals, schools, libraries, parks, dance halls, bowling alleys, swimming pools, tennis courts, and skating rinks. Blacks using public transportation were confined to separate sections of streetcars, trains, and buses. Those visiting the residence of any white person were forbidden to pass through the front door. Nor were they allowed to shake hands with whites, for such an act suggested equality. Some white-owned stores did permit black patronage, but clerks in those establishments generally waited on white customers first. In clothing stores blacks were not permitted to try items on for size, for their touch was deemed "contaminating." Indignity followed them even to the grave, as black and white burial grounds were strictly segregated throughout the South.[2]

The social humiliation inflicted on black Americans was exacerbated by the squalor in which they typically lived. As of 1940, estimates of the national black poverty rate ranged between 71 percent and an astonishing 87 percent, or about twice the white level.[3] In the South, conditions were even worse. Blacks in such cities as Atlanta, Mobile, and Columbia earned scarcely one-third as much as their white neighbors.[4] In rural areas, black family earnings were often no more than one-*eighth* the national average.[5] Nearly half of all southern blacks were employed in agriculture, most either as laborers or sharecroppers. The latter, too poor to pay rent for the fields they cultivated, gave their landlords a portion of their harvested crops instead of money. Unfortunately, such arrangements frequently left the sharecroppers deeper in debt each year.[6]

Southern blacks were not only economically, but also politically, powerless. Though the Fifteenth Amendment to the Constitution stated that no citizen's right to vote could be "denied or abridged . . . on account of race," in the 1890s the South instituted such measures as poll taxes and literacy tests as prerequisites to voting, thereby making it virtually impossible for blacks to cast their ballots. While mandatory for all voters, poll taxes affected whites much less than blacks, who were overwhelmingly poor and thus could rarely pay the required sums. Similarly, literacy tests were beyond the capacity of most blacks, who had received no formal schooling before 1865, and only the most rudimentary education thereafter.[7]

These circumventions of the Fifteenth Amendment lasted through the first several decades of the twentieth century, all but eliminating the black franchise in the South. In many southern districts, only 2 to 3 percent of black men met the voting standards.[8] Adding to the legal obstacles of poll taxes and literacy tests was the ever-present threat that white racists might physically harm those blacks "uppity" enough to exercise their ballot—a threat that persisted into the early 1960s.[9]

The prevalence of white-on-black violence made the South a relatively dangerous place for African Americans throughout the first half of the twentieth century.[10] This danger found its most fearsome expression in the activities of white-hooded Ku Klux Klansmen who, in the early 1920s, numbered between two and five million, thus constituting the largest fraternal nativist organization in American history.[11] Meanwhile the criminal-justice system discriminated against blacks blatantly, leading many of them to develop well-founded negative attitudes toward the law and its enforcers. Because only a few large cities occasionally allowed blacks to sit in the jurors' box, most southern juries were all-white.[12] Moreover, there were no black judges and few black attorneys. As late as 1947, the only southern law school that admitted blacks was at Howard University in the District of Columbia.[13] The vast majority of police officers were white as well, and their aggressive—often brutal—treatment of African Americans struck dread into the hearts of the latter.[14] The police and courts alike were especially punitive with blacks convicted of crimes against whites.[15] As one writer puts it, "Southern blacks lived in danger and in terror; they could count on neither the police nor the courts to protect them from violence and other forms of crime."[16]

Few contemporary Americans realize that segregation actually originated, in part, as a means of shielding blacks from the radical white racism that pervaded the South during the latter decades of the nineteenth century. At that time many southern whites, humiliated by their relatively recent Civil War defeat and enraged by the resulting economic gains of Reconstruction-era blacks, vented their anger in brutal racial assaults. Such people, explains scholar Dinesh D'Souza, considered "the concept of free blacks . . . a scandal, like beasts wandering about without owners"[17]—and consequently sought to beat them back into submission. To protect blacks from these attacks, the southern ruling elite of the late 1800s passed the Jim Crow laws that would separate the races for decades to come.[18] Segregation, writes D'Souza, "offered an attractive alternative to lynching. It permitted whites to avoid what they perceived as offensive or contaminating contact with free blacks, and it allowed blacks to develop their allegedly modest talents in peace and among their own kind."[19] The 1896 *Plessy v. Ferguson* Supreme Court ruling, which pronounced "separate but equal" public facilities constitutional, placed an official seal of approval on the practice of segregation and opened the floodgates for further legislative restrictions to racial mixing.[20]

Conditions for blacks in the North were, though not nearly ideal, considerably better than in the South. While northern blacks encountered plenty of prejudice and discrimination, they at least had "an elementary sense of personal security."[21] They were treated with far more respect than their southern counterparts, as demonstrated by the fact that they could run for political office and were actually encouraged to vote.[22] They were accorded the dignity of being called "Mr." and "Mrs."[23]—rather than "boy," "uncle," "girl," or "auntie," as was customary in the South.[24] They were not, as were southern blacks, constantly reminded of their own second-class status by signs designating public facilities as "white" and "colored" (although some northern restaurants and schools did bar blacks).[25] Neither were they required to enter white-owned homes via the back door, nor to move to the back of any line that formed in a store or office, nor to refrain from shaking hands with whites.[26] In short, they were not compelled to display "the submissive and guarded manners" of southern blacks.[27]

More intimate forms of human interaction, however, were considered unacceptable between blacks and whites even in the North. White aversion to interracial sexual contact, for instance, was strong, though less acute than in the South. Indeed nineteen states outside the South passed laws prohibiting interracial marriages, and even where

such unions were legal they were socially unacceptable among both
blacks and whites—and thus were rare. As of 1958, only 4 percent
of white Americans approved of mixed-race marriages. Most also
disapproved of racial mixing at public pools and beaches, largely because of the sexual undertones of such settings.[28] Northern barber
shops and beauty parlors rarely served both blacks and whites,[29] because many white patrons were reluctant to be touched by the same
scissors, combs, and razors that had come into contact with black
people.

The Great Migrations Alter Black Life Forever

While northern blacks clearly lived much better than their southern counterparts, early-twentieth-century African Americans were predominantly southerners, just as most of their forefathers had been in
the days of slavery. In 1910, fully 89 percent of our country's 10
million blacks still lived in the South, where poverty and toil defined
their lives.[30] Clearly, if they were to make significant social and economic strides, a move northward would be crucial. The outbreak of
World War I in Europe provided the impetus for that move, which
became a watershed event in African American history.

The war temporarily arrested foreign immigration to the U.S.,
thereby stopping the influx of European-born laborers to northern
cities. Then, when our country joined the war in 1917 and thousands of white American factory workers enlisted, a serious labor
shortage ensued. In desperate need of help, northern industrial employers made jobs available to African Americans for the first time.
Beckoned by the promise of a better life, nearly 500,000 southern
blacks migrated to the urban North by 1920. The war's end temporarily restored the flow of European immigrants, but restrictive legislation in the 1920s again stemmed their tide and increased the
demand for indigenous labor. Consequently, by 1930 another 750,000
blacks had moved northward in search of better employment opportunities.[31]

Notwithstanding the sudden influx of blacks to the North,
between 1914 and 1940 the proportion of African Americans residing in the South declined by only about 10 points, from 89 percent to
a shade under 80 percent—a considerable, but not monumental,

reduction.[32] The outbreak of World War II, however, set in motion an even greater northward black migration that radically transformed African Americans from a rural to an urban people. Nearly sixteen million white American men joined the war effort,[33] and their newly vacated jobs had to be filled quickly. That fact, along with the suddenly heightened demand for military-equipment production, opened myriad opportunities for black workers, who boarded trains and buses in droves and headed north for those better jobs. War plants went on twenty-four-hour shifts, and Detroit's auto factories were now feverishly churning out planes, tanks, and jeeps. The unemployment rate for nonfarm workers, which had stood at 55 percent in 1939, plunged to less than 2 percent by 1944.[34] The massive northward move of blacks during these years became known as the Second Great Migration—a phenomenon that would persist until the mid-1960s. Between 1940 and 1970, about 4.4 million blacks left the South.[35]

While so many southern blacks eagerly pursued opportunities in the urban North, millions of others moved from southern farms to southern cities.[36] Whereas in 1940 about 43 percent of all black men were agricultural workers, within two decades that figure shrank to a mere 14 percent.[37] During that same period, the proportion of blacks living in urban areas nationwide grew from 49 percent to 73 percent.[38] Because opportunities for organized action were much greater in cities than in rural settings, this urbanization of black America was crucial to the victories of the civil rights crusades of the 1960s.[39] As scholars Stephan and Abigail Thernstrom write, "The tremendous growth of the black population in southern cities laid the foundation for the emergence of an aggressive civil rights movement with an urban base in postwar years."[40]

Though most contemporary Americans view the 1960s as the decade when the struggle for racial justice began in earnest, there were in fact some significant civil rights developments years earlier. In 1941, for instance, President Roosevelt issued an executive order banning discrimination in government employment and establishing the Fair Employment Practices Committee to investigate and arbitrate charges of bias.[41] Seven years later the Supreme Court outlawed racial discrimination in the sale of private homes.[42] In 1957 Congress passed a civil rights bill empowering the Justice Department to prosecute anyone—chiefly southern local officials—who interfered with any black citizen's voting rights. A new Civil Rights Division was established in the Justice Department to enforce this law, and the U.S. Civil Rights Commission was created to examine discrimination charges.[43]

Moreover, between 1945 and 1964 twenty-six states and many cities established fair-employment commissions and passed antidiscrimination laws to regulate hiring and contracting.[44] During the same period, and to some degree because of such legislation, black Americans made remarkable gains in scholastic achievement, college enrollment, family income, and life expectancy. Between 1930 and 1950, the proportion of black youngsters attending elementary and high school increased steadily from 60 percent to 75 percent, while black college enrollment rose from 27,000 to more than 110,000. Also by 1950, black families nationally were earning half as much as white families for the first time in American history.[45]

It should be remembered that while the civil rights ordinances discussed in the preceding two paragraphs were certainly helpful to the African American community, the pre-1960 economic progress of blacks was largely a result of the great migrations triggered by the two world wars. Because northern black families earned about twice as much as their southern counterparts in the post-World War II years,[46] the increased concentration of blacks in the North naturally elevated their income average nationally. Whereas in 1940 only 10 percent of all black men held the types of white-collar or skilled manual jobs that were reasonably good indicators of middle-class status, by 1960 this figure had swelled to 23 percent.[47] Between 1940 and 1950 the earnings of the average black man, in real dollars adjusted for inflation, grew by a remarkable 75 percent (about twice the rate at which white incomes grew), and increased by another 45 percent during the 1950s. In other words, black men in 1960 were earning two-and-a-half times more, in real terms, than they had earned twenty years earlier.[48] The picture was much the same for black women, whose 1960 earnings were 2.3 times higher than their 1940 earnings had been.[49]

Black incomes during this period grew not only in absolute terms, but also in relation to white incomes. In 1960 black males were earning 58 percent as much as white males—markedly better than the 43 percent figure of 1940.[50] Similarly, black females in 1960 were earning 61 percent as much as their white counterparts, a far cry from the mere 40 percent level of 1940.[51] Black *family* incomes, meanwhile, which in 1940 were just 41 percent as high as the white average, rose to 56 percent of the white average by 1960.[52] The black poverty rate, which had exceeded 75 percent in 1940, plunged to 39 percent by the 1950s.[53]

Overall rates of home ownership also reflected the growing prosperity of African Americans. Whereas in 1940 only 23 percent of black dwellings were owner-occupied, by 1960 the figure had climbed to 38 percent, representing a jump of 65 percent. Rates of white home ownership also grew during those years, but at a slower pace (from 46 percent to 65 percent—a 42 percent rise).[54]

Another important barometer of a people's general condition is life expectancy, and blacks gained considerable ground on whites in this area as well. In 1940 black life expectancy at birth was just 53.1 years, fully 11 years lower than the white figure. By 1960 the black average had risen by 10.5 years, while the corresponding white figure had increased by only about half that much.[55]

By any measure, black prosperity grew at an unprecedented rate between the start of World War II and 1960. As one historian writes, "It is not an overstatement to say that no ethnic group in American history has ever improved its position so dramatically in so short a period, though it must be said in the same breath that no other group had so far to go."[56]

"A New Sense of Dignity and Destiny"

Around the middle of the twentieth century, there were hints that integration would be the trend of America's future. Membership in the National Association for the Advancement of Colored People (NAACP) increased tenfold during World War II,[57] reflecting a growing awareness—among both blacks and whites—of the urgent need for greater racial justice. Two years after the war's end, Jackie Robinson broke major league baseball's color bar. A year later President Harry Truman announced that segregation would be eliminated from our country's armed forces.[58] Truman also appointed blacks to numerous government posts in his administration.[59] Not surprisingly, many whites, particularly in the South, were reluctant to accept black Americans' ever-growing inclusion in once exclusively-white realms. Nevertheless, white racial attitudes were gradually but indisputably evolving in every region of the country. Consider the following:

• In 1942, opinion polls found that the proportion of whites favoring school integration was just 30 percent, and a paltry 2 percent in the South. By 1956, however, these figures had grown to 49 percent and 15 percent, and by 1963 they stood at 62 percent and 31 percent.[60]

• In 1942, about 44 percent of all whites, and only 4 percent of *southern* whites, favored the racial integration of passengers on streetcars and buses. By 1956, these numbers had swelled to 60 percent and 27 percent, and in 1963 they reached 79 percent and 52 percent.[61]

• In 1942, scarcely 35 percent of whites nationwide, and 12 percent of whites in the South, were comfortable having a black person of the same income and education move into their block. By 1956, the corresponding figures had grown to 51 percent and 38 percent, and in 1963 they stood at 64 percent and 51 percent.[62]

• Between 1942 and 1956, the proportion of all whites who viewed blacks as their intellectual equals rose from 41 percent to 77 percent; in the South the shift was from about 21 percent to 59 percent.[63]

• Between 1944 and 1963, the overall proportion of whites who felt that blacks "should have as good a chance as white people to get any kind of job" doubled, from 42 percent to 83 percent.[64]

Clearly, from the outset of World War II through the early 1960s white Americans' racial attitudes grew decidedly more enlightened. This was reflected not only in polls, but also in the fact that Lyndon Johnson, when contemplating a possible run for the presidency in 1960, publicly pushed for the passage of new civil rights legislation—well aware that no longer could a candidate perceived to have segregationist ideals win a national election in the United States.[65] In short, the steady and inexorable transformation of white attitudes toward blacks had set the stage for the golden years of a civil rights movement that would make powerful appeals to our nation's conscience. Those appeals could not be ignored.

An event of historic significance occurred on December 1, 1955, when Rosa Parks refused to yield her seat to a white passenger on a Montgomery, Alabama bus. In response to Ms. Parks's arrest, Martin Luther King, Jr. led Montgomery's black residents in a year-long boycott of the city's buses—a campaign that put a great financial strain on the bus company, three-fourths of whose regular patrons were black.[66] As the months passed, the Montgomery story grabbed headlines in a number of national newspapers, thereby raising Americans' awareness about racial issues as never before. Consequently, the flow of financial contributions to civil rights organizations increased dramatically.[67] Donations poured in from all over the world, though most came from church groups—particularly black churches—in the United States.[68] Finally, on December 21, 1956, a court order officially desegregating Montgomery's buses took effect.[69] "There is a new Negro in the South," a proud Dr. King declared, "with a new sense of dignity and destiny."[70]

Throughout 1956, in large part because of King's charismatic presence and gifted oratory, media coverage of racial issues grew to unprecedented levels. *Time*, *Life*, and *Newsweek* tripled their coverage of civil rights topics that year.[71] Civil rights reform was on America's mind, as evidenced by a massive wave of demonstrations in the late 1950s and early 1960s. These rallies were led by such organizations as the National Association for the Advancement of Colored People (NAACP), the Congress of Racial Equality (CORE), and the newly formed Southern Christian Leadership Conference (SCLC).[72] Boycotts, sit-ins, voter-registration drives, and protest marches spread like wildfire across the South. In 1960 alone, some 70,000 students staged sit-ins in about 100 southern cities, occupying seats in such traditionally segregated facilities as lunch counters, restaurants, and libraries. And the media noticed. Whereas during 1959 *The New York Times* had given coverage to just 10 civil rights demonstrations in the entire country, in 1960 that figure grew to a stunning 414.[73]

May 1963 was a most significant month in the civil rights movement's history. The SCLC, headed by Dr. King, had recently recruited hundreds of high-school students and trained them in the methods of nonviolent resistance. Then on May 2, about 1,000 of those youngsters staged an anti-segregation march in Birmingham, where 600 of them were arrested and jailed. The next day, when 1,000 more students marched toward Birmingham's business district for yet another rally, the city's infamous police chief Eugene "Bull" Connor made a crucial tactical mistake—ordering his men to use nightsticks and German shepherds to drive away the marchers, and sending firefighters to blast them with water from powerful hoses and "monitor guns."[74] The three major television networks broadcast the horrifying scenes of mayhem into millions of American homes. These televised images of brutality urgently drove home the need for civil rights reform in a way that the printed word could not have done. As one journalist put it, a "television picture of a snarling police dog set upon a human being is recorded in the permanent photoelectric file of every human brain."[75] More than ever before, people understood the worthy objectives of a movement whose time had come. Over the next ten weeks, 758 civil rights demonstrations took place in 186 American cities, with many white participants.[76] The summer of 1963 alone saw fifty southern cities agree to desegregate their public facilities.[77] Without a doubt, the psychological transformation that civil rights leaders had hoped for was well underway.[78]

The Great Betrayal

Because he recognized the evolving racial attitudes of white Americans, Dr. King based his appeals for racial justice on the increasingly self-evident premise that it was morally imperative. Committed to helping perpetuate the remarkable social and economic gains that blacks had made during the 1940s and 1950s, King foresaw an America where one day character would matter more than skin color, and where racial unity would render segregation nothing more than a distant, unhappy memory. And indeed the continuing evolution of white attitudes during the past three decades demonstrates beyond any doubt that King's confidence in that vision was well founded. Virtually all contemporary polls of white Americans show that well over 90 percent now favor integrated schools and public accommodations; that almost all oppose employment discrimination against members of any race or ethnicity; that more than six in ten approve of interracial marriages;[79] and that more than 90 percent would be willing to vote for a black presidential candidate.[80] These numbers bear little resemblance to those of ages past.

For the most part, however, King's successors in the civil rights movement have rejected his dream of a color-blind society. As Dinesh D'Souza observes, "It is no exaggeration to say that a rejection of Martin Luther King, Jr.'s vision of a regime in which we are judged solely based on the content of our character is a virtual job qualification for leadership in the civil rights movement today."[81] Author Andrew Kull concurs that "the color-blind consensus, so long in forming, was abandoned with surprising rapidity."[82] A few examples will serve to illustrate just how far from King's ideals some of today's leading activists and liberal scholars have strayed:

• Eleanor Holmes Norton, former chair of the Equal Employment Opportunity Commission (EEOC), advises that we "stop quoting dead saints" like King.[83]

• Jesse Jackson uses the term "intellectual terrorism" to describe the suggestion that King, were he alive today, would oppose racial preferences for blacks in employment and education.[84]

• Legal scholar Charles Lawrence urges blacks to lobby for racial preferences and to "combat the ideology of equal opportunity."[85]

• Lawrence's colleague Patricia Williams supports "some measure of enforced equality" of results, rather than "blindly formalized constructions of equal opportunity."[86]

• In *Rethinking the American Race Problem*, Roy Brooks contends that "there is nothing intrinsically wrong with using race in lawmaking or policy formulation."[87]

• Philosopher Bernard Boxill writes that while southern segregation laws were "certainly wrong," other "color conscious policies like busing and affirmative action could be correct."[88]

• Benjamin Hooks, the NAACP's former executive director, says, "The Constitution itself has recognized that there is color in this world. So from time to time we must use those [racial] categories to achieve the Constitution's goals."[89]

• Mary Frances Berry, who chairs the U.S. Civil Rights Commission, claims that "civil rights laws were *not* passed to give civil rights protection to *all* Americans."[90]

• Afrocentric scholar Molefi Asante charges that "integration makes us cultural hostages [and] threatens our existence as a people."[91]

Because such views have diffused widely throughout the black community, it is hardly surprising that, as historian David Garrow observes, "there is less integrationist sentiment in black America now than at any time since King's death."[92] Along the same lines, scholar David Bositis sees "something of a movement in the African American community away from integration."[93] Black columnist Michael Meyers concurs that "Dr. King's integrationist approach to tearing down America's racial walls is no longer in vogue."[94]

Clearly, King's vision of justice and interracial harmony bears little resemblance to that of his successors, who, masquerading as crusaders dedicated to promoting goodwill, regularly advocate policies and hurl accusations that engender black-white hostility. With near unanimity, they steadfastly refuse to acknowledge that the racial attitudes of whites today differ in any significant way from those of the Jim Crow South. From this point in the text onward, therefore, most references to contemporary "civil rights leaders" appear in quotation marks, for such individuals are rarely justified in claiming that title. If indeed they lead anyone anywhere, it is into the abyss of racial strife. Armed with a stockpile of pernicious myths, they have polluted the minds of millions of our countrymen during the past thirty years, damaging black-white relations every bit as profoundly as the lynch mobs of the 1800s once did. Skillfully and incrementally, their myths have seduced African Americans with the enticing power of victim status— encouraging blacks to blame their social, educational, and economic woes exclusively on the white race. Conversely, these same myths have saddled white Americans with useless, misplaced guilt—leading them to try, like the mendicant friars of old, to expiate their alleged sins through numberless acts of contrition and moral self-flagellation. This combination of blame and guilt has polarized the races in our country to an alarming degree.

Today's "civil rights" establishment, exploiting Americans' inclination to sympathize with the oppressed, has developed an entire industry devoted to recognizing ever-increasing numbers of victims and transforming their lowly status into an emblem of virtue. Consequently, our nation has become filled with professional victims who eagerly embrace the belief that life, in its unfairness, has deprived them of the blessings bestowed on the seemingly luckier, happier individuals around them. For the professional victim, there is distinction in being handicapped, honor in being pitied, and power in inflicting guilt upon others. He wears his pain proudly—secure in his belief that the angels are with him, and comforting himself with myths that affirm his victimhood.

The Myths Defined

There are three principal myths that have forestalled the improvement of American race relations in this latter part of the twentieth century. The first contends that most white people, continuing in the tradition of a bygone era, oppose equal employment and educational opportunities for blacks. This myth further tells us that in order to succeed, blacks in the United States must work harder and longer than their white counterparts—purportedly because the suffocating white racism of past generations persists largely unabated. Those who propagate this notion are not content to confine their condemnations to *genuine* instances of racism, but claim instead that racism is *everywhere*.

A second, related myth holds that were it not for the injustices inflicted upon them by whites, blacks in this country would be relieved of most of the ills plaguing them. It is said, moreover, that a vast reservoir of white bigotry periodically "spills over" and expresses itself in acts of violence against blacks. To support such contentions, many "civil rights leaders" can recite from memory a lengthy list of widely publicized white-on-black crimes allegedly motivated by racism. Asserting further that blacks themselves are incapable of racism, these activists characterize the black community's antiwhite sentiments as nothing more sinister than the justifiable emotions of an oppressed people longing for freedom.

A third myth asserts that all past white-on-black wrongs— however long ago they occurred—continue to hinder blacks to this day. Accepting this premise, many claim that reparations in the form of preferential treatment or monetary payments constitute reasonable remedies for, among other things, the horrors of slavery. Maintaining not only that present-day blacks ought to be compensated for injustices inflicted upon their ancestors, advocates of reparations further claim that contemporary whites should be punished for the transgressions of their own forefathers. Such a view deems black anger at whites— ostensibly founded on a desire to retaliate for past affronts—understandable, if not righteous.

Belief in the foregoing myths is by no means limited to blacks. Indeed it is every bit as common among white students and professors in university classrooms as among the board members of the NAACP; as prevalent among liberal white politicians as among members of the

Congressional Black Caucus; and as popular among white clergymen and social scientists as among their black counterparts. These myths constitute the dominant social vision of our time, and thus it is that many take them as articles of faith rather than as fables.

There are two principal classes of people who generate and disseminate our nation's racial myths. First there are those who, by their own long-term exposure to these fictions, have been molded into resolute believers. Such individuals' lack of clarity, however, is by no means due to want of intellect or education; many of them have earned high academic honors and hold positions of considerable prominence. They are simply blinded by their passionate devotion to a misguided ideology. A second class of myth makers, meanwhile, consists of opportunists representing themselves as messiahs whose leadership will steer the afflicted to a better place. Myths bemoaning societal inequities are the tools of their trade. The less their myths resemble reality, the harder these opportunists work to distort people's perceptions into conformity with those myths. They are essentially useless characters whose employment depends entirely upon their ability to lie effectively.

The destructive potential of lies, of course, has been recognized throughout human history. More than two thousand years ago the philosopher Plato advocated the elimination of particular myths from children's education—based on his belief that those tales, written by the early Greek poets, would corrupt the morals of the young. Specifically, he objected to stories that portrayed the Olympian gods as shameless, intemperate beings who regularly abused and deceived one another. In Plato's view, such tales implied that scandalous behavior, being presumably "godlike," was worthy of human imitation. In the following excerpt from his *Republic*, the characters Socrates and Adeimantus exchange thoughts about what the content of education should be:

SOCRATES: Then shall we simply allow our children to listen to any stories that anyone happens to make up, and so receive into their minds ideas often the very opposite of those we shall think they ought to have when they are grown up?

ADEIMANTUS: No, certainly not.

SOCRATES: It seems, then, our first business will be to supervise the making of fables and legends, rejecting all which are unsatisfactory; and we shall induce nurses and mothers to tell their children only

those which we have approved, and to think more of moulding their
souls with these stories than they now do of rubbing their limbs to
make them strong and shapely. Most of the stories now in use must
be discarded.

ADEIMANTUS: What kind do you mean?

SOCRATES: If we take the great ones, we shall see in them the pattern of
all the rest, which are bound to be of the same stamp and to have
the same effect.

ADEIMANTUS: No doubt; but which do you mean by the great ones?

SOCRATES: The stories in Hesiod and Homer and the poets in general,
who have at all times composed fictitious tales and told them to
mankind.

ADEIMANTUS: Which kind are you thinking of, and what fault do you
find in them?

SOCRATES: The worst of all faults, especially if the story is ugly and
immoral as well as false—misrepresenting the nature of gods and
heroes, like an artist whose picture is utterly unlike the object he
sets out to draw.

ADEIMANTUS: That is certainly a serious fault; but give me an example.

SOCRATES: A signal instance of false invention about the highest matters is that foul story, which Hesiod repeats, of the deeds of Uranus
and the vengeance of Cronos; and then there is the tale of Cronos's
doings and of his son's treatment of him. . . .

ADEIMANTUS: It is true: those stories are objectionable.

SOCRATES: Yes, and not to be repeated in our commonwealth. . . . We
shall not tell a child that, if he commits the foulest crimes or goes to
any length in punishing his father's misdeeds, he will be doing nothing out of the way, but only what the first and greatest of the gods
have done before him.

ADEIMANTUS: I agree; such stories are not fit to be repeated.

SOCRATES: Nor yet any tales of warfare and intrigues and battles of
gods against gods, which are equally untrue.[95]

Socrates identifies what he deems the worst of all sins: "misrepresenting the nature of gods and heroes, like an artist whose
picture is utterly unlike the object he sets out to draw." Today the
American perspective on race parallels this travesty by misrepresenting the nature of human beings. "Civil rights activists," politicians, and
academicians regularly portray white people as fundamentally racist
creatures reluctant to grant their black countrymen equal rights—
legally, socially, or economically. Some of this reluctance is attributed
to overt racial hatred, while much is said to stem from a subtle form of
prejudice that whites unwittingly harbor in their hearts—presumably

as a consequence of being part of the "white power structure." By contrast, blacks are portrayed as eternal victims who constantly need increasing doses of legally mandated protection from white malice—in the form of special privileges, lowered standards, and compensation for past injustices. This view of blacks originates not only from a belief in natural white wickedness, but also from the condescending notion that blacks are incapable of succeeding on their own. As a consequence of this view, great numbers of black Americans feel certain that they are maltreated at every turn—"seeing" racism everywhere, rather than only where it truly, lamentably exists. "Racist" has surely become our nation's most misapplied epithet, directed at a multitude of people and events undeserving of its condemning connotations.

Popular assertions about racism should not be accepted uncritically. We need to distinguish what is demonstrably true from what is patently false, remaining open to the possibility that some ostensibly learned "experts" may occasionally advance the most deluded, worthless nonsense imaginable. It requires courage to cast the accumulated myths of a lifetime to the wind. Our natural desire for simplicity, certitude, and the approval of others occasionally causes us to defend even our most flawed worldviews as if our very lives depended on them. Dead belief systems are difficult to bury, for in doing so we enter a world we do not recognize; we watch the carefully crafted towers of our understanding crash down in ruins; and we lose an integral piece of the only reality we have known, reinforced and imprinted on our minds by a thousand voices, internal and external. We fear such change.

The racial myths that are now an established part of our culture did not capture our minds with either suddenness or ceremony. As the Grand Canyon was formed over eons by the friction of countless water droplets against the rocky earth, so has our nation's racial mythology been sculpted word by word and sentence by sentence—the repetitions of which have been so frequent that most Americans have grown numb to their presence, no longer noticing their own minds being carved up and reshaped. Now, sadly, we find a great chasm dividing white from black, and separating our "common knowledge" from common sense.

Some myths can serve us well for a time. They may be our first, noble attempts to explain what we do not fully understand. Prior to the discoveries made by Copernicus and Galileo, for instance, prevailing wisdom held that the sun orbited the earth; that the stars were embedded in clear, rotating, crystalline spheres which encircled the universe; and that the moon was as perfectly smooth as a polished stone. When scientific evidence disproved all these falsehoods, the leading teachers of the day put forth a great and passionate resistance to the new information. It has always been difficult for "experts" to acknowledge their errors, and both Copernicus and Galileo feared the wrath of such people. So afraid was Copernicus, in fact, that he delayed for years the publication of his masterpiece postulating a sun-centered solar system—unwilling to openly advance his then-heretical theory until virtually on his deathbed. And Galileo, under threat of torture, recanted what he knew beyond any doubt to be true. In modern America, we can ill afford to conceal or recant our understanding of one particularly demonstrable reality: Our mainstream "civil rights leaders" have been lying to us for an entire generation, engendering interracial enmity of immense proportions. Their fictions have flourished in a relatively unchallenged atmosphere because any critic bold enough to expose their smokescreens is called a "racist" if he is white, and an "Oreo" or "Uncle Tom" if he is black. This is enough to silence most people. It is indeed tragic that at the very point in history when America dedicated itself to achieving full racial justice, many of those claiming to represent the black community committed themselves to sabotaging that process. The great black educator Booker T. Washington described such individuals many decades ago:

> There is a class of colored people who make a business of keeping the troubles, the wrongs, and the hardships of the Negro race before the public. Some of these people do not want the Negro to lose his grievances, because they do not want to lose their jobs.[96]

Chapter 2

A Racist Nation

A long habit of not thinking a thing wrong, gives it a
superficial appearance of being right, and raises at first
a formidable outcry in defense of custom. But the tumult
soon subsides. Time makes more converts than reason.
— Thomas Paine[1]

Most contemporary "civil rights leaders" identify racial injustice as an ugly yet omnipresent feature of life in the United States. White bigotry, they contend, is unlikely ever to release its stranglehold on the dreams of black Americans. Consider, as an example of this doctrine, the words of black law professor Derrick Bell:

> The fact of slavery refuses to fade, along with the deeply embedded personal attitudes and public policy assumptions that supported it for so long. Indeed, the racism that made slavery feasible is far from dead in the last decade of twentieth-century America; and the civil rights gains, so hard won, are being steadily eroded. Despite undeniable progress for many, no African Americans are insulated from incidents of racial discrimination. Our careers, even our lives, are threatened because of our color.[2]

These statements portray a country steeped in racism, unyielding to the positive changes promised by the civil rights advances of the

1960s. "Racism," Professor Bell explains, remains "an integral, permanent, and indestructible component of this society."[3] According to Bell, white people's attitudes have changed so little since the days of slavery that he would not be surprised if blacks in "this racist land" were someday again shackled in irons. "Slavery is," he writes, "as an example of what white America has done, a constant reminder of what white America might do."[4] Claiming that "few whites are ready to actively promote civil rights for blacks,"[5] Bell laments:

> Black people will never gain full equality in this country. Even those herculean efforts we hail as successful will produce no more than temporary "peaks of progress," short-lived victories that slide into irrelevance as racial patterns adapt in ways that maintain white dominance. This is a hard-to-accept fact that all history verifies. We must acknowledge it, not as a sign of submission, but as an act of ultimate defiance.[6]

Indeed, Bell deems defiance and perpetual vigilance the only means by which blacks can endure their unending struggle against the white "oppressor class."[7] "African Americans must confront the otherwise deadening reality of our permanent subordinate status," he says. "Only in this way can we prevent ourselves from being dragged down by society's racial hostility. Beyond survival lies the potential to perceive more clearly both a reason and the means for further struggle."[8] Asserting that white Americans "achieve a measure of social stability through their unspoken pact to keep blacks on the bottom,"[9] Bell identifies racism as the principal cause of virtually every problem the black community faces. "The fact," he writes, "that, as victims, we suffer racism's harm but, as a people, cannot share the responsibility for that harm, may be the crucial component in a definition of what it is to be black in America."[10]

According to Bell, hard work and perseverance can scarcely enable blacks to transcend the imposing hurdle of white racism. Successful blacks, he tells us, owe their prosperity more to good fortune than to any system that welcomes their participation or rewards them for their labors. "We rise and fall less as a result of our efforts," he says, "than in response to the needs of a white society that condemns all blacks to quasi citizenship as surely as it segregated our parents and enslaved their forebears." He complains that blacks are "tolerated in good times, despised when things go wrong, [and] as a people . . . are scapegoated and sacrificed."[11] Maintaining that white malevolence knows no bounds, Bell assures us that even if scientists were to invent a magical pill whose consumption would make all blacks perfectly law-abiding, whites would destroy it so as to prevent such an effect. Why? Because black crime, he explains, benefits many whites—such as those who profit from the manufacture of prison uniforms.[12] The eventual black response to such pervasive white wickedness, Bell predicts, will be the rise of charismatic new leaders "who urge that instead of [blacks] killing each other, they should go out in gangs and kill a whole lot of white people."[13]

On July 20, 1991, the taxpayer-funded Empire State Black Arts and Cultural Festival was held in Albany, New York. Guest speaker Dr. Leonard Jeffries, who at that time was chairman of the African American Studies department at City College of New York (CCNY), was scheduled to lecture on the merits of African-centered education. Using this theme as a springboard, however, Jeffries launched into an extended diatribe against whites in general, directing his harshest comments at Jews and Italians. He spoke of "a conspiracy, planned and plotted and programmed out of Hollywood" by "people called Greenberg and Weisberg and Trigliani" to denigrate blacks in the movies. "Russian Jewry," he elaborated, "had a particular control over the movies, and their financial partners, the Mafia, put together a financial system of destruction of black people."[14]

Jeffries also claimed that information about African accomplishments had been systematically removed from school curricula by "very nice, very friendly white folks and their achieving Negro partners."[15] He further referred to Diane Ravitch, an assistant secretary of education who had been critical of Jeffries, as a "sophisticated, debonair racist" and a "Texas Jew."[16] "The white boy can't be trusted," added the fiery professor.[17]

Among Jeffries's beliefs is the notion that melanin, the substance regulating skin pigmentation, is associated with racial superiority. Black people, he maintains, are inherently better than whites because their skin contains more melanin. "Let me clarify my views," he blusters. "Western civilization is nothing more than an institutionalized, sophisticated form of barbarism. . . . Wherever the white man has gone, he has left his three D's: domination, destruction, and death."[18] In 1986 Jeffries went so far as to applaud the explosion of the *Challenger* space shuttle—on grounds that whites had thereby been prevented, at least temporarily, from "spreading their filth throughout the universe."[19] Remarkably, Jeffries's ideas somehow impressed the New York State education commissioner, who appointed him—long after the professor's views about whites were widely known—to help rewrite the public school curriculum in American history and social studies.[20] These same views, it should be noted, also won Jeffries a large following of black students at CCNY.[21] In August 1991, when there was speculation that he would be dropped as the school's department chairman, some 3,500 black demonstrators rallied in support of Jeffries.[22]

Ralph Wiley, author of *What Black People Should Do Now*, sees white racism virtually everywhere:

> [America] needs saving, for here is an underlying stain born of an assumed power. Men—all men, but specifically white men—grow up with an implicit belief that they are born to wield power over others weaker than they. And if these men find they have no power, then they must find the weakest of all and wield what they can. Monsters are thus created.[23]

White people, Wiley tells us, tolerate blacks only to exploit their contributions to white society:

> The United States of America is a place where the citizenry, both native and naturalized, learn to think and act as if they want nothing to do with me or my kind if they want to get ahead, even though black people nurture them, empower them, profit them, turn over to them their best ideas, give them a stylish resiliency they seem to utterly lack otherwise.[24]

Characterizing black Americans as virtual prisoners in a racist land, Wiley writes, "I wonder how [freedom] feels? I am trapped and can only say 'Nooo' and hope my scream is loud enough to discourage the monsters and keep them back until I am strong enough, powerful enough to fight my way free. Powerful enough to slip the noose from my neck and put out the fire on my flesh."[25] He goes so far as to suggest that the dreaded AIDS virus is the centerpiece of a white conspiracy to exterminate the black race. Consider his reaction to basketball star Earvin "Magic" Johnson's 1991 announcement that he had contracted the virus:

Just like that? Explain this. How can it be? I watched the news with dread and revulsion. In the press conference Earv seemed much too calm for a man who had just been given a death sentence. He advocated safe sex. "It's not sex that's killing us," I thought. "It's a virus. Where did it come from?" Later the vice president, Dan Quayle, came out and said Earv should have advocated abstinence. I thought, "F—— you, white man. Even your priests do not abstain from sex with young boys, and all you can say is 'abstain'?"

Earv was HIV-positive. Earv was a good man. Rage, fear, hatred all rose up in me because the rest of us could go at any time, but not Earv. Earv stood for something. Another part of me was not enraged or fearful or hateful. Another part of me admired the tactics even as they were killing me. The virus was doing what I believe it was made to do—destroy the black people, the black men, and intravenous drug users, and gays, and anyone who is among the undesirables, but most especially the black men.[26]

Wiley also holds some strong opinions about Marion Barry, Washington, D.C.'s black mayor who, during the 1980s, was involved in numerous personal and political scandals—including a crack cocaine habit, improprieties with women, extensive mismanagement, and political corruption of epic proportions.[27] Barry nonetheless remained in office for twelve years, thanks to his virtually unanimous support from black voters—a support buttressed by his claims that any investigations into his personal life were racially motivated. He regularly denounced his critics in the "white press" for attempting to destroy his political career via "a new style of lynching."[28] The bubble finally burst in 1990, however, when the Federal Bureau of Investigation (FBI) used a woman to lure Barry into a hotel room to be secretly videotaped smoking crack,[29] after which he was promptly arrested. Wiley laments the mayor's plight: "I'm very sympathetic to any story of sin and redemption involving a black man in America. I feel I have to give Barry every chance to redeem himself. . . . What happened to Marion was pitiful. It was similar to what could happen to any black man."[30]

Following his arrest, Barry characterized the FBI's action as a "political lynching" and even accused the government of trying to kill him with crack that was "90 percent pure."[31] Benjamin Hooks, then the NAACP's executive director, saw Barry's arrest as part of a "pattern of harassment of black elected officials" everywhere.[32] Washington's three black weekly newspapers unanimously defended

Barry, asserting that the mayor had been "set up" by racist whites.[33] Many Washington blacks, in fact, suspected a white conspiracy, which they called "The Plan," whose alleged purpose was to deprive the black community of political power. One of the first steps in this plot, as they saw it, was the removal of Mayor Barry from office. Another step, they claimed, called for whites to plant drugs and guns in black neighborhoods so that black men would kill one another.[34] While these unsubstantiated speculations attracted considerable numbers of believers, Barry's documented vices were of little interest to his supporters. As black columnist Carl Rowan explained, "The mayor may be a cocaine junkie, a crack addict, a sexual scoundrel, but he is our [black people's] junkie, our addict, and our scoundrel, and we aren't going to let you white folks put him in jail."[35]

Notably, Barry's fall from grace seemed only to elevate his standing in the black community. In April 1990, after his stay in a drug treatment center, he attended a conference of 400 black mayors and received a standing ovation when keynote speaker Jesse Jackson called him to the podium. When the cheers finally died down, Jackson, apparently with no sense of irony, proceeded to deliver a discourse on drug policy.[36] Barry himself later held a press conference during which he criticized federal officials for not having done enough to help him battle Washington's cataclysmic crack epidemic.[37]

Cornel West, an Ivy League professor of religion, philosophy, and African American studies, brands the United States a "racist patriarchal" nation[38] where "white supremacy" still defines everyday life.[39] "White America," he writes, "has been historically weak-willed in ensuring racial justice and has continued to resist fully accepting the humanity of blacks."[40] This has resulted, he claims, in the creation of many "degraded and oppressed people [who are] hungry for identity, meaning, and self-worth."[41] Professor West attributes most of the black community's problems to "existential angst derive[d] from the lived experience of ontological wounds and emotional scars inflicted by white supremacist beliefs and images permeating U.S. society and culture."[42] He explains that "the accumulated effect of the black wounds and scars suffered in a white-dominated society is a deep-seated anger, a boiling sense of rage, and a passionate pessimism regarding America's will to justice."[43] "It goes without saying," he adds, "that a profound hatred of African people . . . sits at the center of American civilization."[44]

A National Urban League report paints a similarly bleak picture, claiming that black Americans are "besieged by the resurgence of raw racism, persistent economic depression, and the continued erosion of past gains."[45] The report adds:

> Typical of the moral blinders donned by the nation in recent years is its indifference to the continued existence of racism and racial disadvantage that permeate our society and degrade national life and aspirations. Racism continues to live on despite the pious pronouncements that we are now a color-blind society. It can be seen in the daily drumfire of local reports about racially inspired outrages that show old forms of racism thriving alongside the more subtle forms of discrimination that have become more popular.[46]

The Urban League document goes on to explain that "white Americans remain largely ignorant of—or indifferent to—the plight of black citizens."[47] It condemns "the perpetuation of injustices against blacks and other minorities" that allegedly result from the "Justice Department's failure to enforce the spirit as well as the letter of civil rights law."[48] Finally, it exhorts Americans to repudiate the spreading cancer of racism:

> Racism, in any of its insidious forms, exacts a toll on those who practice it, those who tolerate it, and those who suffer from it. We call upon our national leadership, in both public and private domains, to repudiate racism as a tolerable element within our country's moral fiber and to condemn discriminatory acts and attitudes that serve to degrade our image as a land of freedom, justice, and opportunity.[49]

Some of our country's most prominent black editorialists seem to find white racism lurking around every corner. Earl Caldwell, for one, describes black Americans as "the constant target of racial slurs, insults, and violence, coming from many fronts."[50] Richard G. Carter echoes this belief when he laments "how deep the roots of racism remain in our midst [today]. It's enough to turn the stomach of all decent Americans."[51] Along the same lines, E.R. Shipp calls racism "the most serious obstacle to the social progress of blacks in this country and the greatest threat to [their] personal freedom."[52] "In the United States," she adds, "racism flows as naturally as mother's milk from one generation to the next, perpetuating the notion that entitlement or exclusion is dictated by one's skin color."[53] According to Shipp, even the most ambitious, responsible blacks are doomed to be abused in this allegedly racist land. "Even if you [blacks] do all those things that should make you acceptable," she writes, "[such as] earn college degrees, hold down a job or two, pay your bills on time, do volunteer work, praise God with regularity, you can never be sure when you will be punished for [the crime of] Living While Black."[54]

Carl Rowan charges that "a majority of white Americans continue to believe that they are entitled to have an 'inferior' race of people to do the menial duties, to perform the drudgery of life."[55] "Racism," he says, "remains a terrible curse on this society, and . . . nothing in sight suggests that that curse will soon vanish."[56] Rowan further asserts that "racism has not been as virulent [as it is today] throughout America since the Civil War, with short fuses burning on a thousand powder kegs."[57] After the February 1999 conviction of white racist John William King for the murder of a black Texas man, Rowan wrote that the killer's deed could not be dismissed as a mere "social aberration."[58] Rather, he explained, it was part of a "wide white-supremacy phenomenon" and reflected "the larger and more insidious bigotry that is at work in the larger American society."[59]

"We are the victims of racism in this society," asserts black Democratic representative Louis Stokes.[60] Joseph Lowery, president of the Southern Christian Leadership Conference, warns that white bigotry "is gaining respectability again. There's a resurgence of racism and you find it at almost every level of life."[61] White Americans, he believes, have changed very little since the Kerner Commission asserted in 1968 that "white racism is essentially responsible for the explosive mixture which has been accumulating in our cities."[62]

Benjamin Chavis, former executive director of the NAACP, laments the "vestiges of American apartheid" that prevent blacks from acquiring "a fair share" of the economy. Advocating "a movement for political parity and economic equity," he exhorts blacks to "struggle" for nothing less than "the complete liberation of people of color worldwide."[63] Racism, he says, is "worse today than it was in the '60s."[64] At a Martin Luther King, Jr. event in January 1999, NAACP chairman Julian Bond announced, "Everywhere we see clear racial fault lines which divide American society as much now as at anytime in our past."[65]

Unquestionably, the most influential black "leader" in contemporary America is Louis Farrakhan, who heads the black Muslim group Nation of Islam (NOI). In December 1993 Farrakhan told a black New York audience of more than 20,000 that America's continuing racial inequity lay at the heart of the black community's drug and crime problems. Given a standing ovation for calling the United States an evil nation, he asserted that pervasive white racism makes our society a breeding ground for black crime.[66]

The following month Farrakhan again spoke before an enthusiastic audience of more than 10,000 in New York. Billed as an event "for black men only," this gathering flatly barred whites from attending. Explaining the ban on whites, Farrakhan assistant Munir Muhammad said, "Generally, we deal with our own," though he added, "Hispanics, we don't have a problem with."[67]

According to Farrakhan, whites are "devils" who are "evil by nature."[68] "The God who taught me calls white men the skunks of the planet earth," he says. "They are so wicked and so filthy that God calls them the skunks of the planet."[69] The militant Farrakhan vows that he "will fight to see that vicious [white] beast go down into [a] lake of fire."[70] Regularly referring to Jews as "bloodsuckers" who exploit the black community,[71] he deems Judaism a "gutter religion" and claims that Jewish doctors are engaged in "a diabolical plot to exterminate black people" by deliberately injecting them with the AIDS virus.[72] Notwithstanding such statements, Benjamin Chavis considers Farrakhan "neither anti-Semitic nor racist."[73]

Because much of Farrakhan's rhetoric focuses on what he calls the sinful, oppressive nature of the white race, many of his followers share his view of whites. Consider the words of Sharod Baker, a staunch Farrakhan supporter, who says, "I don't think there's anything wrong with saying I hate [white people]. They have caused me harm over and over, and I wish they were dead."[74] Each year droves of disciples like Baker join the Nation of Islam, which actively recruits new members in black urban areas and on black college campuses. Moreover, the NOI is perhaps the most powerful black movement in our country's prisons.[75]

Indeed, Farrakhan is no mere fringe extremist with a cult following. He draws enormous, standing-room-only crowds of black listeners wherever he speaks. A 1992 lecture he gave in Atlanta actually outdrew a World Series game played there that same night.[76] In a recent National Black Politics survey, 67 percent of black respondents called Farrakhan a good leader. According to a *Time*/CNN poll, some 70 percent of blacks believe that he says things Americans should hear; 67 percent consider him an effective leader; 63 percent believe that he speaks the truth; 62 percent deem him generally good for the black community; more than half call him a good role model for black youth; and only 34 percent see him as "a bigot and a racist."[77] In 1996 the National Newspaper Publishers Association, which represents 200 black-owned publishers, gave Farrakhan its "Newsmaker of the Year" award—for which one criterion was the demonstration of "a higher level of moral authority."[78] In light of Farrakhan's being recognized as a legitimate black cultural icon, it is scarcely surprising that many African Americans have assimilated his negative opinions about whites—and about Jews in particular. A 1998 Anti-Defamation League survey found that blacks were four times more likely than whites to harbor anti-Semitic attitudes.[79]

Farrakhan supporters commonly explain that while his rhetoric may sometimes be offensive, it also has a "positive side." They note, for example, that he often urges blacks to take responsibility for improving their own lives, rather than waiting for help from "racist" white America. They further observe that the NOI has achieved a degree of success, albeit modest, in converting gangsters and addicts into dignified, well-dressed individuals.[80] Yet it is doubtful that Farrakhan's apologists would use the same yardstick to measure the "positive" aspects of a *white* supremacist, segregationist group. One wonders, for instance, whether they would have praised the Ku Klux Klan chapter which, several decades ago, established an institution for homeless children, gave food and money to the poor, and conducted a support program for widows.[81]

Farrakhan's most widely publicized appearance to date was his October 16, 1995 address at the Million Man March in Washington, D.C., which drew at least several hundred thousand black men. Though officially billed as a "day of atonement," a significant portion of the event focused on America's historical and allegedly continuing assault on the black race. "The real evil in America," Farrakhan told the crowd, "is the idea that undergirds the setup of the Western world, and that idea is called white supremacy."[82] Guest speaker Maulana Karenga concurred that "the increasing racism and the continuing commitment to white supremacy in this country" represented a troubling trend.[83] New York congressman Charles Rangel asserted, "Black men are not the problem. Black men are the victims."[84]

"Now we have the burden of two Americas: one-half slave and one-half free," declared Jesse Jackson, another featured speaker at the march.[85] Explaining that blacks were "yearning to breathe free," he exhorted those in attendance to break out of their "shackles" because no one would "free" them voluntarily. "Slave masters never retire," he said. "Oppressors never retire."[86] Jackson named, as the principal perpetrators of this "oppression," law-enforcement officials who "chastise the [black] mothers, . . . chase the daddies, [and] lock up the children."[87] "We [blacks] are under attack by the courts, legislatures, mass media," he added. "We're despised. Racists attack us for sport to win votes. We're attacked for sport to make money. But I tell you today, rabbit hunting ain't fun when the rabbits stop running and start fighting back."[88]

The day before the Million Man March, a number of Nation of Islam allies in our nation's capital sponsored, as a preview to the following day's activities, an event billed as the Black African Holocaust Nationhood Conference. Serving as master of ceremonies was Harvard law student Malik Zulu Shabazz, who told the hundreds in attendance that blacks were little more than outcasts of American society. Whites, he said, "made . . . colleges and institutions, black and white, not to free us, but to make us better servants of white folks. Where's your proof? Look at our condition. . . . The matter of fact is we [are] still niggers in America."[89] Author and guest speaker Tony Martin, meanwhile, lauded the "hatred of oppression and . . . [hatred of] racism which has always been part of [black people's] legacy in this country."[90] Said another speaker, "It's time for the black world's rise and the white world's demise."[91] Such sentiments were enthusiastically received with standing ovations and "Black Power" salutes.

Former Chicago mayoral aide Steven Cokely also spoke at the Nationhood Conference, calling for a "revolution" that would destroy the "illegal *Con*stitution" that undergirds America's "unjust government."[92] "Why I am here this weekend," he proudly declared, "is so that I can help further instigate, agitate, magnify towards a destruction of all that has come from the illegal government called America."[93]

Billing himself "the warrior lawyer," attorney Alton Maddox followed Cokely to the podium. "I am happy to be here," he told the audience, "because this is where the white man does not want us to be. . . . And I will go anywhere in defiance of that lying, low-down cracker [disparaging slang term for white person]. Anywhere!" Suggesting to those in attendance that their "freedom" hinged on their willingness to engage in violence, Maddox explained, "The price of victory is blood. You gotta spill some blood if you wanna be free."[94]

Maddox also directed a few words to any white Americans who might have been watching the telecast of his speech: "I want to say something to the white folks. We [blacks] fully endorse the language and the mannerism of the honorable Louis Farrakhan." The entire audience stood, at that point, to give Maddox a loud ovation, after which he continued: "Because he [Farrakhan] is addressing the pain and suffering of black people for more than 400 years. . . . It's justifiable anger of the black man and the black woman. The mistreatment, the degradation that our people had to suffer in the hells of North America for 400 years. You are [sic] better be glad that the only thing we are doing is calling you [whites] 'bloodsuckers'!"[95]

The highly anticipated climax of the proceedings began when Malik Zulu Shabazz introduced the final scheduled speaker—former NOI spokesman Khalid Abdul Muhammad. With the audience standing and cheering, Shabazz said, "We wanna bring on a man who gives the white man nightmares. We wanna bring on a man who makes the Jews pee in they [sic] pants at night. He's like black Raid on white roaches."[96] Muhammad then stepped to the microphone and addressed the frenzied crowd:

> I came [today] to place the blame squarely where it belongs. I didn't come to pin the tail on the donkey. I came to pin the tail on the honkie. . . . We want to try the white man today. We want to hold court on this devil today, hold court on this cracker. . . . And we will find this cracker guilty beyond any reasonable doubt, with moral certainty, and with no recommendation for mercy. . . . We gonna keep this cracker on death row with no possibility for a stay of execution. . . . [W]e must stand tall to free all black political prisoners. . . . There must be a time and a generation that will rise up, that will not just march, will not just protest, but [will] stand up [a] million strong and bum-rush this cracker and take our political prisoners from this no-good, low-down, dirty white man. . . . [T]he white man is the coldest, most vicious one that has ever lived . . . [on] the planet earth.[97]

Muhammad had first gained significant public notoriety as the result of a speech he delivered on November 29, 1993 at New Jersey's Kean College. In that three-hour denunciation of whites and Jews, he made the following comments:

> Brothers and sisters, the so-called Jew—and I must say the "so-called" Jew—because you are not the true Jew. . . . You are a Johnny-come-lately Jew who just crawled out of the caves and hills of Europe just over 4,000 years ago. You are not from the original people. You are a European strain of people who crawled around on all fours in the caves and hills of Europe, eating juniper roots and eating each other. You knew nothing about fire. You knew nothing about . . . science, or nothing about embalming. You left your dead right in the cave with you, and you slept with your dead for 2,000 years, smelling the stench coming up from the decomposing bodies. You knew nothing about bathrooms and toilets and rest rooms and sanitation systems. You did your number one and your number two, your pee pee and your doo doo right in the caves and hills of Europe. You slept in your urination and your defecation generation after generation for 2,000 years. You knew nothing about fire. You knocked your animals in the head with clubs and boulders . . . and all of you would just gum and eat the fur, the dirt, the filth, and suck the blood from the raw meat, and you still eat your meat raw to this very day.[98]

In that same 1993 address, Muhammad complained that black students were "catching so much hell here . . . on the Kean College campus and in the surrounding Union [County] area, a Jew stronghold."[99] Addressing Jews directly, he said, "How arrogant you are, no-good bastards. . . . Jesus was right, you're nothing but liars. The Book of Revelation is right, you are from the synagogue of Satan. You say I am anti-Semitic. If you are a Semite, I am [anti-Semitic], God damn it. I am against whatever you are. You're just a damn lie. We [blacks] are dominant, strong. You are recessive, weak."[100]

"Jews . . . are our enemy," Muhammad continued. "They use us . . . to clear the path for their own advancement." Making a play on words, he referred to the "Jewnited Nations" and "Columbia Jewniversity" in "Jew York City." He called Jews "the slumlords in the black communities" and suggested that German Jews had brought the Holocaust upon themselves.[101] Ridiculing also the pope of the Roman Catholic Church, Muhammad said, "Go to the Vatican in Rome with the old no-good pope. You know that cracker, somebody need [*sic*] to raise that dress up and see what's really under there."[102]

For sharing his thoughts with the students and professors of Kean College, Muhammad was paid $2,650.[103] His words drew rousing applause from the mostly black listeners,[104] many of whom hoped he would be invited back to dispense more of his "very enlightening, thought-provoking, and above all true" rhetoric.[105] Notably, not a single black member of Kean's faculty or staff felt moved to denounce Muhammad's speech.[106] The reaction of "civil rights leaders," similarly, was silence—with the exception of a few notables like Al Sharpton, a New York Baptist minister who said, "I agree with much of what [Muhammad] said. He is a very articulate and courageous brother."[107]

When some white commentators later rebuked Farrakhan for refusing to condemn his aide's incendiary Kean College address, the NOI kingpin said, "[They] want to use brother Khalid's words against me and divide the house."[108] Nearly two months would pass before even one prominent black "leader"—Jesse Jackson—suggested that Muhammad's rhetoric was in any way racist.[109] Then, taking Jackson's lead, a few members of the Congressional Black Caucus also criticized Muhammad.[110] We may wonder, however, why it took so long for these individuals to speak up. Furthermore, it is unclear why they were careful to find no fault with Farrakhan, urging him only to dissociate himself from his fiery aide and intimating that Muhammad's message was a departure from traditional NOI rhetoric. Yet surely they were aware that this very same Khalid Muhammad had delivered a similar speech in 1991 at Columbia University.[111] Undoubtedly they knew that his Kean College discourse contained nothing with which Farrakhan would disagree. Indeed, during a January 1994 oration before a large black audience, Farrakhan himself drew repeated standing ovations for his scathing denunciations of Jews,[112] who he claimed were "plotting against us [blacks] even as we speak."[113] During the ensuing weeks, he continued to defend Muhammad's rhetoric. "I stand by the truths that he spoke," said Farrakhan, rebuking his comrade only for "the [harsh] manner in which those truths were represented."[114] "Brother Muhammad is like a beautiful black stallion," Farrakhan added, "and it takes God to ride such a gifted horse. He will buck. That's his spirit. He's a warrior. His spirit is one with his people."[115]

After his controversial Kean College address, Muhammad became an increasingly popular speaker among black groups nationwide—making no discernible changes either to the tone or content of his message. In January 1994 he stated that blacks should slaughter all white South Africans, bury them, and then dig them up and mutilate them further.[116] The following month he was a special guest speaker at a Black History Month rally at New Jersey's Trenton State College.[117] Also in February, he spoke at Kent State University in Ohio for a fee of $4,000.[118] Later that month, while addressing a black women's group in Baltimore, he referred to Jews as "slumlords" and "bloodsuckers of the poor."[119] "It's that old no-good Jew," he elaborated. "It's that old imposter Jew, that old hook-nose, bagel-eating, lox-eating, Johnny-come-lately perpetrating a fraud, just crawled out of the caves and hills of Europe, so-called damn Jew."[120] On another occasion he warned that a full-fledged white-on-black holocaust was already in progress.[121]

In March 1994 Muhammad delivered a speech to 500 blacks at Brooklyn's Slave Theater, asserting that Jews "drive their tractor-trailers full of money to their [own] neighborhoods, and our neighborhoods get poorer and poorer and their neighborhoods get richer and richer."[122] Two months later he publicly lionized Colin Ferguson, a black gunman who had shot more than twenty whites aboard a New York train in December 1993. "I love him [Ferguson] as much as America loves General Schwarzkopf, General Westmoreland, General Patton, General MacArthur or General Eisenhower," Muhammad announced.[123] In a similar vein, he told an approving black audience at Howard University, "God spoke to Colin Ferguson and said, 'Catch the train, Colin, catch the train.' "[124] In August 1998 he told a *New York* magazine reporter, "I honestly wanna kill the enemy. I mean, goddamn it, we're supposed to have at least one Colin Ferguson. I would be embarrassed if we couldn't point to one Colin Ferguson that decided one day to . . . just kill every goddamn cracker that he saw."[125]

When personal differences eventually led Farrakhan to expel Muhammad from the NOI, Muhammad quickly found a new calling as a central figure in the militant group known as the New Black Panthers. While Muhammad's sentiments have alienated many over the years, they have also won him legions of admirers in the black community. Attorney Alton Maddox calls him "the conscience of the black liberation movement today."[126]

Not surprisingly, the rhetoric of other NOI spokesmen is no less caustic than Muhammad's. The organization's youth minister Quanell X, for example, openly threatens violence. "All of you Jews can go straight to hell," he said in October 1995. "Black youth do not want a relationship with the Jewish community or the mainstream white community, or the foot-shuffling, head-bowing, knee-bobbing black community. I say to Jewish America: 'Get ready . . . knuckle up, put your boots on, because we're ready and the war is going down.' "[127]

As embodied in the words of Farrakhan, Muhammad, and Quanell X, the NOI's racial attitudes are unambiguous. Nonetheless, Benjamin Chavis, during his tenure as NAACP executive director, proudly announced his organization's "sacred covenant"[128] with Farrakhan and pledged never to "forsake Mr. Farrakhan as my brother."[129] In September 1993, members of the Congressional Black Caucus likewise announced, in front of a large audience, that they too had joined in a "sacred covenant" with America's foremost black "leader."[130]

More Angry Voices

In March 1990 black poet and professor Amiri Baraka—formerly LeRoi Jones—was angered by Rutgers University's refusal to grant him an early tenured appointment to its English faculty. Denouncing the university's decision, Baraka likened his white colleagues to Nazis and Klansmen.[131] At a rally attended by 250 of his student supporters, he blamed "Europhilic elitists and white supremacists" in the English department for blocking his appointment.[132]

Deeming American society inherently evil, Baraka candidly acknowledges his personal hatred for white people. "It might not happen in my lifetime," he says, "but there will come a time when a generation of black people will rise up and destroy this wicked system."[133] In one of his poems, he asserts that blacks are justified in robbing or even killing whites, because the latter "already stole" everything from the former. In the same poem, Baraka describes "the magic dance" of enraged blacks mugging whites in the streets. "Take their [whites'] lives if need be," he writes, exhorting blacks to smash "jellywhite faces" and then dance in celebration of their conquest.[134]

In *The Rage of a Privileged Class*, author Ellis Cose tells readers why middle-class blacks like himself are angry:

> I have done everything I was supposed to do. I have stayed out of trouble with the law, gone to the right schools, and worked myself nearly to death. What more do they want? Why in God's name won't they accept me as a full human being? Why am I pigeonholed in a black job? Why am I constantly treated as if I were a drug addict, a thief, or a thug? Why am I still not allowed to aspire to the same things every white person in America takes as a birthright? Why, when I most want to be seen, am I suddenly rendered invisible? . . . America is filled with attitudes, assumptions, stereotypes, and behaviors that make it virtually impossible for blacks to believe that the nation is serious about its promise of equality.[135]

Such assertions have not diminished at all during the past three decades. "Civil rights leaders" continue to offer constant assurances that America's "original sin" of white racism remains the primary curse of the black community. Consequently, many young blacks, having heard these assurances so often throughout their lives, have grown to despise whites. Consider what occurred a few years ago at Roslyn High School in New York, where black male students regularly denied their white male peers access to a hallway near the gymnasium. Even after a white student described the ongoing intimidation in a letter to the school newspaper, administrators made no effort to end the blockade. One teacher explained that the school's inaction was due to the fact that the offending black students were "disadvantaged" and "need[ed] more attention than most of the white students."[136]

In February 1993 about 150 high-school students in White Plains, New York participated in a "Speak Out" assembly whose theme was "Martin Luther King Twenty-Five Years Later: What Happened to the Dream?" When the students were invited to publicly share their thoughts and concerns about black-white relations, one white youngster made reference to a film about the civil rights movement, titled *A Time for Justice*, which had been presented during a previous assembly. "When a white person was shown lying in a hospital, shot," he recounted, "we heard clapping [by blacks] in the audience. I was very scared about that, and I'm scared right now." A black student then explained that the clapping signified "trying to get even." Another added, "When I finally see a white man getting beat, I instantly clap. It reminds me of my grandparents getting lynched." Still another revealed that he resented white people because they could "get a job much faster than I would."[137]

Indeed, "civil rights leaders" have taught an entire generation of black youth to "see" racism everywhere. In April 1993 dozens of black students at the University of Pennsylvania stole an entire press run of the school newspaper, the *Daily Pennsylvanian*, to express their disapproval of the paper's lone politically conservative column. School president Sheldon Hackney, fearing that he would be thought racially insensitive if he spoke out, refused to condemn the theft.[138] Seven months later the University of Maryland experienced a similar episode when 10,000 copies of its school paper, *Diamondback*, were stolen by black students. The perpetrators of this theft complained that not enough minority models were featured in a *Diamondback* fashion spread; that the paper's report about a car accident which had claimed three black lives was written insensitively; and that one particular article was unduly critical of a black fraternity's hazing practices. The thieves replaced the newspapers with flyers that read, "Due to its racist nature, the *Diamondback* will not be available today— read a book!"[139]

Such incidents have occurred numerous times in recent years, rarely eliciting any rebuke from school officials. On five separate occasions in 1997 alone, for example, University of California at Berkeley chancellor Chang-Lin Tien said nothing to reprimand the thieves who stole all or part of the *Daily Californian*'s 24,000-copy press run whenever the paper contained articles opposing affirmative action.[140] That same year, Cornell University president Hunter Rawlings looked the other way when students seized and burned every copy of a *Cornell Review* issue in which Ebonics, the so-called study of "Black English," was parodied.[141]

Many black professors, it should be noted, are just as inclined as black students to see racism all around them. George Mason University history professor Roger Wilkins, for instance, asserts that white racism pervades America's college campuses. "Despite the strong efforts of the best-intentioned institutions," he writes, "the atmosphere at predominantly white colleges and universities shrieks, 'This is a white space that you occupy only at our sufferance.' "[142] In a similar vein, retired Duke University professor John Hope Franklin laments that white college students "have been encouraged to intimidate, terrorize, and make life miserable for African American students at many of our institutions of higher learning."[143] White Americans, he says, "are a bigoted people and always have been."[144]

It is common even for rich and famous blacks to contend that America mistreats them. Consider the case of the late rap singer Tupac Shakur, who, over the years, ran into much trouble with the law. In August 1992 he was involved in a gunfight during which a small child was shot and killed by a stray bullet.[145] In March 1993 he assaulted a video director in a Los Angeles parking lot, an offense for which he spent fifteen days in jail.[146] Later that year he was arrested in Atlanta on charges of shooting two off-duty police officers during a traffic dispute,[147] and a few weeks later he was indicted for the sodomy and sexual abuse of a young woman in his hotel suite.[148] Notably, Shakur was never bashful about his violent lifestyle and song lyrics. His press kit, in fact, boasted of the turmoil that erupted when a Texas trooper was shot and killed by a teenager who had been listening to the rapper's music.[149]

Notwithstanding Shakur's numerous brushes with law-enforcement personnel, the NAACP nominated him for its prestigious Image Award in 1993. Presumably, the great challenge of trying to overcome the purportedly omnipresent evils of white racism rendered his many transgressions inconsequential. Despite his fame and fortune, Shakur claimed to be as much a victim of racism as less-affluent blacks. "I'm a product of [a] society that openly tells me that my life isn't worth anything," he once said.[150] After Shakur's death, rap music journalist Kim Greene said of him, "He was a thug, but that's what being a black man in America does to you."[151]

In May 1992 rapper Sister Souljah stated that though there might indeed be some good white people, she personally had never met one. She then posited this unusual idea for ending black-on-black urban crime: "[I]f black people kill black people every day, why not have a week and kill white people? You understand what I'm saying? . . . [I]f you're a gang member and you would normally be killing somebody, why not kill a white person?"[152] Souljah encourages young blacks to understand that they are literally "at war" against an oppressive nation that prevents them from getting "what we want in this society."[153] It is noteworthy that former NAACP leader Benjamin Chavis considers Souljah to be "a close friend" of his,[154] while Jesse Jackson calls her a voice "representing the feelings and hopes of a whole generation" of young African Americans.[155]

Many claim that because white racism is so widespread, much black behavior is but an adaptive response to it. Psychologist Richard

Majors, for instance, deems the characteristic aloof swagger or "cool pose" of inner-city black teenagers "a tactic for psychological survival," a coping mechanism designed to insulate their psyches from the choking yoke of white oppression. Enabling them to "appear competent and in control in the face of adversity," the cool pose purportedly affords them a "source of dignity and worth, a mask that hides the sting of failure and frustration."[156]

Dr. Majors explains that the cool pose is characterized by a combination of speech, mannerisms, gestures, and movements that "exaggerate or ritualize masculinity." The "essence of cool," he adds, "is to appear in control, whether through a fearless style of walking, an aloof facial expression, the clothes you wear, a haircut, your gestures, or the way you talk. The cool pose shows the dominant culture that you are strong and proud, despite your status in American society."[157] In an article outlining Dr. Majors's conclusions, *The New York Times* states, "While the cool pose is often misread by teachers, principals, and police officers as an attitude of defiance, psychologists who have studied it say it is a way for black youths to maintain a sense of integrity and suppress rage at being blocked from usual routes to esteem and success."[158] This rage is heightened, according to Majors, by the fact that black males in America are becoming "an endangered species."[159]

In 1994, Hunter College professor John Henrik Clarke asserted that New York City's then-high violent crime rate was a manifestation of antiblack racism. "What used to be the South has moved up North—the bigotry, the murders and the lies," he said. "New York has become little segregated pockets, all pitted against each other. We [blacks] are the targets, unfair targets of the vultures, the police and social agencies. A lot of people have just had it."[160] Along the same lines, the noted black attorney Johnnie Cochran states, "For some time, it has been open season on African American males." He further observes that white people have a "tendency to want to bring down" blacks who have achieved any degree of success.[161] Black newspaper columnist Playthell Benjamin, meanwhile, laments "the rising tide of cynicism" among black youth—a cynicism fed by their "increasing knowledge of the history of American racism, whose legacy of dispossession is the cross they must bear, although most white Americans deny it."[162] "Basically," says publisher and author Haki Madhubuti, "we [blacks] are at war."[163]

People of the "civil rights" vision, black and white, typically claim that white racism touches virtually every aspect of American life. "This is still a profoundly racist country," says author and lecturer Paul Robeson, Jr., "meaning [that] the majority of white people are still racist, to one degree or another. . . . All institutions in this country are, to one degree or another, infected by racism."[164] In a like manner, professor Roger Wilkins declares, "Black people know there is an enormous amount of racism that results in the decimation of their communities."[165] Black professor Henry Louis Gates, Jr. puts it most succinctly: "Racism has become fashionable once again."[166]

Legal scholar Richard Delgado asserts that racism "infects our economic institutions, our cultural and political institutions, and the daily interactions of individuals."[167] State Supreme Court judge Ivan Warner of the Bronx calls "the entire United States" a "racist society."[168] "Everybody of Caucasian descent," adds white political scientist Andrew Hacker, "believes that we belong to a superior strain. Most white people believe that persons with African ancestries are more likely to carry primitive traits in their genes."[169]

Black Nobel laureate Toni Morrison laments that racism "has assumed a metaphorical life so completely embedded in daily discourse that it is perhaps more necessary and more on display than ever before."[170] According to author Kenneth Jackson, "Although the [Ku Klux] Klan is no longer effective, the Klan mentality remains."[171] Elaine Jones of the NAACP Legal Defense and Education Fund agrees that the Klan's views "are shared quietly by many others."[172] Such rhetoric, naturally, fosters great racial antipathy in the black community—a feeling which activist Sonny Carson candidly expressed when he proclaimed himself to be "antiwhite."[173]

Virtually all "civil rights leaders" contend that violent interracial crimes targeting blacks offer compelling evidence of America's racist character. Emmett Burns, a national director of the NAACP, recently lamented that white-on-black violence was "rearing its ugly head again."[174] In August 1991 Al Sharpton led more than 300 black marchers through a mostly white section of Brooklyn, protesting a series of white-on-black assaults that had occurred in that neighborhood during the preceding six weeks. "No justice! No peace!" the marchers chanted as they moved through the Brooklyn streets—carrying not only the red, black, and green flag of black liberation, but also a placard reading, "The white man is the devil."[175] Sharpton has spearheaded many similar marches in more recent times as well, some of them drawing thousands of participants.

After a white Ukrainian immigrant robbed and murdered entertainer Bill Cosby's son in 1997, the slain man's mother Camille theorized that the killer had learned to hate blacks through the racism that was "omnipresent and eternalized in America's institutions, media, and myriad entities."[176] "I believe," she elaborated, "America taught our son's killer to hate African Americans."[177]

Some go so far as to suggest that acts of white-on-black aggression are not necessarily isolated, unrelated events, but may in fact be part of a carefully orchestrated antiblack conspiracy. Theories of whites plotting to destroy the black race have gained considerable popularity in recent years. The National Urban League, for example, alleges that addictive drugs are sold to blacks as part of an extermination campaign masterminded by whites.[178] Along similar lines, *The New York Times* reported in August 1991:

> [P]olling data show that a substantial number of blacks are wondering about conspiracies. As black America gropes for a way to understand the plagues of AIDS, crack, violence and poverty, many black broadcasts and publications have been asking whether white conspirators are plotting blacks' destruction. . . .
>
> Though still a clear minority, some blacks . . . have even embraced the theory that whites created the AIDS virus as a means of racial warfare. Polling data have shown that larger numbers say white conspirators channel drugs into black neighborhoods in order to weaken the population. . . .
>
> [S]ome prominent blacks say the conspiratorial thinking is on the rise. What the theories have in common is the idea that woes like the drug trade stem not simply from white neglect but from white intent—from plans carefully calculated and implemented.[179]

A black newspaper, the *Los Angeles Sentinel*, concluded a 1989 series of AIDS-related articles with a piece entitled, "Blacks Intentionally Infected."[180] That same year, Black Entertainment Television devoted a public-affairs program to the topic, "Black Genocide: Myth or Reality?"[181] In September 1990 *Essence* magazine, whose circulation approaches one million, asked in a headline, "AIDS: Is It Genocide?"[182] In a poll of black Americans that year, roughly 10 percent of all respondents, regardless of educational background, professed to believe with certainty that the HIV virus which causes AIDS "was deliberately created in a laboratory in order to infect black people."[183] Among black college graduates who were asked whether this conspiracy theory *might* be true, the figure was a stunning 31 percent.[184] In 1991 the popular comedian Bill Cosby expressed his own suspicion that AIDS had been developed, presumably by white scientists, "to get after certain people." He admitted that he had no proof but maintained, "I just have a feeling."[185]

Even today, polls continue to show that about one in ten blacks feel certain that AIDS is part of a racist genocidal plot.[186] Activist Steven Cokely, for one, bluntly asserts that Jewish doctors inject blacks with the deadly virus.[187] In December 1998 master of ceremonies Al Sharpton hosted an AIDS Forum in Harlem featuring a dozen guest speakers, all but one of whom professed to believe that the disease was actually engineered by white racists. To the thunderous applause of a black audience grateful that the truth, as they saw it, was finally being told, some of the speakers suggested that whites were using blacks as guinea pigs in secret medical experiments. Others theorized that the ultimate goal was the outright extermination of blacks.[188] Curiously absent from these and similar speculations, however, was any acknowledgment of the fact that between 1985 and 1996, more than half of all Americans who contracted AIDS were white.[189]

Calling white racism a problem that "the entire nation has to deal with,"[190] Jesse Jackson professes to yearn for a future "in which white Americans will have grown, by overcoming their unfounded fears" of black people.[191] He adds:

> Racism is a deeply ingrained congenital deformity in the U.S. It is at the root of our society and it is the rot in our national character. Its contemporary manifestations may be less crude than in the past . . . but they are more manipulative and insidious. The new America utilizes a few black people in essentially racist congregations to prove that the church and its theology are not racist. Take, for instance, the use of black athletes on campuses, as if they are a part of it, when in fact they are used as trained animals to attract prestige and money for the schools. Schools that once locked blacks out are now locking them into the roll [*sic*] of gladiators for entertainment.[192]

Jackson attributes most black problems to the stresses created by racial injustice:

> When people's backs are against the wall, some choose to fight for more education. Some tend to fight back by making the most of their meager income. But some also tend to withdraw in despair and cynicism, feeling that nothing will work. They turn to liquor, drugs, and the pursuit of pleasure in an attempt to escape the pain. Others find their basic fulfillment and gratification in sex without love, discipline, or education, or they make unwanted and unhealthy babies. Some turn to violence, turning on each other instead of to each other.[193]

The "civil rights" vision of the past three decades has taught millions of Americans that most whites are naturally hostile toward blacks—and that blacks, consequently, have comparatively few opportunities to better their own lives. As a result, our country is now filled with the voices—loud and soft, famous and obscure, thundered before large audiences and whispered in private conversations—of blacks who consider white oppression to be their primary obstacle in life. In a 1989 ABC/*Washington Post* survey, 26 percent of blacks agreed that *most* whites shared the racist views of the Ku Klux Klan. Moreover, fully 51 percent believed that *at least one-fourth* of whites had KKK attitudes.[194] Between 1983 and 1994, the proportion of blacks believing that "most white people" wanted to see them "get a better break" dwindled from 33 percent to 25 percent. Meanwhile, the fraction who thought that most whites either wanted to "keep blacks down" or did not care either way rose from 50 percent to 67 percent.[195] A 1995 *Washington Post*/Kaiser Foundation survey of blacks found that 68 percent saw racism as a "big problem" in American society, and that 71 percent thought blacks had "less opportunity" than whites to "live a middle-class lifestyle."[196]

Clearly, ours is a nation pointing an accusatory finger at white racism to explain an enormous array of perceived transgressions. Let us determine whether that finger is pointed in the right direction.

Chapter 3

Deaths Remembered and Lives Forgotten

Half the truth is often a great lie.
—Benjamin Franklin[1]

Late on the night of December 19, 1986, three black men walked into the New Park Pizzeria in Howard Beach, a predominantly white, middle-class neighborhood in Queens, New York. Their car having broken down nearby, the men had come to the restaurant in search of a telephone.[2] When they stepped back outside a short time later, they encountered a group of about a dozen white teenagers who shouted racial epithets and threatened the blacks with a baseball bat and tree limbs. The blacks, in response, flashed a knife at the whites, spat into the face of one, and returned the racial insults.[3] In the ensuing melee, one of the blacks, twenty-year-old Timothy Grimes, was hit on the head with a bat and ran off. The two others later managed to escape through a hole in a nearby fence, but only after having been badly beaten. One of the fleeing blacks, twenty-three-year-old Michael Griffith, ran onto Shore Parkway, where he was struck and killed by a passing car.[4]

The public clamor over this incident was deafening, the media coverage immense. Michael Griffith's death, in the words of columnist Joseph Sobran, "set off a verbal riot in the media—a terrifying wave of editorials, follow-ups, opinion columns, Op-Ed pieces, sermons, [and] analyses."[5] Newspapers, magazines, and broadcast stations across the nation examined the attack in extraordinary depth, their reports liberally peppered with such phrases as: "the cancer of racism"; "Howard Beach is only a symptom"; "alarming increase of racial incidents"; "nationwide pattern"; "climate that encourages racism"; "signals that racism is again respectable";[6] "insensitive to the concerns of blacks"; "worst residual instincts among whites"; and "the historical experience of racial oppression."[7]

"Civil rights leaders" and demonstrators poured into the streets to protest this white-on-black attack, their every step shadowed by legions of reporters and television camera crews.[8] Prominent writers nationwide all had a say about the incident.[9] "People seem to think it's open season on blacks," said the executive editor of the black newspaper *Chicago Defender*.[10] A *Newsweek* headline asked ominously, "Is overt racism once again a national problem?"[11] The corresponding article reported that racially motivated violence "is on the increase nationwide," as demonstrated by "a steady increase in the number of cases involving attacks on blacks moving into white neighborhoods. Around the country, there has been a spate of publicized racial flare-ups."[12] Prominently displayed alongside the *Newsweek* piece was a photograph of crosses burning at a Ku Klux Klan rally in Georgia.[13] A "new racial atmosphere," the article asserted, had "emboldened [white] hate groups" across the United States.[14]

In another review of the Howard Beach episode, *Newsweek* reiterated its claim that white-on-black violence was becoming a major epidemic: "New York's black leaders almost all agree that racial strains are [a significant problem]. They cite a run of incidents that have heightened fear and anger among city blacks the past few years."[15] Similarly, a *New York Times* writer noted that the city had been plagued by white-on-black violence before:

> Last May, a 20-year-old man, Samuel B. Spencer 3d, who was black, was beaten and stabbed to death in an attack that occurred after his bicycle had collided with a car in the Coney Island section. All those arrested in the case were white. [And] in June 1982,

William Turks, 34, a transit worker of Far Rockaway, Queens, was beaten to death by a group of white men.[16]

Attorney Alton Maddox denounced New York's "pattern of racially motivated violence" and called the criminal-justice system "ill-equipped to deal with it."[17] NAACP executive director Benjamin Hooks saw the Howard Beach attack as symptomatic of white racism's disturbing resurgence in America. He blamed President Reagan for this development, explaining that "there is a steady drumbeat from this administration . . . that somehow white males are being mistreated . . . [and] that blacks just have too much done for them."[18] A *New York Times* Op-Ed piece also blamed Reagan, drawing a parallel between the seemingly irrational behavior of the Howard Beach teens and the U.S. economy's escalating deficit. In one of recent journalism's longer logical leaps, the *Times* stated that "President Reagan's deficit, indeed, institutionalizes irrationality."[19]

New York City mayor Ed Koch called the Howard Beach attack "the number one case in the city," likening the actions of the white gang to "the kind of lynching party that took place in the Deep South."[20] Calling for a federal commission to study the "cancer" of racism,[21] Mr. Koch added, "This is the most horrendous incident of violence in the nine years I have been Mayor. We have 1,800 murders a year in this city and they're all bad, but this was the worst murder I believe has taken place in the modern era."[22]

Black civic and political leaders said the attack was evidence that racially motivated violence was a "pervasive problem and not an isolated one."[23] "People are angry and looking for ways to channel their anger," explained Laura Blackburne, counsel for the state conference of NAACP chapters.[24] Activist attorney C. Vernon Mason lamented that in recent times it had become "more acceptable for whites to take the law into their own hands" in conflicts with blacks.[25] The Reverend Calvin Butts, pastor of Harlem's Abyssinian Baptist Church, was "outraged at this overt display of the most vile and ugly kind of racism."[26] Many whites, too, were quick to jump on the passing band-wagon denouncing white racism. New York Civil Liberties Union executive director Norman Siegel proclaimed, "When an act of racial violence occurs, people in the community must speak out, because silence can be read as approving or tolerating racial bigotry."[27]

Two days after the December 19 altercation, thirty carloads

of blacks conducted a protest at the Howard Beach pizzeria where the trouble had all begun. Once congregated, the demonstrators repeatedly intoned, "We shall overcome" and "I am somebody"[28]—implying that societal respect for blacks remained a distant, unrealized dream.

At Michael Griffith's funeral, the Reverend Robert Seay characterized Griffith's killing as a symptom of white America's disdain for the black race.[29] "We wonder why we must continually go through this," Seay told the mourners. "Michael is the victim of a system that perpetuates the inferiority of a certain group of people."[30] Shortly thereafter, Benjamin Chavis announced plans for a large protest to be held later that day. "Our goal," he explained, "is to build up enough momentum to make New York take account of itself."[31]

The protest drew more than 1,200 participants who, once assembled, were told by Benjamin Hooks that the Howard Beach incident was just one of many racially motivated white-on-black attacks that were occurring all over the nation.[32] "These are our streets," shouted one ardent demonstrator. "We should be able to walk wherever we want to."[33] After the Reverend Edward Peters played a cassette recording of a 1963 speech by Martin Luther King, Jr.,[34] groups of marchers chanted in rap style: "Beat, beat back, beat back the racist attacks," and "Segregation here, apartheid there—smash racism everywhere."[35] Yet while New York was engrossed with the marchers and speeches, virtually no one noticed that on that very same day Timothy Grimes—one of the three black victims of the white gang in question—was arrested for stabbing the woman with whom he lived.[36] Within a year, he would also be arrested for pimping a fifteen-year-old girl and shooting his brother in the eye.[37] Was he a man of questionable character? Might his volatile temper have helped escalate the skirmish outside the New Park Pizzeria? Strangely, no one asked.

The Sunday following Michael Griffith's death, the Reverend Timothy Mitchell warned his parishioners that New York City was infested with racism. "What happened to Michael Griffith can happen to any one of us," he said. "The issue is whether we are free to walk around in our city and be seen and protected as God's children."[38]

New York governor Mario Cuomo took the local district attorney off the case and named a special prosecutor.[39] Asserting that Griffith's death represented "new evidence of pernicious violence that's rooted apparently in bias and hatred," the governor pledged to establish a task force on bias-related violence.[40] It was essential, he said, "to take a renewed look at the causes of this form of violence and to develop remedies and strategies, in addition to those already provided in our criminal-justice system, that attack the roots of hatred that result in violence against others."[41] New York's board of education, meanwhile, swiftly introduced a new curriculum intended to promote ethnic and racial harmony. A 246-page study guide called *Roots of Oppression, Seeds of Change*, along with a lesson book titled *The Struggle for Human Rights*, exhorted students to repudiate the evils of racism.[42]

All of the foregoing strategies, statements, and protests were generated, of course, by an incident that "civil rights leaders" and journalists alike attributed to unadulterated white bigotry. Even when black friends of the white Howard Beach assailants denied that the latter were racists, not the slightest dent was put into society's ironclad consensus that the entire affair had been racially motivated.[43] Given this characterization of the case, several mobs of bat-wielding blacks ambushed white victims in retaliation, shouting "Howard Beach! Howard Beach!" during their assaults.[44]

The white youths responsible for Michael Griffith's death were eventually convicted by a jury—not of murder, but of less-serious manslaughter charges, since they did not actually kill the victim themselves. According to attorney C. Vernon Mason, however, these lesser convictions merely reflected "the inability of the majority community to come to grips with their own prejudices in this city."[45] Following the verdict, hundreds of black demonstrators blocked rush-hour traffic in Manhattan and Brooklyn, protesting the "re-emergence of racial intolerance."[46]

Hardly anyone ever heard that on the very night of Griffith's death, in a separate incident only two blocks away from the infamous New Park Pizzeria, several youths viciously beat a white off-duty fireman with a bat, a stick, and their fists—inflicting serious eye, back, leg, and shoulder injuries.[47] Eyewitness descriptions of that gang and its weapons were identical to those of the thugs who attacked Griffith and his companions. Might the same group have been responsible for both incidents? If so, might it be that the attack on Griffith was motivated by something other than race? Not a single "leader" in the black community even posed this question.

The Deafening Silence

In stark contrast to the uproar over Michael Griffith's death in Howard Beach, comparatively few people took notice of the *thousands* of black Americans who fell prey to *black* assailants in the ensuing months and years. With no racial angle to spotlight, the media gave those cases only scant coverage—while the self-appointed "activists" who had been so vocal and visible in Howard Beach were suddenly silent and out of sight. Consider just a few of the black-on-black tragedies they ignored:

• One week after the death of Michael Griffith, twenty-two-year-old Elgin Yates of Connecticut became angered when a teenage male acquaintance disparaged the physical appearance of Yates's girlfriend—sparking a violent argument during which the youngster stabbed Yates to death.[48]

• On February 11, 1991, eighteen-year-old Louis Hairston became involved in an after-school fight with sixteen-year-old Andre Frank in Mount Vernon, New York. The altercation escalated, culminating with a fatal gunshot to the younger boy's abdomen.[49]

• On February 26, 1992, students Tyrone Sinkler and Ian Moore were shot and killed in a corridor of New York's Thomas Jefferson High School by a fellow pupil.[50]

• One April afternoon in 1993, sixteen-year-old Christian Abapka was playing basketball in a Brooklyn schoolyard with his two teenage brothers. During the course of their game, the ball bounced off the rim and onto an adjacent court, where it struck another youth on the head. When Abapka went to retrieve the ball, he was stabbed in the chest and killed by this other youngster.[51]

• Jeffrey Seymour was a Jamaican immigrant who worked as a building superintendent in Harlem. As he finished his chores on June 27, 1993, two teenagers shot him three times in the head and killed him.[52]

• Six weeks later a thirty-two-year-old parolee went on a violent rampage in Brooklyn. On August 12 he sodomized a young woman at gunpoint. Later that day he shot two people, killing one and seriously wounding the other. Two days after that, he shot and killed two men outside a grocery store in Bedford Stuyvesant. Four minutes later and two blocks away, he shot another man in the face during a robbery. Five minutes after that, he shot and killed an unarmed security guard.[53]

• While Elvis Malcolm was returning home from work on October 20, 1993, three men broke into the Bronx apartment he shared with his wife and children. After gagging and binding the youngsters, the intruders demanded money from Mrs. Malcolm, who told them that a downstairs neighbor was holding some cash for her. The thieves promptly put her in a headlock, held a gun to her neck, and led her down the stairs. On the second-floor landing they unexpectedly encountered Mr. Malcolm, shot him dead, and then fled.[54]

• On April 4, 1994, two youths in a Brooklyn subway station shot an honors student to death simply for having looked at them "the wrong way."[55]

• Later that month a drug dealer murdered an eighty-eight-year-old Harlem grandmother by smashing a glass bottle over her head. For the next two days he casually stepped over the dead woman's body and picked through her belongings, which he eventually exchanged for vials of crack cocaine.[56]

• In July 1996 a twenty-seven-year-old intruder murdered three women in a New York City second-story apartment, brutally tortured a fourth, and raped a fifth. One of the two surviving victims managed to escape by jumping out a window. At his court sentencing thirty months later, the remorseless culprit mockingly winked and smiled not only at both survivors, but also at his dead victims' family members.[57]

• In January 1999 four Brooklyn teenagers chased and assaulted fifteen-year-old Michael Bennett following an argument over a neighborhood basketball game in which they had just participated. A fifth assailant then plunged a knife into Bennett's chest, killing him.[58]

The cases mentioned here, of course, are but a tiny fraction of the myriad black-on-black assaults that needlessly spill innocent blood every year. Because these crimes are such common events, they draw little public notice and render even the most vocal black activists mute. In the eyes of such "leaders," *white*-on-black transgressions are testaments to racism, while *black*-on-black offenses are meaningless. Indeed, in the wake of Bennett's killing, the organizer of a local neighborhood outreach program benignly described the assailants as "typical young people" who had simply gotten "caught in the fit of the moment."[59] "All of these young men," he added compassionately, "have little, beautiful things about them that will never be told because everything about them will be gauged through this one senseless act."[60] Such comments were certainly a far cry from the virtually universal depictions of the white Howard Beach youths as cold-blooded, racist killers.

A similar double standard pervades journalism as well. *Newsweek*, for instance, noted that the killing of Michael Griffith "instantly turned the tiny community of Howard Beach into a symbol of racial division in New York City."[61] But if that is true, then what do the black-on-black attacks cited in this chapter—and innumerable others like them—symbolize? Apparently, to *Newsweek* and the media at large, they symbolize nothing. As Patrick Buchanan observes, "Howard Beach . . . has been converted, by ideologues and demagogues, into a synonym for white racism, because of a single fatal incident. Meanwhile, 10,000 felonies emanating from Harlem [presumably] tell us nothing about Harlem."[62]

From Anger to Indifference

While many in the black community remain largely indifferent to black-on-black assaults, they are quick to erupt with outrage at almost any rumor—however unsubstantiated—of an *interracial* attack against a black. Consider a July 1993 incident in Brooklyn, when a twenty-five-year-old black man entered a Korean-owned market and ordered a sandwich, demanding that the worker wash his hands before touching any food. After the men argued for a moment, the customer pulled a gun from his waistband and tried to shoot the market owner. The weapon misfired, however, and when the gunman pulled the trigger a second time, a stray bullet struck and killed a black bystander. In the confusion following the incident, a rumor circulated through the neighborhood that a *Korean* had shot the black victim— prompting dozens of local blacks to rush to the store in protest. The tension abated only after community-affairs police officers, fearing a riot, hurriedly spread the word that the killer was in fact black.[63]

For Brooklyn's black community, the slaying of a black man, when thought to have been perpetrated by a member of another race, was cause for fury—perhaps even violence. Yet the moment it was learned that the killer was black, all indignation vanished. Black columnist Joseph Perkins describes such glaring examples of selective outrage as "one of the great hypocrisies"[64] of the black community:

> When white victimizes black there is protest. The churches are packed. The streets are filled. But when black victimizes black there is silence. The pews are empty, the streets vacant.
>
> The explanation of this phenomenon is that black-on-black crime has no political currency. It cannot be traded upon the way that white-on-black crime can.
>
> As long as black Americans can be portrayed as victims of societal and institutional injustice, we [blacks] can make claims on the system.
>
> To listen to Jesse Jackson, Benjamin Chavis and other prominent black leaders in the wake of the [Rodney] King verdict [see chapter 5 for details], one almost came away with the impression that America had returned to the days when black lynchings were commonplace.
>
> "It makes me weep to think that we have to always continually go through this much drama to get some justice," said a misty-eyed Jackson. "We've learned when you get some justice, you have to fight for the rest," said a defiant Chavis.[65]

Perkins further points out that while "leaders" like Jackson and Chavis depict white racism as black America's greatest problem, they refuse to discuss "the dirty little secret"[66] of black-on-black crime:

> The prospect of a black being physically attacked by a white is far less likely than a black being killed—not just assaulted—by a person of his own race. Consider that in 1992, the FBI reported 1,689 racially motivated attacks against blacks. This number is troubling, but not nearly so profoundly as the 8,000 or so black homicides last year, roughly 95 percent of which were committed by other blacks.
>
> Whenever there is a so-called hate crime against a black person, it is treated as front-page news. If it is sensational enough, maybe Jesse [Jackson] and Ben [Chavis] will come to town. But when there is a black-on-black murder, the story is relegated to the back pages, if that. It is too routine an occurrence to rate more than a passing notice. . . . The threat of a black being victimized by a white is fairly remote. The chances of blacks falling prey to one of their own is 10 times greater.[67]

After the Howard Beach attack, "civil rights" defenders solemnly reminded whites that segregation was over—and that blacks were entitled to walk in any part of town without fear of attack. The implication, of course, was that blacks who entered certain white neighborhoods did so at great personal risk. But as Perkins explains, black Americans are actually in far greater danger when they walk through *black* neighborhoods:

> Just visit South Central Los Angeles or south Dallas or southeast Washington, D.C. The black residents of these neighborhoods are afraid to move about. They fear that if they stop at a traffic light, they might be rousted from their car by a "jacker." That if they stand on the wrong corner, they might catch an errant bullet from a drive-by shooting.
>
> The black inner cities have become urban jungles and young black males the predators. While black men aged 15 to 24 constitute 1 percent of the U.S. population, they commit [30][68] percent of the nation's murders. A young black man growing up in the ghetto has a better chance of dying from a bullet than from heart disease, auto accidents, suicide or cancer—the leading causes of death for virtually every other segment of the population.
>
> [While] the black community [is] prepared to protest, to riot even [when a white person violates one of its members], nary a voice is raised in sympathy to the thousands of blacks who lose their lives year by year at the hands of their violent young men.[69]

Like black-on-black transgressions, white-on-white offenses are also uninteresting to most journalists and community "leaders." Consider, for instance, the lack of public outrage elicited by a barbaric white-on-white attack in New York's Prospect Park in 1987. A man and woman were sleeping outdoors under a blanket one August morning, when three teenagers poured gasoline over them and lit them on fire. Mayor Koch contrasted the scant attention this case received to the uproar over the Howard Beach affair:

> It brings to mind the terrible incident that occurred when a group of twelve whites attacked three black men who appeared in their neighborhood, chasing one onto a highway and to his death. The outrage then was clear and public, as it should have been. Ministers, priests, rabbis, activists, and editorial writers all joined in, and they and I expressed horror at the incident as vigorously as we knew how.
>
> What shocks me now is the lack of outrage at the Prospect Park incident. Is it because both the victims and the accused perpe-

trators are of the same race and that the incident, therefore, could not be viewed as a racial matter? Are we at a point at which we can only be outraged at viciousness if it can be placed in a racial setting? What should infuriate us is evil acts, not the color of the actors.[70]

Predictably, attorney C. Vernon Mason disparaged Mr. Koch's comments. "It is totally unnecessary, unfair, and insensitive," said Mason, "to try to compare some sick individuals [those involved in the Prospect Park burning] with the kind of racially motivated incidents that have occurred too often in this city. I don't know why [Koch's] advisors would permit him to say something like that."[71] In Mason's view, whites who attack blacks are racist predators, while people who attack someone of their own race are merely "sick."

The attack on Michael Griffith and his companions in Howard Beach may or may not have been racially motivated. Of greater import, however, is *why* that incident was singled out for the massive publicity it received from journalists and "civil rights" groups alike. A white-on-black assault of that nature is a relatively rare occurrence in modern-day America (see statistics in chapter 4). *Why*, then, was so unusual an event portrayed as an important social indicator, while incidents infinitely more common are routinely ignored?

Chapter 4

The Double Standard of Bloodshed

Ignorance is preferable to error; and he is less remote
from truth who believes nothing than
he who believes what is wrong.
—Thomas Jefferson[1]

"Whose streets? Our streets! What's coming? War!" This was the chant of the indignant protesters marching along Flatbush Avenue in Brooklyn's Bensonhurst section on August 31, 1989—the "Day of Outrage." Nearly 8,000 people—most of them African Americans—had assembled to express their anger over the death of Yusef Hawkins, a local black teenager who had been shot and killed by a gang of young whites eight days earlier.[2] Leading the demonstration was Sonny Carson, a convicted kidnapper-turned-"community organizer."[3] Also in the throng's vanguard were twelve marchers carrying two symbolic coffins, one in memory of Hawkins and the other in tribute to former Black Panther Huey Newton, who had been gunned down in Oakland the week before. Though Newton was killed by a paroled black criminal in a drug dispute,[4] the demonstrators nonetheless viewed him as a martyr for the cause of civil rights.

As the demonstration progressed, the crowd's collective

mantra took the form of "No justice, no peace."[5] "Our right," shouted one marcher, "is to fight for our freedom. If there is no justice, there will never be freedom in New York City."[6] "People have had enough," cried another.[7] Before long, the protesters pushed themselves into a police line designed to prevent them from blocking rush-hour traffic over the Brooklyn Bridge. Many threw bricks and bottles at the officers, injuring 44 of the 300 policemen on hand.[8]

Prominent blacks from coast to coast rushed to denounce the killing of Yusef Hawkins. According to Dr. Carolyn Goodman, the mother of a civil rights worker slain twenty-five years earlier, the taking of Hawkins's life was "certainly much reminiscent to what went on openly in the South. My feeling is we have to use every form of protest that we have, whether in the streets, the council chambers, the courts."[9] "[T]he clock has run out," she added, "and we've got to move on every front."[10] Benjamin Hooks agreed that public protests were "very necessary in this situation."[11] "In 1989," he cautioned, "we cannot let it appear that any section of the country is off-limits to blacks. When I was growing up in Memphis, there were any number of neighborhoods where blacks could not walk through, couldn't even think about sitting down in. We dare not allow that any more."[12]

The Reverend Herbert Daughtry asserted that black people nationwide were engaged in a desperate struggle against white tyranny. "The wonder of it all," he said, "is that New York has not exploded."[13] When asked to comment on why the Bensonhurst protesters had injured dozens of police officers, he refused to blame the unruly crowd. "I don't know who threw the first what, who swung the first what," said Daughtry. "But it needs to be put in the context of all the years that we [blacks] have been subjected to the denials, the oppression, the brutality, and the killings."[14] Suggesting that the actions of the white Bensonhurst assailants spoke for white America generally, he condemned not only Yusef Hawkins's actual killers, but all of Western civilization—with its "contempt for and destruction of African humanity."[15] In a long letter to *The New York Times*, Daughtry wrote, "Humanity wrapped in ebony hue is [in the eyes of society] of less value than white humanity. Therefore, it can be denied basic human and legal rights. It can be brutalized. It can be killed—as in Bensonhurst—and nothing is supposed to happen to the culprits."[16] He lamented that recent years had brought an "escalation of bias-related violence [against blacks] from both the public and private sectors."[17] The black community's tolerance for white assaults was virtually spent, he warned, closing his letter with this ominous paragraph:

> New York is a powder keg. African Americans have had enough. We have exercised superlative patience. We have boycotted, marched, demonstrated, begged and prayed. It is incredible that black ministers are still willing to go to the scenes of racial murders and pray. Something has got to give. A change must come. No people can be expected to continue to absorb this kind of pain and not explode.[18]

Jesse Jackson, claiming that the killing of Hawkins had created "a political crisis" in New York City,[19] viewed the incident as an indication that the civil liberties of blacks everywhere were under assault. On September 19 he exhorted a crowd of cheering high-school students in Bensonhurst to reaffirm the victories of early civil rights leaders who had sacrificed their lives in the black struggle for equality.[20] "You are the only ones who can assure that their death was not in vain," Jackson told the youngsters.[21] "This was a racially motivated killing characteristic of the Deep South in its worst days," he said on another occasion.[22] Repeatedly fed such rhetoric, the black community inflated to monstrous proportions the social significance of Hawkins's death. A Harlem rap concert honoring the young man's memory drew at least 10,000 people.[23]

During the first week of the 1989 school year, nearly every class in the New York City public-school system participated in discussions and assemblies focusing on the fate of Yusef Hawkins.[24] By September 18 the board of education had furnished all city teachers with lesson plans for a "multicultural" curriculum "aimed at prompting students to discuss and analyze racial problems, in particular the Bensonhurst slaying."[25]

In a *New York Times* guest editorial, a young black man told of his personal struggle to survive the purportedly unceasing assaults of America's white racists.[26] He cited his inability to walk in many parts of New York City without fearing for his safety—"just because I am an African American."[27] Convinced that there were "gangs of white people just waiting to kill me," he worried that his black skin might in fact be his "death warrant."[28] He even wondered whether whites secretly desired to intern all blacks in extermination camps.[29]

When the white teens responsible for Hawkins's death went on trial, groups of black demonstrators gathered outside the court-house to demand justice. One protester burned an American flag and denounced "the racism in America and this here lynching going on."[30] "We African people are tired of being murdered," said another. "Do you know how many millions of blacks have been killed?"[31] Activist Viola Plummer warned, "From this day forward, for every black child that we bury, we are going to bury five of theirs."[32]

What really happened that August night in Bensonhurst when Yusef Hawkins was killed? A gang of young white men armed with baseball bats viciously attacked four blacks who they thought had come to visit a local white girl. During the beating one of the attackers, Joseph Fama, yelled, "To hell with beating them up, forget the bats, I'm going to shoot the nigger." He then drew a gun and shot the six-teen-year-old Hawkins to death.[33]

Was this killing racially motivated? Perhaps so, though there is considerable evidence to the contrary. While the incident was consis-tently portrayed as one in which the whites were looking to assault any blacks they could find, they were in fact agitated over the possibility that their "turf" was being "invaded" by a *specific* group of blacks. Prior to attacking, they repeatedly asked each other, "Are these the guys?"[34] By the time Fama drew his gun, most of the whites—realiz-ing that Hawkins and his companions were not the individuals they were seeking—implored Fama not to shoot, but to no avail. The purely racial explanation is further discredited by the fact that one of the young men who had helped the group round up bats for the attack was Russell Gibbons, a black.[35]

For argument's sake, however, let us momentarily assume that the attack *was* racially motivated. What, then, does such a criminal act, by whites against a black, tell us about our society? As author and social commentator Jared Taylor explains, it simply tells us "that with-out a doubt, there are some whites in America who do ugly things to blacks. However, in a nation of a quarter of a billion people, there will always be a few whites who do ugly things to blacks."[36] It does *not* tell us that most white Americans are racists who, if given a chance, would gladly deprive blacks of their civil rights, if not their lives. "If America were seething with white racism," writes Taylor, "this sort of thing would presumably be happening all the time. It is because it *so rarely happens* that Howard Beach and Bensonhurst became huge sensations. They were proof, they were The Real Thing, racism at its murderous worst. They were what the believers in white wickedness are hunting for."[37]

One month after Yusef Hawkins's killing, the Bronx was the site of an almost identical crime committed by *blacks*—which news reporters largely ignored. A white driver got out of his car to use a public telephone on East Tremont Avenue and was confronted by two blacks who said, "What are you white guys doing [here]? You don't belong here." An argument ensued, during which one of the blacks drew a gun and shot the white man in the stomach. A local black minister, when asked later to comment on this incident, groped for explanations other than racism. "I don't know that that's racism as I define it," he said. "There's a difference between racism and revenge."[38] Perhaps the black assailants, from his perspective, were carrying out retribution for the historical injustices their ancestors had suffered. In this view, black lawbreakers are freedom fighters, not criminals.

Black-on-White Crimes Ignored

One evening in July 1988, as a twenty-three-year-old white named Danny Gilmore drove his pickup truck through a black Cleveland neighborhood, a black man on a moped inadvertently bumped Gilmore's truck and fell to the ground, uninjured. Almost instantly, some forty local residents converged on the scene of the accident and brutally beat Gilmore. The victim managed to break free momentarily, but as he tried to flee he collapsed in front of his truck. At that point one of the attackers, encouraged by the cheering crowd, boarded the vehicle and proceeded to crush the hapless Gilmore to death under its wheels. This gruesome incident received little local coverage and no national attention.[39]

In the summer of 1990 Brian Watkins, a twenty-two-year-old white man from Utah, was visiting New York City with his parents. In a Manhattan subway station on the night of September 2, a gang of black and Hispanic teenagers ran toward the Watkinses—shouting, laughing, and demanding money from them. One of the youths slashed Brian's father with a box cutter and took his wallet. Another knocked Mrs. Watkins to the ground and kicked her head, while a third stabbed Brian in the chest, killing him. The attackers were arrested later that night in the nearby Roseland Ballroom, where they had gone dancing after the murder.[40] New York's black mayor, David Dinkins, reacted to the incident by lamenting the city's problem with "crime and violence," but made no reference to any possible racial motives for the killing. Similarly, black police commissioner Lee Brown characterized the attack as nothing more than "senseless violence" with "no rhyme or reason to it."[41]

In January 1991 a black man named Robert Herbert and three black companions agreed among themselves to kill the first white person they saw. The unfortunate victim of their gruesome pact was a college student from Boston named Mark Belmore, whom they stabbed to death. This story received only brief local media coverage,[42] while the apostles of "justice," predictably, had nothing to say. Also scarcely reported was the arrest, one month later, of a black Indiana man named Christopher Peterson for the shotgun murders of seven whites. Candidly acknowledging that he had "a deep-rooted hatred for white people,"[43] Peterson explained that he had killed for purely racial reasons.

In 1991-1992, Hulon Mitchell, leader of the black, Miami-based Yahweh sect, was tried and convicted of some of the most astonishing antiwhite murders in American history. Mitchell taught a "Killing Class" during which he instructed his students to seek out and destroy "white devils."[44] "One day, Yahweh is going to kill the white devil off the planet," he proclaimed. "We're going to catch him and we're going to kill him wherever we find him. All over America, white heads are going to roll!"[45] A former sect member testified in January 1992 that he himself had killed three whites on orders from Mitchell—explaining that the Yahweh leader did not care whom he killed, so long as his victims were white. In total, sect members murdered at least seven people, beginning in 1986. These victims, whose ears or fingers were usually brought back to Mitchell as trophies,[46] were killed out of pure racial hatred. We can well imagine the national media circus that would have ensued had it been discovered that a *white* group was practicing the ritualistic, racially motivated murder and mutilation of *blacks*.[47] It should be noted, moreover, that the Yahweh trial was in progress concurrent with that of the four Los Angeles policemen who had beaten the now-famous Rodney King. Yet while King became the most talked-about man in America and was depicted as the ultimate victim of civil rights violations, the abominations of the Yahweh sect remained largely local news. Few outside of Miami ever heard about the case.[48]

On November 3, 1992, a black carjacker raped thirty-five-year-old Gail Shollar of New Jersey as her young daughter watched in horror. He then stabbed the woman forty times, disposed of her mangled corpse, and kidnapped the child. At his trial in 1995, he smirked and cursed at the dead victim's kin.[49]

On April 2, 1993, a thirty-nine-year-old German tourist named Barbara Meller-Jensen arrived in Miami with her two young children, rented a car, and proceeded to head for a vacation resort in Miami Beach. Unfortunately, she lost her way and drove into a blighted black neighborhood off Interstate 95. Seeing that Mrs. Jensen was obviously lost, two black outlaws in the vehicle behind hers knew they had come upon an easy prey. Using a tactic commonly employed by roadway robbers, the men intentionally bumped their car into Mrs. Jensen's.[50] When the woman stopped to inspect her vehicle for damage, they beat her, robbed her, and crushed her to death under the wheels of their car while her children looked on.[51] Within a few days this unspeakable tragedy was forgotten by the media and faded from public memory.

Russian-born Ifkiya Malayev immigrated to the U.S. in 1991 with his wife and two children. An engineer by trade but unable to secure employment in that field, he took a job driving a New York City taxi until, on April 19, 1993, he was robbed and shot to death by a black passenger.[52] Once again, an incident of black-on-white crime was uninteresting to journalists and "community activists" alike. A similar indifference attended an October 1992 tragedy in which three black Miami teenagers shot a German tourist while she and her family drove out of a McDonald's parking lot, leaving the woman's legs permanently paralyzed.[53]

In June 1993, white high-school drama teacher Allyn Winslow, biking in Brooklyn's Prospect Park, was accosted by four black teenagers who shouted, "Give us the bike, man! Give us the bike!" When the panicked man tried to flee, he was killed by five gunshots in the back. Once apprehended, the youths confessed to the crime and even admitted to police that they often went to the park to steal bicycles.[54] Notably, however, not a single "civil rights leader" questioned whether Winslow's murder was racially motivated.

In January 1998 a fifteen-year-old black member of the notorious Blood gang shot and killed Vitaly Bereslavsky, a hardworking Latvian immigrant in Brooklyn. The killer then robbed his dead victim of the two dollars in his pocket, and promptly spent the money on cupcakes and fruit punch at a nearby bodega. When investigators later asked him to explain his motives for the crime, the remorseless youth replied tersely, "I was hungry."[55]

One night in 1990 three black men committed a crime that closely paralleled the infamous Howard Beach attack. Angered by an earlier altercation in which they had exchanged racial slurs with a white man, the three blacks vented their rage by brutally beating another white, twenty-one-year-old Robert Massaro of Milwaukee. When the victim managed to break away, his attackers chased him into a lake, where he drowned.[56] This incident received little publicity and the assailants were lightly punished—their penalties consisting of a $500 fine, three years of probation, a community-service provision, and less than a year in prison.[57] The contrast to the political and social tumult created by the Howard Beach case could not have been more striking.[58] Black "leaders"—who had loudly denounced the "soft" punishments given to the white Howard Beach youths—were silent after Massaro's assailants were sentenced.

One May night that same year, a group of seven Tampa, Florida blacks encountered some white teenagers with whom they had previously fought. Most of the whites quickly fled, but the blacks managed to corner one of them and beat him to death with wooden two-by-fours, shouting with every blow, "Don't ever f—— with us again."[59] Like the Howard Beach case, this incident involved a gang surrounding a victim and assaulting him with wooden clubs. In Howard Beach, however, the white attackers did not beat Michael Griffith to death—whether by choice or as a consequence of his escape. Griffith, of course, was later killed accidentally by a passing car. The intent here is not to excuse the actions of that white gang, but rather to show the extreme double standard regulating media depictions of interracial crimes. Whereas the accidental death of a black man in Howard Beach was deemed a national crisis, a black gang's *intentional* clubbing to death of a white man in Tampa was barely reported at all.[60]

While Michael Griffith, Yusef Hawkins, Howard Beach, and Bensonhurst became virtual household words that remain familiar to millions of Americans even to this day, few people remember the names and grisly fates of the white victims named in this chapter. Their cases received only short-lived media coverage before vanishing from public consciousness. They were not repeatedly eulogized as casualties of interracial savagery. The cruelties inflicted on them inspired no "days of outrage." There was no suggestion that the brutality they suffered was a consequence of widespread black enmity toward whites. The selectively outspoken black "leadership" was silent. We did not hear Benjamin Hooks, or anyone like him, lament that parts of this country seemed to be "off-limits" to whites. Nor did we hear Herbert Daughtry, or anyone like him, ask whether whites might "explode" in response to black assaults on them. There were no editorials suggesting the possibility of a black conspiracy to effectively imprison whites behind bars of fear, if not to exterminate them. All was quiet, as if no one noticed that black-on-white—and, for that matter, black-on-black—attacks are far more commonplace than the white-on-black variety.

Burning with Hatred

Journalism's double standard displayed itself again in September 1993, when two interracial attacks in Florida were covered in remarkably dissimilar ways. In one case, two whites were convicted of having forced, at gunpoint, a black man named Christopher Wilson to drive to a deserted field, where they poured gasoline over him and lit him on fire.[61] Because virtually every media reference to this case noted its interracial nature, most Americans who ever heard about the incident—whether from television, radio, or newspaper—were well aware that it involved two whites who had tried to kill a black.

By contrast, consider how journalists reported a Miami incident that occurred the day after Christopher Wilson's attackers were convicted. Only minutes after having arrived from Germany with his pregnant wife, tourist Uwe-Wilhelm Rakebrand, while driving from the airport to a hotel, had his rental car repeatedly rammed from behind by a van. Realizing that he was the target of would-be robbers, Mr. Rakebrand did not stop. The pursuing van then pulled up alongside his car, and a passenger fired a single gunshot into Rakebrand's back, killing him.[62] When a black suspect was later arrested for the shooting, news reports made no mention of his race, identifying him only as a nineteen-year-old male. Nor was there any media speculation about possible racial motives for the crime. Even when it was learned that two black accomplices were still at large, not a single reporter identified their race—at a time when physical descriptions might arguably have helped the public lead police to the guilty parties.

On the very same day that it reported Mr. Rakebrand's murder, *The New York Times* carried a story about a California incident in which three whites were charged with killing a black woman in "a beating with racial overtones."[63] The bold headline read, "3 Charged in Black Woman's Beating Death."[64] While this murder may in fact have been racially motivated, we must wonder why news reporters and "civil rights leaders" customarily disregard that possibility when analyzing black-on-white attacks.

Even when separate crimes are virtually identical, race determines which ones will draw the most attention from demagogues and journalists alike. Compare Christopher Wilson's case to that of Brooklyn's Norma Reilly, a twenty-five-year-old black woman who died in 1990 when some local black gang members poured gasoline into her van and set it on fire while she slept inside the vehicle.[65] Miss Reilly's story made the papers for just one day and was strictly local news.

Similarly, there was not the slightest public outrage following a May 1995 incident in which five black Harlem teenagers spotted a homeless man asleep on a park bench, poured gasoline over his body, lit him on fire, and fled. Remarkably the victim survived, and less than a week later the same youngsters again found him sleeping in the park. They took this occasion to pound the man's head with five-pound cobblestones, rendering him comatose for two months and leaving him permanently brain-damaged. When detectives eventually apprehended the culprits and asked what their motives had been, they casually explained that it had all been "just for fun."[66] News reports of the attacks never identified the victim's race, and once again the "civil rights" crowd was silent.

Nor did even a single "activist" publicly condemn the October 18, 1995 killing of Richard Will, a white man who was doused with lighter fluid and set afire by a group of black youths in a Chicago suburb.[67] A black sociology professor from Northwestern University, in fact, ruled out racism as a possible motive, explaining that the attack on Will merely reflected the "growing level of hostility in poor black neighborhoods that the larger white society sees them as faceless."[68]

In much the same way, many also blamed "society" for the 1997 arson by which twelve-year-old Malcolm Shabazz killed his own grandmother Betty, the widow of Malcolm X. At Mrs. Shabazz's funeral, for instance, eulogist Maya Angelou urged mourners to have compassion for the young killer—reminding them, to loud applause, that he was a child of God whom society had "made" into a troubled, violent youngster.[69]

Color Them White

While black-on-white and *intra*racial crimes typically draw sparse journalistic, social, and political attention, reports of *white-on-black* transgressions evoke a multitude of loud and impassioned responses. Consider the great din triggered by New York's infamous 1992 "sneaker polish attack." Two black youngsters—a boy aged fourteen and his twelve-year-old sister—reported that while walking to school in the Bronx one morning, they had been punched, kicked, and robbed by four white teenagers. The girl recounted that one of the attackers had told her, "You're not getting out of here, you black bitch, until you give me some money." The culminating degradation occurred, said the victims, when their faces were sprayed with a white substance, believed to be sneaker polish, while the assailants shouted, "Y'all are going to be white today."[70]

This incident sparked immediate and extraordinary indignation throughout the city. Mayor David Dinkins, visibly angry, held a press conference at which he characterized the attack as "truly heinous."[71] It was "especially troubling," he said, "because the victims and the perpetrators are so young."[72] Lamenting that the assailants had been "taught to hate" by irresponsible parents,[73] the mayor vowed to "leave no stone unturned" in hunting down those responsible for this "dastardly deed."[74] A reward was offered for information leading to the identification and arrest of the guilty parties.[75]

Throughout the following day, the mayor consulted with city officials to devise a strategy that might "stop those who would spread hate."[76] Bronx borough president Fernando Ferrer organized a team of city officials and clergy to help local schoolchildren cope with whatever anguish the sneaker polish affair was causing them.[77] At Ferrer's suggestion, several Bronx ministers sermonized the following

Sunday about the evils of racism. Also at the borough president's urging, 100 extra police officers patrolled the area where the attack was said to have occurred.[78]

Searching for clues and witnesses, city police interviewed more than 100 people in the two days following the children's report of the attack.[79] Criminal-justice officials called for new laws that would make racially motivated "hate crimes" subject to harsher punishment.[80] "Words of condemnation and messages of good will are not enough," said the executive director of the New York Civil Rights Coalition. "This problem must be addressed more forcefully and systematically."[81] A group called the Partnership of Faith gathered at City Hall to denounce a "virus [of racism] that has turned into a disease that has grown into an epidemic in the city."[82] Al Sharpton led a demonstration outside the 49th Precinct police station and announced his intention to put "pressure on the police to make an arrest" in the case.[83]

Three days after the sneaker polish attack was first reported, a *New York Times* front-page story focused on the emotional suffering of the victimized boy. The article described "a 14-year-old boy [who] has been cloistered away for three days, wrestling with the fear and anger left by four young white men who attacked him and his sister, squirting them with white paint and yelling racial epithets."[84] Readers were informed that "what weighs in [the victim's] heart the heaviest . . . is a wave of anger he says he feels toward an entire race of people."[85] "I feel a certain way about white people now," the boy somberly told the *Times* reporter. "I don't want to feel this way, but that's how I feel: angry, angry that this had to happen."[86] He claimed to have been so traumatized by the incident that he would have to change schools.[87] With "each day his attackers go uncaught," the news writer explained, "the youth's anger simmers."[88] "I have white friends," said the boy, "but to speak truly right now, I don't know what to feel about them."[89] It seemed like the ultimate dilemma: a fair-minded black youth struggling not to form any prejudices against the white race, even though a few of its members had abused him. A concerned Mayor Dinkins called the victims' family and offered them the aid of city counselors.[90]

The sneaker polish incident made national news.[91] Coverage of the case even reached the Caribbean island of St. Thomas, homeland of the victims' mother.[92] It was a story of monumental proportions—a veritable gift from heaven for those searching for white racism. How disappointed they must have been when it was revealed, a month later, that the children had concocted the entire story.[93]

Yet while this particular tale of white bigotry was untrue, it nonetheless inspired numerous acts of black retaliation. Six racially motivated beatings, stabbings, and robberies of whites occurred almost immediately after accounts of the story made headlines.[94] In one case, two black New Yorkers raped a fifteen-year-old white girl.[95] In another incident, two teenage girls—one black and one white—were walking together along a Brooklyn street when a group of some thirty black youths attacked and robbed the white girl while they ridiculed her black friend for keeping company with a white.[96] In the Bronx, meanwhile, a group of twenty black teens robbed two light-skinned Hispanic girls specifically because they thought the girls were white.[97]

In addition to these retaliatory attacks, a number of other serious black-on-white crimes occurred in New York during the time that the sneaker polish furor was dominating the headlines. In one case, approximately fifty black Brooklyn teenagers terrorized pedestrians in lower Manhattan, stealing coats and slashing one man's chest with a knife.[98] In an episode near Columbia University, nine young blacks ran through the streets, viciously assaulting people.[99] In yet another incident, two black muggers shot and killed a Russian immigrant.[100] None of these crimes received more than a passing mention in the press. Nor did they lead to school counseling sessions or extra police patrols. Public officials and community leaders were silent. The contrast to the immense public outrage over the sneaker polish allegations of the very same week could not have been starker.[101]

The Silence Continues

Even when black-on-white attacks are clearly motivated by racism, they generally draw little public attention. Just a few weeks after the sneaker polish hoax, for example, a gang of black Brooklyn teens threw rocks at a bus carrying sixty young Jewish children, smashing its windows and shouting racial insults at the terrified passengers.[102] Two months later, another group of black Brooklynites hit a Hasidic man on the head with a bottle and yelled, "Heil, Hitler" as he ran away.[103] In October 1993 five black teens harassed some eighth-grade Jewish boys at a Bronx playground—punching them, calling them "dirty

Jews," and stealing their belongings.[104] All of these cases were largely overlooked by journalists and "civil rights leaders" alike.

Also in October 1993, a gang of black teenage girls brutally beat a thirty-five-year-old white woman in Harlem, breaking some of her ribs and damaging her kidneys while shouting racial epithets and ordering her to "get out of Harlem."[105] Predictably, this unprovoked assault did not cause the champions of "justice" to grumble about white people not being free to walk safely in certain parts of the city. There was also silence in February 1993, after a forty-two-year-old white artist named Bonnie Bear was robbed and murdered by two young blacks in TriBeca, New York.[106] Nor did "community activists" have anything to say about the tragic 1991 demise of Christian Prince, a white Yale University sophomore who was slain in Connecticut by a black teen who had bragged to his friends that he was going to rob a "cracker."[107]

"C'mon, It'll Be Fun."

Less than a week after Uwe-Wilhelm Rakebrand's murder in Miami, another foreign tourist was slain in Florida—thirty-four-year-old Gary Colley of Great Britain. On the night of September 14, 1993, Colley pulled his rental car into a rest stop about thirty-five miles east of Tallahassee and went to sleep—only to be awakened shortly thereafter by two black gunmen demanding money. When the frightened traveler tried to drive away, one of the blacks shot him in the neck and killed him—making Colley the ninth foreign white tourist slain in Florida in less than a year.[108]

As a result of those nine killings, the state of Florida cancelled its $2 million advertising campaign based on slogans like "One Florida, Many Faces" and "C'mon, It'll Be Fun."[109] Indeed, such ads were an embarrassment in light of the recurrent violence against tourists. Curiously, however, no community leader dared mention that three-fourths of all assaults on foreign tourists in the U.S. are committed by black men aged eighteen to twenty-four.[110] Nor did anyone note that all nine of Florida's tourist murders that year had involved white victims and black perpetrators. Presumably the motives of those nine killers were loftier and less objectionable than the "racist" motives of the occasional white who victimizes a black, as in Howard Beach or

Bensonhurst. When it is black victimizing white, skin color is regarded as no more significant than eye color. When it is white victimizing black, skin color *is* the story.

"A Husky-Looking Man Dressed in White"

On the evening of December 7, 1993, a thirty-five-year-old black man named Colin Ferguson was riding a crowded train during rush hour in Long Island, New York. Suddenly, without warning or provocation, he drew a handgun and began methodically shooting passengers,[111] killing six and wounding seventeen others.[112] While all local news broadcasts that evening led with this story, and every New York newspaper gave it front-page headlines the following day, not a single report mentioned the gunman's skin color. Clothing color, however, was somehow deemed newsworthy by *The New York Times*, which provided the media's most detailed description of the shooter as "a husky-looking man dressed in white."[113] Other publications merely identified him as a "gunman" or a "suspect."[114] The victims, too, remained curiously nondescript in all media reports.[115]

Ferguson's weapon, by contrast, was described in great detail. The New York *Daily News*, for instance, revealed that the 9-millimeter handgun weighed exactly 21 ounces and held "15 rounds [of ammunition] in a standard clip."[116] An entire article, complete with photograph, illustration, and statistics, was devoted to 9-millimeter guns.[117] The intent here is not to imply that such an article was inappropriate or unnecessary, but rather to note that no comparable description of the gunman appeared anywhere in print.

Once in custody, Ferguson openly acknowledged that he had acted for purely racial reasons.[118] Such unabashed candor forced the media to report, in the news broadcasts of December 8 and the newspaper stories of December 9, not only that the gunman was black, but that every one of his victims was either white or Asian. Even with this revelation, however, many chose to classify the crime as the random, inexplicable act of a madman, not the work of a racist.[119] Media pundits nationwide characterized Ferguson's actions as "senseless,"[120] suggesting that he had acted under the compulsion of some cognitive or neurological abnormality rather than with carefully orchestrated malice. A *New York Times* editorialist wrote, "The usual imperative of those who would contemplate an event like [the] Long Island Rail Road massacre is to 'make sense' of it. While the wish is reasonable, no more sense can be made of such a thing than of a typhoon or cyclone. Forget the gunman's declared motive of racial hatred: when someone with a semiautomatic weapon starts perforating citizens *en masse*, the question of motive evaporates."[121]

Compare this with the kind of analysis given to the Howard Beach and Bensonhurst cases, or to the Christopher Wilson burning, or to any other instance of white-on-black crime in memory. Whereas in those notorious cases "civil rights leaders" and social commentators were virtually unanimous in attributing the perpetrators' violence to racism, Colin Ferguson was, for the most part, exempted from such charges; the slaughter he engineered was widely accepted as the bitter fruit of a crazed man's mental imbalance.

Ferguson, it should be noted, had learned the lessons of our racial hucksters very well; that is, he "saw" racism everywhere. His private writings outlined elaborate plans to avenge the perceived injustices inflicted upon him by the likes of the "Chinese racist Mister Sue," "Adelphi University's racism," "racism by Caucasians," and "the filthy Caucasian racist female."[122] Although Ferguson had willingly immigrated from Jamaica to the United States and was free to return to his homeland at any time, he chose instead to stay in this country— apparently to engage in a bit of "freedom fighting" against its inhabitants.

In the aftermath of the carnage aboard the LIRR train, Nassau County Executive Thomas Gulotta stated, "The person who committed this crime was an animal who turned that [railroad] car into a death chamber."[123] Jesse Jackson, warning that such rhetoric might encourage a violent white backlash against blacks, rebuked Gulotta for his harsh characterization of Ferguson and admonished him to "stop playing that George Wallace role, stop playing that Orval Faubus role."[124] "Calling people racial names, animal names," added Jackson, "is provocative. It creates a general danger."[125] Like most "civil rights leaders," however, Jackson failed to see in himself the very qualities he condemned in others. It never occurred to him, for instance, that he ought to moderate his own irresponsible overuse of the inflammatory epithet "racist," which he and his ilk so frequently direct against whites whom it does not accurately describe. Not only is the misapplication of *that* term surely responsible for much black hatred of whites, but it is in fact consistent with the very belief system that caused Ferguson to mow down twenty-three innocent people.

Notably, when white serial killers of recent years—men such as Joel Rifkin, Charles Manson, David Berkowitz, Jeffrey Dahmer, and John Wayne Gacy—have been publicly called "animals" and "monsters," Jackson has not objected. In fact, *the day after* Jackson scolded Gulotta for his comments, a female relative of one of Rifkin's victims was quoted in a major New York newspaper calling Rifkin "a monster"[126]—yet Jackson said nothing to censure her. Neither did he protest in October 1994 when former New York City mayor Ed Koch, on his daily WABC radio program, time and again referred to a gang of white thugs who had recently mauled a police officer as "animals."[127] Nor did Jackson object in May 1997 when nationally syndicated talk-radio host Bob Grant repeatedly characterized the white killer of a young New Jersey girl as a "monster," or the following month when Grant applied the same designation to Timothy McVeigh—the white man responsible for the Oklahoma City bombing of 1995.[128]

In the aftermath of the LIRR massacre, Jackson asserted that it was time not for vengeance but "for reconciliation and redemption."[129] He exhorted white Americans to remember that after the slaying of Martin Luther King, Jr. twenty-five years earlier, blacks "did not succumb to the preoccupation for revenge" on King's killer, but instead "focused on redemption."[130] Presumably it had slipped Jackson's mind that following the King assassination, at least 125 American cities went up in flames or were overrun by riots. Perhaps he had forgotten that more than 55,000 National Guard and army troops were required to quell the violence nationwide.[131]

Dismissing any suggestion that Ferguson's murderous outburst reflected widespread black racism, Jackson explained that the gunman's crime "was not a race rampage," but merely the impulsive act of someone unaware of the gravity of his own actions.[132] Although Ferguson had fired his gun exclusively at whites and Asians, Jackson called the shooting spree a manifestation of "the 'Russian roulette' of *random* violence" for which there was no rational explanation.[133] "When Jeffrey Dahmer killed and ate a bunch of [mostly black] people in Milwaukee," said Jackson, "we didn't take that as evidence of where white America is. So why should Colin Ferguson tell us anything about black America?"[134]

Later that year, however, Jackson's reluctance to generalize by race vanished when a white South Carolina woman named Susan Smith, who had repeatedly told law-enforcement authorities that a black carjacker had kidnapped her two young sons, finally confessed that she herself had drowned the children in a lake. While news of this tragedy horrified most Americans, Jackson could focus only on the "racism" that initially had caused Ms. Smith to blame a black man for her children's disappearance. Jackson demanded, in fact, that white officials apologize to the black community for having believed the woman's false charge.[135]

The voice of Jackson was joined by others. Northwestern University sociology professor Alcorn Morris proclaimed, "This case demonstrates once again the stereotypical view of black men in America, that they are . . . dangerous, that they should be imprisoned. It was the same view that guided lynch mobs during the days of segregation in the South."[136] Along the same lines, black psychiatrist Alvin Poussaint saw Ms. Smith's lies as part of "a long history of scapegoating black men for the ills of the nation." He depicted Smith not as an aberration, but rather as being "in tune with the racism in society."[137]

It seems that in the eyes of people like Pouissaint, Morris, and Jackson, racially motivated crimes are a predominantly white phenomenon. The Reverend Joseph Lowery agrees, as evidenced by his assertion that hate crimes are only those incidents in which people "set out deliberately to violate the rights of blacks."[138] Such a definition presupposes that blacks are incapable of racism—presumably because they "have no power" over whites in our society. Other notables who share the view that blacks cannot be racists are film director Spike Lee, author Joel Kovel, liberal activist Paula Rothenberg, rapper Sister Souljah, and the onetime affirmative action officer for the New York State Insurance Fund, Carolyn Pitts. Ms. Pitts, in fact, believes that *all* whites are racists, whether they realize it or not.[139] The National Urban League's Whitney Young once explained that black people's "antiwhite feelings" cannot be equated with white racism, because that would be "to equate the bitterness of the victim with the evil that oppresses him."[140] Black scholar Coramae Richey Mann contends that because blacks "lack institutional power," it is "definitionally impossible for [them] to be identified as racist."[141]

Of course, if one accepts the notion that racism cannot exist without the "power" to oppress, one must also believe that a virtually impotent organization like the Ku Klux Klan is not racist—clearly a preposterous position. Held in contempt by most white Americans, the Klan today is virtually defunct. Close to bankruptcy,[142] this group which once boasted millions of members and wielded significant political power, now has no established alliances with mainstream white leaders or organizations.[143] Nor can any Klansmen be found among newspaper editors, legislators, district judges, or the directors of major corporations. Contemporary Klan leaders are capable of attracting only a handful of white racists to their meetings, and the organization's steadily declining membership of about 4,000 is many times smaller than that of, among other groups, Louis Farrakhan's Nation of Islam (NOI), whose constituency approaches 150,000.[144] Farrakhan's group, meanwhile, enjoys the strong support of numerous black leaders and mainstream "civil rights" groups—particularly the NAACP and the Congressional Black Caucus, both of which recently formed "sacred alliances" with the NOI. Moreover, Farrakhan's influence extends far beyond NOI membership, as he demonstrated in October 1995 by mobilizing hundreds of thousands of black men to attend a rally in our nation's capital. Nonetheless, "civil rights leaders" ask us to believe that the NOI, because it is composed of people who purportedly lack "power," is not a racist entity.[145]

Sociologist and economist Thomas Sowell eloquently disputes the notion that racism is an exclusively white trait:

> A more tendentious definition of racism has emerged in the late twentieth century to exempt racial minorities themselves from the charge. Racism was now said to require *power*, which minorities do not have, so that even the most anti-white, anti-Jewish, or anti-Asian sentiments . . . were automatically exempt from the charge of racism. No such proviso that power was required for racism ever existed before. That this new and self-serving escape hatch remained largely unchallenged has been one index of the level of moral intimidation surrounding racial issues. . . . In the ordinary sense of the word, minorities of all colors have shown themselves capable of as vicious racism as anybody else, whether in or out of power. The hostility, boycotts, or violence of African-ancestry people against people from India has been common from Kenya to South Africa, as well as in Jamaica and Guyana. Such behavior differs in no essential way from the behavior labelled "racism" when it is the African-ancestry population being abused by people of European ancestry.[146]

A Wellspring of "Rage"

Notably, not all "civil rights" mouthpieces limited their explanations for Colin Ferguson's massacre to insanity. Morris Dees, a former aide to President Jimmy Carter, blamed "a rising sense of frustration among blacks that the promises of the civil rights movement are not coming to pass."[147] Along the same lines, one of Ferguson's attorneys, the late William Kuntsler, announced that his client suffered from "black rage." Whites, warned Kuntsler, must "stop oppressing the black man or be prepared to meet his expressed rage."[148] Ferguson's other attorney, Ronald Kuby, added that "white people have to learn to understand how bitter some black people are about their treatment in this society—and the fruit of white racism is hatred."[149] A *National Law Review* survey found that 68 percent of black Americans agreed that white racism could have driven Ferguson to his rampage.[150]

Instead of depicting Ferguson as a racist, newspapers painstakingly researched his past, looking for clues as to why he had apparently "snapped." *The New York Times* devoted almost a full page to the gunman's life history.[151] Yet even when it was revealed that Ferguson had been raised not in poverty but in an upper-middle-class Jamaican family, those who hunt for racism were not deterred from "finding" the roots of his crime in the soil of white evils. Sociologist Don Robotham, for one, received significant publicity for explaining that Ferguson had been "shattered" by his "particularly traumatic" exposure to American racism.[152]

Ferguson's horrible deed inspired expressions of sympathy, understanding, and even approval from numerous voices in the black community. Professor Sam Pinn of Ramapo College called the shooting spree a justified political act—like the Watts and Los Angeles "rebellions."[153] Wilbert Tatum, who edits the black newspaper *The Amsterdam News*, saw the shootings as part of a sociopolitical mosaic that included New York's mayoral election of the previous month, in which white candidate Rudolph Giuliani had defeated black incumbent David Dinkins. "It [the shooting spree] ties in with so many things," wrote Tatum. "The election, . . . the unrest, anger and resentment, the feeling that the white media played a role in the loss of Dinkins."[154] Observing that Ferguson "lived near Crown Heights," Tatum wondered "what he has seen, what terror has been visited upon

him."[155] The implication was that local Jews had harassed and intimidated Ferguson to the brink of insanity.

NAACP counsel Laura Blackburne told a radio audience that
she "grieved" for Ferguson "because he is as much a victim as the rest
of us. How could we permit a man to walk around with such bottled
up rage?"[156] In a similar vein, Clayton Riley, a talk-show host on black
radio station WLIB in New York, reminded his audience that Ferguson
was "no more enraged about a whole lot of things than I am and a
whole lot of other people are."[157] Asserting that the LIRR massacre
was retribution for past white-on-black sins, a caller to Riley's program said, "These people who enslaved our fathers, enslaved our mothers—they earned it."[158] On other radio programs, meanwhile, many
black callers theorized that white racism had simply broken Ferguson's
spirit. "It just shows you," lamented one Jamaican caller, "how the
system here can destroy people's minds psychologically. . . . He was
not used to the racism that exists in America. . . . We can't just blame the
person."[159]

Clearly, the notion that Ferguson was justifiably enraged at
white society resonated powerfully within the black community. When
a shackled and handcuffed Ferguson was led to a prison cell after his
arrest, other black inmates gave him a standing ovation as he passed
their cells.[160] Ten days later, Louis Farrakhan referred to Ferguson's
crime in the course of a speech to an all-black audience of nearly
25,000 people. "A young black man got on the Long Island Railroad
the other day," said Farrakhan, "and went off and shot down six Caucasians and wounded many more." His audience responded, at that
point, with a standing ovation.[161]

When Is It Racism, and When Is It Not?

In contrast to their relative silence following Ferguson's mul-
tiple murders, "civil rights leaders" reacted vocally to the June 1991
assault on seventeen-year-old Alfred Jermaine Ewell, a black student
at Lawrence High School in Atlantic Beach, New York. After a group
of whites beat and seriously injured Ewell with a baseball bat, *New
York Times* headlines the following day focused exclusively on the
racial aspect of the incident. "Three Arrested in Beating of a Black,"
read one caption.[162] "Atlantic Beach Struggles to Explain Assault by

Whites on a Black Youth," read another.[163] Al Sharpton immediately organized a march to protest the attack. "We are going to raise their consciousness level," he announced. "We are making a collective call for justice."[164] The guilt of the whites who perpetrated this brutal act is not in question here. The significant issue is the double standard by which crimes are appraised, depending upon the respective races of assailants and victims.

Consider also the manner in which *The New York Times* reported two instances of interracial crime on September 27, 1994. In an article about a black man who had raped a twenty-year-old white woman in New York's Central Park, there was not the slightest speculation about possible racial motives for the attack.[165] By contrast, race was the entire focus of a *Times* story about four whites who had beaten a deaf black woman and her teenage son with aluminum bats.[166]

When a thirteen-year-old Bridgeport, Illinois black was savagely beaten by a group of white teens in March 1997, the "civil rights" cartel was predictably incensed. "This town [Bridgeport] is still one of the most racist cities in the United States," said Chicago's Reverend Al Samson, who led a march to protest the beating.[167] "Hatred abounds," added Jesse Jackson, noting that the brutal assault had occurred almost twenty-nine years to the day after Martin Luther King, Jr.'s assassination. Jackson exhorted President Clinton to convene a conference addressing the racial attitudes that had led to the beating, and the president personally telephoned the victim's family to express his concern.[168]

By contrast, Jackson and his fellow agitators said nothing in January 1994 after black carjacker Edward Summers shot two eighteen-year-old white men—Scott Nappi and Michael Falcone—in the back of the head, execution style.[169] Reserving their eloquent denunciations for white transgressions only, the apostles of "justice" presumably found it inconceivable that the black gunman was even capable of being a racist. This one-sided view of racism has diffused widely through the black community, wherein today almost any rationalization for black-on-white crime is preferable to theories that postulate racist motives. Typical was this appraisal by one black who speculated, "I figure it was pressure [that caused Summers to murder]. Sometimes you get so stressed out."[170] Journalists, too, were reluctant to note the interracial nature of Summers's crime. On the day of the shootings, not a single news broadcast mentioned the race of either the assailant or his victims.

In late March 1994 *The New York Times* reported that a gang of five youths had assaulted and robbed twelve elderly women in Brooklyn during a three-week period. One of the more seriously injured victims was a seventy-year-old who suffered a fractured skull and hip. Benignly describing the area in which these crimes occurred as "an integrated, working-class project that also is home to many elderly people,"[171] the *Times* apparently deemed it irrelevant that all five attackers were black and all twelve victims were white. Also unreported was the fact that one of the gang members candidly revealed that he and his fellow thugs had actually made a pact not to rob any blacks. "We would only take white women," explained the youth.[172] Had this been a *white* gang specifically targeting *black* grandmothers, a great hue and cry undoubtedly—and rightfully—would have resounded across the country. But since these crimes were black-on-white, there were no calls for calm by political leaders, no pained newspaper editorials, no television news flashes, no demands for a special prosecutor, no protest marches.

Even when race is clearly the *only* motive underlying a black-on-white assault, the self-professed ambassadors of "goodwill" are usually silent. In May 1997, for instance, a twenty-six-year-old black member of a Nation of Islam offshoot viciously beat a white New York woman named Laura Zirinsky, repeatedly kicking the victim's head and injuring her so badly that she required emergency brain surgery to save her life. At the time of the attack, the perpetrator was carrying a notebook filled with antiwhite writings advocating a race war. Nonetheless, not a single "civil rights leader" in the country publicly said a word about the incident. Nor did the story receive more than a brief mention in the media.[173]

In 1989 a white female jogger in New York's Central Park was raped and beaten nearly to death by a gang of about thirty black and Hispanic teenagers. Fracturing her skull with a lead pipe and mutilating her face with a brick, the assailants left the woman for dead. She lost three-quarters of her blood in the attack and was so badly mangled that even her boyfriend was able to recognize her only by a familiar ring on her finger. When investigators later asked one of the attackers why he had tried to smash the victim's skull, he candidly replied, "It was fun." Despite the fact that several of the youths had agreed, prior to their attack, to "get a white girl," most pundits and community activists discounted any possibility that racism had been the motivating factor.[174] And even though a number of the defendants gave videotaped confessions, black newspapers generally denounced their trial the following year as a racist charade.[175] Harlem pastor Calvin Butts complained, "The first thing you do in the United States of America when a white woman is raped is round up a bunch of black youths, and I think that's what happened here."[176] Of the thirty or so assailants, most were never punished. When the victim, still disfigured and unsteady, went to the courthouse to testify, groups of black demonstrators taunted her, calling her a "filthy white whore" and claiming that her boyfriend was the real rapist.[177] Black columnist William Raspberry provided a rare voice of reason:

> The woman lies near death in a New York hospital, victim not merely of her own foolish daring but also of a singularly bestial attack: vicious, brutish, unprovoked. And I keep wanting the black leadership to say something about it.
>
> Is that silly? What would I want them to say? The 28-year-old woman went jogging in Central Park—*at night,* for heaven's sake—and got in trouble. What's the black leadership got to do with that? What would I want them to say, and in what forum?
>
> I suppose I just want them to say that they—that we—are outraged; that we demand justice; that we care about that woman, though she is white and her attackers are black children.
>
> It's easy enough to understand why they aren't talking. To begin with, it isn't one of their issues. Moreover, the attackers are members of their constituency and the victim is not. And finally, they may fear that to speak out as black leaders would spread the guilt from the young savages who did the deed to blacks generally.
>
> After all, it wasn't "black America" that beat, stabbed, gang-raped and battered this hapless woman and left her for dead. It was a group of some 30 children, themselves victims, no doubt, of some social atrocities, who did this savage thing. Why should black leaders buy into the savagery by having anything to say about it one way or another?
>
> And didn't the victim, while not precisely "asking for it," pretty much bring the horror upon herself? She did resist the advice of friends and the common wisdom of New Yorkers: stay the hell out of Central Park at night.
>
> All true. But it is also true it wasn't "white America" that assaulted the three black men who strayed into Howard Beach,

chasing one to his death in the path of a car. It was a mob of white teenagers.

Still, the black leadership demanded that white leaders speak out about the incident, if only to demonstrate that they weren't all represented by that club-wielding mob. And white leaders did speak out.

As for the notion that the so far unnamed victim of the recent attack should never have gone on a nighttime jog in Central Park—no matter how realistic that advice might be—is not very different from saying those black guys shouldn't have been walking in that all-white, blue-collar section of Howard Beach. There shouldn't be places in America where people are forbidden to go because of their race.

I wish the black leadership would say that. I wish we could get over the notion that we have to defend (or at any rate keep silent about) the bad actors among us, even though I understand why we do it.

Sometimes it is simply because they are black and their critics are white; sometimes it is because we fear that for us to turn on even the most blameworthy of blacks would license racists to turn on all of us. As a matter of fact, the opposite is true. But in any case, it is beside the point.

It may also be beside the point that we don't know what to do about children who, with or without the excuse of poverty, have become such cold-eyed and remorseless monsters. We don't know how to "fix" people who have reached adolescence or adulthood without having internalized any recognizable moral code, and we don't know how to keep from churning out more of them. But surely our vocal disapproval of their savagery is one place to start.

We need to make it clear that we are outraged by brutality, not just white brutality. We need to find the words to say we care about victims, not just black victims. To keep silent in the face of atrocities committed by blacks erodes the moral value of our outrage when the atrocities are committed by whites.

It is in the interest both of justice and our progress that we espouse common standards against which we can establish sound social policy and hold people accountable for their behavior. And just as Martin Luther King, Jr. found the courage to speak out against the violence of both the Klan and the Black Panthers, it must start with the leadership.

Those race spokesmen, self-appointed and otherwise, who have made it their special mission to attack societal injustice must find the courage to measure that injustice by a single yardstick.[178]

The Rationale of Black "Leadership"

Today's "civil rights" messiahs focus considerable attention on the racial injustice that existed in this country during the eras of slavery and segregation. Reminding us that Africans originally arrived in North America against their will, these "leaders" reason that contemporary black-on-white violence often springs from a retaliatory rage that blacks feel over inequities visited on their ancestors. In this view, black-on-white crimes are deemed acts of vengeance rather than racism. When whites harm blacks, on the other hand, such analysts assure us that the animating force is nothing more complex than pure, cold racism.

But this double standard, which presupposes the exclusive historical innocence of blacks and, conversely, the exclusive historical guilt of whites, does not stand up to scrutiny. The planted axiom is that present-day rage and violence are generated by events that happened to other people—years, generations, or even centuries earlier. Such reasoning ignores the fact that human history is, among other things, a vast stockpile of sins to which every race has contributed. By no means has the history of blacks been marked by greater benevolence or justice than the history of whites. Contrary to the claims of those who would blame whites for all the world's evils, black history too is filled with examples of gruesome barbarism and ruthless oppression. A more complete discussion of this fact occurs in chapters 11 and 12—the purpose being not to rank comparatively the sins of each race, but simply to illustrate the intellectual dishonesty of placing the moral burdens of the past upon the shoulders of contemporary whites while ignoring the historical transgressions of blacks.

The "civil rights" vision of recent decades equalizes past white sinners with their present-day descendants, holding the latter liable for moral debts they themselves did not incur. Moreover, it draws no distinction between the descendants of unjust men and the progeny of just men. For example, it ascribes inherited guilt not only to descendants of slaveholders, but even to whites whose forefathers were among the 360,000 Union soldiers who lost their lives fighting the Civil War—a conflict whose central issue was the question of slavery.[179] Neither does this vision look with favor upon contemporary whites whose ancestors helped conduct slaves to freedom via the Underground

Railroad, or whose forebears were active in the abolition movement of the eighteenth and nineteenth centuries.

Quietly underlying this principle of inherited guilt is one of humanity's most sinister instincts: the tendency to impute *collective* guilt or inferiority to all members of a particular race, religion, or class.[180] Drawing no distinction between saints and devils of similar pigmentation or heritage, collective views of culpability and inadequacy have formed the cornerstones of the cruelest movements in world history. Marxists, for instance, saw evil embodied in the form of capitalists; Nazis, in the form of Jews; Inquisitors, in the form of heretics. Notions of racial inferiority, meanwhile, justified for many the perpetuation of the transatlantic slave trade. In each of these instances, the sins or deficiencies ascribed to the unfortunate victims provided their persecutors with intellectual justifications for sweeping slaughters, prison camps, abominable tortures, or forced servitude.

In our own day, the widely embraced concepts of collective white guilt and black innocence—so central to modern "civil rights" dogma—have done enormous damage to American race relations. Many white Americans, some of whom are named in this chapter, have lost their lives at the hands of black assailants seeking "retribution." Nevertheless, the defenders of "justice" persist in portraying all blacks as victims of white oppressors. Black professor Shelby Steele explains the anachronism of such a view:

> Racial victimization is not our [blacks'] real problem. If conditions have worsened for most of us as racism has receded, then much of the problem must be of our own making. To admit this fully would cause us to lose the innocence we derive from our victimization. And we would jeopardize the entitlement we've always had to challenge society. We are in the odd and self-defeating position in which taking responsibility for bettering ourselves feels like a surrender to white power.
>
> So we have a hidden investment in victimization and poverty. These distressing conditions have been the source of our only real power, and there is an unconscious sort of gravitation toward them, a complaining celebration of them. One sees evidence of this in the near happiness with which certain black leaders recount the horror of Howard Beach, Bensonhurst, and other recent instances of racial tension. As one is saddened by these tragic events, one is also repelled by the way some black leaders—agitated to near hysteria by the scent of victim power inherent in them—leap forward to

exploit them as evidence of black innocence and white guilt. It is as though they sense the decline of black victimization as a loss of standing and dive into the middle of these incidents as if they were reservoirs of pure black innocence swollen with potential power.[181]

A "National Epidemic"?

A week after Bensonhurst's 1989 Day of Outrage, a participant in another local protest march asserted, "The death of Yusef Hawkins was an atrocity against humanity." We can only wonder how this speaker would have classified the deaths of Danny Gilmore, Barbara Meller-Jensen, Brian Watkins, Allyn Winslow, and the other white victims mentioned in this chapter. Attorney Alton Maddox, meanwhile, characterized Hawkins's death as a chilling reminder for blacks to struggle ever more vigilantly for justice. "I make no apologies for increasing tension," he told a cheering crowd of demonstrators, "because we can only have progress through struggle. Justice for Yusef Hawkins will be served by how often we march in the streets, and we will march week after week after week." Maddox knew, of course, that since white-on-black assaults are relatively rare (see statistics later in this chapter), he would need to get maximum mileage out of what had occurred in Bensonhurst. And Al Sharpton, for his part, uttered perhaps the most revealing statement of all: "We want people to see the death of Yusef Hawkins as part of a national epidemic."[182] But merely calling something an epidemic does not make it one. Notwithstanding Sharpton's efforts to portray the white race as the enemy of black progress today, an honest search for the true enemy needs to be directed elsewhere.

The True Picture

What are the facts? What are the crime rates of black Americans, and who are their chosen victims? How often are blacks themselves victimized, and by whom? How do these figures compare to those of whites? According to the *Uniform Crime Reports* prepared annually by the FBI, blacks, who make up roughly 13 percent of the U.S. population, commit some 42 percent of all violent crimes—

including 40 percent of weapons violations, 59 percent of robberies, 42 percent of rapes, and 54 percent of murders.[183] These offenders are particularly concentrated among the young. Contemporary black males aged fourteen to twenty-four are among the most dangerous demographic groups in American history. Constituting just 1 percent of our country's population, they commit at least 30 percent of its murders each year. A mere ten years ago the corresponding figure was 17 percent.[184]

Given these statistics, it is not surprising that nearly half of all prison inmates in the United States are black.[185] In some urban areas, the figures are much higher. The prison populations of New York City and Washington, D.C., for example, are 91 percent and 99 percent black, respectively.[186] Among the District of Columbia's black male residents, an astonishing 85 percent are arrested at some point in their lives. On any given day in that city, 42 percent of black men aged eighteen to thirty-five are in some way involved with the criminal-justice system—either behind bars, on probation or parole, awaiting trial, or wanted by the police. The corresponding figure for black men in neighboring Baltimore is 56 percent.[187] Among black males in their twenties nationwide, at least one out of every three are either in prison, on probation, or on parole.[188] Some estimates range as high as 40 percent.[189] To many people, merely stating such facts is equivalent to race-bashing. First Lady Hillary Clinton, for one, claims that media reports about the misdeeds of black outlaws perpetuate negative "stereotypes" about black criminality.[190] White author Maurice Berger, denying that black criminality is even a problem worthy of concern, derides "the myth of the danger" that is "associated with blackness."[191] Ralph Wiley puts it somewhat more crudely. "When they [whites] want to say *niggers*," he asserts, "they say *crime*."[192] Presumably Mrs. Clinton, Mr. Berger, and Mr. Wiley believe that the disproportionately high black crime rate should elicit neither notice nor comment.

Not only are blacks far more likely than whites to commit violent crimes, but they are also significantly more prone to be victims of such offenses. Black males, for example, are about twice as likely as white males to be robbed or assaulted, and seven times more likely to be murdered.[193] Notably, the situation has worsened in recent years. The rate at which black males fall prey to homicide has doubled since 1960;[194] for those aged fourteen to seventeen the corresponding rate has tripled since 1976.[195] Among black males aged fifteen to thirty-four, homicide is now the leading cause of death.[196] Black females are killed far less frequently than black males, but are still sent violently to early graves at five times the rate of white females.[197] Overall, blacks comprise about half of all homicide victims in the United States each year.[198] Residents of Washington, D.C., a predominantly black city, are more likely to be gunned down than are residents of such notoriously dangerous places as El Salvador, Northern Ireland, or Lebanon.[199] The life expectancy of black men in central Harlem is shorter than that of men in the destitute nation of Bangladesh.[200]

This high incidence of antiblack violence, however, has almost nothing to do with whites. Though our racial racketeers continuously bemoan an omnipresent bigotry that allegedly threatens blacks every moment of every day, white-on-black attacks are in fact relatively uncommon in this country. Of all black homicide victims in the United States, 94 percent are slain by other blacks.[201] Of the 1.3 million violent crimes committed each year against blacks nationally, about 81 percent are perpetrated by fellow blacks.[202] Put another way, the 87 percent of the U.S. population that is nonblack accounts for just 6 percent of murders and 19 percent of all violent crimes against blacks.

How can we reconcile these facts with the statements of "civil rights" crusaders who ascribe virtually all black troubles to the malevolence of whites? After all, it was not *black*-on-black crime that caused Benjamin Hooks, among others, to damn the purported existence of white neighborhoods "where blacks could not walk through." Nor was Herbert Daughtry thinking of intraracial black crime when he characterized his people as longtime victims of "the oppression, the brutality, and the killings." Neither was it black-on-black violence that compelled Dr. Carolyn Goodman to say that "the clock has run out, and we've got to move on every front." Nor was this what Jesse Jackson urged all blacks to be vigilant against in order to assure that the tragic deaths of some early civil rights leaders were "not in vain." Neither was it black-on-black brutality to which the *New York Times* guest editorialist referred when claiming that many parts of his city were off-limits to him—"just because I am an African American" whose black skin could possibly be his "death warrant." Nor was it the high incidence of blacks victimizing blacks that Alton Maddox planned to condemn "week after week after week." Neither was this what prompted the angry demonstrator outside the Bensonhurst courthouse to announce, "We African people are tired of being murdered." Nor was black-on-black homicide what Al Sharpton was alluding to when he deemed the death of Yusef Hawkins "part of a national epidemic" that demanded "a collective call for justice."

Each of these speakers willfully chose to ignore the monumental crisis of black-on-black crime and focused instead on the alleged problem of *white*-on-black assaults—as if such incidents were legion. Contrary to "civil rights" rhetoric, however, law-abiding black Americans live in perpetual fear of *black*—not white—predators. Black sociologist Ronald Taylor articulates this fear when describing a recent visit he made to his old Hartford, Connecticut neighborhood, where he was shocked to see young black men selling drugs on street corners. "I was frightened," he says. "And I was embarrassed that I was frightened. These men are my own people, and I don't recognize them."[203] With equal dismay, a resident of an all-black, crime-ridden New York City precinct—wherein more than 120 people were murdered in 1993 alone—lamented the rampant violence plaguing her neighborhood at the time. "I feel like the world is coming to an end these days," she said, "because every time I turn around, someone I know or someone in the neighborhood is getting killed. I just hope I'm not next."[204] A Harlem resident reported that same year, "There are a lot of shootings back here, constantly, nonstop. But you can't run to the window [to look] because they might shoot in."[205] These individuals were not expressing their terror of white men in white hoods ambushing them in the night, but of the *black* outlaws responsible for virtually all the carnage in their communities. Indeed, black fear of *intra*racial violent crime has skyrocketed during the past decade.[206] A 1996 national survey found that fully 52 percent of blacks (as compared to 31 percent of whites) were afraid to walk alone at night in their own neighborhoods.[207]

The real source of the black community's most serious problems was poignantly illustrated in 1994 when Rosa Parks, the brave woman who helped draw national attention to the need for genuine civil rights reforms in the 1950s, was attacked in her Detroit home by a black intruder.[208] Had her assailant been white, the incident undoubtedly would have been spotlighted by "civil rights leaders" as a symbol of white America's contempt for a black heroine. Things being as they were, however, not a single self-anointed champion of "justice" denounced this shameful instance of black-on-black predation.

Other renowned black figures have also been victims of intraracial violence, yet their cases have rarely made newspaper headlines. For example, few people heard that Dr. Carlos Russell, a Brooklyn College professor and the founder of Black Solidarity Day, was terrorized and beaten by some black thugs in his Brooklyn neighborhood in November 1995.[209] Even worse was the plight of the Reverend James Woodruff, a prominent Anglican priest who was recently paralyzed from the neck down by a black assailant's bullet.[210] Unfortunate individuals like these suffer in virtual anonymity because neither "civil rights" activists nor the media publicize their attacks. When there are no whites to blame, the distress of black victims is utterly meaningless to most black "leaders."

Amazingly, many professional race-hustlers imply that *whites* compel blacks to commit crimes against one another. As Professor Derrick Bell puts it, "Victimized themselves by an uncaring society, some blacks vent their rage on victims like themselves."[211] Louis Farrakhan, meanwhile, claims that whites are secretly pleased by black-on-black carnage because they need a constant supply of fresh kills for organ donations. "You've become good for parts," he told a black audience in Ohio.[212] In January 1994, black politicians, academicians, and clergymen convened in our nation's capital for the National Black Leadership (NBL) Search Session on Violence—a conference whose attendees largely blamed white America for every conceivable black ill. As Courtland Milloy of the *Washington Post* observed, "Our most articulate black leaders spent most of their time [at the NBL affair] searching for ways not to use the words 'personal responsibility.' " He noted that Washington mayor Sharon Pratt Kelly had told a cheering black audience that African Americans do not produce the guns or drugs that are decimating their neighborhoods—her implication being that white conspirators funnel those agents of destruction into the ghettos. "The enthusiastic applause she received," wrote Milloy, "sounded like some subconscious effort to drown out the inner voice that might ask: 'Who pulls the trigger? Who smokes the crack?' "[213]

Because black-on-black crime has become so rampant, a handful of "civil rights leaders" have at long last begun, however hesitantly, to confront it. In 1993, for instance, Jesse Jackson told a black audience in Chicago, "There is nothing more painful to me at this stage in my life than to walk down the street and hear footsteps and start thinking about robbery—then look around and see somebody white and feel relieved." But when a number of black pundits immediately criticized Jackson for his comments, he quickly issued a "clarification" and explained that he had been misunderstood.[214] The truth, however, is incontrovertible, and even its staunchest foes accidentally acknowledge it on occasion.

While Mr. Jackson must be commended for finally speaking out against black-on-black transgressions, he (along with all other "civil rights" crusaders) has remained strangely silent on the topic of blacks victimizing *whites*. Might Jackson and his fellow demagogues fear that an honest discussion of black-on-white crime would discredit the principal premise upon which today's entire "civil rights" vision is founded—the *exclusive* victimization of blacks? Could it be that these "leaders" do not want Americans to know that large numbers of whites fall prey to black assailants each year? In short, are discussions about black-on-black crime a convenient distraction from any meaningful dialogue about black-on-*white* crime? Black writer Wayne Edwards muses:

> The current cry against "black-on-black crime" itself smacks of delusion. Crime is crime. And to qualify it on the basis of race is indicative of insincerity. The underlying message is that black-on-black violence is "bad for the race" while black-on-"other folks" violence is acceptable. . . . Imagine for a moment a white politician decrying "white-on-white violence." How would that play within the black community?[215]

Crimes That Cross Racial Lines

From listening to the heralds of white racism, one could easily form the impression that whites are the most frequent perpetrators of interracial crime. Consider, for example, the words of one writer on this topic:

> During the second half of the 1980s, racial violence against blacks increased nationwide. In 1988 a white supremacist movement of violent skin-headed youths, whose weapons included knives, baseball bats, and their own steel-toed boots, sprang up spontaneously in cities throughout the nation. According to academic administrators, there is a "growing pattern of bigotry and animosity towards minority students" at predominantly white schools.[216]

In a similar vein, black columnist E.R. Shipp portrays white-on-black crime as a far greater problem than the converse:

> Remember Howard Beach, where black men were attacked simply because they were in a "white" neighborhood? Remember Bensonhurst, where a black teenager was killed because he was black? Remember firebombings in Canarsie when black families tried moving into certain blocks? [Today] there are places—neighborhoods, Wall Street law firms, country clubs—where blacks are not allowed. I know white people will say they can't go to black neighborhoods in New York, but that's usually only because they haven't tried.[217]

Echoing the theme of black victimization, Professor Cornel West calls African Americans our country's "exemplary targets of racial hatred."[218] Professor Walter Stafford cites the "astounding" amount of white-on-black violence in New York City.[219] A recent *New York Times* article concurs that "the evidence for the danger to young black men, especially those from urban areas, is mounting."[220] Psychologist Richard Majors says that black, inner-city youths seem to be an "endangered species."[221] Dr. Robert Staples, a professor of sociology at a University of California medical school, speaks of "a sort of genocide targeting young black males."[222] "There's not a systematic conspiracy," he explains, "but the most recent figures show that over the last decade black men are the only group of Americans actually to have an average decrease of two months in life expectancy. Every other group, including black women, gained from three to six years."[223] According to professor of African American studies Vivian Gordon, "Black men are a hunted and endangered species. You kill off the male and leave the woman vulnerable and without a partner. They [whites] have done everything to devastate us by devastating our men."[224] Dr. Alvin Poussaint wonders "why there haven't been more blacks who have exploded because of the mistreatment that they have received at the hands of white people."[225]

A 1987 report by the New York Governor's Advisory Committee for Black Affairs (GACBA) states, "[T]he black community must have greater protection from crime. . . . While crime has caused fear, despair, and hardship throughout many segments of society, it has had a disproportionate impact upon the black residents . . . [who] are disproportionately affected by violent crime."[226] "Racially motivated or targeted violence," the report continues, "may arise in the context of organized hate groups such as the Ku Klux Klan, neo-Nazis, the Order, the Aryan Nation, or others whose purpose and ideology is premised on racist or supremacist ideologies. It is groups such as these that come to the public mind most often when incidents of racially motivated and/or targeted violence arise."[227]

The GACBA document further cites the conclusions of sociologist Dr. Harvey Brenner, who attributes antiblack hate crimes to "the national and regional economic situations, and especially the rates of unemployment, [which] represent the dominant influence on violence against minorities."[228] In other words, Dr. Brenner maintains that when whites are out of work or struggling financially, they tend to vent their frustration on blacks. Consistent with this theory is the opinion of Dr. Mary Frances Berry, chairman of the U.S. Civil Rights Commission. "The primary explanation for racially motivated violence against blacks," says Dr. Berry, "has been the need of a segment of the white population to preserve [its] belief in the inferiority of blacks, and to maintain the social and political subordination of an historically outcast group by any means, including violence."[229]

The mainstream media, of course, have largely echoed the dogmas of the "civil rights" cabal. In a 1994 New York Times Op-Ed piece, black novelist Ishmael Reed discusses the damaging "stereotypes" that are created when "pictures of black teenagers charged with antisocial behavior" are "plastered all over the newspapers and TV." Sixty percent of all hate crimes, says Reed, are committed by white teens.[230] Similarly, a September 1994 column by New York Daily News writer Amy Pagnozzi depicts the commission of hate crimes as a principally white affair. While she discusses assaults that are white-on-black, white-on-Hispanic, Italian-on-Mexican, Irish-on-Mexican, Italian-on-Chinese, and Italian-on-Puerto Rican, Pagnozzi makes no reference at all to nonwhite-on-white transgressions.[231]

Likewise, black author Ralph Wiley seems to believe that whites are responsible for the lion's share of interracial brutality. "Black people have a hard way to go in Milwaukee," he writes. "Blacks are but 5 percent of Wisconsin's population, yet were 55 percent of the murder victims between 1984 and 1990."[232] Wiley postulates that the greatest threat to blacks is posed by frustrated, unsuccessful white people who try to compensate for their own underachievement by tyrannizing indigent, uneducated minorities.[233]

Clearly there are many prominent voices trumpeting the notion that perpetrators of interracial violence are disproportionately white—and, by extension, that *black-on-white* crime is so rare as to scarcely warrant a mention. But those making this claim present crime statistics in a most misleading manner. For example, the New York GACBA states unequivocally that notwithstanding the purported scourge of white-on-black violence, most personal crimes are *intra*racial incidents.[234] The implication is that if whites are afraid to walk into a black neighborhood, it is only because they *misperceive* violent crime as tending to cross racial lines.[235] As criminologist William Wilbanks explains, "academics often chastise the white public for fearing an unfamiliar black person, since 'everyone knows' that crime is *intra*racial and thus whites have more to fear from fellow whites than from blacks."[236]

Technically this "common knowledge," as expressed by the aforementioned academics and the GACBA, contains a grain of truth. White victims of violent crime *do* usually (about 68 percent of the time) identify other whites as their attackers, just as *black* victims of violence most often (81 percent of the time) identify other *blacks* as *their* attackers.[237] But the U.S. population is about 73 percent white and just 13 percent black.[238] It would be virtually impossible for any group whose members comprise roughly one-eighth of the total population (as blacks do) to account for a majority of all crimes committed against a group that is almost three-fourths of the population. By contrast, it would not be difficult at all for the larger group—by virtue of its vastly greater numbers—to account for a majority of all attacks against the smaller group.

Yet nothing of the kind occurs in our country. Though whites outnumber blacks by nearly six to one, black criminals account for 94 percent of homicides and 81 percent of all other violence against blacks. Statistically, then, only a small proportion of crimes against blacks are perpetrated by whites. In fact, white criminals target black victims in just 3 percent of their attacks.[239] *Black* outlaws, conversely, attack interracially with startling regularity. Fully *54 percent* of their violent crimes are directed against white victims.[240]

This huge statistical disparity exists in every major category of interracial felonies. White robbers, for instance, target black victims in just 8 percent of their robberies, while black robbers target white victims in 64 percent of their robberies. Whites guilty of assault select black victims 3 percent of the time, while black assailants select white victims 52 percent of the time. White rapists pick out black victims in no more than 5 percent of their rapes, while black rapists pick out white victims in 59 percent of their rapes.[241] Statistically, any given black is about 50 times more likely to commit a violent crime against a white than vice versa.[242] Black-on-white muggings are 30 times more common than white-on-black crimes of the same description;[243] black-on-white robberies are 24 times more common than vice versa;[244] and black-on-white *gang* robberies are 52 times more common.[245]

Although the white population in the U.S. is almost 6 times larger than the black population, about 2.7 times as many whites are killed by blacks as vice versa.[246] According to the Southern Poverty Law Center, nearly 50 percent of all homicides that can clearly be traced to racial motives are committed by blacks, who are but 13 percent of the population.[247] The FBI reports that fully 63 percent of all hate crimes can be classified as "antiwhite."[248] Of the 1.7 million interracial crimes that occurred in 1993 involving both blacks and whites, 89 percent were committed by blacks against whites.[249]

These numbers are staggering. If America were teeming with white racism, surely most perpetrators of interracial crime would be white. Instead, however, the evidence strongly suggests that a dispro-portionate share of racism actually resides within the *black* commu-nity. Though "civil rights leaders" strive to portray white-on-black crime as commonplace, their rhetoric rings hollow. Indeed, these demagogues have proven themselves to be, above all else, our nation's tellers of tall tales, the myth makers of modern America, the quintessential frauds of our time. With tortured faces and ostensibly anguished hearts, they regularly remind us that a scant century ago it was commonplace for blacks in this country to be lynched; occasionally, in fact, they liken those lynchings to modern-day white-on-black attacks, thereby im-plying that little has changed in the past hundred years or so. Mean-while they turn a deaf ear to the screams of the multitudes, both black *and* white, being victimized by black assailants on a daily basis. Con-sider that the peak year for white-on-black lynchings in our nation was 1896, when 161 people lost their lives in that awful manner.[250] Today it takes just a few months for that total to be surpassed by the black-on-black murders in at least half a dozen different American cities.[251]

While the black community in the United States is being decimated by a *self-inflicted* genocide, "civil rights" groups focus almost exclusively on *white* transgressions. A thousand members of the NAACP, for instance, marched through downtown Chicago in July 1994 to protest an incident in which several black youths claimed to have been denied service at a local Burger King restaurant. NAACP executive director Benjamin Chavis sternly warned white America, "If you mistreat one African American, you have to deal with all of us. Our strength is our unity."[252] Thus, a relatively minor dispute in a fast-food establishment was elevated to a major crisis by an organization that ignores millions of black-on-black and black-on-white *felonies* each year. This blatant double standard is nothing short of disgraceful.

As noted earlier, American journalists have, for the most part, bought into the "civil rights" vision. In June 1990, for example, *The New York Times* printed "Black Men: Are They Imperiled?"—an article discussing the high rate at which black males are victimized by homicide.[253] Nowhere did it mention that the vast majority of those who prey upon blacks are black themselves; that if blacks are in fact imperiled, it is by one another. Presumably, the *Times* writer deemed such details inconsequential.

Similarly, a *New York Times* reporter covering the 1992 "sneaker polish" hoax in the Bronx (see pages 64-65) noted the "extraordinary public attention" being focused on that "particularly cruel" attack,[254] which she characterized as part of a "string of well-known crimes that have tainted New York's reputation as a melting pot—the Howard Beach killing, the slaying of Yusef K. Hawkins."[255] Yet she never mentioned that both citywide and nationwide, only a small percentage of white assailants target black victims, whereas more than half of black assailants choose white victims. Instead, she asked readers to believe that only *white-on-black* violence offered compelling evidence that "the melting pot" of racial harmony was boiling over. Such a contention, of course, was pure intellectual dishonesty.

Notwithstanding the fact that the vast majority of interracial violence is black-on-white, many people view white fear of black crime as evidence of racism. For instance, in February 1999 Cardinal John O'Connor of New York urged members of his Saint Patrick's Cathedral congregation to examine the bigotry possibly lurking in their own hearts. "If I am walking a lonely street at night," he asked rhetorically, "do I fear the approach of a white man as I fear the approach of a black man? Let's be brutally honest."[256] But O'Connor's implication (that white fear of black crime is rooted in racism) does not address the fact that *blacks* fear black crime as much as whites do. Consider that in a 1991 national survey, fully 59 percent of African Americans (and just 52 percent of whites) agreed with the statement that blacks, as a group, are "aggressive or violent."[257] Consistent with this finding, another recent study (cited earlier in this chapter) showed that some 52 percent of blacks were afraid to walk the streets of their own neighborhoods at night.[258] Given these thorny but vital realities, it hardly seems sensible to reflexively ascribe *anyone's* fear of black crime to racism. Rather, it is reasonable to assume that such fear is, in most cases, merely a realistic response to the disproportionately high rate at which black men currently commit crimes.

Is the Justice System Racist?

The vast majority of blacks believe that the American criminal-justice system—from the police to the courts—discriminates against them. A 1981 Florida poll found that 97 percent of blacks considered the system racist, while a more recent *USA Today*/CNN/Gallup poll puts the figure at 66 percent[259]—still alarmingly high. Black "leaders" and the black media, meanwhile, are virtually unanimous in asserting that the system is racist, and the clamor of these opinion shapers drowns out most voices of dissent. Los Angeles congresswoman Maxine Waters, for one, claims that "the color of your skin dictates whether you will be arrested or not, prosecuted harshly or less harshly, or receive a stiff sentence or gain probation or entry into treatment."[260] She warns that by imprisoning disproportionate numbers of black males, "we are risking an entire generation of African American young men because of an unjust justice system."[261] Along the same lines, author Daniel Georges-Abeyie writes that racism "is the single most damaging reality of the criminal-justice system—a reality that is responsible for the disrespect, distrust, and fear that black people hold for the law."[262] An NAACP report speaks of "race, police, and violence" as "inseparable in this country." Racism, the report asserts, "informs every aspect of policing" in the United States.[263] A Catholic pastor in New York contends that one of the justice system's principal objectives is "putting young black males in jail by any means necessary."[264] Jesse Jackson, decrying America's "jail-industrial complex," maintains that blacks are overrepresented in prison populations not because of their criminal activity, but because the justice system holds them to a different standard than whites.[265]

Clearly, charges of racism in law-enforcement are brought forth with regularity by political, academic, and religious leaders. When black New York assemblyman Arthur Eve learned in 1990 that blacks in his state were at least ten times more likely than whites to be in prison or under court jurisdiction, he swiftly concluded that "New York is the most racist state in America."[266] In the early 1990s, a brochure put together by the Dinkins administration in New York City informed its readers that there "won't be peace" until the police stop running "young men of color . . . off the streets."[267] Activist Sonny Carson decries the criminal-justice system's "conspiracy" against black youth.[268] Professor Cornel West charges that "whites have often failed to acknowledge the widespread mistreatment of black people, especially black men, by law-enforcement agencies."[269] White political scientist Andrew Hacker cynically concludes that "despite constitutional safeguards, police and prosecutors and judges still find it relatively easy to ensure that one out of every five black men will spend some part of his life behind bars."[270] The Reverend Calvin Butts asserts that law-enforcement officials indiscriminately round up and incarcerate black men—even those who have done nothing wrong. Drawing a parallel between today's prisons and the plantations of the old South, Butts likens blacks currently behind bars to the slaves of yesteryear. "We have to tell them [whites] to let our people go," he proclaims.[271] In a similar vein, the Reverend Herbert Daughtry declares that police officers pose a greater danger to blacks than do organized hate groups.[272] Through sheer repetition, these allegations have been transformed into accepted "facts," though there is *no* evidence to support them.

Following the lead of "civil rights" messiahs, the media generally are quick to publicize stories seeming to prove the racism of America's justice system. In constant pursuit of sensational headlines, journalists are ever-ready to trumpet tales of inconsistent, discriminatory sentencing patterns. In June 1991, for instance, *The New York Times* reported that a judicial commission had "spent three years and $1 million sifting evidence ranging from scholarly studies to bathroom graffiti to jailhouse jargon [and] concluded that the New York State court system is 'infested with racism.' "[273] Upon closer examination, however, it becomes clear that this "study" had major flaws and was, in fact, little more than a propaganda piece serving the heralds of white racism everywhere. Consider, for example, that "the panel reasoned that since the court system is a crowded, rough, and sometimes humiliating place for those caught up in it, and since a disproportionate number of those accused of crimes are black and Hispanic, the system must be regarded as racist."[274] In other words, those evaluating the judicial system presupposed that any racial or ethnic imbalance in arrest and incarceration statistics must *necessarily* have been due to racism, rather than to the unequal rates at which members of various groups committed crimes. Thus, eschewing logic, the panel "proved" that arrest patterns were discriminatory simply by stating that members of different groups were arrested at different rates.

At the very end of the *Times* article, the following was revealed:

> Much of the report dwells on a minority member's perception of the court system, such as a black entering a courtroom where all the court officers are white. "One of the great problems we have is the problem of perception," Judge [Sol] Wachtler said in an interview. "Perception becomes reality when it comes to bias or prejudice. If there is the perception that a justice system is not treating all the citizens fairly, then the justice system is not going to work."[275]

A significant portion of the report, then, was based purely on the personal perceptions of minority defendants—perceptions jaundiced not only by the unpleasant experience of being tried and sentenced, but also by the "civil rights" establishment's constant depiction of the justice system as racist.

Another widely publicized study, published in 1989, reported that in nearly two-thirds of Georgia jurisdictions, black criminals were twice as likely as whites to go to jail for the same offenses—making for sensational speculations about the evil forces at work in southern courtrooms. Yet journalists never mentioned that the researchers had ignored the influence of prior convictions on sentencing. Because all legal systems in the world punish repeat offenders more severely than first-timers, any study of incarceration patterns that disregards prior convictions is virtually worthless.[276] This very obvious fact, however, was apparently not understood by many in the media. The same faulty analysis was evident in a January 1999 *New York Times* article reporting that "black prison inmates generally serve more time for the same crime than white inmates: 26 months for blacks for all types of crimes compared with 24 months for whites." Once again, the effect of prior convictions was ignored.[277]

What *do* we know about comparative sentencing patterns? *Do* black offenders receive stiffer penalties than white offenders for equivalent crimes? The most exhaustive, best-designed study of this matter—a three-year analysis of more than 11,000 convicted criminals in California—found that the severity of sentences depended heavily on such factors as prior criminal records, the seriousness of the crimes, and whether guns were used in the commission of those crimes. Race was found to have no effect whatsoever. In fact the researcher, Joan Petersilia, was forced to admit that these results contradicted the conclusions she had drawn from an earlier study—when she had not taken prior convictions and the use of firearms into account.[278]

The criminal-justice process is comprised of a number of stages or "decision points" at which law-enforcement personnel (such as police and judges) must decide how to proceed (i.e., whether to make an arrest, whether to convict or acquit a defendant, or whether to impose a harsh or mild sentence). Contrary to popular mythology, there is *no* evidence of racial discrimination at any of these decision points. Black overrepresentation is almost entirely at the arrest stage—reflecting the simple fact that the "average" black breaks the law more frequently than the "average" white. (See the forthcoming section titled "The Police" for a comprehensive explanation of this point.) Not only are the outcomes at all other decision points nearly identical for both races, but the slight differences that do exist tend to favor *blacks*. Moreover, there is no evidence to support the stereotype that southern states are likely to have inordinately large black-white disparities in arrest, conviction, and execution rates—presumably because of bigoted white sheriffs, judges, and juries. No such pattern exists. In fact, a number of southern states have racial gaps smaller than the national average.[279] Further, the arrest rates of blacks living in cities that are politically black-controlled are no lower than the arrest rates of blacks in white-controlled cities.[280]

There *is* evidence, however, that certain *individual* decision-makers are more likely to be lenient with whites than with blacks. Anecdotal accounts of their decisions, loudly and repeatedly publicized by "civil rights leaders," form the basis of the myth that blacks cannot get fair treatment in American courts. But there are, in fact, *other* individual decision-makers with an *equal* tendency to be harder on *whites* than on *blacks*, and this "cancelling out effect" results in no overall racial variance.[281] For instance, while one judge in Fulton County, Georgia recently meted out severe sentences to 56 percent of black defendants but only 24 percent of white defendants in his courtroom, another judge in the very same county imposed harsh sentences on 67 percent of whites but only 11 percent of blacks. Overall, then, "the court" did not discriminate.[282]

Similar examples of individual discriminators can be found on juries as well. While black "leaders" and citizens alike frequently malign white jurors for their verdicts in cases involving blacks, there have also been many questionable decisions by black jurors in cases involving whites. In some American cities, black jurors are unlikely to believe any testimony given by white police officers and are reluctant to convict black defendants even when there is formidable evidence of their guilt. Indeed, as long ago as the 1970s Bronx district attorney Mario Merola observed that it was virtually impossible to convict a black defendant in his borough because minority jurors largely rejected the testimony of white police officers.[283] "When I started in this office," another Bronx prosecutor recently told *The New York Times*, "the strongest case [we] could have . . . was when all [our] witnesses were police officers. Now, sadly, it's the weakest."[284] "If you have a case involving cops," adds a fellow prosecutor, "you [the prosecutor] are almost certain to lose."[285]

Consider that in the Bronx, where more than 80 percent of jurors are black or Hispanic—as are the overwhelming majority of defendants—47.6 percent of felony cases result in acquittals. This is a rate nearly three times higher than the national average.[286] The story is much the same in Washington, D.C., where 95 percent of defendants and 70 percent of jurors are black. Defendants go free in 29 percent of the city's felony trials—almost double the national acquittal rate.[287] Other cities with substantial minority populations reflect similar statistics.[288] According to Paul Butler, a black criminal-law professor at George Washington University, many black jurors simply believe that black defendants "are better off out of jail, even though they're clearly guilty." Black jurors, Butler contends, actually have a "moral responsibility . . . to emancipate some guilty black outlaws."[289]

Butler's philosophy was clearly on display in the February 1995 trial of Curtis Rower, a black Atlanta man who had shot and killed a thirty-nine-year-old white woman in front of her two young children. The evidence against Rower, who confessed to the crime, was so overwhelming that the defense did not even attempt to raise a reasonable doubt as to his guilt. "He is absolutely, unequivocally, without further discussion, as guilty as a man could be of taking another person's life," defense attorney Edwin Marger conceded. But Marger also tried to evoke the jurors' sympathies by portraying his client as an underprivileged black man living "in a world apart, a subculture, in a country with great bounties." During deliberations, black jury foreman Henry Parks announced that he believed none of the evidence against Rower. The defendant, Parks explained, was the victim of a poor upbringing, the product of circumstances which the white jurors did not understand. The case ended in a mistrial.[290] Similarly, a 1995 Baltimore jury that included eleven blacks refused to convict defendant Davon Neverdon of murder, despite the compelling testimony of four eyewitnesses.[291]

In 1992 Edward Evans, a young black man from Washington, D.C., was arrested for the gunshot murder of a local white man. Not only did two of Evans's friends testify in court that they had actually seen him shoot the victim, but one of them reported that Evans hated white people and had long been intent on killing a white man. In spite of such powerful evidence, however, black juror Velma McNeil refused to convict. During deliberations, she told fellow jurors that the judicial system was systematically biased against blacks. After forcing a mistrial, McNeil emerged from the courtroom and openly embraced a member of the defendant's family.[292]

Most tragic of all are those cases where obviously guilty defendants are acquitted. Consider the case of Joel Lee, a white Maryland man who, on September 2, 1993, was confronted by a group of black males demanding money from him. When the terrified Lee was slow to comply, one of the blacks shot him in the face and killed him. After the gunman was apprehended, his defense attorney offered to have him plead guilty in return for a forty-year prison sentence. But prosecutors and the victim's family, unwilling to settle for anything less than a life sentence with no possibility of parole, insisted on taking the case to court. In the trial, not only did several eyewitnesses give incriminating testimony against the gunman, but some of his friends revealed that he had bragged to them about his awful deed. After all the evidence was presented, a jury of eleven blacks and one Pakistani deliberated for nine hours, at which point one juror sent a note to the judge that read, "I feel as though it is becoming a racial issue to some of my fellow jurors. If possible, please excuse me from this jury duty." The judge denied the request, and the next afternoon the jury announced its verdict: not guilty on all charges.[293] In much the same way, the 1990 Washington trial of accused murderer Darryl Smith ended in acquittal when a minority juror who "didn't want to send any more young black men to jail" swayed the rest of the panel to his point of view.[294]

While racial discrimination clearly has occurred in many court cases, against both blacks and whites, there is no evidence of *systemic* antiblack bias in our modern-day criminal-justice system. In studies that consider all relevant variables—the defendant's prior criminal record, the severity of the crime in question, the offender's demeanor with police, whether a weapon was used, and whether the crime in question was victim-precipitated—no differences have been found in sentencing patterns, either in relation to the victim's race or the offender's race.[295] It is noteworthy that in the 1930s—long before the passage of our country's major civil rights legislation—black Americans were four times more likely than whites to serve time in prison; by 1979 this number had grown to eight times more likely. Did America become more discriminatory, or could it be that prison statistics do not have much to do with discrimination?[296]

The Police and the Courts

Why is the average black far more likely to be arrested than the average white? Is it because African Americans actually commit a disproportionate share of crimes, or are they the victims of discriminatory police arrest patterns? Thanks to the National Crime Victimization Surveys (NCVS) conducted annually by the Census Bureau, the answer to these questions is clear.[297] Victims and witnesses of violent crimes such as robbery, rape, and assault are usually able to see an attacker well enough to at least identify his or her skin color—along with other distinguishing characteristics like sex, height, weight, hair color, and clothing. Since these descriptions are generally what enable the police to make arrests in such cases, even the most racist officer has very little room for discretion; he cannot arbitrarily arrest a black person if witnesses identify a white offender. NCVS data show that statistically, the average black is far more likely than the average white to be identified, by a victim or witness, as the perpetrator of a violent crime. This racial gap, moreover, is approximately equal to the racial gap in actual arrest rates. In other words, blacks are arrested for violent crimes in proportionately higher numbers than whites not because of police racism, but simply because they commit those crimes at higher rates than whites.[298]

Conversely, in property crimes such as burglary or auto theft, which are far less likely to have witnesses, and for which a great deal of proactive investigation is necessary to find and arrest a suspect, a racist police officer would have a much greater opportunity to arbitrarily, unjustly arrest blacks. Therefore, if police racism were indeed responsible for the comparatively high overall arrest rate of blacks, we would expect to find a greater racial imbalance in arrests for property crimes than for violent personal crimes. Such is not the case, however; the racial gaps for property crime arrests are significantly *smaller*. Correcting for the unequal population sizes of black and white Americans, the black-white arrest ratio for burglary is 3.92 to 1, for larceny-theft 3.97 to 1, for auto theft 4.01 to 1, and for arson 2.96 to 1. To put it another way, the average black is approximately three to four times more likely to be arrested for property crimes than is the average white. By contrast, the black-white arrest ratios for personal crimes (where police have almost no room to allow their own prejudices to influence their arrest patterns) are 6.76 to 1 for murder, 6.66 to 1 for rape, 11.95 to 1 for robbery, and 5.06 to 1 for aggravated assault.[299] Clearly, there is no evidence of systemic police discrimination against blacks in making arrests. In a recent review of the literature, the politically liberal author Michael Tonry was forced to conclude that "black incarceration rates are substantially higher than those for whites . . . [because] black crime rates for imprisonable crimes are substantially higher than those for whites."[300]

Despite such facts, however, critics of the police persist in alleging unfair treatment. One study that is frequently cited as "proof" of police bias examined nearly 5,700 police encounters with civilians in various metropolitan areas around the country, and found that blacks were arrested in 21.4 percent of their run-ins with police, while whites were arrested 13.1 percent of the time—a disparity of 8.3 percent.[301] Though this gap led many to conclude that blacks were being discriminated against, in truth the offender's race was not nearly the best predictor of whether a police officer would make an arrest. Several variables—the offender's demeanor with police, the seriousness of the crime, and whether a weapon was used—were much better predictors than race. For example, more than 37 percent of "antagonistic" offenders were arrested, as compared with only 12.8 percent of "civil" suspects, regardless of race. Moreover, when the crimes in question were felonies, 42.5 percent of suspects were arrested, whereas for misdemeanors the likelihood of arrest was just 13.7 percent—again, regardless of race.[302] But since blacks commit, per capita, many more violent felonies than do whites, it is reasonable to assume that the black offenders examined in this study were more likely than their white counterparts to be implicated in such serious crimes; it is also reasonable to assume that these felons were more prone to exhibit antagonistic behavior toward police officers than were misdemeanants. Finally, the 8.3 percent disparity in arrest rates before such additional considerations is too small to account, in any meaningful way, for the fact that blacks are arrested, per capita, about four and a half times more commonly than whites.[303]

If it were true that racial discrimination by white police officers contributes to the high arrest rate of blacks, it would logically follow that the arrest decisions of black officers should differ significantly from those of their white colleagues. Since black officers would not be expected to paint all members of their own race with the broad brush of bigotry, one might expect them to arrest blacks at a lower rate than do white officers. There is no evidence of such a difference, however. Black and white officers have very similar arrest patterns.[304]

Another current hotbed of controversy is the issue of police brutality, which the vast majority of blacks in the U.S. consider more likely to be directed at them than at whites.[305] Community activists—ever-eager to recite lists of cases in which blacks were treated roughly by white officers—point to such incidents as undeniable proof of racism among law-enforcement personnel. These anecdotes, trumpeted by loud and angry voices, form the foundation of black Americans' belief in their own vulnerability to police abuse. "There is a widespread feeling among [blacks]," writes black columnist Bob Herbert, "that they are living in a police state, and that many of the cops are a threat to the very lives of their children. The anger and resentment over this is growing by the day."[306] A March 1999 *New York Times* poll of New York City residents found that 63 percent of blacks classified police brutality against minorities as "widespread."[307] In the same poll, 81 percent of blacks said that police officers generally favored whites over blacks.[308]

In truth, however, there is considerable literature suggesting that black suspects are treated no worse than white suspects—when their demeanors toward the police are similar and their crimes are equivalent.[309] One study in particular found not only that black suspects were less likely than white suspects to be handled roughly by the police, but also that black *citizens in general* were less likely than their white counterparts to have the police use excessive force against them for any reason.[310] Research further shows that both white and black police officers are more likely to use excessive force against antagonists of their own race than against those of another race.[311] Black officers as a group, for instance, are more likely than their white colleagues to shoot black suspects. While this may be partly because black officers more frequently patrol black neighborhoods, black and white officers who work only in black neighborhoods are equally likely to shoot black civilians.[312]

The author of a lengthy report examining the link between race and police arrest patterns cites the findings of eight different studies to support his contention that police officers handle black offenders more roughly than white offenders. Yet not one of those studies presents any evidence that *comparable* black and white suspects are treated differently by the police. Differences are found only when the treatment of *all* black criminals is compared with the treatment of *all* white criminals, regardless of their crimes. This is because black offenders are statistically overrepresented in violent crimes that are likely to elicit a dramatic police response. By contrast, when we classify criminals into groups that differ only by race (i.e., when we do not compare black murderers with white misdemeanants, but with white murderers), we find that the police treat blacks and whites in basically the same manner.[313] It takes courage to examine facts carefully, to compare like with like, and to avoid the temptation to twist truth into "proving" what one wants to prove.

Notwithstanding the weighty evidence that contradicts their

every allegation, "civil rights leaders" relentlessly crusade to convince the world that police racism is rampant. They complain, for instance, that some 50 percent of all criminal suspects killed by police officers are black—presumably a suspiciously high figure for a group that constitutes barely one-eighth of the U.S. population. Yet they neglect to mention that 50 percent is actually a very reasonable figure in light of the fact that blacks commit almost half of the violent crimes which are virtually certain to bring a perpetrator into contact with the police; that more than 60 percent of those slain suspects are themselves carrying firearms when the police gun them down;[314] and that 85 percent of all police officers slain in the line of duty are white men whose killers are usually black.[315] Finally, no one grumbles over the fact that black civilians are responsible for about three-fourths of all justified, self-defense killings of other civilians—and that the great majority of those slain in such cases are also black.[316] Why do the champions of "justice" give the benefit of the doubt to black civilians who kill black criminals, but rush to condemn white police officers who kill black criminals?

Knowing the truth about such issues can literally be a matter of life and death, for there are many who use charges of police racism as pretexts for violence. For example, the 1992 Los Angeles and Washington Heights riots (see chapter 5) saw dozens killed, hundreds more injured, and property destroyed on a massive scale—all because blacks and Hispanics in those communities were persuaded to believe that the criminal-justice system was racist. As criminologist William Wilbanks explains, black Americans' contempt for the justice system produces a "justification" to disobey the law. "Some blacks receive the message," says Wilbanks, "that they are not actually offenders when they commit a crime but [are] victims of an unjust system."[317]

This message, of course, emanates from many high places in the black community. According to Al Sharpton, much black crime is merely retaliatory violence. "We must not reprimand our children for outrage," he says, "when it is the outrage that was put in them by an oppressive system."[318] Similarly, in the wake of a 1980 black riot in Miami, the Urban League president suggested that the city's "white power structure"—political and judicial—had created a racial atmosphere in which refraining from rioting was "too much to ask of any [black] human being."[319] Unfortunately, the constant drumbeat of such nonsense has poisoned millions of American minds, making it possible for the myth of a racist justice system to gain wide acceptance even in the absence of empirical evidence to support it.

Consider that in 1983 the liberal-leaning National Academy of Sciences found "no evidence of a widespread systematic pattern of discrimination in sentencing."[320] In 1985 the *Journal of Criminal Law and Criminology* concluded that a disproportionate number of blacks were in prison not because of a double standard of justice, but because of the disproportionate number of crimes they committed.[321] That same year, federal government statistician Patrick Langan conducted an exhaustive study of black and white incarceration rates and found that "even if racism [in sentencing] exists, it might explain only a small part of the gap between the 11 percent black representation in the United States adult population and the now nearly 50 percent black representation among persons entering state prisons each year in the United States."[322] A 1993 study by the National Academy of Sciences arrived at the same conclusion.[323]

In a 1987 review essay of the three most comprehensive books examining the role of race in the American criminal-justice system, the journal *Criminology* concluded that there was little evidence of anti-black discrimination.[324] Four years later a Rand Corporation study found that a defendant's racial or ethnic group bore little or no relationship to conviction rates; far more important than race were such factors as the amount of evidence against a defendant, and whether or not a credible eyewitness testified.[325] In 1993 a Justice Department study tracked the experience of more than 10,000 accused felons in our country's seventy-five largest cities and found that black defendants actually fared *better* than their white counterparts. Indeed, 66 percent of black defendants were actually prosecuted, versus 69 percent of white defendants. Among those prosecuted, 75 percent of blacks and 78 percent of whites were convicted.[326] Likewise, a 1996 analysis of 55,000 big-city felony cases found that black defendants were convicted at a lower rate than whites in twelve of the fourteen federally designated felony categories.[327] This finding is consistent with the overwhelming consensus of other recent studies, most of which indicate that black defendants are slightly *less* likely to be convicted of criminal charges against them than white defendants.[328]

Moreover, there is no evidence that white judges as a group are more likely than black judges to send blacks to prison or to give them longer sentences.[329] The previously cited 1991 Rand

Corporation study of robbery and burglary defendants found almost no relation between a defendant's race or ethnicity and his likelihood of receiving a severe sentence.[330] Two years later a study of federal sentencing guidelines found no evidence of racially disparate punishments for perpetrators of similar offenses. The seriousness of the crime, the offender's prior criminal record, and whether weapons were used accounted for *all* the observed interracial variations in prison sentences.[331] In 1995 statistician Patrick Langan analyzed data on 42,500 defendants in the nation's seventy-five largest counties and found "no evidence that, in the places where blacks in the United States have most of their contacts with the justice system, that system treats them more harshly than whites."[332] This is true for youngsters as well as adults. There have been hundreds of post-1969 studies of minorities in the juvenile-justice system, and barely two dozen show even the slightest evidence of possible racial discrimination.[333] As Princeton professor John DiIulio, Jr. writes:

> The evidence on the race-neutrality of incarceration decisions is now so compelling that even topflight criminologists who rail against the anti-drug regime, mandatory sentencing laws, three-strikes laws, and other policies with which they disagree are nonetheless careful to contend that racial biases are "built into the law," are "America's dirty little secret," or constitute "malign neglect." In other words, they do everything but challenge the proposition that blacks and whites who do the same crimes and have similar criminal records are now handled by the system in the same ways.[334]

Racial Profiling

No issue in contemporary criminal justice arouses more passion than racial profiling, a term referring to the police consideration of race in determining whether to search the property—particularly the vehicle—of a suspect who has violated a specific law, major or minor. Consider that during an eighteen-month period in 1997 and 1998, whites accounted for 59 percent of the 87,489 drivers whom police stopped for traffic violations along the New Jersey Turnpike, while blacks accounted for 27 percent. Of those 87,489 stops, about 1,200 resulted in the officers searching the vehicles involved. But only 21 percent of the cars searched were driven by whites, while fully 53 percent were driven by blacks.[335] These disproportions caused the guardians of "equity" to complain that police racism was rearing its ugly head on the roads of the Garden State. Al Sharpton sarcastically quipped that "all blacks become suspects" simply because of their skin color.[336] President Clinton called racial profiling "the opposite of good police work where actions are based on hard facts, not stereotypes. It is wrong, it is destructive, and it must stop."[337]

Notwithstanding such statements and the strong emotions that underlie them, there is utterly no reason to characterize racial profiling as a racist policy. Rather, it is founded on one of modern criminology's most important ideas, and one that has revolutionized police practice—the belief that serious crimes can be prevented by aggressively targeting minor offenses as well. For example, when William Bratton headed New York City's Transit Police in the late 1980s, part of his strategy for controlling subway violence was to have his officers make arrests for such small infractions as fare beating, panhandling, graffiti, smoking, and boisterous behavior. Within two years, the city's subway felonies had dropped by more than 30 percent, in large part because *one-sixth* of all fare evaders stopped by the police were either carrying a weapon or were wanted for other crimes on outstanding warrants. Thus, as *The Wall Street Journal* reports, "By paying attention to behavior that most people regard as not worth bothering about, the Transit Police prevented some violent crimes on the subways."[338]

The same principle applies to felons on the highways: Many people who break major laws are also likely to violate minor ones, such as traffic regulations. Indeed, stopping motorists for driving infractions has resulted in the seizure of many illegal drug shipments—and even the apprehension of Oklahoma City bomber Timothy McVeigh, who first attracted police attention because his pickup truck had no license plate.[339]

Some important civil liberties issues are raised, of course, by allowing the police to cast a wide net. For instance, cracking down on subway fare beaters also snares (and embarrasses) some passengers who are merely in a great hurry to keep important appointments. Similarly, many otherwise respectable motorists may be subjected to intrusive and fruitless vehicle searches simply because they made an illegal turn or drove faster than the speed limit. Yet the fact that blacks are searched in disproportionate numbers is not a function of police racism, but of the unfortunate fact that blacks are several times more likely than whites to commit those serious crimes that law officers hope to uncover (see chapter 4 for statistics). On the New Jersey Turnpike during 1997 and 1998, about 10.5 percent of the searches of white-driven vehicles led to arrests or the seizure of contraband—usually drugs or weapons. Of the minority-vehicle searches, 13.5 percent produced arrests or the seizure of contraband.[340] This disparity is not as small as it may seem at first glance. The latter figure is fully 29 percent higher than the former, meaning that searches of minority-driven cars were almost one-third more likely to uncover something illegal.

Racial profiling, it should be pointed out, does not affect only blacks. The very term "profiling" first drew public notice by way of the FBI's behavioral-science unit, which developed the most famous of all criminal profiles—that of serial killers as predominantly white, male loners.[341] Moreover, many *white* drivers in certain black ghettos arouse police suspicions as possible drug traffickers—simply because the officers know, from experience, that white traffickers frequently deliver their shipments to dealers in those neighborhoods.[342]

It is also noteworthy that officers do not profile suspects by race alone. Among other things, they look for signs that a motorist has driven many hours without stopping—which drug transporters often do, for fear of leaving their cargoes unattended even for a brief time. Loose-fitting clothing, day-old beard stubble, and food wrappers on the car floor can be important clues. In addition, vehicles accoutred with potent air fresheners (commonly used to fool drug-sniffing police dogs) may arouse an officer's suspicion.[343]

Consider further that because the vast majority of our nation's felons are young men, male suspects under the age of thirty are much likelier than anyone else to be searched by the police. This does not indicate that police officers dislike men and young people—any more than racial profiling reveals bigotry. Asking the police to disregard what they know about the common characteristics of criminals—whether those traits involve race, age, or sex—is asking them to abandon reason. Clearly it would make no sense to require officers to search the belongings of men and women, or of people in their twenties and their seventies, in proportionate numbers. Why, then, should we blame the police for responding to the unpleasant but stubborn fact that African Americans, at the present time, commit a grossly disproportionate share of serious crimes? Los Angeles police chief Bernard Parks, who is black, puts it this way: "It's not the fault of the police when they stop minority males or put them in jail. It's the fault of the minority males for committing the crime. In my mind it is not a great revelation that if officers are looking for criminal activity, they're going to look at the kind of people who are listed on crime reports."[344]

Crack in the System

In recent years many critics of the justice system have noted that the penalties for possession of crack cocaine, which is most often used by poor blacks, are "excessive"—while penalties for possession of powder cocaine, whose users are typically affluent whites, are comparatively mild.[345] Though these critics generally suggest that the harsh anti-crack penalties were instituted by "racist" Republicans intent on incarcerating large numbers of blacks, the *Congressional Record* shows that such was not at all the case. In 1986, when the federal anti-crack legislation was being debated, the mostly-Democratic Congressional Black Caucus strongly supported it and actually pressed for even harsher penalties.[346] In fact, a few years earlier CBC members and other Congressional Democrats had pushed President Reagan to create the Office of National Drug Control Policy.[347]

Those who denounce the federal crack penalties conveniently fail to mention that the vast majority of our country's cocaine arrests are made at the state (not the federal) level, where sentencing disparities between cases involving powder and crack cocaine do not exist.[348] Furthermore, drug possession accounts for only 2 percent of all offenses that propel individuals into federal prisons. And those most likely to be incarcerated for drug convictions are not mere users, but *traffickers*, who are largely career criminals with very long rap sheets. In federal drug-trafficking cases, the average quantity of cocaine possessed by an offender is 183 pounds.[349]

Such facts, of course, hardly deter our "civil rights" mouthpieces from denouncing the "racist" double standard of justice for cocaine-related offenses. But notably, these critics view the alleged inequity solely from the *criminal's* perspective. That is, they overlook the fact that the harsher penalties for crack violations harm only a small subset of the black population—namely, drug dealers and users—while benefiting the great mass of law-abiding people in black neighborhoods.[350] Also overlooked is the fact that black Americans are actually *less* likely to be arrested for drug offenses than for crimes of violence.[351] Thus even if federal courts punished crack violations as lightly as powder cocaine infractions, the black prison population would scarcely shrink at all.[352]

The Death Penalty

While those who maintain that the American justice system is racist often decry the "discriminatory" application of the death penalty, almost no capital punishment statistic even remotely suggests antiblack racism. Some figures, in fact, could be interpreted as showing bias against *whites*. For example, a study commissioned by the NAACP's Legal Defense and Education Fund found that white convicted murderers in Georgia during the 1970s were 80 percent more likely to receive a death sentence than their black counterparts.[353] This is consistent with the fact that white murderers *nationwide* are more likely to be sentenced to death than black murderers (11.1 percent vs. 7.3 percent).[354] Moreover, whites who kill whites are slightly more likely to be sentenced to death than blacks who kill whites (11.5 percent vs. 10.4 percent);[355] and whites who kill blacks are slightly more likely to be on Death Row than blacks who kill blacks.[356] Of course, due to our court system's nearly interminable appeals process, only a small percentage of the criminals sentenced to death are actually executed in any given year. Consider that between 1977 and 1993, a period during which more than 400,000 Americans were killed in violence, just over 4,000 convicted killers were sent to Death Row.[357] Of those 4,000, only 227 were in fact executed—124 whites, 88 blacks, 14 Latinos, and 1 American Indian.[358] In other words, 55 percent of the murderers executed during those years were white and 39 percent were black, even though blacks committed well over half of all murders nationwide. Currently, about 58 percent of the prisoners on Death Row are white and 40 percent are black.[359]

Plainly, these facts cannot be reconciled with rhetoric about the death penalty supposedly favoring whites over blacks. Hard evidence exposes such rhetoric as nothing more than a lie—promulgated by frauds and responsible for generating great black resentment toward whites. Consider the words of Representative John Conyers, a prominent member of the Congressional Black Caucus, who laments that "blacks account for 40 percent [of Death Row inmates], while they account for only 12 percent [actually 13 percent] of the U.S. population."[360] Mr. Conyers seems strangely unaware that blacks are actually quite *under*represented on Death Row, given that they commit more than half of our nation's murders.

Because, obviously, no honest case can be made for the notion that black killers in general are disproportionately sent to Death Row, capital punishment's opponents have had to find creative ways of "proving" that the American justice system values white lives more than black lives. Perhaps the most commonly cited "proof" is the fact that someone who murders a white person is more likely to be sentenced to death than someone who murders a black person (11.1 percent vs. 4.5 percent).[361] In fact, a well-known statistical analysis conducted by Georgia State University professor Joseph Katz found that blacks who killed whites in Georgia during the 1970s received the death penalty 11 percent of the time, whereas blacks who killed *blacks* were sentenced to death just 1 percent of the time.[362]

Yet while these numbers may, at first glance, appear to incriminate the justice system, we must keep in mind that convicted killers cannot be executed in accordance with the whims and prejudices of judges and juries; that the law in fact requires that certain aggravating circumstances be proven before any murderer can be put to death. Among these circumstances are armed robbery, kidnapping, rape, mutilation, execution-style shooting, torture, and extreme physical brutality.[363] Notably, the Katz study found that black-on-white murders occurred in conjunction with one or more of these variables far more frequently than did black-on-black murders.[364] Fully 67 percent of black-on-white homicides, for instance, also involved armed robberies—as compared to just 7 percent of black-on-black homicides.[365] Black-on-black killings, moreover, were most commonly drug-, gang-, or family-related—categories that typically do not qualify for the death penalty.[366] In addition, 73 percent of those black-on-black incidents were "hot-blooded" killings that occurred between acquaintances or relatives fighting at home or in their neighborhoods. Black-on-*white* killings, by contrast, tended to be the more "cold-blooded," calculated, and brutal types of crimes that society punishes most severely.[367] The added question of whether aggravating circumstances were equally predictive of a death sentence for whites who killed blacks could not be answered by the Katz study, which simply did not review enough such cases to justify any statistical conclusions. White-on-black murders have been comparatively rare in the United States for many years, and only 22 of the nearly 2,500 homicides examined in the study involved whites killing blacks.[368]

Virtually all reliable research on capital punishment confirms the Katz study's finding that the death penalty does not discriminate against blacks. No careful scholarly study in recent years has demonstrated that a defendant's race plays a significant role in the outcome of murder trials.[369] In their exhaustive 1994 review of the literature, professors Stanley Rothman and Stephen Powers controlled for all relevant variables and found no evidence of racial discrimination in post-1972 capital sentencing.[370] Nor is there any evidence that black murderers serve longer prison terms than comparable white murderers.[371] It is time for Americans to realize that the "civil rights" brigade has been lying to them for a generation.

Misdirected Blame

Impervious as they are to hard facts and common sense, most of our "civil rights leaders" never tire of preaching that America's prison population is disproportionately black because the justice system discriminates. It is most remarkable that these apostles of "candor" and "truth" choose to blame racism, rather than the black family's disintegration, for the fact that a comparatively high proportion of black males are currently locked behind bars. Unwilling to acknowledge a link between the black incarceration rate and the 70 percent black out-of-wedlock birth rate,[372] they ignore the fact that growing up without a father is, statistically, a more reliable forecaster of a boy's future criminality than either race or poverty.[373] They are seemingly unmoved by the fact that regardless of race, 70 percent of youngsters in state reform institutions, 72 percent of adolescent murderers, 60 percent of rapists, and 70 percent of long-term prison inmates were raised without fathers.[374]

White-Collar Crime

There are those who assert that white offenders are underrepresented in violent crime statistics simply because they are immersed in the intrigues of white-collar crime. Exemplary of this view are the following remarks by white political scientist Andrew Hacker:

> In fact, we know much less about offenses by whites, since their crimes tend to be office-based, or involve insurance claims or tax evasion, fewer of which are uncovered or apprehended. . . . There is reason to believe that larcenous proclivities exist in members of every race but since more alternatives are open to whites, they have less need for thievery that threatens physical harm.[375]

Plausible though these assertions may seem, they are utterly without substance. Evidence simply does not support the notion that whites direct their energies toward white-collar crime more than blacks do. Rather, blacks are about three times more likely than whites to be arrested for forgery, counterfeiting, embezzlement, and receiving stolen property. These disproportions—though virtually ignored in the literature on race—have existed for decades.[376] It is dangerous beyond measure to base our assumptions on hearsay, anecdote, and mythology.

"A Real Clear Message"

On December 22, 1984, four black teenagers with prior criminal records surrounded and demanded money from a white subway passenger in New York named Bernhard Goetz. Realizing that he was in danger, Goetz, who was secretly carrying a loaded gun, drew his weapon and shot each of the would-be robbers. No one was killed, but one of the teens, Darrel Cabey, was rendered permanently paralyzed by the bullet that struck him. After the shooting, Goetz fled the train and went into hiding, thereby setting in motion a massive manhunt that ended ten days later when he voluntarily surrendered to police. While the national media gave this case extensive coverage, "civil rights leaders" everywhere portrayed Goetz as a racist who enjoyed "hunting" for black males. A grand jury, however, upon considering the facts of the case, refused to charge Goetz with attempted murder and indicted him only for possessing an unlicensed weapon—an offense for which he spent eight months in prison. But the case dragged on for several years after that because Cabey sued Goetz for damages in a civil trial and won a $43 million judgment in 1996. Cabey's attorney, Ronald Kuby, applauded the verdict for sending "a real clear message to all the bigots out there, all the racists with guns, all the people who consider the lives of young black men to be worthless. These lives are worth a lot and so you better keep those guns in the holster."[377]

Notably, Kuby did not say whether Cabey and his friends may themselves have injected race into the incident—by targeting Goetz mainly because he was white. Nor did the attorney speculate as to whether *black* gunmen considered the lives of young black men worthless. Presumably he expected Americans to believe that the Goetz case, which involved a white man who was minding his own business until he was accosted by a group of thugs, was more socially significant than the epidemic of black violence that had long been destroying thousands of lives, black *and* white, each year. Journalists and "civil rights leaders" apparently shared Kuby's view, giving the case such enormous publicity that millions of Americans soon became familiar with the name Bernhard Goetz.

Almost no one recognizes the name Austin Weekes, however. On the night of April 13, 1980, this twenty-three-year-old black man was riding a Brooklyn subway when two white teenagers confronted him, spat at him, and asked, "What are you looking at, Nigger?" At that point, the terrified Weekes pulled an unlicensed pistol out of his bag and shot one of the youths through the heart, killing him. Weekes then fled the train and remained in hiding until 1986, when he was found, arrested, and charged with second-degree murder for the 1980 shooting. While in police custody, Weekes wept as he explained that he had started carrying a gun just days prior to the shooting because he had recently been mugged. A Brooklyn grand jury, sympathetic to his predicament, chose not to indict him.[378] In contrast to the Goetz incident, this case received comparatively little media coverage. No "civil rights leaders" suggested that Weekes was "a racist with a gun" who had gone "hunting" for whites aboard the subway. Knowing that a black-on-white shooting would not stoke the fires of their crusade, our usually vocal demagogues remained quiet, waiting four more years for their shining moment in the sun when Bernhard Goetz reacted to some subway predators exactly as Austin Weekes had.

Chapter 5

Rage

A false conclusion once arrived at is not easily
dislodged. And the less it is understood,
the more tenaciously it is held.
                                    —Morris Kline[1]

Rodney King, a parolee who had recently been incarcerated for armed robbery, was drinking heavily the night of March 3, 1991, consuming a large quantity of high-alcohol beer. Shortly after midnight, he got into his car with two drinking buddies and headed for a liquor store to replenish his supply of booze. Driving with a blood-alcohol level more than twice the legal limit, he sped along a Los Angeles freeway at 80 mph, his radio blaring, singing loudly with his friends.[2]

When a police car's flashing lights appeared behind him, King, who was violating his parole by driving while intoxicated, knew that he would surely be sent back to prison if caught.[3] Thus he tried to escape, reaching speeds of up to 115 mph as his companions pleaded with him to stop the car.[4] When he was finally caught, King ignored police commands that he lie down on the ground—and instead smiled, danced, and waved to a police helicopter overhead.[5] He threw a kiss and wiggled his rear end at a female officer who had ordered him, at gunpoint, to lie down.[6] Four policemen tried to handcuff him, but the six-foot, three-inch, 250-pound suspect threw them off his back and punched at them wildly. Surmising that King was under the influence of PCP, a drug that can cause psychotic behavior and empower its user with extraordinary strength,[7] the officers tried unsuccessfully to subdue him with a 25,000-volt electric stun gun.[8] While a choke hold might have been the most effective method of bridling King, the Los Angeles Police Department had banned its use in 1982 after some drug users died from it. The officers' only recourse, therefore, was to use their nightsticks.[9] The blows they delivered to King were videotaped by an amateur photographer who later made the tape available to news reporters.

For a full year, a short segment of that tape was replayed countless times on television stations across the country. Virtually everyone in America became familiar with the image of Rodney King absorbing the blows of police batons. Politicians and law-enforcement officials nationwide asserted that justice demanded nothing less than the eventual conviction of all the officers involved. "We will not tolerate the savage beating of our citizens by a few renegade cops," said Los Angeles mayor Tom Bradley.[10] "The people of this city," he added, "have been slapped in the face by the attitude and bigotry of these officers."[11] In a similar vein, Los Angeles police chief Daryl Gates stated that "a few thoughtless officers have failed to have a reverence for the law . . . failed to understand their job to protect and serve."[12] "I am confident," said L.A.'s former police chief Ed Davis, "that the officers who beat Rodney G. King . . . will be charged and convicted by their own actions. . . . [T]he videotape of the incident is quite compelling enough to vault its stars into state prison."[13]

Yet the majority of the video, which was about four minutes long, was never seen by most Americans.[14] Portions of it clearly showed King resisting arrest and lunging aggressively at the officers, who could neither subdue him nor be certain that he was unarmed.[15] One may reasonably wonder why news telecasts, which so frequently aired the twenty seconds of tape showing excessive police force, gave virtually no exposure to the footage of King defying police authority. One might also wonder why nearly all media references to the incident characterized it simply as "the beating of black motorist Rodney King." Given King's criminal history and his behavior on the night in question, "motorist" hardly seems the most fitting term to describe the man.[16]

Moreover, reporters covering the story consistently referred to the four policemen who beat King as white. To this day, few Americans are aware that one of those officers was actually Hispanic.[17] Nor do many people realize that King had two black companions in his car on that fateful night, both of whom cooperated with the police, and neither of whom was harmed.[18] Shortly after the incident, in fact, King himself expressed his belief that race had *not* been a factor in the treatment he had received—a most significant statement which journalists chose to *ignore*.[19] (Of course, King would later change his story and claim that the officers had used racial epithets against him during the beating.)[20] The media's portrayal of the incident, in conjunction with the "civil rights" establishment's lamentations about an unjust American "system," filled many in the black community with indignation.[21]

In March and April 1992, the four policemen who beat King stood trial for the serious charges of assault with a deadly weapon and assault under color of authority.[22] Inexplicably, the media failed to clarify for the public the precise nature of these charges. While most Americans thought that the issue was simply whether the police had used undue force, the actual question was whether the officers had tried to inflict *serious bodily harm* on King. Indeed, one Oregon judge explained that under the laws of that state, an equivalent charge would have been attempted murder.[23] Consider the difficulty of proving such a charge in King's case. The paramedic who treated him immediately after the altercation said she saw only minor injuries, the worst of which was a cut on his face (though hospital x-rays later revealed a fractured right cheekbone and fibula).[24] Consider also that on his way to the hospital, King laughed, used obscenities, and resisted medics' attempts to treat him.[25] Apart from the question of whether the officers had used excessive force, the fact remains that King was not *seriously* injured in any way.

In all, the jurors heard twenty-nine days of testimony and viewed the entire videotape—not just the brief portion that the rest of America saw—and were unconvinced that the police had tried to seriously harm King. Consequently, on April 29 three of the defendants were fully exonerated, while the fourth was acquitted on all but one count. Of course, had the officers been charged with simple assault, the prosecution's burden of proof would have been much lighter and the likelihood of guilty verdicts far greater.[26] But this was an irrelevant detail to the many L.A. residents who had absorbed, for most of their lives, the rhetoric of "civil rights" orthodoxy. Their sense of outrage was further fueled by the statements of public officials like President George Bush, who lamented that the jury decision "has left us all with a deep sense of personal frustration and anguish."[27] Willie Brown, who was then the Speaker of the California Assembly, saw the verdicts as "a confirmation of years and years and years of racism within the criminal-justice system."[28] Slightly more than an hour after the verdicts were read, isolated pockets of violence broke out in South Central Los Angeles. When the police response was restrained and tentative, chaos quickly spread throughout the city.[29] For the next several days, we witnessed the worst American riots of the twentieth century.

Faces in the Crowd

Many of the rioters' victims were poor Asian and Hispanic immigrants who spoke little English and could not, by any stretch of the imagination, be said to represent the "white establishment" that had exonerated Rodney King's assailants. One such victim was Marisa Bejar, a Mexican woman who was driving with her husband and seven-month-old baby when the violence started. As her car was hit by a torrent of rocks, bricks, and wood, a gash that would require thirteen stitches was opened on the woman's face. A black man then leaned into the car, struck Mr. Bejar on the head, demanded all of his money, and threatened to kill him if he resisted. While other blacks in the vicinity shouted obscenities at their prey, a teenager threw a large sign at the car's rear window, shattering the glass and injuring the Bejar baby.[30]

Another Mexican family, the Vacas, also had their car bombarded by rocks. When the frightened driver veered and crashed into a nearby truck, a black mob rushed toward the car and pulled two men and a woman from the vehicle, beating and robbing them. One of the attackers candidly explained that he had joined in the violence simply because the victims were Mexican, "and everybody else was doin' it."[31]

Fidel Lopez, a self-employed Guatemalan construction worker, felt the full force of the rioters' brutality. A group of blacks stopped him in his pickup truck, pulled him out onto the street, spray painted his face black,[32] robbed him of $5,000 worth of building supplies, and destroyed his truck.[33] When Lopez tried to flee, several men pounded his head with a stereo speaker and kicked him into unconsciousness,[34] nearly severing his left ear.[35] The assailants then poured gasoline on the battered victim and sprayed his genitals with black paint. "He's black now, he's black now," they shouted with glee.[36] Lopez was so badly injured by the beating that he was unable to work for months afterward and became financially destitute. A year and a half later he still suffered from frequent headaches, back and chest pain, vomiting, and severe dizziness. In addition, his speech was significantly more halting than it had been before the attack—indicating that he had suffered some brain damage—and he was deaf in his left ear. "They destroyed me physically and economically," he said.[37]

The rioters showed no mercy for even the most defenseless victims. Mexican American Sylvia Castillo, for instance, was seriously injured by a black assailant who threw bricks and bottles at her while shouting, "Bitch, you are going to die."[38] "[We're] f——ing up everything white and Mexican that comes through here," yelled another.[39]

Fifty-two-year-old truck driver Larry Tarvin was one such "white thing." At a congested L.A. intersection, a group of blacks pulled the five-foot, seven-inch, 130-pound trucker out of his vehicle and stomped him mercilessly, inflicting fractured ribs, a cracked pelvis, and permanent facial scars on the battered victim. As Tarvin lay in the street, bleeding heavily, an onlooker shouted, "No pity for the white man. Let his white ass down. Now you know how Rodney King felt, white boy."[40]

Another unfortunate white victim was thirty-two-year-old Matt Haines, who was riding a motorcycle with his nephew when a gang of some fifteen blacks knocked the pair off the bike and beat them. Haines was shot in the head and killed in the attack, while his nephew was shot three times in the arm.[41]

Horrible as these incidents were, the white male who became the most widely recognized symbol of black retribution for the King verdict was Reginald Denny, a trucker who unwittingly entered an area where violence had broken out. Several black rioters hurled rocks through Denny's window and yanked him out of the vehicle, onto the street, where they began to kick him. One assailant threw a five-pound oxygenator at Denny's head, stepped on the victim's face, and struck him three times on the head with a claw hammer. Another man hurled a brick into Denny's temple, crushing part of his skull, and then performed a victory dance at the site of the attack. Others who came to join the onslaught also danced in celebration. Several of them threw liquor bottles at Denny, spat at him, and jumped on his head—leaving his face fractured in at least ninety places and his left eye dislocated.[42] While the victim lay unconscious in the street, a local crack user picked Denny's pockets with one hand while holding a liquor bottle in the other.[43] As one black policeman put it, "young men and women were . . . hollering and taking over the streets like it was a Nazi gala."[44]

In all, the 1992 Los Angeles riots left 58 people dead, more than 2,300 injured (227 of them critically), a billion dollars in property damaged or destroyed, and at least 5,300 buildings burned.[45] In L.A.'s Koreatown section, 80 percent of all businesses were damaged in some way.[46] There were smaller-scale violent outbreaks in other cities as well, with blacks attacking whites in Richmond, San Jose, Atlanta, Las Vegas, New York, and elsewhere. Yet a careful search of news reports did not reveal a single instance of white-on-black retaliation for any of these incidents.[47]

The "People's Rebellion"

Many prominent voices in the black community refused to condemn the rioting. Jesse Jackson, for one, deemed it an understandable reaction to societal racism. "Desperate people do desperate things," he explained.[48] Along the same lines, black author Walter Mosely declared, "America is a brutal land. Its language is violence and bloodshed. That's why [Rodney] King was beaten. That's why another [Martin Luther] King was assassinated."[49] Popular rap singer Sister Souljah saw the violence as retribution for the "white supremacy" which, "in the real world," caused black people to "die on a daily basis."[50] Los Angeles activist Paul Parker told NBC television's *Dateline* that he considered the rioters "heroes" who had courageously "stood up for black people." When asked if he felt any sympathy for Reginald Denny, Parker candidly replied, "No. I saw the white race being bloodied and beaten."[51] Benjamin Chavis, who would later become executive director of the NAACP, rejected the very term "riot"—characterizing the unrest as a "people's rebellion" against white injustice.[52] Similarly, a Berkeley professor of American history explained that L.A.'s destruction had actually been set in motion by "the clubbing of black America."[53] Professor Cornel West agreed, calling the riots a "multiracial, trans-class, and largely male display of justified social rage."[54] "The Los Angeles upheaval," he elaborated, "was an expression of utter fragmentation by a powerless citizenry."[55] Indeed, rage was the most widely offered explanation for the chaos that had gripped the city. The *Los Angeles Times* printed a week-long series of feature articles entitled "Understanding the Riots," which largely ascribed the violence to black rage induced by white racism, police harassment, and economic inequities.[56]

Los Angeles congresswoman Maxine Waters held "economic, social, cultural, and political" factors responsible for the disorder,[57] explaining that the looters were, for the most part, merely poor women "who wanted shoes for their children and bread."[58] Blaming the federal government's "neglect" of America's inner cities,[59] she was by no means the only Democrat to charge that the Reagan and Bush administrations had cut aid to the country's urban poor. Yet hard evidence shows that between 1980 and 1992, federal spending on social welfare programs actually *grew* from $538 billion to $774 billion (in constant 1992 dollars).[60] In fact, social welfare spending had been skyrocketing for nearly three decades, increasing more than sixfold (in real terms) since 1965.[61] Whereas in 1965 such spending had amounted to just 5.5 percent of the U.S. Gross Domestic Product, it reached 13.2 percent by 1992[62]—making it the largest single item in the federal budget.[63] In 1992, federal aid to state and city governments nationwide was $150 billion—the highest total in American history up to that time.[64] In 1991, the year in which Rodney King was beaten, Los Angeles County received more federal assistance than any other county in the United States.[65]

Waters further asserted that racial injustice was rampant in America. "Get angry and let these people know it," she exhorted blacks. "You do have power."[66] Like Professor West, she claimed that the L.A. tumult could rightly be called a "rebellion" or "insurrection," but not a riot. "Riot implies to me wild, crazed, uncalled-for actions," she explained, "and I'm not so sure that's quite appropriate for what took place in Los Angeles."[67] It was "unfortunate," she said, that "it takes things like this rebellion to wake people up."[68]

Bill Clinton, then the governor of Arkansas, shared Waters's compassion for those who had "rebelled." Attributing the violence primarily to capitalism's inequities, he called it "heartbreaking to see some little children going into the stores . . . and stealing from their neighbors, but they live in a country where the top 1 percent of Americans have more wealth than the bottom 90 percent."[69]

To Understand or to Punish?

Were the L.A. rioters basically good but disgruntled citizens who were "pushed over the edge" by perceived injustice, or did they in fact welcome the opportunity to exploit the breakdown of law enforcement? Certainly, film footage of their escapades often showed them laughing, cheering, even dancing while victims were brutalized.[70] Looters, meanwhile, expressed delight as they walked off with armfuls of stolen property. In one such scene, captured on videotape, a man robbing a store told his accomplices, "Bring all that sh——out. . . . Y'all can thank Rodney King for this. . . . Go back there and get the rest—Yeah."[71] Other film clips showed parents, with their children at their sides, methodically placing bundles of purloined merchandise into the trunks of their cars. The claims of Congresswoman Waters notwithstanding, the looters largely ignored such basic necessities as food and clothing. Instead they focused on alcohol and entertainment equipment, making liquor stores and electronics shops particularly popular targets.[72] "You could smell the liquor on people's breath from several feet away as they walked by," said one news reporter. "You already had anger and frustration at the intersection—and when you fueled it with alcohol it turned to insanity."[73] Indeed, these plunderers were no strangers to mood-altering substances. A *Los Angeles Times* survey estimated that two-thirds of the looters regularly used alcohol or drugs.[74]

Police department files in 1992 classified almost half of all black Los Angeles males aged twenty-one to twenty-four as gang members.[75] These young men, of course, contributed greatly to the city's destruction. Though most of them ascribed their participation in the riots to their personal sense of outrage over the unpunished beating of Rodney King, they generally had histories of violence long predating the King affair. In fact, it is reasonable to assert that by sacking the city, L.A.'s gangsters were simply pursuing their favorite pastime—albeit on a scale larger than usual. As one member of a gang unit at the county probation department put it, "They didn't care about Rodney King. Guys like King had been beaten up [by thugs] for decades in these neighborhoods. They were just using the verdict as an excuse to party."[76]

The very question of whether some rioters may have been motivated by genuine rage is, in the final analysis, irrelevant. Many people who perpetrate evil—from arsonists to serial rapists to cold-blooded killers—feel some degree of rage. The same is true on a larger scale. When the Nazis, for instance, tried to force their will upon the world, they too felt rage about many things—the humiliation imposed on Germany by the Versailles Treaty, the economic hardships their country was suffering, and the perceived evil of Jews.[77] Yet rage does not justify depravity.

There are times, moreover, when violence is predicated not on anger but on pure barbarism—as demonstrated by the L.A. rioters who laughed and danced while they robbed stores and attacked defenseless people. Consider also some sizable disturbances that have occurred following *happy* occasions. In Detroit and Chicago, thousands of city residents reacted wildly—destroying property and assaulting people—after their home teams won National Basketball Association (NBA) championships in recent years. Indeed, after the Chicago Bulls won their first NBA title in 1991, more than 100 of their "fans" were arrested for looting and reckless endangerment.[78] When the Bulls repeated their feat the following year, not only did the arrest total climb to over 1,000, but 107 police officers were injured while trying to quell the mayhem.[79] After the Bulls won their third successive championship in 1993, almost 700 people were arrested citywide—137 of them on felony charges—and two innocent bystanders were killed.[80] Some of these jubilant demonstrators sprayed the streets with gunfire, while others dragged people out of their cars and stabbed them.[81] Similar acts of senseless violence have frequently occurred in Europe following emotionally charged soccer games.

"Civil rights leaders," academicians, and members of the media commonly depict sadistic marauders who terrorize entire cities as reservoirs of sociological information, specimens to be examined so that society might learn how to better address its own "injustices." This perspective was demonstrated in May 1993 when reporters gave extensive coverage to an event of dubious merit—the National Urban Peace and Justice Summit, a conference at which gang members from twenty-six cities across the U.S. met in Kansas City, Missouri, purportedly to pledge a truce. "Gang Members Reach Agreement at Summit," read a typical newspaper headline.[82] In addition to whatever pacts were entered into—bargains that were, incidentally, kept secret by all the negotiators—some of the topics on the summit agenda included the "economic development of urban areas, police brutality, and political empowerment."[83] Largely escaping the media's notice was the irony of violent outlaws solemnly professing devotion to the economic prosperity of the very neighborhoods they themselves had systematically destroyed with an infusion of drugs and crime. Likewise unnoticed was the paradox of these most brutal individuals voicing their alleged concerns about *police* brutality.

Journalists who sidestep controversy, however, are not nearly as contemptible as self-serving politicians who seek, at any price, to curry favor with potential voters. Consider, for example, the fact that newly elected president Bill Clinton invited black leaders from two of America's most infamous gangs, the Crips and the Bloods, to attend not only his 1993 inauguration, but also an inaugural luncheon held in honor of "outstanding individuals."[84] If our elected officials are so frightened of being labeled "racists" that they lack even the good sense to dissociate themselves from society's most vicious enemies, then truly we are a people in deep trouble.

In October 1993 Jesse Jackson, Benjamin Chavis, and Louis Farrakhan gathered in Chicago to speak at yet another national conference of gang leaders. During his address, Jackson inspirationally informed the motley crew of felons in his audience that they represented the "new frontier of the civil rights struggle."[85] "This ain't no gang meeting," he later told reporters. "We're having an urban-policy meeting."[86] The conference participants, taking Jackson's lead, announced that they preferred to be called "street organizations" rather than the more pejorative "gangs." Their principal objective, they claimed, was "to get political power so we can enjoy economic power in this society."[87]

Young people receive a particularly warped message when "leaders" like Jesse Jackson laud criminals and thugs as vanguards in the march for social justice. As one writer explains:

When you have institutions and adults who endorse, with great
fanfare, that which is obviously pathological, two very great schisms
take place in the minds of the watching young. First, they lose the
ability to distinguish between good and bad. Secondly, in their
confusion, they are drawn to the darkest elements of society while
seeking to mimic what those in authority told them, by example, is
acceptable.[88]

Victims and Racists

From the moment the videotape of Rodney King's beating
was made public, millions of Americans—black and white alike—
saw him as a prototypal victim of white tyranny. He was, as one
black writer observed, "elevated to the status of Rosa Parks and
Martin Luther King."[89] Following the acquittal of the four Los Angeles police officers in April 1992, college campuses nationwide were
flooded by student protesters denouncing the jury verdict. Some 500
demonstrated at Yale; nearly 1,000 marched at the University of Massachusetts.[90] Celebrities, too, took pains to show their support for
King. With much fanfare, outfielders Darryl Strawberry and Eric Davis
invited King as a special guest to a Los Angeles Dodgers' baseball
game.[91] And politicians, whenever they felt the need to capitalize on
their purported understanding of black concerns, referred to King's
beating and the subsequent jury verdict as troubling examples of
society's lingering racism.

The police officers who in 1992 were exonerated in the King
case stood trial again the following year, this time on charges that they
had violated King's civil rights. As the day of the verdict neared, the
mayor and police chief of Los Angeles held a press conference in
which they pleaded with residents to refrain from violence in the event
of an acquittal.[92] In New York City, public-service television announce-
ments calling for racial tolerance were aired on all three major networks, and city officials begged for calm.[93] A pessimistic Benjamin
Chavis rushed to Los Angeles just prior to the verdict "to be with
those young brothers and sisters while they're being encircled right
now."[94] Then, on April 17, 1993, the jury pronounced two of the
policemen—including the lead officer, Sergeant Stacey Koon—guilty
of violating King's civil rights. Both officers were sentenced to two
and a half years in prison.

Why had these men been tried a second time? As one commentator explains, it was "because our leadership class, all the way to the top, reacted in panic to the Los Angeles riots, virtually promising a new trial, convictions, and jail terms if only the mob would stop pillaging. Koon [was] a sacrificial lamb, a political offering to appease the mob."[95] Judge John Davies, who handed out the thirty-month sentences, conceded as much when he announced his reasons for not imposing longer prison terms. "The second indictment and the second prosecution," he said, "has the specter of unfairness."[96]

Judge Davies, it should be noted, ruled that the officers had in fact acted in accordance with police department regulations until the last nineteen seconds of their altercation with King. It was just prior to those final seconds, said Davies, that they should have stopped hitting the uncooperative suspect with their batons. But it was those nineteen seconds that imprinted their image on the collective American memory. It was those few moments that brought Rodney King fame and fortune—and brought Stacey Koon bankruptcy, imprisonment, and the loss of an honorable career.[97]

"An honorable career?" one might ask. What could be honorable about a man who presided over such a flagrant abuse of power? Is Koon not clearly a racist without whose presence Los Angeles minorities are now safer? Perhaps these questions can best be answered by the following account of an incident that occurred in L.A.'s crime-ridden 77th precinct just a few months prior to the King affair, as reported by the *Los Angeles Times*:

> A black transvestite prostitute with open sores around his lips was seized by a heart attack and fell to the floor of the police station locker. As other officers stood back aghast, . . . Koon dropped to his knees and administered mouth-to-mouth resuscitation in a futile effort to save the man. An autopsy revealed what officers had feared—the dying prostitute had AIDS.[98]

Why had Sergeant Koon, a father of five children, risked his life to try to save that man? In Koon's own words, the reason was simple: because the black prostitute was, like all people, "made in the image and likeness of God."[99] These are hardly the words and actions of a racist. Indeed, it can reasonably be argued that Koon's selfless concern for others—whatever their color—far exceeds that of his pious critics.

By July 1995 Rodney King had been arrested six times since the night of his 1991 beating: once for speeding, twice for drunken driving, twice for spouse abuse, and once for trying to run over a police officer who had caught him enlisting the services of a transvestite prostitute.[100] During a 1994 trial in which King sued the city of Los Angeles for $9.5 million in "beating-related damages," he testified that while he was being struck by the nightsticks, he "felt stripped of my human decency and my will as a human being."[101] Presumably his "human decency" had been intact earlier on that 1991 night as he sped along the road in a drunken stupor at 115 mph. When he taunted the arresting officers, wiggled his rear end at them, refused to comply with their orders, and finally lunged at them, his "human decency" was apparently still unsullied. Moreover, King's memory mysteriously improved by the time the 1994 trial began. Whereas he had testified three years earlier that he could not recall whether the officers had used any racial epithets during the beating, he was now confident that they had. Such inconsistencies, however, had no effect on many people's perception that King—even with his long arrest record—was nothing more than an innocent victim of a racist posse in blue uniforms. King's attorney described his client as "a decent man that has become a symbol of a wrong to a people."[102] "This is a race case," he added. "I don't know how you can separate the Rodney King incident from black people, from African American people, from how we feel."[103]

In March 1994 King became a wealthy man when Los Angeles paid him $3.8 million as compensation for the baton blows he had endured three years earlier. Yet despite his victory in court, King remained the eternal victim, complaining that the award was too small.[104] Meanwhile, other lawbreakers were carefully observing just how profitable a few bruises could be. Soon after the King settlement, a number of L.A. outlaws committed petty crimes and then led police officers on high-speed car chases, hoping that they would be stopped, arrested, and roughed up a bit—so that they too might hit pay dirt.[105]

The Anonymous Victims

Rodney King, of course, was not the only person ever to have been treated roughly by the police, but his case was deemed more newsworthy than most simply because it featured white officers and a black victim. Other racial combinations, by contrast, draw virtually no public notice. Consider what occurred one February 1985 day when twenty-year-old Paul Fava and a friend were standing on a Bronx subway platform, waiting to board a train to South Street Seaport. Across the platform, a group of teenagers were shattering overhead light bulbs, prompting a passerby to call the police. But before Officer Marvin Yearwood and his partner arrived at the scene, the mischievous youths had boarded a train, leaving only Fava and his companion in the station. Yearwood, a thirty-two-year-old black transit cop, rushed toward Fava with his gun drawn, ordered him against the wall, and killed him with a bullet to the back of the head. The officer was eventually acquitted of criminally negligent homicide, but was removed from the police force because of his clear overreaction in the Fava case. Not surprisingly, few people ever heard about this tragedy. Garnering much more attention at the time was the recent death of Eleanor Bumpers, a deranged, knife-wielding black woman whom a *white* Bronx policeman had gunned down in self-defense three weeks earlier.[106] Whereas Ms. Bumpers's killing sparked angry protests by "civil rights" watchdogs throughout the city, Paul Fava died virtually unnoticed.

On January 3, 1992 in Miami, a twenty-three-year-old black man named Antonio Edwards was sitting in his parked blue Cadillac with two friends. His car, which was facing the wrong direction on a one-way street, was deemed suspicious by passing police officers because it matched the description of a vehicle used in a fatal shooting earlier that day. At least seven officers converged on the scene, pulled Edwards from the car, handcuffed him, and threw him to the ground. Black officer Carl Seals then applied a choke hold on the suspect for several minutes, inadvertently cutting off the young man's air supply and causing him to fall into a coma, from which he was not expected to recover.[107] Certainly this incident was as clear an example of excessive force as the Rodney King beating. Not only did Edwards sustain a far more serious injury than King, but police later learned that Edwards's car was not even the one involved in the earlier shooting—meaning that he was an innocent man, unlike Rodney King. Nonetheless, there were no riots, no marches, no voices raised in public protest. Today the name Antonio Edwards means nothing to America, whereas the name Rodney King is known to all. While King lives in perfect health and immense wealth, Edwards lies comatose in a Miami hospital bed, where he will likely remain in vegetative obscurity until the day his breathing ceases—because his injuries cannot be traced to the brutality of a white man.

On January 10, 1993, a white Rhode Island policeman was suspended without pay because, during a traffic stop the previous day, he had punched a sixteen-year-old named Frank Sherman. Three months later the officer walked into an auto body shop where Sherman and three friends were working and shouted, "You're all going to die." He then proceeded to shoot each of the young men point-blank, killing three of them and critically wounding the other.[108] Reprehensible though this crime was, however, it prompted no public outrage or charges of brutality—simply because the killer and all his victims were white. In short, the story had no racial angle for journalists and charlatans to exploit.

Neither did many people hear about the three New York correction officers who were charged with the fatal 1999 beating of inmate Thomas Pizzuto in Nassau County Jail. The defendants—two whites and a Hispanic—allegedly pummeled Pizzuto to quiet his incessant demands for heroin addiction treatment.[109] Because the victim was white, however, the protectors of "civil rights" had nothing to say about the incident.

The beating of Rodney King had the unusual feature of having been videotaped and subsequently shown innumerable times to a nation conditioned to believe in omnipresent white racism. Similarly, in April 1996 a television news helicopter videotaped a pair of white Los Angeles policemen using their nightsticks to hit two Mexicans whose pickup truck they had stopped along an L.A. freeway. The tape showed one deputy repeatedly clubbing the male driver on the back and shoulders for about fifteen seconds, even after the man had fallen to the ground, while another deputy struck a female passenger twice on the back with his nightstick and pulled her to the ground by her hair. The driver sustained an elbow fracture and was taken to a hospital for treatment, while the woman required no immediate medical attention.

Mexico's Ministry of Foreign Relations reacted angrily to the incident, sending a letter to the U.S. Department of State expressing "indignation" over the Los Angeles Police Department's "flagrant violation of human rights." The American Civil Liberties

Union, along with black and Hispanic advocacy groups, called the beating symptomatic of a nationwide pattern of racially motivated police abuses. "This is something that we know goes on every day in the lives of immigrants, African Americans, and poor people in general," said Robert Lovato, executive director of the Central American Refugee Center in Los Angeles. "It's been a disease we haven't been able to rid ourselves of."[110]

Lost amid the accusations of brutality and racism, however, was the fact that the truck driver had circumvented a Border Patrol checkpoint, ignored orders to stop, and then led police on a high-speed chase for *eighty miles*, sometimes reaching speeds of 100 mph—while nineteen additional Mexicans in the truck bed threw beer bottles and pieces of metal at the pursuing police car. At least twice during the chase, the truck driver sideswiped other moving vehicles in an effort to divert police attention. When the truck finally stopped, all nineteen passengers quickly fled into the roadside brush, thereby leaving the officers vulnerable to an ambush, and making the quick incapacitation of the driver and his sidekick all the more imperative.[111] But these details were irrelevant to the champions of "civil rights."

In great contrast to the media uproar over this episode, almost no attention was paid to a September 1993 incident in which a surveillance camera videotaped two white guards at a New York State prison repeatedly striking a handcuffed white inmate on the head and legs, causing him to groan in pain with each blow. Accounts of this beating inspired no community protests, no riots, no impassioned calls for "justice." The victim's name—Jason McDade—is unfamiliar to most Americans.[112] Without a white-on-minority angle to exploit, the usually vocal demagogues felt no compulsion to parade themselves before the cameras and microphones.

In December 1993 a newspaper photographer snapped a picture of a black police officer handcuffing a white female suspect and then latching her hands to the base of a mailbox on a Washington, D.C. sidewalk. For nearly twenty minutes the woman was forced to sit on the frigid ground begging, to no avail, for the officer to free her.[113] Though this incident was quickly forgotten by the media, consider what might have transpired if the participants' racial backgrounds were reversed. Under such circumstances, the image of the frantic, pleading woman undoubtedly would have received such immense public exposure that everyone in the country would have known her name and face five minutes into that evening's newscasts. Instead, to most Americans she is a nameless, faceless entity.

In August 1994 an onlooker videotaped a policeman not only knocking a teenager to the ground and repeatedly striking him on the head with a nightstick, but then handcuffing the youth and using the baton to drag him roughly across the ground.[114] Though this incident occurred in the very same city where Rodney King had been beaten three years earlier, few Americans ever heard about it, and fewer still saw even a single telecast of the videotape. Since the civilian was Hispanic and the police officer was black, there were no guilty whites upon whom journalists and the "civil rights" cabal could rivet the nation's attention.

There was also silence following a brutal 1995 altercation between several white police officers and a black prisoner in their custody. On August 16, at New York's Rockland County Correctional Facility, inmate Reginald McFadden stuffed a towel into the toilet bowl of his cell, causing the water to overflow. When Sergeant Richard Mallon entered the cell to investigate, McFadden assaulted him so violently that it required seven policemen to subdue the prisoner. Four officers suffered head and back injuries in the struggle, which lasted ninety seconds and was recorded on a prison surveillance video.[115] Yet few Americans ever even heard of this tape's existence. White police officers hitting a black suspect makes big news in America, but a black prisoner attacking white policemen does not arouse the slumbering defenders of "justice" and "decency."

Sometimes brutality is filmed in instances where no police are involved. In 1993, for example, a security camera videotaped, with vivid clarity, the robbery of a Vietnamese-owned jewelry store in Washington, D.C. The tape showed four black men ransacking the store, pistol-whipping a female employee, and shooting the owner in the stomach.[116] Why, we may wonder, did this event receive only minimal media coverage? Why was the videotape not shown hundreds of times, over the course of many months, on nationwide television? Why was this horrible interracial crime, fully captured on tape, not exploited as a barometer of black racism? Clearly, the media have a double standard for determining what is newsworthy.

Police As Killers, Police As Victims

In many minority neighborhoods today, residents are openly hostile to law-enforcement officials. Consequently, the killing of even the most dangerous black or Hispanic criminal by a white police officer is apt to evoke a flood of outrage in those communities. Consider what occurred one August day in 1991, when two New York policemen responded to reports of shots being fired on Brooklyn's East 21st Street. When a Hispanic suspect pulled a gun on Officer Emanuel Gonzalez, white officer Jeffrey Hutton reacted quickly and shot the gunman several times, killing him and saving Gonzalez's life. Predictably, however, Hutton received no thanks from community residents for having removed an armed and dangerous predator from their midst. Instead, 150 demonstrators immediately protested the "excessive" use of police force.[117]

On August 27, 1988, black New Jerseyite Samuel Williams, who was wanted on six outstanding drug and weapons warrants, threatened white police officer Paul Letizia with a steel rod, prompting Letizia to shoot and kill him. Williams's death triggered immediate outrage among local blacks and Hispanics, who transformed the slain thug into a martyred saint and protested his killing with two days of rioting and looting.[118] When a grand jury later heard all evidence pertinent to the case and concluded that the officer had acted properly under the circumstances,[119] none of those who had rushed to judgment apologized for having done so.

Police officers who risk their lives each day to help rid society of its avowed enemies—whatever their color—do not receive, from the "civil rights" cartel, even the slightest shred of sympathy when they are wounded or killed in the line of duty. Rather, the self-anointed voices of social conscience remain silent at such times, devoting their energies instead to rationalizing the behavior of hoodlums whose racial or ethnic background they share. Consider the case of Newark detective John Sczyrek, who arrested two black men on narcotics possession charges in August 1992.[120] When the case went to trial ten months later, Sczyrek, scheduled to testify, was entering the courtroom when he was gunned down by a cousin of one of the suspects.[121] Since the killer was black and the victim was white, the community reacted to Sczyrek's death with equanimity. There was no soul-searching about possible racial motives for the crime. There were no rallies held to protest the shooting. No black "leader" denounced the gunman.

In December 1994 four black men armed with semi-automatic weapons robbed a Brooklyn bicycle shop, tying up the store owner and rifling the cash register. When white police officer Raymond Cannon arrived and attempted to intervene, he was shot twice in the face and killed.[122] But because his death had little headline value in the marketplace of racial myths, his murder was heralded by silence, not protests.

On April 27, 1988, Sergeant John McCormick went to conduct a drug search at the cocaine-filled Manhattan residence of a twenty-two-year-old Hispanic woman. When he entered the apartment, the woman ran into a rear bedroom and fired several gunshots through the doorway, killing McCormick.[123] Since the victim was white, minority "leaders" neither mourned his death nor condemned his killer.

Another tragic case was that of New York City police officer Edward Byrne, who in February 1988 lost his life violently in South Jamaica, Queens—a predominantly black area that had been overrun in the preceding months by the spread of crack dealing and its associated ill effects.[124] As he guarded the house of a drug-case witness whose home had twice been fire-bombed by dealers, four black men drove up alongside Byrne's vehicle and shot him dead. Predictably, black "leaders" neither denounced this murder nor called for the punishment of the killers. In fact, they did not even hold the actual gunmen responsible for Byrne's death, but instead reproached the American "system" for having "created" these criminals and others like them. In a major press conference, a coalition of local black clergymen expressed their personal opposition to capital punishment—even for perpetrators like those who had killed Officer Byrne. "Too many of those who occupy the death rows of our prisons are poor and/or black or Hispanic," said the Reverend Larry Dixon.[125]

On October 17, 1989, two blacks and two Hispanics broke into a Manhattan McDonald's restaurant at 3:15 a.m. Inside were five janitors and a tile setter doing their jobs. While the gun-wielding intruders forced the janitors into a back room and ordered them to open a safe, the tile setter was able to run outside and enlist the help of three policemen. When the officers arrived at the scene, two of the robbers fled up a ladder and onto the roof. Officer Anthony Dwyer pursued them but was pushed, in the ensuing struggle, into a deep shaft between two buildings, where he lay writhing in agony for more than forty minutes before dying.[126] Naturally, Dwyer was not publicly mourned by a single "leader" in the black or Hispanic communities. No "civil rights" group said a word to praise his courage or lament his death. Yet how much attention would this case have received if the outcome had been reversed—if the officer had thrown one of the robbers off the roof to *his* death? How long would have been the lines of protesters demonstrating their outrage over such an incident? But events being as they were, all was relatively calm in the city.

Things were similarly tranquil in August 1998, when a seventeen-year-old, black, career criminal shot and killed black police officer Gerard Carter in Staten Island, New York. As columnist Michael Meyers observed, "It is mind-boggling, but a sign of the times, that no civil rights dirge is played to mourn the death by execution of this model citizen."[127]

There was little calm, however, on August 3, 1995, when eighteen-year-old Carlos Santos fell from a fourth-floor window of a Washington Heights, New York drug den, and then claimed that a police officer inside the building had intentionally pushed him through the window. News of this incident spread through the neighborhood like wildfire, the flames of which were further fanned when Santos's mother falsely told reporters that her son was paralyzed as a result of the fall.[128] The police, meanwhile, vehemently denied that any officer had pushed Santos out of any window, but their denials were predictably ignored by the Washington Heights community. A crowd of more than 100 screaming demonstrators marched through the streets,[129] many of them throwing bottles at police officers.[130] Presumably the protesters never thought to withhold judgment until the facts of the case could be reliably established. Instead they assumed, with their customary haste, that the police department was hiding the truth. How inconvenient they must have found it when, three days later, Carlos Santos confessed that he had lied about the incident; when he admitted that in fact he had fallen accidentally; and when he further disclosed that he had fabricated his original story due to pressure from area residents urging him to blame the police.[131] Thus any injuries and property losses that might have occurred in the unrest following Santos's fall were utterly senseless. The price of mythology can be high indeed.

A 1994 incident in a black section of Lexington, Kentucky

provides yet another example of a minority community's readiness to explode at a moment's notice. On the morning of October 25, five policemen tried to arrest eighteen-year-old Antonio Orlando Sullivan for his involvement in a gang-related street shooting of a few weeks earlier. When the officers arrived at the suspect's home, however, he hid inside a closet and for several minutes was unresponsive to orders that he come out. When the young man finally did emerge from behind the door, white officer Philip Vogel, whose gun was drawn throughout the tense standoff, shot and killed him. Though Vogel, a twenty-two-year veteran of the police force, claimed to have pulled the trigger accidentally, hundreds of local blacks immediately took to the streets—overturning police cars and throwing rocks and other objects at whites.[132] Dismissing any possibility that the shooting of Sullivan was in fact inadvertent, the demonstrators presumed instead that it was the malicious act of a racist. Yet even if we agree, for rhetorical purposes, that their presumption was correct, we must wonder why this killing inflamed people's passions more than most other murders in Lexington or any other American city. Why should the slaying of this man have been more significant to the black community than the thousands of black-on-black murders that occur nationwide each year? Why did this particular incident in Lexington warrant a violent response, when the reckless gunfire a few weeks earlier by this very same "martyr" had elicited no community reaction whatsoever?

The type of outrage exhibited in Lexington was noticeably absent following the July 12, 1986 shooting of white New York City policeman Stephen McDonald. As the officer was questioning three black youths for suspicious behavior near a Central Park boathouse,[133] the eldest suspect, Shavod Jones, pulled a pistol from his waist and fired at McDonald three times, damaging the officer's spinal cord and rendering him permanently paralyzed from the neck down.[134] Predictably, no "civil rights leader" in America uttered a word of protest.

Though Jones already had a long criminal history which included incidents of assault and armed robbery,[135] New York City's black police commissioner, Benjamin Ward, could not bring himself to speak harshly of the youth. When a local district attorney suggested that juveniles who attempt to kill police officers should be tried and sentenced under the strictest Class A felony statutes, Ward disagreed. The criminal-justice system, he said, "should be more willing to give a second chance to someone like that."[136] Apparently, Ward did not classify the periods following Jones's numerous prior convictions as "second chances." Moreover, he repeatedly referred to Jones as a "child" with a troubled emotional history,[137] implying that the youngster's actions needed to be understood in the context of his tumultuous past. One wonders why the white youths in Howard Beach and Bensonhurst were not afforded this same paternalistic understanding by public officials.

While Jones was in prison, his sentence was lengthened considerably as punishment for his violent behavior against prison employees and fellow inmates. Due to a bureaucratic error, however, he was mistakenly released in March 1994—about 600 days too early. When prison officials realized their mistake, they retrieved Jones from his Harlem home and once again placed him behind bars.[138] Notably, the young man's acquaintances were filled with sympathy for him. A female friend characterized his re-imprisonment as "ridiculous,"[139] while a next-door neighbor asserted that law-enforcement officials were "trying to mess with [Jones's] mind."[140] Another neighbor, Craig Ford, speculated that Jones would suffer "psychological damage" from the "cruel and unusual punishment" of being locked up again. Jones "knows what he did was wrong," Ford explained. "When it happened, he was just a kid."[141]

Crisis in Washington Heights

On July 3, 1992, Officer Michael O'Keefe and his two partners on a police anticrime unit were patrolling West 162nd Street in New York's Washington Heights. Noticing a tall, muscular Hispanic man pacing the sidewalk and pulling his jacket over a bulge in his waistband, the officers concluded that he was carrying a gun. O'Keefe got out of the car at the corner of 163rd Street and set out after the suspect—six-foot, one-inch, 200-pound Jose "Kiko" Garcia. The other officers, meanwhile, drove around the block to flush Garcia from the opposite direction.[142]

As Garcia was entering an apartment building, Officer O'Keefe ordered him to stop, at which point the suspect put up a violent struggle. The two men battled for almost four minutes before the bigger, more powerful Garcia gained the upper hand and drew his .38 caliber gun. O'Keefe instinctively pushed aside Garcia's arm, grabbed his own pistol, and fired. The suspect buckled, staggered, then turned toward the officer and aimed his gun again. At that point, O'Keefe shot the man a second time, killing him.[143]

Public reaction to news of the killing was swift and passionate. Rumor spread through the local Dominican community that O'Keefe had, without provocation, pitilessly murdered an innocent person. Newspapers displayed photographs of Garcia's relatives weeping over the young man's untimely death.[144] Contrary to police assertions of Garcia's known drug-involvement, a number of area residents publicly eulogized their dead neighbor with high praise, painting a verbal portrait of a kind, gentle man. "He [Garcia] had no problems with anyone," said one acquaintance. "If someone was hungry, he'd give them $10 to get food."[145] "He didn't know why he was being beat up here," claimed the Garcia family's attorney. "The kid was never arrested; he wasn't a drug dealer."[146]

In conjunction with such glowing depictions of Garcia, self-proclaimed eyewitnesses emerged from the woodwork to charge that Officer O'Keefe had ambushed a defenseless, innocent man. "Undercover police hit [Garcia] on the knee," said one local. "After they break [*sic*] his legs, they pulled him in and shot him three times."[147] "They shot him like a dog," asserted another, "but worse than a dog. Because Americans, they respect their dogs, but they don't respect their Dominican[s]."[148] Garcia's aunt rejected the police department's contention that her nephew was armed at the time of the altercation. "No man who has a revolver is going to die like a chicken on the floor," she reasoned.[149] Area resident Juana Madera, who claimed to have witnessed the shooting from a nearby staircase, said that Garcia was lying flat on his back—possibly unconscious—when O'Keefe "kicked him onto his stomach and pulled out a pistol," shooting him three times in the back.[150] "The cop looked like he was high," she told a news reporter.[151]

The community's anger grew with every rumor, every allegation, and every grieving relative's testimony about their beloved Kiko's unblemished character. "We're sick of abuse," complained one local Dominican.[152] "We're in the United States," said another, "but we still lack a lot. We are marginalized."[153] Area residents initially protested Garcia's death by setting fires and dumping debris onto their neighborhood streets for two days. On the third day city councilman Guillermo Linares, carrying the Dominican flag, led marchers along

Broadway in a display of "outrage." He lost control of the demonstrators, however, when they began overturning cars, setting buildings on fire, throwing rocks and bottles at windows, and assaulting police officers.[154] With each passing hour thereafter, incidents of vandalism and violence increased in frequency throughout Washington Heights. Protesters threw garbage out of their apartment windows and onto the streets below.[155] Hordes of arsonists swarmed and terrorized the city.[156] On one particular day, more than 1,000 demonstrators ransacked an area spanning 79 city blocks.[157] In all, the disturbances continued for six days, during which 131 vehicles were damaged or destroyed, 14 buildings were burned, 90 people were injured (74 of them police officers), and one person was killed.[158] "There's no other way for the government to listen to us," explained an angry protester. "There have been too many abuses."[159]

Political and community leaders reacted meekly to the violence. Mayor Dinkins, for example, legitimized the rioters' rage by asserting, "There is much anger in the community, *understandably*,[160] about the death of Jose Garcia."[161] Pleading for—rather than demanding—their cooperation, he told a crowd of listeners, "We want justice, but we want peace. Justice we will have, but peace I beg you for."[162] The mayor also met with Garcia family members to promise them not only a thorough investigation of the shooting,[163] but also that the city would pay for Garcia's funeral.[164] Garcia's sister reported afterward that Dinkins "said he was very sorry and was going to help us as much as possible."[165] The mayor's timorous approach was mirrored by his press secretary, who said, "The thing we want to do right now is figure out a way to calm things down."[166] For how long would this contemplative, restrained course have been followed if a *white* mob had been plundering large sections of the city?

Once all the facts of the O'Keefe-Garcia conflict were established, it became clear that the latter's apologists were lying. Reports from the medical examiner and the Garcia family's pathologist confirmed that Garcia had only two bruises on his body—one on the nose and the other on the head—supporting O'Keefe's contention that he had struck his adversary twice with his police radio.[167] This evidence contradicted the "eyewitness" testimony of Juana Madera, who had claimed that Garcia was savagely, repeatedly beaten on the head, shoulders, hands, and knees.[168] In addition, four minutes of tape-recorded police radio transmissions proved that O'Keefe was in a panicked state during the altercation, desperately calling for help—again contradicting Madera's claim that he had stood over an injured Garcia and methodically, cold-bloodedly shot him.[169] Moreover, bullet fragments, impact marks, and wounds on Garcia's body all showed that Garcia was standing up when he was shot, rather than lying on his back as some witnesses had claimed.[170] As these facts surfaced one by one, Madera finally admitted that she had not even seen O'Keefe shoot Garcia.[171]

With each new piece of evidence that came to light, it became more apparent that Garcia bore no resemblance to the paragon of virtue his relatives and neighbors had described. Police evidence records contained photographs and a videotape of Garcia fraternizing with known drug-dealers[172]—not surprising in light of the fact that he himself worked for a drug ring basing its operations in Juana Madera's apartment.[173] Indeed, law-enforcement officials had long known Garcia to be a gun-toting outlaw,[174] and a warrant was actually out for his arrest at the time of his death.[175] An autopsy showed not only that Garcia's septum was perforated—a classic symptom of heavy cocaine use[176]—but also that cocaine was in his system when he died, a finding corroborated by the Garcia family's pathologist.[177]

The Washington Heights tumult was, in sum, a six-day riot in which a community's rage about alleged police brutality "spilled over" into violence. Yet the incident that ostensibly set off the mayhem had transpired in a wholly different manner than the rumor-filled street version. Had Kiko Garcia been a white man, his neighbors undoubtedly would have cheered his death as a welcome event freeing them from the tyranny of a worthless thug. Instead, he was made a martyr because his killer was a white police officer.

The day Garcia died, a Connecticut man named Scott DiNapoli knocked a woman unconscious at a shopping center and took her to his home, where a passerby who spotted her frantically banging on a window ran to call the police. When Lieutenant Don Thirdkildsen arrived at the scene, DiNapoli moved toward him with a knife, leaving the officer no recourse but to shoot and kill him.[178] Since everyone involved in this episode was white, there were no public demonstrations protesting DiNapoli's death. Absolutely no one questioned whether Thirdkildsen may have pulled the trigger too soon. In fact, other than for a brief newspaper account, the incident was largely ignored by journalists and the general public.

Condemnation and Forgiveness: A Double Standard

By portraying whites as uniquely racist, "civil rights leaders" have effectively united blacks and Hispanics against a common "enemy." Though professing an allegiance to social justice and interracial understanding, these self-anointed guardians of "brotherhood" have instead created countless thousands of black and Hispanic racists. Nowhere is the bitter fruit of their antiwhite rhetoric more apparent than in the very different standards to which minority communities hold white, as opposed to nonwhite, criminals. Consider the tragic case of Valerie Santiago, a seven-year-old girl who lived in a Bronx apartment with her mother, Gloria—a known drug and alcohol abuser. One day in 1992 a male acquaintance named Domingo Sierra gave Gloria forty dollars with which to purchase drugs for him. When she did not return within a half hour, however, Sierra went to the woman's apartment and kidnapped little Valerie, whom he proceeded to rape, strangle, and then bury under a pile of empty cannisters in a weed-covered lot.[179] Hispanic leaders said nothing about this senseless waste of life, presumably drawing a measure of comfort from the fact that at least the child had not been murdered by a white man with racist motives.

When twenty-two-year-old pre-med student Cynthia Rivera was visited by tragedy in 1992, Hispanic activists were again silent. The young woman was in her Bronx apartment with her grandmother and a teenage boy when two intruders suddenly burst through the door, forced the three occupants into a bathtub filled with water, and attempted to electrocute them by throwing appliances into the tub. When this plan failed, the assailants proceeded to stab the boy and grandmother more than thirty times apiece, killing them. Next they turned their attention to Miss Rivera, stabbing her twenty-seven times and leaving her for dead. Miraculously, however, she survived the attack and later provided crucial testimony that helped convict the perpetrators, Edwin Ortiz and Thomas Cruz.[180] But since both assailants were Hispanic, the community did not decry their bestial cruelty.

In July 1993, by contrast, Dominicans in Washington Heights erupted with outrage after a twenty-year-old motorcyclist named Alfredo Soto was accidentally struck and killed by a police car pursuing a suspect. Intimating that the officer had collided with Soto deliberately, area residents likened the incident to a murder.[181] Bands of protesters threw rocks at police officers, set garbage cans ablaze, and injured several firefighters with a Molotov cocktail. But instead of denouncing such acts of barbarism, Councilman Guillermo Linares and Human Rights Commission leader Rolando Acosta tried to defuse the community's rage by expressing sympathy and promising that "justice" would be done.[182] Remarkably, no one asked whether Soto, by illegally driving his motorcycle without a helmet, might have been to some extent responsible for his own death. Nor did anyone appear concerned by the fact that Soto's driver's license had been previously suspended *seventy-two times*.[183] Is it not reasonable to question whether a man with such a driving record might have been at least partially to blame? As always, the instantly outraged community never even thought to ask.

Not all car accidents trigger violent demonstrations, of course. One April 1993 day in New York's Crown Heights, a black driver who had accumulated some two dozen traffic tickets during the previous four years was traveling more than twice the speed limit in a 30 mph zone. Losing control of his vehicle, he drove onto a traffic island and struck an entire family of Hispanic pedestrians, killing a two-year-old boy and critically injuring the child's five-year-old brother.[184] Yet this accident ignited no public outrage. Since the driver was not white—or, worse yet, a white policeman—no one saw any reason to suspect a malicious intent. Thus all remained calm—a far cry from the uprising sparked by Alfredo Soto's death three months later.

Nor did many take notice in January 1993 when a black gunman robbed and killed two Hispanic grocery store owners in Brooklyn, pitilessly shooting the victims execution-style.[185] While cruel, deliberate murders like these elicit only silence from minority communities, a traffic accident in which a white police officer *un*intentionally strikes and kills a Hispanic motorcyclist sparks indignation and protest. It does not portend well for a society when its members selectively denounce killings based on the skin colors of those who carry them out.

The widespread hatred and distrust of the police in minority neighborhoods is a testament to the steady diet of lies that "civil rights leaders" have fed the public for so long, thereby creating entire communities convinced that law-enforcement officials are their enemies. Indeed, the messiahs of "justice" are not the least bit reluctant to suggest that police officers are responsible for a disproportionate share of urban-area murders. Al Sharpton, for one, holds that "the real mobsters in our community often wear blue uniforms and carry night-sticks."[186] Along the same lines, the Reverend Herbert Daughtry charges that the police are more apt to unjustly kill black civilians than are Klansmen or Skinheads.[187]

The natural consequence of such rhetoric was displayed in a shocking 1993 incident on a Washington Heights street where, one October night, a number of automobiles were illegally double- and triple-parked. When a police tow truck came to remove these vehicles, area residents cursed and threatened the officers. During the arguing, a local Hispanic man slipped away, went up to the roof of a six-story apartment building adjacent to the scene of the dispute, and dropped a thirty-pound bucket of spackle onto the head of white policeman John Williamson, killing him instantly. In stark contrast to the community's grief and outrage over the death of drug dealer Jose Garcia, those who witnessed the killing of Officer Williamson cheered and applauded.[188]

In January 1994 the New York City police department received a call reporting a robbery in progress at Muhammad's Mosque, a Harlem meeting place for Nation of Islam members.[189] When officers arrived at the scene, however, they discovered that the call had been a setup. Mosque members, enraged that "outsiders" had entered their building without permission, attacked the uniformed "intruders," injuring eight of them.[190] Following the melee, Al Sharpton and attorney C. Vernon Mason organized a rally "in support" of the mosque,[191] brazenly demanding that the police department apologize for its "attack on the entire black community."[192]

Racism, of course, is not altogether absent from police departments—just as it is not wholly absent from work forces in any other field. "Civil rights leaders," however, tend to paint a most distorted picture of reality—virtually never praising the police for their crime-fighting efforts, yet seizing every opportunity to accuse them of wrongdoing. In October 1994, for instance, Jesse Jackson and Al Sharpton used scrub brushes and disinfectant to clean the sidewalk adjacent to a Harlem police station wherein a number of officers had recently been charged with corruption. The intent, Jackson explained, was to symbolically "clean out some of the germs in this precinct."[193] Meanwhile, *on that very same day*, a gang of white Brooklyn teenagers savagely assaulted a fifty-six-year-old white patrolman, their blows causing the man's face and head to become so swollen and disfigured that fellow officers failed to recognize him.[194] Jackson and Sharpton, naturally, had nothing to say about this brutal attack. But had that same gang of hoodlums beaten a black drug dealer, such "spokesmen" would have flooded the airwaves with indignant outcries.

This double standard speaks volumes about the true agenda of so many black "leaders," whose motivations contrast sharply with those of, among others, Chinese community leaders. Sociologist and economist Thomas Sowell explains:

> [T]he leaders of American Chinatowns have urged the police to treat street hoodlums roughly—including vigorous use of billy clubs—even though the hoodlums might be Chinese and the police white. Black community leaders, however, follow opposite policies— vying with each other in decrying police use of force. Both sets of leaders respond to their respective incentives, which are quite different. Businessmen as unpaid civic leaders with no political careers in prospect have an incentive to reduce crime and other community problems by whatever means seem most effective. But blacks pursuing political or protest organization careers cannot afford to let their rivals seem blacker-than-thou. The differences are differences of incentives rather than of race.[195]

One black outlaw well-schooled in the lessons of the "civil rights" cabal was Larry Davis. Known to be a violent, armed drug dealer, Davis wounded six officers in a 1986 shootout with New York City police—at a time when he was already a suspect in several murder, kidnapping, and car theft cases. In his subsequent trial for the shootout, Davis claimed that he had fired at the officers only to defend himself against their attempts to "assassinate" him. A jury of ten blacks and two Hispanics believed Davis's story, acquitting him on nine counts of attempted murder and six counts of aggravated assault. For his daring escapades and success in beating the most serious charges against him, Davis developed a reputation as a sort of folk hero in his South Bronx neighborhood. "I was supposed to be page 12 in the *Daily News*," he boasted. " 'Black youth killed by police.' But I refused to die."[196]

In truth, of course, if a black man had been killed under such disputed circumstances, particularly by a white policeman, stories of his death would have been front-page, national news—the stuff of which demonstrations, denunciations, and even riots are made. Only the most foolish officer would risk forfeiting his good reputation, his career, or even years of his life to a prison sentence, by shooting a black suspect unnecessarily. All policemen know that shooting any black—for whatever reason—is likely to draw considerable public attention and evoke cries of "racism" from many places in the black community. For evidence of this, one need only look at the example of William Lozano, a Miami officer whose January 1989 shooting of a black suspect triggered three nights of citywide rioting that led to one death, dozens of injuries, hundreds of arrests, and millions of dollars in property damage.[197] Though Lozano was sentenced to seven years in prison for the shooting, a 1991 appeals court overturned that decision upon learning that the original jury had convicted him out of fear that an acquittal would have triggered more mayhem.[198]

It is quite likely that police officers, ever-haunted by the looming threat of public condemnation and rioting, sometimes hesitate to shoot even armed suspects who pose a serious threat to them. What of Anthony Dwyer, John McCormick, and Raymond Cannon? Were they reluctant to use their guns for fear of the consequences they might face for firing a fatal shot? "Civil rights leaders" virtually never raise such questions, preferring instead to characterize police departments as little more than state-sponsored militias whose principal mission is to shoot as many minorities as possible. In December 1994, for example, Al Sharpton led a march through the heart of New York City to protest what he called an abundance of police abuses aimed at blacks. "We've taken enough," declared the fiery activist.[199] On another occasion—following a 1997 police shooting of a machete-wielding black teenager in Washington Heights—Sharpton vowed, "We [blacks] are not going to keep burying our children and acting like it's their [own] fault."[200] On a 1994 talk-radio program with a predominantly black audience, Sharpton gave this response to a caller who urged blacks to shoot police officers: "Whatever [anti-police] violence comes down, it has been incited by white police misconduct."[201] Clearly, this statement is bereft of any concern for the more than 1,300 American police officers who have been killed in the line of duty since 1990—not to mention the half a million others to be injured on the job during that same period.[202]

Echoing Sharpton's views, the Reverend Herbert Daughtry asserts that police brutality drives many blacks "to the conclusion that the youth of African ancestry are an endangered species." He has on occasion publicly recited the names of blacks who were "killed by people we pay to protect us."[203] Early in 1990, after David Dinkins had been New York City's mayor for a few months, Daughtry was shocked to learn that there had been an increase in the number of civilians killed by police officers during that early part of Dinkins's term. Apparently amazed that city police were still shooting people now that the mayor was black, Daughtry concluded that the trend must have been a "legacy" from the administration of Ed Koch, the white mayor who had preceded Dinkins in office.[204] Such thinking equates law enforcement with white racism.

In the eyes of most "civil rights leaders," law-enforcement officers do very little right. Consider what occurred in New York during Khalid Abdul Muhammad's September 5, 1998 "Million Youth March"—which featured a deep roster of guest speakers shouting incendiary remarks about the police. March organizer Erica Ford, for one, told the crowd, "The police are our number one enemy, brothers and sisters. . . . We can't get these people off our backs."[205] Malik Zulu Shabazz concurred, "Police brutality is out of control, and the fascist police force is out of control, and we must unite to defeat them, and destroy them by any means necessary."[206] Khalid Muhammad himself encouraged listeners to physically attack police officers before leaving the premises. "Get to whaling on their asses here today," he said.[207]

Not surprisingly, a number of the attendees followed those instructions. When police interrupted Muhammad's hate-filled diatribe shortly after four o'clock, the hour at which a city permit required the march to end, a number of youths in the crowd began to throw railings and other objects at the officers. Jesse Jackson, however, depicted the *police* as the instigators. "I think the [marchers] showed an amazing amount of sobriety," he said, "and that, toward the end of the event, police started the problem."[208] NAACP president Kweisi Mfume agreed, "It was regrettable that those young people whose sole purpose [for attending the march] was to lift themselves up were subjected to that treatment. There was a clear overreaction on the part of the police department."[209] A number of black "leaders" went so far as to call for "civil rights" investigations of the officers,[210] whose efforts to break up the proceedings at the agreed-upon hour were allegedly "racist."

Such negative attitudes toward the police are transmitted from one generation to the next, corrupting countless young minds with the false notion that law officers are their enemies. In mid-1998, for instance, NAACP members in Ossining, New York were quick to ascribe the shooting of an armed black suspect by three local policemen to the officers' bigotry. Though the circumstances that had led to the shooting were initially in dispute, dozens of black school-children took their cue from the protesters and, one July evening, gathered at Ossining's Community Center to make banners condemning the police. "I think those cops need to go to prison," said one nine-year-old boy, "because what they did wasn't right."[211] "It wasn't fair that they shot [him]," offered a ten-year-old girl. "They lied and said all this stuff. . . . It made me feel angry."[212] "I don't think it [the shooting] was right," said a third child. Even if he [the suspect] did have a gun, they shouldn't have shot him."[213] As such statements plainly illustrate, the shrill rhetoric of blustering imposters has made the presumption of police guilt a foregone conclusion in the malleable minds of many minority children.

Police shootings of criminals, it should be pointed out, are not nearly as common as many "civil rights leaders" would have us believe. In 1996, for example, 14 blacks were killed by New York City police—most while the victims were in the process of committing serious crimes.[214] In a city where hundreds of thousands of felonies occur each year, and where more than 363,000 individuals were taken into police custody in 1996 alone,[215] 14 dead suspects is by no means a number of epidemic proportions. That same year, 506 African Americans citywide were killed by persons—virtually all of them black—other than police officers.[216] The story has been much the same in other years as well. In 1995, 13 blacks were killed by the police while 588 were killed by civilians, and in 1994 the corresponding numbers were 15 and 777, respectively.[217] In 1998 fewer than 1 percent of the city's 39,000 police officers discharged their weapons even a single time, and scarcely 10 percent draw their guns even once over a twenty-year career.[218] It is indeed disgraceful that the self-anointed guardians of "justice" routinely ignore the putrid stench of death permeating a crime-ravaged black community, while selectively denouncing the few white policemen who happen to shoot black suspects.

Occasionally, of course, police officers do overreact to situations, behave unprofessionally, or use excessive force. Consider a 1999 incident in which four white New York City officers mistook Amadou Diallo, a law-abiding African immigrant, for an armed criminal and riddled his body with bullets. Forty-one shots were fired in all, nineteen of them hitting the suspect and killing him instantly.[219] "Civil rights leaders" wasted no time before accusing the police of racism. On several occasions, Al Sharpton led thousands of protesters in marches against police brutality.[220] "Crime has gone down . . . everywhere but [at] the NYPD," said the outspoken activist. "Police brutality is a crime."[221] Jesse Jackson condemned New York mayor Rudolph Giuliani for "having helped set a climate that seems to glorify police misbehavior and a callous disregard of the citizens."[222] Khalid Abdul Muhammad called the NYPD "an organized death corps," and urged city blacks to kill whites in retaliation. "It's time to speak the language of those whose language is killing, maiming, lynching and genocide," he said. "This is the time for you white people to realize that you are doing evil. You will be having funeral processions in the white community. . . . They shoot one of ours forty-one times. We'll shoot forty-one of theirs, one time. . . . There's medicine in the murder. There's healing in the killing."[223] The Center for Constitutional Rights called Diallo's killing an "execution . . . reminiscent of the behavior of death squads in Central America in the 1960s."[224]

Many local blacks expressed similar contempt for the police and mayor alike. "Why do you treat a black man like a dog?" one protester angrily asked Giuliani.[225] Two others shouted at the mayor, "You coward. You are the devil. Murderer. Bloodsucker."[226] Yet another called him "a monster."[227] "It's a shame," added Dr. Matthew Adams of Grace United Methodist Church, "that New York City has become the Mississippi of 1964."[228]

Curiously, none of these critics addressed the fact that the supposedly racist officers who shot Diallo reported the incident to police headquarters immediately after it happened, making no attempt to deny their role in the shooting. As black columnist Michael Meyers wrote, "Who can believe . . . that these cops . . . were intent on adopting murder as a tactic to control street crime? If they were, where was the attempt at coverup? In earlier times, such rogue cops would've simply placed 'a spare' (weapon) on the scene or in the dead man's hands."[229] Nor did the critics mention that those same officers, once they realized they had shot an unarmed, innocent man, broke into tears at the scene—one of them sickened with grief to the point of vomiting. In short, even if the Diallo shooting was an example of bad police work, there is no reason to assume that it was motivated by racial malice.

Moreover, none of the critics mentioned that under Giuliani's watch, police shootings of civilians were significantly rarer than during the preceding administration of black mayor David Dinkins; that in 1998, in fact, the number of shootings per thousand officers was the lowest the city had seen in twenty-five years; and that New York's ratio of police shootings to total population was lower than that of any other American city.[230] Consider that in mostly black Washington, D.C., where two-thirds of law-enforcement officers are black, police shoot black suspects at *double* the rate of New York cops.[231] Also left unaddressed was the fact that New York City's "average" white suspect who resists arrest is actually *more* likely to be shot by the police than his "average" black counterpart. Indeed 13.5 percent of whites who attempt to flee the police are shot during pursuit, twice the rate at which black and Hispanic suspects are shot in similar circumstances.[232] Such realities are a major inconvenience to people intent on depicting the police as a band of racists.

Neither did the mayor's detractors note that minorities had been the prime beneficiaries of the steep plunge in New York City's overall murder rate since Giuliani took office in 1994. Brooklyn's mostly black 75th Precinct, for instance, was the scene of 110 murders in 1993 but only 37 in 1998. Similarly, the 34th Precinct in Washington Heights had 50 murders in 1993 but just 9 in 1998. If citywide murder rates had held steady at 1993 levels, rather than falling as they did, then 308 more whites, 2,299 more blacks, and 1,842 more Hispanics would have been killed by the end of 1998.[233] Though these numbers went largely unpublicized, they are a remarkable testament to the overwhelmingly positive effect that New York's police have had on the city's minority life in recent years.

While Amadou Diallo's name became virtually a household word throughout the United States in early 1999, few Americans ever heard about thirty-two-year-old John Perrin of Las Vegas, who was shot fourteen times and killed by police officer Bruce Gentner during an April 12 pedestrian stop. Throughout the ensuing weeks of investigation that led a coroner's jury to eventually clear Gentner of any wrongdoing, not one "civil rights leader" in the country called attention to the case. Because both Gentner and Perrin were white, the story was strictly local news.[234] Meanwhile, *that very same month*, Al Sharpton flew to Riverside, California to lead hundreds in a protest over a local prosecutor's decision not to indict four white police officers who had fatally shot an armed black woman. Newspapers nationwide covered the event.[235] Two weeks later Sharpton was back in New York, protesting a white policeman's accidental shooting of a suspicious black teen who had tried to run from three uniformed officers seeking to question him.[236]

Another case that dominated news headlines for some time was a 1997 incident involving black New Yorker Abner Louima—who was brutally sodomized by a white policeman with a wooden stick.[237] The guilty party, Justin Volpe, was convicted in a May 1999 trial, thanks largely to incriminating testimony provided by two fellow white officers.[238] Disgraceful as Volpe's actions were, however, there is no reason to believe that *racism* was his motive. Not only had he never given any prior indication that he disliked blacks, but his girlfriend at the time of the Louima incident was a black woman whom he had been dating steadily for two years. In short, bad police work—even brutality—is not necessarily evidence of a racist heart.

Contrary to the bleatings of most "civil rights leaders," police abuse of *any* type is exceedingly rare in this country. In 1997 the Justice Department conducted a first-of-its-kind study which found that *fewer than 1 percent* of Americans who had ever come into contact with the police met with actual or threatened physical force. And in those cases where force was used, respondents said it was usually because they themselves had provoked the officers.[239] A statistical analysis of New York City criminal-justice records shows a similar pattern. In 1996, there were fewer than 5,000 civilian complaints filed against the NYPD—about one for every 85 or 90 arrests—and nearly all the complaints turned out to be baseless.[240] These data, naturally, received little media publicity.

It is notable that even the most vocal critics of law-enforcement officials willingly accept police protection when facing potential danger themselves. In December 1995, for example, Al Sharpton was guarded by police after receiving a series of death threats for his perceived role in having instigated the arson of a Jewish-owned clothing store in Harlem (see chapter 8). The previous year, rap singer Ice T, whose song "Cop Killer" glorifies those who gun down policemen, exhibited similar hypocrisy. During an autograph-signing session promoting his book *The Ice Opinion*, he was guarded by the very same officers whose killing he had celebrated in song.[241]

The selfless bravery of police officers who risk their lives to help people in trouble goes utterly unacknowledged by most of those so eager to accuse them of racism. Such was the case, for instance, when a six-year-old black boy was trapped inside a blazing Brooklyn apartment in December 1993. As the child's panicked mother and six siblings watched, four white policemen broke through the apartment door and searched for him[242]—only to be forced out three times by the choking smoke. Finally, on the fourth attempt, they found the boy and rescued him from a rear bedroom.[243] No "civil rights leader," of course, had even a word to say about the incident. Such events, after all—no matter how common—are not easily reconcilable with the dearly held doctrine of unbridled white racism.

Chapter 6

Mythology Run Amuck —and Tragedy

The quality of ideas seems to play a minor role in mass movement leadership. What counts is the arrogant gesture, the complete disregard of the opinion of others, the singlehanded defiance of the world.
—Eric Hoffer[1]

When a lie is incessantly repeated by prominent scholars and social commentators alike, it eventually gains legitimacy with the population at large. Via such repetition, the myth of rampant white malevolence victimizing blacks has become axiomatic to millions of Americans. A long parade of "civil rights leaders"—tirelessly condemning white racism while ignoring *black* racism—have taught blacks to loathe and distrust whites. This instruction has led to much needless tragedy.

On the evening of August 19, 1991, two seven-year-old black children—Gavin and Angela Cato—were playing on a sidewalk in the Crown Heights section of Brooklyn.[2] At about 8:20 p.m., a twenty-two-year-old Lubavitcher Jew named Yosef Lifsh drove his station wagon through a red light near the corner where the Cato children were playing.[3] His vehicle struck another car and was sent skidding onto the sidewalk, killing the boy and seriously injuring the girl.[4]

Notwithstanding the accidental nature of the crash, the busy intersection was quickly flooded with angry blacks[5]—some of whom, one observer noted, "started beating [Lifsh] in the face."[6] Within a few minutes two ambulances arrived at the scene almost simultaneously—one of them a city-operated Emergency Medical Services (EMS) unit, and the other a private, Hasidim-owned Hatzolah vehicle.[7] When the Hatzolah paramedics observed the Cato children already receiving treatment from EMS workers, they turned their attention to Lifsh and two fellow Lubavitchers who had been riding with him.[8] But when black youths in the vicinity began to attack the Hatzolah crew,[9] police instructed the latter to immediately take the three Hasidim away.[10]

Throughout the neighborhood, rumor spread that the Cato children were denied medical treatment until after the Jews had been cared for.[11] As *The Amsterdam News* reported, "Black residents of Brooklyn's Crown Heights neighborhood are steaming mad that a car full of Jews was escorted to an ambulance and whisked away after the car crushed the life out of a seven-year-old and pinned a second child underneath, resulting in critical injuries."[12] Other rumors held that Lifsh had fled the scene of the accident.[13] Some even charged that he had run over the children out of utter disregard for black lives, if not intentionally. Community "leaders" did nothing to dispel such unfounded notions. To the standing ovation of a large black audience, for example, Al Sharpton announced that it was not merely a car accident that had killed Gavin Cato, but rather "the social accident of apartheid."[14] The contentious activist then challenged local Jews— whom he derisively characterized as "diamond merchants"—to "pin their yarmulkes back and come over to my house" to settle the score.[15] Finally, he claimed without proof that Lifsh had run over the Cato children while in a drunken stupor.[16] Stirred by such false accusations, hundreds of Crown Heights blacks took violently to the streets. At least 500 youths pelted Jewish homes with rocks and set vehicles on fire, shouting, "Jew! Jew!"[17] Some vandalized police cars, others looted stores,[18] and still others threw bricks and bottles at law officers.[19] "The first Jew that comes down that street," threatened one rioter, "is a dead man."[20] A sign above the site where Gavin Cato was killed urged blacks to bring the "white Jew" to justice.[21]

Three hours after the boy's death, a twenty-nine-year-old Hasidic man named Yankel Rosenbaum, unaware of the accident that had claimed Cato's life, was walking alone on a Crown Heights side-walk when he was ambushed and beaten by a gang of at least twenty blacks, one of whom stabbed and mortally wounded him. "These [assailants] were looking for any Jew," a local Hasid later lamented.[22] "He [Rosenbaum] was killed for no other reason than he was Jewish and white and for vengeance," observed another. "Vengeance for an incident that was an accident, and there was no reason for vengeance."[23]

Arrested for Rosenbaum's murder was sixteen-year-old Lemrick Nelson, who was caught by police as he ran from the scene of the attack. After a bloody knife with the inscription "Killer" was found in the suspect's pocket,[24] he was brought before the dying victim, who positively identified Nelson as the person who had stabbed him.[25] Indeed, laboratory tests would later reveal that the blood on Nelson's knife matched Rosenbaum's.[26] Such were the initial facts of the Crown Heights incident.

Al Sharpton, among others, was sympathetic to the "retalia-tory" violence that had killed Rosenbaum. "We must not reprimand our children for outrage," said Sharpton, "when it is the outrage that was put in them by an oppressive system."[27] Two days after Rosenbaum and Cato lost their lives, Sharpton, Sonny Carson, and attorney C. Vernon Mason organized a rally protesting the boy's death.[28] The participants, in the tradition of today's "civil rights" dis-ciples, were equipped with an abundance of rage but little capacity for reason. Even after city officials informed them that police can de-tain drivers who hit pedestrians only in cases involving drunkenness or speeding—and that Lifsh was guilty of neither—the protesters re-mained angry that Lifsh had not been arrested. With virtual unanimity they asserted that had the driver been black, he would have been jailed.[29] As they marched toward the 71st Precinct station house, a number of them suddenly veered north, running *en masse* toward Lubavitcher headquarters, where they burned an Israeli flag. A group of some 200 black youths then ran down Eastern Parkway, throwing rocks and bottles, demolishing cars, and vandalizing a firehouse.[30]

City authorities were intimidated by the rioters. "We are in a tense situation," said Mayor Dinkins. "It's painful"—hardly the words of a man prepared to resolutely enforce the law.[31] In fact, the mayor *prevented* police officers from using the force necessary to quell the violence, instructing them not to retaliate against the barrages of rocks and bottles aimed their way.[32] "New York's finest have been transformed into New York's lamest," complained police union president Phil Caruso. "Lame not only because of the severe nature of the injuries sustained—but because of the relatively lethargic, virtually inert response that police officers under an actual state of siege have been allowed to put forth."[33] "If police officers are placed under a life-threatening attack," he added, "they should use their nightsticks or firearms to fend against such attacks."[34] Mayor Dinkins referred to these statements as "not at all useful."[35]

Assaults on the police continued for three nights, as did the attacks on Jewish homes. One particularly fearless group of rioters smashed the windows of a parked car and then attacked the responding police officers with rocks and bottles.[36] "It was fun, throwing bottles at the cops," a local teenager candidly stated. "I just don't like white people," said another.[37] On August 24, with the black community's passions raised to a fever pitch, Al Sharpton led 400 shouting protesters through the heart of the Crown Heights Hasidic community in yet another demonstration of outrage. "No justice, no peace!" cried the marchers.[38]

The restraint imposed upon the police, and the resulting escalation of mob violence, led to two fatalities in addition to Yankel Rosenbaum's. In one case, an Italian man was murdered when his black killers mistook him for a Jew.[39] In another incident, an elderly Holocaust survivor, terrified that rioters would break into her building at any moment, jumped to her death from the window of her third-floor apartment.[40] She had survived Adolf Hitler and the Nazis, only to succumb five decades later to the pogrom in Crown Heights. In all, more than eighty Jews were attacked during three days and nights of unrest. Hundreds of cars were vandalized and hundreds of Jewish homes were damaged.[41] It was not until the fourth day after Gavin Cato's death that the mayor permitted police to vigorously enforce the law, thereby ending the violence at last. All told, 38 innocent civilians and 150 police officers had been injured.[42]

Perhaps the most astonishing feature of the Crown Heights riots is that they were triggered by a purely accidental—and not at all unusual—occurrence. Indeed, over 42,000 deaths result from motor vehicle accidents in the United States each year. This is equivalent to 115 deaths per day, or about one every 12 minutes. Moreover, traffic accidents annually cause 1.6 million injuries nationwide—meaning that 4,400 people are hurt every day, or one every 20 seconds.[43]

Rational people understand, then, that car accidents are far from rare, but reason takes a distant back seat in our current racial climate. The self-righteous hordes of "civil rights" apostles draw no distinction between an accident and a premeditated murder. Judging every incident by the skin colors of those involved, they permit no relevant facts to put a crimp into their crusade for "justice." The determined Sharpton, for instance, actually traveled to Israel to search for Lifsh, as if the latter were a criminal. When angry Israeli onlookers taunted Sharpton with shouts of "Go to hell," he replied, "I *am* in hell."[44]

Further Cultivation of the Lie

While a grand jury deliberated on whether there was sufficient evidence to indict Yosef Lifsh on criminal charges, Mayor Dinkins publicly speculated that a non-indictment would "certainly not be well received in the African American community."[45] When it was eventually announced that no formal charges would be brought against Lifsh, the mayor told a black audience that the legal intricacies pertaining to indictments in cases like this "certainly [cannot be explained] to a layman." In fact, he added, "I'm not sure you can explain it to too many of us who are lawyers."[46] Meanwhile, Cato family attorney Colin Moore portrayed the grand jury deliberations as nothing more than a racist charade whose outcome had been predetermined. With such comments shrouding in mystery the grand jury process, black suspicions of a racist justice system soared to new heights. As one area resident said, "If a black man had been arrested, that black man would still be in custody, and you know it. It's not fair. It's not right. Yet you say it is justice. That's no justice to me."[47]

Out of the rubble of false rumors, meanwhile, local blacks constructed a variety of stories "explaining" how white racism was destroying black lives on a daily basis. Consider, as an example, one woman's patchwork account of what had happened to Gavin Cato:

> I'm so upset that they left the little baby to die. That's what we are so angry about, that the ambulance came and took out the Jew guys, that the police directed them to take care of the Jew guys. And now, the Jew guy, he is off and free, and the baby is dead. You saw the little kid pinned underneath the car. An accident will always happen, but they left him. How could you do something like that?[48]

Other Crown Heights blacks likewise fashioned their own versions of reality. Where they were short on facts, they were long on interracial distrust. A prominent member of the local Haitian community, for instance, complained about "the way black people are looked at, the assumptions about black people. That black people are no good, stupid, gross. That we are different—whatever they mean by different."[49] According to eighteen-year-old Khalil Moore, "The Jewish community looks at America as a step up, [but] the black community looks at America as being someplace that has been taken away from them."[50] In a similar vein, fifteen-year-old Nafeesha Pasha lamented, "They [the Hasidim] have all the police, but we [blacks] can't get the police for an emergency. They get the good schools."[51] Said another observer, "I think the Jews want to take everything."[52] "If we don't get justice," warned a vocal protester, "we will call for Black Power, then revolution."[53] "We are sick and tired of being treated like animals," said yet another.[54] One distraught woman, ostensibly fearing for the safety of black youngsters everywhere, cried to Deputy Mayor Bill Lynch, "I'm tired of death! I'm tired of death!"[55] Speaking as if there had been an epidemic of black children killed by Jews, she seemed unaware that those responsible for virtually all of the murders in her community were black.

Trial and Verdict

In October 1992 Lemrick Nelson stood trial for the murder of Yankel Rosenbaum. Despite the compelling evidence against him, the defendant was found not guilty by a jury composed mostly of blacks and Hispanics.[56] Portraying his client as a "sacrificial lamb" on the altar of a racist city, Nelson's defense attorney, Arthur Lewis, Jr., convinced the jurors that corrupt police officers had framed the youngster.[57] Moreover, Lewis suggested that Rosenbaum had actually provoked the attack that killed him[58]—an opinion echoed by Sonny Carson, who told a WLIB radio audience that Rosenbaum "tried to taunt people and got beat. . . . [T]he brothers who did that were defending themselves."[59]

In the hours before the jury verdict was announced, tension filled the city. Fearful that violence would erupt if Nelson were convicted, hundreds of extra police officers stationed themselves on the streets of Crown Heights while the reading of the verdict was delayed for more than two hours.[60] When word spread, however, that Nelson had been acquitted, the officers loosened their riot gear and removed the security barricades.[61] As columnist Eric Breindel noted, "[T]he cops knew—as did everyone else in New York—that Hasidic Jews weren't about to stage a riot. The precautions were necessary only when the possibility existed that Nelson would be found guilty. That might have led to a full scale . . . riot. But acquittal? No danger."[62] In the plaza outside the courthouse, blacks reacted euphorically to the verdict, cheering and raising their arms in triumph.[63] "My son was forgiven by God," the defendant's father proclaimed—a curious statement in light of the fact that he presumably believed in the boy's innocence.[64]

Later that evening, more than 1,000 Hasidic Jews gathered for a peaceful demonstration outside their Lubavitcher headquarters.[65] As police stood by to defuse any potential confrontations between these protesters and neighborhood blacks, many black onlookers resented the officers' presence. "Who do you think [the police] are here to protect?" asked one man sardonically. "Not us," replied a young black woman. "If black people responded like this, running through the streets, they would get their heads beaten in."[66]

The night after Lemrick Nelson was acquitted, his attorney celebrated the favorable verdict by treating his client and the jurors to dinner at a New York restaurant—where jury members toasted Nelson *even though his presence in the mob that had attacked Yankel Rosenbaum was never in dispute.*[67] Not surprisingly, "civil rights leaders" nationwide said nothing about the insensitive nature of this celebration. Consider, however, what might have been said—by media pundits and the self-proclaimed defenders of "justice"—if the California jury that acquitted the Los Angeles police officers in the first Rodney King trial had dined with the defendants immediately after that verdict.[68]

Selective Outrage

As previously noted, the Crown Heights riots of 1991 erupted in response to an *accident* that involved neither malice nor premeditation. By contrast, only silence had attended a very *intentional* murder on a Crown Heights subway platform five years earlier. It was July 2, 1986, when a group of black youths wielding planks and pipes crushed the skull of Israel Rosen, a forty-nine-year-old Orthodox Jew visiting from Australia.[69] Though the victim lay in a coma for several months before dying on New Year's Day 1987, few Americans ever heard about his horrible fate. His death received but a brief mention in the press, as the media's attention at the time was largely focused on the killing of Michael Griffith in Howard Beach (see chapter 3).[70]

Crown Heights was again visited by violence on April 27, 1991, when a black gunman shot four nonwhite males in a grocery store, killing three of them and rendering the lone survivor permanently disabled.[71] Two months later, sixteen-year-old Raphael Rympel was shot twice in the chest and killed by a black assailant on a Crown Heights playground.[72] In February 1992 a black career-criminal broke into the Crown Heights home of Phyllis LaPine, a thirty-eight-year-old Hasidic mother of four, stabbing her thirty-five times and leaving her to die in front of her two-year-old daughter.[73] Dreadful though these incidents were, news reporters paid little attention. Politicians did not wring their hands in frustration. The posturing champions of "civil rights" were silent. Where were the professional protesters? Where was their outrage?

While murders occur with startling regularity in many American cities, traffic accidents like the one that killed Gavin Cato are even more common. Rarely, though, do they ignite public protests or violence. Even in cases where drivers are negligent, reckless, or wantonly cruel, journalists and community activists alike have little to say—so long as the victims are not minorities killed by white drivers. Consider just a few of the myriad tragedies that the headlines largely forgot:

• In October 1987 a black Chicago man driving in a drunken stupor ran over and killed a twenty-one-year-old white woman named Marcia Lehmberg—a National Merit Scholar and an accomplished musician. Miss Lehmberg's future had seemed full of promise prior to that fateful day when she chose the wrong time and place to cross the street.[74]

• In May 1993 a white Manhattan man was run over and dragged eight blocks by a white driver whose blood-alcohol level was far above the legal limit. The victim's left ear was torn off, the left side of his body was mangled, and he was rendered unable to breathe without a respirator.[75]

    • On May 1, 1994, an intoxicated black driver named Abraham Meyers ran over two white teenage girls and their parents in a Queens, New York crosswalk.[76] The mother and both daughters were killed, while the father was left in serious condition with leg fractures.[77]

    • Two and a half weeks later, a black driver with a long history of traffic violations and license suspensions ran over and killed white college professor James Wynne on a New York City street.[78]

    • In June 1994 a white Brooklyn ambulance worker named Christopher Prescott was treating an injured victim at the scene of a traffic accident when a drunken black driver crashed a Jeep into a nearby vehicle and pushed it into Prescott's work area. Prescott was killed, his partner suffered two broken legs, and the patient—who had sustained only minor injuries from the original accident—was left in critical condition with head and chest injuries.[79]

    • Not even the *intentional* 1993 killing of a seventy-two-year-old white man named George Skouras troubled the messiahs of "justice." While Skouras walked with his wife in a New York parking lot one July day, a white man in a station wagon drove up to the couple, reached out of his car window, and attempted to snatch the woman's purse. When Mr. Skouras tried to protect his wife's bag, the driver deliberately crushed him to death under the wheels of his car.[80]

    Because none of these cases involved white perpetrators and minority victims, "civil rights leaders" and their malleable flock of disciples coolly turned their attention to other matters. Yet consider, by contrast, what occurred in September 1993 after a Crown Heights Jew drove into a fifty-three-year-old black pedestrian named Antoine Chemene, breaking the woman's ankle. When an unfounded rumor spread through the neighborhood that the driver had killed the victim and then gone into hiding, angry blacks quickly filled the city streets—a number of them throwing bottles in protest. It was a scene ominously reminiscent of the tense atmosphere that two years earlier had erupted into the Crown Heights riots, though this time a large police presence helped avert a similar catastrophe.[81]

    Notably, just an hour after Ms. Chemene's misfortune, Crown Heights was the scene of further trouble. A twenty-two-year-old black woman named Barbara Augusma was enjoying the festivities of a

West Indian American Day carnival when, without warning or provocation, she was shot in the head and killed.[82] Because the gunman
was black, however, community activists and their devoted entourage
of supporters responded with nothing more than a collective yawn.

When Children Die in Accidents

Undoubtedly, the black community's sorrow over Gavin Cato's
death was heightened by the fact that the victim was but an innocent
child. Yet we are left to wonder why there are no similar outpourings
of anguish when *nonwhite* drivers injure or kill children of *any* race
or ethnicity. There was utter disinterest, for example, on July 13, 1993,
when a livery cab driven by a Hispanic man struck and killed five-
year-old Taima McCullaugh on a Manhattan street, after which the
driver sped away—only to be later captured by police on the other
side of the city.[83] Despite his contemptible disregard for the child's
welfare, this man went uncriticized by the black community and its
"leaders." No one suggested that he may have struck the girl with
premeditation. Nor did anyone accuse him of indifference to the value
of a black child's life. Because he was not white, his motives were not
at issue.

Eleven months later, an unlicensed Hispanic driver was speeding along a Bronx street when he lost control of his unregistered,
uninspected vehicle and ran over three small Hispanic children on the
sidewalk.[84] Community "activists" responded only with silence.

In July 1990 a stolen car suddenly veered onto a Brooklyn
sidewalk and struck a four-year-old boy, dragging him nearly seventy-five feet to his death. But because the child and his killer both
were black, this tragedy made no headlines.[85]

In May 1993 a motorist whose license had been suspended
sixty-three times hit two black children, aged two and four, while speeding along a Brooklyn road. Though the older child died of his injuries
within a few hours,[86] the driver's black skin made the story relatively
uninteresting for racial arsonists and news reporters alike.

Four months later an eight-year-old Hasidic boy from Crown
Heights was run over and seriously injured by a van after stepping
down from his school bus. The accident occurred only 100 feet from
the spot where Gavin Cato had been killed two years earlier, yet this

time there was not the slightest hint of public protest—simply because the driver of the van was black. "Witnesses calmly stood by in the aftermath of the accident," read one newspaper account, "a peaceful contrast to the violence that erupted two years ago."[87]

Meanwhile, *white* drivers who hit pedestrians can evade charges of racism only if their victims are also white. In April 1993, for instance, a white, eight-year-old Brooklyn child suffered irreversible brain damage and fell into a coma when struck by a Jewish driver whose license had previously been suspended more than forty times.[88] Despite the man's abominable driving record, there was virtually no public clamor over the incident.

When Children Are Brutally Slain

In light of the widespread fury triggered by the purely accidental death of Gavin Cato, one might logically expect even greater outrage in cases involving the *deliberate* brutalization of children— regardless of race. But when killers are black, that expectation invariably goes unfulfilled. Indeed, even the most gruesome black-perpetrated murders of black youngsters are routinely ignored by "civil rights leaders" and their constituencies. Consider just a few such cases that received little, if any, attention:

• In October 1990 a Harlem man beat his girlfriend's two-year-old daughter to death simply because the child had been dancing in front of a television screen, blocking the man's view.[89]

• In May 1993 a Jersey City man stabbed his wife and then fled to Brooklyn with his four-year-old stepson. When the terrified boy was unable to stop crying, the man strangled him to death and dumped his body into a garbage chute.[90]

• That same month a forty-year-old ex-convict kidnapped a young New Jersey girl and took her to his boardinghouse, where he raped and murdered her.[91]

• Several weeks later a newly paroled New Jersey man abducted a six-year-old girl from her aunt's backyard. After sexually assaulting the child, he strangled her to death and dumped her body under the porch of an abandoned house.[92]

• In March 1994 Nicole Edmondson of East Orange, New

Jersey left her four-year-old son home alone for more than seven hours while she attended classes at a local community college. During that time, two teenage boys broke into the woman's apartment, tied a leather belt around the child's neck, and strangled him to death.[93]

None of these abominations evoked even a whisper of public protest, yet a white driver's accidental killing of a black child on a Crown Heights sidewalk was cause for rioting.

Chapter 7

America: "Rapist of Blacks"?

An error cannot be believed sincerely enough
to make it a truth.
— R.G. Ingersoll[1]

Most contemporary "civil rights leaders" depend, for their livelihood, on the continued existence of societal injustices, both real and imagined. Consequently, they have an enormous psychological and financial interest in perpetuating the notion that ours is a racist country. They possess neither the courage nor the integrity to acknowledge what black professor Shelby Steele expresses so eloquently:

> I believe that black Americans are infinitely freer today than ever before. This is not a hope; this is a reality, an extremely hard-won reality. . . . [T]he American black, supported by a massive body of law and the not inconsiderable goodwill of his fellow citizens, is basically as free as he or she wants to be. For every white I have met who is a racist, I have met twenty more who have seen me as an equal. And of those twenty, ten have only wished me the best as an individual. This I say, as opposed to confessing, has been my actual reality. I believe it is time for blacks to begin the shift from a wartime

to a peacetime identity, from fighting for opportunity to the seizing of it. The immutable fact of late twentieth-century life is that it *is* there to seize.[2]

Does white racism still exist in America? Of course it does, occasionally manifesting itself in injustice and cruelty. Sadly, racism is likely to plague humanity forever. All races of people in all ages of history have demonstrated an inclination toward intergroup hostility, and we should not be surprised to find examples of it in our own society. Particularly in a country with a population as large and diverse as ours, it is almost unimaginable that a day will ever come when racists are completely eliminated from our midst.

The fact that racists live among us, however, in no way proves that our society is intrinsically racist. Indeed, the overwhelming majority of white Americans today not only reject the notion of their own racial superiority, but strongly support integration and the full protection of equal rights for minorities.[3] (See chapter 14 for a more detailed discussion of polling data regarding current white attitudes toward blacks.) Nonetheless, present-day "civil rights" mouthpieces largely refuse to acknowledge the white community's attitudinal transformation of recent decades. In order to retain their positions as navigators on a purportedly noble mission, these "leaders" obstinately deny the goodwill of most whites and portray the black struggle for equality as an arduous, ongoing crusade. To further their own agenda, they will even elevate a hoax into a rallying point.

On November 28, 1987, in a wooded area of Wappingers Falls, New York, two ambulance paramedics found a sixteen-year-old black girl named Tawana Brawley inside a plastic garbage bag—seemingly in a dazed, unresponsive state. Her hair was matted and chopped unevenly, her clothing smeared with feces, and her chest covered with racial slurs written in black letters. She was wearing a pink sweatshirt, a dark sweater wrapped around her head and neck, one shoe, and a pair of denim pants with scorch marks on the inner thighs.[4] Horrible as all this was, the circumstances seemed even uglier when Miss Brawley reported that she had been repeatedly raped and sodomized for four days by six white kidnappers, one of whom wore a police badge.[5] She further alleged that she had been forced to perform oral sex on the men, at least one of whom urinated into her mouth.[6] It was among the most disturbing tales in recent memory, evoking the anger and pity of virtually all who heard it.

There was immediate, profound soul-searching by journalists and a horrified public. "For blacks, especially," *The New York Times* reported, ". . . this is a troubling time."[7] Hundreds of protesters from near and far attended marches held on the victim's behalf to publicly condemn acts of racial hatred.[8] Behind the scenes, meanwhile, "civil rights" activists scrambled to get involved in the case. Al Sharpton, for one, quickly assumed the role of special advisor to Miss Brawley and thereafter worked closely with the girl's attorneys—C. Vernon Mason and Alton Maddox. Lamenting that their client had fallen prey to "certain elements that have constantly antagonized the black community, including the Ku Klux Klan and law-enforcement personnel,"[9] the Brawley team demanded that New York governor Mario Cuomo appoint a special prosecutor to the case. In compliance, the governor assigned to that role Attorney General Robert Abrams, who promptly called the Brawley case "the highest priority investigation in my office."[10] Mr. Abrams was unable to accomplish much, however, when Miss Brawley's advisors refused to let her speak to even one law-enforcement official investigating the incident. Alleging that the American criminal-justice system treated blacks unfairly,[11] they instructed the girl to defy a grand jury subpoena requiring her to testify.[12]

In December the U.S. Justice Department initiated a civil rights investigation into Miss Brawley's attack,[13] making every effort to assure a skeptical black community that the girl would get a fair hearing. Said a spokesman for the Subcommittee on Criminal Justice, "Effective prosecutions from the Federal Government would serve as effective deterrents for hate crimes, which we see increasing across the country. We're concerned that local black communities don't feel they can have confidence in local or state officials to investigate these kinds of crimes."[14]

"This is a case that is never going to die," Alton Maddox proclaimed in February 1988. "Within a week, everyone in the country will be focusing on this case."[15] "I'm made out to be the bad guy," he added, "because my position is that the system has to be sensitive to everyone. It amazes me how the system can somehow become insensitive when the victim is black."[16] C. Vernon Mason, meanwhile, claimed that "everybody in Wappingers Falls knows who [raped Miss Brawley]—even I know who did it. The Brawley family will not cooperate until arrests are made."[17] In response, Attorney General Abrams unequivocally denied that anyone—let alone everyone—knew who had attacked the girl.[18]

Also in February, entertainer Bill Cosby and the publisher of *Essence* magazine, Ed Lewis, announced that they were offering a $25,000 reward for information leading to the arrest of the perpetrators.[19] Meanwhile, the topmost levels of state government continued to give the Brawley case the highest priority. Governor Cuomo met at length with the girl's attorneys and tried earnestly to satisfy their demands.[20] "We know someone has violated her in a terrible way," said Cuomo. "We need to know who did it, and we need to see that that individual or individuals are punished as the law provides."[21] It appeared, at first, that the governor had succeeded in winning the trust of Maddox and Mason, who finally agreed to let their client testify "at the appropriate time."[22]

Within a week, however, the Brawley advisors abruptly rescinded this agreement.[23] As a spokesman for Attorney General Abrams observed, "They seemed to want some commitment that we would pursue strategies other than [obtaining] the cooperation [and testimony] of Tawana Brawley."[24] Prior to this impasse, most observers had attributed Miss Brawley's silence to the advice of her lawyers. Yet now those same attorneys characterized their own refusal to cooperate as deference to the wishes of their client.[25] It became increasingly unclear who was advising whom. Mr. Abrams's efforts to negotiate a solution, meanwhile, went unappreciated by the Brawley team, which now accused the attorney general of "aligning himself with the culprits."[26] Moreover, Dutchess County police officers were besieged with death threats after Sharpton, Mason, and Maddox publicly charged that "high level" local law-enforcement officials were involved in the crime.[27]

More accusations followed. Sharpton, for instance, suddenly demanded that Abrams be removed from the case because of an alleged "relationship" between the attorney general and the Dutchess County sheriff, who was, according to Sharpton, "a suspect in this case."[28] Thus, after having initially pressed for Abrams's intimate involvement in every phase of the legal proceedings, the Brawley advisors now pronounced him unfit to play any role at all. Sharpton insisted that there was "absolutely no way" that his client would talk to Abrams.[29] "That's like asking someone who watched someone killed in the gas chamber to sit down with Mr. Hitler," said the outspoken activist.[30] Whereas just five days earlier Sharpton had expressed his "respect for Mr. Abrams" as a "liberal politician" whose "record in civil rights is unquestioned,"[31] he now likened the attorney general to the Nazi tyrant of the 1940s. For good measure, Maddox charged that Abrams had masturbated while staring at a photograph of Miss Brawley.[32] Sadly, Abrams proved to be intimidated by the trio's reckless accusations and obstructions of the evidence-gathering process. Reluctant to take a tough stand against their slanderous rhetoric, he tried instead to placate them. "I understand," he said, "the skepticism that exists in the black community about certain institutions in this country, about whether blacks can truly get justice."[33]

As the case dragged on, week after week, members of the "civil rights" brigade remained unwilling to publicly criticize the Brawley advisors' reprehensible behavior. Governor Cuomo speculated that skeptical black onlookers were keeping their doubts about the case private, for fear "that they'd be called 'Uncle Toms' " were they to jump off the Brawley bandwagon.[34] Indeed, it was only on condition of anonymity that one black attorney conceded, "Among black civil-rights lawyers there is a lot of concern about this case. There is suspicion that they [Miss Brawley and her advisors] don't want this case to go forward because the case is not what it appears to be on the surface."[35]

While black critics of the Brawley team spoke only anonymously or in measured, muffled tones, a number of prominent "civil rights leaders" openly praised Sharpton, Mason, and Maddox. The Reverend Calvin Butts of Harlem suggested that "what they [the advisors] are doing now is in the best interests of Tawana Brawley and in the best interests of a new standard of justice for black people. In order to do this, like in Howard Beach, they have had to take some fairly drastic action."[36] Along the same lines, high-ranking NAACP representative Laura Blackburne said, "I think it's clear they want to be sure this will be handled in the most serious, most aggressive possible manner."[37]

By late February 1988, three months after the alleged kidnapping and rape, Miss Brawley still had given no information to law-enforcement officials.[38] Thus a grand jury was empanelled to hear testimony regarding the case[39]—inexplicably prompting C. Vernon Mason to accuse Cuomo of having no interest in bringing Miss Brawley's attackers to justice.[40] Sharpton, for his own part, charged that the grand jury was racially insensitive because only two of its twenty-three members were black.[41] Presumably he deemed it irrelevant that fewer than 100 blacks lived in all of Wappingers Falls—meaning, therefore, that blacks were in fact statistically *over*represented on the grand jury.[42]

Three and a half months after the alleged rape, the Brawley attorneys at long last came forth with a concrete accusation naming one of the assailants. At a news conference in Manhattan's Grand Hyatt Hotel, Alton Maddox declared, "Stephen Pagones [Dutchess County's assistant district attorney] was one of the attackers." Also accusing District Attorney William Grady of trying to cover up Pagones's involvement in the crime, Maddox exhorted Governor Cuomo "to make an immediate arrest" of the two "suspects."[43] Though he adduced not a shred of evidence to substantiate his allegations, Maddox vowed that unless both men were jailed, he "would not even consider" allowing his client to testify.[44] When asked if he could prove the charges, Maddox replied, "We don't want to outline to Mr. Pagones what evidence we have. He's still a law-enforcement official and is in the position to retaliate against the family."[45]

In June, nearly seven months after the alleged rape, Perry McKinnon, an aide to Al Sharpton, stepped forward to make a remarkable series of disclosures. A former police officer, private investigator, and director of security at a Brooklyn hospital, McKinnon revealed that "Sharpton acknowledged to me early on that 'The story do sound like bull—— but it don't matter. We're building a movement. This is the perfect issue. Because you've got whites on blacks. That's an easy way to stir up all the deprived people, who would want to believe, and who would believe—and all [you've] got to do is convince them—that all white people are bad. Then you've got a movement.' "[46] In a statement foreshadowing the Crown Heights riots of three years later, McKinnon said that Sharpton was "building an atmosphere" for a race war.[47] "Sharpton told me," McKinnon continued, " 'It don't matter whether any whites did it or not. Something happened to her . . . even if Tawana done it to herself.' "[48]

The other Brawley advisors, McKinnon explained, were no more honorable than Sharpton. Alton Maddox, for instance, "didn't want to know any facts about the case. He said he was going to approach it on the political front. You see, Alton Maddox hates all white people. This whole Tawana Brawley situation is not about Tawana Brawley."[49] None of the advisors, said McKinnon, even attempted to "gain proper evidence before making accusations."[50] To prove his truthfulness, McKinnon submitted to a lie detector test administered on camera, and passed all questions.[51] (It is worth noting that nearly a decade later, when the Brawley advisors testified in a civil defamation suit brought against them by Stephen Pagones, none of them could cite even a single specific measure they had taken to verify their allegations.)

Despite mounting evidence that the Brawley case was a hoax, the major media continued throughout 1988 to spotlight it as one of the great outrages of modern America. In June the television program *Donahue* broadcast live from a Brooklyn Baptist church, giving the Brawley advisors and an audience stacked with supporters a forum in which to bang the drum of white racism.[52] Two weeks later C. Vernon Mason asserted, without evidence, that the white ambulance drivers who initially found Miss Brawley in the woods that November 1987 day had actually wanted her to die.[53]

In August, Jesse Jackson characterized the Brawley episode as "part of a larger and growing case of racial antagonisms and a loss of confidence in the judicial system."[54] "You cannot separate the agony and estrangement in the Brawley case," he explained, "from the behavior of elected officials . . . or what happened in Howard Beach."[55] Presumably, Jackson expected Americans to believe that white assailants posed a greater threat to the black community than did black assailants.

The Fraud Revealed

In the autumn of 1988, after conducting seven months of painstaking investigation, interviewing 180 witnesses, examining more than 250 evidence exhibits, and compiling 6,000 pages of testimony, the grand jury released its report concluding that the entire Tawana Brawley story had been fabricated.[56] "We know the facts," said Attorney General Abrams. "We have solved the case. The allegations that [Brawley] made are false."[57]

The evidence against Brawley was weighty indeed. Medical tests performed on the girl shortly after the paramedics hospitalized her found no evidence that she had been attacked in any way.[58] There were no bruises, cuts, or other signs of trauma to her mouth or vaginal area. Microscopic and chemical tests for semen and urine proved negative, contradicting her claim that the attackers had forced her to perform oral sex and urinated into her mouth. She had no injuries other than a slight scratch on her right breast and a small bruise behind her left ear, and showed no evidence of malnourishment or exposure despite allegedly having spent ninety hours outdoors in freezing weather. Nor were there any traces of plant material on her clothing.[59]

In truth, Miss Brawley had probably spent little, if any, of her four-day absence outdoors. Not only had a neighbor spotted the girl entering her family's former (and temporarily vacant) Wappingers Falls apartment during that period, but police investigators also found several key pieces of evidence inside that apartment.[60] Among those items were a denim jacket that Brawley had been wearing at the time of her disappearance, and charred cotton fibers matching those discovered under her fingernails by medical examiners.[61] Moreover, another neighbor had seen her crawling into a plastic bag in the woods just prior to the paramedics' arrival.[62] In short, everything pointed clearly to the only conclusion possible: Tawana Brawley had not been raped. At least a million dollars of taxpayer money had been spent to investigate a colossal hoax.[63]

While racially motivated white brutality was the centerpiece of the Brawley allegations, it is likely that the girl's phony story was in fact inspired by her fear of a *black* person—specifically, her mother's boyfriend Ralph King, whose long history of violence included the 1969 murder of his former wife. More recently, King was known to regularly carry a gun, sell drugs, and associate with alcoholics and drug addicts. In addition, he had been involved in many violent quarrels with Tawana Brawley. In 1986, for instance, when the girl was arrested for shoplifting, law officers had to forcibly stop King from beating her at the police station. Sadly, Miss Brawley could hardly hope to find solace in the arms of her mother, who had also beaten her many times for running away and spending nights with male companions.[64] On that November 1987 day when she disappeared from Wappingers Falls, the girl was most likely afraid to go home and be punished for some transgression. Thus she fabricated a story that the American public had been primed to believe by decades of racial mythology. Her tale was, as Sharpton understood, the perfect symbol of white racism in America.

Predictable Denials

Even after the fraud had been exposed, vocal black "leaders" persisted with their familiar mantra. "We will continue to fight," Al Sharpton told a radio audience. "It did not end today [with the grand jury decision]. It just began today."[65] In unison with Mason and Maddox, Sharpton denounced Governor Cuomo and Attorney General Abrams as racists who had allowed the grand jury to "cover up" the evidence against Stephen Pagones.[66] Then the three advisors, along with Miss Brawley and some 200 supporters, blocked New York City traffic in a gesture of protest against the legal system's alleged abuse of blacks. "We're here to honor black women who have suffered in the criminal justice system," said Sharpton. "We will stop this town every week until you learn how to respect the African queens who live among you."[67]

Black columnist Earl Caldwell would call the Brawley case "a huge chapter of black rage and white denial."[68] Along the same lines, the Reverend Saul Williams of Dutchess County said, "From a historical standpoint, I'm not ready to trust the grand jury. They were not out to prove that [Brawley] was attacked. They were out to prove that she was not. I have to believe her until something in me is made not to. America is a rapist of blacks."[69] Legal scholar Patricia Williams considered the case a tragedy for all black Americans—regardless of whether anything had actually happened to the girl. "Tawana Brawley," said Williams, "has been the victim of some unspeakable crime. No matter who did it to her—and even if she did it to herself. Her condition was clearly the expression of some crime against her, some tremendous violence, some great violation that challenges comprehension. And it is this much that I grieve about. The rest of the story is lost, or irrelevant in the worst of all possible ways."[70] According to Otis Brown, president of the Atlanta chapter of the NAACP, "It doesn't matter to me whether Brawley did it or not, because of all the pressure these black students are under at these predominantly white schools. If this will highlight it . . . I have no problem with that."[71]

Some whites expressed sympathy for Miss Brawley as well. Anthropologist Stanley Diamond reasoned that "it doesn't matter whether the crime occurred or not, [since it was] the epitome of degradation, a repellant model of what actually happens to too many black women."[72] In a similar vein, attorney William Kuntsler said, "It makes no difference whether the attack on Tawana Brawley really happened, because a lot of black women are treated the way she was treated."[73]

In 1990, when an appellate court punished Alton Maddox for his role in the Brawley hoax by revoking his law license, the recalcitrant attorney declared, "This is not a time for racial harmony. It's time to up the ante. It's time to turn up the temperature in the streets. . . . They're going to see more of me. They're going to beg me to take my license back because they can control a man in the court-room. There are no controls in the streets." He predictably called the court's ruling "racist" and reaffirmed his intention never to reveal what he supposedly knew about the Brawley case. "If the condition for my getting my license back is to give . . . information about Tawana Braw-ley, I will never practice law in New York State again," he said.[74] The more obvious it became that Maddox had defrauded the public, the more defiant he grew.

Not surprisingly, Sharpton was similarly obstinate. For more than a decade after Miss Brawley first made her false allegations, he continued to reiterate his "belief" that she had been brutalized by a group of whites. In February 1989, for instance, he told a *Spin* maga-zine interviewer, without proof, that Stephen Pagones had privately confessed to the crime. Sharpton further asserted, falsely, that Brawley's gang-rape allegations had been confirmed by medical tests whose results were in C. Vernon Mason's possession. And finally, for good measure, he lamented that the girl had tragically fallen prey to a barbaric "white-supremist cult ritual."[75] When Pagones sued him for defamation in 1997, Sharpton portrayed himself as a wrongly perse-cuted man of honor who, like Martin Luther King, Jr., placed the pur-suit of justice above all else. Mysteriously, however, he could "no longer recall" having made a number of his slanderous accusations against Pagones and other law-enforcement officials years earlier.[76] When asked whether he had made even the slightest attempt to verify Miss Brawley's allegations about Pagones before going public with them, Sharpton self-righteously retorted, "I would not engage in sex talk with a fifteen-year-old girl."[77] In other words, he had been quite willing to put Pagones through a torturous, high-profile, ten-year or-deal—which would both bankrupt the young attorney and destroy his marriage—without ever knowing for sure whether Brawley's shock-ing charges were even true.[78] He proudly explained, moreover, that he had handled the Brawley affair no differently than any other case. "I'm a civil rights leader and this is what I do," said Sharpton.[79] No words could have described more precisely—or more pathetically— what so many of our nation's "civil rights leaders" have become.

Double Standards

It has become routine for members of the "civil rights" cabal to overlook their own deceitfulness while self-righteously denouncing the lies of others. Consider a 1989 Boston case in which a white man, Charles Stuart, devised a plan to kill his pregnant wife in order to collect life-insurance money. He drove his wife to a black neighborhood, fatally shot her, and then shot and wounded himself—later telling law-enforcement officials that a black gunman had done this horrible deed. When it was eventually learned that Stuart was in fact responsible for both his wife's death and his own superficial wound, attorney C. Vernon Mason characterized the hoax as an attempt to take advantage of the public's readiness to believe the worst about blacks:

> He [Stuart] was certainly aware of the advantages he would be given by making an accusation against a black person. He created a person; no person existed. It was just a matter of labeling someone who was vulnerable. He knew he could falsely charge a black person and get an outpouring of sympathy from the white community. And he also knew that the system would work in concert with that conspiracy. He knew how to take advantage of whiteness in a racist society.[80]

We can only marvel at the mental gymnastics by which Mason was able to simultaneously condemn Stuart's lie and defend his own role in the Brawley hoax—which, it should be noted, was by no means the sole fraud of his law career. Over the years, Mason represented hundreds of black clients who specifically sought out his services because of his reputation as a representative of the disadvantaged. Unfortunately for those clients, however, their trust in Mason was misplaced. In January 1995 this "civil rights" attorney—who masterfully portrayed himself as the downtrodden's champion—was convicted of sixty-six counts of professional misconduct and was disbarred from the legal profession. His offenses included "a pattern of neglect, dishonesty, fee gouging, client abandonment, fraud, deceit, and misrepresentation."[81] Indeed, while claiming to be part of the remedy for society's alleged abuse of blacks, he was actually part of the problem. While calling constant attention to the purported evils of whites, this charlatan was busy fleecing the very people he claimed to protect.

Those Whose Cries Go Unheard

Unlike the Brawley fiasco, most of the thousands of rape cases investigated each year in this country receive little, if any, publicity. Consider the brutal attack of Brooklyn's Crystal Stevens, whose ex-boyfriend beat and raped her repeatedly one May night in 1992.[82] After the terrifying ordeal was over, Miss Stevens filed rape charges against her attacker, whose friends promptly threatened to kill her in retribution. Four months later, one of them attempted to follow through on this threat, pushing Miss Stevens onto a train track where three subway cars ran over her—severing her right leg, her left kneecap, and parts of both hands. Eighteen hours of surgery saved the woman's life, but for six months thereafter she had to lie flat in a "halo" brace so as to prevent her smashed vertebrae from cutting her spinal cord.[83] Horrible as this case was, it garnered virtually no public notice—simply because the victim and her attackers alike were black. Predictably, the self-proclaimed champions of black honor, who had been impossible to silence when condemning Tawana Brawley's "degradation," were never heard from.

One January 1992 morning, two black men abducted a fifteen-year-old white girl from a Brooklyn bus stop—taping her eyes shut, driving her to a remote location, and raping her. When the terrified victim asked the men why they had singled her out for this crime, they candidly answered, "Because you are white and perfect."[84] The dearth of media coverage that attended this awful attack was a sharp contrast to the massive publicity given the Brawley hoax.

In April 1994 a forty-three-year-old Russian woman was jogging near New York's Coney Island beach when she was ambushed by a group of five black teens who dragged her under a boardwalk, brutally beat her, and then took turns raping her at gunpoint.[85] The city's daily newspapers carefully avoided identifying the assailants as black,[86] while community activists said nothing about the incident.

Six months later, a white Brooklyn woman sitting in her parked car was suddenly attacked by two black teenagers and their Hispanic companion. After taking turns raping and sodomizing the victim, the assailants stole her wallet and fled.[87] While we cannot be certain whether this was a crime of racism or simply a crime of convenience, it is noteworthy that journalists and social commentators alike chose to ignore the story's racial element—something that is rarely over-looked when attackers are white and victims are minorities.

In 1992 a white North Carolina woman named Melissa McLoughlin was abducted and repeatedly raped by a group of seven blacks who later dumped the hapless victim into a tub of bleach, shot her five times, and left her to die alongside a quiet road. Though the killers later acknowledged that their motives for the crime were purely racial—explaining that they were responding to "400 years of white oppression"[88]—the news media virtually ignored this story. Few out-of-staters heard about it.

By contrast, when several white St. John's University students were indicted for the sexual assault of a young black woman in 1991, the story received extensive coverage and became a focal issue for "civil rights leaders" nationwide. When the case went to trial later that year and resulted in acquittals for three of the accused men,[89] the prophets of "justice" were incensed. Representative Charles Rangel likened "this unbelievable verdict" to "what used to happen in the South with a black victim."[90] With similar disgust, the Reverend Herbert Daughtry called the verdict not only "a blatant manifestation of sexism and racism," but actually "one of the greatest miscarriages of justice the world has ever seen."[91] "The jury [had] to decide," he explained, "[whether to] convict these young, white, athletic, Ameri-can-dream-type boys or cause this irreparable pain to this family [and] this black girl from Jamaica. Given the social order in which we live, they couldn't rise to the occasion and render a just verdict."[92] One can only wonder why Mr. Daughtry's crusade against "irreparable pain" never led him to speak out about the agony suffered by Crystal Stevens and the other victims mentioned in this chapter. Presumably, pain is irreparable only if inflicted by a white person upon a black.

For many African Americans, the St. John's verdict merely confirmed their suspicions that the entire criminal-justice system was racist. As a *New York Times* writer covering the trial observed, "Blacks saw [in the trial] an opportunity to right a historic wrong: white men, from the time of the slave trade, viewing black women as fair game."[93] While many undoubtedly viewed the case this way, the rightful purpose of trials is certainly not to redress the wrongs of distant history, but rather to allow individual cases to be judged on their pertinent, particular merits.

"Rapist of Blacks"?

To what extent can it be said that America is a "rapist of blacks," as the Reverend Saul Williams colorfully, if figuratively, asserted? Certainly it is true that black women are victimized by this awful crime with troubling frequency—thousands of times in any given year. Yet those assaults have little to do with white racism. In truth, white rapists who target black victims are far outnumbered by black rapists who prey upon whites. In 1988, for instance, there were *fewer than 10* reported cases of white-on-black rape nationwide, but more than 9,400 reports of black-on-white rape.[94] Three years later some 100 white rapists attacked black victims, while more than 20,000 black rapists attacked white victims.[95]

Even before the civil rights advances of the 1960s, white-on-black rape was a rarity. Studies conducted in 1958 and 1960 found that only 3.6 percent of all rapes were white-on-black. Notably, black-on-white rapes were also relatively uncommon in those years, accounting for just 3.2 percent of sexual assaults.[96] Since that time, however, the incidence of black-on-white rape has skyrocketed while the white-on-black variety has remained rare. Throughout the 1970s, black-on-white rape was at least ten times more common than white-on-black.[97] A 1974 study in Denver revealed that whereas 40 percent of the city's rapes were black-on-white, there was not a single reported case of white-on-black rape.[98] Today black rapists choose white victims for about 59 percent of the sexual assaults they commit.[99]

Given these facts, it becomes apparent that Reverend Williams's bold assertion is nothing more than a lie—a catchy but meaningless slogan designed to convince black Americans that whites degrade them on a regular basis. Having been dutifully shielded from the truth by such "civil rights leaders" and the media, most Americans are unfamiliar with interracial rape statistics and thus are easily misled. But in the final analysis, Williams and his ilk have nothing more enlightening to say than Tawana Brawley herself, who in 1997 asserted that "what happened to me happens to *hundreds of thousands* of women every day" in America.[100] In the mosaic of rape cases in the United States, the Tawana Brawley story—even if it *had* been true—would have comprised only one tiny fragment among many thousands. Yet it was treated as if it were the largest, brightest, most important piece in the entire pattern.

Chapter 8

"Bloodsuckers" and "Interlopers"

Man prefers to believe what he prefers to be true.
—Francis Bacon[1]

On the afternoon of January 18, 1990, a forty-six-year-old black woman named Giselaine Fetissainte walked into Red Apple, a Korean-American grocery store located in the Flatbush section of Brooklyn, to do some shopping. Shortly thereafter a dispute arose between Mrs. Fetissainte and the grocers. According to the customer, store manager Bong Ok Jang accused her of theft and insisted on looking inside her bag before he would allow her to leave the store. When the woman balked, Mr. Jang allegedly grabbed her by the neck, slapped her face several times, and knocked her to the floor—inflicting head, neck, and abdominal injuries.[2]

The Korean merchants' version of the story was markedly different. Mrs. Fetissainte, they said, went to the cash register with her merchandise but disputed the amount due. When the cashier asked for more money, the irate customer allegedly responded by messing up a register display, hurling peppers, and spitting at the cashier. When Mr. Jang put his hands on the woman's shoulders and asked her to leave, she purportedly dropped to the floor and began to scream.[3]

Rumor quickly spread through the area's black community that Mrs. Fetissainte had been "savagely beaten"—perhaps into a coma.[4] Though the facts were very much in dispute, the incident touched off a long and bitter boycott of Red Apple by black protest groups. Every day, from early morning until late at night, demonstrators stood outside the store and frightened away all potential patrons. Referring to Koreans as "bloodsuckers" and "yellow monkeys,"[5] the protesters distributed leaflets urging blacks not to shop "with people who don't look like us."[6]

Activist Sonny Carson soon expanded the boycott to include also Church Fruits, another Korean-owned store which, according to the demonstrators, had a business relationship with Red Apple.[7] With nearly all potential customers afraid to cross the picket lines, the markets' revenues dwindled to almost nothing. Their combined daily receipts—which before the boycott had averaged about $9,000—now ranged between $10 and $30.[8]

Most amazing of all was the fact that virtually no one in New York, other than residents of Flatbush, even heard about the boycott during its first three months. The media, ever-reluctant to report incidents that show blacks to be racists, ignored the story until late April 1990.[9] We can well imagine, of course, the zeal with which reporters would have covered a story of white or Asian protesters boycotting a black-owned market, chanting antiblack slogans, and specifically discouraging passersby from patronizing African American businesses.[10] In all likelihood, the entire nation would have been aware of the story.

Deeply Rooted Bitterness

Accusing Korean store owners of treating black customers with less respect than other patrons,[11] many Flatbush blacks characterized the Red Apple altercation as "totally racial."[12] Their grievances, however, extended far beyond that incident. Some alleged that banks were more willing to approve loans to Korean and Vietnamese immigrants than to blacks.[13] Others resented the fact that Korean-owned markets far outnumbered black businesses in Flatbush.[14] As one local black remarked, "This is our community, but isn't it odd that none of these markets are owned by blacks? Something is wrong with this picture. If someone would just give me a chance, I'd open up a produce market that put these other stores out of business."[15] Notably, he did not identify the "someone" who had theretofore thwarted his ambition.

Other local blacks asserted that Korean businesses took money from the black community while "giving nothing in return"— apparently unaware that as much as 60 percent of some Korean grocers' merchandise came from black suppliers.[16] Comfortably oblivious to such facts, the boycotters vowed to continue their crusade until both of the targeted markets were permanently closed.[17] Forgiveness, they explained, did not occupy a high position on their agenda. "We've been forgiving for 400 years," said one protester. "They attack one black woman, they attack them all."[18] With similar indignation, Sonny Carson warned that blacks would not "tolerate continued assaults by people who don't live in our community, don't employ people in our community, and don't have our best interests at heart. In the future, there'll be funerals, not boycotts."[19] As Deputy Mayor Bill Lynch observed, the boycott seemed "to have taken on a life of its own."[20]

Most of the city's previous black boycotts of Korean-owned stores had ended in closings or transfers of ownership. A four-month campaign against the Brooklyn market Tropic Fruits, for instance, resulted in a settlement requiring the owner to sell his business, issue a written apology, donate money to black organizations, and attend "sensitivity training" classes. In recent years other black groups have organized similar boycotts of Korean businesses in Philadelphia, Chicago, Los Angeles, and Washington, D.C.[21]

Ben Limb, president of the Korean American Lawyers Association, called the Red Apple altercation an "isolated incident."[22] But the peddlers of the Great Myth see no interracial dispute as isolated. In their eyes, even an unsubstantiated rumor about a merchant-patron squabble qualifies as evidence of widespread, pernicious racism— and thus may set off months of outrage. Because a peaceful resolution would have robbed their storm of its thunder, the boycotters predictably rejected a judge's suggestion that a city mediator be utilized to help settle the conflict.[23] Further, they disregarded a court order requiring them to stay at least fifty feet from the markets while picketing.[24] When a second judicial order reaffirmed the fifty-foot rule, Sonny

Carson called the judge a racist and stormed out of the court.[25] Black police commissioner Lee Brown actually appealed the order and refused to enforce it.[26] Mayor Dinkins, meanwhile, was careful not to rebuke the protesters, lest he arouse the wrath of black groups in Brooklyn.[27] Instead of ordering police to keep the picketers outside the mandated fifty-foot radius, the mayor explained that "tremendously delicate diplomacy" was in order.[28] Not until the boycott was four months old, in fact, did he even acknowledge that it might have been racially motivated.[29] How long would such a campaign of intimidation and financial destruction have been allowed to persist if a *white* or *Asian* group had been chanting anti*black* slogans and flouting court orders while picketing a *black*-owned business? How long would it have taken for such a boycott to be characterized as racist?

The Mayor's Myths

On May 11, after 113 days of the illegal boycott had virtually destroyed Red Apple and Church Fruits, Mayor Dinkins, in a televised speech, made this hollow pledge: "We will never allow any group or any person to turn to violence or the threat of violence to intimidate others, no matter how legitimate their anger or frustration may be."[30] Then, presumably to demonstrate his sensitivity to the black community's grievances, he urged black New Yorkers to "repress" their own "rage" over the fact that they themselves "have never been free from fear of attack."[31] Invoking the name of Yusef Hawkins, a black Bensonhurst youth killed by a group of whites under racially charged circumstances nine months earlier (see chapter 4), the mayor asserted that "no verdict can undo the damage . . . done on that devastating night last August [when Hawkins was killed]."[32] "The hate that was unleashed upon . . . Hawkins," Dinkins added, "can never be called back. The pain that ripped through his body, his family, and the city can never be fully healed, and his sacrifice must never be forgotten."[33] We are left to wonder, of course, if any of the vast number of crimes committed by *blacks* against *nonblacks* were equally worthy of remembrance; if any of *those* crimes required society to respond with an equal measure of self-restraint; and, for that matter, why no black-on-*black* crimes had "damaged" the city as severely as the murder of Yusef Hawkins allegedly had.

In the same address, Mr. Dinkins explained that a number of "frustrating" social, psychological, and economic factors were causing the boycotters to disobey the law. "As such frustrations build and pressures mount," he said, "people are more likely to lash out. In tough times, child abuse increases, alcohol abuse rises and the bonds of civility and decency fray."[34] Apparently the mayor was unaware that during the Great Depression of the 1930s, when poverty and hopelessness plagued American life as never before or since, violent crime rates were far lower than today—for whites and blacks alike. Indeed it was not until the 1960s, a period of economic prosperity, that crime rates soared.[35]

The notion that economic deprivation leads to lawlessness is one of modern America's grandest delusions—discredited by many millions of people through the ages who have demonstrated that the choice between civility and barbarism is made in accordance with moral values, rather than compelled by economic circumstances. The concurrent presence of indigence and high crime rates in our country's inner cities by no means proves that poverty causes crime—*but more likely suggests that the moral depravity underlying criminal behavior frequently causes poverty*. If a felon feels no moral restraint against harming his fellow man; if he has no desire to work for a living; if he feels no responsibility to care for the children he fathers; and if he places little or no value on education—then it is his own corrupted value system, and not an unjust society, that hinders him.

The intent here is not to suggest that people in poverty tend to be immoral, but rather that immoral people who happen to be destitute ought not blame their social pathologies on poverty. Human history is replete with examples of impoverished people—of all racial backgrounds—who have endured almost unbearably "tough times" without descending into criminal activity. During the 1960s, for instance, the residents of San Francisco's Chinatown were among America's poorest people—with the most unemployment, the worst housing conditions, the least education, and the highest rate of tuberculosis in their city. Yet despite such hardships, only *five* people of Chinese ancestry went to jail in the entire state of California in 1965.[36]

Jewish immigrants to America during the late nineteenth and early twentieth centuries also repudiated criminality despite having to face extreme economic privation. Historian Max Dimont describes them:

The majority of these immigrants had arrived penniless, all their worldly belongings wrapped in a bundle. . . . Most of [them] arrived in New York. Some made their way into other cities, . . . but the majority remained in New York, settling in the Lower East Side of Manhattan, [which was] a neighborhood of the poor. Sociologists, with their impressive charts showing the number of toilets (or lack of them), the number of people per room, the low per capita income, paint a dismal picture of the Lower East Side Jewish slum. But their charts do not capture its uniqueness. Though it bred tuberculosis and rheumatism, it did not breed crime and venereal disease. It did not spawn illiteracy, illegitimate children, or deserted wives. Library cards were in constant use.[37]

Grievances Without End

Two days after the mayor's televised speech, a group of at least a dozen Brooklyn blacks mistook three Vietnamese men for Koreans, shouted racial slurs at them, and assaulted them with knives, bottles, and a baseball bat.[38] Though one of the victims suffered a fractured skull,[39] there were no community protests on his behalf. Nor did the Flatbush boycotters see any reason to condemn the attack or to take any focus off their seemingly interminable crusade. "We are stronger than ever," one of them proclaimed. "We will never give up."[40] "Boycott! Boycott!" the group echoed repeatedly.[41] As it became increasingly clear that solutions and reconciliation were the last goals this "movement" sought, attorney Stephen James, who represented the picketers, resigned from the case because they would give him no latitude to work toward a settlement.[42]

In September, when the boycott was eight months old, an appellate court unanimously reaffirmed the fifty-foot rule. This time Police Commissioner Brown enforced the order, a task that required some 400 police officers.[43] With the demonstrators finally at a safe distance, more customers began to cross the picket line. On September 21 Mayor Dinkins himself, in a long-overdue gesture of support, shopped at both Red Apple and Church Fruits[44]—prompting one protester to shout, "Nothing can stop us! We ain't going to listen to Uncle Tom Dinkins."[45] Mrs. Fetissainte's attorney Colin Moore, meanwhile, called the mayor's action "regrettable" and "not helpful to the negotiating process."[46] "For the mayor to condemn this method [of protesting]," he added, "is for him to condemn the methods by which black people, including himself, gained power."[47] Presumably Mr. Moore equated the civil rights demonstrations of the 1960s, which awakened our nation's conscience to some very real injustices, with an illegal mob's intimidation of American citizens nearly three decades later. Like most contemporary "civil rights leaders," he failed to understand that the mere act of protesting does not make its ostensible cause just.

The very next day, the protesters violated the fifty-foot rule—chanting, among other slogans, "Death to all white men."[48] Later that month, in an effort to ease tensions in the community, Red Apple owner Bong Jae Jang hired a black employee—notwithstanding the fact that the boycott's financial toll had rendered Jang unable to pay even his two family members who worked at the store.[49] The boycott lingered into early 1991, although by then increasing numbers of people were crossing the picket line. In February the grocer was at long last vindicated when a jury found him not guilty of Mrs. Fetissainte's assault charges. Just a few hours after the acquittal, however, protesters again stationed themselves outside Red Apple's door and resumed their picketing. A number of them actually entered the store, surrounded Jang, and pointed imaginary guns (signified by their fingers) at him, chanting, "Die. Die."[50] Unable to endure any more, Jang sold his shop and moved away.[51]

"Because They Are Different"

One of the low points of the long Red Apple ordeal came one June day in 1992 when Governor Mario Cuomo strolled around Queens, New York, stopping to visit various Asian merchants to impart to them "a greater understanding of the historical burden borne by blacks."[52] To the employees of one grocery store, he said:

> We are cognizant of the fact that for a long period of time we deprived [blacks] not just of their civil rights, we deprived them of their human rights. And so, in a kind of weak attempt to in some way compensate for that, we constructed special programs called affirmative action programs. I don't understand people who resent it. Because they are different. Because the Italian-Americans were not

locked in chains and dragged here from Naples and then tied to machines and made to haul them like beasts of burden.[53]

Mr. Cuomo's assertion that blacks "are different," of course, drips with the condescending paternalism typical of white liberals who routinely blame "society" for every black problem. Their thinking is no different from that of the disgruntled black Flatbush resident who claimed that he gladly would have opened a market of his own if only "someone" would have given him "a chance." Was it really racism that had produced the dearth of black-owned businesses in that Brooklyn neighborhood, or was it the victim mindset fostered by "civil rights leaders" and academics who preach as an article of faith that life's best opportunities are reserved for whites and, to a lesser extent, Asians?

In stark contrast to the lingering outrage triggered by the altercation in Red Apple, a 1993 incident involving another Asian storekeeper and some black New Yorkers was quickly forgotten by the city's black community. Siew Yeo, a thirty-year-old immigrant from Singapore, worked as a cashier at Lee's Chinese Kitchen in the Bronx. One November day, three black teenagers burst into the store, waved a revolver in Mrs. Yeo's face, demanded that she hand over the money in her cash register, and fatally shot her when she was slow to follow orders. The victim, who had planned to attend a party the following day to celebrate both Thanksgiving and her third wedding anniversary, was survived by her husband and two-year-old son.[54] No protests were held in her memory.

Nor were there any protests following the January 1995 killing of Soon Sin, a frail, sixty-three-year-old Asian woman who was shoved off a subway platform and onto the tracks below, where she was run over by a passing train. The culprit, a black man named Reuben Harris, laughed as he told law-enforcement officials what he had done.[55] Again, "civil rights leaders" nationwide were silent.

Apostles of Their Own Delusions

The rhetoric accompanying racially motivated crusades can have grave consequences indeed—as in the case of a 1995 black boycott of Freddy's clothing store, a Jewish-owned shop in Harlem.

The boycott started when Freddy's owners announced that because they wanted to expand their own business, they would no longer sub-let part of their store space to a black-owned record shop.[56] On a WWRL radio program, Morris Powell, leader of the boycott and the head of Al Sharpton's "Buy Black" committee, referred to these Jewish merchants as "crackers."[57] On the streets, meanwhile, Powell and his fellow protesters told passersby, "Keep [going] right on by Freddy's, he's one of the greedy Jew bastards killing our people. Don't give the Jew a dime. . . . Freddy the Jew has to go, one way or another."[58] Some demonstrators went so far as to openly threaten violence. Said one man, "F—— white people. F—— the Jews. Remember Yusef Hawkins of Bensonhurst. We will do the same to Freddy."[59] Another yelled, "We're going to come back with twenty niggers and loot and burn the Jews."[60] Still another warned, "I will be back to burn the Jew down. Burn, burn, burn."[61]

Never far removed from any black boycott, Al Sharpton provided some additional soundbites for the media. "We will not stand by," he told a radio audience, "and allow them to move this brother so some white interloper can expand his business on 125th Street."[62] "There is a systematic and methodical strategy," he added, "to eliminate our [black] people from doing business on 125th Street. . . . One of our brothers . . . is now being threatened."[63] Sharpton urged blacks to join "the struggle [that] brother Powell and I are engaged in."[64] Among those supporting that struggle was Conrad Muhammad, a key spokesman for Louis Farrakhan's Nation of Islam.[65]

In Harlem and other black communities nationwide, signs reading "Buy Black" and "Black-Owned" adorn the premises of many business establishments.[66] Were *whites* to display similar signs urging patrons to "buy *white*," they would rightfully be denounced as racists by every "civil rights" group in the country. Yet when *black* businesses call for such "solidarity," their motives are not questioned. According to the Reverend Calvin Butts of Harlem, in fact, blacks are not even capable of racism—allegedly because they have no "power to inflict oppression."[67]

In the Freddy's clothing store drama, however, black boycotter Roland Smith certainly did wield considerable power. When he entered Freddy's on December 8, 1995, he ordered all blacks to exit the store and then proceeded to shoot three whites and a Guyanese Indian who remained. He thereafter set the building on fire, killing himself and seven others—mostly Hispanic employees—in the process.[68] Having listened for so long to the incessant, hate-filled messages of "civil rights leaders," Smith had become an angry, hateful racist himself. He was among the legion who, in the words of black columnist Michael Meyers, zealously "transform themselves into the apostles of their own delusions."[69]

Chapter 9

In the Name of Diversity

Of all tyrannies, a tyranny sincerely exercised for the good of its victims may be the most oppressive. . . . Those who torment us for our own good will torment us without end, for they do so with the approval of their own conscience.

—C.S. Lewis[1]

Claiming that the United States reserves most of its best educational and career opportunities for whites, "civil rights" activists and their devotees commonly blame societal racism for fueling the "black rage" that sometimes explodes into violence. As former New York City education chancellor Ramon Cortines puts it, "Many young people have such rage because of the way they feel they've been treated by society [that] they're willing to blow somebody else away."[2] What proof is there to substantiate this charge? What evidence suggests that a racist "white power structure" endeavors to keep blacks subservient? These questions are explored in this chapter.

For many years the United Negro College Fund (UNCF) has produced television advertisements soliciting contributions to support black colleges and their students. Against the backdrop of the familiar UNCF motto—"A mind is a terrible thing to waste"—these ads typically feature a young black person dejected because he or she lacks the funds to pay for a college education. Viewers are essentially told that without massive financial assistance, countless blacks would literally be barred from college for lack of money. But ads that tug at the heartstrings and tickle the tear ducts do not necessarily reflect reality, and indeed the facts tell a story very different from the UNCF commercials. Unbeknownst to most Americans, black students and professors are in fact the most prized and sought-after commodities in higher education today. In order for a school and its students to be eligible for federal financial aid—which at some institutions totals hundreds of millions of dollars[3]—that school must first obtain accreditation,[4] for which a chief requirement is a substantial black presence in the student body and on the faculty.[5]

There are six agencies in the U.S. responsible for school accreditation. The largest and most powerful is the Middle States Association of Colleges and Secondary Schools, under whose jurisdiction are approximately 600 colleges and universities, 1,800 high schools, and 900 elementary schools.[6] Until 1988, Middle States and other accrediting agencies were interested primarily in evaluating the quality of a school's resources and professors. They wanted to know, for example, how many volumes were in a school's library, whether that school had sufficient funds to support the academic programs it offered, how many Ph.D.s were on the faculty, and how many articles those instructors had published in the leading journals of their fields.[7] In 1988, however, Middle States added new accreditation criteria aimed at bringing more minorities into classrooms and administrative offices. The new policy stated that "to be eligible for accreditation, an institution must . . . have a governing board which includes a diverse membership broadly representative of the public interest and reflecting the student constituency. [Members] should represent different points of view, interests, and experiences as well as diversity in age, race, ethnicity, and gender."[8]

It is appropriate at this point to devote a paragraph to a discussion of the term "minorities." While its dictionary definition pertains to groups whose members are comparatively few in number, in "civil rights" parlance the word is synonymous with "victims"—usually referring exclusively to blacks and Hispanics, though occasionally including American Indians, Vietnam War veterans, persons with disabilities, and women. It almost never refers specifically to people of Polish, German, Russian, or Jewish heritage, though each of those groups constitutes but a small fraction of our nation's inhabitants.[9] Nor does it often refer to people of Japanese, Chinese, or Korean ancestry, none of whom comprise even 1 percent of the U.S. population.[10] Asian Americans—because of their relative scholastic excellence—are rarely included on lists of minorities entitled to benefit from special admissions and hiring programs at American colleges. As Thomas Sowell observes, "minority" has become a "politically corrupted" word that no longer denotes a statistically smaller part of the population, but rather "people you feel sorry for."[11]

To comply with the strict new guidelines of Middle States and other accrediting agencies, thousands of colleges and academic departments nationwide made the hiring of nonwhite professors a top priority. In 1988, for instance, the University of Wisconsin announced its intention to increase its number of minority faculty members by 75 percent.[12] Shortly thereafter Yale promised a 40 to 60 percent increase,[13] while Hampshire College reserved half of its academic appointments for minorities.[14] With similar zeal, California legislators passed laws mandating that at least 30 percent of all new professors at community colleges statewide be nonwhite.[15] The University of Vermont, meanwhile, pledged to hire four to eleven minorities every four years.[16] Duke was even more specific, vowing to add at least one black to each department within five years.[17] Bucknell set aside funds specifically for recruiting minority professors in whatever fields they could be found,[18] while Purdue went so far as to promise extra funding for its first five departments to hire nonwhite instructors.[19]

Though such efforts may seem laudable, real problems arise when we examine the pool of qualified applicants competing for those faculty positions. The racial distribution of Ph.D. recipients in recent years attests to the fact that there simply are not enough credentialed black and Hispanic professors in the applicant pool to fill the number of positions earmarked for them. In 1992, for instance, blacks nationwide earned just under 1,100 doctorates, Hispanics nearly 900, and whites more than 23,000. As is the case in most years, about half of all the black doctorates were in a single field—education—while most of the rest were in social work and sociology. Blacks earned only 4 doctorates in mathematics, 5 in computer science, 7 in physics and astronomy, 17 in chemistry, 48 in engineering, and 61 in the biological sciences. Not a single black in the United States earned a doctorate in the highly specialized fields of algebra, geometry, logic, atomic physics, geophysics, paleontology, oceanography, biomedical engineering, nuclear engineering, cell biology, endocrinology, genetics, microbiology, geography, statistics, classics, comparative literature, archaeology, accounting, or business economics.[20]

The comparatively low number of black and Hispanic Ph.D.s, many of them clustered in just a few disciplines, makes it difficult to infuse college faculties with significantly greater nonwhite representation. Adding to this difficulty is the fact that minority Ph.D.s frequently forego professorial opportunities in favor of careers in private industry, where they are aggressively recruited for positions paying substantially more than teaching jobs. A 1986 survey of some 500 blacks in doctoral programs found that fewer than half planned to teach.[21]

With so few minority Ph.D.s pursuing careers as professors, colleges have found it increasingly necessary to raid one another's faculties in desperate attempts to meet their own "diversity" goals—thereby creating an endless cycle of black and Hispanic instructors coming and going through our nation's campuses. Consider what occurred at the University of Wisconsin (UW), whose administrators recently resolved to add at least twenty nonwhites to the faculty each year for half a decade. In the first year of this plan, UW managed to recruit eighteen new minority professors—but lost more than that many to other schools.[22] Bidding wars for minorities have become so intense that black Ph.D.s teaching on the collegiate level now earn, on average, $2,000 more than their white counterparts with equivalent credentials and experience.[23]

The Long Road to Quotas

Attempts to diversify faculties, student bodies, and work forces in this country began, quite nobly, with the intent of making employment and educational opportunities available to everyone—including members of those groups that traditionally had been excluded. In 1954 the Supreme Court issued two landmark rulings toward this end—in *Brown v. Board of Education* and *Bolling v. Sharpe*—banning the legally authorized segregation of white and black schoolchildren. But because the vast majority of whites in the South were outraged at these Court rulings, southern states were particularly slow to desegregate their schools. As of 1964 in the eleven ex-Confederate states, a paltry 1.2 percent of black public school students attended schools with *any* white pupils at all.[24]

Notwithstanding the South's foot-dragging approach to desegregation, the *Brown* and *Bolling* rulings enabled future plaintiffs to legally challenge persisting segregation in all realms of public life. Moreover, as racial issues occupied an increasingly central position in the minds of Americans, the court of public opinion slowly but inexorably evolved in a more progressive direction:

• Whereas in 1956 the proportion of whites favoring school integration was just 49 percent nationally and 15 percent in the South, by 1963 these figures had grown to 62 percent and 31 percent, respectively.[25]

• In 1956 some 60 percent of whites nationally, and 27 percent of southern whites, favored racial integration on streetcars and buses. By 1963 these numbers had swelled to 79 percent and 52 percent.[26]

• In 1956 about 51 percent of whites nationwide, and 38 percent of whites in the South, were comfortable having a black person of the same income and education move into their block. By 1963 the corresponding figures had grown to 64 percent and 51 percent.[27]

• In 1944, a decade before *Brown*, only 42 percent of whites believed that blacks "should have as good a chance as white people to get any kind of job." By 1963 the figure stood at 83 percent.[28]

The growing popularity of the nondiscrimination ideal led to the greatest civil rights initiative in American history—the passage of the 1964 Civil Rights Act. This legislation outlawed segregation in all facilities designed to serve the general public, both publicly and privately owned. Such entities as buses, streetcars, hotels, libraries, swimming pools, dance halls, movie theaters, and bowling alleys could no longer lawfully keep blacks out or confined to separate areas. In addition, the new law forbade discrimination in employment and public education, denying federal funds to "programs that operated in a discriminatory manner."[29] The Civil Rights Act was later supplemented by the 1965 Voting Rights Act (banning poll taxes and literacy tests as prerequisites for voting) and the 1968 Fair Housing Act. At long last, the United States had developed a body of law guaranteeing blacks the rights and protections that historically had been denied them.[30]

These civil rights victories uniformly mandated equality under the law for all people—a principle central to our nation's loftiest ideals. And while those ideals had never before been fully realized, the process of tearing down racial barriers was actually well underway long before the 1960s. As noted in chapter 1, between 1945 and 1964 no fewer than twenty-six states passed laws and established special commissions to prevent race-based employment discrimination.[31] In a similar spirit, a 1957 civil rights bill gave the Justice Department the authority to prosecute southern officials attempting to prevent any citizen from voting. Not only was a Civil Rights Division created in the Justice Department, but the U.S. Civil Rights Commission was established to oversee the investigation of discrimination charges.[32] Though many whites resisted such progress, by the sixth decade of this century an ever-growing number of them were in favor of granting basic civil rights to blacks.

Notably, the meaning of the term "civil rights" has undergone a radical transformation during the past generation. Originally it meant plainly "that all individuals should be treated the same under the law, regardless of their race, religion, sex, or other such social categories."[33] In no way did it connote preferences for people belonging to any particular group. As legislators prepared to vote on the 1964 Civil Rights Act, Senator Hubert Humphrey, a key advocate of the bill, took great pains to assure his colleagues that the new law would "not require an employer to achieve any kind of racial balance in his work force by giving preferential treatment to any individual or group."[34] The statute's wording, in fact, could not have been clearer on this matter—explicitly stating that only *intentional* discrimination would be illegal.[35] Indeed, Senator Humphrey made it "wholly clear that inadvertent or accidental discriminations" were perfectly acceptable.[36] In accordance with American legal tradition, the new legislation placed the burden of proof squarely on the accuser—meaning that defendants (i.e., employers) would be presumed innocent until proven guilty.[37]

In the early 1960s the term "affirmative action" made its seemingly innocuous entrance into the American lexicon. Its precursors were such phrases as "positive effort" and "affirmative program," which by 1960 were already in wide use among "civil rights" crusaders, particularly liberal Democrats.[38] In 1961 a National Urban League official announced that "being color-blind . . . is no longer a virtue. What we need to be is positively color-conscious."[39] A year later the Congress of Racial Equality (CORE) began pressuring employers to give hiring preferences to blacks as compensation for past discrimination, while Urban League president Whitney Young bluntly recommended, for similar reasons, "a decade of discrimination in favor of Negro youth."[40] The NAACP also joined the chorus of those pushing for preferences, just a few years after having passionately advocated color-blind jurisprudence in the *Brown* case.[41]

Then, shortly after the 1964 Civil Rights Act was passed, President Lyndon Johnson issued Executive Order 11246, which required federal contractors to adopt color-blind hiring practices. Calling for *equal* treatment rather than special preferences based on race, this order mandated that contractors "take affirmative action to ensure that applicants are employed, and that employees are treated during employment, without regard to their race, color, religion, sex or national origin."[42] To comply with the order, employers were to take such "positive steps" as posting advertisements for job openings in places and publications where nonwhites would be likely to see them— all for the purpose of equalizing *opportunities*.[43] But 11246 never proposed equalizing *outcomes* by means of racial preferences.

Before long, however, the distinction between equal opportunities and equal outcomes would not only blur, but would actually shift in favor of the NAACP, CORE, and Urban League ideal. In the mid-1960s the Equal Employment Opportunity Commission (EEOC) changed the legal standards by which employment discrimination was to be judged, tacitly endorsing the notion that unequal outcomes were *prima facie* evidence of unfair labor practices.[44] Soon thereafter, both private and public institutions "began an elaborate process of adjusting scores and lowering standards in order to give racial preference to minorities, particularly blacks, to raise their representation."[45] This process began cautiously and secretively, without public knowledge. It was driven principally by the courts and the federal government's newly created civil rights divisions, among which were the EEOC, the Office of Federal Contract Compliance Programs (OFCCP), and the Office of Civil Rights. The latter, in fact, had a presence in both the Departments of Justice and Education.[46] These new agencies were staffed, for the most part, with black activists and white liberals. The policies they endorsed were generally signed into law behind closed doors, without democratic debate, by judges and bureaucrats.[47] In light of the civil rights movement's color-blind ideal that had just recently won the minds of most Americans, advocates of racial preferences well understood that only under a veil of secrecy could their proposals gain a foothold in the United States.[48] As Stephan and Abigail Thernstrom explain, "The move toward race-conscious, preferential policies was quiet, gradual, and subtle—not the sort of tale that makes for headline news. Regulatory guidelines and executive orders governing such matters as federal-contracting rules are low-visibility items."[49] In short, the public had no idea that such enormous changes were furtively taking place.[50]

The trend toward preferences continued in the ensuing years. In 1968 the Nixon administration's Labor Department announced its Philadelphia Plan, which set specific "goals and timetables" for hiring in that city's construction industry.[51] That same year, the OFCCP issued its own guidelines containing the terms "goals and timetables" and "representation."[52] These guidelines, whose stated objective was to achieve "full and equal employment opportunity," encouraged preferential hiring but were not outright calls for quotas.[53] Within two years, however, the Labor Department codified a "goals and timetables" requirement for all federal contractors,[54] and by 1971 the OFCCP made it clear that the central purpose of such "results-oriented procedures" was to "increase materially the utilization of minorities and women."[55] From that point onward, employers would be required to achieve proportional racial representation within specified time periods. As the term "equal opportunity" gradually gave way to "affirmative action," the definition of the latter changed completely. No longer meaning "positive steps" taken to publicize employment opportunities in minority neighborhoods, affirmative action became synonymous with filling racial quotas. Exemplary of this change was San Francisco State College's October 8, 1971 shift "from the idea of equal opportunity in employment to a deliberate effort to seek out qualified and qualifiable people among ethnic minority groups and women to fill all jobs in our area."[56] That same year, a Department of Health, Education, and Welfare official explained that affirmative action required employers to "consider other factors than mere technical qualifications."[57] The era of eroded standards for the sake of "diversity" was well underway.[58]

As exemplified by the gradual blending of "equal opportunity" and "affirmative action," a hallmark of the decade between 1964 and 1974 was the constant change of meaning that key terms in "civil rights" parlance underwent. Another such term was "desegregation," originally defined as the color-blind, open-door policy of admitting students into schools without regard to race. The 1964 Civil Rights Act warned, in fact, that federal funds would be withheld from schools that failed to desegregate in this manner. But a scant four years later the Supreme Court, ruling that desegregation was not enough, ordered schools to *actively integrate* their student bodies. Calling for the assignment of students to schools *with* regard to their race— purportedly as a "remedy for past unconstitutional segregation"[59]—such forced integration was anything but color-blind.[60] As author Dinesh D'Souza puts it, "Invoking proportional representation as the standard of justice, courts navigated around the seemingly clear language of the law to coerce integration in the name of enforcing desegregation, and to use the terms interchangeably to disguise this transition."[61] In 1971, as a logical extension of this policy, the Court ruled that for the purpose of achieving racial "balance," students were to be bussed to designated schools—even if those schools were located a considerable distance from the children's homes.[62]

Next it was time for the prophets of "justice" to redefine discrimination—the very concept whose existence had necessitated the civil rights movement in the first place. Endorsing this redefinition, the landmark 1971 *Griggs v. Duke Power Company* Supreme Court decision mandated that employers make all hiring decisions *with*, rather than *without*, regard to race.[63] Whereas before *Griggs,* discrimination had referred to some action taken against an individual because of his or her race or ethnicity, after *Griggs* it meant nothing more than a "lack of a politically acceptable statistical percentage."[64] If a given company's work force, or a particular school's student body, consisted of proportionately fewer blacks than were living in the surrounding area, that statistical disparity would now be deemed evidence of discrimination.

Also in 1971, the Supreme Court ruled that no company's employment criteria could include such assets as literacy or a high-school diploma—because those criteria would have disproportionately disqualified blacks.[65] Whereas the 1964 Civil Rights Act was designed to prevent disparate *treatment*, now the courts were punishing disparate *impact*.[66] Employers were increasingly required to rectify all "deficiencies in the utilization" of minorities, thereby transforming the guarantee of equal *opportunity* into a mandate for equal *results*.[67] An "unbalanced" work force was now sufficient reason to suspect discrimination, and employers accused of this transgression would be considered *guilty until proven innocent*.[68] "We have vetoed the presumption of innocence," one EEOC chairman acknowledged.[69]

In 1972, when the EEOC was granted legal power to sue private companies, it began systematically threatening to file discrimination lawsuits, the specter of which intimidated one company after another into hiring by race. The threats were aimed first at major corporations such as AT&T, General Electric, and General Motors—the usual result being a consent decree mandating that the accused discriminator not only cough up millions of dollars in back pay, but also implement an aggressive minority-hiring program. "Once we get the big boys," predicted EEOC chairman John Powell, "the others will soon fall in line."[70]

In two major decisions near the end of the 1970s—*Regents of the University of California v. Bakke* and *United Steelworkers v. Weber*—the Supreme Court ruled that for the ostensible purpose of "remedying" past inequities that had favored whites over blacks, it was now permissible to discriminate against whites. In fact, *even where no past discrimination could be proven*, educational institutions and employers were encouraged to use race as a "plus factor" favoring nonwhites in admissions and hirings.[71]

Affirmative action thereafter became increasingly widespread, year after year, until the 1989 *Ward's Cove Packing Company v. Atonio* case, wherein the Supreme Court not only shifted the burden of proof in discrimination lawsuits back onto the plaintiffs, but also gave employers more freedom to use aptitude tests to evaluate job candidates.[72] But this was only a temporary setback for the supporters of affirmative action, who scored a major victory two years later when the Civil Rights Restoration Act of 1991 overturned *Ward's Cove* and largely restored *Griggs*, once again making employers accused of discrimination guilty until proven innocent.[73]

More recent developments in civil rights law are discussed later in this chapter, as well as in chapter 10. Among the most important of these is Proposition 209, passed in 1996 to ban race and gender preferences from California's public agencies and universities. Two years later the state of Washington enacted a similar measure called Initiative 200. Though advocates of preferences predictably characterized these laws as racist attempts to discriminate against nonwhites, such charges were utterly unfounded. Initiative 200, for instance, stipulates only that the state "shall not discriminate against, or grant preferential treatment to, any individual or group on the basis of race, sex, color, ethnicity, or national origin" in education, employment, or contracting.[74] Like Prop 209, whose language is virtually the same, it is the very *antithesis* of discrimination.

The Painstaking Effort to Recruit Minorities

The recruitment of minority professors is big business in American higher education. The president of New York's Mercy College spoke for most of his peers when recently pledging his own "commitment to increased cultural diversity within faculty ranks."[75] To help colleges achieve their "diversity objectives," numerous minority-oriented publications listing academic job openings have sprung up during the past decade. The demand for black and Hispanic employees is so great, in fact, that these publications can charge much higher fees for advertising space than their circulations would normally command.[76]

A monthly periodical called the *Affirmative Action Register* is filled with help-wanted notices encouraging minorities to apply for various high-level positions at U.S. colleges and universities. Virtually all schools characterize themselves in these ads as Affirmative Action/ Equal Employment Opportunity (AA/EEO) establishments—thereby demonstrating the tortured language and contradiction that are the perpetual handmaidens of preferential policies. Equal opportunity, of course, in its literal sense, refers to an arrangement in which individuals—regardless of their racial or ethnic backgrounds—are evaluated by prospective employers solely on the basis of their qualifications. Affirmative action, on the other hand, is currently synonymous with preferential consideration given to people for no reason other than their belonging to a particular group—ethnic, racial, gender, sexual orientation, etc. But while such a policy is obviously the opposite of equal opportunity, colleges compose their recruitment ads as if the two concepts were interchangeable, as if equal opportunity and racial preferences were the same thing. In 1993, for instance, when announcing its intent to hire a women's volleyball coach, Alabama's Troy State University identified itself as "an AA/EEO Employer [that] encourages applications from blacks, females, and other minorities."[77]

Similarly, Northern Michigan University professed itself to be an "Affirmative Action/Equal Opportunity Employer" when its chemistry department solicited applicants for a tenure-track faculty position in biochemistry. "NMU is deeply committed to develop a diverse applicant pool," read the ad. "Women and minorities are especially encouraged to apply."[78] Another NMU ad announcing the need for a science and mathematics director stated, "In recent years NMU has established the goal of ethnic and cultural diversity as a major, ongoing priority of the university and hence is seeking a diverse applicant pool in this search. We strongly encourage women, minorities and others to apply who may contribute to this diversity and who generally meet the basic qualifications of the position."[79] Do these sound like policies one would expect to find in a nation intent on oppressing its minorities?

During its search for a president in 1993, Metropolitan State University in Minnesota stipulated that the successful candidate would be required to provide "leadership in advancing the goals of affirmative action and equity in education and employment."[80] The school's recruitment ads, however, failed to specify which of those contradictory goals was more highly valued. That same year, the University of Wisconsin-Whitewater, then searching for an associate dean, identified itself as an AA/EEO employer that especially encouraged applications from "women, minorities, Vietnam-era veterans, and persons with disabilities."[81]

Some ads are little more than bizarre contradictory concoctions. When California's Foothill DeAnza Community College was seeking a chancellor in 1993, it proudly characterized itself as an "equal opportunity, affirmative action" institution that "does not discriminate on the basis of race, color, gender, religion, age, national origin, disability, or sexual orientation. Applications from, and nominations of, women and ethnic minority candidates are encouraged."[82] Austin Community College and Colorado Mountain College also used exactly this verbiage in their respective ads to recruit presidential candidates that year.[83] Why are advertisements like these not regarded as improper? Why is it deemed permissible to specifically seek out minorities or women but unjust to target whites or men?

In the January 1993 *Affirmative Action Register*, Kent State University's geology department "strongly encouraged" female and minority candidates to apply for an assistant professorship.[84] The University of Massachusetts at Boston, meanwhile, made it known that minorities were "especially encouraged to apply" for an opening in the biology department.[85] Similarly, the State University of New York at Oswego announced that it was "actively seeking to enhance the diversity of its faculty. Women, persons of color, and disabled candidates are encouraged to apply."[86]

Each year thousands of such ads flood the pages of education periodicals. The theme is constant—minority hirings are of the highest priority. Kentucky's Morehead State University, for example, asserts that it aggressively seeks "candidates who will augment the diversity of its faculty, staff and administration."[87] The University of Maryland boasts that it "takes very seriously its commitment to diversity and affirmative action, and strongly encourages the application and nomination of both female and minority candidates."[88] The College of Science at California State Polytechnic University professes a strong dedication to "affirmative action efforts to diversify" its faculty—never explaining, of course, how "diversity" might help cultivate excellence in science.[89]

In a recent *Chronicle of Higher Education,* Case Western Reserve University, which was seeking a chemistry department chairman, announced that "applications from women and minority candidates are particularly welcome."[90] That same month Iowa State University specifically solicited "applications from women and minorities";[91] Tufts University invited professors "from diverse backgrounds" to join its faculty;[92] and the University of Mississippi reassured potential nonwhite applicants of its "strong institutional commitment to the principle of diversity."[93]

A 1993 Charles County Community College ad, complete with the familiar AA/EEO label, urged minorities not only to apply for a professorial position in the mathematics department, but also *to identify themselves as minorities.*[94] Could any exhortation contradict more blatantly the intent of the 1964 Civil Rights Act? How does having applicants identify their racial or ethnic backgrounds contribute to the achievement of a color-blind, unbiased selection process? Moreover, what possible connection could there be between one's minority status and his or her effectiveness as a mathematics teacher?

Because such ads are part of the public record, they stop short of openly acknowledging that whites are, in many cases, not even eligible to be hired. The *private* correspondences of college presidents and department chairs, however, tend to be much more candid, and for this reason are typically marked, "Confidential—Internal Use Only."[95] Consider the following excerpt from a 1971 letter written by the head of a state-college economics department to his counterpart at a major state university:

> All of the . . . state colleges have been requested to implement a program of active recruitment of qualified faculty of minority background, especially Negro and Mexican-American. Since I am unable to determine this type of information from the resumes you have sent me, I should very much appreciate if you could indicate which of your 1972 candidates are either Negro or Mexican-American.[96]

Examples of such clandestine communications abound, and clearly they are nothing new. In 1972 the head of the sociology department at a southern state university not only specified that "all unfilled positions in the University must be filled by blacks or females,"[97] but actually told a professorial candidate that "it will only be possible to consider you for a position in the event that you are black."[98] In 1973 the dean of an Illinois state college made it clear that "only those applications from members of minority groups" would be "actively considered" to fill a teaching vacancy in the chemistry department. His preference, he wrote, was to hire a "Black or Chicano."[99] That same year, a memorandum from the English department chair at the University of Massachusetts read, "At present we are authorized, in accordance with the University's strong commitment to Affirmative Action recruitment, to interview only candidates from ethnic minorities."[100]

In the mid-1970s, Columbia University president William McGill sent this memorandum to his deans and department chairs, asking them to comply with affirmative action guidelines:

> The academic and personal qualifications of each individual to whom a Columbia appointment is offered must continue to be the only criteria for selection. . . . [A]t the same time, it is my belief that

academic excellence is not one-dimensional. An increased number
of members of minority groups and women within the instructional
ranks will add significantly to the strength and vitality of Columbia
University.[101]

As philosophy professor Alan Goldman observed at the time, "McGill
seems to be suggesting that, in the present context, being a minority-
group member or woman should itself be considered a qualification
for being a teacher at Columbia."[102]

Also in the 1970s, the Department of Health, Education, and
Welfare (HEW) demanded to know why a particular Ivy League university had no minority students in its religious studies graduate program. When informed that a reading knowledge of Hebrew and Greek
was required for admission to the program, HEW representatives retorted, "Then end those old-fashioned programs that require irrelevant
languages. And start up programs on relevant things which minority
group students can study without learning languages."[103] In compliance with this directive, the university initiated a massive recruitment
campaign targeting nonwhites.[104]

In 1984, when the provost of San Francisco State University
(SFSU) authorized the English department to hire two new professors, he made it clear that "candidates recommended to me [must] be
nonwhite. Let me underscore that the stipulation is an absolute condition."[105] A few years later, during a push to locate minority professors
for another SFSU department, the head of the hiring committee advised its members to "save time and energy by not examining any applications from white males."[106] Still another department evaluated
four "persons of color" as "hirable," while judging several white candidates as "also well qualified but not hirable."[107] Similarly, when a
white Ph.D. applied in 1989 for a job teaching Stanford University's
"Culture, Ideas, and Values" course, he was told that "only racial
minorities" were being considered for the position.[108] That same year,
the head of Wayne State University's faculty search committee decided that each of two vacant teaching positions in the sociology department "*must* be filled by a minority person."[109] Likewise, Ohio
Wesleyan University recently specified that it was seeking "black
applicants for a tenure-track position."[110]

Incredible though it may seem, the pursuit of "diversity" has
replaced the pursuit of excellence as the highest consideration at

most colleges and universities. School administrators now deem the purported moral rectitude of having a racially "balanced" faculty sufficient justification for accepting mediocrity among its ranks. Consider Miami University of Ohio's 1986 decision to institute minority-preference hiring. Stipulating that even "minimally qualified" minority candidates could be hired,[111] university administrators made no pretense of even attempting to find the best available person for each position. A decade and a half earlier, Cornell University had implemented a similar policy that not only called for "the hiring of additional minority persons and females," but explained that "in many instances, it may be necessary to hire unqualified or marginally qualified persons."[112] What could be more demeaning to the members of any ethnic or racial group than to be treated as if they were incapable of meeting the same standards as everyone else?

In Praise of Race and Gender

Despite academia's herculean efforts to recruit black professors and administrators, many "civil rights leaders" continue to claim that racism pervades university hiring practices. Characterizing critics of racial preferences as enemies of justice, these "leaders" maintain that affirmative action is not only desirable but necessary to counter the pernicious effects of "institutional" racism. They find it inconceivable that opponents of preferences might actually be motivated by a concern for standards rather than by bigotry. As one black professor puts it, "When you see the word 'qualifications' used, remember this is the new code word for whites."[113] In a similar vein, legal scholar Johnnetta Cole asserts that white opposition to affirmative action is a "sophisticated expression of racism."[114]

In April 1990 black professor Derrick Bell took a leave of absence from his teaching post at Harvard Law School, hoping that his action would pressure the university to hire a black woman as a tenured faculty member. Black female law students, he explained, were in desperate need of similarly pigmented "role models" with whom they could identify. Although 45 percent of Harvard Law's faculty appointments since 1980 had gone to minorities and women, none of them were both black *and* female—hence Professor Bell's objection.[115] Harvard students staged two sit-ins in the office of Robert

Clark, dean of the law school, to demonstrate their support for Bell's position. "I'm coming from the perspective of a black woman," one female protester explained, "and we need black women role models."[116] Said another, "They [Harvard] have had years to find a black woman [professor], but they just want to keep the status quo, what they call the comfort level of white men. The fact remains that we are getting only a white male corporate view of the law."[117] The relatively small supply of credentialed black professors, coupled with the intense competition among so many colleges to secure their services, was apparently irrelevant to the Harvard protesters. In fact, it is unlikely that they were even aware of such realities.

Dean Clark responded to the demonstrators by affirming that while Harvard was indeed dedicated to recruiting more minority and female professors—as evidenced by the school's hiring record during the preceding decade—he would allow neither Professor Bell's strike nor the student sit-ins to rush the administration into making any particular appointments. When Clark asserted that no attempt to increase "diversity" should override Harvard's commitment to academic excellence, one female protester called his position "highly insulting to blacks" and symbolic of "the elitism of Harvard."[118] Along the same lines, black columnist Carl Rowan charged that "merit" was nothing more than "the code word privileged whites use to protect their special hutches at Harvard and hundreds of other universities."[119] A group of Professor Bell's supporters went so far as to file a lawsuit against Harvard, claiming that even if the school's hiring practices were not discriminatory by design, they were discriminatory "by default."[120]

In contrast to the manner in which Dean Clark handled the Derrick Bell affair, most college administrators quickly capitulate to the demands of protesting black students. Demonstrators who stage sit-ins and take over administrative offices are usually rewarded for their activism with apologies and promises of atonement for their schools' alleged sins. Such atonement takes many forms: the immediate hiring of additional black professors, the development of black studies programs, the creation of black student organizations, an increase in minority-enrollment quotas, and the construction of black-student dormitories or cultural centers.[121]

Because the mindset of Professor Bell and the Harvard protesters has come to dominate American higher education, a climate of pronounced race-consciousness now pervades our nation's college

campuses. A natural outgrowth of this development is a recently published book entitled *The Multicultural Student's Guide to Colleges:
What Every African-American, Asian-American, Hispanic, and
Native-American Applicant Needs to Know About America's Top
Schools*. For each of nearly 200 colleges and universities, this book
catalogues the number of nonwhite students and professors on campus, the retention rate of minority students, the names of ethnic-theme
houses and black student unions, information about racial and ethnic
studies programs, and details about special scholarships reserved exclusively for nonwhite students. In all, the book contains more than
700 pages of information about such "minority concerns."[122]

Searching for Racism

Because minorities comprise nearly half of its student body,
the Old Westbury branch of the State University of New York (SUNY)
proudly proclaims itself "the flagship of racial diversity for the SUNY
system." Nonetheless, the "racial pride" minutemen on campus remain ready to be offended at a moment's notice. For instance,
when President L. Eudora Pettigrew recently decided to eliminate
the school's performing arts program, which emphasized African American dance and jazz, 200 students occupied the library in protest.[123]

Indeed there are many who can "find" white racism just about
anywhere. Professor Eric Hirsch, for example, denounced Columbia
University's 1990 decision to mete out stronger penalties to protesters
blocking access to school buildings. Reasoning that because black
students had led the three most notable prior takeovers of Columbia's
Hamilton Hall, Hirsch concluded that the new rules were racist because they were "likely to affect mainly blacks."[124]

In 1990 New York's Baruch College, whose student body
was fully 64 percent nonwhite, had its accreditation renewal delayed
when the Middle States Association of Colleges found an unaccept-
ably high minority-dropout rate and "a paucity of minority representation" among the school's professors and administrators.[125] While no
one could cite any way in which Baruch had intentionally harmed, neglected, or excluded minorities, the college was forced to immediately
recruit more black and Hispanic professors—a task that necessitated lowering traditional hiring standards.[126] The school further

agreed to: (a) form a special panel that would address the issue of minority-student retention; (b) establish a faculty committee that would "evaluate the extent to which the base curriculum prepares students to function in a multicultural college and work environment"; and (c) offer minority lecturers extra time to obtain doctoral degrees.[127] Not only are such efforts to "diversify" very costly, but they are made for the express purpose of trying to retain the very teachers and students who "civil rights leaders" claim are neither valued nor respected in American higher education. Meanwhile, it seems to trouble no one that black colleges have traditionally been the staunchest enemies of "diversity" in the United States. Taking virtually no measures to increase white representation on their faculties or in their student bodies, some of these schools have actually gone to great lengths to preserve their monochromatic makeups. In the late 1980s, for example, Louisiana's mostly black Southern University went to court to fight a proposal that would have set aside 10 percent of its admissions slots for whites.[128]

Knowing that an "insufficient" representation of minority students can affect accreditation and federal funding, colleges from coast to coast put forth a great effort to attract black and Hispanic applicants. Stanford University, for instance, mails letters each year to 15,000 nonwhite high-school graduates with high Scholastic Aptitude Test (SAT) scores, inviting them to apply.[129] Some schools offer minority students such incentives as refunds of application fees, free trips to their campuses, tickets to rap concerts or sporting events, and even academic scholarships.[130] Other schools simply pay cash, often in the form of grants that need not be repaid, to nonwhites who register with them.[131] Harvard, for one, gives black students almost unlimited financial aid regardless of their need,[132] while black students in Pennsylvania are guaranteed full-tuition scholarships if they study for advanced degrees anywhere in the state.[133]

In this frenzy to enroll minorities, academic standards for admission have become flexible commodities. The high-school grades and standardized-test scores traditionally required by American universities do not apply to blacks, who are regularly accepted with credentials far lower than those required of whites and Asians.[134] Because the obvious injustice of such a double standard is troublesome even to many advocates of racial preferences, a host of critics have emerged during the past two decades to denounce all standardized tests as "biased" against blacks—and therefore invalid.

Is Testing Biased?

The Scholastic Aptitude Test, administered to high-school juniors and used as a measure of their potential for collegiate success, has engendered great controversy in recent decades. Although for the past thirty-five years it has proved to be the best available predictor of academic performance[135]—an even better predictor, in fact, than high-school grades, interviews, and teacher recommendations[136]—many claim that this test discriminates against blacks, whose average scores in most years are some 200 points lower than those of whites.[137] According to educator James Crouse, the SAT "has an adverse impact on blacks and lower-income kids."[138] "Standardized tests are used from the cradle to the grave," agrees Gerda Steel of the NAACP, "in ways that keep certain segments of the population from realizing their aspirations. Most of all they limit the access of blacks and other minorities to higher education."[139] Amherst College president Tom Gerety flatly calls it "simple-minded, incorrect, and even racist" to believe "the ridiculous notion that 'qualifications' and test scores are synonymous."[140] Richard Seymour of the Lawyers' Committee for Civil Rights describes standardized tests as "an engine for the exclusion of minorities."[141] Charging that low SAT scores prevent many blacks from attending the colleges of their choice, critics like these ignore the fact that the test *does not underestimate, but in fact slightly overpredicts*, the collegiate success of blacks.[142] Even for students who attend historically black colleges, the SAT and other standardized tests predict college grade-point-average exceptionally well.[143]

After scrutinizing years of test questions, critics of the SAT have been able to identify only a handful of items that seem genuinely biased. In recent years the College Board, which administers the exam, has endeavored to eliminate all questions that presume middle-class or suburban life experience—inserting in their stead items dealing with African American experiences and passages written by black authors. These measures, however, have had no effect on test scores.[144] Curiously, the SAT's detractors never comment on the fact that Asian students outperform whites on the test. It is worth asking why the self-professed champions of "fairness" never suggest that the SAT might have a *pro-Asian* bias that discriminates against *whites*.[145]

Of course, even if the SAT *were* biased, its critics' primary charge would nonetheless be baseless—simply because low-scoring

blacks are *not* disqualified from admission to the colleges and universities of their choice. As noted earlier, schools consistently admit blacks
with SAT scores far below those required of whites and Asians.[146]
Among students at the University of Virginia in 1988, the white SAT
average was 246 points higher than that of blacks[147]—virtually
matching UCLA's 250-point racial gap of 1990.[148] In the early
1990s at the University of California at Berkeley, incoming whites and
Asians had SAT scores about 300 points higher than those of their
black counterparts.[149] As of 1994, black undergraduates were entering Stanford University with a mean SAT score of 1,164—good
enough to put them in the top one-sixth of test-takers nationally, but
far below the 1,335 average of their white classmates.[150] Nationwide
between 1990 and 1994, whites and Asians taking the SAT averaged
945, while blacks averaged 740.[151]

Socioeconomic factors are often cited as the causes of these
gaps in performance. Those who oppose the SAT commonly claim
that blacks from poor backgrounds lack the social and educational
experiences necessary for excelling on such exams. One New York
newspaper, for instance, reported in February 1999, "Research continues to demonstrate the link between wealth and academic performance. The United Negro College Fund found that 53 percent of
college-bound black students taking the SAT in 1996 had family incomes below $30,000, compared with 18 percent of whites."[152] This
implies, of course, that if economic inequalities were eliminated, differences in test scores would diminish or disappear altogether. Plausible though this theory sounds, however, it is discredited by hard
evidence. Nonblack students from families with yearly incomes of
under $10,000 score 44 points higher than the overall black aver-
age.[153] White students from families earning $10,000 to $20,000
outscore black students from families earning $70,000 or more.[154]
Asian American students whose families earn $6,000 or less score
higher on the math SAT than black students whose family incomes are
$50,000 or more.[155] Stanford sociologist S.M. Dornbush, intrigued
by the scholastic excellence of impoverished Asian American students, found that they simply "work a heck of a lot harder" than their
peers to raise their SAT scores and school grades.[156]

Dornbush's findings about study habits are consistent with those
of a 1992 survey which found that 21 percent of black twelfth-grad-
ers watched five or more hours of television per weekday, more than

triple the viewing time of their white peers. In addition, 20 percent of blacks reported spending at least an hour per day playing video games, nearly twice the corresponding percentage for whites.[157] In another recent study, Harvard researcher Ronald Ferguson found that black high-school students "watch twice as much TV as white kids—three hours a day as opposed to one and a half hours a day."[158] A 1996 survey of fourth graders yielded similar results: 69 percent of blacks but just 37 percent of whites watched four or more hours of television daily, and blacks were three times likelier than whites to watch at least *six* hours of TV per day.[159] The respective television viewing habits of black and nonblack children may well reflect deep cultural differences in attitudes toward education. In national studies asking students to name the lowest grade they could receive without angering their parents, blacks consistently name lower grades than whites or Asians.[160] The intent here is neither to criticize blacks nor to praise Asians and whites, but simply to point out that some widely held assumptions about the causes of scholastic underachievement are baseless.

The comparatively poor study habits of black children are at least partially, if not totally, a by-product of the greatest crisis currently afflicting the black community—a 70 percent out-of-wedlock birth rate. The high incidence of single-mother black homes disproportionately predisposes black children to the many problems associated with fatherlessness. Studies show that children born to unwed mothers—whatever their race—are much likelier than youngsters from intact families to be abused or neglected, to experience impaired cognitive and verbal development, and to exhibit emotional or behavioral troubles.[161] Obviously, such conditions greatly hinder children's ability to do their schoolwork.

Critics of the SAT, however, routinely ignore such stubborn realities—preferring, as noted earlier in this section, to trace all black scholastic troubles to socioeconomic causes. By extension, these faultfinders commonly ascribe the racial gap in SAT scores to what they deem the "inadequate" funding of the big-city public schools that most black test-takers attend. Such schools, the critics claim, are starved for money, whereas white students are likelier to attend comparatively wealthy suburban schools. Yet such assertions are utterly unfounded. Research actually shows that the higher the percentage of minority students in a school district, the *higher* the per-pupil expenditures.

Mostly-minority school districts spend fully 15 percent more on each student than districts where minority enrollment is below 5 percent. Moreover, per-pupil spending in the central cities of metropolitan areas—regardless of race—is identical to spending levels in the surrounding suburbs.[162]

Harming Victims and Beneficiaries Alike

Double standards in the admissions process have lamentable consequences not only for those students rejected because of their race, but also for those who are preferentially admitted. Because the latter are often enrolled in schools for which they are academically underprepared, their college careers are commonly beset with failure. Consider the example of Berkeley, where in one recent year the average composite SAT scores of incoming black freshmen was 952. While this was well above the national average of 900, it was far below the 1,232 average of Berkeley's first-year white students and the 1,254 average of its Asian freshmen.[163] That same year, the median high-school grade-point-average (GPA) of Berkeley's entering black freshmen was 3.52, significantly lower than the 4.0 median of their white and Asian counterparts.[164] In fact, from the early 1970s to the mid-1990s it was standard procedure for blacks to be admitted to Berkeley with comparatively weak scholastic credentials. It is not surprising, then, that their dropout rate during that period was about 70 percent—much higher than that of their nonblack peers.[165] Sadly, this pitiful scenario pervades American higher education. Fully two-thirds of blacks who started college after 1979 have dropped out and failed to graduate.[166] In a recent study examining the performance of students at some 300 major colleges and universities, the respective graduation rates of white and black students were 57 percent and 34 percent—meaning that the corresponding dropout rates were 43 percent and 66 percent.[167] Notably, the high proportions of preferentially admitted students failing to graduate is not unique to the United States; similarly high attrition rates have plagued the intended beneficiaries of group-preference programs in other nations as well.[168]

Common sense, of course, tells us that black students who meet their schools' normal admissions criteria should fare better academically than those recruited mainly for their skin color—and indeed experience bears this out. Between 1982 and 1987, for example, 42 percent of blacks admitted to Berkeley under normal standards graduated, while only 18 percent of those admitted on affirmative action did the same. The picture was similar for Hispanics: Those admitted under the regular standards had a 55 percent graduation rate, as compared to 22 percent for the affirmative action "beneficiaries."[169]

The strong connection between SAT scores and graduation rates suggests that any school which admits a particular subset of students under artificially low standards does those students a great disservice, virtually condemning them to scholastic failure. Among Berkeley's entering freshmen in 1988, fully 88 percent of those with SAT scores in the 1,300s eventually graduated. For students with scores in the 1,100s, 900s, 800s, and 700s, the corresponding graduation rates were 83 percent, 72 percent, 62 percent, and 58 percent— whatever their race.[170] With regard to black students in particular, the pattern is just as clear. Blacks with SAT scores between 851 and 1,000 have a 77 percent graduation rate from colleges whose overall SAT average is 900. By contrast, blacks who score between 700 and 850 on the SAT graduate from those same schools only 56 percent of the time, and blacks whose SAT scores are below 700 have just a 38 percent chance of graduating.[171]

It should further be noted that the negative consequences of placing students in colleges for which they are unprepared persist long after their schooling is over. One study found that by the age of thirty-two, blacks who had dropped out of upper-echelon colleges were earning about 25 percent less than blacks who had *graduated* from *less-selective* colleges. In other words, schools that tried to demonstrate racial "virtue" by admitting underqualified black students actually did considerable long-term harm to those very students.[172]

In the U.S. today, approximately fifty-eight colleges and universities are considered "elite" schools, typically admitting only applicants who score at least 1,200 on the SAT; that is, an average of 600 on both the verbal and quantitative (math) portions of the test.[173] But only 1 to 3 percent of black test-takers meet that requirement in any given year.[174] In 1995, for instance, just 1,764 of our country's 103,872 college-bound blacks (1.7 percent) scored 600 or better on the verbal part of the test.[175] The corresponding proportions of whites and Asians scoring that high were 9.6 percent and 10 percent, respectively.[176] Asians performed even more impressively on the math

SAT—scoring *650* or better nearly 26 percent of the time, whereas whites and blacks registered such scores at rates of just 13.4 percent and 2 percent, respectively.[177] There are currently about 6.5 times as many whites as blacks taking the SAT, but the white/black ratio of students scoring 600 or better on either portion of the test approaches 40:1.[178] Even if we assume that every black scoring at least 600 on just *one* portion of the test elected to attend one of the elite fifty-eight schools, in most years there would barely be enough qualified black candidates to supply each of those institutions with 60 first-year black students. Yet Harvard has admitted 100 or more black freshmen every year since 1970,[179] and Berkeley admitted 831 black freshmen in 1989 alone.[180]

We know, of course, that only a small percentage of black students with SAT scores above 1,200 enroll at the elite fifty-eight schools, while the great majority distribute themselves among the rest of our country's thousands of colleges and universities. Consequently, upper-echelon schools intent on meeting their affirmative action quotas have no choice but to lower their academic standards for incoming black freshmen. Second-level schools, in turn, lower their own traditional standards and settle for black students more suited for third-rung schools. As a result of this "shifting" process, black students all across the United States are mismatched with schools for which they are academically unprepared. Meanwhile, other students are denied admission to those same schools simply because they are white or Asian.

The racial disparity in SAT performance exists not only among students who score 600 or more on either part of the exam, but also among those who manage to break the more modest 500 barrier. In 1994, only 15 percent of black high-school seniors nationwide scored 500 or better on the math portion of the SAT, and just 8 percent scored that high on the verbal portion. The corresponding figures for white students were 56 percent and 30 percent, and for Asian students 61 percent and 28 percent, respectively.[181]

Black students lag behind other groups not only in SAT scores, but also in high-school GPAs. In one recent year just 5.5 percent of college-bound black seniors compiled academic averages of B-plus or better, compared to 16.5 percent of whites and 22 percent of Asians.[182] This dearth of high-achieving black students, however, has not deterred university administrators from setting ever-increasing goals for black enrollments. University of Maryland president William

Kirwan, for instance, proclaims that his school has a "special obligation to attract larger numbers of African American students."[183]

Our country's best engineering schools generally require math SAT scores of 700 or better, but in most years fewer than 6 out of every 1,000 black test-takers score that well. By comparison, whites and Asians register these scores at rates of 58 per 1,000 and 142 per 1,000, respectively.[184] Thus if engineering schools are to meet affirmative action goals for black enrollments, they have no alternative but to lower their standards. Consider the case of Massachusetts Institute of Technology (MIT), which gets the nation's top 1 percent of engineering students. While the math SAT scores of blacks admitted to MIT are in the top 10 percent nationally, they are in the *bottom* 10 percent among MIT students.[185] In fact, MIT takes in more than four times as many black students as a purely academic admissions standard would allow.[186] Not surprisingly, then, many of the school's black students struggle with their studies and drop out.[187] Were they to attend less-competitive schools whose academic demands are not quite so exacting, they would stand a far greater chance of graduating and going on to successful professional careers. Instead they are used as pawns in the affirmative action game, while white and Asian students, who do not similarly "benefit" from racial preferences, graduate at much higher rates.[188] As George Mason University economics professor Walter E. Williams writes:

> [A]ffirmative action programs in college recruitment do not come close to being even a zero-sum game where blacks benefit at the expense of Asians [and whites]. It is more like a negative-sum game, where everybody is worse off. In other words, [affirmative action programs lead] to the rejection of Asian and white students with a higher probability of graduation in favor of black and Hispanic students with a significantly lower probability of graduation. Thus, white and Asian students are being sacrificed to the benefit of no one.[189]

Along the same lines, law professor Lino Graglia describes the folly of placing students (whatever their race) into academic environments for which they are unprepared:

> A frequently noted effect [of affirmative action] is virtually to guarantee that the preferentially admitted students are placed in schools

for which they are greatly underqualified. It is as if professional baseball decided to "advantage" an identifiable group of players at the beginning of their professional careers by placing them in a league at least one level above the one in which they could be expected to compete effectively. The admission of an identifiable group of greatly underqualified students is a prescription for frustration, resentment, loss of self-esteem, and racial animosity.[190]

It should be noted that the negative consequences of affirmative action extend well beyond the emotional difficulties described by Professor Graglia. As Princeton dean of admissions Fred Hargadon explains, lowered standards have given minority students the dangerous message that they need not work hard at their studies.[191] Editorialist John Leo concurs, "A number of awful lessons are being taught by the current aggressive pursuit of black students—that blackness has a higher commercial value than personal traits or achievement, and that blackness may be able to buy acceptance of a lower work ethic."[192] Leo further observes that "all this well-intentioned special treatment has had a devastating effect on campus race relations."[193] In a similar vein, Professor Graglia notes that because white students "have become convinced that ordinary standards just don't apply to blacks,"[194] affirmative action "is virtually a formula for escalating racial consciousness and tension."[195]

Minorities Bought and Sold

The case of New Jerseyite George Watson provides a classic illustration of the insincerity inherent in affirmative action. In 1993 Watson was a black high-school senior coveted by colleges nationwide because he was a B student who scored 690 on the mathematics portion of the SAT. Consequently, he received unsolicited application materials from more than 100 schools—some offering to waive their customary application fees, others inviting him for all-expenses-paid visits to their campuses. One university promised him a $20,000 scholarship even though his parents were affluent and did not need financial assistance.[196] Harvard, meanwhile, sent Watson a letter informing him that it would waive its January 1 application deadline for him. When he phoned the Harvard admissions office to learn more, the woman who handled his call claimed to know nothing about such an arrangement. But when Watson then identified himself as black, she suddenly understood.[197]

Another black student, Fred Abernathy, had a similar experience. Though more than half of his peers nationwide had outscored him on a standardized exam known as the American College Test (ACT), Abernathy was flooded with college invitations in the spring of 1995. After weighing his many options, he decided to enroll at the University of Illinois's highly selective College of Engineering. But the majority of his white classmates there had scored in the 98th or 99th percentile on the ACT. Thus Abernathy, like many other blacks on campus, quickly found himself adrift in an academic environment for which he was grossly underprepared. Not surprisingly, almost half of the school's blacks were dropping out each year, whereas the white graduation rate was close to 90 percent.[198] Not for a moment, however, did this stubborn reality cause school officials to consider abandoning their use of preferential admissions standards.

Because the competition to enroll black students is so fierce, many colleges quietly bend their financial-aid guidelines to attract blacks in greater numbers.[199] Some do this, as noted earlier, by offering grants that are, for all practical purposes, bribes—even to the wealthiest of students. Much like professional sports franchises trying to outbid each other for the services of free agents, schools vie with one another to lure blacks to their campuses. As a result, many black students—even the scholastically mediocre—can virtually have their pick of America's finest universities. Consider that in 1992, fully 78 of the first 172 black high-school seniors accepted by Harvard chose instead to take full scholarships from other schools. Many of those 78 students hailed from families with yearly incomes exceeding $150,000, an amount that ordinarily would have made them ineligible for any type of financial aid. Clearly, they were offered scholarships not because of need—nor even because of scholastic excellence—but simply because they were black.[200] Princeton's Fred Hargadon concedes that colleges often overstep the bounds of propriety in their attempts to attract black applicants. "There's a very delicate balance to maintain," he says, "when diversifying student bodies. Some schools seem to have crossed the line."[201]

Affirmative Action Everywhere

Because of the current obsession with "diversity," almost every American college and university now employs affirmative action officers and supplemental "specialists" in racial- and ethnic-group relations.[202] This is true not only of traditional four-year colleges that offer instruction in a variety of disciplines, but also of more-specialized schools. *The New York Times* reports, for instance, that "diversity clearly is the issue of the day at business schools,"[203] where professors take particular care to ensure that student teams formed for group projects are ethnically diverse,[204] and where classes on diversity are often part of the core curriculum.[205] Moreover, the agency that handles business school accreditation has formed a special task force which periodically sponsors diversity forums attended by representatives from academia and corporate America.[206]

Medical schools, too, place a premium on diversity, admitting nonwhite applicants under much lower standards than white applicants. In most years, the average Medical College Admissions Test (MCAT) scores of blacks accepted by medical schools are lower than those of whites who are *rejected*.[207] This erosion of standards has been in progress for decades. In the 1970s, Harvard Medical School decided to reserve 20 percent of its admissions slots for minorities—regardless of their MCAT scores. When disproportionate numbers of black and Hispanic students subsequently did poorly in the required science courses, Harvard not only dropped those requirements but replaced its traditional letter-grading system with a less rigorous pass-fail arrangement. When these measures failed to reduce the minority dropout rate, Harvard announced that students would thereafter be eligible to graduate by doing nothing more than passing the national boards. Then, when it was found that minorities failed the boards in disproportionate numbers, they were given five opportunities to pass. Eventually the requirements were waived altogether.[208]

At another top medical school in the early 1970s, faculty members lobbied for the admission of more black students—even the academically mediocre—by quota. When the dean expressed his concern that this course of action would bring in many poorly prepared students incapable of surviving the school's demanding curriculum, the professors told him, "You just let them in. We'll see that they graduate."[209] Contemplate how such policies must affect the quality of the doctors who come out of our medical schools. As Harvard professor Stephan Thernstrom points out, "Over 80 percent of the minority physicians with strong enough grades and test scores to merit admission [to medical school] without preferences [go] on to become board-certified, matching the record of whites and Asians. By contrast, a mere *32 percent* of minority medical school graduates with the weakest college academic records [manage] to achieve certification in their specialty."[210]

For many years, of course, advocates of affirmative action have dismissed any suggestion that quotas and preferential policies ascribe greater importance to "diversity" than to excellence. Former EEOC chairman Clifford Alexander, for one, says that affirmative action "has nothing to do with finding unqualified black men or women. It is about finding qualified black people who are there in abundance but who, either inadvertently or by choice, have been overlooked."[211] Historian John Hope Franklin agrees that the policy "makes no compromise with respect to ability."[212]

Such claims, however, cannot be reconciled with how affirmative action really works. Consider the case of Allan Bakke, who in the early 1970s was twice rejected by the University of California at Davis medical school— despite having registered MCAT scores that placed him in the top 3 percent of test-takers nationally.[213] Bakke was the unfortunate victim of a UC Davis policy that reserved 16 percent of all first-year medical school seats for blacks and Hispanics only—to the exclusion of even the most superior white candidates. Thus it happened that the minorities accepted in preference to Bakke had a combined undergraduate grade-point-average of only C-plus, as well as MCAT scores that ranked in the bottom third of all test-takers. Bakke eventually sued the university for discrimination and won his case in state court. UC Davis then brought the case before the Supreme Court, which, while ruling in Bakke's favor, also stipulated that schools *could* consider race as one factor in the admissions process.[214]

When Bakke was first rejected by UC Davis, the student admitted in his place was an African American named Patrick Chavis, who was later lionized by affirmative action's proponents as someone who went on, after graduating, to become a heroic "poor-folks' doctor" in a "mostly black and Hispanic, down-at-the-heels, inner-ring suburb of Los Angeles."[215] He was, in short, depicted as a testament to the potential benefits of racial preferences. In 1997, however, Dr. Chavis had his medical license suspended after having been found negligent and incompetent in the treatment of three separate patients.[216] One of them was a forty-three-year-old black woman who died while Chavis performed cosmetic surgery on her, a procedure for which his only training had been one-half of a four-day course at the Liposuction Institute of Beverly Hills.[217] While supporters of affirmative action may argue that is unfair to judge their prized policy by one such isolated failure, they themselves have long sung the praises of the policy's isolated successes—most prominent among whom was Dr. Chavis. Indeed, Senator Edward Kennedy frequently characterized Chavis as someone for whom race-based preferences had been a springboard to a career in service of the poor.[218] Similarly, Tom Hayden often praised Chavis's exemplary record of "providing primary care to poor women."[219]

Like medical schools, most major law schools—including New York University, Harvard, Cornell, and the Universities of Virginia and Illinois—have programs specifically designed to recruit minorities.[220] In fact, black students are admitted to America's top law schools at a whopping 17.5 times the rate that a color-blind process would allow.[221] In one recent year only seventeen black law school applicants in the entire country had scholastic credentials as good as those of the average student admitted to Georgetown Law School. Yet Georgetown Law takes in about seventy blacks each year.[222] Obviously, there are two very distinct sets of admissions standards.

Any black applicants who demonstrate even moderate ability are virtually assured admission to the law school of their choice. In 1994, for instance, UC Berkeley School of Law admitted every black applicant with a GPA of at least 3.50 and a Law School Admissions Test (LSAT) score of 90 or above; by contrast, only 42 percent of similarly qualified whites were admitted. That same year, UCLA Law School admitted 61 percent of black applicants with GPAs between 2.50 and 3.49 and LSAT scores between 60 and 89.9; white and Asian students with those same credentials were admitted at rates of 1 percent and 7 percent, respectively.[223]

As we would expect, this double standard has consequences that in the long run are not good for the many black students stranded in educational environments for which they are ill-suited. Between 1977 and 1988, some 73 percent of white law school graduates in California passed the bar exam on their first try, as compared to just 30 percent of their black peers. In New York between 1985 and 1988, the first-time pass rate for whites was 73 percent, while for blacks it was 31 percent. In Florida in 1991, the corresponding figures were 76 percent and 46 percent, respectively.[224] A 1998 national study of 27,000 recent law school graduates found that 92 percent of whites and 61 percent of blacks passed the bar exam on their first attempt.[225] All told, preferentially admitted black law students are *three times more likely* to fail the bar exam than blacks admitted on the basis of academics and LSAT scores alone.[226] In other words, students whose scholastic abilities are congruent with the demands of their schools stand a good chance of gaining something worthwhile from their educational experience. By contrast, students whose schools exploit them as symbols of "diversity" usually find that, when all is said and done, they have thrown away thousands of tuition dollars to tackle curriculums they simply could not master.

Nonetheless, for fully three decades law school admissions committees have cared more about cultivating "diverse" student bodies than about the long-term problems faced by preferentially admitted students. As early as 1969, only five of the forty-three blacks accepted by Yale Law School met normal admissions criteria. Dean Louis Pollack explained at the time that Yale's admissions officers rejected the "uncritical application of the normal indices of past academic performance," and thus were apt to select many minority students with "high promise not reflected in formal academic terms."[227] Unfortunately, he could not specify how this "high promise" might be identified and measured empirically.[228]

In 1976, only 39 black law school applicants in the United States met the traditional academic requirements of our country's leading law schools.[229] In order to fulfill their diversity objectives, then, these schools admitted myriad black students who were underprepared for the educational challenges they would face. To justify such admissions, school administrators predictably cited an abundant body of literature discussing the importance of "leadership," "commitment," and "character"—presumably the qualities for which most of the black students were accepted. The results, however, were dismaying: Black GPAs at the top ten American law schools that year ranked only in the 8th percentile[230]—leaving us little choice but to question the ability of admissions committees, or anyone else, to use arbitrary impressions as accurate measures of potential achievement. Sadly, very little has changed in the past two decades. In 1997, of the 2,707 law school applicants whose college grades and LSAT scores equalled or bettered those of Berkeley's average law student, just 16 were black.[231]

Despite their unimpressive track record in identifying (on the basis of nonacademic criteria) students of "high promise," universities across the country now attach great importance to such criteria solely to create a veneer of respectability for sham admissions policies. Admissions committees everywhere boast that they evaluate each applicant as a "whole person"—considering such factors as how well a student has overcome adversity or utilized past opportunities.[232] Says one admissions director, "We are trying to assess character and other personal qualities such as energy, self-discipline, and generosity."[233] Harvard's admissions committee—confident in its own capacity to "identify the nuances" of each applicant's "character and ability"—staunchly defends its practice of admitting minority students who demonstrate "academic *competence*" in preference to white students who exhibit "academic *superiority*."[234] "We want to serve the best students from all backgrounds," explains Harvard's dean of admissions, "and we're trying to choose people who will be leaders later on. . . . If we're driven exclusively by academic qualities, we would have a much less rich and interesting student body than we currently have."[235]

Higher education's recent emphasis on nonacademic admissions criteria has greatly diminished the degree to which scholastic achievement is rewarded. Perfect GPAs and high standardized-test scores no longer guarantee one's admission to college ahead of students with comparatively poor grades and test scores hundreds of points lower. Consider the case of Amherst College, which in 1987 rejected more than half of all applicants with verbal SAT scores of 750 or better, while admitting 26 students who scored below 400 on the same test.[236] That same year, Stanford University rejected over half of all applicants with verbal SAT scores exceeding 700, yet admitted more than 100 others who scored below 500. Similarly, Duke rejected 35 applicants who scored at least 750 on the verbal test, but accepted 293 who scored under 550.[237] MIT, meanwhile, accepted fewer than 40 percent of all applicants who scored 750 or better on the quantitative SAT—whereas two decades earlier fully 65 percent of similarly qualified candidates had been accepted. This decrease at

MIT, it should be noted, was not due to any decline in the number of high-scoring applicants. In 1987 there were actually more high-achievers applying to MIT than ever before; they simply were not being accepted as automatically as they once had been.[238]

Not only have admissions committees failed to reliably identify students whose academic potential is visible only through the mists of nonacademic considerations, but there is no evidence that such students tend, more than anyone else, to excel in their post-collegiate endeavors.[239] Thomas Sowell raises an even more fundamental point:

> Putting aside the very large question whether any admissions committee could possibly accomplish the task of assessing how well individuals have utilized their varying opportunities, the question remains: What purpose would that serve anyway? It might well be more of a personal achievement for a boy from an utterly blighted family, growing up in desperate social conditions, to have taught himself the rudiments of reading and writing than for a privileged lad from an expensive boarding school to have mastered Einstein's theory of relativity. But is college admissions a reward for past moral merit or an assessment of future intellectual accomplishment? It is by no means clear that most admissions committees have chosen the latter—or have even distinguished the two in their own minds.[240]

Even if we accept, for argument's sake, the premise that a student's extracurricular achievements, special talents, and personality traits *should* be heavily weighted by admissions committees, we must still wonder why the overwhelming majority of students admitted for such nonacademic qualities are black. Are we to believe that only *black* applicants demonstrate leadership, commitment, altruism, civic pride, and an ability to overcome handicaps? Admissions committees certainly seem to believe this, for these are precisely the traits that account for black applicants nationwide being admitted to colleges at much higher rates than academically superior whites.

At Rice University, the 52 percent acceptance rate of black applicants in 1995 was more than double the rate for whites.[241] At the University of Virginia that same year, black applicants were admitted 54 percent of the time—and all others just 37 percent of the time. The corresponding figures at Amherst College were 51 percent and 19 percent, and at Bowdoin College 70 percent and 30 percent, respectively.[242] In a recent study of the admissions statistics for five very selective universities, black applicants were far more likely to be accepted than whites of equivalent credentials. For example, among applicants whose SAT scores ranged between 1200 and 1249, the admission rates for blacks and whites were 60 percent and 19 percent, respectively.[243] Another study of the nearly 20,000 admissions decisions that were made in Florida's state-supported law and medical schools between 1995 and 1997 concluded that race was "a major factor" in admissions. "Significant numbers of white and Hispanic applicants," read the report, "are denied admission who present qualifications that would give a better than 90 percent chance [of] acceptance if they were black."[244]

This pattern is virtually universal in American higher education. Most notable, perhaps, is the fact that these preferences do not occur merely at the margins; that is, race is not simply a "plus factor" that is considered only when the overall records of competing applicants are otherwise equivalent. Rather, black students are vaulted into colleges ahead of whites who have vastly superior credentials—all for the purpose of achieving predetermined numerical objectives.[245] Incredible though it may seem, admissions committees commonly consider a student's race to be *more* important than his or her academic ability. At the University of Michigan, the admissions system gives applicants 20 points for being black or Hispanic, but only 12 points for scoring a perfect 1,600 on the SAT.[246]

As noted earlier in this chapter, the federal dollars that a school receives are, to a large degree, predicated on its having a "diverse" student body. Because this prerequisite has become so firmly entrenched in higher education, our political leaders are reluctant to tamper with it. In 1998 Congress voted down an amendment that would have cut off federal aid to any public college or university that considered race or ethnicity in its admissions process. Such an amendment, of course, would have turned the current system on its head, effectively forcing an end to affirmative action in academia. The measure was defeated, however, by a vote of 249 to 171.[247]

Those Who Lose

It should be noted that not *all* beneficiaries of affirmative action do poorly in college. Consider the case of Yale's black law professor Stephen L. Carter, a highly accomplished scholar who candidly acknowledges that when he applied to Harvard Law School years ago, the admissions committee, unaware that he was black, rejected him. Carter further recounts that shortly thereafter the committee, upon learning that he belonged to a "preferred" minority group, apologetically asked him to consider enrolling at Harvard after all. "We [mistakenly] assumed from your [excellent] record that you were white," explained a Harvard professor at the time.[248] Could any statement illustrate more graphically the condescension and low expectations with which academia views black students?

Racial preferences are morally offensive regardless of which group is their intended beneficiary. At Harvard in 1982, for instance, *whites* were admitted with average SAT scores 112 points lower than those required of Asians.[249] Between 1983 and 1987 Brown University actually took measures to limit Asian admissions, for fear that purely academic criteria would have led to an "overrepresentation" of such students—and thus a shortage of whites and blacks. Consequently, even while Asian students' high-school grades and SAT scores improved, their rate of admission to Brown declined.[250] The story was much the same at Berkeley, which for many years formulated an academic index for each applicant—taking into account high-school grades, SAT scores, and honors achievements. The highest possible index was 8,000. While blacks were consistently admitted with scores as low as 4,800, whites had to score at least 7,000 to be accepted. But Asians had the highest hurdle to jump—simply because they outperformed both whites and blacks academically, and thereby posed a threat to Berkeley's carefully engineered racial "balance." Thus Asians whose indexes exceeded 7,000 stood only a 50 percent chance of being accepted.[251]

Even some secondary schools have, in recent years, set stricter standards for Asian applicants than for others. At San Francisco's Lowell High School, recognized as one of our nation's finest schools, prospective students take an entrance examination for which the highest possible score is 69. Prior to California's 1997 ban on affirmative action, Chinese American students had to score 66 or better to be admitted, while 59 was sufficient for whites, and 54 for blacks and Hispanics.[252]

It should also be noted that in a few cases affirmative action has been applied to benefit *whites* over *blacks*. Indeed, in 1995 a federal judge ordered Alabama State University (ASU), which was virtually all-black, to spend $1 million per year on scholarships for white applicants only—so as to attract students whose presence would "diversify" the ASU campus. Consequently, in the 1996-1997 school year ASU gave out 671 scholarships to white students—one for almost every white enrolled. As a general rule, of course, affirmative action lowers standards for its beneficiaries, and ASU was no exception. To be eligible for many of these white scholarships, students needed only a C average—and in some cases were not even required to have a high-school diploma. Inevitably, then, hundreds of more-qualified black students were denied admission to ASU simply because of their skin color—truly an ironic, disgraceful twist of history.[253]

The flip side of the Alabama State coin, meanwhile, is illustrated by an episode that transpired at Berkeley in the 1980s:

> Student A was ranked in the top third of his [high school] class, student B in the bottom third. Student A had College Board scores totaling 1,290; student B's scores totaled 890. Student A had a good record of citizenship; student B was expelled last winter for breaking a series of major school rules. Student A was white; student B was black. Berkeley refused student A and accepted student B.[254]

In 1992 the University of Texas Law School aroused the ire of its own "Student A," Cheryl Hopwood, who applied there for admission after graduating from California State University at Sacramento with a 3.80 GPA and scoring very well on her LSAT. A most resilient individual, Ms. Hopwood had overcome much adversity in her life prior to pursuing a law career. When she was a young girl her father died, and she was raised thereafter under difficult circumstances by her mother. She held a job throughout her high-school years and later paid her way through college.[255] On both academic and nonacademic grounds, she was a seemingly ideal applicant. Yet because she was white, she was denied admission to the law school.

Texas Law's customary practice was to set aside 15 percent of its seats for blacks and Mexican Americans, who were accepted under much lower standards than all other students. Not only were these preferred applicants given practically automatic admission, but most were awarded scholarships—even in cases where there was no financial need. Every black applicant with credentials similar to

Hopwood's received a $7,000 scholarship and free tuition. University officials acknowledged that had Hopwood been black, she would have "in all probability" been admitted. In fact, in the year she applied, Texas Law rejected 668 white applicants before rejecting a single black. Among candidates who scored between 189 and 192 in the law school's academic rating system, 89 percent of Mexican Americans were admitted, as were 100 percent of blacks. Of white applicants with equivalent credentials, only 6 percent were admitted.[256]

Along with Ms. Hopwood, three other white students who were also denied admission filed suit against Texas Law, claiming "reverse discrimination." In August 1994 a federal judge ruled that although the school's policies were technically unconstitutional, it did not have to admit the four plaintiffs. The school's only violation, said the judge, was its use of separate admissions committees to evaluate the applications of white and minority students—merely a "procedural flaw." While the university would thereafter be required to utilize just one admissions committee, it would not be prevented from accepting minority students under lower standards than whites. The University of Texas president reacted happily to the court decision. "It's a real victory for affirmative action policies in universities," he said, "because it concludes that they are necessary, that they are constitutionally required, and that they are proper. We are very, very happy."[257]

This 1994 verdict was overturned two years later, however, when the U.S. Court of Appeals for the Fifth Circuit ruled that Texas Law's use of race as a factor in admissions was unconstitutional.[258] Notably, the 1996 decision applied not only to schools in Texas, but also in Mississippi and Louisiana—the other states covered by the Fifth Circuit.[259] The Department of Education, however, was slow to accept the appellate court's ruling—threatening for more than a year to withhold millions of dollars in federal aid from Fifth Circuit schools that failed to attract "enough" nonwhite students.[260]

Many who outwardly praise affirmative action are privately troubled by the policy's obvious injustices—and therefore seek to silence anyone bold enough to point out those failings. Consider what occurred in April 1991 after a white Georgetown law student, Timothy Maguire, discovered that his black classmates had been admitted to the law program with far lower LSAT scores and GPAs than those required of whites. Maguire created enormous controversy when he submitted to the student newspaper an article exposing this double standard. Black students on campus, outraged that anyone would dare suggest that Georgetown favored black applicants over whites, branded him a racist.[261] The Black Law Student Association, demanding that Maguire's degree be withheld, browbeat him into a public apology. And for fear of receiving similar treatment, numerous attorneys refused to defend Maguire in lawsuits that were brought against him.[262]

Judith Areen, dean of Georgetown Law, denied that the school had a preferential admissions policy for blacks—explaining that the selection process took into account many factors, some of which overrode strictly academic considerations. She noted, for instance, that a required essay in which prospective students wrote their reasons for wanting to attend Georgetown was of critical import. In response to Areen's explanation, one incisive commentator mused, "We are to understand, apparently, that there is an inverse correlation between high LSAT scores and GPAs [on one hand], and [on the other hand,] an ability to write an essay on why one wants to be a law student at Georgetown. [And presumably] this peculiarity manifests itself disproportionately in the case of black applicants."[263]

Yet most pundits accepted Areen's explanation. The *New York Times* editorial page rebuked Maguire for his "obsession with numbers." Meanwhile, the highest-ranking members of our country's legal-education establishment concurred with Areen's assertion that critics of the law school admissions process were ignorant of its complexities. In a joint press release, some of these officials explained, "Besides the LSAT and undergraduate GPA, several other considerations are taken into account. [These include] personal statements from applicants, letters of recommendation, work experience, and the applicant's prior success in overcoming personal disadvantage."[264] In other words, all types of subjective factors were considered in evaluating candidates—factors allowing for nearly infinite leeway in the selection process. Schools were thereby able to guarantee the desired racial composition for their entering freshman classes—though race was conspicuously absent from all public explanations of the "complex" admissions process.

The uproar that attended the Maguire case illustrates the taboo against pointing out even the most blatant examples of racial preferences. The rare person who dares to speak up is generally vilified by his peers. Consider, as further evidence of this, the firestorm of criticism aimed at University of Texas law professor Lino Graglia in September 1997, after he said in a news conference that black and Mexican American students were "not academically competitive" with white students at America's top universities. Their scholastic short-comings, he suggested, were "the result primarily of cultural effects" that attach no stigma to academic failure.[265] After Graglia made these comments, spokesmen for Texas Law expressed dismay over his "offensive and painful words."[266] The university's three top officials quickly issued a statement condemning the professor's "abhorrent" sentiments while reaffirming their own desire for a school that was "fully representative of the marvelously rich diversity of the people of Texas."[267] Nearly the entire faculty, moreover, signed a statement denouncing Graglia's remarks, while black student leaders filed racial-harassment complaints and state lawmakers called for the professor's dismissal.[268] "He should not continue to represent the state of Texas or educate the future leaders of our state," said Representative Hugo Berlanga.[269] Jesse Jackson attended a campus rally for "diversity" and said that Graglia's comments reflected a "fascist ideology."[270]

None of Graglia's critics, of course, substantively addressed what he had said, but merely jockeyed with one another to offer the swiftest and most dramatic expression of outrage at his "insensitivity." Not one of them dared acknowledge that for decades thousands of academically uncompetitive minority students have been admitted to colleges for the express purpose of filling racial and ethnic quotas. Consider the case of Berkeley, which after almost a decade of accepting nonwhites under the lowered standards of affirmative action, proudly announced in 1988 that it had achieved multiracial "parity." What Berkeley did *not* announce, naturally, was that it had achieved this parity by systematically discriminating against highly qualified white and Asian candidates. "Merit is no longer the predominant factor in admissions," conceded one Berkeley official.[271] "We've got to have affirmative action," explained another. "Otherwise, the whole freshman class will be composed of Caucasians and Asians."[272] While acknowledging that Berkeley's policy was clearly discriminatory, these individuals nonetheless deemed it "the price we have to pay for diversity."[273] Along the same lines, a Harvard law professor calls racial preferences "simply an incidental consequence of addressing a compelling social need."[274] Florida Regents spokesman Keith Goldschmidt candidly declares, "There are race-conscious policies in the state university system and it's something we're proud of."[275]

In 1990, only four-tenths of Berkeley freshmen were admitted to the school on academic merit alone. The rest were selected principally for their contributions to "diversity"—usually in preference to white and Asian students with impeccable academic qualifications. Just one-third of the class, in fact, was white.[276] Prior to 1997, fully 20 percent of the applicants whom Berkeley rejected each year had perfect 4.0 high-school GPAs.[277] In 1989 alone, Berkeley turned down more than 2,500 white and Asian applicants with straight-A averages but did not reject a single black with similar credentials.[278] Today blacks hold some 3,000 of the 48,000 freshman seats at America's twenty-five highest-ranked universities, or 6.3 percent. Yet if SAT scores alone determined admissions, the figure would be scarcely 1.5 percent.[279]

Artificial "Propping Up"

Once an educational institution accepts black students—underqualified though some may be by traditional standards—it works diligently to ensure that they stay in school and eventually graduate. Excessively high minority-dropout rates can jeopardize not only a university's reputation, but its accreditation status as well. To reduce minority attrition, many professors evaluate the work of black and Hispanic students more leniently than that of their white and Asian classmates—a practice which liberal sociologist David Reisman terms "affirmative grading."[280] Some colleges have simply watered down their curricula to make it difficult for *any* students to fail.[281] Indeed, A's and B's account for about 83 percent of all grades at Princeton University. At Stanford the figure is 80 percent.[282] Until 1995, in fact, Stanford professors gave no grades below C-minus, and students were permitted to drop courses as late as the eve of their final exams without paying any academic penalty.[283]

Other schools, meanwhile, have developed extensive remedial programs designed to help bring minority students up to par. Whereas thirty years ago only 6 percent of colleges provided remedial English instruction for scholastically underprepared students, today fully 78 percent of colleges offer such courses.[284] Nationwide, there are currently some 300,000 instructors teaching remedial classes at the college level.[285] Obviously, these efforts to keep marginal students in school are costly. Texas A&M University, for instance, spends nearly $8 million annually on minority recruitment and retention programs.[286] In Florida, the cost of remedial education for college students is about $50 million per year.[287]

Because it is imperative that they maintain "diverse" student bodies, some schools use monetary incentives to motivate black students to perform well. At Penn State University, blacks are paid $580 if they maintain a C average, while those with a B average or better are given twice that amount.[288] This type of reward system is condescension at its ugliest. As Thomas Sowell puts it:

> What all the arguments and campaigns for quotas are really saying, loud and clear, is that *black people just don't have it*, and that they will have to be given something in order to have something. . . . Those black people who are already competent . . . will be completely undermined, as black becomes synonymous—in the minds of black and white alike—with incompetence, and black achievement becomes synonymous with charity or payoffs.[289]

Graduate schools employ the same types of affirmative action policies as undergraduate, business, medical, and law schools—quietly bending admissions guidelines so as to favor nonwhite applicants. Consider how little importance many of these schools attach to the Graduate Record Examination (GRE), a three-part test widely used to evaluate the skills of students applying for graduate studies programs. In one recent year, while the national average score on the verbal part of the exam was 499, the black average was 370; while the national average on the quantitative portion was 516, the black average was 363; and while the national average on the analytical section was 522, the black average was, again, 363.[290] Black scores on the GRE are lower than those of any other ethnic group taking the test.[291] Undaunted by these facts, however, graduate schools across the country continue to set ever-increasing goals for black enrollments. How are such objectives to be achieved without drastically lowering standards and making a mockery of merit?

While many critics of the GRE charge that the test is culturally biased, there is no credible evidence to support this claim. Were there bias in the exam, it would surely manifest itself most clearly on the verbal portion, where students are tested on their reading comprehension, language skills, and familiarity with literature. The quantitative and analytical portions of the test, on the other hand, measure knowledge and abilities that have nothing to do with culture. Yet black students actually perform better on the verbal part of the test than on the other parts. Meanwhile Asian students, who are the most culturally distinct of all groups taking the GRE,[292] score only 20 points below the national average and 109 points *higher* than the black average on the verbal portion. As Dr. Walter E. Williams incisively asks, "If the examination is culturally biased, how is it that people of a culture far more alien [than that of blacks] to the American culture score close to the national mean [on the verbal test]?"[293] Incidentally, on the quantitative portion of the test Asians exceed the national average by 59 points, while on the analytical portion they match the national average exactly.[294]

Although no one has been able to show how the GRE discriminates against any demographic group, graduate schools nationwide—desperate to remain sufficiently "diverse"—largely overlook the low scores of black applicants. Moreover, special services and publications have emerged in recent years to capitalize on this desperation. The Minority Graduate Student Locator Service, for example, is a computer-based search service that helps graduate schools and fellowship sponsors reach a larger pool of black and Hispanic applicants.[295]

Help from Many Places

Each year thousands of scholarships and fellowships earmarked exclusively for nonwhite students are made available by private organizations, individual colleges, publicly and privately held corporations, the federal government, and state governments. While some of these awards are structured to cover general educational expenses without regard to the recipients' fields of study, others are designated specifically for students in particular academic disciplines. Indeed, minority students of architecture, accounting, dentistry, nursing, literature, the performing arts, and music are eligible for many awards that are off-limits to whites.[296] The myriad sources from which nonwhites can obtain financial assistance for their schooling are catalogued in such books as *Higher Education Opportunities for Minorities and Women*;[297] *The Minority Student's Complete Scholarship Book*;[298] *The Black Student's Guide to Scholarships*;[299] *The Hispanic Scholarship Directory*;[300] *The Higher Education Moneybook for Women and Minorities*;[301] the *Directory of Financial Aid for Minorities*;[302] the *National Directory of Minority Organizations*;[303] and *The Big Book of Minority Opportunities*.[304] In addition, there are separate publications that list financial-aid resources reserved for nonwhites pursuing careers in engineering, law, business, education, journalism, medicine, and science.[305]

Through a variety of broad-based programs, the federal government takes a very active role in helping minorities get a college education. The Minority Science Improvement Program, for instance, provides government grants ranging in value from $19,000 to $472,000 to support science, mathematics, and engineering students in predominantly black and minority colleges.[306] The Minority Participation in Graduate Education Program, meanwhile, awards federal grants of more than $75,000 apiece to nonwhite students pursuing advanced degrees in any field.[307]

Each year our country's black colleges receive nearly $1 billion in federal aid. Of the thousands of colleges and universities in the United States, only the 107 black colleges are given special federal grants to cover operating expenses. Under the White House Initiative on Historically Black Colleges, twenty-seven major federal agencies and departments are required to give grants and loans to these schools.[308]

Nearly 90 percent of all private colleges make some scholarships—whose average value is $6,800 per year—available only to nonwhites.[309] Duke, Rice, and the University of Virginia are just a few of the prestigious schools that earmark certain scholarships for blacks only.[310] Harvard Graduate School gives all minorities full scholarships regardless of financial need.[311] New Jersey's Rutgers University—renowned for its aggressive recruitment of minorities—awarded scholarships to no fewer than 244 nonwhite freshmen in 1992 alone.[312] Florida Atlantic University (FAU), in a recent effort to increase black enrollment, waived all tuition expenses for black students. This measure, said FAU president Anthony Catanese, demonstrated that the school was "serious about recruiting."[313]

Eighty-nine colleges participate in the Minority Engineering

Program, through which nonwhite students in that field receive money, tutoring, counseling, and other special services. Notably, students of Japanese and Chinese ancestry are not eligible.[314] Because they typically outperform their peers—black *and* white—Asians are not considered "disadvantaged" minorities who require the helping hand of affirmative action, however impoverished their backgrounds may be.

The University of Chicago and twelve campuses of the Big Ten Universities have instituted a Summer Research Opportunities Program designed to encourage minority students to attend graduate school. Off-limits to whites, this program offers each participant research experience under the individualized guidance of a professor. In 1990 alone, 571 students took advantage of this opportunity.[315] Yale has instituted a similar minorities-only program.[316]

Each year the University of Michigan's Minority Summer Institute pays all travel and living expenses for thirty nonwhite students who receive six weeks of preparation for doctoral business programs. In addition to the all-expenses-paid feature of this summer-study opportunity, each participant is awarded $2,500 just for showing up.[317]

Since 1993, the U.S. Department of Education has donated nearly half a million dollars to the speech program at New York's Mercy College.[318] This money covers full-tuition scholarships, stipends, and other support services for minorities studying to become teachers of the speech- and hearing-handicapped.[319]

Under the state of Pennsylvania's $15 million Graduate Opportunities Tuition Waiver Program, thirty universities statewide offer full scholarships to black students for their graduate education. A comparable program exists in Florida.[320]

Contrary to popular mythology, corporate America contributes huge sums of money every year to minority-education initiatives. The General Electric Foundation, for instance, has instituted a $20 million program, open only to nonwhites, to train students for professorial careers in business, science, and engineering.[321] IBM finances fellowships for minorities studying physics, chemistry, engineering, mathematics, and computer science.[322] General Motors, in an agreement with the NAACP, has pledged to donate $500,000 to fund the law school education of nonwhite students. Ford and Chrysler have made similar promises.[323] One of America's largest philanthropies, the Ford Foundation, supports numerous predoctoral and postdoctoral fellowships for minorities who are "underrepresented" in the social and physical sciences.[324] A legion of minority scholarships are available from the National Action Council for Minorities in Engineering (NACME), whose funding is provided by numerous corporations. In one recent academic year, some 4,200 students at 144 schools received more than $3 million in NACME awards.[325]

Indeed, the sources of funding for minority-education programs are virtually numberless:

• Under the auspices of the Jackie Robinson Foundation, more than 100 minority students who demonstrate "high academic achievement, financial need, and leadership potential" receive scholarships each year.[326]

• The United Negro College Fund awards up to 1,200 scholarships annually to students at forty-one black colleges and universities.[327]

• The Committee of Institutional Cooperation (CIC) offers two-year fellowships to minority students of the social sciences and humanities at eleven universities. Each award covers full tuition costs and provides an additional $8,000 stipend per academic year.[328] The CIC also offers four-year awards to nonwhites pursuing Ph.D.s in anthropology, economics, geography, history, political science, psychology, and sociology.[329]

• The National Science Foundation sponsors special three-year fellowships to minority graduate students in science and engineering. These awards are not available to students of European, Japanese, or Chinese extraction.[330]

• The Earl Warren Legal Training Program issues grants earmarked for black law students.[331]

• The Council for Career Development for Minorities gives fellowships to black and Hispanic students aspiring to become career counselors or job-placement officers at mostly-minority colleges.[332]

• The American Psychological and Sociological Associations offer minority fellowships valued at more than $6,500 apiece to Ph.D. students of those disciplines.[333]

• The Fund for Theological Education awards special fellowships to black graduate students of religion, clearly stipulating that all candidates "must be black."[334]

• The Congressional Black Caucus Foundation sponsors fellowships—whose values range from $12,000 to $15,000—for black applicants wishing to work in the offices of U.S. congressmen.[335]

• The American Political Science Association offers graduate fellowships worth $6,000 apiece to black students in that field.[336]

• A special consortium for minorities enrolled in MBA programs sponsors fellowships that pay all tuition costs for two years plus modest stipends to cover living expenses.[337]

• The Mendenhall Fellowship Program for Minority Scholars provides stipends, housing, office space, library privileges, and computer support for nonwhite Ph.D. candidates.[338]

• The Council for Opportunity in Graduate Management Education gives financial support to minority students working toward advanced degrees at Cornell, Harvard, MIT, Stanford, and a number of other prestigious institutions.[339]

• The National Achievement Scholarship Program for Outstanding Negro Students gives more than $2 million to black college students each year. These awards are underwritten by grants from various corporations, foundations, colleges, and private contributors.[340]

The list, of course, could go on and on. The programs mentioned here—and hundreds more like them—are part of a large network of policies that seek ever-greater *inclusion* of blacks in academia.

As noted earlier, colleges commonly offer generous financial-assistance packages to attract black students—including many with mediocre academic records or hailing from affluent families. In the early 1990s there was much debate regarding the propriety of these racially exclusive scholarships—until U.S. Education Secretary Richard Riley decreed in 1993 that such awards were legal, desirable, and to be "encouraged." To every college president in the country, Riley sent a letter explaining that race-based scholarships could help correct the "improper actions of the past" by "providing equal opportunity and . . . enhancing a diverse educational environment."[341]

The Clinton administration concurred with and expanded on Riley's position, announcing that race could be the determining factor not only in *awarding* scholarships, but also in *denying* them.[342] One victim of this ruling was Daniel Podberesky, a Hispanic student who compiled a perfect 4.0 high-school GPA and scored over 1,300 on the SAT. Despite his impressive scholastic accomplishments, however, this young man's 1990 application for a scholarship under the University of Maryland's Banneker Program was denied, purportedly because that program was reserved for black students of similarly outstanding credentials. In truth, however, Banneker recipients are required only to have a 3.0 high-school GPA and a score of 900 or better on the SAT.[343] Podberesky, then, was more than qualified academically. He was simply underqualified racially. A federal appeals court ruled in October 1994 that the black-only Banneker scholarships were unconstitutional[344]—a decision that the U.S. Supreme Court let stand in May 1995.[345] It remains to be seen whether these court decisions will establish a precedent for further challenges to race-based scholarships at other universities and in other states.

Examples of double standards in the awarding of scholarships abound. Consider the policy of the National Merit Scholarship Corporation (NMSC), which annually gives cash grants to our country's most gifted high-school graduates. Six thousand students win the NMSC's regular scholarships each year, but there are almost no blacks among them. To make amends for this apparently embarrassing situation, the NMSC now reserves 700 scholarships for "outstanding Negro students," who need not meet the standard criteria.[346]

Never Enough

Notwithstanding academia's back-bending efforts to recruit black students, many high-profile figures staunchly maintain that antiblack bias pervades American higher education. Former Georgetown basketball coach John Thompson, for example, claims that college admissions standards disproportionately deny educational opportunities to black students.[347] In a similar vein, when a 1994 study by the American Council on Education (ACE) revealed that the yearly number of black men receiving doctorates had dwindled by 19 percent during the preceding decade, NAACP official Wade Henderson declared, "It certainly confirms our fears that black males are an endangered species in academia."[348] Moreover, the ACE urged academic institutions, the federal government, and private foundations to do whatever they could to encourage black students to stay in school.[349] Incredible though it may seem, the supposedly informed authors of this study were apparently ignorant of the extraordinary measures that colleges had already taken to maximize African Americans' participation in higher education.

Blindly following the lead of "civil rights" mouthpieces, many black college students are convinced that the academic world discriminates against them. A 1993 *U.S. News and World Report* feature on campus race relations notes that black students "believe that whites have greater access to university financial aid."[350] A similar sense of victimization was displayed in 1989 when more than 400 black students from Ivy League and Boston-area colleges convened at Harvard University for a four-day conference focusing on minority-education issues.[351] One female in attendance, a Harvard sophomore, complained that many of her white peers thought that universities often admitted blacks under artificially low standards. "The only thing people hear," she said, "is that affirmative action helped get us here, and that's not the complete story. It's not that affirmative action is bringing in inadequate people to better schools. It's that people who have equal ability are now being considered for entrance into the better schools."[352] Along the same lines, another Harvard sophomore tried to dispel white "misconceptions" about affirmative action. "I personally feel we are here because we have something unique about us," he explained. "Our blackness is something unique, but I don't find that to be the most important factor."[353] While it is troubling to hear young people resort to such self-delusion in order to protect their fragile egos, affirmative action virtually guarantees that many black students will find themselves in just such a position. Preferential admissions policies, by their very nature, create suspicion in the minds of students—both black and white—that many of the blacks on any given campus might not have gotten there solely on the strength of their academic abilities.

Quotas Enveloping Education

"Diversity," it should be noted, is a major issue not only on the collegiate level, but as early as kindergarten and the first grade. Schools that educate significant numbers of black and Hispanic children go to great lengths to secure the services of as many minority teachers as possible—ostensibly to provide their students with "role models" of the same race or ethnicity. So great is the demand for nonwhite instructors, in fact, that the executive director of the American Association of Colleges for Teacher Education recently went so far as to propose that black teachers be paid more than their white peers.[354] Unfortunately, the sacrificial lamb in most efforts to match teachers and students by race is quality. In order to hire and retain more minority teachers, among whom academic excellence is in *comparatively* short supply, school districts nationwide have lowered their qualification standards significantly. When California administered a basic competency exam to prospective teachers in 1983, only 26 percent of black test-takers registered passing grades—a far cry from the 76 percent of whites who passed the same exam. In Florida that year, blacks and whites passed a comparable test at rates of 35 percent and 90 percent, respectively.[355] The corresponding figures in Arizona were 24 percent and 73 percent, in Texas 10 percent and 62 percent, and in Georgia 34 percent and 87 percent. Similar black-white disparities were found in numerous other states as well,[356] and those gaps have actually grown over time. As of 1995, twenty-six states were administering certification tests to aspiring teachers,[357] with about 90 percent of whites but only 35 percent of blacks passing.[358]

Not surprisingly, a host of critics allege that teacher-competency tests are nothing more than tools to drive African Americans out of the profession. Black educator Faustine Jones-Wilson, for instance, calls these exams "still one more way of reducing the number of minority teachers under the guises of 'excellence' and 'accountability.' "[359] Apparently in agreement with such charges, many school administrators deem it more important to find suitable "role models" than to hire teachers who demonstrate competency and knowledge on the standardized tests.[360] School systems in Detroit and Atlanta, among others, have revamped their teaching staffs from nearly all-white to virtually all-nonwhite in order to reflect the racial composition of their student populations.[361] Moreover, about 10.1 percent of our country's public school principals are black, a figure about one-third larger than the 7.4 percent share of teaching posts held by blacks. "Since principals are drawn from the ranks of teachers," explains Dr. Stephan Thernstrom, "this substantial disparity suggests that school authorities in a great many American communities . . . have given fairly strong preferences to black candidates seeking to pursue administrative careers."[362] Unfortunately, such measures have not led to any improvements in student performance.[363]

Despite the frenzy to match minority-group students with teachers of like heritage, there is in fact no evidence that youngsters perform better under such conditions.[364] American students of Japanese and Chinese extraction, for instance, have done superbly—many without ever having seen an Asian teacher. Similarly, as long ago as the late nineteenth century the children of destitute Jewish immigrants in New York did phenomenally well under Irish Catholic teachers.[365] It has been consistently demonstrated that students' personal motivations and parental support are far more important to educational success than are the physical characteristics of classroom teachers. Incidentally, it is worth asking why no one dares suggest that *white* students require *white* teachers as role models. "Civil rights leaders" nationwide would surely denounce such a proposal as racist. This double standard presumes that white pupils can benefit from being exposed to black or Hispanic teachers, but that the converse does not hold for minority children.[366]

The New York City school system, for all practical purposes, abandoned the merit system in a 1990 attempt to have the ethnic and racial makeup of its teacher force approximate that of the city at large. It was decided, among other things, that any local school board which did not hire "adequate" numbers of minorities would be subject to suspension. The city's board of education president was realistic enough to admit not only that finding enough good minority teachers to fill the prescribed quotas would be difficult, but also that the policy was unlikely to benefit the students. Nonetheless, he favored the move as a means of avoiding the *appearance* of discriminating against blacks.[367] The fact that it required *actual* discrimination against whites did not trouble him in the least.

Such discrimination against white teachers is nothing new. In the early 1980s, the Boston public school system had to lay off 1,300 teachers. Normally, those with the least seniority would have been let go first, but a federal judicial order allowed experienced white teachers to be laid off while the school district actually *hired* new black teachers.[368] During the same time period in Jackson, Michigan, the customary "last-hired, first-fired" guidelines were discarded, and minority schoolteachers were retained in preference to their more experienced white colleagues. A United States district court supported this arrangement on grounds that minority instructors could serve as the types of role models that historically had been denied to black and

Hispanic students. Yet there was no evidence that the Jackson school district had ever discriminated against minorities. The court ruling, then, basically held that discrimination against whites was an appropriate means by which to "remedy" the fact that few minorities had chosen to be schoolteachers in Jackson.[369]

Efforts to pair nonwhite instructors with nonwhite children are founded largely on the premise that such teachers can help their students develop self-esteem more effectively than white teachers. Indeed, many contemporary educators trace almost all minority students' failures to the notion that white society robs such children of their pride and dignity—which supposedly flourish if exposed to successful same-race authority figures. Similar deluded notions about how students acquire self-respect comprise the philosophical basis for Afrocentric education, which teaches that Africa was the scene of humanity's first major achievements in philosophy, mathematics, science, architecture, and literature—only to have its people's accomplishments in those fields "stolen" by white Europeans. Such ludicrous education obscures historical accuracy under the dark shadows of fictions ostensibly designed to imbue black students with pride in themselves and in their heritage.

Afrocentrism teaches, for instance, that ancient Africans developed a complex "national system of reservoirs";[370] that early African myths about the origins of the universe were "very close to modern physics";[371] that twenty-three centuries ago Africans had accurately calculated the speed of light, an achievement which eluded Western scientists until the twentieth century;[372] that the Dogon people of medieval Mali made use of powerful telescopes, as evidenced by their tribal dance which precisely paralleled the orbit of the star Sirius B—a star that is impossible to see with the naked eye and which NASA did not discover until the 1980s;[373] that Africans "understood the structure of the planetary system" thousands of years ago;[374] and that such modern inventions as cannons, long-range missiles, ship propellers, automatic hammers, and gas engines "have the roots of their development in early African uses of power."[375]

The scope of Afrocentrists' extraordinary claims is virtually boundless. They teach that ancient Egyptians not only knew how to harness electricity, but actually built power-driven airplanes that they used "for travel expeditions and recreation";[376] that many of Aristotle's ideas were "stolen" from African texts;[377] that Europeans such as

Napoleon shot the noses off Egypt's great statues for the express purpose of destroying all evidence that ancient Egyptians were actually broad-nosed blacks rather than of Middle Eastern appearance;[378] that Judaism and Christianity are "largely plagiarized from African blacks";[379] that Jesus Christ himself was black;[380] that Africans invented both democracy and the modern judicial system;[381] that Africans were using the antibiotic tetracycline in Nubia fourteen centuries ago;[382] that while European medicine was mired in medieval ignorance, East Africans were performing Caesarian sections "with one hundred percent success";[383] that fifteenth-century Africans were performing such delicate surgical procedures as "cornea transplants";[384] and that African tribal wars were "not much more than a frightful game" with "a highly humane aspect"—their main objective being "to overcome or frighten away the adversary, not to kill at all."[385] Two Afrocentric schools in Milwaukee go so far as to teach that "black Egyptians once had wings and flew freely around the pyramids until the Europeans arrived and killed off all the natural fliers."[386] Administrators at both schools justify such instruction on the grounds that it supposedly helps the students develop self-esteem.

It is notable that despite their ardent denunciations of racism, Afrocentrists fully concur with *white* racists that skin color predetermines human worth; they disagree only about which race is superior. "The Afrocentric message," observes Dinesh D'Souza, "is basically the one that Hitler delivered in the 1930s: we were great once, we have been humiliated, let us recognize the evil ones who have stolen our birthright, let us confront them and recover our inheritance, by any means necessary."[387]

In the early 1990s a number of urban school systems—those of Atlanta, Baltimore, Indianapolis, Milwaukee, Pittsburgh, Richmond, and Philadelphia, among others—adopted Afrocentric curriculums. In 1993 Detroit announced that it would institute "a new Afrocentric curriculum in all 261 [of its] schools."[388] These developments, of course, will only deepen the ignorance of unwitting, impressionable children.

Racial considerations have become paramount in virtually every aspect of American education—in some cases affecting even a teacher's freedom to reprimand or punish uncooperative students. In 1992, for instance, the Cincinnati public school system adopted a tough, new disciplinary code mandating stiffer penalties for disruptive or dangerous youngsters. Two years later, however, a judicial review found that this policy was having a disparate racial impact on black students (who, on the whole, had more behavior problems than whites). As an alternative, the court proposed a settlement requiring teachers to keep written records of the race and gender of every student whom they punished in any way. If, over time, the disciplinary record of any particular teacher proved to be racially "unbalanced," then his or her performance evaluation, salary, and job security might be affected.[389]

It should be noted that efforts to ensure racial balance often take the form of policies regulating which schools students may attend. A 1995 survey of 103 urban school districts found that fully 45 percent were under court order "to maintain racially balanced schools."[390] For the larger districts in that group, the figure was a whopping 69 percent. In addition, many other districts had voluntarily adopted desegregation programs without court-imposed mandates.[391]

Some General Observations

Racial preferences are, in the final analysis, nothing more than double standards that reward some people and penalize others for the color of their skin. And while the discriminatory nature of these policies is generally couched in such euphemisms as "goals" and "timetables," the inevitable effect of affirmative action is a fairly rigid quota system. In the words of philosophy professor Alan Goldman:

> What is a positive 'goal' for one group must be a negative 'quota' for its complement; this is simply a logical truth. . . . As long as there is some proportion of the total reserved for some participant, it seems that we have a quota. . . . It is hard to avoid the conclusion that the additional purpose to be served by the numerical goals is to apply pressure for [discrimination against whites] despite official disclaimers of such intent.[392]

Although affirmative action's ostensible purpose is to promote greater diversity, it focuses not on a diversity of ideas or skills, but rather of skin tones. As Professor Lino Graglia puts it, "Affirmative action enforcers do not check schools for diversity of views or experience in the student body; they check only for the presence of blacks and—to a much lesser extent—members of other preferred groups."[393] Graglia summarizes the injustices of such a policy:

> Racially preferential admission is an inappropriate means of compensation for several reasons. First, our historical assimilationist national policy has been to insist upon the general irrelevancy of one's membership in a particular racial group as a basis for government action. Second, lack of qualification for a course of study can be rationally addressed only by taking steps to remove the lack, not by overlooking it and proceeding as if it did not exist. Finally, it is plainly unjust that the cost of racially preferential admissions should be largely borne by the particular individuals whom the racially preferred replace, even though they bear no particular responsibility for the disadvantage for which compensation is supposedly being made.[394]

Clearly, racial preferences do not end discrimination but merely shift it onto the members of different groups. This plain truth was best expressed by black Supreme Court Justice Thurgood Marshall, who, in defense of affirmative action, once told Justice William Douglas, "You [white] guys have been practicing discrimination for years. Now it's our turn."[395] Such a statement was indeed a far cry from Marshall's eloquent 1954 NAACP brief for *Brown v. Board of Education*, in which he had stated, "Distinctions by race are so evil, so arbitrary and invidious that a state, bound to defend the equal protection of the laws must not invoke them in any public sphere."[396]

Proponents of affirmative action, who would unanimously denounce any legalized policies that specifically favored whites over blacks, flatly deny that preferences favoring *blacks* are equally wrong. Professor Gertrude Ezorsky, for example, explains that whites who are denied jobs or school admissions by affirmative action ought not be classified as victims of "reverse racism" or "reverse discrimination"—because those denials are not rooted in the premise that white people are genetically inferior to others.[397] Presumably, Professor Ezorsky feels that this distinction should console those whites who lose employment or educational opportunities to less-qualified but more-properly pigmented candidates. Moreover, her references to "*reverse* racism" and "*reverse* discrimination" are founded on the planted axiom that *ordinary* racism and discrimination are *white* characteristics. Her premise, with its obvious and enormous implications, has been accepted blindly and without intellectual scrutiny by the American people.

Affirmative action's critics, meanwhile, commonly note that the policy produces an angry backlash in those whites who are the displaced pawns of quotas. Less widely recognized, however, is that it breeds *black-on-white* animosity as well. By treating blacks as wounded victims whom whites would eagerly exploit if not for the protective arm of racial preferences, affirmative action reinforces the notion that American institutions are, in their natural state, basically unfair to minorities. In short, it persuades blacks to consider themselves unqualified to succeed on their own merit and, simultaneously, entitled to receive special privileges because of their skin color. It would be difficult, if not impossible, to concoct a policy more certain to exacerbate racial tensions.

Hope for the Future

A few recent developments in affirmative action law have had notable effects on the racial and ethnic makeups of the student bodies at colleges in several states. As noted earlier in this chapter, an appellate court ruled in 1996 that the consideration of race in school admissions was unconstitutional in Texas, Mississippi, and Louisiana. Consequently, black enrollments declined substantially at numerous schools in those states. The University of Texas (UT) Law School, for instance, took only 4 blacks and 26 Hispanics into its first-year class of 1997—a sharp drop-off from the school's previous average of about 100 minorities in each entering class.[398] Meanwhile, black representation among freshmen on UT's undergraduate campus fell by 50 percent.[399] In California, where racial preferences in college admissions were banned by the 1996 passage of Proposition 209, the results were similar. At Berkeley Law School, black enrollment among first-year students declined by 81 percent in 1997, the year in which the color-blind policies first took effect.[400] Statewide, only 229 blacks and Hispanics were accepted by California law schools that year— less than half the 1996 total of 473.[401]

Of course, Prop 209 affected undergraduate enrollments as well. At Berkeley, the freshman class that started college in the 1998 fall semester was the first entering class whose demographic makeup was affected by the new law. That semester, blacks comprised 10.5

percent of all entering freshmen, as compared with 21.9 percent the year before.[402] Whereas 547 blacks had been part of the 1997 freshman class, the 1998 figure was only 224.[403] The story was similar at UCLA, where black freshman enrollment dropped from 518 in 1997 to 304 in 1998. The corresponding numbers at UC San Diego were 374 and 226; at UC Davis 504 and 354; and at UC Santa Barbara 442 and 374.[404]

Not surprisingly, these statistics prompted the indignation of preferential policy advocates who characterized Prop 209 as proof that white America was intent on denying blacks the opportunity to attend college. Jesse Jackson, urging Americans to "pursue the dream of an inclusive society,"[405] charged that California schools were "cleansing" themselves of black students.[406] In a similar vein, television personality and editorialist Cokie Roberts called the decline in black representation at Berkeley "not just wrong," but "dangerous."[407] "The white students who were admitted," she wrote, "will miss an important part of their educational experience."[408] Minority communities, she added, would not only be left with a dearth of successful role models for their young people,[409] but would "have less access to the rights and services they deserve."[410] Theodore Mitchell, vice-chancellor of UCLA, lamented what he called "the real danger . . . that the University of California system will become a segregated system."[411] Berkeley chancellor Robert Berdahl called the drop in his school's black freshman enrollments "grim," adding that "it isn't easy to put a positive light on this."[412] Dana Inman, director of Berkeley's Black Recruitment and Retention Center, warned black students considering applying to her school that "it's a very hostile environment here and . . . we [blacks] are not welcome here because they're not letting us in."[413] Inman's colleague Jimar Wilson added that "if the university does not want people like me anymore, that means I'm unwanted."[414]

Many students shared the sentiments of these opinion shapers. Said one Berkeley senior, affirmative action's elimination "sends a strong message that the school is going to cater to a certain population and not open itself to the diverse population that is out there."[415] A prospective applicant of Mexican descent added, "Since I was a little kid I've wanted to go to Berkeley. With affirmative action gone, part of me wishes I was born a little earlier. There are people with much worse grades who got in last year. But it's going to be harder for me."[416] These statements drip with not only with a sense of entitlement, but with an utter absence of concern for merit.

Curiously, none of these affirmative action boosters chose to point out that under the new race-neutral standards, *not a single* California student—white, black, or any other color—had protested that he or she was denied admission to law school because of race.[417] In other words, the merit-based system had eliminated from students' minds the nagging suspicion that not everyone was being judged by a single standard. Moreover, no one in the "civil rights" crowd mentioned that although black enrollment had in fact dropped at some schools, it had simultaneously *risen* at others. For example, while Berkeley Law admitted fewer blacks in 1997 than in prior years, black representation in Berkeley's journalism program *tripled*. Meanwhile the black presence at UC San Diego's law school grew substantially, the number of blacks in UC Riverside's graduate school doubled, and black undergraduates at UC Irvine increased by 47 percent over two years. Similarly, though the number of blacks attending the University of Texas at Austin declined in 1997, the University of Houston had 15 percent *more* blacks than the previous year.[418] The new rules, then, did not in any way bar minority students from attending college, but simply required them to redistribute themselves among institutions and fields of study where they met the same academic standards as their white and Asian peers.[419]

Contrary to this reality, however, our racial racketeers consistently claim that black Americans will never be able to participate fully in academia without the aid of preferences and lowered standards. And while this prediction's inherent premise clearly degrades blacks, it is quite obviously the philosophical underpinning of affirmative action. Viewing blacks as damaged—and therefore incompetent—victims, "civil rights" advocates rarely, if ever, suggest that true justice and equal opportunity might best be achieved by maintaining high standards for all. Indeed, the belief that we are demonstrating "compassion" by not requiring blacks to perform up to the level of whites and Asians is one of modern America's most destructive myths. In the names of nondiscrimination and fairness, affirmative action is firmly rooted in discrimination, injustice, and condescension.

The same critics who condemned Prop 209 also denounced a similar bill, known as Initiative 200, that became law in Washington state two years later.[420] Likewise, they disapproved of a 1998 federal appeals court decision striking down racial preferences at the prestigious Boston Latin High School. Because that ruling expanded the affirmative action debate into the realm of public school systems, its implications for the future are potentially far-reaching. Hundreds of school districts nationwide are currently under court orders to implement racial preferences that facilitate desegregation, and the Boston decision may set a precedent for ending such policies everywhere. "This puts a further stake in the heart of the diversity rationale," lamented Terence J. Pell of the Center for Individual Rights in Washington.[421] "I'm very concerned that [this decision] could lead to racial isolation, resegregation, and less educational opportunity for minority children," added Jeff Simering, director of legislation at the Council of the Great City Schools.[422]

Policies that presume blacks incapable of succeeding without preferential treatment deny the enormous store of intellectual resources in the black community. They are policies founded on the mindset that Booker T. Washington identified when he wrote, long before affirmative action was ever contemplated, "When a white boy undertakes a task, it is taken for granted that he will succeed. On the other hand, people are usually surprised if the Negro boy does not fail. In a word, the Negro youth starts out with the presumption against him."[423] Washington maintained that hard work, not preferential treatment, was the key to black success. "Every persecuted individual and race," he wrote, "should get much consolation out of the great human law, which is universal and eternal, that merit, no matter under what skin found, is in the long run, recognized and rewarded. This I have said here, not to call attention to myself as an individual, but to the race to which I am proud to belong."[424]

While some may deem such sentiments nothing more than fanciful musings from which inconsequential idealism is woven, there is compelling evidence that blacks—treated not as victims but as competent human beings—are quite capable of performing at an intellectually high level. Consider the case of Chattanooga, Tennessee's six Paideia schools—named after the Greek word meaning "the upbringing of a child." Founded in the 1980s by Mortimer Adler and a number of fellow educators, these schools require all pupils in each class to study the same rigorous curriculum and to attain high levels of mastery. The results have been nothing short of spectacular. In this largely minority district—once regarded as "an academic basket case"[425]—

student scores are now among the highest in the state. Imbued with a genuine love for study, some 98 percent of these students later go on to attend college. Parents have been known to camp out for more than a week in the long enrollment lines to secure a place for their children in these schools.[426] Other Paideia schools have sprung up in Florida, Kentucky, North Carolina, Virginia, Arkansas, Colorado, Illinois, Ohio, New York, Washington, and Alaska.

The Paideia schools, it should be noted, are by no means unique in their achievements. There have been many black schools—both public and private, and some in the very heart of America's poorest ghettos—where students' standardized-test scores have exceeded the national average.[427] Consider, for instance, the storied success of Chicago's Westside Preparatory School, founded by Marva Collins, which became a testament to the benefits of a demanding educational environment. Teaching a mostly black, inner-city population, Ms. Collins pushed her students far beyond the intellectual limits usually thought possible for small children. She exposed students as young as four and five years old to the works of such authors as Shakespeare, Tolstoy, and Twain. To children a bit older, she introduced the likes of Aristophanes, Plato, Voltaire, Dostoyevsky, Sophocles, and Chaucer.[428]

As long ago as 1899, the mostly lower-class black teenagers attending Washington, D.C.'s Dunbar High School (which was originally named the M Street School) achieved higher standardized-test scores than two-thirds of the city's white pupils. From its 1870 inception through the mid-1950s, Dunbar was renowned as an extraordinary school, its quality evidenced by the fact that a majority of its students went on to higher education at a time when few blacks elsewhere did. A rigorous curriculum coupled with strict requirements for attendance and punctuality were Dunbar's hallmarks.[429]

On the college level, Georgia Institute of Technology (GIT) recently adopted a philosophy similar to that of Dunbar, Westside Prep, and the Paideia schools. In 1989, GIT's minority-education office concluded that its traditional remediation program had failed to improve the academic performance of black and Hispanic students because it expected too little of them. Resolving to raise expectations, school officials instituted a Challenge Program requiring minority students to achieve the same levels of mastery as their white peers. Under this initiative, incoming black and Hispanic freshmen were put through a rigorous, five-week summer course that demanded their hard work and dedication. Within a short time, the school's nonwhite attrition rate dropped to almost zero, while the overall performance gap between minority and white engineering students disappeared. Today more than 70 percent of GIT's black and Hispanic engineering majors eventually graduate—a rate twice as high as that of their nonwhite counterparts at other schools. The results have been so dramatic, in fact, that a number of colleges nationwide are now instituting their own Challenge Programs.[430] GIT's outgoing president, John Patrick Crecine, explained the remarkable improvement in student performance: "The change was in us and what we told them we expected of them. In the past we told them they were dumb, that they needed fixing, and we had them in remedial programs."[431]

Georgia Tech's new academic atmosphere is rare in the education of American minority students. Far more typical are scenarios like that of a Washington, D.C.-area university which recently advised all incoming black and Hispanic freshmen not only to register for the school's multicultural tutoring program,[432] but also to take a light course load—based on the assumption that "they won't do well if they take a difficult program."[433]

Black students *deserve* to be held to the same high academic standards normally reserved for whites and Asians. In the long run, artificial "propping up" only *harms* its recipients, whatever their race. Shelby Steele eloquently describes the mindset of dependence and entitlement that is the curse of any program allocating aid to people based on the color of their skin:

> Blacks . . . [are] seen as generally "less than" others. Their needs are "special," "unique," "different." They are seen exclusively along the dimension of their victimization, so they become "different" people with whom whites can negotiate entitlements, but never fully see as people like themselves. . . . This, of course, is not racism, and yet it has the same effect as racism since it makes blacks something of a separate species for whom normal standards and values do not automatically apply.
>
> Nowhere is this more evident today than in American universities. At some of America's most elite universities, administrators have granted concessions in response to black student demands . . . that all but sanction racial separatism on campus—black "theme" dorms, black student unions, black yearbooks, homecoming dances, and so on. I don't believe administrators really believe in these

separatist concessions. Most of them are liberals who see racial separatism as wrong. But black student demands pull them into the paradigm of self-preoccupied white guilt whereby they see a quick redemption by offering special entitlements that go beyond fairness. In this black students become invisible to them. Though blacks have the lowest grade-point-average of any group in American universities, administrators never sit down with them and "demand" in kind that they bring their grades up to par. . . . [T]here is little difference between giving black students a separate graduation ceremony or student lounge and leaving twenty dollars in the tip plate on the way out the door.

What demonstrates more than anything the degree to which university administrations (and faculties) have been subdued by this paradigm is their refusal to lead black students, to tell them what they honestly think, to insist that they perform at a higher level, and to ask them to integrate themselves fully into campus life. This marks the difference between self-preoccupied guilt and the guilt of genuine concern. . . . The former grants entitlements, [and] the latter . . . demands black development.

[P]olicies whereby institutions favor black entitlement over development . . . have, I believe, a dispiriting impact on blacks. Such policies have the effect of transforming whites from victimizers into patrons and keeping blacks where they have always been—dependent on the largesse of whites. This was made evident in a famous statement by Lyndon Johnson at Howard University in 1965: "You do not take a person who, for years, has been hobbled by chains and liberate him, bring him up to the starting line of a race and then say, 'You're free to compete with others,' and justly believe that you have been fair."

On its surface this seems to be the most reasonable of statements, but on closer examination we can see how it deflects the emphasis away from black responsibility and toward white responsibility. . . . [It portrays blacks as] passive recipients of white action. The former victimizers are challenged now to be patrons, but where is the black challenge? . . . Nowhere in this utterance does President Johnson show respect for black resilience, or faith in the capacity of blacks to run fast once they get to the "starting line." This statement . . . had the two ever-present signposts of white guilt—white self-preoccupation and black invisibility. . . .

[A]ffirmative action . . . offers entitlements, rather than development, to blacks. A preference is not a training program; it teaches no skills, instills no values. It only makes a color a passport. But the worst aspect of racial preferences is that they encourage dependency on entitlements rather than on our own initiative, a situation that has already led many blacks to believe that we cannot have fairness without entitlements. . . .

Preferential treatment, no matter how it is justified in the light of-day, subjects blacks to a midnight of self-doubt. . . . [I]t indirectly encourages blacks to exploit their own past victimization as a source of power and privilege. Victimization, like implied inferiority, is what justifies preference, so that to receive the benefits of preferential treatment one must, to some extent, become invested in the view of one's self as a victim. In this way, affirmative action nourishes a victim-focused identity in blacks. The obvious irony here is that we become inadvertently invested in the very condition we are trying to overcome. Racial preferences send us the message that there is more power in our past suffering than our present achievements— none of which could bring us a *preference* over others.

When power itself grows out of suffering, then blacks are encouraged to expand the boundaries of what qualifies as racial oppression, a situation that can lead us to paint our victimization in vivid colors, even as we receive the benefits of preference. The same corporations and institutions that give us preference are also seen as our oppressors. At Stanford University minority students— some of whom enjoy as much as $15,000 a year in financial aid— recently took over the president's office demanding, among other things, more financial aid. The power to be found in victimization, like any other power, is intoxicating and can lend itself to the creation of a new class of super-victims who can feel the pea of victimization under twenty mattresses. Preferential treatment rewards us for being underdogs rather than for moving beyond that status. . . .

But, I think, one of the worst prices that blacks pay for preference has to do with an illusion. I saw this illusion at work recently in the mother of a middle-class black student who was going off to his first semester of college. "They owe us this, so don't think for a minute that you don't belong there." This is the logic by which many blacks, and some whites, justify affirmative action—it is something "owed," a form of reparation. But this logic overlooks a much harder and less digestible reality, that it is impossible to repay blacks living today for the historic suffering of the race. If all blacks were given a million dollars tomorrow morning it would not amount to a dime on the dollar of three centuries of oppression, nor would it obviate the residues of that oppression that we still carry today. The concept of historic reparation grows out of man's need to impose a degree of justice on the world that simply does not exist. Suffering can be endured and overcome, it cannot be repaid. Blacks cannot be repaid for the injustice done to the race, but we can be corrupted by society's guilty gestures of repayment.

Affirmative action is such a gesture. It tells us that racial preferences can do for us what we cannot do for ourselves. The corruption here is in the hidden incentive *not* to do what we believe preferences will do. This is an incentive to be reliant on others just as we are struggling for self-reliance. And it keeps alive the illusion that we can find some deliverance in repayment. The hardest thing for any sufferer to accept is that his suffering excuses him from very little and never has enough currency to restore him. To think otherwise is to prolong the suffering. . . .

[P]referential treatment does not teach skills, or educate, or instill motivation. It only passes out entitlement by color, . . . [but] entitlement by color is not a social program; it is a dubious reward for being black.[434]

Chapter 10

The Disaster of
Preferential Policies

*A universal human stupidity is the belief that our
neighbor's success is the cause of our failure.*
—Charles V. Roman[1]

"Too white and too male" was how a female commissioner at
New York's Human Resources Administration characterized the list
of HRA employees eligible for promotions in 1993.[2] To "rectify" the
racial makeup of the list, she and her fellow HRA officials manipu-
lated civil service rules so that blacks and Hispanics could be promoted over whites who outscored them on an exam normally used to
determine career advancement. "This is sheer racism," said George
Silberman, a white supervisor who was denied promotion. "They're
passing over people who they say don't meet their standards of sensitivity, when every manager who has evaluated me for the past four or
five years has been black or Hispanic and all my evaluations have
been outstanding." A black president of the Social Service Employees Union concurred that the HRA was principally concerned with
"diversity" and simply "didn't care about the quality of people's service."[3]

Mr. Silberman, like so many of his colleagues, was a casualty of racial quotas—the messy by-product of affirmative action, a policy which during the past quarter of a century has affected millions of workers in both the public and private sectors. An amazing case involving the Boston Fire Department (BFD) in the mid-1970s illustrates the extent to which race had already, by that time, supplanted competence as a primary hiring consideration. A pair of white identical twins, Philip and Paul Malone, each failed the BFD's qualification test in 1975 and consequently were dropped from the applicant pool. Two years later they took the test again—at a time when the fire department was under pressure from a court-ordered affirmative action plan to hire more minorities. In a devious attempt to exploit this judicial mandate, the Malones now classified themselves as black—claiming to have discovered in 1976 that their great-grandmother, who was long dead, was of African ancestry. Their exam scores this time around were 57 and 69 percent, respectively—far below the 82 percent cutoff point for white applicants, but more than sufficient for black applicants. Thus the fire department immediately hired the "black" Malone twins.[4]

Another classic example of affirmative action's workings involved the San Francisco Fire Department (SFFD), which had a longstanding tradition of periodically testing large groups of applicants and hiring those who scored best. The test had two parts—one physical and one written—with the latter accounting for 60 percent of each applicant's score.[5] In 1982 a court determined that there were not enough minorities in the department and ordered that more be hired to "correct" this shortage—even though there was no evidence that the existing racial imbalance was due to any past discrimination. In response to the court order, the SFFD aggressively recruited and preregistered a multitude of blacks for the test. But because only 20 percent of them actually followed through and took the exam, the number of minorities who received passing grades fell far short of the court's prescription. Thus the fire department, desperate to hire as many nonwhites as possible, lowered its cutoff score for the written test by 14 percent. When this lowered standard still yielded too few minorities with passing grades, the results of the written test were disregarded altogether. White, black, and Hispanic applicants were then ranked on the basis of the physical test alone—but only against others of the same racial and ethnic backgrounds. The department then hired equal numbers of candidates from each of the three lists, even though many of the minorities who were hired in this manner scored substantially lower than whites who were rejected.[6] This practice of ranking job candidates only in relation to other applicants of the same race or ethnicity is called race-norming, which by the mid-1980s had become standard procedure for some forty state governments and countless private companies.[7] Before it was outlawed in 1991, race-norming had been used to adjust the job-application scores of at least sixteen million people.[8]

Following the discovery of the SFFD's overall racial imbalance, it was also found that whites in the department historically had been promoted in significantly greater numbers than blacks—not because of any chicanery, but simply because the former tended to outscore the latter on tests used to determine promotions. Yet even though no intentional discrimination could be proven, a court now mandated that the SFFD promote more blacks—so as to "rectify" the existing imbalance. Thus a special grading system was devised, allowing blacks to be promoted even over whites who scored much higher. Moreover, blacks who had failed the old, "discriminatory" test were now given jobs *and* back pay—based on the logic that they "should" have passed the first time.[9]

Indeed, racial and ethnic-group preferences have become commonplace in fire and police departments across the United States. In 1985, an appellate court in Cleveland ordered that white and minority firefighters be promoted in equal numbers—notwithstanding the fact that whites tended to score much higher on exams designed to measure the job-related knowledge and skills of each applicant. Rejecting the idea that affirmative action should be used only to compensate *specific* individuals who had been personally discriminated against,[10] the court instead ruled that just being nonwhite was enough to qualify a person for special treatment—even if that person had not suffered a single discriminatory act in his or her life. More recently, a Hispanic lieutenant in Miami candidly explained that his city's fire department hired 60 percent Hispanics "regardless of qualifications. . . . They just have people take a test, and they pick minorities [even] from the bottom of the list."[11] Meanwhile, California's diversity-conscious San Jose Fire Department hired only one of the more than 2,000 white males who applied for jobs in 1992, though many of them had better qualifications than the 21 minorities who were hired.[12]

Two years later, the Los Angeles Fire Department did not even feign an effort to judge all applicants by a single standard. Under great pressure to hire more blacks and Hispanics, the LAFD simply turned away 10,000 whites who wanted to take the firefighters' exam in 1994.[13]

What impact must such policies have on white employees' perceptions of, and suspicions about, the minorities who work alongside them? Could anything be more degrading to those minorities? And above all, what kind of society are we creating when we accept an arrangement by which marginally qualified people are hired over those more qualified, simply because of their skin color or ethnic background?

Because white job applicants frequently score higher on employment tests than their minority rivals, advocates of preferences often allege that the tests themselves discriminate in favor of whites and are therefore invalid. Consider the case of the Newark Fire Department, which traditionally administered a written exam and a three-part physical test to rate prospective firefighters. This system went unchallenged until 1991, when the apostles of "equity" pointed out that whites were consistently outscoring blacks and Hispanics on two portions of the physical test—a platform climb and a tunnel crawl. Reasoning that this "disparate impact" had caused nonwhites to be underrepresented in the department, a federal judge concluded that the overall test was somehow flawed. As a "remedy," he ordered that all future applicants be judged only by their scores on the written exam and the obstacle course, where there was no racial or ethnic disparity in performance.[14] Similar logic formed the basis of a federal court's order that the Detroit Police Department use a rigid race-norming formula to determine all promotions. In accordance with this order, black and white candidates were thereafter ranked on separate lists and were promoted in equal numbers.[15]

Sometimes police and fire departments initiate aggressive minority-hiring campaigns in reaction to public criticism or pressure from the "civil rights" cabal. Such was the case a few years ago in New York City, where blacks comprise 25 percent of the population but only 13.4 percent of the police force.[16] Despite the NYPD's explanation that, for whatever reasons, comparatively few blacks tend to apply for police jobs, many critics have charged that blacks are systematically excluded from the department by racists within it. In response to such allegations, then-police commissioner Raymond Kelly postponed the October 1992 police entry examination for six months so that recruiters might have more time to attract black applicants.[17]

Race: the Measure of All Things?

Because traditional measures of merit must be discredited in order for preferential policies to be deemed morally justifiable, it is not surprising that proponents of affirmative action now characterize even the most reasonable job standards as "biased." Consider, for instance, that in most cases employers cannot automatically reject applicants with past criminal convictions or dishonorable discharges from the military. The Equal Employment Opportunity Commission (EEOC) has ruled that disqualifying job candidates on either basis is unfair to blacks, because blacks are statistically more likely than whites to have such marks on their records.[18] According to the EEOC, hiring decisions based on these criteria would have a disparate impact on African Americans and thus may be considered racist. This tortured logic demonstrates that the EEOC has wandered far from the path of common sense—forcing employers to treat each applicant not as an individual but as a representative of his or her particular race. Such thinking is clearly the antithesis of what Martin Luther King, Jr. envisioned. It would be laughable, were it not so tragic, to hear the very people professing loyalty to Dr. King's dream espousing policies that desecrate the spirit of that dream.

A job applicant's prior criminal history is by no means the only personal information that most employers must disregard when making hiring decisions. The EEOC has also declared it unlawful to deny employment on the basis of an applicant's general appearance, dress, manner of speaking, credit history, previous arrests for gambling, status as an unwed mother, or even *personal work habits*—unwittingly implying that nonwhites are incapable of measuring up to society's traditional norms.[19] It would be difficult to imagine a more condescending view of minorities, yet this very perspective underlies preferential policy programs all over this country.

Equating random statistical inequalities with intentional discrimination, the EEOC uses an 80 percent formula to enforce proportional representation. Suppose, for example, that in a given geographic area blacks comprise 10 percent of all residents. Under the 80 percent rule, an employer in that area must ensure that at least 8 percent of his recruits are black. In other words, the proportion of recruits who are black must equal at least four-fifths the percentage of blacks in the larger population.[20] A company's failure to abide by this formula alerts EEOC officials that "something is wrong" with its hiring practices.[21] Even a firm that employs an abundance of nonwhites in blue-collar jobs may be investigated for discrimination if a disproportionately low number of minorities hold *white*-collar or supervisory positions.[22] Former EEOC chairman Eleanor Holmes Norton set this foreboding tone when she warned employers that her office would sue them if their work forces were not racially "balanced."[23]

It should be noted that the EEOC has grown, since its establishment in 1964, from a five-member entity to its current size of nearly three thousand full-time employees with an annual budget of $220 million.[24] Focusing heavily on "goals and timetables," this agency requires businesses to "remedy" the underrepresentation of employees from "protected classes."[25] If an employer fails to "balance" his work force within a specified time period, he can expect large cash penalties and the loss of contracts. The EEOC will simply conclude, in such cases, that "[t]he effectiveness, thoroughness, and frequency of whatever efforts the [employer] was making . . . fall short of what is necessary."[26] As Professor Nathan Glazer observes, the only safe solution for an employer is proportional hiring. "Every employer worth his salt," writes Glazer, "knows that . . . the EEOC . . . and the rest of the agencies are urging [him to hire by quotas], while they simultaneously explain that they have nothing of the sort in mind."[27] As of 1989, the EEOC had settled more than 250,000 complaints in favor of plaintiffs, and filed nearly 90,000 cases in federal courts.[28]

For skeptics who doubt that the EEOC actually wants companies to enforce strict racial quotas, a recent case involving the Chicago-based Daniel Lamp Company should prove instructive. Located in a predominantly Hispanic neighborhood, this company employed twenty-six workers—twenty-one Hispanics and five blacks—in the early 1990s. Based on the demographics of the surrounding region, however, EEOC officials calculated that Lamp should have employed precisely 8.45 black workers. Thus, as a penalty for having "discriminated," the company was ordered to give $123,000 in back pay to a number of black applicants who were previously denied jobs.[29]

Similarly, in 1994 the federal government pressured the

University of California at San Diego (UCSD) into paying $600,000 to twenty-seven previously rejected black job applicants. This money was paid even though the school's vice-chancellor, who was black, insisted that race had played no role in UCSD's hiring decisions. The problem, he explained, was that the job applicants in question simply lacked the requisite skills.[30] That same year San Diego's Marriott Hotel agreed to pay $627,000 to thirty-four black women whose job applications had been turned down. The settlement required Marriott not only to offer the women jobs immediately, but also to give them on-the-job training and credit for whatever vacation time and sick leave they might otherwise have accrued.[31]

Few Americans realize just how intimately the federal government is involved in the administration of preferential policy programs. The U.S. Labor Department, for instance, flatly denies government contracts to companies that do not practice affirmative action.[32] Every public school system and every business—public, private, and non-profit—with fifteen or more employees must file EEOC forms detailing the racial makeup of its work force.[33] Eighty-six percent of the entire nonfarm private-sector labor force is affected by this EEOC regulation.[34] To monitor compliance, the Labor Department dispatches hundreds of inspectors to aggressively pressure employers to rectify situations where there are "not enough" nonwhites.[35] Any company that is instructed to hire more minorities must, according to federal guidelines, develop "diversity" objectives that are "significant, measurable, attainable, and planned for specific results."[36] Contracts may be cancelled if the goals and timetables are not met. Each year thousands of discrimination cases are filed in federal courts with EEOC clearance, and thousands more are resolved through what author Dinesh D'Souza aptly calls "strong-arm negotiation."[37]

A watchdog sub-agency within the Labor Department is the Office of Federal Contract Compliance Programs (OFCCP), always on the lookout for companies with an underrepresentation of minority employees. To satisfy OFCCP requirements, every company with federal contracts exceeding $50,000 must follow race-preference regulations,[38] as must every local government, police department, and college that receives federal money.[39] More than 400,000 corporations that do business with the U.S. government must file with the OFCCP and abide by the regulations in its 700-page rule book.[40] Each year the OFCCP conducts compliance reviews of at least 4,000 of these firms, most of which are investigated not because anyone has complained of discrimination, but because the agency's computer checks indicate an "under-utilization" of minorities.[41] If an OFCCP officer deems a company's affirmative action program inadequate, he may conduct an on-site, unannounced inspection of the premises.[42] The OFCCP currently has about 800 employees and an annual budget of $50 million.[43]

Affirmative action's voluminous regulations and the bureaucracies they spawn impose a heavy financial burden on society and require countless thousands of hours to administer. For example, an average OFCCP construction-industry audit takes 52 hours to complete. Nonconstruction audits require about 141 hours apiece, while university audits demand some 427 hours each.[44] All told, there are currently 160 separate federal-government preferences, requiring thousands of agencies and more than 100,000 government lawyers, investigators, and agents to enforce.[45] Indeed, affirmative action has become a monstrous money pit that swallows up rivers of taxpayer dollars on a daily basis. American companies are forced to spend some $30 billion annually on remedial training for employees hired solely for the sake of "diversity." Additional billions are lost due to the comparative ineptitude of workers hired under artificially low standards. According to a report in *Forbes* magazine, the impact of preferential policies "may easily have already depressed the GNP [Gross National Product] by a staggering four percentage points—about as much as we spend on the entire public school system."[46]

Affirmative action is just as wasteful in education as in business. Consider the San Francisco public school system, which, after being sued repeatedly by the NAACP in the late 1970s, signed a desegregation consent decree that set rigid guidelines for the racial composition of each school's student body. Since that time, the city has spent more than $250 million on efforts to enforce racial quotas in its schools. In the 1993-1994 school year alone, consent-decree spending was $32.7 million, or 7 percent of the total education budget. Yet no academic benefits have resulted from these expenditures. Currently, the average grade for black students in the city's public schools is D-plus, and San Francisco ranks 54th out of 57 counties statewide in achievement-test scores.[47]

Set-Asides and Related Policies

The 1980s saw not only the rise of race-norming, but also of "set-aside" schemes under which federal, state, and local governments reserved a predetermined percentage of contracts for companies owned by nonwhites or women—regardless of whether any white male-owned companies could have provided the same services less expensively or with higher quality. As of 1989, some 36 states and 190 local governments had such programs in place.[48]

Set-asides typically earmark at least 10 percent of all contracts for minority-owned firms, which in turn are required to give 100 percent of their subcontract work to other minority-owned companies. This requirement applies even in places where there are few, if any, nonwhite subcontractors available to bid on the work. One corporate executive, for instance, explains that his firm was unable to bid for two multimillion-dollar projects "because we were unable to obtain any response whatsoever from qualified minority contractors to do any subcontract-type work."[49]

This preoccupation with racial quotas formed its roots decades ago. As long ago as 1971, an official from the Department of Health, Education and Welfare announced that "government contractors [must] consider other factors than mere technical qualifications."[50] In other words, wasted money and shoddy work could be tolerated so long as the end result was greater "diversity." Because set-asides allot contracts based on minority status—rather than on efficiency, quality, or cost—they are breeding grounds for duplicity. White-run businesses have often fraudulently claimed black ownership so as to take advantage of set-asides. Many black-owned companies have been established for the same purpose—even if they lacked the ability and resources to adequately complete the jobs on which they placed bids.[51]

A 1989 Supreme Court ruling restricted set-asides on the state level but had no effect on Section 8(a) of the Small Business Act, which grants companies owned by "economically disadvantaged" minorities access to government service contracts without competition.[52] By definition, of course, white-owned firms are not disadvantaged.[53] Thus while 8(a) may, at first glance, appear to be a noble effort to help the truly needy, closer scrutiny reveals it to be nothing more than a preferential policy that rewards people for having nonwhite skin. Though 8(a) stipulates that each of its beneficiaries must have a net worth of less than $250,000 (excluding home and business equity), this restriction is regularly ignored. A recent audit found that some 70 percent of all 8(a) beneficiaries had net worths exceeding $1 million. Thus a program purporting to aid the "disadvantaged" actually helps those who are already relatively affluent. In 1994 alone, 8(a) granted $5.5 billion worth of contracts to 5,400 minority-owned businesses.[54]

By eliminating competition, 8(a) all but guarantees that tax-payer money will be squandered on a grand scale—as in 1995, when the Department of Defense reserved fully 35 percent of its construction projects for minority-owned firms, two-thirds of which were not even required to submit competitive bids.[55] Set-aside programs are also utilized by the Departments of Energy and State, the National Aeronautics and Space Administration (NASA), the Federal Communications Commission, and virtually every division of the U.S. government.[56] Unfortunately, 8(a) is susceptible to the same abuses that plague most other set-aside arrangements. All types of fly-by-night operations have been formed for the sole purpose of exploiting the program, turning quick profits and then closing up shop. A recent survey of companies that the Small Business Administration listed as "current" 8(a) beneficiaries found that 22 percent either could not be reached or had ceased operations.[57]

In 1991 the U.S. Congress passed a Civil Rights Act designed to strengthen affirmative action programs and ban job standards that were anything above the bare minimum. The new law decreed that employers with fifteen or more workers would be considered "guilty until proven innocent" of discrimination if their labor force did not statistically resemble the demographic makeup of the surrounding community. Consequently, any employer with a "racially unbalanced" work force must now show that the job qualifications he requires are not excessive. He must be able to demonstrate not only a business purpose for his standards, but also that those standards could not be replaced by others "that would be just as efficacious for the business purpose but have a lesser racial impact."[58] If he cannot prove his case, he is subject to large punitive damages and may be ordered to keep detailed records of how many blacks he interviews and hires for future job openings. In fact, even if he is *acquitted* of discrimination charges, he may nonetheless have to pay a penalty if his hiring criteria are anything more than minimal.[59] Faced with the terrifying prospect of frivolous discrimination suits that could spell their financial ruin, business owners know that hiring by race is the only safe course to follow.[60] Moreover, because the law specifically exempts businesses with fewer than fifteen employees, small companies actually have an incentive to limit their growth so as to avoid potential problems.[61]

The 1991 Civil Rights Act, it should be noted, also struck a rhetorical blow *against* quotas by banning race-norming. The practical significance of this ban, however, was largely nullified by the new law's added stipulation that disparate impact would thereafter be illegal. In other words, employers would still be required to maintain racially balanced work forces—but to do so via some method other than race-norming. Many firms, therefore, stopped administering standardized tests and began relying more heavily on subjective criteria that allowed greater freedom to select job applicants by race.[62] Meanwhile, Americans were apparently expected to overlook even the most blatant examples of racial preferences. For instance, when a California transit executive observed that some "inept" minorities had been hired under affirmative action, he was promptly suspended from his job and was given "sensitivity and awareness training."[63]

Incredibly, the very legislators who wrote the 1991 Civil Rights Act exempted themselves from the suffocating standards foisted upon all other Americans. Senator Warren Rudman of New Hampshire, making his case for the Congressional exemption, warned that the bill would surely encourage frivolous lawsuits against Congress. Thus he deemed it "absolutely essential that, as to our legislative employees, we have an absolute right without outside review by anyone of what we do."[64] Senator George Mitchell agreed that he and his colleagues should be unencumbered by the mandates of civil rights legislation:

> It has been said here many times tonight that we want to make the Senate the same as everyone else, that we want to treat Senators the same as everyone else, that we want to have the Senate treated the same as the private sector. Mr. President, not a single Senator believes that. Not a single Senator wants that.[65]

Defining Discrimination

People in public office commonly find it difficult to abide by the rules they set for the rest of society. This is well illustrated by the case of Ruth Bader Ginsburg, President Clinton's 1993 Supreme Court appointee, who has consistently supported judicial rulings equating minority underrepresentation in a given company's work force with illegal discrimination. During her Senate confirmation hearings, Justice Ginsburg was asked by Senator Orrin Hatch:

> Suppose a small business in a major city that was majority black had never hired a black person, even though that business, in over a decade, had hired more than fifty people. Further suppose that a disappointed black job applicant filed a discrimination suit, but he or she was unable to provide any direct evidence of intentional discrimination by the employer. Would such statistics, standing alone, in your view justify an inference of racial discrimination?[66]

Ginsburg replied that such a statistical disparity was most certainly evidence of discrimination, which, she explained, could be a subtle transgression. Senator Hatch then informed Ginsburg that if an employee in this scenario were to file a discrimination lawsuit based on the aforementioned statistics alone, the business owner would not only be required to defend himself against the charge, but would be considered guilty until proven innocent. Noting that the average defense in such cases costs $80,000, Hatch explained that even groundless suits could financially ruin an honest, ethical business. Finally, the senator pointed out that Justice Ginsburg herself, over the course of thirteen years as a judge in predominantly-black Washington, D.C., had hired fifty-seven law clerks, not a single one of whom was black. He elaborated:

> Now I find no fault with that because I know you had no desire to discriminate. Even though your court sits in the middle of a majority black city, Washington, D.C. The crucial point to keep in mind, however, is that when the concept of discrimination is divorced from intent and we rely on statistics alone, a small business man or woman might find him or herself spending hundreds of thousands of dollars to fend off suits, and in fact, that is what's happening around this country right now.[67]

Discrimination lawsuits—even those with no merit—can financially devastate not only small businesses, but large corporations as well. Consider Liberty National Bank and Trust Company of Louisville, Kentucky, which in 1989 made a determined effort to recruit as many black clerks and tellers as possible. Of the 200 employees the bank hired that year, 16 percent were black—a proportion exceeding that of blacks in the Louisville work force as a whole. Nonetheless, when the Labor Department learned that fully 32 percent of all Liberty National job applicants in 1989 were black, it deemed the 16 percent figure inadequate and ordered the bank to give jobs and more than $250,000 in "lost earnings" to some of the very same blacks who previously had been rejected.[68] Thus, Liberty National was punished even though its aggressive pursuit of black employees had been, if anything, discriminatory against *whites*.

Employers charged with discrimination can suffer huge financial losses even if they disprove the allegations against them. For example, by the time a court cleared Sears Roebuck of any wrongdoing in a 1985 discrimination lawsuit filed by the EEOC, the company had already paid more than $20 million for its legal defense—against unfounded charges.[69] As noted earlier, most companies have opted to avoid the risk of incurring such expenses by simply hiring according to skin color—regardless of whether such a policy requires them to employ a certain number of underqualified or incompetent workers.[70]

Some businesses, unlike Sears, elect to settle their lawsuits outside of court. Typical was a 1991 arrangement in which Northwest Airlines, which was charged with discrimination based solely on the numerical underrepresentation of nonwhites in its work force, agreed to: (a) finance scholarships for black trainees; (b) spend $3.5 million on programs that would accelerate the hiring and promotion of African Americans; and (c) pay hundreds of thousands of dollars to blacks who claimed discrimination. Notably, the company did all this while maintaining that it had not discriminated; the settlement was simply a comparatively cheap, quick alternative to a costly trial.[71] Many other corporations have gone this same route in recent discrimination cases brought by the EEOC: General Electric settled for $32 million, Ford for $23 million, and General Motors for more than $42 million.[72]

These amounts, however, were dwarfed by Texaco's $176 million settlement of a 1997 lawsuit brought by six black employees. The suit was founded largely on the contents of some secretly recorded audiotapes of a high-level Texaco official supposedly referring to blacks as "jelly beans."[73] "You can't just have we and them," he was heard telling his colleagues. "You can't just have black jelly beans and other jelly beans. It just doesn't work."[74] Expert analysis of the tapes, however, quickly revealed that the "black jelly beans" remark, far from being racist, was nothing more than a derisive reference to the diversity training classes that Texaco had long been requiring its employees to attend—classes in which the instructors sometimes used different-colored jelly beans mingled together in bags as a means of illustrating "diversity issues." In fact, the supposedly offensive phrase had only become popular among Texaco executives after Roosevelt Thomas, Jr., the former president of the American Institute for Managing Diversity, had recommended it to them. Another taped remark about "the black jelly beans" being "glued to the bottom of the bag" was certainly insensitive, but no more so than Jesse Jackson's crude references to New York as "Hymietown" several years earlier. Yet with the self-righteous hypocrisy typical of contemporary demagogues, Jackson became Texaco's chief critic during the 1997 flap.[75]

Once we sift out the distortions and false reports, we find that the most disturbing element actually on the tapes was evidence seeming to suggest that company officials conspired to destroy documents pertinent to an employment discrimination suit that Texaco was fighting. Certainly such a charge, if true, warranted severe punishment, and indeed the final settlement terms were among the most exacting ever imposed on an American corporation. Texaco agreed, among other things, to set a 29 percent "goal" for minority employment; to finance additional internship and scholarship programs earmarked for nonwhites; to give an immediate 10 percent raise in salary to all blacks on the payroll; and to make a $70,000 lump-sum payment to *each* of 1,348 current and former employees—whether or not they had ever suffered even a single act of discrimination on the job.[76] Predictably, "civil rights leaders" pointed to the Texaco case as evidence that racism was still deeply entrenched in American business. It is curious, however, that not one of them lauded the large settlement as proof that racial discrimination has become morally intolerable to most Americans, and is thus punished severely. Nor did they tone down their outrage in May 1998 after a jury acquitted the Texaco executives of the conspiracy charge.[77]

Equal Opportunity and "Representation"

It is logically wrong and morally reprehensible to equate random statistical disparities with intentional discrimination. While real discrimination certainly occurs in America, its victims have powerful, legal means of redress. The courts have been punishing this transgression for a long time and will continue to do so.[78] Recent years, in fact, have seen discriminators penalized more heavily than ever before. Prior to the passage of the 1991 Civil Rights Act, discrimination cases were heard by federal judges who limited plaintiffs' awards to back pay and attorney fees.[79] The 1991 legislation, however, allowed for jury trials and large punitive damage awards.[80]

For the past three decades, perhaps the single greatest impediment to improved race relations has been the "civil rights" establishment's perverse redefinition of such words as "discrimination," "racism," "representation," and "disadvantaged." Determined to convince Americans that white malevolence is ever-expanding, the self-anointed messiahs of "justice" have cloaked their discussions of these terms in demagogic rhetoric. Thomas Sowell explains:

> The automatic equating of statistical disparities with "disadvantage" can . . . outlive historical reality for those groups that have in fact been historically disadvantaged in every sense. Because patterns of behavior differ so greatly among social groups, advantaged and disadvantaged cannot be reduced to merely statistical meanings. Some groups from various parts of the world have indeed been seriously disadvantaged relative to others, but there is no way to determine that, if the word "disadvantaged" becomes simply a synonym for substandard end-results, [or] if all substandard performances are covered by the blanket word "disadvantage".[81]

Statistical disparities occur naturally in every field of human endeavor—even where there is no trace of discrimination. For example, the National Basketball Association (NBA) and National Football League (NFL) are mostly comprised of black players. Were we to extend the logic of "civil rights leaders," we would be forced to conclude that whites and Asians are somehow "disadvantaged" by unfair NBA and NFL policies that favor blacks over all others. It is reasonable to wonder why the champions of "justice"—who ostensibly equate numerical imbalances with discrimination—never argue for affirmative action programs that might increase nonblack representation among professional basketball and football players.

The sports world offers many examples of statistical inequalities that occur without discriminatory intent. In the NBA, eight of the top ten career scorers are black, as are nine of the top ten career rebounders and shot-blockers.[82] By contrast, all major National Hockey League records are held by white players. Meanwhile, major league baseball's various statistical categories are dominated by players of different racial and ethnic backgrounds. Black players historically have hit significantly more home runs per times at bat than whites, and nearly twice as many as Latins; three of the four highest career home run totals were compiled by black players; the only three players ever to steal 100 or more bases in a season were black; seven of the nine best one-year slugging percentages belong to two players of German ancestry—Babe Ruth and Lou Gehrig; the ten highest single-season strikeout totals for pitchers were recorded by whites; and eight of the top ten career hit totals belong to whites.[83] Imagine the absurdity of trying to attribute each of these curiosities to various types of discrimination. Would anyone really suggest that players from ethnic groups that are underrepresented in particular statistical categories should receive preferential treatment from umpires and referees, so as to compensate those athletes for the "discrimination" they have presumably suffered? Should team owners make a conscious effort to acquire more players from underrepresented groups, even if it would mean diminishing their teams' overall quality?

Reaching Out in All Directions

Corporate America's aggressive pursuit of minority employees takes numerous forms. Many companies recruit extensively from black colleges,[84] publicize employment opportunities in periodicals geared toward blacks and Hispanics,[85] and even compile directories of minority organizations that might lead to contacts with potential nonwhite employees.[86] Since the 1970s, in fact, most major corporations and a host of smaller ones have implemented specific, wide-ranging strategies for recruiting minorities.[87] General Foods and Bristol-Myers Squibb, for instance, have programs devoted exclusively to finding and placing nonwhite job candidates.[88] With similar intent, AT&T has developed Project View, a program that introduces minority engineering majors to the research being done at Bell Labs and usually leads to summer jobs for the participating students.[89] In 1990, some 65 percent of DuPont's college recruits were women or minorities.[90] The following year, 43 percent of US West's newly hired college graduates were nonwhites,[91] as were 42 percent of all sales hires at General Mills in 1992.[92]

Large and small companies alike send representatives to minority job fairs and career days in hopes of attracting blacks and Hispanics to join their work forces. The catalogue of companies that regularly take part in such events is virtually endless. A few of the more well-known participants are Ameritech, Campbell Soup, Kellogg, Levi Strauss, Bell Atlantic, Metropolitan Life, Sony, Upjohn, Coca Cola, Dow Chemical, Borden, MCI, Procter & Gamble, Philip Morris, the *Washington Post*, Avon, Merrill Lynch, and Allstate.[93]

One of the most effective and popular methods by which companies recruit black employees is through their funding of internship programs, many of which are exclusively for nonwhite high-school and college students.[94] Interns are given temporary jobs with the sponsoring companies, are frequently paid competitive salaries,[95] sometimes receive monthly rent subsidies,[96] and may even be awarded scholarship money to cover future tuition costs.[97] The typical employer maintains close contact with his or her interns after their work periods are completed, hoping to hire them for permanent jobs after college. Blacks and Hispanics, of course, are particularly coveted for internship programs in today's diversity-conscious atmosphere. In 1991, more than 50 percent of US West's interns were minorities.[98]

A host of fellowship programs are also geared primarily toward black and Hispanic students. AT&T, for one, sponsors a Co-operative Research Fellowship Program that provides minority students with a yearly stipend of more than $13,000 plus money to cover the cost of tuition, books, and other educational expenses.[99] General Foods awards fellowships worth up to $50,000 apiece to help its minority employees earn graduate degrees, and then appoints these individuals to full-time management positions with the company.[100] Walt Disney Studios earmarks a number of fellowships for nonwhite writers and specifically requests that agents submit material written by minorities. Warner Brothers and 20th Century-Fox also have outreach programs that target black recruits.[101]

Because meeting affirmative action goals is one of corporate America's highest priorities, companies regularly review—and, where necessary, accelerate—their own progress in hiring, training, and promoting nonwhites.[102] The chairman of Polaroid recently expressed the sentiments of most corporate executives when he announced that his company was striving to be "the employer of choice for minorities."[103] Along the same lines, TRW's ambitious goal is to hire nonwhites at twice the rate of their present availability in the marketplace,[104] while Merck & Company proudly asserts that "hiring minorities for executive-level positions is an important part of the recruiting process."[105] A survey of *Fortune* 500 chief executive officers reveals that more than 70 percent engage in race-based hiring and only 14 percent hire strictly on merit.[106] Because the competition to acquire black workers is so intense, diversity-conscious companies are often forced to lure blacks away from rival firms.[107] Nearly half of CEOs surveyed complain that they have lost good minority employees to other companies.[108]

In an effort to keep their black and Hispanic workers from looking for greener pastures elsewhere, many companies have established minority-employee organizations that sponsor mentorship and self-help programs, produce newsletters, organize fund-raising activities, and provide a forum in which nonwhites in the labor force can air their grievances. At Atlantic Richfield, minority workers receive specialized self-development courses for both their personal and professional growth.[109] Borden has a Career Options Program that provides nonwhites with training in various departments, thereby increasing their overall marketability.[110] Other companies periodically conduct workshops where black employees can voice concerns about their work climate, reward system, and career options.[111] At General Foods, an Ethnic Diversity Council sponsors lectures, panel discussions, and other events designed to "[make] minorities feel more welcome while also sensitizing nonminority employees to issues that are important to minority co-workers."[112]

Under affirmative action guidelines and the EEOC's definition of discrimination, employers must not only *hire* substantial numbers of minorities, but must also *promote* significant numbers to management positions.[113] The Mead Corporation, Xerox, Kellogg, and Borden are just a few of the industrial giants that reserve their largest executive bonuses for those managers who hire and promote the most nonwhites.[114] The Equitable Company has instituted a special program for the express purpose of hiring and developing black managers. "Because of the program," says one Equitable executive, "we went from six black vice presidents in 1980 to twenty-nine black vice presidents in 1990."[115] Chevron Corporation formulates individual career-development plans for each of its minority employees, with the goal of producing as many nonwhite managers as possible.[116] In 1989 Motorola vowed to promote at least two nonwhites to the vice president level each year through 1996.[117] Kentucky Fried Chicken asks head-hunting firms to provide separate lists of white and black job candidates, so as to facilitate race-based hiring for its senior executive positions.[118] Pacific Gas & Electric reports that approximately 22 percent of its current managers are minorities,[119] while at Amtrak and Levi Strauss the figures are 20 percent[120] and 35 percent,[121] respectively. At Xerox, 14 percent of all executives at the vice president level or above are black.[122] Indeed, American companies spend vast resources on the recruitment, training, and career advancement of nonwhite employees. Charges that blacks are frequently denied jobs because of their skin color rightfully belong to a bygone era. Words that rang true in past generations are now just echoes of hollow myths.

Though "civil rights leaders" tend to characterize corporate America as discriminatory and socially irresponsible, virtually every major firm in our country participates in programs specifically designed to help minority communities:

• The Prudential funds a number of youth-development programs for urban minorities.[123]
• Each year United Parcel Service (UPS) sends twenty-five of its managers to volunteer several weeks of their time for inner-city civic organizations—doing "everything from dishing out food in soup kitchens to reading stories to children of migrant workers."[124]
• Dayton Hudson Corporation sends representatives to Detroit's mostly-black public schools to teach students how to interview for jobs, write resumes, and find employment. The company also hosts career fairs geared toward blacks, and funds a free tutoring program for black schoolchildren.[125]
• PepsiCo recently granted $2 million to the Pepsi School Challenge programs in Dallas and Detroit, which work to decrease nonwhite students' dropout rates.[126]
• Pacific Gas and Electric runs a tutorial and mentoring program for minority schoolchildren.[127]
• Federal Express provides technical equipment, individualized tutoring, and counseling services for students at the mostly

black Booker T. Washington High School in Memphis, Tennessee.[128]

• Philip Morris delegates black managers to serve as mentors for students at black colleges.[129]

• IBM has developed a Faculty Loan Program, through which fifty-five nonwhite employees are "loaned" each year to minority colleges—receiving full pay and benefits while instructing students in computer science, mathematics, engineering, and business administration.[130]

• TRW supports minority engineering programs at several universities.[131]

• Quaker Oats has been recognized by the American Bar Association for its commitment to improving opportunities for black and Hispanic lawyers.[132]

• Procter & Gamble sponsors many large-scale family reunions across the country, but financially supports only those of black families.[133]

Almost all large companies give regularly to black organizations and charities, with donations ranging in size from modest to enormous:

• In recent years Exxon has given hundreds of thousands of dollars to black colleges and the United Negro College Fund.[134]

• In 1991 alone Hewlett-Packard contributed more than $530,000 to minority-education programs across the United States.[135]

• Avon recently gifted $500,000 to the Schomburg Center for Research in Black Culture,[136] while Eastman Kodak donated $1 million to the United Negro College Fund.[137]

• Honeywell Corporation has poured millions of dollars into minority-education programs throughout the 1990s.[138]

• Dayton Hudson contributed some $2.7 million to black and Hispanic organizations in 1991,[139] a feat which Clorox duplicated the following year.[140]

• *The New York Times* annually donates upwards of $5 million to minority cultural and educational organizations.[141]

• Each year McDonald's and IBM give millions of dollars to the United Negro College Fund,[142] while the Prudential gives approximately $16 million to urban minority-development programs.[143]

• Not only do many arts councils earmark both public and private funds for black dance, theater, and art groups,[144] but the

National Endowment for the Arts actually penalizes grantees that do not have significant nonwhite representation.[145]

Many corporations contribute huge sums of money to scholarship funds reserved exclusively for nonwhite students:

• Between 1989 and 1993, the DeWitt Wallace/*Reader's Digest* Fund donated $37 million to "Pathways to Teaching Careers," a program providing scholarship money for minorities interested in becoming schoolteachers. This money paid for the schooling of more than 2,500 aspiring teachers at forty-six colleges and universities.[146]

• AT&T sponsors an engineering scholarship program, open only to women and minorities, that fully covers students' educational and living expenses for four years.[147]

• MCI has created a minority scholarship program at the University of Colorado for students of computer science and engineering.[148]

• Atlantic Richfield funds numerous scholarships for nonwhite students attending Texas and California colleges.[149]

• PepsiCo recently granted $1 million to finance minority scholarships at Arizona State University's College of Business.[150]

• Quaker Oats funds minority scholarships at several universities, among which are Loyola, Fisk, DePaul, and the University of Tennessee.[151] Bristol-Myers Squibb does the same for black and Hispanic marketing majors at Cornell, Duke, Harvard, and Columbia Universities.[152]

• Colgate-Palmolive, in conjunction with the National Dental Association, has established scholarships for black students enrolled in dental health-related programs.[153]

• Procter & Gamble covers full tuition expenses for selected minority students of chemical technology at the Ohio School of Applied Science.[154]

• Chevron has contributed scholarship money for nonwhite engineering students at more than fifty universities, while General Motors sponsors scholarships to eight black colleges each year.[155]

• Exxon has created a Minority Scholarship Program for mathematics, science, and engineering students.[156]

• Eastman Kodak provides scholarships and summer internships for minority students in cooperation with the Urban League Scholars Program.[157]

Apart from such charitable donations, most large companies make special efforts to purchase many of their supplies and services from minority-owned firms, and these transactions amount to more than $20 billion annually.[158] The following table shows how much money some of our country's industrial giants paid to nonwhite suppliers in 1992.

Dollars Spent Through Minority Purchasing Programs in 1992[159]

Allstate	$49 million
American Airlines	$155 million
Ameritech	$127 million
Amtrak	$80 million
Anheuser-Busch	$100 million
ARCO	$200 million
AT&T	$208 million
Avon	$50 million
Bell Atlantic	$100 million
Borden	$70 million
Burger King	$60 million
Campbell Soup	$64 million
Chevron	$150 million
Chrysler	$575 million
Clorox	$8.5 million
Coca Cola	$100 million
Colgate-Palmolive	$25 million
Coors	$40 million
Corning	$3.1 million
Dow Chemical	$35 million
DuPont	$220 million
Exxon	$150 million
Federal Express	$30 million
General Motors	over $1 billion
Hewlett-Packard	$70 million
J.C. Penney	$325 million
Johnson & Johnson	$80 million
Kellogg	$16 million

McDonald's	$400 million
Merck & Co.	$45 million
Metropolitan Life	$50 million
Pacific Gas & Electric	$300 million
PepsiCo	$87 million
Pfizer	$60 million
Philip Morris	$215 million
Polaroid	$30 million
Sara Lee	$30 million
Sprint	$20 million
Time Warner	$60 million
UPS	$10 million
Warner-Lambert	$25 million

Of course, such companies are motivated to do business with minority-owned firms by more than an altruistic devotion to "diversity." Obviously, they are also eager to establish reputations that the "civil rights" cartel will not assail. Out of the fertile soil of this obsession with race, new businesses have sprung up to capitalize on the panic. One such entity is Univex, a black-run operation that introduces executives to minority suppliers for a minimum retainer of $4,000 per month.[160] The National Minority Supplier Development Council provides a similar service, charging $30,000 annually to each of 3,000 public and corporate clients.[161] There are also many regional groups that perform the same function.[162]

Yet while corporate America relentlessly strives to increase black participation in its day-to-day activities, activists and academics continue to tell their familiar tales of extensive antiblack discrimination. Jesse Jackson, for instance, laments "the corporate lockout"[163] which he says has kept blacks "out of banking and textiles and [the] auto [industry] and food markets and telecommunications."[164] Explaining that "the walls" must "come down," whether they be "in South Africa or South Carolina,"[165] he exhorts "Wall Street corporations" to "open up the marketplace" and "let us [blacks] in."[166] Along the same lines, law professor Derrick Bell contends that "racial discrimination in the workplace is as vicious (if less obvious) than it was when employers posted signs 'no negras need apply.' "[167] "It has begun to seem," he adds, "that blacks, particularly black men, who lack at least two college degrees, are not hired in any position above the most menial."[168] Columnist Carl Rowan shares Bell's view of America as a wasteland for black opportunity. "A white high-school graduate," says Rowan, "may still get a better job and earn more than a black person with a college degree."[169] An equally pessimistic Gertrude Ezorsky writes in her book *Racism and Justice*:

> [A]lthough black-white inequality of educational attainment has been substantially reduced in some respects, such as in the amount of schooling received and the level of reading, nevertheless requirements for a college diploma and for adequate test scores continue to exclude blacks from employment and from postgraduate schools that provide training for desirable positions.[170]

The Diversity Industry

Because the employment, promotion, and retention of black employees are high priorities for American business, a large industry has been created by people marketing their services as "diversity consultants." These "specialists" are paid as much as $10,000 per day to teach managers and employees how to "value diversity."[171] They conduct "diversity training" seminars, "cultural awareness" workshops, and "sensitivity" classes—all ostensibly designed to reduce racial and cultural tensions in the workplace. In practice, however, a major function of such events is to promote guilt among white workers and employers alike. The teaching sessions—which consist of lectures, case studies, discussions, role plays, videotapes, and various "awareness experiences"—can last anywhere from a few hours to several days.[172] Though corporate executives commonly boast that these sessions deepen interracial understanding among employees, in truth the central message of many diversity seminars is that whites are—whether or not they realize it—the principal cause of bad race relations.[173]

Urged to publicly confess their own hidden prejudices and bigoted impulses, white participants in such seminars are often told that racism is nothing broader than "the systematic oppression of people of color."[174] They are further taught that their own racism is much like an onion, composed of many layers which they must continuously strive to "shed" throughout their lives—whether or not they consciously see themselves as racists. Consistent with this notion, posters bearing such slogans as "I don't want to be a racist . . . but I think I might be" are put on display.[175] One organizer of "racism awareness" programs bases his lessons on the premise that most white Americans deem "people of color" inferior.[176] Another candidly asserts, " 'White male' is what I call the newest swear word in America."[177] Yet another explains that whites are inherently racist and thus "need to be re-educated."[178] In a recent faculty sensitivity session at the University of Cincinnati, a blond female professor was forced to withstand the ridicule of her peers for being "a member of the privileged white elite" whose three college degrees were not earned but were a "genetic entitlement."[179] Similarly, in a student workshop at the University of Wisconsin, a "race-relations specialist" hammered home the notion that *all* whites are racists, evoking "the repentant sobs of white students."[180] Along the same lines, a University of Cincinnati trainer once told a white male student that the recent death of the young man's father had been, on balance, a good thing, for it had "removed one more racist influence" from the son's life.[181] In the minds of many diversity consultants, it seems, the need for sensitivity is a one-way street.

Some of the activities that take place at these seminars—which purport to address both racism *and* sexism—are nothing short of shocking. At a Federal Aviation Administration workshop, for instance, all men in attendance, regardless of race, were pressured to walk through a line of female co-workers who, as instructed, fondled the males' genitals and "rated their sexual attributes"[182]—an exercise supposedly intended to "sensitize" the men to the type of harassment they presumably were prone to inflict upon women. Another exercise required all black employees to gather in a private room and discuss the "oppression" that they suffered on a daily basis in America's "white-dominated society." They were then instructed to rejoin their nonblack colleagues and verbally attack a white man.[183]

Diversity consulting and sensitivity training have developed into a billion-dollar industry affecting nearly three-fourths of the American work force.[184] Among the more well-known corporations that require their employees to undergo such training are: Allstate, Sprint, US West, TRW, General Mills, Federal Express, Corning, Coca Cola, Hallmark, Chevron, Chrysler, The Equitable, Dow Chemical, Sara Lee, Procter & Gamble, MCI, Merrill Lynch, Bell Atlantic, Xerox, Clorox, UPS, Avon, General Electric, Borden, Sony, J.C. Penney, Levi Strauss,

Johnson & Johnson, McDonald's, Coors, General Motors, Hewlett-Packard, Philip Morris, and Colgate-Palmolive. Of course, this is only a partial list.[185] Long-term use of diversity consultants can cost a corporation hundreds of thousands of dollars. One consulting company, in fact, offers a five-year package costing more than $2.5 million.[186]

After diversity consultants have finished "educating" everyone, employers must somehow abide by affirmative action regulations on their own. To accomplish this, more and more corporations are hiring full-time diversity managers. At least half of all *Fortune* 500 companies now employ such specialists to help department managers and executives deal with "diversity issues" like the fulfillment of hiring and promotion quotas.[187]

Nothing New

Racial preferences for nonwhites have been firmly entrenched in American business for a generation. As long ago as 1973, AT&T enacted a court-ordered affirmative action plan designed to achieve "full utilization of minorities and women at all levels of management and non-management . . . at a pace beyond that which would occur normally; to prohibit discrimination in employment because of race, color, religion, national origin, sex or age; and to have a work environment free of discrimination."[188] Paradoxically, then, the framers of this plan decided that the best way to achieve an environment free of discrimination was simply to discriminate against whites. While the plan permitted AT&T to continue its longstanding custom of administering aptitude tests to prospective employees, it also mandated that minorities be hired in significantly greater numbers than ever before—even if this meant hiring "basically qualified" nonwhites in preference to more-qualified whites.[189] "No Bell Company," read the admonition, "shall rely upon the minimum scores required or preferred on its pre-employment aptitude test batteries as justification for its failure to meet its intermediate [racial representation] targets for any job classification."[190] In essence, this meant that even if minority applicants performed very poorly on the tests, that was no reason for AT&T not to hire them. Skin color itself was a job qualification—even more important than ability.

When an employer evaluates job candidates, he considers their previous work experiences and forms some general impressions about their overall abilities. Some employers also administer basic competency tests such as the General Aptitude Test Battery (GATB), which since 1947 has been recognized as an excellent measure of the cognitive skills necessary for a wide variety of occupations. Over the years, however, the GATB has drawn much criticism because white test-takers have consistently outscored their black counterparts. To "remedy" this situation, the U.S. Labor Department mandated in 1981 that race-norming be used to tabulate the scores.[191]

Whenever companies test prospective employees even for minimal competence, problems arise if "too few" minorities pass. Consider the case of Prudential Insurance, which between 1978 and 1984 rejected about 8,000 nonwhite job applicants, many of them because of their failure to meet minimum standards on a test of reading and math abilities. Because blacks failed this test in disproportionately large numbers, the Labor Department initiated an investigation of the company's hiring practices. Prudential, of course, was well aware of the government's propensity to equate random statistical imbalances with intentional discrimination. The daunting prospect of a potential government suit—and the possible loss of $50 million worth of business with federal agencies—frightened the company into making some major concessions. Prudential agreed not only to spend an estimated $3 million on math and reading remediation classes for the same job candidates it had previously rejected, but also to offer full-time jobs to at least 600 of those individuals.[192]

Standardized employment tests have had a long, controversial history in this country. In the middle part of the twentieth century, most employers felt justified in administering such tests to job applicants for the purpose of evaluating their reading, writing, mathematical, and reasoning skills. As of 1963, in fact, some 90 percent of American businesses had testing programs for white-collar, clerical, supervisory, production, and even assembly-line jobs. That same year, however, when the Motorola Corporation rejected the job application of a black Illinois man because of his poor performance on a multiple-choice test of general cognitive abilities, he filed a grievance with the Illinois Fair Employment Commission (IFEC). Pronouncing the test unfair to "culturally deprived and disadvantaged groups," the IFEC ordered Motorola not only to hire the man, but also to permanently stop using the exam to evaluate prospective employees.[193]

In 1964, however, Congress struck a blow for employers, ruling that they could administer and "act upon the results of any professionally developed ability test provided that such test . . . is not designed, intended or used to discriminate because of race."[194] Senate floor leaders confirmed that employers were not required to abandon the use of tests where, "because of differences in background and education, members of some groups are able to perform better . . . than members of other groups."[195] As Senators Joseph Clark and Clifford Case explained, "An employer may set his qualifications as high as he likes, he may test to determine which applicants have these qualifications, and promote on the basis of test performance."[196]

Nonetheless, in 1966 the EEOC issued guidelines stating that whenever an employment test resulted in a lower passing rate for minorities, the employer would be considered guilty of discrimination unless that test could be "validated" in accordance with EEOC-defined procedures.[197] Employers now had to prove not only that their existing standards were absolutely necessary for job performance, but also that no alternative measures could reliably screen prospective workers and simultaneously yield more minority hirings.[198] These requirements proved to be so exacting that for more than ten years no employer was ever able to successfully prove his case.[199] Thus, by effectively outlawing disparate impact, the EEOC removed intent as a necessary element in defining discrimination.[200] In the 1971 *Griggs v. Duke Power Company* case, a unanimous Supreme Court ruling confirmed that employers could no longer administer tests that had a disparate impact on minorities unless those tests could be justified by clear "business necessity."[201] Consequently, throughout the 1970s a host of tests were scrapped for such reasons as: failure to determine the tests' validity for blacks as well as whites; inadequate analysis of job requirements; invalidated cutoff scores; insufficient proof that the qualities tested were essential to job success; failure to find alternative means of judging job applicants; and cultural bias.[202] By 1975, only 45 percent of American employers were still testing job applicants.[203]

It should be noted that the stated reasons for eliminating so many standardized tests were largely smokescreens; the only "problem" was that minorities tended to score lower than whites. Indeed, the most reliable research on testing shows that "measures of general cognitive ability are substantially correlated to success on the job in virtually every situation that has been competently measured."[204] In fact, the more complex the job, the better the standardized measures of cognitive ability predict performance.[205] A 1982 study by the National Academy of Sciences thoroughly scrutinized a wide array of such tests for evidence of cultural bias and "strongly discounted the notion that there even is such a thing."[206]

It should not be forgotten that selecting employees by valid measures of cognitive ability—rather than by less reliable, nontest criteria—can have a profound effect on the overall quality of a work force. Higher standards tend to produce better employees, while lower standards have the opposite effect. For this reason it is impossible to establish, for any test, a minimum "cutoff score" (above which all candidates are eligible) without severely compromising job performance and overall work-force efficiency. It is estimated that among white-collar government employees, hiring on the basis of test scores would generate some $600 million in increased productivity per year.[207] Similar increases would undoubtedly occur in the private sector as well. Consider that when U.S. Steel lowered its hiring standards so that more minorities would qualify for jobs, the result was a dramatic decline not only in the "mastery" scores of trainees, but also in their later job-performance ratings.[208]

Reign of Terror

American corporations go to extraordinary lengths to avoid any conflicts with black organizations that might accuse them—however unjustly—of racial insensitivity. Compared to the prospective nightmare of having to endure negative national publicity, companies find it much easier, and ultimately less expensive, to steer clear of all controversy by enforcing racial quotas and donating money to the "correct" organizations. Capitalizing on corporate America's fear of racial friction, the NAACP has become adept at intimidating firms into "fair share agreements" that call for increases in black hirings, black promotions, and the use of black-owned vendors. At least seventy companies have been bullied into such accords[209]—receiving, in exchange for their payoffs and pledges, assurances that the NAACP will not frivolously accuse them of discrimination.[210]

Sadly, the NAACP has become an ugly caricature of what once was a respectable civil rights organization. It has been corrupted not only by its refusal to acknowledge the anachronism of its crusades, but also by its own swollen sense of self-importance—an arrogance spawned by the tremulous genuflections of American business. In August 1993, for example, NAACP leaders criticized Hughes Aircraft's record of minority hiring, even though that company's work force was among the most diverse in the information systems industry.[211] Like most corporations, however, Hughes tried to appease its critics rather than engage in open, public debate. "The NAACP is an important organization," bleated Vice President David Bradley. "We are interested in knowing how we might improve."[212]

The terror that the NAACP strikes into the hearts of business leaders was again illustrated by a 1993 incident involving AT&T. Appearing in the company's in-house magazine was a cartoon—considered racially offensive by some "civil rights leaders"—depicting a long-distance telephone caller in Africa as a monkey. Unfortunately, AT&T's magazine editors had failed to foresee the cartoon's potential for offending the supersensitive. Wilting under the heat of criticism from NAACP officials and such paragons of "sensitivity" as Al Sharpton, company president Robert Allen apologized for the cartoon and dutifully announced new plans to "accelerate diversity" at AT&T.[213]

Apologies, however, were not enough for the defenders of "dignity," who saw the cartoon as evidence that AT&T's leaders essentially equated blacks with monkeys. "The apology is notwithstanding," said Sharpton. "We want more than an apology. We want to meet with the chairman of the board. . . . It's time to find out who's minding the store and whether there are enough blacks working for the company."[214] Despite the fact that AT&T had contributed generously for decades to black educational and advocacy organizations, Sharpton and Jesse Jackson, Jr. led a protest demonstration outside the company's New York headquarters.[215] Joseph Lowery of the Southern Christian Leadership Conference and members of the Congressional Black Caucus met with President Allen to demand that AT&T step up its efforts to hire and promote black workers.[216] Following the meeting, Allen sheepishly asked the NAACP to help him "enhance" his company's "relationship with the African American community, as well as with the African people in the Caribbean [and in] Africa."[217]

McDonald's was yet another corporate giant to succumb to "civil rights" blackmail. Several years ago, leaders of the NAACP's Los Angeles chapter initiated a boycott against the restaurant chain, alleging that it discriminated against blacks in its hiring, purchasing, and franchising policies.[218] After meeting with NAACP representatives to negotiate a settlement, McDonald's officials announced that they would: (a) aggressively recruit minority employees, managers, and franchisees; (b) establish at least 100 new black-owned restaurants during the next four years; and (c) purchase more supplies and professional services from black-owned firms.[219]

Like the NAACP, Jesse Jackson has repeatedly threatened to lead boycotts against companies with "insufficiently diverse" work forces—invariably frightening his targets into major affirmative action concessions.[220] The Congressional Black Caucus, meanwhile, wields economic and political clout of a different kind. Much of its multi-million-dollar "war chest," funded primarily by corporate America, is used to promote the campaigns of black political candidates nationwide.[221] Would such a race-specific allocation of resources be tolerated in this country if its avowed purpose were to help exclusively *white* candidates?

Affirmative Actions's Enormous Domain

America's obsession with "diversity," and its concomitant abandonment of high standards, has become a national disgrace. The fear generated by potential charges of racism is unlike anything this nation has heretofore seen. Even the most powerful government entities have meekly submitted to the tyranny of preferential policies. At the Department of Housing and Urban Development (HUD), for example, managers can obtain an "outstanding" rating only if they aggressively "promote diversity." To qualify for this designation, they must either facilitate the career advancement of those with "diversity status," or be active members of minority, feminist, or homosexual organizations.[222]

When the U.S. State Department discovered that comparatively few black Americans speak foreign languages, it removed foreign-language ability from its list of hiring criteria.[223] Though the department hires no whites who score below 70 on its qualification exams, blacks can be hired with scores in the mid-50s.[224] In fact, since 1979 it has placed blacks who narrowly fail their entrance exams into a "near pass" category that allows them to still be hired.[225]

The story is much the same at the Federal Bureau of Investigation, which gives blacks five extra points on its exams simply because they are black.[226] Without this manipulation of scores, the bureau would be unable to meet its "diversity goals." All FBI merit awards, bonuses, performance reviews, promotions, training programs, and coveted assignments are carefully apportioned with racial "balance."[227] Moreover, the bureau takes pains not to discipline "any group of employees at a statistically significant higher rate than any other group."[228]

In 1998 the U.S. Marine Corps adopted a quota policy aimed at "diversifying" its officer ranks. This "12-12-5 Plan" mandates that officers of various racial and ethnic backgrounds be represented in proportions roughly equal to those of the general population—12 percent blacks, 12 percent Hispanics, and 5 percent Native Americans, Asian Americans, Alaskan Natives, and Pacific Islanders.[229]

Early in his presidency, Bill Clinton proved himself to be an enthusiastic advocate of quotas. His proposed health-care plan of 1993 called for the creation of a National Council of Graduate Medical Education, which would have barred medical students from entering those specialties wherein their racial and ethnic groups were already "overrepresented."[230] The following year, the Clinton administration ruled that employers could take race into account when deciding whom to lay off or fire. This was something brand new in American history. In defense of their unprecedented position, administration officials predictably intoned pious sermons on the importance of maintaining "racial diversity" in the workplace.[231]

The case that raised this issue involved the Piscataway, New Jersey school board, which, for budgetary reasons, found itself in the position of having to lay off either Sharon Taxman, a white teacher, or Debra Williams, Taxman's equally qualified black co-worker. After much deliberation, the board decided to terminate Taxman and keep Williams for the purpose of maintaining a "diverse" faculty. In other words, Taxman was let go for purely racial reasons. When Ms. Taxman filed a discrimination lawsuit against the school board, she won at every turn in the lower courts, thereby setting the stage for the case to be heard by the Supreme Court in 1997. Amid speculation that the Court would declare race-based firing unconstitutional, "civil rights" groups, in a move orchestrated by Jesse Jackson, raised enough money from corporate donors to pay 70 percent of a $433,500 out-of-court settlement which effectively removed the case from Supreme Court consideration.[232] While few Americans protested Jackson's behind-the-scenes manipulations, we can well imagine the public outrage that would attend a similar effort by *white* groups to derail a *black* plaintiff's discrimination lawsuit. Given that the Taxman case could have dealt a virtual knockout blow to racial preferences, the Clinton administration was pleased with the out-of-court settlement.

Within a year it seemed likely that yet another case, this one involving the Boston Latin High School, might soon be the subject of a potentially historic Supreme Court ruling. Boston Latin's policy was to admit half of its new students each year exclusively on the basis of school grades and entrance-exam scores, and half on a mix of merit and race. But in 1998 a white plaintiff named Sarah Wessmann charged that because of this policy, she had been denied admission in favor of less-qualified minority students. Though she initially lost her case in a lower court, the U.S. Court of Appeals later reversed that verdict, finding the school's race-based policy unconstitutional. When the school board eventually voted to appeal this second decision to the Supreme Court, the NAACP and U.S. Education Department stepped in. Fearful that a Court ruling in Wessmann's favor would establish a legal basis upon which *all* affirmative action programs could be declared unconstitutional, they convinced the board to pursue the case no further. Explaining his rationale for dropping the appeal, the Boston School superintendent candidly acknowledged, "This is not a case that would be isolated to Boston. The whole country would have to live with the decision."[233] Once again, the Clinton administration was relieved that racial preferences had dodged a legal bullet.

To be sure, President Clinton's stance on "diversity" has never wavered. In 1995, while trying to fill the vacant position of U.S. Attorney in Mississippi, he nominated, in succession, four black candidates for the job. The first three had to withdraw their names from consideration when routine investigations into their backgrounds revealed tax problems, at which point the president settled on the fourth candidate, Buck Buchanan. Through this entire selection process, Clinton chose not to nominate Josh Bogen, a white Mississippi attorney with impeccable political and civil rights credentials—certainly far stronger than Buchanan's. Grady Tollison, Jr., a former president of the Mississippi Bar Association, was angered by the president's refusal to consider Bogen for the job. "I find it offensive," said Tollison, "that someone like Josh Bogen, who's been on the right side of the issues and who has sacrificed so much and is so qualified is now being rejected. I'm a lifelong Democrat, but I also believe we shouldn't say, 'Let's get an African American at all costs.' Bogen is being rejected apparently for one reason, because he's white. That's not right."[234]

Unfortunately, however, it is not unusual for the appointment of public officials to fall under affirmative action's wide umbrella. As settlement for a civil rights lawsuit in 1992, for example, Louisiana officials pledged to appoint twenty-five black judges.[235] A year later the Common Council of White Plains, New York announced its preference to fill a vacant judgeship with either a minority or a woman. "It's been my view over the years," explained White Plains mayor Alfred Del Vecchio, "that the . . . judgeships should be representative of all genders, all colors, and all races."[236] In other words, there should be quotas.

In July 1995, when President Clinton sensed voters' growing resistance to race-based preferences, he issued a statement expressing both his opposition to numerical quotas *and* his belief that "affirmative action has been good for America."[237] "I don't favor the unjustified preference of the unqualified over the qualified of any race or gender," he assured the American public.[238] These comments, of course, not only revealed the president's apparent ignorance of the fact that affirmative action has become *literally synonymous* with quotas and preferences, but also sidestepped the fundamental concerns of the policy's detractors. Even the staunchest critics of racial preferences generally recognize that few people would condone the hiring of completely *un*qualified job applicants over well-qualified competitors. The real issue is that affirmative action commonly elevates *less*-qualified individuals above *more*-qualified rivals.

Our country's obsession with "diversity" has affected even the process by which we elect our political leaders. In 1982 Congress approved a proposal to systematically redraw voting districts nationwide so as to create a host of new districts wherein blacks or Hispanics constituted a clear majority of the voting population.[239] Proliferating most rapidly after the 1990 census, these newly configured

entities were not comprised of specific towns or municipalities—
but rather were delineated by the residential patterns of minorities.
Thus, the redrawn districts often looked like one absurdly shaped,
multi-tentacled monster bordered by another.[240] The 12th District in
North Carolina, for instance, extended 200 miles along a narrow strip
abutting Interstate 85 and connecting a number of black neighborhoods.[241]

This restructuring of voting districts, known as racial gerrymandering, gave black and Hispanic candidates "virtual pre-paid
tickets to the U.S. Congress"[242]—thanks to the nearly unanimous support they traditionally receive from voters of like race or ethnicity.[243]
In 1986 and again five years later, the Supreme Court upheld redistricting.[244] Then in 1995, by a 5 to 4 vote, the Court altered its position, stating that the use of race as a predominant factor in defining
district boundaries was unconstitutional.[245] Not surprisingly, most "civil
rights" activists opposed this latest Court ruling. Some, in fact, not
only supported gerrymandering, but actually suggested that light- and
dark-skinned blacks should be assigned to separate districts.[246]

Preferential Policies and the Mass Media

Racial preferences have been deeply entrenched in the broadcasting industry for many years. As early as 1978, affirmative action
laws were passed to encourage nonwhites to buy radio stations.[247]
Minority broadcasters thereafter received extra points from the
Federal Communications Commission (FCC) when applying for
broadcast licenses.[248] In 1987 the FCC went a step further, officially requiring TV and radio stations to hire more nonwhites. Subsequent to that directive, if a minority-group's representation in a
particular station's work force was significantly lower than in the
surrounding population, that station's broadcast license could be re-
voked.[249] A broadcaster facing a possible loss of license was permitted to defend his hiring practices, but an unsuccessful defense could
cost him the entire value of his broadcast rights. His second (and
certainly less risky) option was simply to sell his broadcast rights to a
minority buyer, at 75 percent of market value, while his case was
under review.[250] In 1990 the Supreme Court ruled that not only were
such race-conscious measures constitutional, but that the increased

"diversity" of broadcasters was a valid federal objective.[251] Eight years later the FCC changed its course somewhat, announcing that although it would no longer revoke licenses from stations where minorities were "underrepresented," it would still require broadcasters to "demonstrate that they are reaching out in their communities to pull together a diverse applicant pool."[252]

In recent decades, a host of minority plaintiffs have made fortunes suing radio and television stations for discrimination. Though most of these charges have been groundless, broadcasters have traditionally tried to avoid long and expensive court battles by simply paying the plaintiffs to withdraw their complaints. One organization in particular, the National Black Media Coalition (NBMC), has filed literally thousands of discrimination complaints with the FCC. In 1988 almost all of the NBMC's $500,000 budget came from payoffs it received in exchange for dropping its mostly frivolous accusations. When the FCC ruled in 1990 that broadcast stations could no longer pay plaintiffs to withdraw their complaints, the NBMC altered its tactics and began to charge broadcasters for help in locating prospective black employees.[253]

Prior to an April 1995 change in the tax laws, any broadcaster who voluntarily sold a station to a minority-owned organization automatically received a tax break from the Internal Revenue Service. This meant that blacks often won bids for stations even when they made much lower offers than their white competitors. Consider that *The New York Times*, when it sold a cable television subsidiary to a group with 20 percent minority ownership, received a $50 million tax break—more than enough money to compensate the *Times* for accepting the purchaser's comparatively low bid. As author Jared Taylor incisively asks, "Was that really a good enough reason for our government to add $50 million to the budget deficit?"[254] Of course, minorities who bought stations under these rules were under no obligation to run them. Purchasers could simply acquire stations at the bargain rates available only to minorities—and immediately sell them to white buyers at market prices, thereby racking up quick profits.[255] In 1990, for instance, a group of black businessmen led by Charlotte's then-mayor Harvey Gantt bought a discounted television license under the FCC's minority-preference bidding system. Four months later the group sold that same license to whites at the full market price, pocketing a $3 million profit.[256]

Another longstanding minority-preference program gave huge tax advantages to African Americans who bought radio or television stations. Ostensibly instituted to help "economically disadvantaged" minorities, in practice these tax breaks were nothing more than rewards for having black skin. Consider, for example, a group of black investors who purchased a Buffalo, New York television station in 1985, took advantage of the tax benefits, and eventually sold the station at a substantial profit. Among the "economically disadvantaged" constituents of this group were Colin Powell, O.J. Simpson, Patrick Ewing, Julius Erving, the actor Mr. T, and several members of entertainer Michael Jackson's family.[257] This program was repealed in early 1995—to the doleful strains of "civil rights leaders" lamenting the alleged resurgence of Jim Crow.

Perhaps affirmative action's most universal characteristic is its tendency to corrupt. For instance, many minorities found it lucrative to bid on broadcast stations and then withdraw those offers in exchange for payoffs from competing white bidders. In one 1980s case, black millionaire Vernon Jordan applied under the minority category for two Washington, D.C. radio stations. A white-owned company eventually purchased them, but only after paying Jordan $765,000 to retract his offer.[258]

In the newspaper industry, the incidence of racial preferences has skyrocketed in recent years. Virtually all major publications now have minority-recruitment staffs and in-house diversity units. As a result, nonwhites currently hold more than 10 percent of all newspaper jobs in the U.S.—approximately double the 1985 figure. In fact, many publications boast even higher numbers. At the *Washington Post*, 18 percent of the professional staff is composed of minority journalists.[259] The *Philadelphia Inquirer*, meanwhile, has developed a five-year quota plan requiring that half of all newsroom hires be minorities.[260] In 1994 almost 40 percent of newspaper interns nationwide were nonwhites.[261]

In November 1998 the American Society of Newspaper Editors announced that "the nation's newsrooms must reflect the racial diversity of American society."[262] There are currently at least five major groups actively promoting affirmative action in the newspaper industry: (a) the National Association of Black Journalists; (b) the National Association of Hispanic Journalists; (c) the Native American Journalists Association; (d) the Asian American Journalists Association; and (e) Unity: Journalists of Color.[263] Characterizing minority journalists as "the foot soldiers of diversity," the Ford Foundation recently donated $500,000 to the Unity organization.[264]

Many newspaper employees—from entry-level clerks to upper-echelon executives—candidly acknowledge that an obsession with "diversity" now dictates the hiring and firing practices of their industry. An executive at one New York weekly recently announced his intention to "begin getting rid of these middle-aged white men."[265] At a 1993 *Los Angeles Times* staff meeting, Washington bureau chief Jack Nelson announced that he would thereafter hire only women and minorities. When asked whether such a policy constituted discrimination, he replied, "No. It's affirmative action."[266] That same year, *New York Times* executive director Max Frankl boasted that he had all but stopped "the hiring of nonblacks and [had] set up an unofficial little quota system."[267] Along the same lines, a *Washington Post* reporter observes, "It's definitely a huge advantage in the business to be a minority. . . . There is just a different standard. White people have to knock their heads against the door and be really exceptional. Whereas, if you're black, they recruit you, they plead with you, they offer you extra money."[268] There are some jobs, designated as "black slots," for which the *Post* will not even consider white candidates. These positions sometimes remain vacant for months while *Post* recruiters "comb the country for a suitable black hire."[269] Not surprisingly, there is palpable racial tension in the *Post* newsroom.[270]

The Death of Common Sense

Preferential policies touch the everyday workings of municipal agencies and private companies in countless ways. As *Business Week* succinctly puts it, affirmative action is "deeply ingrained in American corporate culture"[271]—often to preposterous lengths. In 1990, for instance, the head of New York Telephone's Affirmative Action Division sent a letter to several thousand firms with which his company regularly conducted business. "It is our intention," he wrote, "to insure equal opportunity in all aspects of business operations, including purchasing of goods and services." He then requested that all vendors reveal what percentages of their companies were owned or operated by nonwhites.[272] How could such data possibly aid the cause of color-blind, nondiscriminatory equal opportunity?

In one defense contractor's office, it was recently determined that while there were "enough" white and Hispanic employees on the payroll, more blacks were "needed." Consequently, all applications from nonblacks were automatically discarded. "If we had been honest," acknowledged one personnel secretary, "the sign outside would have read, 'Jobs Available—only blacks need apply.' "[273]

The long reach of affirmative action often borders on the incredible. In 1993 New York City commissioned a study—at a cost of more than $750,000—to determine the ideal racial and ethnic "balance" of workers in city agencies. By examining each demographic group's representation in New York's overall population, the researchers stipulated exactly how many whites, blacks, Asians, Hispanics, and Native Americans each particular agency should hire. The absurdity of such an endeavor was illustrated by the study's conclusion that the city's law department ought to have six American Indian attorneys in management.[274] "Six Native American lawyers, we're supposed to have?" asked an incredulous Lorna Goodman, Chief of Affirmative Litigation. "I find that extraordinary! How many [Native Americans] graduate from New York-area law schools?"[275] Indeed very few do, but this reality seemed not to trouble the researchers, who were concerned only with developing a theoretical formula by which all skin tones would be adequately represented.

Sometimes, even the most reasonable solutions to lingering dilemmas cannot be explored because those remedies may offend the sensibilities of the "civil rights" crowd. Consider that taxpayers currently spend about $2 billion each year to cover the defaults on college student loans. In an effort to address this problem, several members of Congress recently proposed the seemingly sensible idea that the government should make no further loans to students attending any school where the default rate exceeded 25 percent. Yet when studies revealed that many historically black colleges were well above the 25 percent figure, all consideration of the plan abruptly ceased.[276]

In 1989 affirmative action even touched the world of classical music when state legislators withheld $1.3 million in subsidies to the Detroit Symphony Orchestra (DSO)—because only one of its ninety-eight members was black. The DSO was informed that in order to receive these funds, it would have to hire more black musicians immediately. Some legislators even threatened to picket the orchestra's concerts until it became more "diverse." Thus the DSO, facing the prospect of considerable financial loss, promptly hired a black bass player without an audition and agreed to hold no future tryouts without black applicants. It should be noted that all previous DSO auditions had been conducted "blindly," with candidates playing their instruments behind a screen so as to eliminate any chance of bias by the judges. Ironically, then, in order to abide by state politicians' prescriptions for ending "discrimination," the orchestra was in effect required to discriminate along racial lines for the first time in its history. Blind auditions were abandoned because they had a "disparate impact" on blacks.[277]

The DSO's dearth of black players is not at all unusual. Indeed, only 1 percent of the musicians in our nation's major orchestras are black, and twelve of the top thirty-six orchestras have no blacks at all.[278] Are we to believe that all of these orchestras systematically discriminate by race, or could it be that their racial makeup—much like that of National Basketball Association teams, really has nothing to do with discrimination? Is it inconceivable that members of different racial and ethnic groups might have differing interests and skills? Should people not be free to pursue the ventures they choose without third-party observers deciding who ought to be participating in this field or that?

Notably, there is one publicly funded employer conspicuously exempted from all affirmative action regulations—Louis Farrakhan's Nation of Islam (NOI), to which the federal government awards some $30 million worth of security contracts each year. In return for this money, the NOI stations a number of security guards at various inner-city housing projects around the country. The government grants these contracts on a noncompetitive basis, making no attempt to locate other organizations that might provide the same service less expensively.[279] Farrakhan's group, of course, flatly refuses to "diversify" its work force and will employ literally any black in preference to a white—as evidenced by the twenty-nine convicted black felons on its Baltimore payroll alone. Yet remarkably, the NOI's blatant violation of federal regulations goes largely unnoticed in this country. "Civil rights leaders"—ever on the lookout for *white* bigots—ignore the issue entirely.

Even recent immigrants to the United States, so long as they are nonwhite, qualify for affirmative action advantages over native-born whites.[280] This is true not only for nonwhites whose ancestors may have suffered discrimination in America, but also for those whose forebears never even set foot on this continent. Indeed, affirmative action has degenerated into little more than a frenetic search for minorities upon whom to bestow racial or ethnic preferences. Consider the ludicrous situation wherein the California Highway Patrol has occasionally gone to *Mexico* to advertise job vacancies—so as to meet its hiring quotas for Hispanics.[281]

Tragic Repetitions of History

Supporters of affirmative action in the United States are undaunted by the policy's long track-record of disastrous consequences. Not having learned the lessons of history, they press forward—with all the fearless resolve of crusaders confident in their sacred cause—to repeat history's mistakes. Blinded by their purported desire for "justice," they ignore the fact that preferential policy programs in other societies have consistently polarized populations and, in many cases, irrigated landscapes with rivers of blood.[282]

India

Home to nearly a billion people, India is the world's largest multi-ethnic society—socially fragmented along religious, caste, regional, ethnic, and linguistic lines. Some 180 languages and 500 dialects are spoken nationwide, and intergroup hostilities have traditionally been intense. Clashes between India's Muslims and Hindus, for instance, "have produced some of the great bloodbaths of human history."[283]

Into this already-volcanic brew of disparate peoples and traditions, government-imposed preferential policies began injecting potent doses of toxic venom as early as the 1860s. Consider what transpired in northeastern India's state of Assam, which was under British rule throughout the late nineteenth and early twentieth centuries. During that colonial period, educated Bengali immigrants (who were brought to Assam by the British) became overrepresented among

Assam's lawyers, doctors, teachers, journalists, and government administrators. Meanwhile another immigrant group, the Marwaris, became prominent in Assam's industry and finance. Jealous of the success enjoyed by both of these groups, the native Assamese, who were largely peasant farmers, sought to improve their own position via group preferences. In the 1860s Assamese nationalists pressured political authorities into changing the official language of the schools from Bengali to Assamese, and by the 1920s they had persuaded the British to stem the flow of Bengali and Marwari migrants into Assam. Eventually the Assamese—largely through protests, threats, and outright violence—were able to secure preferences in state government employment. Thereafter they demanded that their native tongue be made the *exclusive* language of Assam's government institutions— a proposal that predictably infuriated the Marwaris and the Hindi-speaking Bengalis. Intergroup tensions over these issues festered and grew for many years, and when political activists in the mid-1960s denounced Marwari employers for hiring too few Assamese workers, Marwari businesses throughout Assam fell prey to arsonists and rioters.[284]

When the Assamese made additional demands for the primacy of their language in 1972, they found themselves increasingly embroiled in violent clashes with Bengali activists. Government proposals for compromise were obstinately rejected by the Assamese, whose demands for preferences eventually spread to the private sector, further heightening intergroup hostilities and sparking many riots. In 1983, Assamese mobs slaughtered more than 1,000 defenseless Bengali Muslims.[285]

The story has been much the same elsewhere in India. During the early 1960s in the state of Maharashtra, calls for preferences favoring Maharashtrians over "outsiders" in both public and private industry led to extreme levels of group polarization. Out of this hostile climate emerged a political movement called Shiv Sena, which strove to compel employers to reserve for Maharashtrians 80 percent of all jobs in Bombay. The movement's leader, Bal Thackeray, through his many "exposés" of "immigrant dominance," masterfully roused the xenophobic instincts of young and uneducated Maharashtrians. To drive home their agenda, Shiv Sena activists organized boycotts, ran candidates for political office, and periodically resorted to mob violence—killing more than 200 and leaving at least 10,000 homeless in

1984 alone. The perpetration of such atrocities, however, did nothing to diminish the movement's popularity. Some Shiv Sena rallies drew as many as 200,000 people.[286]

The Assamese and Maharashtrians, it should be noted, each constituted a numerical majority of their respective states' populations; they sought group preferences for themselves because various immigrant groups had outperformed them educationally and economically. But India has also seen the institution of preferences in favor of *minority* groups that traditionally had underachieved, usually through no fault of their own. Consider the case of the "untouchables," a designation used to identify the members of at least 1,000 local castes throughout the country who historically have been granted few, if any, basic human rights.[287] In 1950 the Indian government, in an effort to improve the wretched condition of these "backward classes," set aside for them more than one-fifth of all openings in employment and college admissions. But the fulfillment of these quotas required that the largely unskilled and poorly educated beneficiaries be judged by a uniquely lax set of standards—thereby arousing the ever-escalating resentment of the upper castes. In the late 1970s, for instance, when many untouchable applicants failed to score even the barest acceptable minimum of 35 percent on their medical school entrance exams, the qualifying requirement was reduced to a meager 15 percent. Before long, engineering schools followed suit, accepting lower-caste candidates who scored as low as 10 percent on their admissions tests— far below the 70 percent required of all other aspiring engineers. Not surprisingly, almost none of these newly preferred engineering students were able to maintain the minimum grade average needed to continue in school, and more than 85 percent dropped out without a degree.[288]

Sadly, the pro-untouchable preferences spawned a violent societal backlash against their beneficiaries. Bloody protest riots broke out repeatedly in the 1970s—often for the barest of causes. In 1978, for instance, when a university was renamed in honor of the late leader of a newly preferred group, more than 300 villages were overrun by riots that destroyed nearly 2,000 homes—all in response to a purely symbolic gesture.[289] Similarly, a 1981 dispute over seven medical school slots reserved for lower-caste members led to riots that killed forty-two people.[290] Four years later, a plan to increase the number of admissions slots reserved for untouchables in medical and engineering schools led to months of rioting and at least 200 deaths.[291]

Undaunted by these tragedies, in 1990 Indian prime minister V.P. Singh announced plans for further dramatic increases in job and school set-asides for lower-caste people. But as India was already flooded with many more university graduates than the job market could absorb, Singh's decision sparked anger among members of non-preferred groups throughout the country.[292] Before long, Indian streets were littered with the casualties of brutal clashes between advocates and opponents of set-asides. Seventy people were injured by rioting in the northern city of Delhi,[293] six were killed at a demonstration in Patna,[294] and dozens more lost their lives to violence elsewhere. Twenty-four towns found it necessary to impose curfews to curtail the unrest.[295] In 1995 an inadvertently omitted comma in a government roster of quota-eligible tribes led Gowari caste members to believe that they would be denied the group preferences they had expected to receive. In response, more than 40,000 Gowaris in Maharashtra staged a chaotic protest in which 113 people were trampled to death.[296]

As in the United States, preferential policies in India have bred widespread corruption. Many Indians, for example, have tried to exploit group preferences in employment and education by fraudulently claiming lower-caste membership. "Counterfeiters do a brisk business," reports the *Washington Post*, "in false lower-caste certificates that allow upper-caste applicants to take advantage of job or education quotas."[297] But the most notable—and predictable—result of India's preference programs has been the country's increased group polarization, evidenced by such extreme measures as the creation of private caste armies.[298]

Sri Lanka

Situated off the southeast tip of India, the island of Sri Lanka (known as Ceylon until 1972) is home to approximately eighteen million people—74 percent of whom are members of the Sinhalese ethnic group, and 18 percent of whom are Tamils.[299] Until the middle of the twentieth century, these two groups, marked by differing languages and religions, were unequally represented in various lines of work. While the Sinhalese were concentrated in lower-paying, unskilled occupations, Tamils tended to pursue careers in comparatively lucrative professional fields. In 1948, Tamils held one-fourth of all civil service jobs and comprised 32 percent of the country's doctors, 40 percent of its engineers, and 46 percent of its accountants. In higher education, Tamils were represented among medical and engineering students in proportions more than twice as high as their presence in the general population.[300] Notably, their impressive professional and scholastic achievements were due not to any preferential treatment, but largely to the 152 years (1796-1948) of English-language education that they, as a group, had received from British colonial rulers and Christian missionaries. This instruction had effectively prepared them to take advantage of employment opportunities in the British colonial government and the professions. The Sinhalese, by contrast, had received comparatively little schooling of a comparable nature, and thus were generally unequipped for technical occupations.[301] Nonetheless they exhibited no overt resentment toward their Tamil neighbors, and the two groups coexisted peacefully into the 1950s. Mid-twentieth-century observers characterized Sri Lanka as "an oasis of stability" where "religious and racial harmony" were "present in a high degree."[302] Preferential policies put an end to that idyll.

In 1956 the radical Sinhalese figure S.W.R.D. Bandaranaike scored a stunning victory in the national election for prime minister. Under his leadership, the government not only made Sinhalese the island's official language, but also instituted a number of group preferences favoring Sinhalese people in both education and employment. The country's leading teacher-training college, for instance, was thereafter reserved for Sinhalese students only,[303] while other universities began accepting Sinhalese applicants under far lower standards than their Tamil rivals. By the early 1970s, entrance-examination scores had been rendered virtually meaningless, as even the lowest-scoring Sinhalese students were being admitted to institutions of higher learning ahead of the highest-scoring Tamils. In 1974 strict quotas were established to further restrict Tamil admissions into collegiate science and engineering programs. By 1975 Tamils constituted only 17 percent of medical students and 14 percent of engineering students nationwide, whereas six years earlier they had been 49 percent and 48 percent, respectively. Moreover, Tamils were driven out of the army, the civil service, and the teaching profession.[304]

Moderate Tamils attempted to negotiate with the government but found it impossible to strike any bargains with the many Sinhalese demagogues who had inflamed their people's ethnocentric passions. When Tamil moderates were eventually replaced by more-militant leaders promoting complete secession from the Sinhalese,[305] violence by both ethnic groups became widespread. The mid-1970s saw the rise of Tamil guerilla movements responsible for robberies, arson, and hundreds of murders.[306] When Sinhalese army units were sent to restore order in the Tamil regions, they regularly avenged Tamil atrocities by indiscriminately slaughtering innocent civilians. By 1983 Sri Lanka's once-amicable groups were embroiled in a civil war that continues to this day and has already claimed at least 51,000 lives.[307] In short, the country's affirmative action programs—implemented with good intentions and under the banner of "justice"—has succeeded only in fomenting a most dreadful form of racism. Like the contents of Pandora's box, that racism, once released, could no longer be constrained. As Thomas Sowell puts it, the people of Sri Lanka discovered that racism "could not be turned on and off like a faucet."[308]

Nigeria

Nigeria's 104 million people are divided into some 250 tribes or ethnic groups, the largest of which are the Hausa and Fulani of the north, who together comprise roughly 30 percent of the country's population. Next in size are the Yorubas of the southwest and the Ibos of the southeast. These four major ethnic groups, like the Tamils and Sinhalese of Sri Lanka, have historically been represented unequally in different occupations. The Ibos and Yorubas have tended to pursue careers in lucrative, technical fields, while the Hausa-Fulani have been employed mostly in low-paying, unskilled positions. This situation did not result from any systematic discrimination but from historical happenstance. During the colonial period, Christian missionaries to Nigeria confined themselves to the southern section of the colony, bringing education, medical care, and other beneficial features of Western culture to that region alone. Thus the Ibos and Yorubas, because of their access to education, came to be overrepresented among Nigerian physicians, technicians, merchants, artisans, clerks, semiskilled workers, and college students. At all educational levels, northerners constituted only a tiny fraction of the student population. In 1926, just 5,210 of Nigeria's 138,249 primary-school children were in the north—though the north was more populous than the south. Similarly, not even one of the nation's 518 secondary-school students at the time was a northerner. By 1957 the north still had fewer than 10 percent of Nigeria's schoolchildren.[309]

After Nigeria gained its independence in 1960, northern political leaders began to institute preferential hiring and job-training programs that specifically discriminated against southerners. When no northerners were available to fill vacant positions, even expatriates were preferred to southerners. As the scope of discriminatory policies expanded, Ibos and Yorubas were increasingly excluded from retail trade, land ownership, college admissions, and government jobs.[310] Not surprisingly, these policies, and the divisive ethnic appeals undergirding them, led to colossal levels of group polarization and sporadic eruptions of mob violence. In 1966 the Ibos staged a military coup, to which northerners retaliated with a counter-coup. Thereafter it became commonplace for screaming mobs of northerners to attack their hated southern enemies with bayonets, clubs, poison arrows, and shotguns. After tens of thousands of Ibos had been systematically massacred in this manner, they staged a mass exodus and seceded from the rest of Nigeria, forming the independent nation of Biafra in 1967. Two and a half years of civil war followed, in which at least a million people died.[311] There is perhaps no more graphic illustration of the potential dangers of preferential policies than the tragic story of Nigeria.

Malaysia

Malaysia, located in Southeast Asia, has a population that is roughly three-fifths Malay and one-third Chinese. Though the Malays have been politically dominant over the years, their Chinese neighbors traditionally have controlled the higher echelons of Malaysian industry and education. As of 1970, Chinese entrepreneurs and investors owned the majority of Malaysia's domestic corporate interests and more than 80 percent of its retail establishments. At the same time, some 80 percent of the country's college students were Chinese. Between 1960 and 1970, almost 1,500 Chinese students nationwide received bachelor's degrees, compared to only 69 Malays. In the more demanding fields of science, mathematics, and engineering, the disparities between the two groups were even greater. Indeed, more than 400 Chinese earned engineering degrees during the 1960s, while only 4 Malays did the same.[312] These imbalances, it should be noted, were not caused by anti-Malay discrimination. As college admissions at that time were based solely on examination results, the Chinese achievements were due entirely to hard work and study. Malay leader Dr. Mahatir bin Mohamad candidly described the Chinese as a "hardened and resourceful" people. "Whatever the Malays could do," said Mohamad, "the Chinese could do better."[313]

Throughout the 1960s, Malaysian political leaders grew increasingly troubled by the scholastic and economic gulf between the Chinese and Malays. To "correct" the situation, the government implemented a "New Economic Policy" designed to achieve "racial balance." Affirmative action programs giving Malays preferences for loans, college admissions, government jobs, and private-sector activities were instituted and greatly expanded well into the 1970s. But unfortunately these preferences failed to lessen intergroup hostilities. Rather, the Malays became more race-conscious than ever, repeatedly unleashing bloody riots against the Chinese.[314]

Historical Ethnic Differences

Germans

Affirmative action advocates in the United States are reluctant to concede that entire cultures—like individual human beings—often differ from one another fundamentally in interests, values, and work habits. One of human history's most self-evident realities is that different groups of people traditionally have been drawn to, and have prospered in, differing pursuits. Consider the example of the Germans, who in eighteenth-century America established a reputation for being relentlessly hard workers whose farm labor was of a much higher quality than that of most contemporaries.[315] In skilled trades as well, Germans were considered superior to people of other nationalities. Their proficiency in glass blowing, wagon making, and gunsmithing was widely recognized, as were their contributions to the printing, brewing, piano, and construction industries.[316] More than any particular skills, however, what guided Germans to success in America was a set of values—in particular, their esteem for hard work, thrift, and education.[317] Their social and economic ascent was fueled by persistent toil, not political activism or welfare programs implemented on their behalf.

People of German ancestry have experienced similar success in virtually every country to which they have migrated. In Brazil, for instance, "their economic contributions [have been] out of all proportion to their numbers."[318] By 1950, Germans owned more than half of all the industrial enterprises in the southern Brazilian states, while Brazilians of Portuguese ancestry, who comprised the majority of the population, owned only one-fifth.[319] In Australia, too, Germans have made significant contributions in science, the arts, and the piano and wine industries. There, as elsewhere, they quickly developed a reputation as "sober, industrious, frugal, honest, and law-abiding people."[320]

Irish

In stark contrast to their German counterparts, Irish immigrants were not, for the most part, entrepreneurs. Eighteenth- and nineteenth-century observers described them, rather, as "habituated to working for others, not striking out on [their] own."[321] Nor did education occupy a lofty position in the Irish hierarchy of values. Considered "hostile" to literacy, Ireland was the only nation in Europe not to build a single university during the Middle Ages.[322]

The nineteenth-century Irish were infamous for their untidy living habits, not only in their homeland, but in England and America as well. Even in urban communities, they were accustomed to keeping farm animals in their homes—a practice that generally resulted in filthy, unsanitary living quarters.[323] Alcoholism, too, was a prominent feature of Irish life, both in Ireland and overseas. As early as the sixteenth century, travelers to Ireland noted widespread drunkenness throughout the country. To this day, in fact, Irish citizens spend a higher percentage of their personal incomes on alcohol than do the people of any other European nation.[324] In modern America, the Irish "drink more, and more frequently, than any other ethnic group."[325]

Given the degree to which alcohol permeated Irish social life, it is not surprising that violence continuously plagued Irish communities of the 1800s, where the impulsive brawls of "the fighting Irish" were legendary.[326] In nineteenth-century America, Irish neighborhoods developed a reputation as especially dangerous places—from New York to New Orleans to Milwaukee.[327] Throughout their early history in Britain as well, the Irish were renowned for their fighting and drunkenness[328]—prompting British contemporaries to describe them contemptuously as people of "laughing savagery."[329]

Their reputation for such behavior made Irish immigrants undesirable as neighbors to early-nineteenth-century Americans. When Irish families moved into an already established neighborhood, members of other ethnic groups often packed up and left in disgust or fear. Landlords actually preferred renting to black rather than Irish tenants, and employers were reluctant to hire anyone of Irish ancestry. Help-wanted advertisements frequently read, "No Irish need apply," or "any color or country except Irish."[330] In the mid-1800s, Irish immigrants suffered the taunts and violence of such groups as the Know-Nothings, a powerful movement of anti-Catholic exclusionists.[331] Francis Walker, who headed the American Economic Association during that period, characterized the Irish as "beaten men from beaten races, representing the worst failures in the struggle for existence."[332] One writer of the period mused, "The best remedy for whatever is amiss in America would be if every Irishman should kill a Negro and be hanged for it."[333]

Both at home and abroad, the Irish of the 1800s generally lived in squalor. Even American slaves enjoyed better food and living conditions than did the peasants of Ireland. The average life expectancy for an American slave was thirty-six years; for the Irish peasant, a mere nineteen years.[334] W.E.B. Du Bois wrote that when black slaves were freed in the post-Civil War era, they were—though destitute—"not as poor as the Irish peasants."[335] The abolitionist and former slave Frederick Douglass, when visiting Ireland in the 1840s, was so appalled by the poverty there that he was almost "ashamed to lift my voice against American slavery."[336] Along the same lines, one visitor to Ireland in the 1830s wrote, "I have seen the Indian in his forests and the negro in his chains, and thought, as I contemplated their pitiable condition, that I saw the very extreme of human wretchedness; but I did not then know the condition of unfortunate Ireland."[337] Irish immigrants to America were no better off. Penniless and packed together in filthy slums, the majority were unskilled laborers heavily concentrated in the most difficult, menial, and dangerous jobs.[338]

The status of Irish Americans has improved dramatically over the past century. By the early 1980s they had equalled the American national average in both income and I.Q.—thereby completing one of history's "great social transformations of a people."[339] The Catholic Church, whose hierarchy in the United States came to be dominated by people of Irish ancestry, played a major role in this transformation. By promoting education and discouraging violence and drinking, the Church helped the Irish assimilate into American society.[340] It is noteworthy that when the Irish began to discard some of their more disagreeable behaviors, they won the respect of many who formerly despised them.

Italians

Like other ethnic groups, Italians historically have had their own unique set of cultural attributes, among which are a strong emphasis on hard work and frugality.[341] In Brazil and Argentina, nineteenth-century Italian immigrants developed reputations for being willing to take whatever jobs were available, while others—native Argentines, for instance—disdained "menial" labor.[342] Said one Argentine contemporary during that period, "Phenomenal is their [Italians'] fervor for work: all wish to get rich, and quickly."[343] This work ethic was the driving force behind the great economic strides that Italians made not only in South America, but in the U.S. and Australia as well.

Italian immigrants commonly began life in their new homelands under appalling conditions and had few, if any, possessions.[344] In nineteenth-century Brazil, Italian indentured laborers "were subjected to many abuses—frauds, sexual assaults on women and girls, and floggings of male workers, all reminiscent of the system of slavery that had only recently been abolished."[345] In the United States, most pre-1900 Italian immigrants were young males living packed together in cramped quarters—as many as ten people per room in some places.[346] Few of them came to America with any significant amount of formal education. Fully half worked at unskilled, manual jobs, and almost none had white-collar or professional occupations. In the western U.S., Italian laborers were concentrated in vineyards, wineries, and farms, while in urban areas they flocked to construction jobs. From their meager wages, many saved enough money to bring their families over from Italy; by 1910, in fact, their wives and daughters constituted more than one-third of New York's garment-industry labor force.[347]

Higher education, meanwhile, played a small role in Italian American life well into the twentieth century. As late as 1969, only 6 percent of Italian Americans over the age of thirty-five were college graduates.[348] For most, the preferred paths to upward mobility were via blue-collar work and small-business ownership. By toil and thrift, they made remarkable economic progress over the span of just a few decades. Whereas in 1910 their incomes were less than half the national average, by 1968 they exceeded the national average.[349]

Japanese

It is by no means axiomatic that groups which historically have been mistreated will forever lag behind others socially or economically. As Thomas Sowell explains, "Groups with a demonstrable history of being discriminated against have, in many countries and in many periods of history, had higher incomes, better educational performance, and more 'representation' in high-level positions than those doing the discriminating."[350] Consider, for example, the Japanese. Following Japan's attack on Pearl Harbor in 1941, approximately 120,000 people of Japanese ancestry living in the United States—most of them American citizens—were subjected to mass internment in prison camps, where they were kept behind barbed wire fences and were under constant military guard until December 1944. During their detention, their belongings were either stolen or sold off, resulting in property losses of at least $400 million[351]—a figure that today would be many times that amount. While legitimate national-security concerns may have necessitated the internments, the fact remains that what was done to Japanese Americans during World War II was far more severe than anything done to any other American minority group at that time or since.

After their release, they began the arduous work of putting their lives back together, a task they accomplished with impressive speed. By 1959 they had equalled the average income of whites, by 1969 they were earning nearly one-third more than the average American family,[352] and as of 1990 their incomes were 50 percent above the national average.[353] It should be noted that their rise to prosperity was rooted not in political activism, but in such factors as low rates of out-of-wedlock births and broken homes; a great capacity for hard work; a higher-than-average percentage of households with more than one income earner; and an above-average tendency to study mathematics and science in school, thereby preparing themselves for employment in high-paying, technical fields.[354]

Acculturation and increased social acceptance were important by-products of Japanese Americans' extraordinary economic gains. By 1980, three-fourths of them spoke only English, and their rate of intermarriage with whites was rising steadily.[355] Consider further the observations of Dr. Thomas Sowell:

> The military aggressions of Japan in the 1930s and 1940s generated anti-Japanese sentiments in many countries, usually to the detriment of the Japanese living in those countries. The far greater acceptance of the Japanese overseas in the postwar years, after the fears and hostilities aroused by Japan's military threat had passed, suggests that hostility to the local Japanese was not purely racial or due simply to locally generated economic rivalry or social friction. . . . The remarkable reversal of public attitude toward the Japanese over the years—especially in Australia, Peru, and the United States—suggests that behavior and performance are more effective ways of changing other people's minds than moral crusades or emotional denunciations.[356]

Jews

Perhaps no group has better demonstrated an ability to endure hardship than the Jews, who throughout their existence have been subjected to some of the most horrific cruelties in the annals of human history. During the Crusades, for instance, the rising religious fervor of Christians inspired angry mobs to massacre Jewish "unbelievers" by the thousands.[357] Throughout the Middle Ages, Jews were repeatedly victimized by "confiscatory taxation, mass expulsions, orgies of mob violence, looting, and systematic destruction of property."[358] Some European countries went so far as to issue edicts requiring Jews to live in quartered-off sections of towns or cities, separate from all other people.[359] Many of these ghettos were fully enclosed by walls with gates that were locked at night, so as to keep the purportedly menacing inhabitants away from Christians.[360] Indeed, Jews were often blamed for calamities that could not otherwise be explained. For example, during the Black Death that killed perhaps half the European population during the mid-1300s, many claimed that Jews had created the plague by poisoning the drinking water in Europe's wells. In retribution for this alleged treachery, legions of Jews were slaughtered in Germany, Belgium, Switzerland, France, and Spain.[361]

In the Muslim world, Jews were not only subjected to open humiliation, but were forced to convert under pain of execution.[362] Thousands more fell prey to the recurring riots and massacres of fourteenth- and fifteenth-century Spain.[363] In 1492 a royal decree expelled all Jews from Spain and confiscated their property.[364] Seventeenth-century eastern Europe was marked by "almost uninterrupted massacres of Jews,"[365] at least 100,000 of whom were slaughtered in Poland alone between 1648 and 1658.[366] The Greek Orthodox Cossacks of that period ravaged Jews with startling savagery, sawing them to pieces, flaying them alive, roasting them to death over slow fires—even slitting infants in half with their swords.[367] After more than two additional centuries of continued persecution, nearly a third of eastern Europe's Jews fled their homelands as the 1800s drew to a close—an exodus shadowed by that of Russian Jews trying to escape the increasingly bloody pogroms in their own country.[368] And of course, the most well-known examples of atrocities aimed at Jews were carried out in Adolf Hitler's extermination camps, where millions were murdered in the 1940s.[369]

In the late 1800s Jewish immigrants arrived in America with less money than most other newcomers and lived in extreme poverty, huddled together in tiny quarters. Yet they quickly developed a reputation for working long hours for little pay, and gradually saved enough money to start their own small businesses or finance their children's schooling.[370] Unlike their Italian counterparts, they placed a premium on formal education. As early as 1916, Jews constituted a large percentage of the students at several New York City colleges and eventually became "overrepresented" in such professional fields as dentistry, medicine, and law.[371] Moreover, they developed a vibrant spirit of entrepreneurship. When discrimination excluded them from many occupations, they started enterprises of their own—eventually dominating the garment and motion picture industries.[372]

Today more than 40 percent of the world's Jews live in the United States. Theirs has been a remarkable story of struggle and triumph. By 1969, Jewish family income in this country was 72 percent higher than the national average.[373] Not surprisingly, many "civil rights leaders" point to Jewish prosperity as proof of America's alleged inequities. They assert, for instance, that Jews in the U.S. earn much more than Hispanics because the former face less discrimination than the latter. But this assertion fails to explain why Jews *throughout Latin America* are also more prosperous than the native Hispanic populations of that region.[374] It requires intellectual integrity to look beyond discrimination as a knee-jerk explanation for all intergroup inequalities.

Chinese

Chinese immigrants in numerous countries have demonstrated an extraordinary ability to overcome imposing social obstacles and to break the shackles of poverty via the sheer force of hard work. As Thomas Sowell writes:

> The cultural advantages that enable some groups to advance faster—and particularly to advance from poverty to affluence—need not be specific skills. The Chinese who immigrated into Southeast Asia or to the United States usually had little to offer besides a monumental ability to work hard and long, and to save their money. Even with groups who had useful job skills—such as the eastern European Jews who entered the garment industry in the United States—their greatest success came ultimately in other fields, using new skills acquired by education or experience. Attitudes and work habits are often more crucial—and take longer to acquire—than do specific skills. The Chinese's aptitude for arduous and painstaking work—demonstrated in numerous manual occupations in Southeast Asia and the United States—readily produced scientists and mathematicians in both places, when the opportunities arose. But groups without such traits seldom choose science and mathematics as fields of study, even when they are financially able to reach the college or university level.[375]

Dr. Sowell describes the extreme discrimination that Chinese immigrants have faced—and thrived in spite of—in various parts of the world:

> Throughout Southeast Asia, for several centuries, the Chinese minority has been—and continues to be—the target of explicit, legalized discrimination in various occupations, in admission to institutions of higher learning, and suffers bans and restrictions on land ownership and places of residence. Nowhere in Malaysia, Indonesia, Vietnam, Thailand, or the Philippines have the Chinese ever experienced equal opportunity. Yet in all these countries the Chinese minority—about 5 percent of the population of Southeast Asia—owns a majority of the nation's total investments in key industries. By the middle of the twentieth century, the Chinese owned 75 percent of the rice mills in the Philippines, and between 80 and 90 percent of the rice mills in Thailand. They conducted more than 70 percent of the retail trade in Thailand, Vietnam, Indonesia, Cambodia, the Philippines, and Malaysia. In Malaysia, where the anti-Chinese discrimination is written into the Constitution, is embodied into preferential quotas for Malays in government and private industry alike, and extends to admissions and scholarships at the universities, the average Chinese continues to earn twice the income of the average Malay.[376]

Through much of American history, immigrants of Chinese ancestry were well acquainted with racism's sharp sting. In 1790 they, along with blacks, were excluded from citizenship when Congress forbade the naturalization of anyone who was not a "free white person." When blacks finally were granted citizenship eighty years later, the Chinese were not. The low esteem in which Chinese people were held was expressed by California's 1879 constitution, which specifically denied voting rights to "natives of China, idiots, and insane persons."[377] It was not until 1943 that the Chinese were permitted to become American citizens.[378]

Chinese immigrants to the United States began arriving in significant numbers during the 1850s, settling principally in California. Nearly all of them were men, and most remained celibate for years because white American women, for whom consorting with Asians was considered a social disgrace, would have nothing to do with them. Some eventually returned home to seek wives, but only after firmly establishing themselves in this country.[379] Because of their readiness to work long hours for meager wages, they aroused the resentment of many native-born Americans. Consequently, the California legislature levied a host of exacting taxes and fees upon all Chinese residents of the state.[380]

In the 1860s thousands of Chinese immigrants toiled at the backbreaking work of building our nation's railroads. A decade later many of them found jobs in the canning, cigar, and clothing industries. Others, meanwhile, worked at draining the swamps and marshlands of California—an enterprise that made it possible to build the city of San Francisco.[381] During this period, Chinese overseers herded boatloads of unskilled laborers to the New World and worked them mercilessly.[382] In response, President Ulysses S. Grant openly opposed Chinese immigration to the U.S. because the newcomers were often brought here under conditions similar to those of the black slaves who had just recently been freed.[383] The 1870s also saw legions of Chinese men shipped as virtual slaves to the Caribbean, where they were bought and sold like animals in what were called "man markets."[384]

From 1882 to 1943, the U.S. government allowed no Chinese immigrants to enter the country.[385] Meanwhile, those already here faced constant discrimination but nonetheless gained a reputation for being exceptionally hard workers. They were particularly concentrated in California's shrimp-fishing and agricultural industries until discriminatory taxes, legislation, and violence eventually drove them from those occupations.[386] Because they were barred from most types of employment and had few alternatives open to them, many Chinese Americans started their own laundry businesses; by 1920 more than one-fourth of all Chinese men in the United States were laundry workers. Many others were restaurant workers, personal servants, houseboys, cooks, and farm laborers. Less than 1 percent had professional occupations.[387] From their low wages in these various endeavors, they saved whatever money they could and steadily improved their economic status.

In more recent times, formal education has become a central feature of Chinese tradition. In fact, Chinese American students have developed a reputation for behaving better and working harder than their white peers. On the collegiate level, Chinese Americans tend to specialize in the most difficult and lucrative fields, such as medicine, science, and engineering.[388] Of all American ethnic groups today, the Chinese have the highest proportion of their population working in professional and technical occupations.[389] By 1959 they had already exceeded the average national income,[390] and by 1990 their median family earnings were 61 percent above the national average.[391]

West Indians

West Indian blacks first immigrated to the United States early in the nineteenth century, though it was not until the first quarter of the twentieth century that they began to arrive in large numbers. When the Indies were plagued by widespread poverty and unemployment in the early 1900s, people of the islands were attracted to the U.S. by its growing industrial economy and its opportunities for social mobility.[392] But West Indian immigrants had great difficulty adjusting to the hardships of black life in America, frequently finding discrimination in this country to be worse than in their homeland. While many of these newcomers were highly skilled and educated, most could find no employment in their chosen professions and consequently resorted to starting their own businesses. Groups of West Indian investors commonly pooled their savings to purchase rental-apartment buildings or to finance new business ventures.[393] This inclination toward entrepreneurship still persists among West Indians, who currently own more than half of New York City's black businesses. They are particularly prominent in the publishing, real estate, advertising, banking, clothing, and taxi industries.[394] While they comprise only 1 percent of all blacks in the United States,[395] West Indians are represented in professional, white-collar, and skilled occupations at double the per capita rate of American-born blacks and slightly higher than that of the U.S. population as a whole.[396] Moreover, their average income exceeds both the national average and the Anglo-Saxon average.[397]

Compared to other immigrant groups, the black West Indians who settled in early-twentieth-century America were extraordinarily literate. Ninety-nine percent of all West Indian arrivals to the U.S. between 1911 and 1924 could read and write English. By contrast, one-fourth of European-born immigrants during those years were unable to read or write any language, and in some groups illiterates were a majority. Southern Italian newcomers, for instance, had an illiteracy rate of 54 percent.[398] Of Portuguese, Lithuanian, and Polish immigrants, scarcely half could speak English.[399]

From the moment they first set foot on American soil, West Indians were recognized by their contemporaries as hardworking, frugal people—quickly gaining a reputation for their "drive, ambition, thrift, and cleverness."[400] Black American journalist George S. Schuyler admired them for their "enterprise in business, their pushfulness."[401] James Weldon Johnson, a major figure of the Harlem Renaissance, described West Indians as "sober-minded" people who had "something of a genius for business,"[402] noting that in these respects they differed "almost totally" from "the average Negro of the South."[403] A popular slogan in Harlem during the 1920s and 1930s asserted that when a West Indian "got ten cents above a beggar, he opened a business."[404]

Historically, relations between American and West Indian blacks have been antagonistic. Economic competition between the two groups, along with cultural and political differences, have provoked considerable mutual acrimony. American blacks frequently describe West Indians as "overly aggressive, clannish, radical, and arrogant." West Indians, on the other hand, tend to characterize American blacks as undependable workers who lack ambition.[405] For this reason, many West Indian business owners are reluctant to hire American-born blacks.[406]

The Limits of Discrimination

Without visible victims on whose behalf they could claim to fight, "civil rights leaders" would find themselves as irrelevant as discarded tissues blowing in the wind. Relentlessly, therefore, they continue to trumpet tales of victimization—even where none exists—claiming all the while that their ultimate goal is "justice." The remarkable success stories of the ethnic groups discussed in this chapter, however, expose the shortcomings of a vision which defines all inequality as the fruit of exploitation; which presumes that discrimination against a particular group leads inevitably to that group's substandard achievement; and which dismisses any possibility that the members of such a group could ever rise to prosperity.

Just as the substandard performance of some groups is by no

means proof, in itself, that they have been discriminated against, neither can the overachievement of other groups be regarded as *prima facie* evidence that they have benefited from societal biases in their favor. Asian Americans, for example, whose history in this country has been fraught with extreme discrimination, are today significantly overrepresented among U.S. college students—particularly at the most prestigious schools and in the more demanding fields of study.[407] In fact, some 47 percent of Asian Americans aged twenty-five to forty-four are college graduates, a rate two-thirds higher than that of white Americans in the same age bracket.[408] Further, the scholastic success of Asian Americans has come in spite of the fact that even today many schools discriminate against them in admissions policies, holding them to tougher standards than either their black or white peers (see page 221 for explanation).[409] As Thomas Sowell notes, Asians have neither "the power to 'exclude' the majority of the American population from American colleges and universities, nor to discriminate against them in admissions, choice of fields, or academic success."[410]

Sowell discusses the logical problems inherent in any attempt to characterize all group differences as the effects of discrimination:

> Tempting as it is to imagine that the contemporary troubles of historically wronged groups are due to those wrongs, this is confusing causation with morality. The contemporary socioeconomic position of groups in a given society often bears no relationship to the historic wrongs they have suffered. Both in Canada and in the United States, the Japanese have significantly higher incomes than the whites, who have a documented history of severe anti-Japanese discrimination in both countries. The same story could be told of the Chinese in Malaysia, Indonesia, and many other countries around the world, of the Jews in countries with virulent anti-Semitism, and a wide variety of other groups in a wide variety of other countries. Among poorer groups as well, the level of poverty often has little correlation with the degree of oppression. No one would claim that the historic wrongs suffered by Puerto Ricans in the United States exceed those suffered by blacks, but the average Puerto Rican income is lower than the average income of blacks.
>
> None of this proves that historic wrongs have no contemporary effects. Rather, it is a statement about the limitations of our knowledge. . . . To pretend to disentangle the innumerable sources of intergroup differences is an exercise in hubris rather than morality.[411]

The plain truth is that statistical disparities between groups are now, and always have been, commonplace around the world.[412] It is by no means a foregone conclusion that affirmative action is an appropriate means of "correcting" such imbalances. Would it really make sense, for instance, to "rectify" the overrepresentation of blacks in the National Basketball Association? Would some important social need be addressed by mandating that Asians, Europeans, Polynesians, or Arabs be admitted to the league in roughly equal proportions to their numbers in American society? "Civil rights leaders" do not ask such questions concerning areas that blacks dominate. Yet they complain regularly about the "injustice" of unequal racial distributions in fields where blacks are underrepresented. Indeed, Jesse Jackson favors affirmative action in all sectors of American life. He proposes that for the nearly $600 billion that black Americans spend each year, they should be guaranteed a corresponding share of the service and manufacturing contracts that companies award.[413] "We must have a plan to achieve equal results," he asserts.[414]

Social commentator George Gilder rejects the notion that preferential treatment holds the key to upward mobility or social justice:

> [E]very successful ethnic group in our history rose up by working harder than other classes, in low-paid jobs, with a vanguard of men in entrepreneurial roles. But the current poor, so it is supposed, can leapfrog drudgery by education and credentials, or be led as a group from poverty, perhaps by welfare mothers trained for government jobs. These views depict the current poor as a race . . . alien to the entire American experience, . . . radically different in motive and character from whites.[415]

Gilder describes the crippling mindset created by affirmative action programs which, though ostensibly intended to help the "downtrodden," serve only to dissolve ambition for work and self-improvement:

> A program to lift by transfers and preferences the incomes of less diligent groups is politically divisive—and very unlikely—because it incurs the bitter resistance of the real working class. In addition, such an effort breaks the psychological link between effort and reward, which is crucial to long-run upward mobility. Because effective work consists not in merely fulfilling the requirements of labor

contracts, but in "putting out" with alertness and emotional com-mitment, workers have to understand and feel deeply that what they are given depends on what they give—and they must supply work in order to demand goods. Parents and schools must inculcate this idea in their children both by instruction and example. Nothing is more deadly to achievement than the belief that effort will not be rewarded, that the world is a bleak and discriminatory place in which only the predatory and the specially preferred can get ahead. Such a view in the home discourages the work effort in school that shapes earnings capacity afterward.[416]

Gilder's ideas echo those expressed long ago by Booker T. Washington, who wrote that "progress in the enjoyment of all the privileges that will come to us must be the result of severe and constant struggle rather than of artificial forcing."[417] Gilder contends that our national leaders have a duty to speak truthfully on matters of race, and to finally move beyond the rote recitation of platitudes that blame all black problems on white racism:

> The refusal of American leaders to tell the truth about blacks is more important when it comes to black poverty. The prevailing ex-pressed opinion is that racism and discrimination still explain the low incomes of blacks. The proposition is at once false and insidi-ous. Not only does it slander white Americans, it deceives and de-moralizes blacks. Not only does it obstruct the truth, it encourages, by its essential incredibility, the alternate falsehood, held in private by many blacks and whites, that blacks cannot now make it in America without vast federal assistance, without, indeed, the very govern-ment programs that in fact account for the worst aspects of black poverty and promise to perpetuate it. Finally, the liberal belief in bigotry as an explanation for the condition of blacks leads to still more preposterous theories about the alleged poverty of other groups, from women to Hispanics, and to a generally manic-depres-sive vision of the economy, in which poverty is seen both as more extreme and more remediable [by external intervention] than it is. . . .
>
> To get a grip on the problems of poverty, one should . . . forget the idea of overcoming inequality by redistribution. . . . [Any] effort to take income from the rich, thus diminishing their investment, and give it to the poor, thus reducing their work incentives, is sure to cut American productivity, limit job opportunities, and perpetuate poverty.[418]

Like Gilder, Ken Hamblin, the black host of a Denver talk-radio program, deems preferential policies destructive to African Americans:

> Quotas and affirmative action are killing us. It's a system that says if you're black, then we won't expect so much from you, we won't challenge you. Well, dammit, I think it's time we start demanding, challenging, expecting. We've come to a point where every time a white person sees a black person in a job, they assume it's affirmative action. Do you know how demeaning that is? . . . You whites have done your job. You got rid of slavery. You marched for the end to segregation in the South, got rid of the poll taxes. Thank you very much. Now let us go. Let us achieve. Let us fail. We are capable of being held accountable.[419]

Few individuals articulate the pitfalls of affirmative action as capably as public speaker Emanuel McLittle, the president of Destiny Communications based in Selma, Oregon. In a 1993 debate with Jesse Jackson, McLittle gave this reply to Jackson's assertion that preferential policies were needed to counteract antiblack discrimination:

> I am troubled by the whole trend that we hear coming not only from you, [Mr. Jackson,] but from many of those people who pretend to speak for black America, that imply that blacks cannot achieve, cannot make it without the liberal arm of affirmative action. Not only did I make it without affirmative action, I never heard of it. I never heard of anything like affirmative action during those years in the sixties and seventies when I burned the candle at both ends to go through school at night, during the day, and worked at the same time to support a wife and two children. Nobody gave me anything—ever—and not only am I furiously opposed to that whole notion that every black American is somehow . . . a magical recipient of special programs advanced by the civil rights leadership, but I am equally disappointed to hear the joining implication that, without help, we can't make it alone. . . .
> You seem to be void of the whole notion that in [the 1990s] black Americans are as mature and as developed and as wealthy as other peoples. You seem to negate [this] and always render us [blacks] to a status of childlike infants—politically, economically, socially, spiritually—a people who constantly need help. And I'm puzzled why it is that your help is always generated from liberal whites. . . . We are grown-up Americans now. And we lead—many

of us—the most powerful and the most wealthy cities in this country . . . and our police chiefs in those cities are black. Our boards of education are black.

You talk a great deal about historical wrong. Well, historical wrong is just that—historical. It is in the past. Much of what you have [criticized] on the air, as a spokesman for black America, has been in the past. You do not seem to be able to realize that many of us have gone beyond even many whites in this country. Many of us are extremely wealthy, including yourself. You are not exactly a poor man. And, from wherever you got your money and wherever you got your fame, you have achieved it as a black man. And many of us have made these accomplishments in life. It is time for those of us—whether you call us on the right or call us on the left—it is time for those of us who disagree with this whole victim point of view to be heard, Mr. Jackson. And it is time for us to be heard in the same light, in the same volume, in the same power that Jesse Jackson's point of view is heard.[420]

We cannot deny, of course, that American history has been blemished by many unfortunate examples of discrimination—none more severe than that suffered by blacks. Yet "civil rights leaders" serve no one's best interest by denying that our country has made enormous progress in eradicating the injustices of the past. Nor do they serve anyone by refusing to concede that history's victims—however greatly they may have suffered—are beyond the reach of our ability to help them. However pure our intentions, and however keen our desire to see justice served, we cannot correct historical wrongs by compensating the descendants of past victims. Such gestures, Thomas Sowell explains, are founded on an "*illusion* of compensation"[421]— neither helping the original victims nor punishing the original culprits:

> [T]o transfer benefits between two groups of living contemporaries because of what happened between two sets of dead people is to raise the question whether any sufferer is in fact being compensated. Only where both wrongs and compensation are viewed as collectivized and inheritable does redressing the wrongs of history have a moral, or even a logical, basis.
>
> The biological continuity of the generations lends plausibility to the notion of group compensation—but only if guilt can be inherited. . . . No one would advocate that today's Jews are morally entitled to put today's Germans in concentration camps, in compensation for the Nazi holocaust. Most people would not only be

horrified at any such suggestion, but would also regard it as a second act of gross immorality, in no way compensating the first, but simply adding to the sum total of human sins.[422]

Surely people who abolish evil traditions are to be admired. Pockets of civilized societies all over the world have, to their great credit, outlawed such abominations as slavery, cannibalism, human sacrifice, the burning of suspected witches, and the torture of political prisoners. But efforts to redress historical wrongs by compensating the *descendants* of those who were victimized—and by punishing the *descendants* of those who transgressed—tend only to bring further injustices to the present. Dr. Sowell explains:

> What must be understood first about history is that it is irrevocable. Attempts to redress the wrongs of history must face the intractable fact that whatever may be done will apply only to the future, not to the past. Most of history's victims or villains are beyond the reach of human power. Symbolic expiation creates new incentives and constraints for the future, and the specific consequences of this need serious consideration.
>
> History is a bottomless pit of wrongs. . . . We cannot simply equate past victims with current members of the same group. . . . While we cannot do anything about the past, we can at least avoid jeopardizing the future with futile symbolic attempts to undo history.[423]

Restoring Sanity

Because debates about affirmative action generally center around the issue of its moral acceptability, the policy's actual effectiveness in improving the overall status of black Americans is not often questioned. People on both sides of the dialogue tend to assume that racial preferences, whatever their philosophical merits or shortcomings, have contributed greatly to the black economic advances of the past generation. Atlanta mayor William Campbell articulated this position in 1996 when he said, "Everybody who is a person of color in this country has benefited from affirmative action. There's not been anybody who's gotten into a college on their own, nobody who's gotten a job on their own, no one who's prospered as a businessman or businesswoman on their own without affirmative action."[424]

The mayor's dramatic assertion, however, is utterly unfounded. Affirmative action has in fact been of remarkably little benefit to those for whom it was originally intended—the poor. Within those groups earmarked for preferential treatment, the relative position of poor individuals has actually *declined* under affirmative action.[425] This is in large measure due to the nature of the penalties that await anyone found to be violating affirmative action laws. Employers, keenly aware of the possibility that they will face discrimination charges if they should ever have to fire a black worker, are hesitant to risk hiring those marginal cases that affirmative action is purportedly intended to help.[426] One company, for instance, was sued by the EEOC after firing a black employee who had been late or absent nearly once in every three working days over an eight-month period. "When we fired him," the employer explained, "I had to provide reams of data comparing lateness and absenteeism by observed skin color for all apprentices within his particular trade over a fifty-two-week period."[427] Without a doubt, the ever-looming threat of such frivolous lawsuits gives employers little incentive to take a chance on hiring those blacks who most need an opportunity to prove themselves in the business world. Consequently, the prime beneficiaries of preferences are minority-group members who have already established a successful track record. As Professor Stephen L.Carter puts it, "What happened in black America in the era of affirmative action is this: Middle-class black people are better off and lower-class black people are worse off."[428]

While middle-class blacks have undeniably realized tremendous social and economic gains since preferential policies became widespread in the early 1970s, there is no evidence that those policies created—or even contributed to—the gains. Black economic progress was well underway, and proceeding at a brisk pace, long before affirmative action even came into being. It was in the 1940s and 1950s, in fact, that black poverty had begun to decline, that the racial income gap had begun to shrink, and that black college enrollment and professional advancement had started their dramatic upswings. Surprisingly, these trends did not pick up speed following the civil rights reforms of the 1960s, but simply continued their steady, unremitting climb. Nor did black progress quicken after the rise of racial preferences in the early 1970s.[429] It is intellectually dishonest, then, to credit affirmative action programs for setting in motion advancements that had already gained considerable momentum well before those programs even existed. Few Americans are aware that by 1971, black couples with two working spouses were earning 5 percent *more* than white couples of the same description in every part of the United States except the South. Notably, this was *before* affirmative action became widespread and, more importantly, *before* it became synonymous with racial preferences.[430] As scholar and author Charles Murray writes, "There's hardly a single outcome—black voting rights, access to public accomodation, employment, particularly in white-collar jobs—that couldn't have been predicted on the basis of pre-1964 trend lines."[431]

Nonetheless, rivers of money are poured with great urgency into preference programs, whose direct and indirect costs in 1991 alone totaled some $115 billion and may have depressed our country's Gross National Product by as much as 4 percent. Incredible though it may seem, we have spent trillions of dollars on affirmative action programs over the past twenty-five years "to create an outcome that would have happened even if the government had done nothing."[432]

By assuming that white bigotry is the black community's predominant obstacle, and that racial preferences are a necessary safeguard against that bigotry, affirmative action does not speak to the most serious problems afflicting black Americans. Black columnist Joseph Perkins names some of those problems: "As long as there are 6.5 million blacks lacking high-school diplomas, [more than 750,000][433] blacks in correctional institutions, 157,000 black teenage mothers and 510,000 teenage drug abusers, it is only wishful thinking to expect the race as a whole to ever achieve parity with whites."[434]

Professor Cornel West, like most other supporters of affirmative action, claims that without preferences "it is a virtual certainty that racial . . . discrimination would return with a vengeance."[435] But West and his ilk ignore the very relevant fact that white opinions about anti-black discrimination no longer resemble—even remotely—those of decades and centuries past. Indeed, white attitudes toward blacks have been studied extensively for fifty years, and all reliable research shows a revolution of the mind virtually without precedent in our nation's history.[436] Public opinion polls indicate that as early as 1975 white support for equal employment opportunities exceeded 90 percent and today is practically unanimous.[437]

Arguments supporting racial preferences also fail to acknowledge that if a white employer were to hire poorly qualified whites in preference to well qualified blacks, he would pay a price for his discrimination. That is, his business would suffer a diminution of overall efficiency, productivity, profitability, and public esteem. In much the same way, if a white banker were to reject, for racist reasons, the loan applications of qualified black candidates, he too would pay a price for his bigotry—by losing potentially profitable loans. A car salesman would pay a similar price for refusing to sell automobiles to black customers because he disliked blacks.

Because a competitive market puts a price on discrimination, the private sector historically has discriminated far less than has government. The regulation that once required southern blacks to sit in the back section of buses illustrates this point. Blacks were not relegated to those seats because bus companies wanted them to sit there, but because of Jim Crow laws passed by politicians. When these laws spread throughout the South about a century ago, private bus companies not only opposed them but actually challenged them in court. Even after their efforts to have the laws repealed were unsuccessful, companies were slow to enforce seating regulations, for fear of alienating potential black customers and thereby losing revenues.[438] It was not until bus companies were threatened with government lawsuits, and their employees were arrested for noncompliance, that the buses of the South became segregated.[439]

Such a scenario is not at all unique to the United States. In most countries around the world, discrimination has been greater in government-controlled industries than in the private sector. In fact, it is quite common for people in private industry to furtively circumvent governmental edicts requiring them to discriminate. For instance, when South Africa was ruled by its white minority, violations of apartheid laws were common in competitive market sectors. In clear breach of housing regulations, hundreds of thousands of blacks lived in areas that the government had designated "for whites only." Similarly, hundreds of construction companies quietly hired "too many" blacks—including many in positions higher than the laws allowed.[440] Clearly, neither South African employers nor landlords were eager to forego the benefits of hiring or renting to desirable black individuals. It was only after the government began to mandate discrimination and punish noncompliance that they felt compelled to discriminate.

Governments tend to discriminate more than private-sector businesses not because the former are composed of morally defective people, but because discrimination costs them nothing. Unlike privately owned companies, a government—federal, state, or local—suffers no financial consequences if its discriminatory policies are inefficient and wasteful; it can simply increase or reapportion its tax revenues to off-set the losses.[441] By contrast, inefficiency and waste can cost private businesses their very existence. Given these facts, one would expect crusaders for minority advancement to favor competitive markets and repudiate government controls. To the contrary, however, today's "civil rights leaders" overwhelmingly favor the latter, as evidenced by their near-unanimous support for affirmative action.[442] In fact, they generally characterize proposals to end or scale back racial preferences as "assaults" on "civil rights."

    Though private-sector discrimination does, of course, occur, the messiahs of "justice" wrongly depict it as a uniquely white transgression. Consider how the Urban Institute shamelessly misrepresented the findings of its 1991 investigation of discriminatory hiring practices. In that study, researchers recruited twenty male college students, ten black and ten white, and then matched them in black-white pairs whose constituents were virtually identical in appearance, deportment, and qualifications. Both members of each pair then applied, individually, for the same entry-level jobs with a variety of private-sector companies in Chicago and the District of Columbia. The Institute monitored the results of their more than 400 separate applications. In 67 percent of all cases, neither candidate was offered a job; in 13 percent of cases, both were offered positions; in 15 percent of cases, only the white candidate received an offer; and in 5 percent of cases, only the black candidate got an offer. Hailing these findings as incontrovertible proof of racism in the workplace, the Institute neglected to mention that black interviewers in the study were just as likely as white interviewers to hire applicants of their own race.[443] Nor did it mention that in some of the cases where neither applicant was offered a position, other black job-seekers with no connection to the study may in fact have been hired. As Stephan and Abigail Thernstrom write in *America in Black and White*, "In light of the small sample size . . . and other methodological flaws, it is hard to take that small differential seriously. If it is attributable to discrimination at all, rather than chance variation, it is discrimination at a level that can barely be detected."[444]

    A similar 1991 report in Denver received far less publicity, perhaps because it in no way supported the notion that antiblack discrimination pervades the workplace. In that study, black and white job candidates met with the same reaction from interviewers 78 percent of the time, while blacks were favored in 10 percent of the cases, and whites were favored in 12 percent—yielding no statistically significant evidence of discrimination. Moreover, the Denver researchers found that more employers favored Hispanic applicants over whites than vice versa.[445]

Is there a legitimate place for affirmative action in America today? Perhaps there is—but only if the policy is practiced as it was originally intended. That is, while it may be reasonable to ask employers to take "positive steps" to publicize job openings in minority communities, compelling those same employers to hire in strict accordance with racial quotas is quite a different matter. Similarly, while it is sensible to ban racial discrimination in the workplace, it is imprudent to mandate that the racial makeup of an employer's work force mirror that of the larger community—thereby allowing him little latitude for hiring the workers he wants. While it is morally imperative to protect every *individual* from discrimination based on race or ethnicity, there is no justification for imposing quotas that trample on individual rights in order to ensure proportional *group* representation. While it is appropriate for consumers to place a cost on discrimination by organizing boycotts against companies that truly discriminate by race, it is unfair for any government to dictate by legislation whom a company must hire. And while it is proper to compensate individuals for discrimination that they themselves have suffered, it is illogical and unjust to compensate any person for discrimination suffered by total strangers in another place and time—perhaps even another century. If affirmative action is to be of any real benefit to American society, it must return to being synonymous with equal opportunity rather than quotas. Its contemporary critics, for the most part, are not racists motivated by a desire to deny minorities a chance for upward mobility. Rather, they are people who reject the folly of replacing one historical wrong with another.

"A Brutally Violent Act"

A June 1995 Supreme Court decision provided some genuine hope of ending racial preferences in the United States. In a 5 to 4 vote, the Court ruled that federal affirmative action programs would thereafter have to "be justified by evidence of particularized discrimination in a specific sector rather than a general assumption of widespread racism or sexism."[446] The Court further decreed that most federal set-aside programs were unconstitutional.[447] While these rulings stopped far short of dealing a death blow to affirmative action, they ushered in an era during which preferential policies would constitute the centerpiece of a passionate national debate. The executive and legislative branches of our government now shoulder the burden of deciding where and when affirmative action is justified.[448]

Predictably, advocates of affirmative action have maintained a strong, united front in combatting initiatives to end racial preferences. Most anti-affirmative action proposals around the country have failed to win full floor action in state legislatures.[449] President Clinton has been among those most reluctant to let preferential policies end. Though he pledged in 1995 to eliminate all of the 160 federal affirmative action programs that did not meet the Supreme Court's new guidelines, none of those programs had been ended as of October 1998.[450] When Californians voted in November 1996 to pass Proposition 209, whose purpose was to abolish public-sector group preferences in their state, the president characterized the measure as *unconstitutional.*[451] "I don't know why," said Mr. Clinton, "the people who promoted this in California think it's a good thing to have a segregated set of professional schools."[452] It is indeed astonishing that our country's highest elected official could so pervert the English language as to characterize a popular mandate against race-based school admissions as "segregation."

President Clinton, of course, is not alone in misrepresenting the intent of legislative and judicial efforts to create a level playing field for college admissions. When black and Hispanic applications to American medical schools dropped by 11 percent in 1997, many boosters of affirmative action blamed the decline on Proposition 209 and the *Hopwood* court decision, which together had outlawed public-sector race preferences in California, Louisiana, Mississippi, and Texas. The president of the American Association of Medical Colleges saw the black drop-off as "an ominous sign for the medical community and our nation, which badly needs a physician work force that is both diverse and reflective of our society as a whole."[453] Hector Garza, vice president for access and equity programs at the American Council on Education, warned that "the threat to affirmative action in many states is sending the signal to minority students that they are unwelcome."[454]

Supporters of affirmative action commonly paint their white opponents as bigots who would willingly reinstitute legalized antiblack discrimination. Presumably we are to believe that racism, rather than a desire for justice, causes whites to oppose race preferences in hirings and promotions by a ratio of nine to one.[455] As columnist Carl Rowan puts it, affirmative action's critics are animated by nothing more complex than "apoplectic spasms of bigotry" and a desire to "roll the clock back to a time of segregation and rabid racial discrimination."[456] Jesse Jackson characterizes those same people as modern-day incarnations of slaveowners and segregationists.[457] New York congressman Charles Rangel likens attempts to end race-based preferences to Hitler's crusade to exterminate Jews.[458] Legal scholar Patricia Williams claims that such terms as "quotas," "preferences," and "reverse discrimination" are white people's "con words" designed to conceal the "seeds of prejudice."[459] In April 1999, Vice President Al Gore told a cheering audience of NAACP members, "Critics of affirmative action . . . talk about [wanting] a color-blind society. Give me a break. They use their 'color-blind' the way duck hunters use their duck blind. They hide behind it and hope the ducks won't figure out what they're up to."[460]

The preceding statements demonstrate that Thomas Sowell is quite correct in observing, "If you have always believed that everyone should play by the same rules and be judged by the same standards, that would have gotten you labeled a radical sixty years ago, a liberal thirty years ago, and a racist today."[461] Consider that in October 1996, as Californians prepared to vote on affirmative action's future in their state, *advocates* of preferences actually paid $4,000 to David Duke, the former Klansman, to represent the anti-affirmative action position in a college debate. Clearly, their intent was to depict their adversaries as racist—even Klannish.[462] Along the same lines, black Atlanta mayor William Campbell said in July 1999, "Just because . . . right-wing hate groups dress themselves in suits instead of robes doesn't mean [opposition to affirmative action is] still not racism."[463]

Not surprisingly, these same advocates are inclined to portray *blacks* who oppose affirmative action as traitors to their race. Film director Spike Lee, for example, denounces Michael Williams, a black opponent of race-based college scholarships, as an Uncle Tom who deserves to be "dragged into the alley and beaten with a Louisville Slugger [baseball bat]."[464] The Reverend Amos Brown asserts that Ward Connerly—a black Board of Regents member who led the 1996 fight to pass Proposition 209 in California—is so contemptible as to not "even deserve to be called an Uncle Tom."[465] In a similar vein, California state legislator Denise Watson charges that Connerly "wants to be white,"[466] while Jesse Jackson refers to him as a "house slave" and a "puppet of the white man."[467]

Jackson also condemned Supreme Court Justice Clarence Thomas's 1995 decision to support more stringent standards for race-preference programs, characterizing Thomas's vote as "a brutally violent act" which "in effect, stabbed Dr. [Martin Luther] King, . . . paving the way back toward slavery."[468] Along with Al Sharpton, Jackson led a prayer vigil outside Thomas's home to protest the judge's decision.[469] "At night," said Jackson, "the enemies of civil rights strike in white sheets, burning crosses, . . .[whereas] by day, they strike in black [judicial] robes."[470] Carl Rowan sarcastically suggests that "if you give [Justice] Thomas a little flour on his face, you'd think you had David Duke."[471] San Francisco mayor Willie Brown calls Thomas not only "a shill and cover for the most insidious form of racism," but also a man whose views are "legitimizing of the Ku Klux Klan."[472] Brown adds that Thomas "should be reduced to talking only to white conservatives" and "must be shut out" by the black community.[473]

Joining the choir of crusaders for "justice," Charles Rangel sang a most familiar tune in response to the Supreme Court's 1995 restrictions on the racial gerrymandering of voting districts. "The only time you're going to see us [blacks]," he asked, "will it be in prisons? Will it be with the homeless? Will it be in the inner cities?"[474] Disparaging the Court's attempt to diminish the role of race in American political life, Rangel quipped sarcastically, "There's a disease called color-blindness that overnight has swept . . . this nation."[475] No statement could demonstrate more dramatically how far today's black "leadership" has strayed from Martin Luther King, Jr.'s dream.

Chapter 11

The Beloved Homeland

It's not ignorance that's so bad, but it's all the things we know that ain't so.

—Will Rogers[1]

On June 15, 1993, more than 700 black New York City school-children gathered at the United Nations to take part in a Day of the African Child celebration. They wore homemade African clothing, waved the flags of African nations, and sang African songs during festivities designed, ostensibly, to deepen the youngsters' appreciation for their heritage. A number of guest speakers eulogized some 100 black South African students who had been slain in 1976 while protesting their government's mandate that the Dutch-derived Afrikans tongue become the official language of the schools. Spectators applauded enthusiastically when one South African teen stepped to the microphone and described the struggle for liberation that was taking place in his homeland, where, under apartheid, blacks had been treated as second-class citizens for much of the twentieth century.[2]

Incidents like the 1976 student killings made South Africa the focal point of American demonstrations and boycotts throughout the

1980s, when thousands of political leaders and ordinary U.S. citizens from coast to coast participated in the "Free South Africa" protest movement.[3] Singing such inspirationals as "We Shall Overcome," they marched, displayed anti-apartheid banners, and proudly allowed themselves to be arrested for such infractions as assembling too close to the South African embassy.[4] Among those arrested were high-profile figures like TransAfrica founder Randall Robinson, Coretta Scott King, Mary Frances Berry, Dick Gregory, Harry Belafonte, Stevie Wonder, Amy Carter, the Reverend Joseph Lowery, and U.S. representatives Walter Fauntroy, Charles Hayes, John Conyers, Parren Mitchell, and Ron Dellums.[5] College students, meanwhile, organized anti-apartheid rallies on campuses all over the United States,[6] protesting not only white rule in South Africa, but also their own schools' South African investments.[7] In response to these protests, most American colleges and universities sold whatever stocks they owned in companies with business ties to South Africa.[8]

Against this backdrop of worldwide condemnation, a cultural boycott against South Africa virtually eliminated all performances there by foreign entertainers, who took their shows instead to neighboring Zimbabwe and Swaziland.[9] Additionally, American protesters and "civil rights" groups pushed for strict economic sanctions against the South African government.[10] In reaction to public pressure, U.S. corporations sold their South African holdings and drastically scaled back their operations in the land of apartheid.[11] Explaining his company's decision to stop selling its products in South Africa, Apple Computer vice president Michael Spindler candidly said, "Apple rejects the apartheid policies of the current. . . government."[12]

During apartheid's final years, American politicians publicly dissociated themselves from anything even remotely suggesting sympathy for South Africa, lest they be accused of racial insensitivity. In July 1990, for instance, New York governor Mario Cuomo's campaign committee pulled $1 million out of Chemical Bank, which had recently been blacklisted by an anti-apartheid organization. Further, the governor announced his support for a law prohibiting state pension-fund investments in any companies conducting business in South Africa.[13] In a similar spirit, numerous American states and cities sold whatever shares they held in firms with South African ties.[14] New York and Boston combined for $700 million worth of such divestitures in December 1984.[15] Most money-center banks stopped lending to the South African government and its public agencies[16]—with some banks refusing even to extend credit to private South African borrowers. "We abhor the apartheid system," explained the president of one such bank.[17] "Civil rights" groups went so far as to brand South Africa an outlaw nation. The NAACP, in fact, petitioned the United Nations to expel South Africa from its General Assembly.[18]

While the anti-apartheid protests in the U.S. and elsewhere surely had noble intentions, one must wonder why South Africa was singled out above all other African nations for worldwide censure. Though undeniably unjust, apartheid was mild in comparison to the many forms of black-on-black tyranny that have plagued the African continent since the dawn of human history. Indeed, for many centuries recurring wars of indescribable savagery have decimated vast regions south of the Sahara, forcing tens of millions to flee their homelands.[19] Even the very recent black-perpetrated slaughters afflicting Liberia, Burundi, Rwanda, and Nigeria (discussed later in this chapter) dwarf the evils that occurred under South Africa's white rule. Moreover, freedom and civil liberties are practically unknown in Africa's black-ruled nations. Political repression is omnipresent. Terrified of government reprisals, most Africans "live in a cocoon of fear—afraid even to whisper innocuous political comments."[20] The citizens of Ghana have coined the phrase "culture of silence" to describe the suffocating atmosphere of intimidation pervading their country.[21] Untold numbers of Africans have been imprisoned, tortured, or put to death for crimes no greater than speaking out against government policies. As of 1990, only four of Africa's forty-five black-ruled countries allowed their citizens to conduct political protests without the threat of violent retribution.[22] Even under apartheid, blacks in South Africa had greater freedom of expression than blacks almost anywhere else on the continent.[23]

Recent decades have seen Africa's tyrannical governments virtually extinguish their countrymen's intellectual and creative impulses. Writers and philosophers are scarce south of the Sahara.[24] Even newspapers with long traditions of praising their nations' political leaders have been shut down for printing an occasional criticism.[25] From coast to coast, editors, journalists, poets, scholars, and professors have mysteriously "vanished" after expressing ideas contrary to those approved by their governments.[26] As Dr. George Ayittey, author of *Africa Betrayed*, puts it, "African writers lay their lives on the line for every sentence they write and publish or for every view they espouse in public."[27] The demise of literature in Uganda typifies Africa's intellectual atrophy:

> Uganda was one of Africa's most literary countries— Kampala was stocked with bookshops. Makerere University had a well-established drama troupe and Oko p'Bitek's poems were widely read. But economic collapse and political terror silenced the writers and emptied the bookshops. Many of Uganda's best writers are dead.[28]

It is hardly surprising that in such an atmosphere, African journalism has declined precipitously during the past thirty years. Whereas in the mid-1960s there were 299 daily newspapers in Africa, by the early 1980s only about 150 remained.[29] During that period, the continent's total newspaper circulation dwindled from three million to two million, with nine countries actually retaining no newspapers at all.[30]

Ninety-five percent of black Africa's population is composed of peasants, a great mass of humanity possessing almost no political power. As of 1990, only four sub-Saharan countries allowed free elections.[31] Twenty-three others were ruled by military dictatorships, while eighteen operated under a one-party system where candidates ran unopposed and then declared themselves "presidents-for-life."[32] "Some African leaders get themselves emotionally identified with their country, which they consider their personal property," observes Lieutenant General Emmanuel Erskine, the former commander of United Nations forces in Lebanon. Their belief "that they should rule until death," adds Erskine, "is the single major phenomenon creating serious political crisis on the continent. Not even bulldozers can dislodge some of these leaders from office."[33] Of the more than 180 African heads of state to hold power since 1960, fewer than twenty relinquished their authority voluntarily.[34] Professor Ayittey explains, "Government, as it is understood in the West, does not exist in many African countries. What exists is a 'mafia state,' a government hijacked by a phalanx of gangsters, crooks and scoundrels [who] extract resources from the poor peasantry to enrich themselves."[35] One Nigerian commentator expressed his own distress over these political conditions:

It is only in Africa where you still find life-presidents in the twentieth century. People live in perpetual fear of their rulers, yet we call for unity against apartheid in South Africa. African leaders portray their countries as flowing with milk and honey, yet an average African citizen today is on the verge of economic ruin.[36]

Indeed, the sins of Africa's political tyrants have produced full-scale economic disaster. Of the world's thirty-six poorest nations, twenty-four are in black Africa—despite the region's wealth of natural resources.[37] Africa has 40 percent of the world's potential for hydroelectric power, 50 percent of its gold, 90 percent of its cobalt, 50 percent of its phosphates, 40 percent of its platinum, 8 percent of its petroleum reserves, 12 percent of its natural gas, more diamonds and chromium than any other region of the globe, and millions of acres of untilled farmland.[38] Nevertheless, as of 1992 the sub-Saharan nations, populated by half a billion people, had a combined Gross Domestic Product of just $135 billion—a total roughly equal to that of Belgium, whose population was but 10 million.[39] As one African-affairs analyst puts it, "Onerous state controls, unstable currencies, runaway government expenditures, confiscatory taxes, political instability and crumbling infrastructure have conspired to create an environment inimical to development."[40] According to the Index of Economic Freedom, published jointly by the Heritage Foundation and *The Wall Street Journal*, Africa is "the least economically free continent" on earth.[41] Yet while most Africans live in dire poverty, their government officials loot countless millions of dollars from them each year.[42]

Though the oppression strangling black Africa has been far more debilitating than apartheid ever was, groups such as the Organization of African Unity (OAU), which regularly denounced South African civil rights violations, have traditionally ignored the transgressions of black governments. Consider the OAU's position on Uganda, where more than 800,000 people were murdered under the regimes of Idi Amin and his successors during the 1970s and 1980s.[43] When Amin was slaughtering 150 peasants a day, the OAU not only remained silent, but actually *elected Amin to be its president.*[44] A local Anglican bishop condemned such hypocrisy:

The OAU's silence has encouraged and indirectly contributed to the bloodshed in Africa. I mean, the OAU even went so far as to go to Kampala for its summit (in 1975) and make Amin its chairman. And at the very moment the heads of state were meeting in the conference hall, talking about the lack of human rights in southern Africa, three blocks away, in Amin torture chambers, my countrymen's heads were being smashed with sledge hammers and their legs being chopped off with axes.[45]

Thankfully, recent years have seen foreign donors—mostly Western nations—pressure a number of traditionally repressive African governments to begin embracing capitalism and democratic elections. But progress in that direction has been slow, tenuous, and frequently interrupted by bloodletting. It remains to be seen how successful these first, tentative steps toward freedom will be.[46] Between 1990 and 1995, the number of African democracies rose from four to fifteen, but then dropped to thirteen in 1997 when military regimes overthrew democratically elected governments in Congo and Sierra Leone.[47]

Surveying the Continent

Along coastal West Africa is the Republic of Liberia, a country of more than 2.6 million people, where in 1989 fierce tribal conflicts led to armed warfare pitting President Samuel Doe's Krahn and Mandingo tribesmen against the Gio and Mano troops loyal to the rebel Charles Taylor.[48] As the fighting intensified, military personnel on both sides perpetrated a host of atrocities, pitilessly slaughtering thousands of unarmed civilians.[49] In some instances, warriors destroyed entire villages and left vast stretches of the countryside virtually depopulated. They used knives and cutlasses to butcher men, women, and children. One July 1990 bloodbath saw Doe's troops massacre 600 Gio and Mano refugees inside Saint Peter's Lutheran Church in the Liberian capital of Monrovia.[50]

While mutilation, dismemberment, and cannibalism were trademarks of Doe's military reign of terror, his rebel opponents were no more merciful toward their victims. In one typically gruesome chapter of the war, rebel soldiers near the front lines killed 300 refugees and wounded 755 others, beheading and disemboweling many of them.[51] A United Nations representative described one small piece of the horror: "I saw [the bodies of] a mother who was trying to protect her son and [at] the same time had a baby on her back. The mother was shot, the baby's skull had been slashed open, and there was no brain in it."[52] It is speculated that the dismembered parts of these ravaged corpses were used in witchcraft rituals, which are common in West Africa.[53]

By April 1994 the war in Liberia had resulted in at least 150,000 deaths, nearly half of which were due to starvation.[54] Though ships filled with food supplies from around the world were sent to Monrovia, the warring parties prevented relief workers from delivering their cargoes to the dying masses.[55] With no prospect of help in sight, more than 1.5 million Liberians fled the country.[56]

Doe's regime was notorious for its rampant corruption.[57] Thievery by government officials was open and widespread. Doe himself "repeatedly conned the United States out of countless millions of dollars."[58] Further, he "rigged elections, the constitution, even the date of his own birth so he could retain the presidency."[59] In 1992, however, he was captured, tortured, and killed by troops loyal to Prince Yormie Johnson, the leader of a rebel faction.[60] Yet even in Doe's absence, life in Liberia remains difficult. Fierce combat continues to plague the country, education and health services are virtually nonexistent, and the economy is in ruins.[61]

Along the northern shore of the Gulf of Guinea is Nigeria, composed of a mostly rural and poverty-stricken population that numbers roughly 107 million.[62] There are more than 250 ethnic groups in the country, four of which—the Hausa, Fulani, Yorubas, and Ibos—dominate its economic and political life.[63] As noted in chapter 10, the traditional hostilities between these groups were exacerbated by the government-instituted preferential policies of recent decades. In the violent ethnic conflicts of the 1960s, Hausa soldiers slaughtered thousands of Ibo civilians.[64] In 1967 the beleaguered Ibos seceded from Nigeria, forming the Republic of Biafra.[65] Two and a half years of civil war ensued, during which at least a million Biafrans died— many of starvation.[66] Particularly tragic was the plight of Ibo children. Their bellies swollen and their black hair turned red by protein deficiency, they were flocked into "orphanages" where they died by the thousands.[67] When burials were possible, the dead generally were dumped into mass graves.[68] A January 1970 Ibo surrender brought an end to the war, at which time Pope Paul VI called on the victors to prevent further genocide. They answered his plea, however, with calculated defiance—displaying antipapal banners during ostenta-tious victory parades. It was only an international aid campaign spearheaded by the United States that spared the Biafrans addi-tional calamity.[69]

The years since the civil war's end have not been kind to Ni-geria. As one writer puts it, this "comatose giant of Africa may go down in history as the biggest country ever to go directly from colonial subjugation to complete collapse, without an intervening period of successful self-rule."[70] Because there are so many ethnic groups living in close proximity, some of them subdivided into mutually hostile Mus-lim and Christian sects, street violence is rampant throughout the coun-try. Armed robbery and murder are a constant worry for anyone who dares to venture outdoors.[71] With health care nonexistent, the surviv-ing victims of violence must treat their wounds without professional assistance.[72] Unemployment and inflation are out of control, and an-nual per capita income is just $375.[73] Transparency International, a private watchdog group based in Berlin, ranks Nigeria's government as the world's most corrupt.[74] Drunken soldiers commonly seize in-nocent people's belongings without cause.[75] Editors and journalists are routinely arrested—even "liquidated"—for criticizing the govern-ment in print,[76] and political prisoners are more numerous than ever before.[77] The country's four oil refineries are nonfunctional, and the funds intended for their repair have been stolen. Consequently, the world's seventh-largest oil-producer cannot even supply gasoline to its own people.[78]

South of Nigeria is Angola, the home of 10.6 million people.[79] Marked by fierce ethnic antagonisms, this nation was torn asunder by a brutal civil war that raged from 1975 to 1991—in some years killing as many as 150,000 souls.[80] After a brief peace, fighting resumed in 1992 and persisted into 1994—a period during which more than 1,000 people died each day from war-related causes, mostly famine.[81] A 1994 peace accord mitigated the conflict somewhat, but intermittent combat continued through January 1999, when all-out war erupted again.[82] Naturally, the many years of bloodshed have taken a huge toll on Angola's economy, distribution system, and infrastructure. For a full generation, the government has funneled nearly every available penny into the war effort—as demonstrated by a 1993 budget that allocated $12 million to education, $18.5 million to health, and $475 million to the military.[83] Among the long war's many dreadful legacies are at least fifteen million land mines that remain hidden under Angolan soil—rendering a third of the country's territory unusable,[84] making farming in most other areas perilous at best, and adding constantly to the list of 70,000 victims who have already lost limbs in mine explosions.[85]

Northeast of Angola is Burundi, one of the world's poorest nations—plagued for decades by an abysmal quality of life and the ever-present threat of violence. The Tutsi ethnic group—though a numerical minority making up just 14 percent of Burundi's population—has dominated the country politically and economically since the sixteenth century.[86] By contrast, the Hutu majority, comprising 85 percent of the population, has traditionally held almost no power in governmental and economic affairs.[87] The inequality existing between these groups is perhaps best expressed by the *Current History Encyclopedia*, which characterizes Burundi's social structure as "a mirror image" of South Africa's former apartheid system.[88] In recent decades thousands of Hutus, unwilling to endure the extreme discrimination aimed at them, have fled the country.[89] Those unable to escape, however, have suffered almost unimaginable misery, as Burundi's ethnic tensions have periodically exploded into some of the most horrific atrocities in human history. In 1972, for instance, when a Hutu uprising killed some 2,000 Tutsis,[90] Tutsi troops responded by putting to death more than 200,000 Hutus within six weeks[91]—many of them by starvation and torture.[92] Another Hutu insurgency in 1987 resulted in about 1,000 Tutsi deaths, prompting the Tutsi-dominated army to massacre at least 100,000 Hutus in retaliation.[93]

Most disciples of the American "civil rights" establishment are familiar with South Africa's 1960 Sharpeville Massacre, an incident in which some white policemen, surrounded by a mob of angry blacks, sprayed gunfire at the crowd and killed sixty-nine people. This may be the most infamous event that ever occurred in South Africa.[94] By contrast, few Americans understand that *black*-on-black atrocities such as those in Burundi—motivated principally by ethnic hatred—constitute a large part of African history. With their highly selective vision, our usually keen-eyed activists have carefully overlooked the transgressions of black Africans, preferring instead to direct world attention exclusively to the injustices of South African apartheid. Such "leaders" understand, of course, that any candid discussion of black-on-black brutality would not only undermine their effort to portray whites as the singular cause of black troubles worldwide, but would also make it clear that black racism and tribalism have had a long, bloody history quite apart from any white influences.

Not surprisingly, then, when Burundi was plagued by yet another eruption of ethnic violence in 1993, the "civil rights" cabal was silent again. In October of that year, Tutsi troops killed President Malchior Ndadaye, a Hutu who had been elected to office four months earlier.[95] When his death was announced, thousands of enraged Hutu peasants immediately took to the streets, seeking revenge. Armed with spears, machetes, and knives, they scoured the countryside for Tutsis they could kill[96]—in some places setting entire villages on fire. Not even young children were spared. At a gas station in the town of Kibimba, at least two dozen Tutsi schoolchildren were burned alive.[97]

Before long, however, the Tutsi army began to retaliate. Truckloads of soldiers surrounded and raided Hutu villages, indiscriminately slaughtering innocent civilians.[98] Thousands of corpses soon littered the landscape, and thousands more were dumped into rivers. Scores of refugees died each day from starvation and disease in makeshift camps.[99] Heavy combat continued into 1994, with an estimated death toll exceeding that of the 1972 genocide.[100] "It is total desolation," lamented Burundi's Interior Public Security Minister, "and the situation is catastrophic."[101] Thereafter, sporadic outbreaks of violence continued through 1999.[102]

Immediately north of Burundi is Rwanda, a nation of deeply-rooted ethnic hostilities and the scene of some of the most brutal conflicts the world has ever known. Rwanda's original inhabitants were pygmies who were succeeded several centuries ago by the hunting and farming Hutu tribe.[103] In the fifteenth century, however, the war-like Tutsis invaded from the north and reduced the Hutus to serfdom, marking the beginning of 400 years of Tutsi dominance.[104] In 1959 the Hutus, weary of their lowly status under Tutsi rule, rose up in violent revolt and seized political control of the country by the following year. This transfer of power prompted many thousands of Tutsis to flee rather than live under Hutu rule.[105]

Rwanda has long been a poor and troubled nation. Its annual per capita income is about $260,[106] life expectancy at birth is scarcely forty years,[107] and human rights violations are common. Police may enter people's homes without warrants, citizens may be detained for long periods without being formally charged with any crime, prisoners are frequently tortured, and freedom of movement within the country is greatly restricted.[108]

Such conditions seem mild, however, in comparison to the devastation that was visited on Rwanda in April 1994 after the country's president, Juvenal Habyarimana, was killed in a suspicious plane crash.[109] Violent anarchy pitting Hutus against Tutsis immediately erupted throughout the country. Armed with machetes, spears, arrows, and automatic weapons,[110] gangs of marauders raped and butchered women and children inside their homes.[111] Defenseless hospital patients were killed in their beds.[112] Not even aid workers, priests, or nuns were spared.[113] In one shameful incident, more than 2,000 refugees in a church compound were mowed down by machine gun fire.[114] In southwestern Rwanda alone, at least 22,000 Tutsis were massacred while seeking sanctuary inside Roman Catholic churches.[115] Before long, tens of thousands of rotting corpses were piled in the streets,[116] while at least that many were thrown into lakes and rivers.[117] All the while, Hutu radio stations fueled the killers' passions. "All Tutsis will perish," the announcers proclaimed. "They will disappear from the earth. We strike them down with arms. Slowly, slowly, slowly, we kill them like rats."[118]

As the fighting intensified, hundreds of thousands of terrified Rwandans took flight to neighboring Tanzania[119]—and at least a million more to Zaire, where legions died from disease in overcrowded, filthy camps.[120] The death toll in Rwanda reached 800,000 within three months[121]—and eventually exceeded a million.[122] At no point, however, did American "civil rights leaders" either denounce or lament the Rwandan carnage. At the time, in fact, they were far more agitated over some allegedly "racist" comments made by a New York Yankees' employee about minority residents of the Bronx.[123] For good measure, Al Sharpton accused white Europeans of privately cheering the destruction that would, by "depopulating" Rwanda, allow them to eventually "take over" the country.[124]

Notwithstanding Sharpton's claims, however, enormous amounts of foreign aid—mostly from Europe and the United States— were shipped to the Rwandan refugee camps.[125] The International Federation of the Red Cross set up hospitals and care centers to treat the wounded and infirmed.[126] Doctors, technicians, and medical equipment were sent by Australia, Sweden, Norway, Ireland,

America, Belgium, Holland, Germany, and Great Britain.[127] These were presumably the same white nations that Mr. Sharpton accused of conspiring to facilitate Rwanda's "depopulation." Curiously, neither Sharpton nor his fellow champions of "justice" had anything to say about the many Rwandan officials who withheld food supplies from the starving masses in an effort to reassert their power.[128]

While the depravity in Rwanda was at its height, a predominantly black team of National Basketball Association stars traveled from the U.S. to South Africa to play some exhibition basketball games and tour the country.[129] Several of the players reacted emotionally to their initial firsthand view of apartheid's former domain. Center Alonzo Mourning, for example, said, "Cape Town is so beautiful and so close to a place where black people are living—I don't know—in conditions that are just unbelievable. It's sad, depressing. Hopefully, with the change in government, with apartheid gone, that will somehow change."[130] "I've been places where there have been economic problems," added coach Lenny Wilkens, "but here, it's oppression. Here, they haven't been allowed to better themselves."[131] In a similar vein, black columnist Curtis Bunn wrote:

> There was anger at knowing that blacks reside in such inhumane conditions because of apartheid, a system under which about five million white South Africans suppressed 24 million black South Africans and other races. And there was frustration in understanding that, while [President Nelson] Mandela is in office and blacks have gained freedom with the abolition of apartheid, the essence of that ugly entity persists. . . . If nowhere else, it exists in the townships. The sight of barely clothed children living in tiny shacks in disease-infested communities brought tears to the eyes of members of the NBA's South Africa tour.[132]

Thus, while South Africa's white oppressors were the focal point of these black Americans' disdain, the uncontrolled, murderous hordes that had butchered countless blacks in Rwanda went uncriticized—simply because they too were black.

To the west of Rwanda is the Democratic Republic of Congo (known as Zaire until May 1997)—where some forty-seven million inhabitants live, for the most part, in the abject poverty spawned by the boundless corruption of their government officials.[133] Consider the actions of Mobutu Sese Seko (formerly Joseph Mobutu), who ruled the country for more than three decades before abdicating in May 1997. Early in his presidency Mobutu solidified his power by "sowing the seeds of suspicion to pit one tribe against another," thereby virtually eliminating his political opposition.[134] While his countrymen earned only $100 per year,[135] Mobutu's salary alone amounted to 17 percent of Zaire's annual budget.[136] Moreover, during his tenure he transferred at least $5 billion from the state treasury to his own foreign bank accounts.[137] With these funds, he purchased dozens of lavish properties around the world—including a fifteen-acre beach resort, a plantation of orchards, a Portuguese vineyard, a thirty-two-room Swiss mansion, and a sixteenth-century Spanish castle.[138] Not surprisingly, such self-indulgent greed made Mobutu thoroughly hated in Zaire.[139]

Though food shortages and steep inflation plagued Zaire throughout Mobutu's reign, he felt no compulsion to curb his own appetite for excess. In 1981, for instance, while visiting the United States to request financial aid, Mobutu and his entourage of nearly a hundred people spent $2 million partying in New York and Florida.[140] In response to this frivolity, the U.S. announced that it would decrease aid to Zaire—a move that Mobutu called "insulting."[141]

To this day, Congo (Zaire) continues to wallow in decay despite its vast potential for prosperity. Possessing enough arable land and hydroelectric potential to feed and power all of Africa, the country has been looted so thoroughly by its leaders that its economy has been all but obliterated:

> The capital's state-run hospitals are closed, and the patients have been sent home. . . . The public sector, by and large, has ceased to function. There is a government, there are ministers and there is even an official budget, but there is an air of fantasy about it all, since the tax collection system has broken down and virtually no custom revenues are coming in. For the most part, the government has taken to paying its bills by printing fresh batches of currency.[142]

In August 1998, shortly after Laurent Kabila overthrew President Mobutu and assumed leadership in Congo, rebel soldiers rose in revolt against Kabila. Before long, troops from seven neighboring nations—Rwanda, Uganda, Sudan, Angola, Zimbabwe, Chad, and Namibia—became involved in the conflict. Combatants on both sides committed a host of unspeakable atrocities. In one December 1998 incident, 600 civilians in the town of Makobola were herded into their houses and burned alive by rebel troops. Adults who tried to escape were gunned down, while babies and small children were thrown into deep pit latrines and left there to die.[143] Meanwhile, in retribution for the aid that Rwandan Tutsi soldiers were giving the rebels, Congolese government troops and vigilante mobs united to hunt down and slaughter thousands of Tutsis—even unarmed *civilian* Tutsis who merely resided in Congo.[144]

Uganda, situated in eastern Africa, was nearly destroyed by the barbarism of its own president, Idi Amin, during the 1970s. Assuming power in 1971, Amin embarked on a reign of terror that utterly demoralized and impoverished his nation. Among his earliest political acts was the mass expulsion of the country's 50,000 Asian immigrants[145]—a move that was actually popular among native Ugandans, who "resented the affluence of Pakistani and Indian shopkeepers and technicians."[146]

From the very beginning of his regime, Amin was notorious for the periodic purges by which he eliminated his enemies; his unpredictable extermination squads struck dread into the hearts of his countrymen.[147] Ever fearful that Amin's secret police would accuse them of some imagined crime, Ugandans huddled quietly in their homes at night.[148] Those arrested were sometimes packed eighty to a cell.[149] Many suspected dissidents were beheaded; others were disemboweled.[150] Some were herded into rooms and blown up with explosives; others were suffocated with their own severed genitals.[151] Some were forced to roll in the blood of mutilated corpses and commit cannibalism on them; others had their heads smashed with sledge hammers.[152] Amin himself often participated in these executions and was known to occasionally drink his victims' blood. At first, the rest of the world "recoiled in horrified disbelief at the tales of bodies—often hideously mutilated—floating in the Nile, of prominent citizens disappearing, and of ghastly scenes of torture and execution in Uganda's dank prisons."[153] The stories could not be ignored for long, however, as tens of thousands of refugees began flooding across Uganda's borders in search of safety,[154] all with similar tales of horror to tell.

Amin's penchant for cruelty was unsurpassed. Shortly after he abruptly divorced his three wives in 1973, one of them, who was pregnant at the time, chose to have an abortion rather than give birth out of wedlock. Amin, enraged by her decision to terminate the pregnancy, ordered his extermination squads to slaughter her and the entire family of the doctor who had performed the abortion. He then had the arms and legs of his murdered wife cut off and reattached to her body, backwards. Showing this hideous sight to the two children the woman had borne him, he said, "See what happens to bad mothers!"[155]

In 1977 Amin issued an edict calling for the arrest of hundreds of Langi tribesmen on the suspicion that they were plotting against him.[156] Once they were in custody, he had them strangled and clubbed to death. Other inmates spent six hours the following day loading the mangled bodies onto trucks. "All the heads had been smashed in," said one eyewitness, "and the floor was littered with eyes and teeth."[157]

Throughout Amin's reign, disposal of the country's innumerable butchered corpses was done in the most expedient manner possible. Thousands were dumped into mass graves in Uganda's untamed forests. Others were dropped into roadside ditches. Still others were hurled into the Nile River to be devoured by hungry crocodiles. Occasionally scuba divers had to be sent into the Nile to remove clustered bodies blocking the intake duct at the Owen Falls hydroelectric plant.[158]

In 1976 and 1977 increasing numbers of school and church groups protested the wickedness of Amin's regime. Sensing the growing unrest, as well as the uncertain loyalty of his army, Amin tried to deflect attention away from himself by claiming that Uganda had been ambushed by Tanzanian troops. "Retaliating" against this "unprovoked attack," he declared war on Tanzania in 1978—only to be defeated and run out of office the following year.[159] During his eight years as president, he and his henchmen had slaughtered approximately half a million black Africans.[160] Even after Amin's overthrow, however, Uganda did not know peace. Deeply rooted ethnic hatreds touched off more intertribal fighting,[161] resulting in at least 300,000 deaths between 1982 and 1985.[162]

Since 1986, the members of a rebel group called the Lord's Resistance Army (LRA) have terrorized northern Ugandan villages, killing adults and kidnapping their children, many of whom they enslave.[163] Boys as young as nine years old are kept undernourished, taught to shoot AK-47s, and forced to walk hours each day as roving soldiers. Girls, meanwhile, are kept as "wives" by LRA commanders.[164] Suspected enemies are dismembered, beheaded, or tied to trees and shot.[165]

As in Uganda, fierce tribalism has existed virtually everywhere in Africa for many centuries. Benin, for instance, is composed of more than forty ethnic groups whose relations historically have been hostile.[166] In Kenya, ethnic fighting in 1992-1993 killed more than 1,000 people and left an estimated 200,000 others homeless.[167] These Kenyan clashes were generally one-sided, as Kalenjin troops loyal to President Daniel arap Moi attacked droves of unarmed civilians. The aggressors chased and burned thousands out of their homes, forcing them to live in camps and churchyards without clothes, food, or money.[168] In August 1997, organized gangs from coastal ethnic groups not only destroyed homes and businesses belonging to people from inland tribes, but also hacked many of those people to death with machetes.[169] Five months later, after President Moi was elected in a vote that divided Kenyans along tribal lines, yet another round of fighting erupted.[170]

Political repression has thrived for decades in the West African nation of Guinea, where in 1958 Ahmed Sékou Touré became president and established his party as the country's sole political entity.[171] During his ghastly tenure, he imprisoned, tortured, and executed anyone thought to oppose him.[172] In all, he took at least 10,000 political prisoners,[173] about a quarter of whom simply "disappeared" in a manner reminiscent of Orwell's "vaporizations."[174] To further solidify his power, Touré also purged the army on a regular basis.[175] Upon his death in 1984, a military coup ushered in a new president and prime minister. Unfortunately for the people of Guinea, however, these new leaders were no less ruthless than Touré in eliminating suspected opponents.[176]

In 1972 Equatorial Guinea was placed under the barbarous regime of President-for-Life Francisco Marcias Nguema. Declaring himself to be the country's only god, he demanded that his own portrait be displayed on every altar in this predominantly Catholic land.[177] The Church's refusal to comply prompted Nguema to murder thousands of his Catholic countrymen in retribution. By the time he was overthrown in 1979, he had slaughtered some 50,000 people, or about one-seventh of the country's population.[178]

The 11.4 million people of Zimbabwe, located in southeastern Africa, have suffered greatly under the nefarious government of President Robert Mugabe. From the moment he assumed power in 1980, Mugabe's plan was to maintain a one-party state, "a truly Marxist-

Leninist party to ensure the charting of an irreversible social course and create a socialist society."[179] When asked to define socialism, he candidly replied, "In Zimbabwe, socialism means what's mine is mine, but what's yours we share."[180] Not surprisingly, under this economic arrangement most of Zimbabwe's population has lived in dire poverty for years. Annual per capita income in the country is but $700,[181] the unemployment rate among high-school graduates is 50 percent, and prospects for the future seem even bleaker. Some 280,000 students now graduate from Zimbabwean high schools each year, only to flood a job market with no more than 12,000 openings.[182]

The early 1980s saw growing numbers of rebels challenging Mugabe's rule. Prominent among them were the Ndebele southerners, from whom the government began to withhold vital food shipments. In Mugabe's attempt to starve these adversaries into submission, he made no effort to differentiate between actual dissidents and members of the general Ndebele population.[183] Indeed, the president and his Shona supporters slaughtered more than 43,000 Ndebele tribesmen between 1980 and 1993, though the total number of dissidents did not exceed 9,000.[184]

The Central African Republic (C.A.R.) is a nation of just over three million people who have suffered under political tyranny of almost unfathomable proportions.[185] A country with a per capita income of $250, a life expectancy of forty-one years, and a literacy rate of 18 percent, C.A.R. was one of the world's most impoverished nations under Jean-Bedel Bokassa's dictatorial rule from 1966 to 1979.[186] The destitution of his countrymen, however, did not prevent Bokassa from living a life of inordinate luxury. He considered all government money to be his own, using it to finance his travels and real-estate purchases all over Europe.[187] On December 4, 1977, he proclaimed himself Emperor Bokassa I and changed his country's name to Central African Empire. To mark the occasion, he held a spectacular coronation ceremony costing $22 million, or one-fourth of the nation's entire yearly revenues.[188] When student protesters began to demand government reforms in the late 1970s, they were put to death. The emperor, who often participated in the executions of suspected dissidents and their families, personally murdered almost 100 students himself.[189]

Despotic abuse of power has rarely, if ever, manifested itself more egregiously than in Ethiopia, located in eastern Africa. From the thirteenth through twentieth centuries, one ethnic group, the Amhara, dominated the country's culture and politics—controlling the monarchy, the church, the military, and virtually all other social and political institutions.[190] In 1917 began the fifty-seven-year rule of President Haile Selassie, a tyrant who allowed Ethiopia's vast peasant class no political or economic rights.[191] Selassie was deposed in a 1974 coup led by Mengistu Haile Mariam, who during the next three years consolidated his power and made Ethiopia a socialist state with close ties to the Soviet Union and Cuba. As intolerant of political opposition as his predecessor, Mengistu required his countrymen to inform the government about anyone thought to be disloyal to the new regime. Parents and children were encouraged to spy on one another for evidence of sedition.[192] Even *imagined* dissidents were put to death on a regular basis. In May 1988, for instance, Mengistu's soldiers entered the town of She'eb, rounded up 400 "anti-government collaborators"—including women, children, the elderly, and the disabled—and proceeded to drive over them with tanks.[193]

In the 1980s Ethiopia was gripped by a brutal civil war into which almost all government funds were poured—even while the country was ravaged by famine. Though Mengistu officially attributed the food shortage to drought conditions, government corruption was the principal cause.[194] A number of foreign countries sent food and medical supplies to aid the dying masses, only to have those cargoes intercepted and stolen by the Ethiopian military.[195] The United States in particular sent large amounts of aid in the famine's early stages, yet was criticized by Mengistu for not sending more.[196] Presumably Mengistu expected American taxpayers to help defray the cost of the $100 million celebration he had held—during the height of the famine—to commemorate the tenth anniversary of Ethiopia's socialist revolution.[197]

Immediately east of Ethiopia lies Somalia, one of the world's poorest nations and home to nearly ten million people.[198] When fighting erupted between government and rebel groups in 1988, thousands of unarmed citizens were killed by combatants on both sides.[199] Government forces murdered an estimated 60,000 civilians in 1990 alone.[200] By early 1991, more than half a million refugees had fled the country, while another 400,000 had been forced to relocate within Somalia itself.[201] The conflict escalated into full-scale civil war throughout 1991 and 1992, devastating large parts of the country.[202]

Somalia's recent history is filled with examples of brutal government repressions—complete with the torture and execution of political prisoners.[203] In 1990, when listeners jeered during a speech by President Muhammad Siad Barre, presidential guards opened fire on the crowd, killing more than sixty people.[204] The ever-present threat of such brutality terrified Somalians throughout Barre's regime. He eventually abdicated in January 1991, leaving several mutually antagonistic, clan-based guerilla groups to compete for control.[205] Today the presidency is vacant and the country has no functioning government.[206]

When droughts in the late 1980s and early 1990s caused a great famine in Somalia, foreign relief efforts were thwarted by the interclan fighting that raged nationwide.[207] The combatants stole relief packages containing food and medicine, "while at the same time the country had become filled with walking skeletons who had but a few days or hours to live."[208] In all, at least 300,000 people died of war- and famine-related causes.[209] It was only with U.S. leadership in "Operation Restore Hope" late in 1992 that the situation began to improve. American soldiers, joined by troops from a number of other countries, were sent to Somalia to ensure the proper distribution of lifesaving resources.[210]

Sudan, situated west of Ethiopia, is an impoverished land of more than thirty-two million inhabitants who deem ethnic-group membership a principal facet of their social identity.[211] They are acutely aware of even the slightest intertribal variations in skin pigmentation.[212] In this land without political freedom, critics of the government are subjected to electric shock, rape, partial castration, whipping, beating, clubbing, shackling, burning with hot irons, denial of food and water, mock executions, and other forms of physical and psychological torture.[213]

For sixteen years Sudan has been immersed in a devastating civil war, pitting the Muslim north against the non-Muslim south, that has claimed at least 1.9 million lives.[214] The vast majority of the casualties are southerners—not rebels, but merely civilians who do not share the regime's radical Islamic ideology.[215] Without the slightest regard for innocent human life, the combatants on both sides are concerned with nothing beyond their own military objectives.[216] Even while famine claimed a million Sudanese lives between 1988 and 1992,[217] government and rebel troops alike bombed relief centers and prevented humanitarian agencies from feeding and medicating the perishing multitudes. Moreover, when the government needed to raise money for the purchase of weapons in 1990, it obtained the necessary funds by *exporting the entire national grain reserve*.[218] Consequently, by June of 1992 some 5,000 children were dying of hunger and disease each day.[219] Today, with the ongoing war making it impossible for most farmers to plant crops, another 2.6 million people face the looming threat of starvation. As one observer reports, "People are reduced to digging up termite mounds to eat scraps the termites have buried."[220] Notwithstanding this monumental national crisis, government forces continue to bomb feeding centers and hospitals.[221]

In Sierra Leone, located along western Africa's Atlantic coast, a rebel movement seeking to wrest power from the country's first democratically elected government systematically butchered thousands of innocent civilians during 1998 and 1999.[222] In a campaign ominously named "Operation No Living Thing,"[223] rebel soldiers killed at least 6,000 in the capital city of Freetown during January 1999 alone. Moreover, they hacked off the limbs of thousands more in a barbaric show of force intended to intimidate would-be resisters.[224] Other rebel tactics included gang-rape, kidnapping, and the imposition of sexual slavery.[225] One unfortunate victim describes his horrible ordeal:

> At about 4 a.m. I heard bombs and gunshots outside my house. The rebels came and banged on the door. They said they would kill us all outside. My wife took five of the six children outside. I stayed inside with one. My wife threw herself on top of two of the children to protect them. They shot my wife, killed two of the children, [and] shot my seven-year-old through the stomach.[226]

Another victim, a forty-six-year-old father of six named Lamine Jusugarka, had both his hands chopped off while his wife had her kneecaps smashed by a hammer-wielding rebel. "We were in the line," Mr. Jusugarka recalls. "One after another. . . . When they finished with you, when they cut your two hands, you run. They say 'Move! If you don't move, we'll fire on you.' Fifty [were dismembered] on that particular day."[227]

When one considers the vast scope of black-on-black atrocities that have afflicted Africa throughout its long history, the myopic vision of "civil rights leaders" who denounce only white transgressions seems particularly hypocritical. Contemplate the words of black author Tony Martin who recently said, "In the whole history of so-called civilized nations, there has never been anything to compare with the lynching of African Americans. For years in [the United States], thousands of our [black] people were lynched and killed, were strung up from trees, were riddled with bullets, were burned at the stake on a daily basis in this country."[228] Certainly, all would agree that lynching, which at its zenith took the lives of 161 black Americans in a single year,[229] was a sinful, appalling practice. Yet we must marvel at the absurdity of anyone deeming crimes of that magnitude more egregious than the wanton slaughter of *millions* of Africans, by other Africans, during a span of just a few years.

Modern Slavery

While there is no white-ruled nation on earth today where slavery is considered anything but an abomination, there are currently hundreds of thousands of black slaves held captive in several African countries. For instance, in Mauritania, located just north of Senegal in northwestern Africa, debt bondage is a common arrangement that forces whole families to work, sometimes for several generations, in futile efforts to pay off loans.[230] With little or no hope of ever attaining freedom, such people's lives lack even the slightest trace of human dignity.[231] Moreover, there are at least 30,000 full-fledged black slaves under the command of Arab masters within Mauritania's borders, plus another 300,000 recently freed slaves who continue to serve their former masters because of psychological or economic dependence.[232] Mauritanian slaves are regarded as nothing more than property that can be sold outright or traded for such commodities as camels, guns, and trucks. Each master not only decides when and whom a slave may marry, but also owns any children that result from such unions.[233] For even the slightest infractions, these slaves are routinely subjected to beatings, the denial of food, or prolonged exposure to the sun with their hands and feet bound together.[234] For more serious transgressions, the "camel treatment" is frequently the penalty of choice. In this procedure, a slave is stretched and tied around the belly of a dehydrated camel, which is then given water to drink until its belly expands enough to tear the victim apart. Another punishment calls for insects to be inserted into a slave's ears, which are then sealed with wax—leaving the victim, whose arms and legs are bound, to go insane from the bugs running inside his head. Yet another torture uses hot coals to burn the slave's genitals.[235]

Slavery is also practiced today in Sudan, whose Islamic fundamentalist government arms the Arab tribespeople living along the border that divides the Muslim north from the animist south. Muslim raiders regularly descend upon southern Dinka villages and transport their captives to northern slave markets.[236] Thus far, tens of thousands of Dinkas have met this awful fate.[237] In 1988 the purchase price for these slaves was about $90 apiece, but by 1990, because of their huge surplus, that figure had dropped to just $15.[238] There are reports of chattel slavery in northern Nigeria, Rwanda, Niger, and the Ivory Coast as well.[239] In Ghana, religious custom holds that for serious offenses like murder and rape, the offender's family must give up one of its young virgins for sexual enslavement in the shrines of traditional priests.[240] In the Central African Empire, Emperor Jean-Bedel Bokassa periodically had hundreds of slaves massacred for his own amusement.[241]

Remarkably, our "civil rights leaders" are silent about such practices. The Congressional Black Caucus (CBC), for instance, has never taken a stand against modern-day African slavery.[242] Louis Farrakhan, who dutifully denounces white-on-black evils wherever he may find them, actually made a 1995 visit to Sudan as an honored guest of the government.[243] In their quest to call attention to the wickedness of modern African slavery, the American Anti-Slavery Group and the human-rights group Pax Sudani Network have repeatedly begged support not only from the CBC and Farrakhan's Nation of Islam, but also from Randall Robinson's TransAfrica organization, Jesse Jackson's Rainbow Coalition, and the NAACP—only to have their pleas ignored.[244] The messiahs of "justice," it seems, are concerned only with *white* sinners and black victims, a double standard that has infuriated many Africans. Indeed, when President Clinton sent Jesse Jackson as a special envoy to Nigeria in 1994, a number of that country's pro-democracy activists initially refused to meet with him and even threatened to stone him.[245]

Consider for a moment some of the awful realities of African life described in this chapter—the depredations visited upon black

Africans by their own countrymen, not just today but since the dawn of time. It would be laughable, were it not so tragic, to hear our self-anointed crusaders for "freedom" ranting about the evils of South Africa's white rule while completely ignoring the far greater atrocities occurring elsewhere on the continent. Illinois representative Charles Hayes, for one, said at a 1984 anti-apartheid rally in Washington, "I just couldn't sit by and not offer my support to try to end the atrocious situation in South Africa."[246] Similarly, Congressman Walter Fauntroy once explained that such demonstrations were "[acts] of consciousness in response to the repressive action of the South African government. . . . Nowhere in the world is the plight [of human beings] more painful than the plight of the people in South Africa."[247] Jesse Jackson, who stood in the vanguard of the fight to end apartheid, went so far as to liken South Africa's regime to that of Adolf Hitler's Nazi Germany.[248] By contrast, when the NAACP's then-executive director, Benjamin Hooks, was asked in the 1980s to comment on the political turbulence and ethnic violence plaguing so many black African countries, he replied that "there is little black Americans could or should do directly to help foster or affect political change in sub-Saharan Africa. I don't think it is our business to meddle in their affairs."[249]

In April 1991 Jesse Jackson attended, along with Coretta Scott King and other champions of "liberty," an African/African American Conference in the Ivory Coast, where delegates united to proclaim their commitment to fighting white racism both in the United States and South Africa. "We are a community of resistance," announced one speaker, "united in a fight against racism, apartheid and forced indebtedness." But no one at the conference talked about the black-perpetrated human-rights violations which even then were destroying more black lives every week than South Africa's white government had snuffed out in all its history.[250] Consider that between 1910 and 1980, a total of about 8,000 blacks were killed in strife against the South African government[251]—a number surpassed in mere days during the 1991 carnage in Burundi alone. Even within South Africa itself, recent decades have seen black-on-black violence exceed the white-on-black variety. In the capital city of Natal, for example, black factional fighting killed thousands in the late 1980s.[252] Between 1990 and 1993, nearly 53,000 South Africans died violently—a large percentage of them black victims killed by other blacks.[253]

Black attacks on both whites and Indians living in South Africa have also become increasingly common in recent years[254]—a fact which the media have all but ignored. "Contrary to what modern-day rhetoric would have us believe," writes Dr. Walter E. Williams, "racial oppression and discrimination find no color group innocent of their practice."[255] Indeed, there are numerous African countries where blacks today discriminate against Arabs, Syrians, Indians, Lebanese, and Chinese. In fact Asians, who were expelled *en masse* from Idi Amin's Uganda, have been similarly forced out of Kenya.[256] Moreover, they currently face severe discrimination in Tanzania, Zambia, Malawi, and elsewhere in eastern and central Africa.[257] In Ethiopia, meanwhile, Muslims have been persecuted since Mengistu's regime. Consider that when a number of Muslim leaders were tortured and killed in Ethiopia's Hararghe province in December 1986, a secret policy document noted that it was "necessary to employ new methods and tactics to destroy the Muslims."[258]

Without a doubt, Africa's most salient and enduring feature is its disunity. Composed of more than 2,000 tribes or ethnic societies—each possessing its own language, culture, and traditions—the continent has known brutality of epic proportions since time immemorial.[259] In 1998 alone there were eleven major armed conflicts, resulting in at least 1,000 deaths apiece, south of the Sahara. As of July 1999, large-scale wars were being waged in eight African countries, while low-intensity conflicts plagued five others. In addition, over 8 million of the world's 22 million refugees were in Africa.[260] Nonetheless, contemporary "civil rights" crusaders find it fashionable to portray their ancestral homeland as an Eden-like paradise—unspoiled until trod upon by the sinful feet of whites. Thanks to such mythology, few Americans realize that African history has been "full of depredations, subjugation, and massive enslavement among peoples who were all black, but whose internal ethnic and tribal differences were as deadly in their effects as similar differences among Europeans."[261] Fewer still are aware that, as attested to by South African archbishop Desmond Tutu, most black Africans were freer under white colonial rule than they are under their own leaders today.[262] Even during the height of apartheid, in fact, more blacks moved *into* South Africa than left it—because the economic and social conditions in other African nations were worse.[263] In April 1987 an Anglican bishop in Kenya condemned the hypocrisy of South Africa's usually-vocal critics who routinely turned a blind eye toward the cruelty of *black* Africans elsewhere on the continent:

> People [in Kenya] are the victim[s] of threats, fear, and tyranny. For how long will these injustices and humiliations continue in our country? What is the point of protesting against injustices in South Africa when there are worse violations of human rights at home? There is no difference whether a violation of human rights is committed by a white man or a black man, that is immaterial. The truth is, some of the violations of human rights in this country are no different from those of South Africa.[264]

When South Africa legalized more than thirty political parties and released Nelson Mandela from prison in 1990, African leaders from coast to coast reacted with euphoria. Zambian president-for-life Kenneth Kaunda, for one, hailed that "glorious day" of liberation and promise.[265] Curiously, however, neither Mr. Kaunda nor his barbarous counterparts elsewhere on the continent felt any similar inspiration to allow political freedom in their own one-party states.[266] As Dr. George Ayittey observes, "Those African leaders cheering the most wildly [over Mandela's release] were the tyrants who have ruined Africa, slaughtered its people, looted its wealth, and imprisoned thousands."[267]

Black author Keith Richburg, the former Africa bureau chief for the *Washington Post*, lived in Africa from 1991 to 1994, during which time he covered, among other events, the Somalian and Rwandan civil wars. When he saw firsthand some of the horrors that have defined African life for so long, he understood, with great sadness, that the land of his forefathers was a most unwelcoming place:

> I'm tired of lying. And I'm tired of all the ignorance and hypocrisy and double standards I hear and read about Africa, much of it from people who've never been there, let alone spent three years walking around amid the corpses. Talk to me about Africa and my black roots and my kinship with my African brothers and I'll throw it back in your face, and then I'll rub your nose in the images of the rotting flesh. . . .
> We are told by some of our supposedly enlightened, so-called black leaders that white America owes us something because they

brought our ancestors over as slaves. And Africa—Mother Africa—is often held up as some kind of black Valhalla, where the descendants of slaves would be welcomed back and where black men and women can walk in true dignity.

Sorry, but I've been there. I've had an AK-47 rammed up my nose, I've talked to machete-wielding Hutu militiamen with the blood of their latest victims splattered across their T-shirts. I've seen a cholera epidemic in Zaire, a famine in Somalia, a civil war in Liberia. I've seen cities bombed to near rubble, and other cities reduced to rubble, because their leaders let them rot and decay while they spirited away billions of dollars—yes, billions—into overseas bank accounts. . . .

So excuse me if I sound cynical, jaded. I'm beaten down, and I'll admit it. And it's Africa that has made me this way. I feel for her suffering, I empathize with her pain, and now, from afar, I still recoil in horror whenever I see yet another television picture of another tribal slaughter, another refugee crisis. But most of all I think: Thank God my ancestor got out, because, now, I am not one of them.

In short, thank God I am an American.[268]

Chapter 12

The Chains of Slavery

Nothing is so firmly believed as that which we least know.
—Montaigne[1]

Many of the rationales that "civil rights leaders" commonly use to justify—and even encourage—black anger at whites are founded on the historical reality that millions of African people were once transported to the New World to live out their lives in servitude. For a country that was, as Lincoln said, "conceived in liberty and dedicated to the proposition that all men are created equal," the institution of slavery was surely a national disgrace.

The first influx of black slaves to the Western Hemisphere occurred in the early 1500s when Spain, having recently conquered a large part of the New World, began shipping Africans to the West Indies to work in the region's flourishing sugar industry.[2] The North American mainland, by contrast, would not see its first African natives until 1619, when the crew of a Dutch frigate landed at Jamestown, Virginia and gave the local colonists twenty black men in return for food and supplies.[3] It would be decades, however, before Africans began to arrive in the American colonies in significant numbers. Through the first half of the seventeenth century, British indentured servants were the principal source of imported labor in North America, far outnumbering African slaves. The latter, in fact, were generally used only as replacements for escaped or freed indentured servants. While most of the black newcomers were poor, a few did manage to thrive economically. The enterprising Anthony Johnson, for example, who came to America in 1622, actually became an importer of both black and white indentured laborers in 1651. But by 1670, both law and custom defined all Africans in the colonies as slaves.[4]

The black presence in North America began to grow rapidly in the 1680s, when the ever-expanding colonies underwent a massive shift from reliance on indentured to slave labor. Because indentured servants were held for only a few years and then freed, there was a constant need to replace them. But while colonial demand for these replacements rose, the number of Englishmen willing to travel under indenture to America dwindled. This development was due to changing conditions on both sides of the Atlantic. England was in a period of renewed political stability and economic prosperity, marked by rising wages and improved employment opportunities. Meanwhile, land in the colonies became more densely settled and thus less readily available—thereby reducing New World opportunities for unskilled immigrants. As the flow of indentured servants to America consequently declined, colonial landowners looked to Africa for substitutes.[5]

By the mid-1700s slavery existed in all thirteen colonies, though in the North it was never so prevalent or economically crucial as in the agricultural South. Between 1774 and 1804 every northern state abolished the practice, thereby rendering it the South's "peculiar institution."[6] With the invention of Eli Whitney's cotton gin in 1793, southern demand for slave labor soared to new heights.[7] All told, between 1510 and 1870 at least 9.6 million, and perhaps as many as 11 million, African slaves were forcibly taken to the New World in bondage.[8] These figures, it should be noted, do not include the million or so who died in transit.[9] Of those who survived the ocean crossing, about 4 million went to the Caribbean islands, more than 3.6 million to Brazil, and some 427,000 to the British North American colonies (and later the United States). Of those 427,000, almost 90 percent arrived prior to the legal abolition of the English slave trade in 1807.[10] The situation of America's northern blacks, of course, was markedly better than that of their southern counterparts by the turn of the nineteenth century. Although poor and social outcasts, blacks in the North were by then technically free. As early as 1810, the number of free blacks in America was more than double the number of slaves.[11]

Slavery in All Places, at All Times

Virtually as old as civilization itself, the institution of slavery existed in the Americas, Europe, Asia, Africa, and the Middle East for thousands of years.[12] As long ago as 3,000 B.C. the Sumerian civilization that flourished along the Euphrates River enslaved its prisoners of war.[13] The Babylonians of the eighteenth century B.C. practiced slavery as well, as did China's Shang dynasty of the same period.[14] In fact, slavery continued to be a feature of Chinese society until the twentieth century A.D.[15] In the seventh century B.C. the Assyrians, who at that time dominated most of the Near East, regularly plundered neighboring states, massacring all resisters and making slaves of those they captured alive.[16] In all these empires, as elsewhere in the ancient world, slavery was an accepted, unquestioned facet of life. It aroused no outrage among either private citizens or public officials, and required no special moral justification.[17]

Ancient Egypt made extensive use of slaves, the more fortunate of whom knew lives of only moderate toil in service of the royal family, the nobility, or the priests. Less fortunate were those slaves put to work in the inhospitable gold and copper mines of northeastern Africa, where legions literally dropped dead from the unbearable heat and scarce water supplies. Egyptian slaves were astronomical in number, as King Ramses III demonstrated in the twelfth century B.C. when he single-handedly gifted 113,000 of them to the various temples of Egypt.[18]

It is worth noting, at this point, that modern-day Africanists and "civil rights" prophets commonly contend that the ancient Egyptians were black. From Egypt's great civilization, they claim, white Europeans "stole" philosophy, astronomy, mathematics, and much more. As Al Sharpton colorfully informed an audience of black students at New Jersey's Kean College, "White folks was in the caves while we was building empires. . . . We built pyramids before Donald Trump even knew what architecture was. . . . We taught philosophy and astrology and mathematics before Socrates and them Greek homos was born."[19] Never, though, do such pundits criticize the supposedly black Egyptians for having practiced slavery some 3,000 years before the first white slavers even set foot in Africa. While praising the early intellectual and architectural accomplishments of those who dwelt along the Nile, these demagogues carefully ignore the Egyptian enslavement of Jews that was well underway as early as the second millennium B.C. This selective vision is one of the great hypocrisies of our time.

The principal ingredients necessary for the development of slavery as an institution are vulnerable people and a demand for their labor. Racism is by no means a prerequisite. Throughout history, in fact, a great many groups all over the world have been enslaved by racially identical conquerors.[20] In ancient Greece and Rome, for instance, slavery flourished without any racial ideology to support it.[21] While Greeks generally enslaved only "barbarians" of foreign ancestry, they attached no special importance to the skin color of their subjects. Virtually all Greek slaves were white and were acquired as the spoils of war.[22] The Greek slave markets were bustling places indeed. In Chios, Delos, Corinth, Rhodes, Aegina, and Athens, countless thousands of human beings were sold into bondage.[23] In Delos it was common for a thousand slaves to be sold in a single day.[24] Following the battle of the Eurymedon in 468 B.C., some 20,000 captured Persians were put up for sale at once.[25] Greek merchant families attained an elevated social status by purchasing slaves, whom they regarded as investments not unlike buildings or plots of land.[26]

Slaves in the Greek world were treated with varying degrees of kindness and cruelty, depending upon where they lived. In many places they occupied the lowest position in the social hierarchy and worked in agriculture, mining, and milling.[27] Among the most wretched were the mine slaves. At the Laurium silver mines in Attica, at any given time between 10,000 and 30,000 slaves, bound in chains, were forced to work in appalling underground conditions under the constant threat of brutal floggings.[28] In Sparta, too, slaves had a difficult existence and consequently threatened violent revolts virtually every year.[29] Slaves elsewhere in Greece, by contrast, lived under better conditions—and in some places were assigned to relatively respected positions as civil servants, clerks, and prison attendants.[30] Some actually received daily wages for their work. Athens in particular was known for its mild treatment of slaves.[31] In fact Athenian slaves, who numbered nearly 100,000 in the fourth century B.C.,[32] lived better than poor freemen in many other Greek city-states.[33]

The Romans, like the Greeks before them, acquired most of their slaves via military conquest. The enormous numbers of captives they took in the Carthaginian, Punic, and Gallic wars resulted in a Roman slave population that exceeded any other in world history up to that time. Plutarch records that on one day in 167 B.C., some 150,000 slaves were sold in a single Roman market.[34] Between the years 58 and 50 B.C., Caesar's western campaigns won 500,000 slaves from Gaul alone.[35] Roman armies also enslaved Sardinians, Syrians, Macedonians, Epirotes, Achaeans, Cilicians, Paphlagonians,[36] Germans, Celts, Galatians, and Jews.[37]

The Germanic peoples of central Europe practiced slavery until about the fifth century A.D. Though they won most of their slaves in war, they also acquired many from long-distance traders near the Black Sea. Not permitted to work alongside free members of the population, German slaves were considered mere pieces of property. They could be whipped, tortured, or killed at their master's whim.[38]

France, Poland, Lithuania, Russia, and Viking-era Scandinavia all knew slavery.[39] In eleventh-century England, slaves comprised fully 10 percent of the country's population.[40] For hundreds of years, Europeans living in the vulnerable coastal settlements of the Balkans were regularly raided and captured by pirates who sold them, by the tens of thousands, in the slave markets of North Africa and the Middle East.[41] While Moors and Spaniards enslaved each other in medieval Spain,[42] the inhabitants of the Black and Caspian Sea regions periodically clashed and sold their respective captives into slavery.[43] During the same period, Christians and non-Christians enslaved one another along the warring Mediterranean frontiers.[44] In the fourteenth century, Pope Gregory XI himself excommunicated all Florentine Catholics and encouraged their enslavement.[45] Prior to the development of a strong Russian state, Turkish raiders sold hundreds of thousands of Russians in the international slave trade.[46] The sixteenth-century Turkish pirate Barbarossa—who for many years ravaged the coasts of Greece, Italy, and Spain—captured and enslaved thousands of Christians in just one raid on the Balearic Islands off Spain's east coast.[47] From a later raid on Venice, he returned home with at least 2,500 children to be raised as slaves.[48] The Ottoman Turks commonly enslaved boys from the European populations they conquered.[49] When Ottoman warriors subjugated Hungary in the sixteenth century, the peace terms they imposed required the Hungarians to hand over 10 percent of their population each decade as slaves.[50] Moreover, legions of Slavs were sold all over Europe and the Ottoman Empire for several centuries. Slavs along Yugoslavia's Dalmatian coast, for instance, were enslaved by other Europeans for at least 600 years.[51] The very word "slave," in fact, is derived from their name.[52]

Following the spread of Islam along the Arabian peninsula, periodic wars between Arabs, Turks, and Christians yielded great numbers of slaves.[53] In the eleventh century, the Egyptian ruler Mustansir owned tens of thousands of white slaves.[54] Two centuries later, conquering armies from central Asia subjugated Russians, Georgians, Circassians, Albanians, and Armenians—selling them to slave traders all over Western Europe and the Muslim world.[55]

The mighty Indian civilizations of Central America and Mexico practiced slavery as well. In Mayan society, people commonly sold themselves and their children into slavery in exchange for food and shelter. When a criminal was given a death sentence, it often brought with it the enslavement of his entire family.[56] Mayan life was replete with brutality. One of the culture's chief priorities was the waging of war, in which the capture, torture, and eventual slaughter of enemy soldiers was a principal objective. Other captives were taken only for ritualistic sacrifice. Indeed some wars were started for the express purpose of obtaining victims to be killed during ceremonies honoring the accession of a new ruler.[57] As one scholar puts it, "While atrocities have occurred around the world, this was a society in which such behavior was not simply accepted, but systematized and celebrated."[58]

Similarly, the Aztecs built a vast empire by conquering myriad weaker tribes and treating them with great cruelty[59]—in many cases completely exterminating them.[60] It was customary for Aztecs to sacrifice captured enemy warriors *en masse*, cutting their hearts out of their living bodies and pouring rivers of blood down the steps of the pyramid wherein the killings took place.[61] The Aztecs also kept enormous numbers of slaves, tens of thousands of whom were periodically sacrificed to the gods.[62] It should be noted that the bitterness spawned by such inhumanity eventually helped facilitate the Spanish conquest; in 1519, Aztec subjects joined forces with Cortés to overthrow their indigenous overlords.[63]

One of the world's largest pre-Columbian civilizations was that of the fifteenth-century Incas, whose dominion at one time stretched more than 2,000 miles from north to south, covering areas of what today are Peru, Ecuador, Chile, Bolivia, Colombia, and Argentina.[64] Along with a king, a nobility consisting of some 40,000 people ruled the empire's millions of inhabitants. Like the Aztecs, the Incas treated their subjects brutally, as evidenced by their elaborate sacrificial rites that sent thousands of captive Indians to their deaths. On some occasions Inca priests actually collapsed with exhaustion from stabbing so many victims.[65]

Further north, long before the first Europeans arrived in the New World, an elaborate slave-trading network developed among the Indians of the Northwest American coast, where slaves constituted as much as 10 to 15 percent of some tribes' populations.[66] According to many historians, Indian slavery in this region was of nearly as much economic importance to its practitioners as was the plantation slavery of the antebellum South. Possessing no human rights whatsoever, slaves of the Northwest coast were considered property in every sense and were subject to sale or disposal at any time. Many were killed ceremoniously, as in the ritual of the Kwakiutl cannibals, who sacrificed and then ate their slaves.[67] Other tribal chiefs routinely killed slaves in potlatch festivities—solely to demonstrate that they were wealthy enough to waste large quantities of their own human property.[68] Slave raiding was common also among the Natchez of the lower Mississippi, the Cherokees of the Appalachian highlands, and the native tribes living along the Atlantic coast, from Florida to Virginia.[69] When the transatlantic slave trade later brought Africans to the New World, some Indian tribes—among them the Cherokees, Choctaws, Seminoles, Chicasaws, and Creeks—took black slaves as well.[70] Though most Indian masters owned just a few slaves, others owned dozens and often treated them terribly.[71] The Cherokees, for instance, were notorious for their cruelty to slaves.[72] Over time, black slavery became an integral part of life for many Indians—as evidenced by the fact that some tribes continued to keep slaves until 1866, a full year after the Civil War's end. At that point, under pressure from the American government, they reluctantly agreed to end the practice.[73]

In the Orient, meanwhile, slavery was deeply entrenched in Asian culture, where smaller and less-advanced groups—such as hill tribes, nomads, and bands of hunters and gatherers—were repeatedly overrun by marauders from more-developed societies with superior weapons.[74] Slavers from what are now the Philippines conducted many large-scale raids throughout Southeast Asia.[75] For almost 1,000 years, between one-third and one-half of Korea's inhabitants were slaves.[76] Similarly, parts of Thailand and Burma were nearly one-third slave between the seventeenth and early twentieth centuries.[77] In India, slavery existed from ancient times until the 1800s. As of 1841, there were nearly nine million slaves on Indian soil.[78]

Slavery in Africa Before the Europeans

Contemporary "civil rights leaders" are generally loath to acknowledge that white Europeans were not the first slavers in Africa; that Arabs in fact had developed an extensive slave trade on the continent long before the European arrival; and that Arabs actually placed whites and Asians in bondage along with light- and dark-skinned Africans.[79] As to black slaves in particular, the 14 million transported by Arab traders to the Islamic regions of North Africa and the Middle East far exceeded the number shipped to the New World in Europe's transatlantic enterprise.[80] Istanbul, the capital of the Ottoman Empire, was for many years one of the largest and busiest slave markets in the world.[81] Female slaves there were paraded, examined, and bid on in humiliating public auctions.[82] Likewise, the large East African slave market in Zanzibar featured "rows of girls from the age of twelve and upwards . . . exposed to the examination of throngs of Arab slave-dealers and subjected to inexpressible indignities by the brutal dealers."[83] Caravans of Arab traders regularly crossed the Sahara with legions of newly captured Africans destined for the marketplace.[84] Their flesh scarred from the lashings of hide whips, long lines of these wretched creatures—many of them women carrying their babies—were chained together at their necks and forced to march more than 1,000 miles across the burning desert.[85] Their condition was pitiable:

> Their arms and legs almost fleshless, their bodies shrivelled up, their looks heavy and their heads bent, while they were marching along eastward into an unknown future, farther and farther away from their homes, separated from wife and child. The slaves were mostly bound together according to their powers of marching, without the least regard to sex.[86]

Slaves unable to keep up with the caravans were left behind to die horrible, lingering deaths from heat, thirst, and hunger.[87] Thousands of human skeletons—mostly the remains of girls and young women—have been found strewn along the old Saharan slave routes. Many of these skeletons were clustered in the vicinity of wells, suggesting their desperate but futile attempts to reach water and stave off death.[88]

What reader's heart is not choked with emotion by such sorrowful descriptions of human misery? Who does not recoil in horror from such vivid narratives of cruelty? Who can refrain from denouncing, in the strongest possible language, such abominations carried out against African people? Reasonable though such questions may be, we must also ask if even one "civil rights" apostle will acknowledge that slavery was in fact widely practiced in black Africa by *black* masters long before either the first Arabs or Europeans arrived there. Indeed, as one writer puts it, "The numbers of people enslaved within Africa itself exceeded the numbers exported, [but] history has largely forgotten them."[89]

For more than 2,000 years the economies of sub-Saharan Africa were tied to the capture, use, and sale of slaves. In the Mali empire of the thirteenth and fourteenth centuries, black rulers controlled large plantations worked by slaves who were subjected to severe abuse and cruelty.[90] The powerful medieval kingdoms of Ghana and Songhai relied heavily on slave labor as well.[91] The first Portuguese explorers in Africa found, around 1480, an extensive slave trade stretching from the Congo to Benin. Medieval African sculptures, with their depictions of slaves bound and gagged for sacrifice, speak volumes from the reaches of distant history.[92] By some estimates, between 30 and 60 percent of all African people were slaves, meaning that the transatlantic trade—though horrible and immoral—was in a sense merely an extension of Africa's already thriving internal slave market.[93] As historian R.W. Beachey explains, "Domestic slavery, as far as we knew, existed among all tribes in Africa, and varied in severity from a nominal connection to the power of life and death exercised by a master."[94] Slavery, in fact, was entrenched far more deeply in Africa than in Europe—largely because Europeans recognized land as the principal source of private wealth, whereas African custom recognized no revenue-producing private property other than slaves.[95]

In his 1854 publication *A Slaver's Log Book*, which chronicles the years 1808 to 1847, slave trader Theophilus Conneau explains:

> In Africa, where coin is not known, the slave is made a substitute for this commodity. Therefore if a man wants to purchase a wife, he pays the amount in slaves; another wishes to purchase a quantity of cattle, he tenders in payment slaves. Fields of cassava, rice, or yams are paid in slaves. The African court also taxes all forfeitures and pecuniary penalties in slaves.[96]

Today's Afrocentrists and "civil rights leaders," of course, largely ignore the fact that African peoples used slaves in all manner of agricultural, domestic, military, and even commercial and governmental enterprises.[97] Instead of criticizing the slave-owning black societies of history, such pundits cite those very societies as examples of high civilization.[98] Consequently, the myth that white Europeans were the first to bring slavery to Africa has gained wide acceptance in America. Certainly the books and films of our popular culture reinforce this myth. Consider, for instance, the scene in the movie *Roots* where Kunta Kinte seems puzzled by the chains of white slavers—as if shackles and bondage were something new to his people. Yet slavery was in fact widely known in the part of Africa from which he came, long antedating any white influences. Explaining the film's historical inaccuracy on this point, *Roots* author Alex Haley candidly said, "I tried to give my people a myth to live by."[99]

Through a long and bloody history, powerful sub-Saharan tribes regularly used their military strength to enslave their weaker neighbors, both for their own use and for sale to European traders. The area near the Niger River, for example, produced a relatively advanced civilization whose insatiable appetite for conquest led to the subjugation of all inland societies within its reach. The slaves who were transported across the Atlantic to the New World originated, for the most part, from such subordinate African tribes already under the domination of stronger ones.[100] European slavers did not need to pursue and capture their victims by force, but could simply purchase them from other Africans who had already taken them into captivity. As author Basil Davidson writes in *The African Slave Trade*, "The notion that Europe imposed the slave trade on Africa is without any foundation in history. . . . Those Africans who were involved in the trade were seldom the helpless victims of a commerce they did not understand. On the contrary, they responded to its challenge. They exploited its opportunities."[101]

The Ibos and Ashanti were among those who sold thousands of their fellow Africans to white slave traders,[102] as did the Benin and Igbo of Nigeria.[103] Likewise, the Akan people of Ghana, who controlled the Gold Coast trade, readily accepted European gold in exchange for slaves.[104] Fifteenth-century Portuguese traders arriving in Senegal and Mauritania found the natives eager to swap slaves for horses—the exchange rate ranging between ten and fifteen slaves per horse.[105] Tribes that sold or traded slaves were motivated largely by a desire for profit. Indeed, upon the introduction of the transatlantic slave trade, West African warrior tribes discontinued their longstanding tradition of slaughtering male prisoners of war—who now had market value. But when white slavers went out of business many years later, these tribes returned to murdering their male captives.[106]

African complicity in the European slave trade is almost universally overlooked by "civil rights leaders"—though that very complicity was a source of great wealth for many sub-Saharan societies. As one African chief in the early nineteenth century candidly explained, "We want three things: powder, ball and brandy; and we have three things to sell: men, women and children."[107] Zora Neale Hurston, a prominent writer of the Harlem Renaissance, observed:

> The white people held my people in slavery here in America. They had bought us, it is true, and exploited us. But the inescapable fact that stuck in my craw was: my people had sold me. . . . My own people had exterminated whole nations and torn families apart for a profit before the strangers got their chance at a cut. It was a sobering thought. It impressed upon me the universal nature of greed and glory.[108]

To most contemporary Westerners, the term "slavery" is associated exclusively with the white subjugation of black Africans. Few Americans realize just how widespread slavery has been around the world, throughout human history, among all races. This lack of awareness is due not just to the prattling of demagogues who selectively denounce only the *white-on-black* slavery of yesteryear, but also to the Western world's unique inclination to condemn, in writings that have touched the minds of millions, its own historical involvement in slavery. The West's voluminous antislavery literature dwarfs any corresponding body of literature elsewhere.[109] It was about two centuries ago that the issue of slavery became, for Europeans, a burning moral dilemma, inspiring a profusion of treatises denouncing it. Non-Western cultures, meanwhile, had no similar aversion to slavery, nor felt any comparable imperative to eradicate it. This was largely because the very concept of freedom simply did not exist in most parts of the world. "There was no word for freedom in most non-Western languages before contact with Western peoples," writes sociologist Orlando Patterson.[110] Thomas Sowell elaborates, "Strange as it may seem today, for centuries the institution of slavery aroused little moral concern anywhere in the world, until an influential group of Englishmen began attacking the practice in the eighteenth century, eventually achieving an end of the trade and ultimately abolition of slavery itself. [The notion] that slavery was wrong was one of many Western ideas imported into the Third World."[111] It is ironic that the West's pained self-criticism over slavery has resulted, among intellectuals, in the condemnation of Western society as uniquely evil, while cultures historically oblivious to slavery's immorality have escaped reproach.

"Civil rights leaders" and Africanists commonly attribute the white enslavement of blacks to a racist doctrine of black inferiority—a doctrine that purportedly allowed whites to pursue their slaving activities unburdened by guilt. But if one argues that slavery resulted from white people's sense of racial superiority over blacks, how then does one explain the innumerable examples of slavery, throughout the ages and spanning the globe, having nothing to do with race? As discussed earlier in this chapter, historically it has been common for people of all hues to enslave others of the same skin color. The strongest incentive for enslavement has never been racial hostility, but the presence of vulnerable people unable to offer much resistance. In Africa white slavers found not only such easy victims, but also many people willing to sell their countrymen into bondage. Thus it was not racism, but the potential for great profit with little risk, that first motivated European traders. The West's racial devaluation of blacks *followed*, rather than preceded, the advent of the transatlantic slave trade, as Thomas Sowell explains:

> Peoples regularly subjected to slave raids might indeed be despised, and treated with contempt both during their enslavement and after

their emancipation, but that was not what caused them to be enslaved in the first place. Although there was no religious basis for racism in the Islamic world, the massive enslavement of sub-Saharan Africans by Arabs and other Moslems was followed by a racial disdain toward black people in the Middle East—but this racial disdain followed, rather than preceded, the enslavement of black Africans, and had not been apparent in the Arabs' previous dealings with Ethiopians. In the West as well, racism was promoted by slavery, rather than vice versa. Both in North America and in South Africa, racist rationales for slavery were resorted to only after religious rationales were tried and found wanting. But that is not to say that either rationale was in fact the reason for enslavement. In many other societies, no rationale was considered necessary.[112]

Varieties of Slave Systems

Throughout human history, slaves in different places have lived under a wide range of conditions—which at times were surprisingly good, and in other cases exceptionally harsh. As noted earlier, for instance, Athenian slaves in the ancient world were, on the whole, treated well. In the antebellum South, many American slaves lived day-to-day lives similar to those of average white working people. Some southern slaves, in fact, were allowed to choose both their own housing and their own employers, a practice that also existed among slaves in ancient Rome and, more recently, in Southeast Asia. In the Ottoman Empire some slaves actually ruled provinces, led armies into battle, and advised the sultan on government policy.[113] Conversely, in numerous places around the world millions of slaves were literally worked to death.[114]

The slave systems of precolonial Africa, like those elsewhere in the world, varied greatly both in structure and severity. Classic plantation slavery was much less common in Africa than in the Western Hemisphere, though it did exist on a large scale in such places as Egypt, Sudan, and Zanzibar.[115] The living conditions of African slaves spanned many points along a continuum,[116] at one end of which were men and women whose status was not far below that of their masters' kin, while at the other end were slaves in the strictest sense—subject not only to possible sale or torture at any time, but also to their masters' sexual appetites.[117] Many African slaves were not even allowed to claim their own children as descendants, thereby losing the highly valued honor of being "remembered with reverence after death" as the ancestors of succeeding generations.[118]

In some tribes, where the lives of slaves were not so difficult, the tangible advantages of freedom might not have seemed obvious to an outside observer until times of trouble. Among the Tuareg of central Sudan, for example, when rainfall was ample and food plentiful, one could scarcely distinguish the slave from the free. Yet during droughts, when basic necessities were scarce, slaves were the last to receive vital resources and often were forced to move away.[119] Similarly, the Sena tribe of Mozambique practiced one of the mildest forms of slavery, but during famines traded slaves for needed provisions.[120]

Slaves in other tribes, meanwhile, were regularly subjected to great brutality even in the best of times. They could be beaten, raped, starved,[121] shackled in irons, or castrated for the slightest cause.[122] Many more faced the constant fear that they would be human sacrifices at funerals and other ritual occasions.[123] Upon the death of their masters, slaves were often slaughtered so that they could "accompany the spirit" of the departed into the netherworld.[124] For the Aboh of Nigeria, it was customary that some forty slaves be killed for this purpose whenever a king was buried.[125] A similar tradition existed among the Efik people who lived where the modern border between Nigeria and Cameroon is now situated. In one particular 1786 sacrifice, held in honor of a recently deceased Efik elder, fifty slaves were beheaded.[126]

Losing their lives by the hundreds in such tortures and sacrifices, and suffering involuntary transfer by the thousands,[127] slaves all over Africa were "treated in ways that no . . . freeman would tolerate for himself or his fellows."[128] Consider the awful penalties with which the transgressions of Aboh slaves were met:

> In 1859 . . . a wealthy Aboh chief had entrusted one of his slaves with a canoe. When it was found to be missing, [the chief] put the slave in chains until . . . the canoe could be found. . . . [T]he slave "lay upon a heap of excrement and other refuse; his legs fettered to a huge block of lumber." In another case, [a chief's] slave was alleged to have committed adultery with his master's wife. . . . [The master] had the slave's vital organs and ears cut

out and his body pierced through with stakes and exhibited at the beach to serve as a deterrent to others.[129]

Even for minor offenses, it was common for Aboh slaves to be whipped, placed in blocks, sold,[130] or otherwise punished:

> A slave [who] was apprehended for petty theft [was executed]. Another slave, who had stolen twelve bags of salt from his master's store, was reportedly "gagged and tied up in the most inhuman manner . . . his body covered with lacerations. . . ." He was finally drowned in the Niger.[131']

Like their counterparts elsewhere, African masters had a variety of motivations for acquiring slaves. For many, it was a way to achieve greater fame, prestige, and wealth.[132] Others were more interested in expanding their kinship group or gaining new field laborers.[133] Still others utilized slaves as foot soldiers who would bear the largest burden of casualties in combat.[134] Indeed, wars often started after a quarrel resulted in the death of a freeman, and continued until the aggrieved group had murdered enough slaves to satisfy its desire for vengeance.[135]

How African Slaves Were Acquired

African tribes procured slaves in a number of different ways, among which were outright purchases and negotiated exchanges.[136] Swahili caravans, for instance, regularly visited the Kenyan interior to buy Kikuyu slaves, which they then exchanged in Kitui for cattle, which they finally traded for ivory in Mumoni.[137] At times, external calamities heightened the need for slave trading, such as when famine-ravaged societies swapped people for cargoes of grain.[138] In many instances people voluntarily placed themselves into slavery because they needed to leave their kinship group—usually due to some unresolvable quarrel.[139] And occasionally when a member of one tribe murdered an outsider, a child from the offending group was sent, as restitution, to spend the remainder of his or her life serving the aggrieved.[140] Adult members of other tribes, meanwhile, frequently bought orphaned or abandoned infants and raised them as slaves.[141]

Kidnapping, too, was a common tactic for acquiring slaves,[142] with bands of raiders ambushing unsuspecting victims and carrying them off unseen.[143] Villagers all over Africa lived in perpetual fear of kidnapping and subsequent enslavement.[144] "Generally when the grown people in the neighborhood were gone far in the fields to labor," explained one former African slave, "the children assembled together in some of the neighbors' premises to play; and commonly some of us used to get up a tree to look out for any assailant, or kidnapper, for they sometimes took these opportunities of our parents' absence to attack and carry off as many as they could seize."[145]

While there were clearly many avenues to slave ownership in Africa, by far the most common were wars and raids in which ambitious, well-armed aggressors overran their weaker neighbors.[146] The Ngoni and Yao tribes terrorized the people of Nyasaland; the Baganda dominated much of Uganda; the Nyoro and Hima tribes of Ankole enslaved Toro women and children; the Tutsis subjugated the Hutus in Rwanda; the Masai of Kenya tyrannized the Kikuyu and Kamba; and the Somali enslaved the Galla of eastern Africa.[147] In the larger, more developed African states the demand for slave labor was particularly strong.[148] The Damagaram kingdom west of Lake Chad, the Tuareg society of central Sudan, and the Wolof and Sereer peoples of West Africa turned slave raiding into big business, feeding their victims into a complex trading network.[149] As historian Frederick Cooper observes, most Africanists in recent years "have preferred to ignore the fact that in Africa, as in most of the world, wealth and power also meant exploitation and subordination. The use of slaves was not the only route to power, and slaves were not the only exploited people, but the complexities of African societies were reflected in the diverse forms of slavery."[150]

Slave raiders typically carried out surprise assaults in the early morning, killing male resisters while capturing women, children, and the elderly.[151] Successful raiders returned to their home villages beaming with pride, forcing their captives to march in front of them while jubilant kinfolk cheered.[152] The raided territories, meanwhile, were left utterly devastated. A nineteenth-century eyewitness account describes the horrors that such attacks typically left behind:

> On our return through the Mbe country [in what is now Kenya], a most harrowing sight presented itself: what only a few days before

were prosperous villages, standing amid fields of grain, were now smoking ruins; bodies of old men, women and children, half-burnt lay in all directions; here and there might be seen a few solitary individuals, sitting with their head buried in their hands, hardly noticing the passing caravan, and apparently in the lowest depths of misery and despair. On questioning several of these unhappy beings, I was informed that the Masai had unexpectedly arrived one morning at dawn, spearing and burning all before them and carrying off some 250 women, and large herds of cattle. Only a few of the unfortunate people had escaped by fleeing to the mountains.[153]

Some tribes in particular developed reputations for their burning lust for conquest. The Wanyamwezi of eastern Africa, for instance, engaged in slaving on a massive scale, not only as agents for Arab traders but also for their own exploitation.[154] The most powerful and populous tribe of their region, the Wanyamwezi were infamous for treating their slaves "as if they were on the level of animals."[155]

In Uganda's Bantu kingdom, where slavery was a longstanding institution, nineteenth-century observers were astounded not only by the large number of slaves in the Bantu king's possession, but also by "the cheapness with which life was held."[156] Bantu slaves were treated with extreme cruelty, and each day a few were mutilated and killed as punishment for the smallest infractions.[157]

Slaves were also plentiful in Buganda, an East African kingdom located just north of Lake Victoria in present-day Uganda. Many Bugandan slaves were female prisoners of war who were distributed—sometimes by the hundreds—among local chiefs.[158] Following the wars of King Suna in the 1860s, female captives were so numerous that Suna presented more than 2,000 of them as token gifts to his mother and wives.[159] Throughout most of the nineteenth century, Bugandan warriors and their Bunyoro rivals repeatedly clashed on the battlefield,[160] each side enslaving their captives and then using them as exchange commodities with Arab traders.[161]

While critics of Western civilization eagerly point out the depravity of white-imposed slavery, they are inclined not only to minimize the evils of *black*-on-black enslavement, but also to overlook the suffering that the latter caused. Indeed these critics have invented the absurd fiction that slavery among black African societies was generally benign and cheerily accepted by all. In truth, however, there is no reason to believe that African slaves who were transferred from one tribe to another suffered any less psychological pain than those who were sold to white or Arab traders. As historians Igor Kopytoff and Suzanne Miers explain, each slave, regardless of his ultimate geographical destination, "was wrenched from his own people, losing his social personality, his identity, and status. He suffered a traumatic and sometimes violent withdrawal from kin, neighbors, and community, and often from familiar customs and language. The change was usually drastic and total."[162]

Life in Africa Apart from European Influences

Tribal warfare and military raids were regular occurrences in Africa long before the first Europeans arrived on its shores.[163] Unlike the idyllic Eden commonly depicted by "civil rights leaders," African history abounds with examples of barbaric societies that ruthlessly overran all neighboring populations.[164] The Zimba were an especially brutal conquering horde that terrorized large parts of East Africa during the sixteenth century,[165] keeping slaves for their own use rather than as articles of exchange.[166] Further south, the Zulus developed shields and spears superior to those of neighboring societies,[167] thereby establishing dominance over a vast geographic area whose northernmost offshoots stretched as far as Tanganyika.[168] Under the leadership of Chief Shaka in the early 1800s, Zulu warriors systematically conquered virtually every group with whom they came into contact, incorporating some tribes into the Zulu nation and completely exterminating others.[169] Renowned for their ferocity, the Zulus commonly scalped, mutilated, or disemboweled their victims.[170] Meanwhile the Matabele, who occupied what is now Zimbabwe, practiced horrible, refined forms of torture and liquidation.[171] Zambia's Bemba tribe was yet another group of marauders whose savagery was related in this gruesome eyewitness account from 1900:

> In nearly every village are to be seen men and women whose eyes have been gouged out; the removal of one eye or one hand is hardly worthy of remark. Men and women are seen whose ears, nose and lips have been sliced off and both hands amputated. The cutting off of breasts of women has been extensively practiced as punishment for adultery but . . . some of the victims . . . are mere children. . . . Indeed these mutilations are inflicted with the utmost callousness;

every chief for instance has a retinue of good singers and drummers who invariably have their eyes gouged out to prevent them running away.[172]

African societies ranged in scale from small nomadic tribes of Bushmen to larger, highly organized kingdoms such as those of the Ganda, Hausa, Lozi, Yoruba, Ashanti, and Dahomey.[173] In what is now the middle portion of Ghana, the Ashanti state was a confederacy of towns, each governed by a council, which "remained united primarily for warfare against outsiders."[174] The Dahomey of western Africa, by contrast, lived under the absolute rule of kings who commanded an army, a network of spies, and a host of executioners. Dahomey kings were feared by their neighbors as powerful, bloodthirsty tyrants.[175] In fact, most of the centralized African kingships had a grim and bloody side, as exemplified by this 1897 description of a human slaughterhouse in Nigeria:

Altars covered with streams of dried human blood, the stench of which was awful . . . huge pits, forty to fifty feet deep, were found filled with human bodies, dead and dying, and a few wretched captives were rescued alive . . . everywhere sacrificial trees on which were the corpses of the latest victims—everywhere, on each path, were newly sacrificed corpses. On the principal sacrificial tree, facing the main gate of the King's Compound, there were two crucified bodies, at the foot of the tree seventeen newly decapitated bodies and forty-three more in various stages of decomposition. On another tree a wretched woman was found crucified, whilst at its foot were four more decapitated bodies. To the westward of the King's house was a large open space, about three hundred yards in length, simply covered with the remains of some hundreds of human sacrifices in all stages of decomposition. The same sights were met with all over the city.[176]

It should be noted that the few politically integrated African kingdoms that developed between the fifth and sixteenth centuries were far outnumbered by neighboring societies whose political disunity left them vulnerable to invasion.[177] Stronger tribes everywhere expanded by subjugating weaker ones.[178] War was almost constant. Tribal differences created hostilities every bit as severe as those in other parts of the world that were based on ethnicity, color, or caste.[179]

Impediments to Civilization

Civilization is, by and large, a product of cultural exchange and shared knowledge. Where geographical barriers forbid such interactions, civilizational development may be limited. Without intercultural contact, people cannot benefit from the ideas, inventions, and knowledge of other societies.[180] Such were the circumstances of black Africa, partitioned from the continent's northern reaches by the Sahara Desert, and from the rest of the world by vast oceans.[181]

In large measure because of this isolation, the written word was a scarce commodity south of the Sahara. The only places with any degree of literacy were the Sudanic empires, the Christian regions of Ethiopia, the Swahili cities on the Indian Ocean, and a few Islamic outposts such as Timbuktu. Even in the great Bantu states of central and southern Africa, professional scribes were almost nonexistent. Consequently, African societies depended principally on oral traditions to retain and transmit knowledge.[182] Without the ability to record information and build on the learning of preceding generations, civilizational advancement was difficult.

Apart from such wealthy and politically integrated kingdoms as Ghana, Mali, and Songhai, most African societies were characterized by great poverty and primitiveness. Possessing almost no technology, they were unable to utilize the power of either wind or water for the purpose of milling grain. While a handful of communities grew somewhat efficient at mining, they had no pumps to allow for deeper digging—thus leaving most of their natural resources untapped.[183] With the wheel and plow virtually unknown in Africa, natives generally "had to rely on the power of a man's arms, legs, or back to perform all their labors."[184] Almost no community south of the Sahara could harness animals to pull plows or wagons until Europeans introduced such techniques in the nineteenth and twentieth centuries.[185] It was also during this period that Europeans taught Africans the concept of replenishing the soil's fertility with green crops and animal manure.[186]

In addition to its relative primitiveness, precolonial Africa was rife with such abhorrent customs as infanticide, the execution of suspected witches, cannibalism, and ritualistic murders.[187] As early as the year 1200 in the Nigerian city of Benin, groups of young women were herded together, sacrificed, and thrown into deep pits—a practice that persisted until at least 1897.[188] In many African societies little effort was made to treat criminals humanely, and lawbreakers were commonly beaten to death, impaled, or mutilated.[189] In some places the concept of equality before the law simply did not exist, and the relative caste statuses of offender and victim determined the punishment for any given crime.[190] None of these distasteful practices, of course, were uniquely African. The intent here is simply to note that modern-day "civil rights leaders" who incessantly criticize the historical sins of the West largely overlook the comparable sins of black Africans.

American Slavery

Regardless of the cruelties that African peoples inflicted on one another, our modern sense of justice tells us that the Western world's imposition of involuntary servitude on them was a moral disgrace. And while nothing can now compensate the millions of departed souls who saw their lives wasted and their spirits broken by enslavement, all Americans would agree that such an abomination should never be repeated. But what can be said to one who believes it is his right—indeed his obligation—to remain bitter at the white race because of its past enslavement of black Africans? What words will answer the individual—black or white—who assigns an inherited guilt to modern-day whites because their skin pigmentation resembles that of yesteryear's European and American slavers?

First of all, those who categorically condemn all present-day whites for being the descendants of slaveowners are, at best, misinformed. Even at the high point of the transatlantic slave trade, the majority of white Americans never owned any slaves. In 1790 roughly one-fourth of all free American families owned slaves, and by 1850 this figure had shrunk to 10 percent.[191] Moreover, most present-day Americans are descendants of people who first came to this country *after* American slavery had been abolished—and who, therefore, never owned slaves.[192] Such facts are, to be sure, somewhat irrelevant if one accepts that descendants are in no way culpable for the sins of their forefathers. Yet even if one wishes to argue that guilt for the transatlantic slave trade *is* somehow heritable, no more than a small percentage of contemporary whites can be charged with the "crime" of having descended from American slaveowners.

Another commonly ignored fact is that even some American *blacks* participated in the exploitation of slaves. Black slave ownership first appeared around 1750 and continued until the Civil War. Some black masters were people of noble intent who had saved enough money to buy, for their relatives and friends, freedom from white masters—though the purchased individuals technically remained slaves because of emancipation restrictions. But many free blacks "debased their African kinsmen, sometimes their own relatives, into chattel slavery. . . . [They] purchased other blacks for no liberating end but simply to enjoy the benefits of being slaveowners."[193] Of the free black families in antebellum New Orleans, fully one-third owned slaves.[194] In 1830 there were more than 3,500 black slaveholders nationwide—principally concentrated in Louisiana, Texas, Florida, Mississippi, and South Carolina. Most possessed no more than a few slaves each, but some owned several dozen, and a few actually owned more than a hundred.[195]

It is worth noting, at this point, the manner in which American slaves were treated. A typical day for slaves consisted of rising before five o'clock in the morning and working between twelve and sixteen hours at monotonous agricultural tasks. Their meals were bland, their living quarters drab, and their religious and social lives "entirely subordinate to their work routines."[196] Most significantly, of course, they were subjected to a legal status that was morally reprehensible in a nation that professed to venerate freedom. Like their counterparts elsewhere, American slaves suffered the indignity of being auctioned in open markets, bred and sometimes branded like cattle, and used as stakes in card and dice games.[197] Many lived each day fearing that their spouses and children might be sold and taken to a distant plantation, never to be seen again.[198] As the black scholar W.E.B. Du Bois wrote early in the twentieth century, one of slavery's most insidious qualities "was in part psychological, the enforced personal feeling of inferiority, the calling of another Master, the standing with hat in hand. It was the helplessness. It was the defenselessness of family life. It was the submergence below the arbitrary will of any sort of individual."[199]

Notwithstanding the facts stated in the preceding paragraph, it should be noted that American slaves received better treatment and had far lower mortality rates than their counterparts elsewhere in the New World. Their basic material needs of life—food, clothing, and shelter—were provided at levels not much below those of the average, working white American;[200] their life expectancy was only slightly lower than that of their masters;[201] and they were not as poor as some contemporary European peasants or laborers.[202] In fact, it is likely that the average southern slave lived better than the vast majority of the world's population a century ago.[203] Caribbean and Latin American slaves, by contrast, died in droves from their murderous work load—a situation that necessitated many large-scale slave importations to replenish the labor force. Their high death rate was further augmented by an inordinately high suicide rate, no doubt caused by their abject circumstances.[204] Consider the comparative population trends of slaves in various regions of the Western Hemisphere. In Santo Domingo more than 800,000 slaves were imported during the eighteenth century, yet by 1790 the country's slave population—even with procreation—was only 480,000.[205] Jamaica imported more than 600,000 slaves between 1701 and 1810, but by the time of the British Emancipation Act of 1833, only 250,000 remained.[206] Cuba also imported at least 600,000 slaves during the eighteenth century, but by 1870 there were barely 200,000 left.[207] These figures stand in marked contrast to the steady rise in the slave population of the United States. The 427,000 Africans who were brought in bondage to North America multiplied in number, by the mid-1800s, to more than four million.[208]

These population trends, to be sure, reflected not only great disparities in the comparative hardships of slave life in different places, but also the varying degrees to which slaves in particular countries were permitted to marry and form families. In the West Indies, where it was relatively inexpensive to import Africans, masters discouraged slave procreation.[209] They preferred instead to purchase new adult slaves when old ones died—rather than incur the long-term expense of raising them from infancy. Thus, comparatively few African females were brought to the Latin and Caribbean countries, making black family life in those regions scarce. In the U.S., by contrast, where it was quite costly to import Africans, masters encouraged the marriage and procreation of the slaves they already owned—so as to develop a continuous supply of young replacements for aging field hands. Not surprisingly, then, the infant mortality rates of slaves in the American South, where plantation owners took care to keep their human property healthy, were much lower than in the Indies.[210] American masters, of course, were motivated at least as much by economics as by compassion, for obviously it was in their financial interest to protect their investments.[211]

Abolition—Humanity's Triumph

Those who criticize the West for its historical participation in the transatlantic slave trade rarely mention that the abolition of slavery was a uniquely Western idea originating in eighteenth-century Great Britain, the largest slave-trading nation of its time. The Quakers were the first organized religious group in Britain to condemn the involuntary servitude to which fellow children of God were being subjected. Before long, a conservative group of evangelicals in the Church of England joined the antislavery crusade. Sparked by the moving exhortations of these passionate preachers, British public sentiment against slavery steadily rose to enormous proportions. By the end of the century slavery's existence had become intolerable to the consciences of British Christians and humanitarians, who deemed it an egregious violation of personal dignity. Rich and poor, working class and nobility—all came to believe that it was time to end this oldest of institutions.[212] In one of the great achievements of human history, Britons united to pressure their own government to legislate slavery out of existence. In an era long before mass communication, mass transit, or mass movements, members of Parliament were amazed to find themselves inundated with petitions demanding slavery's abolition. One particular month, in fact, saw the delivery of more than 800 petitions containing some 700,000 signatures.[213] Such irrepressible public outcry spurred England to end its own slave trade in 1807.[214] Indeed it was not slavery, but rather this unprecedented moral impulse to ban it, that was truly unique in human history. Yet the fact that every nonwhite civilization in the world not only ignored the problem of slavery, but never even considered it to *be* a problem, is somehow dismissed as irrelevant by our "civil rights" messiahs.

Once Britons had eradicated slavery from their own nation, they embarked on the larger goal of eliminating it from the rest of the British Empire and all civilized societies. In 1810 the slave trade was outlawed in Mexico and Venezuela. Chile followed suit in 1811, as did Argentina in 1812.[215] By 1833 plantation slavery throughout the British Empire was ended,[216] and fifteen years later France outlawed the institution in its own territories.[217] The Civil War put a stop to American slavery, and in 1888 Brazil abolished the practice as well.[218] Thus, after thousands of years during which people everywhere had simply accepted slavery as a natural part of the social order, it was eradicated from the entire Western Hemisphere in less than a single century.[219]

It is unfortunate that contemporary "civil rights" crusaders flatly refuse to acknowledge that the transatlantic slave trade was welcomed and supported by those African societies that profited handsomely from selling their fellow blacks to European slavers. The stronger black states of the coastal regions, for instance, "managed to monopolize the traffic with the hinterland [and] prospered amazingly."[220] Numerous kingdoms—among them the Oyo, Dahomey, and Ashanti—gained their might and prosperity entirely from slaving.[221] It is likely, in fact, that the transatlantic slave trade actually created more employment for *African* dealers than for their European counterparts.[222] Though the slave trade is generally described as having uniformly demoralized all Africans, the slave-dealing black societies of the Gold Coast that prospered because of slavery bitterly opposed Britain's abolition efforts.[223] Tribal leaders in Gambia, the Congo, and Dahomey actually sent delegations to London and Paris to argue against abolition.[224] Meanwhile, the rulers and merchants of Senegal demanded that their territory be classified as a French "protectorate" rather than a "colony," so they could legally continue dealing slaves.[225] Neither the African kings nor Arab leaders of the nineteenth century shared the West's moral imperative for ending human bondage,[226] and it was only Great Britain's pressure that eventually caused some of those resisters to free their slaves.[227]

During the middle third of the nineteenth century, African demand for slaves increased tremendously. As Oriental and Occidental purchasers gradually dropped out of the market, there was a profusion of African people left vulnerable to slavers in their own homelands. Because of this surplus, slaves became available at sharply reduced purchase prices, thereby making their ownership more attractive to African buyers.[228] Thus, after 1830 vast stretches of the continent saw a dramatic rise in black-on-black enslavement.[229] In the 1830s the slave population of Zanzibar alone exceeded 100,000.[230] In western Sudan slaves became so numerous that they comprised a majority of the area's population in the second half of the nineteenth century.[231] As of 1870 in Ibadan, the Yoruba city of southern Nigeria, 104 families owned a combined total of more than 50,000 slaves, an average of almost 500 per family.[232] Overall after 1850, black African purchasers acquired more slaves than were exported to the Occident and Orient combined.[233] The typical African master of the period became more determined than ever to squeeze from his slaves all the labor he could—forcing them to work excessively long hours and making their lives almost unbearable.[234]

East Africa's plantation economy peaked between 1875 and 1884, when the Kenyan coast had some 45,000 slaves—44 percent of its total population.[235] The Ethiopian highlands and the areas east of Lake Chad, where slaves had comprised only 4 percent of the region's inhabitants back in 1820, were one-third slave by 1900.[236] Also by the end of the nineteenth century, slaves constituted between one-third and one-half of all people living in the vast Sahelian grasslands stretching from the Atlantic coast of Senegal to the shores of Lake Chad.[237] Near some commercial centers the proportion reached an astounding 80 percent.[238] As of 1900, northern Nigeria's Sokoto caliphate—an area roughly the size of California—contained at least 2.5 million slaves.[239]

The Question of Reparations

Thousands of "civil rights" activists and hundreds of organizations are currently pushing the U.S. Congress to pass legislation mandating monetary reparations to compensate contemporary black Americans for the inequities their ancestors suffered in the transatlantic slave trade.[240] Such restitution, the activists explain, would finally enable blacks to reap some of the economic benefits that slavery's profits gave to the country. They cite numerous factors—all the unpaid labor, the ceaseless toil, the suffering and degradation of the slaves—as indispensable building blocks upon which much of the early American economy was founded. They claim, further, that because black slaves worked so hard for so little, the descendants of those unfortunate individuals should now be given a "fair share" of the current American economy. In the late 1980s a convention of black legislators in New Orleans went so far as to pass a resolution demanding monetary reparations for "those of us who worked for hundreds of years unpaid."[241] Among the prominent individuals and organizations currently advocating such payments are Jesse Jackson, Louis Farrakhan, the NAACP, the National Coalition of Blacks for Reparations in America, and several members of the Congressional Black Caucus such as Representative John Conyers.[242]

Curiously, those who call for American reparations never suggest that the Arab emirates should pay something as well—even though Arab slaving activities in Africa were far more extensive and long-lasting than those of the West.[243] Nor have reparationists expressed even the slightest impulse to compensate the descendants of those African slaves who endured the wretched cruelties of *black* masters in their motherland. In fact, these self-proclaimed apostles of "justice" have never even intimated that *contemporary* African masters—in Mauritania, Sudan, Ghana, Nigeria, Rwanda, and Niger—ought to release and compensate the slaves they hold *today*. Clearly, the "civil rights" cabal would rather depict whites as an evil monolith than work for the welfare of people in bondage.

In order for the proposition of reparations to have any merit, it would be necessary to demonstrate that slavery in fact yielded net economic benefits to the country making the payments. While certainly individual slavers profited greatly from their enterprise, it is doubtful whether, in an overall historical sense, either the United States or Great Britain realized a net profit from the slave trade. Though some have claimed that Britain's industrial revolution was made possible by the wealth generated by slavery, in truth all of Britain's slaving profits amounted to less than 2 percent of the country's domestic investments during that era.[244] Moreover, British military expenditures in the abolition effort were comparable to all the profits that slavery had ever brought to the country.[245] Similarly, it is unlikely that American profits from slavery were any greater than the huge cost of fighting the Civil War—"a war that would not have had to be fought if there were no slavery."[246] If there were no net monetary gains from slavery—when gross profits are weighed against the cost of the abolition struggle—there is no logical economic basis upon which to award present-day blacks reparation payments.[247]

Notwithstanding these facts, it is commonly claimed that slavery made a vital contribution to the economic and cultural development of the West. The planted axiom is that slavery inevitably creates lasting economic benefits for its practitioners. But Brazil, which may have consumed more slaves than any nation in history, and which was the last country in the hemisphere to outlaw slavery, was still economically underdeveloped at the time of its abolition in 1888. The country's later industrial and commercial development was principally the work of European immigrants.[248] To this day, in fact, Brazil's most prosperous and industrialized areas are those southern regions that were settled by German, Italian, and Japanese newcomers.[249] The story is much the same in the United States, where the places that had the most slavery have generally been the poorest.[250] Likewise, the western European nations that were first to abolish slavery led the rest of the world into the modern industrial age.[251]

Those who would argue that reparations should be paid on moral rather than purely economic grounds—as a price tag for the sufferings of slaves—ignore the stubborn reality that guilt is not passed from one generation to the next. As Thomas Sowell points out, if guilt were heritable "then this generation of Jews would be justified in putting this generation of Germans in concentration camps. No one believes that—not Jews, not Germans, nor any other sane adults."[252] Reparationists, of course, unanimously dismiss the fact that long before white slavers ever stepped onto African soil, the ancestors of contemporary black Americans were tyrannized by one or another of Africa's many ruthless tribes. There is scarcely a group of people anywhere, in fact, whose forefathers were not oppressed, attacked, enslaved, or to some degree victimized by another group at one time or another. Human history is a narrative punctuated on virtually every line by brutality, and past horrors cannot be eradicated by present pretensions. Dr. Sowell expresses the futility of attempting to right the wrongs of history through any forms of compensation:

> To say that one has been compensated is to say that things have been set right. But nothing within human power can ever set right the sufferings and degradations of millions of human beings, all over this planet, for thousands of years. Slavery can neither be forgiven nor forgotten, certainly not by those who never suffered it personally—and certainly not in exchange for money or other benefits. Such a political deal would rank with the cynical sale of indulgences in the Middle Ages.[253]

The reparationist view deems it possible to determine precisely the degree to which people's historical suffering preordains not only their own subsequent underachievement, but that of their descendants as well. In truth, however, such calculation is a task far beyond human capacity. History abounds with examples of penniless immigrants in many places starting life anew, taking menial jobs, facing extreme discrimination, and yet eventually rising above the economic level of the natives.[254] Other groups have been enslaved, interned in prison camps, even systematically exterminated—only to go on eventually to great prosperity within a relatively short time. Nonetheless, the "civil rights" crowd stubbornly clings to the obviously false notion that groups of humble or oppressed origins are permanently handicapped by those beginnings.

Like millions of others who suffered the cruel blows of history, the victims of American slavery are all in their graves, far beyond our ability to repay them for what they lost. Yet proponents of reparations deem it a reasonable alternative to compensate those slaves' *descendants* generations later. Meanwhile, they scarcely care that the unfortunate millions who were shipped to America were already slaves in Africa, as were many millions more who remained in their motherland under black masters. Nor do reparationists recognize the debt that contemporary blacks owe to America for finally ending slavery at the cost of hundreds of thousands of Union soldiers' lives nearly fourteen decades ago. They fail to acknowledge the unsettling fact that the transport of African slaves across the Atlantic Ocean was—though a moral abomination that wasted millions of innocent lives—on balance a benefit to those slaves' descendants. Booker T. Washington, who was born a slave but later became the most influential black American educator and statesman of his time, put it this way:

> Think about it: we went into slavery pagans; we came out Christians. We went into slavery pieces of property; we came out American citizens. We went into slavery with chains clanking about our wrists; we came out with the American ballot in our hands. . . . Notwithstanding the cruelty and moral wrong of slavery, we are in a stronger and more hopeful position, materially, intellectually, morally, and religiously, than is true of an equal number of black people in any other portion of the globe.[255]

Early in the twentieth century, the black feminist writer Zora Neale Hurston articulated a similar idea:

> From what I can learn, [slavery] was sad. Certainly. But my ancestors who lived and died in it are dead. The white men who profited by their labor and lives are dead also. I have no personal memory of those times, and no responsibility for them. Neither has the grandson of the man who held my folks. . . . I have no intention of wasting my time beating on old graves. . . . I do not belong to the sobbing school of Negroes who hold that nature somehow has given them a low-down dirty deal and whose feelings are all hurt about it. . . . Slavery is the price I paid for civilization, and that is worth all that I have paid through my ancestors for it.[256]

Chapter 13

Finding Racism Everywhere

Every man, wherever he goes, is encompassed by a cloud
of comforting convictions, which move with him
like flies on a summer day.
—Bertrand Russell[1]

Contemporary America's "civil rights" movement, having squandered the moral authority that attended its birth, has degenerated into little more than an assembly line for the manufacture of racists, both black and white. Blaming white society for virtually every conceivable black ill, those in the movement's vanguard have convinced millions of African Americans that their white neighbors are not to be trusted. By the same token, the prevailing demagogic rhetoric of recent decades has embittered millions of whites—by contending that even their best efforts to foster racial justice are woefully inadequate. These consequences have not occurred by mere chance, but have been willfully brought about by activists whose very livelihoods are contingent upon interracial strife—and who are, therefore, reluctant to concede that black life has improved much since the 1950s. As the NAACP's former chairman Myrlie Evers-Williams puts it, "America [still] reeks of racism."[2] "This is a racist society, and it will be for a long time to come," concurs activist Roger Williams.[3] Legal scholar Kimberle Crenshaw calls racism "the central ideological un-derpinning of American society."[4] Along the same lines, black educa-tor Johnnetta Cole says, "Racism is alive and well in America. We [blacks] have a collective sense that we are still not free."[5] Such people claim to find new examples of white malevolence every day, sometimes in the most surprising places.

According to black columnist E.R. Shipp, many blacks be-lieve that tough anti-crime measures by law-enforcement authorities are nothing more than mandates to "crack black heads"; that calls for welfare reform are made with the intention of "forcing lazy blacks to work"; that capital punishment proponents are primarily interested in executing the disproportionate number of black Death Row inmates; and that politicians' pledges to cut taxes are but thinly veiled attempts to reduce financial assistance to poor blacks.[6] In a similar vein, black New York congressman Charles Rangel characterizes white politi-cians who favor tax cuts and the death penalty as racists. "It's not 'spic' and 'nigger' anymore," says Rangel. "They say, 'Let's cut taxes.' You don't have to be a social scientist to understand that if you're going to reduce taxes, it's going to impact on the poor, and the poor happen to be blacks and other minorities. . . . Tax cuts, plus more death penalty, plus more jails, plus cuts in education, plus cuts in youth programs, is racism."[7]

It is indeed astounding to see how far some can stretch their imaginations to find "evidence" of white racism. Consider the ex-ample of Dr. Ernest Johnson, a psychologist who concludes, from his study of 1,000 Florida tenth-graders, that black teens tend to be an-grier than their white peers. Theorizing that this black anger is bred by white America's many racists,[8] Dr. Johnson does not even speculate as to whether it may result, at least in part, from the constant threat of *black* predators terrorizing their own neighborhoods. Nor does he trace it, even in part, to the fact that scarcely 35 percent of black youngsters currently live in two-parent homes.[9]

Concurring with Johnson is Dr. Elijah Saunders, a black car-diologist at the University of Maryland Medical School, who asserts that "if there were no racism in America, hypertension would be less of a problem for blacks. Hypertension is at near-epidemic propor-tions among blacks and is chiefly responsible for their high mortality rates from heart and kidney disease and stroke. It makes sense to me that racism and black rage are emotional stressors that could worsen any physiological tendency toward hypertension."[10] Remarkably, Saunders does not speculate as to whether *black*-on-black violence—rampant as it is—might account for even a fraction of black Americans' stress-induced cardiovascular disease. Rather, we are presumably to believe that white racists lurking around every corner, practicing their craft, are our country's principal agents of black malaise and hypertension. Incidentally, it should be noted that in 1994 medical researchers discovered that blood-vessel elasticity—essential for cardiovascular health—tends to be greater in whites than in blacks.[11] Thus it may be that racial differences in the incidence of high blood pressure are caused by nothing more sinister than physiology.

But if, as Dr. Saunders claims, black hypertension rates implicate white racism, how then are we to interpret suicide rates? By Saunders's logic, the comparative suicide rates of blacks and whites should reveal important information about the relative degrees of stress afflicting members of each race. A disproportionately high incidence of suicide among blacks, for example, would surely be hailed by "civil rights" messiahs as evidence that racism was casting its deadly shadow over the souls of black Americans. Yet in fact, white men have a substantially higher suicide rate than black men (19.9 per 100,000 population versus 12.5 per 100,000), while the rate for white women is about two and a half times greater than for black women (4.8 versus 1.9 per 100,000).[12] Could it be that whites, feeling overwhelmed by the many black-on-white attacks that occur annually in this country (see statistics in chapter 4), sometimes react by taking their own lives in despair? No one ever asks this question; the very notion is dismissed as preposterous. The intent here is not to advance the theory that black racism leads to white suicides, but merely to suggest that such a conjecture is no more absurd than one attributing black hypertension to white racism.

People of the "civil rights" vision blame white society for a multitude of medical, criminal, educational, and familial problems plaguing the black community. They assure us, for instance, that if black Americans are afflicted disproportionately by AIDS, incarceration, school failure, and fatherless homes, it is because of white racism's debilitating effects. Dr. Saunders's hypertension hypothesis is but a logical extension of this worldview. But as illustrated by their silence on such matters as suicide statistics, proponents of this vision commonly disregard data that conflicts with their treasured theories.

Consider a recent study which revealed that while the smoking rate of young white women stayed constant (at about 27 percent) between 1987 and 1992, it declined dramatically among young black women (from 21.8 percent to 5.9 percent).[13] Notably, these rather startling findings drew little attention from journalists and racial activists, whose analysis of the numbers was limited to benign observations that tobacco advertising campaigns aimed at white women had apparently been effective.[14] Yet we can well imagine the lengthy list of accusations that would have flooded our nation's airwaves and editorial pages had research shown that smoking rates had decreased among *white* women but not among *black* women. All the usual culprits would have been named: the pressures of life in a racist nation, a lack of self-esteem resulting in a subconscious death wish, and the advertising industry's genocidal targeting of black women. But because, in this case, it was whites who were disproportionately involved in self-destructive behavior, there was no hand-wringing, no soul-searching, no impassioned plea for the tobacco and advertising industries to stop "exterminating" smokers.

Nor have the champions of "justice" acknowledged the lingering psychological and economic costs of interracial assaults. Victims of violent crime are ten times more likely than non-victims to suffer from severe depression—and twice as likely to need a doctor's care—even more than a decade after their victimization.[15] Perhaps the greatest debilitation occurs in rape victims, 40 percent of whom later report having suicidal thoughts, and 20 percent of whom eventually attempt to kill themselves.[16] Given the fact that about nine-tenths of interracial attacks are black-on-white (see chapter 4 for details), would it be altogether unreasonable to blame black racism for many of the physical and emotional afflictions that white crime victims must endure for a lifetime? Regardless of how one answers this question, certainly its premise is as reasonable as blaming white racism for black hypertension.

"Racism" as Sport

Former Georgetown University basketball coach John Thompson claims that racism underlies Proposition 48, a regulation instituted in 1986 requiring student-athletes to meet minimum standards of academic competence in order to qualify for intercollegiate athletic competition. Under this rule, graduating high-school students with GPAs between 2.0 and 2.5 must score at least 700 (out of a possible 1,600) on the Scholastic Aptitude Test (SAT), while those with high-school GPAs of 2.0 or lower must score at least 900. With 400 being the lowest SAT score possible, these demands hardly seem excessive.[17] Thompson, however, asserts that because the SAT is "culturally biased," Prop 48 unfairly discriminates against black students. In fact, while the ordinance was under consideration, Thompson demonstrated his displeasure by boycotting one of his team's basketball games and leaving the court during another.[18] Instead of applauding measures requiring students to maximize their study time—so as to best equip them for success in life beyond the playing field and the hardwood— Thompson characterized as victims those who elected to do nothing in the classroom.

In 1995 the National Collegiate Athletic Association (NCAA) instituted a similar plan known as Proposition 16, which also made athletic eligibility contingent upon minimum levels of academic achievement.[19] But four years later, once it was noted that fully 94 percent of whites but just 74 percent of blacks met the new standards, a federal judge ordered Prop 16's rescission because of its "unjustified disparate impact against African Americans"[20]—a decision applauded by John Thompson.

In January 1994, the members of college basketball's Black Coaches Association (BCA) protested an NCAA ruling that reduced, from fifteen to thirteen, the number of basketball scholarships that any school could award to student-athletes.[21] Led by John Thompson, BCA coaches complained that this reduction would deny hundreds of impoverished black American males an opportunity to receive a free college education.[22] Yet while these drillmasters ascribed their protests to purely scholastic concerns, their actions betrayed a much greater preoccupation with winning ball games.[23] During the years just prior to the NCAA scholarship edict, these same BCA coaches had recruited basketball players from countries all around the world: Senegal, Yugoslavia, Canada, Zaire, Nigeria, Gambia, Holland, Burundi, New Zealand, Denmark, and Romania.[24] Though quick to condemn the NCAA for allegedly making things tough on African Americans, they saw nothing wrong with scouring the globe themselves for foreign-born athletes to fill roster spots that otherwise could have gone to native blacks. Sports columnist Phil Mushnick decried the BCA's pretense of virtue:

> If access to education [were] at the core [of the BCA's displeasure over the reduction in athletic scholarships], the BCA's member coaches would not preclude genuine access by scheduling games that take student-athletes thousands of miles from campus for extended periods while [school is] in session. . . . If academic success is the issue, then BCA coaches should've long ago refused to participate in basketball's post-season—it's too close to finals. Or is it that 'access' is a euphemism for 'accident,' as in education by accident?[25]

Thompson and his BCA colleagues have plenty of company in their constant hunt for racism. For instance, *New York Times* columnist William Rhoden lamented in 1994 that Alcorn State University's outstanding black quarterback, Steve McNair, probably would not win college football's prestigious Heisman Trophy that year. Comparing this "injustice" to the pre-1947 color bar in major league baseball, Rhoden wrote, "Unfortunately, Heisman voting is a beauty contest, and black has not always been considered beautiful."[26] But while noting that no black had won the trophy prior to 1961, he neglected to mention that of the last twenty Heisman winners, *sixteen* had been black.[27]

Black newspaper columnist Richard G. Carter saw racism in the New York Knickerbockers' 1989 acquisition of Kiki Vandeweghe, who became the second white player on the Knicks' twelve-man roster that year. A high-scoring, perennial all-star in the NBA, Vandeweghe brought impressive credentials to New York. Though his recurring back problems at the time made it difficult to predict his future effectiveness, team management felt that acquiring Vandeweghe was a gamble worth taking. Carter, however, saw things otherwise, asserting that Knicks' general manager Al Bianchi merely wanted another white face on the team. Moreover, Carter was annoyed by the New York fans' positive reaction to Vandeweghe's arrival. "[E]veryone knows what the presence of white sports heroes can do for the psyche of white fans," he wrote. "It makes 'em feel oh, so good. . . . It was big-time sport business as usual in these United States. Some things never change."[28]

In September 1998, shortly after both Mark McGwire and

Sammy Sosa had broken the single-season home-run marks of Babe Ruth and Roger Maris, white sportswriter Wallace Matthews chastised white Americans for the subliminal racism they had supposedly displayed by rooting harder for the "red-haired" McGwire than for Sosa, a "brown-skinned" Dominican.[29] "It looks a whole lot racist," wrote Matthews. "And jingoistic. And unfair."[30] "Fifty years after Jackie Robinson introduced Major League Baseball to another new talent pool it could dip into," he added, "the game is still racist to the core."[31]

Apparently it never occurred to Matthews that much of the public's anticipation regarding McGwire's assault on the home-run record was attributable not only to the unprecedented frequency with which he had been hitting home runs for three consecutive seasons, but also to his longstanding reputation as a sort of modern-day Ruth whose prodigious moonshots are unrivaled in height and distance. Nor did Matthews seem to consider that McGwire naturally drew much of the public's attention simply because he had led the home-run race for virtually the entire 1998 season, albeit by a slim margin over Sosa. Neither did Matthews appreciate that when McGwire surpassed the totals of Ruth and Maris, he was several homers ahead of Sosa and thus stood alone on baseball's center stage. When Sosa passed Ruth and Maris a few days later, his achievement was, through no fault of his own, simply lacking that same mystique.

Curiously, the race-conscious and nationalistic reactions of *Dominican* baseball fans seemed not to bother Matthews at all. He did not comment on the fact that during Sosa's home-run chase, Dominicans all over America and Santo Domingo were clearly rooting for him to beat out McGwire, adorning their cars and clothing with Sosa's name and likeness.[32] Neither was Matthews offended that thousands of Sosa's countrymen gave their beloved slugger a hero's welcome when he visited his homeland after the 1998 baseball season. Nor did he deem it "jingoistic" when the Dominican baseball league ceremoniously dedicated that year's winter season to Sosa.[33] Neither did he regard it as "racist" when Dominican fans publicly honored other native-born big-leaguers like Moises Alou, Raul Mondesi, Alex Rodriguez, Pedro Martinez, and Vladimir Guerrero.[34] And finally, Matthews made no mention of the fact that Sosa was adored by white, black, *and* brown fans in Chicago, where he played. Incidentally, such reverence was not unlike the *national* adulation that has long been heaped upon another Chicago legend, Michael Jordan, who may well be—to fans of *all* colors—the most revered athlete in American history.

Jesse Jackson professes to detect a great deal of racism in professional sports—most notably in baseball. He complains that there are too few black faces among major league umpires and franchise executives. Of course, he provides not a shred of evidence that blacks have been intentionally excluded, but merely cites their alleged underrepresentation as "proof" of discrimination.[35] Curiously, however, he is untroubled by the fact that blacks and Hispanics—who together make up less than one-fourth of the U.S. population—comprise fully 41 percent of major league baseball players.[36]

Others complain that the National Basketball Association and National Football League do not have "enough" black owners, general managers, head coaches, and team-office employees. Yet these same critics are undisturbed by the fact that the NBA and NFL player pools are 82 percent and 67 percent black, respectively.[37] The apostles of "equity," it seems, object to numerical imbalances only in cases where *blacks* are scarce. Where blacks dominate, questions of discrimination are never raised.

Indeed, "civil rights leaders" choose their crusades carefully. While Jesse Jackson sees no reason to campaign for proportional racial representation on NBA or NFL rosters, he vehemently denounced the 1996 Academy Awards voting, on grounds that not enough blacks had been nominated for the prestigious Oscars. Explaining that because Hollywood had imposed what he called a "white-out," he urged blacks to neither attend the awards ceremonies nor watch them on television. "It doesn't stand to reason," he said, "that if you are forced to the back of the bus, you will go to the bus company's annual picnic and act like you're happy."[38]

Alerted once again by his own keen eye for white bigotry, Jackson condemned the NBA in January 1997 for "stripping" black forward Dennis Rodman "of his dignity" when the league suspended the controversial player for eleven games as punishment for his having kicked a courtside photographer. Presumably, Rodman's dignity had been intact not only when he delivered his costly kick, but also during the previous several years when he had written a bestselling book whose every page was liberally peppered with profanities; when he had dyed his hair a different brilliant color for each game; when he had publicly appeared in women's clothing and makeup on numerous occasions; when he had intentionally head-butted a referee during a ball game; when he had vulgarly cursed out the Mormon religion during a playoff series in Utah; and when he had been suspended at least a dozen times for undermining his various teams and coaches.[39] In short, Jackson asks us to believe that it was not until the NBA's punitive action that Rodman's "dignity" had been sullied.

The "civil rights" cabal's broad definition of racism encompasses virtually anything that a white person might think or say. The late Jimmy "The Greek" Snyder was forced to resign from his broadcasting job after publicly *complimenting* black athletes for being better jumpers than their white counterparts. While he attributed their great leaping ability in part to hard training, he also speculated that blacks' superior leg power stemmed from the days of slavery, when masters purposely bred large, strong males with females of similar description.[40] Unfortunately, Snyder's assertion breached "civil rights" etiquette, which deems it racist for whites to suggest that blacks are better natural athletes—presumably because of some unspoken, joining implication that blacks are inferior to whites intellectually.

Consider also the case of Dale Lick, who in July 1993 was a leading contender for the presidency of Michigan State University (MSU). His candidacy for the position was forestalled, however, when the *Detroit Free Press* printed this remark which he had made four years earlier: "A black athlete can actually out-jump a white athlete on the average, so they're better at the game [of basketball]. All you need to do is turn to the NCAA playoffs in basketball to see that the bulk of the players on those outstanding teams are black."[41] Once Lick's comments were publicized, students, professors, and state officials rushed to denounce his "insensitivity." Bruce Miller, executive director of MSU's presidential search committee, expressed his great "concern" about the brewing controversy. Under pressure from all sides, Lick eventually withdrew his candidacy for the MSU job.[42]

Roger Bannister, the legendary British runner who is now a neurologist, touched off a similar clamor in September 1995 when he said, "As a scientist rather than a sociologist, I am prepared to risk political incorrectness by drawing attention to the seemingly obvious but understressed fact that black sprinters and black athletes in general all seem to have certain anatomical advantages." These comments instantly prompted angry responses from many in the black community.[43]

Curiously, when blacks make observations identical to those of Bannister, Lick, and Snyder, there is not the slightest ripple of public reaction. For example, when NBA standout Charles Barkley was traded from the Philadelphia 76ers to the Phoenix Suns in 1992, he commented on the prospect of playing alongside some high-caliber white players on his new team. "It's been about nine years," he said, "since I played with white guys who can play, back in the Bobby Jones era."[44] On another occasion Barkley remarked upon the fine jumping ability of white basketball player Rex Chapman, saying, "He jumps like a black man."[45] Football player Lawrence Taylor once said that only "brothers" (slang term meaning blacks) could play the cornerback position well.[46] Sprinter Carl Lewis observes that black athletes seem to be "made better" than white athletes.[47] Former baseball great Joe Morgan has candidly stated that the "speed, quickness, and agility" of blacks is "clearly superior" to that of whites. Ex-football star Lynn Swann concurs that "black athletes are just able to do more things than the other athletes." O.J. Simpson once remarked that blacks are physically "geared to speed" in a way that whites are not.[48] In November 1993 Wayman Tisdale, a black forward for the NBA's Sacramento Kings, noted the athleticism of his new white teammate, rookie Bobby Hurley. "Bobby's a lot faster and a better passer than I thought," said Tisdale. "He's like a black kid."[49] In October 1997, reporters pointed out that the Chicago Bulls had looked particularly bad in an exhibition game they had played without stars Michael Jordan, Scottie Pippen, and Dennis Rodman. In response, Rodman attributed the team's lackluster performance to the fact that the lineup featured "less black guys, more white."[50]

Though such comments do not even raise an eyebrow when made by a black, a white expressing similar ideas quickly finds himself the main attraction in a media circus. The same is true of any whites who dare to stereotype blacks as "lacking the [mental] necessities" for managing a baseball team, as former Los Angeles Dodgers' general manager Al Campanis once asserted.[51] The intent here is not to defend Campanis's foolish statement—which ultimately cost him his job—but rather to point out the different standards by which "civil rights" disciples judge blacks and whites.

The sports world was again the scene of racial controversy in

July 1994, when it was reported that Richard Kraft, the New York Yankees' vice president for community relations, had referred to minority residents of New York's South Bronx as ill-mannered "monkeys" and "little colored boy[s]." Television reporters eagerly jumped on the story, asking local black and Hispanic teenagers how they felt about Kraft having called them monkeys. Minority "leaders" were indignant. Bronx borough president Fernando Ferrer characterized Kraft's comments as "blatant[ly] racist," steeped in "bigotry," and symptomatic of anti-minority prejudices pervading the Yankees' front office. These prejudices, he explained, were "the real reason" for the club's interest in moving out of the Bronx. Said Ferrer, "[Kraft has] demonstrated his contempt for the city's fans and especially its fans of color."[52]

In truth, Kraft's *actual* words bore little resemblance to the snippets paraphrased by community "leaders." His reference to "monkeys," for example, was nothing more than an expression of annoyance over the fact that youngsters at local playgrounds frequently hung from basketball hoops and intentionally tore them down. "It's like monkeys," he said. "Those guys can all go up and hang on the rim and crack the rim and bend the hoops. It's a continuous maintenance problem."[53] This is clearly a far cry from maliciously calling blacks and Hispanics "monkeys." Just as running might be called horse-like behavior, or flying might be called bird-like, climbing and hanging can reasonably be called monkey-like. In fact, the "monkey bars" that are often found in playgrounds are named for this obvious reality. That something so self-evident must even be explained is a testament to how widely racial paranoia has swept through our land.

When Kraft made his "little colored boy" remark, he was lamenting the fact that so many black youths in the South Bronx had become involved in crime. Saddened that a generation of youngsters was growing up without proper moral guidance, he said, "I don't know what happens to the little colored boy who goes through school here. . . . I don't know if he loses his roots here."[54] In a related comment, Kraft asserted that such destructive youngsters needed—somehow—to learn better manners. Is it really racist to desire that those who behave poorly might improve their conduct? Would it not be *more* racist to accept their bad behavior as inevitable, presuming them incapable of aspiring to higher standards?

Kraft's benign intentions notwithstanding, public scorn and the rhetoric of community "leaders" led him to resign from his job with the Yankees. Former National League president Bill White, who is black, provided a rare voice of reason:

> I'm disgusted over what happened to Dick [Kraft]. I've known Dick for twenty years and he uses the term "monkeys" toward all kids. As for the "little colored boys" remark . . . hey, since I've been alive we've been called colored, Negroes, blacks, African Americans—they just don't know what to call us. What happened to Dick is a lot of BS. I asked him if I could help get his job back, but he said, "No thanks." I feel very badly for him.[55]

Despite Kraft's contention that his comments were in no way intended to be offensive, the guardians of "justice" clung tenaciously to their ironclad conviction that he harbored a deep-seated contempt for blacks and Hispanics. Compare this to the treatment Charles Barkley received in February 1995 after telling reporters that he hated white people. When Barkley was later asked why he had made such a statement, he indignantly explained that he had been joking. "If you don't like it, f—— you and f—— your family," he told his questioners.[56] "Civil rights leaders," predictably, never mentioned the incident, and before long it was forgotten by the media. The intent here is not to impute a racist motive to Barkley's remark about whites, but simply to spotlight the double standard to which whites and blacks are held.

During a postgame interview in February 1998, Barkley made some further racially charged remarks to a white sports reporter who asked him if he would consider his pro career incomplete should he fail to win an NBA title before retiring. "I know you good ol' boys in the press are gonna rag on me until I win a championship," Barkley replied tartly. "You're what I call the Angry White Males. Most of you guys who write for newspapers are all rednecks. None of you guys ever put on a jockstrap. I'm not gonna let you Angry White Males dictate my career." He then turned to his teammates and said, "You know how I love to [bleep] with these white boys."[57] This incident went virtually unreported by the media.

In March 1996, CBS television sportscaster Billy Packer caused a great stir when he referred to Georgetown University's black basketball star Allen Iverson as a "tough monkey." Though Packer's comment was intended only to praise Iverson's tenacious play, the arbiters of "propriety" were instantly offended. Jesse Jackson, for one, likened Packer to Al Campanis, who, as noted earlier, had once disparaged the intellectual capacity of blacks.[58] A flustered Packer quickly apologized for his choice of words and assured everyone that he had meant no harm.

A year later David Halberstam, the white play-by-play sports-caster of the NBA's Miami Heat, mentioned during a radio broadcast that Heat guard John Crotty (who is black) was a University of Virginia (UV) graduate. The announcer mused aloud that UV founder Thomas Jefferson, were he still alive, would surely have been proud of Crotty's athletic accomplishments. Noting that Jefferson was a slaveowner, Halberstam joked, "If basketball had been invented back then, Jefferson would have had a great team" [comprised of slaves]. Within a matter of days the national media vilified Halberstam as a racist—not only for stereotyping blacks as purely athletic specimens, but also for speaking flippantly about slavery. The NBA fined him $2,500 for his "insensitive" comments, and he nearly lost his job. Contrite and embarrassed, Halberstam solemnly apologized to the black community for his remarks.[59]

In February 1998, University of Arkansas (UA) basketball coach Nolan Richardson, who is black, made a remark that scarcely differed from Halberstam's. During a press conference, Richardson alluded to the abundance of outstanding players in the Southeast Conference, of which UA was a part. "Let's face it," he said. "Where did most of the slave ships stop?" His implication was that the descendants of slaves from the Southeast, being black, were athletically gifted—and therefore proficient at the game of basketball. Unlike Halberstam, however, Richardson made his comment without penalty. He was neither fined nor even asked to "clarify" what would have been deemed a grossly improper statement had a white person said it.[60]

Like their coaches, a number of black athletes are also quick to spot "racism." In December 1998 New York Jets linebacker Brian Cox was fined $10,000 by the National Football League for making two dangerous and illegal tackles against an opposing quarterback. Because the league official who imposed the fine was black, Cox could not blame run-of-the-mill white racism for his troubles. Thus he explained that he was the victim of a more subtle brand of bigotry that "pitted" black players "against" black officials who, so as not to displease their racist white peers, were willing to treat black players unfairly. "Why do we [blacks] always have to be pitted against each other?" he fumed. "I do have a problem with that, because every time we have to be subject to discipline of some sort, it always has to be against a person of color. If they [black league officials] are token, it's worthless. It's just like slave Negro, house Negro mentality, and that's what this is."[61] We should remember, of course, that just a few years earlier the allegedly racist NFL had been fully prepared to drop Tempe, Arizona from consideration as a potential Super Bowl site unless the citizens of that state voted to observe Martin Luther King Day as an official holiday.[62]

Even the music played at sports arenas during athletic events can raise the suspicions of the supersensitive. At a November 1996 hockey game between the New York Islanders and Buffalo Sabres, the rock classic "Play that Funky Music [White Boy]" blared over the arena's sound system during a play stoppage moments after Islander winger Dan Plante had scuffled with black Sabre defenseman Rumun Ndur. The following day a New York newspaper suggested that the playing of this song was, because of the preceding skirmish's interracial component, the "tasteless moment of the night." In truth, however, race had nothing to do with the choice of music. All songs played during each break in the action were pre-programmed, and thus the timing of the offending song was purely coincidental.[63]

It should also be noted that Hispanic athletes, like their black counterparts, are generally permitted to make racially derogatory remarks with impunity. In July 1997, for instance, boxer Hector Camacho asserted that black heavyweight Mike Tyson had "too many niggers around him"—evoking not even the slightest reproof from the foes of "insensitivity."[64] Were a white sports celebrity to say something similar, he would be stigmatized for the rest of his career, if not the rest of his life.

"Racism" Around Every Corner

One day in December 1989, police officers at New York's Port Authority bus terminal, who at the time were conducting an aggressive drug-interdiction campaign, arrested a nineteen-year-old black woman named Annette Evans for carrying several ounces of cocaine in her handbag. At the woman's trial, however, Justice Carol Berkman dismissed all charges against Miss Evans—reasoning that since the vast majority of people arrested by Port Authority police were black and Hispanic, the police force was most likely racist. "Minorities did not fight their way from the back of the bus," said Berkman, "just to be routinely stopped and interrogated on their way through the terminal. . . . The picture that emerges is one of discriminatory law enforcement, law enforcement that does incalculable damage to our civil liberties and which produces at best questionable results for the war on drugs."[65] Lost in the mists of Berkman's lofty reasoning, unfortunately, was the fact that the suspect was indeed guilty of the crime for which she was arrested. Also overlooked by the judge was that *whites*, and not minorities, were being stopped and interrogated by Port Authority police in numbers disproportionate to their actual involvement in drug-related crimes. In 1989 blacks and Hispanics comprised 65 to 75 percent of all suspects questioned by police in the drug-interdiction program, but were more than 99 percent (208 out of 210) of those actually found to be carrying drugs.[66] Whites, meanwhile, constituted 25 to 35 percent of suspects questioned by police, but were fewer than 1 percent of those actually arrested for possession.[67] In other words, many whites were stopped on police suspicion even though they were violating no law. Based on these figures, one could reasonably argue not only that police surveillance of whites was excessive, but that the corresponding surveillance of minorities was unduly lax. Justice Berkman, of course, did not see things this way.

Berkman's reference to statistics that purportedly "proved" discrimination is not at all unusual among advocates of proportional representation. The mountain of mythology surrounding child adoption figures provides yet another example. Because a disproportionate number of children eligible for adoption have historically been black, and most couples wanting to adopt have been white, "civil rights" messiahs have contended for many years that few whites are willing to adopt interracially. In truth, however, many white couples have been eager to adopt and form families with black children. Nonetheless, hundreds of thousands of black youngsters have been shuffled from foster home to foster home, never to know the joy of a stable family life, simply because some "mental-health experts" have determined that white parents would be unable to raise those children properly. Indeed, the National Association of Black Social Workers characterizes the placement of black children into white homes as "cultural genocide." In a similar vein, a report by the Black Task Force on Child Abuse and Neglect warns against the "transculturation" that occurs "when one dominant culture overpowers and forces another culture to accept a foreign form of existence." Asserting that "children need to be with those who are most familiar with their culture, heritage, and family system,"[68] the report concludes that "[b]lack children belong, physically, psychologically, and culturally in black families in order that they receive the total sense of themselves and develop a sound projection for the future."[69] Such statements imply that black children are better off with no family life at all, or with transitory stays in unstable foster homes, than with life in a loving white family. Yet according to longitudinal research conducted over the past two decades, black youngsters suffer *no* adverse effects from adoption by white parents. In fact, a twenty-year study of such children by an American University professor found them to be "better adjusted, far better cared for, and no less conscious and proud of their racial heritage than black children adopted by blacks or remaining in foster care."[70] It was not until 1994, when Congress passed the Multi-Ethnic Placement Act, that the restrictive policies precluding transracial adoptions were loosened.[71]

In 1998 NAACP officials condemned the *Merriam-Webster Dictionary* for including, among its definitions of the word "nigger," the phrase "a black person." Remarkably, the critics chose not to point out that this was just one of several definitions listed; that its inclusion was consistent with *Webster*'s policy of first defining each entry by its oldest usage; and that the word's offensiveness was clearly noted. The dictionary stated not only that the word was "expressive of racial hatred and bigotry," but that it "now ranks as perhaps the most offensive and inflammatory racial slur in English."[72] Nevertheless, the NAACP's paragons of "sensitivity" saw this issue as a potential launching pad for another great crusade against racism. Thus they demanded that *Merriam-Webster* executives make public their "records on procurement, employment, promotion, and the makeup of their board of directors to determine if a culture within the company has made it difficult for them to recognize why this definition is unacceptable to millions of Americans."[73]

A year later the NAACP was again in hot pursuit of "racists" when president Kweisi Mfume announced that because blacks comprise "a significant constituency that is disproportionately affected

by gun violence," his organization would file a lawsuit against gun manu-
facturers. "Easily available handguns," he thundered, "are being used
to turn many of our communities into war zones."[74] In Mfume's view,
the shooting deaths of black victims ought not be blamed on the remorseless cruelty of their mostly black killers who pull the triggers,
but rather on the long, icy fingers of white racism.

Along with "civil rights" champions like Jesse Jackson and his
Rainbow/PUSH Coalition, the NAACP charges that even laws barring convicted felons from voting in political elections are racist.
Forty-six states and the District of Columbia do not permit felons to
vote while in prison, and fourteen states actually prohibit them from
ever voting again—even after having served their sentences. But because blacks are convicted of felonies at considerably higher rates
than whites, and thus are disproportionately sanctioned, the guardians
of "liberty" ask us to believe that such regulations are merely modern
versions of the poll taxes that once prevented southern blacks from
casting their ballots.[75]

Because our racial demagogues have so effectively depicted
the U.S. as a den of white bigotry, virtually any issue can arouse the
suspicions of an understandably jittery African American community.
For instance, many black residents of Orange, New Jersey contend
that their state's lottery system is rigged against them. "While they
have no proof," reports *The New York Times*, "they constantly complain that most winners of large Pick 6 Lotto jackpots come from
areas that are predominantly white."[76] Notwithstanding this widespread perception, statistics show that the number of big winners
from any particular region is commensurate with the number of tickets sold therein—just as one would expect from a random, unbiased
number-selection process. Nevertheless, there are those who simply
refuse to let such facts alter their presumptions. As one black New
Jerseyite blusters, "They don't put Lotto winners in the black areas
and they can't convince me otherwise."[77]

Those who scout for racism have even been known to "find" it
buried inside desk drawers. In January 1998, James Williams, a former
investigator for the Westchester County District Attorney's Office in
New York, filed a federal lawsuit charging the county with having denied him a promotion because he was black. Though a jury found the
county not guilty of discrimination, Williams was nonetheless awarded
$48,000 for the trauma he purportedly suffered when, in March 1995,

while looking through a recently retired co-worker's desk, he found a folder containing some racially offensive jokes. The court ruled that this folder—even though its owner clearly had stashed it in a private place—made the D.A.'s office a "racially hostile work environment" for black employees.[78]

The Blame Game

The inclination of many "civil rights leaders" to blame whites for virtually all black problems often borders on the absurd. In December 1993, for example, the NAACP denounced journalists in the "white press" for supposedly conspiring to destroy the public image of entertainer Michael Jackson, who at the time was under investigation for having allegedly molested a young boy. "This is not only about Michael Jackson," said NAACP West Coast director Shannon Reeves, "but about how the media uses its power to continue to aid in the oppression and degradation of African Americans in this country." Curiously, Reeves said nothing about the media's enormous marketing campaigns which over the years had made Jackson into a megastar. Nor did he issue comment after Jackson agreed to pay his accuser millions of dollars to drop the molestation charges and keep silent about the matter.[79]

Consider also the case of former NAACP leader Benjamin Chavis, who in 1994 was removed from his position after having stolen at least $64,000 from the organization's coffers.[80] Despite the fact that the NAACP's *black* directors voted by a 53 to 5 margin to depose Chavis, he nevertheless blamed his demise on "forces outside the African American community," prominent among which were "right-wing Jewish groups."[81] "This media frenzy," he explained, "is just another ploy to divide and conquer black leaders."[82] Along the same lines, Ron Davies of the Center for Constitutional Rights lamented that Chavis was being "sacrificed on the altar of white supremacy."[83]

In 1992 boxer Mike Tyson was convicted of raping a beauty-pageant contestant. Though Tyson's victim was black, and he was found guilty by a mostly black jury, writer Ishmael Reed likened the fighter's incarceration to a lynching. "As soon as a black man wins the heavyweight championship [as Tyson had previously done]," wrote Reed, "a movement begins among some whites to dethrone him."[84]

Film director Spike Lee accused the justice system of trying to "demoralize" Tyson simply because "he was making too much money" for a black man.[85]

In August 1994 black Illinois congressman Mel Reynolds was indicted on a number of serious charges—including statutory rape, tampering with a witness, and soliciting child pornography. Predictably, however, Mr. Reynolds ascribed the indictments to a societal atmosphere of white racism. "If I were a white congressman with the same background," he said, "would the same thing have happened? I think not."[86] Similarly, black congressman Walter Tucker of California blamed racism for his own indictment on corruption charges.[87] "Look at the list," he said. "There was Marion Barry before me. There was O.J. Simpson [charged with a 1994 double murder] before me. There was Mike Tyson [convicted of rape] and [Michael] Jackson. You may as well call me Mike Tucker."[88]

Indeed, many prominent blacks have adopted "racism" as a one-size-fits-all reply to their accusers—often with no logical basis. Former U.S. Surgeon General Joycelyn Elders claims that today's abortion opponents are the very same people who once fought against civil rights for blacks. Given the fact that a disproportionately large number of aborted fetuses are nonwhite, Elders's comment makes no sense at all. Why would "racist" anti-abortionists work to save nonwhite lives? Would true racists not strive instead to *increase* access to abortion?[89]

With similar carelessness, the Reverend Joseph Lowery sees racism in proposals to close southern black colleges and merge their student bodies with those of larger white colleges. While common sense tells us that real bigots would *oppose* racially integrated schools, the heralds of white racism—such as Lowery—reflexively trace all events to the bedrock of evil white intentions. Curiously, Lowery neglects to mention that the proposals for black college desegregation, which he portrays as a white-supremacist ideal, actually originated with Justice Department officials wishing to eliminate unconstitutional racial segregation.[90]

"Civil rights" watchdogs found racism even in New York City's 1994 "student-scooper" program, which, in an effort to place otherwise idle children into a structured academic environment, authorized police officers to deliver truant students to designated schools. During the first five weeks of the program, police interrogated about 4,000 school-age youngsters, 89 percent of whom proved to be actual truants, and 11 percent of whom had legitimate reasons for being out of school. Of those 4,000 children, 45 percent were Hispanic, 40 percent were black, 9 percent were white, and 6 percent were Asian. Because these figures included a slight overrepresentation of Hispanics and blacks—who respectively constituted 37 percent and 36 percent of the city's schoolchildren—the champions of "fairness" brayed. "There seems to be a disproportionate number of children of color picked up," complained board of education member Esmerelda Simmons. "We need to be sure their civil liberties are not being curtailed."[91] Presumably it never occurred to Ms. Simmons that the numbers may simply have reflected the reality of the streets.

When the New York State Education Department released a 1999 report indicating that disproportionately high numbers of black students were being placed in special-education classes, many minority parents and child-advocacy groups wondered aloud whether the racial imbalance was due to racism. "I have been raising that question for years," said Willie Collins, president of an Ossining, New York Parent-Teacher-Student Association. "Where are the white kids [in special education]? But I never get answers."[92]

Notably, no one seemed concerned over the degree to which the black community's stratospheric incidence of fatherless homes might affect black children's scholastic performance. The Family Research Council reports that regardless of race, children born out of wedlock are far likelier than those born into two-parent homes to: (a) have severe physical, intellectual, emotional, or behavioral problems; (b) experience abuse or neglect; (c) demonstrate a comparatively weak sense of right and wrong; and (d) achieve relatively low levels of cognitive and verbal development.[93] Moreover, these fatherless youngsters are less likely to live in an environment that values education—as evidenced by the fact that homes headed by unmarried teenage mothers are only half as likely as their two-parent counterparts to contain a good variety of children's books.[94] Given the fact that in recent years some 70 percent of black births have been into fatherless homes, there are clearly some logical reasons—unrelated to racism—why comparatively large numbers of black children might need special education.

A November 1998 tempest flared up after white Brooklyn schoolteacher Ruth Sherman read *Nappy Hair*—a book featuring several whimsical illustrations of a young black girl with unruly locks—to her mostly black class. The author, a black woman, wrote the book for the express purpose of helping black youngsters take pleasure in the "nappy" texture of their own hair. Nevertheless, upon learning that Miss Sherman had read the book to their children, a number of black parents accused her of having insensitively, and perhaps maliciously, made fun of African Americans. When some parents threatened her with violence, the distraught and terrified teacher—who was loved by her students—promptly resigned.[95]

Some charges of racism can be very profitable for those who raise them, as illustrated by a recent incident involving the Denny's restaurant chain and its parent corporation, Flagstar Companies. Late on the night of May 30, 1993, a traveling group of 132 blacks stopped to eat at a Denny's in northern Virginia. Because only one cook was on duty at the time, the restaurant manager informed the group that he would be unable to provide its members with adequate service. Interpreting this as a racial affront, the group filed a complaint with the Human Rights Commission. Shortly thereafter Flagstar, in order to avoid costly litigation and negative publicity, agreed in an out-of-court resolution to make cash payments to each member of the group. In addition, the company pledged to donate money to a number of black organizations, none of which was in any way connected to the plaintiffs. Among the recipients of these payoffs were the United Negro College Fund, the NAACP Legal Defense and Education Fund, the Martin Luther King, Jr. Center for Nonviolent Social Change, the Martin Luther King Celebration Committee, and a group called Strengthening the Black Family, Inc.[96]

Also in 1993, a group of eighteen blacks filed a class-action discrimination suit against a Denny's in San Jose, California. Not long thereafter, six black Maryland plaintiffs filed a similar suit alleging that a Denny's employee had deliberately made them wait for service while he attended to a group of later-arriving white customers. Again Flagstar capitulated out-of-court—settling both suits for a combined $54 million. The twenty-four primary plaintiffs from these two cases, along with about three dozen others who jumped into the lawsuits, were awarded between $15,000 and $35,000 apiece. The remaining money was then divided among all blacks in the country who were willing to charge that they had ever received poor service at a Denny's restaurant. When black publications ran full-page ads publicizing the availability of Flagstar's money, the response was overwhelming. Attorneys for the plaintiffs set up telephone hotlines which for four months took applications from thousands of people hoping to board the gravy train.[97]

Denny's is just one of many companies that have settled discrimination lawsuits outside the courtroom. The enormous monetary transfers in such cases are essentially extortion payments to a "civil rights" establishment which, in exchange for cash, merely agrees not to defile the allegedly offending companies' names with further frivolous charges of discrimination. While the Denny's lawsuits were pending, for instance, NAACP officials initiated behind-the-scenes negotiations with Flagstar. Threatening nationwide boycotts and bad publicity, they arranged a $1 billion "fair share" agreement that required Denny's to: (a) substantially increase its number of minority-owned franchises; (b) purchase at least 12 percent of its supplies from black vendors; (c) institute a preferential-hiring program for African American employees; and (d) "contribute" $68,000 to the NAACP.[98]

Jesse Jackson is another who has mastered the art of squeezing money from corporations fearful of losing favor with the "civil rights" establishment. In January 1998, for example, when he conducted a three-day "diversity conference" that exhorted Wall Street firms to hire more executive-level black employees, a number of brokerage houses gave Jackson substantial sums of money as a show of support for his goals. Notably, however, none of those contributors understood specifically how their donations would be put to use— blindly leaving all spending decisions entirely up to Jackson. As Merrill Lynch spokeswoman Bobbie Collins said, "We're comfortable with Reverend Jackson making a decision on how the money will be used." In all, Jackson's seminar raised more than $500,000. About one-fifth of that total, Jackson explained, would be used to defray the costs of the conference, while the rest would be spent "to increase our research capacity [and] strengthen our staff capability."[99]

"Sticks and Stones May Break My Bones . . ."

In a November 1994 faculty meeting, Rutgers University president Francis Lawrence made a brief reference to disadvantaged black students who, he said, lacked "the genetic, hereditary background" to score well on SAT exams. When his comments were made public by reporters three months later, Mr. Lawrence learned just how little margin for error whites are afforded when speaking about race. Demanding that Lawrence resign as president, more than 150 black Rutgers students staged a sit-down protest at center-court during a February 1995 intercollegiate basketball game in the school gymnasium, forcing the remainder of the contest to be postponed. "Hey, hey, ho, ho! Francis Lawrence has got to go!" chanted the protesters.[100]

In October 1989, Brooklyn high-school teacher Jeff Goldstein sparked a great commotion when he told his social studies class that many black Americans were more inclined to denounce South African apartheid than to condemn the far worse forms of oppression taking place in *black*-controlled African nations. Angered by Goldstein's remark, black students on campus responded with disruptive behavior, threats of violence, and a bomb scare.[101] Even though the teacher had said nothing untrue (as evidenced by the information discussed in chapter 11), he was impugned as an "insensitive" racist.

Three months later the chairman of the New York City Council's education committee, Arthur Katzman, lamented that a host of predominantly black schools were plagued by chronic violence, student underachievement, high dropout rates, and low standardized-test scores. He further observed that many black children demonstrated "no liking of learning," triggering protests by outraged black students and their parents. "We want Mr. Katzman removed because of his statements," said one student. "You insulted my children," an angry parent told Katzman.[102]

When *blacks*, however, make statements similar to Katzman's, there is nary a whisper of protest. Contemplate black anthropologist Signithia Fordham's observation that many black students perform poorly in school for fear of incurring the disapproval of their black peers who construe striving for academic success as an attempt to "act white."[103] "Kids are worried about being cut off by their own community," she elaborates, "and uncertain about being accepted by the other [white] community. . . . They choose to avoid adopting attitudes and putting in enough time and effort in their schoolwork because their peers (and they themselves) would interpret their behavior as 'white.' "[104] According to Ms. Fordham, black youngsters are also reluctant to speak standard English, be punctual, attend the opera or ballet, study in the library, do volunteer work, and visit museums—all to avoid the appearance of "acting white."[105]

Concurring with these remarks, a black assistant principal says, "I have run across blacks who do not want to seem white. [They fear that] if they achieve, they might fall into that category."[106] This observation is illustrated by the recent example of an outstanding black high-school student in Washington, D.C. who, while receiving a special scholarship, stepped to the podium and told the parents and teachers in attendance that his black classmates had nicknamed him "whitey" because of his diligent study habits.[107] Similarly, a nineteen-year-old UC Berkeley student recalls that during high school, "I got a lot of criticism about speaking proper speech. . . . They [other youngsters] would say, 'Why do you talk like you're white?' "[108] A successful black middle-school student in Oakland told *Time* magazine in 1992 that her low-achieving black peers, who generally accused studious blacks of acting like whites, often threatened her with violence.[109] Cedric Jennings, a hardworking District of Columbia high-school student, reported a similar experience to *The Wall Street Journal* in 1994. Most of his classmates, he explained, were poor students and considered him a traitor to his race because he studied a great deal. "The charge of wanting to be white, where I'm from, is like treason," said Jennings. "Doing well [academically] here means you better not show your face."[110] In July 1999 *The New York Times* quoted an eighteen-year-old black student who said, "When you're on the streets, you speak Ebonics. . . . When you're in school, you speak proper English. But when you talk too proper, your peers will call you white and say you're a cracker."[111]

John McWhorter, a black professor of linguistics at UC Berkeley, sees a tendency in his black undergraduates "to simply not try as hard as the white and Asian students."[112] "These [black] students," he adds, "are not stupid or willfully lazy—they are simply victims of a fundamental association of school with an 'other' culture sensed as oppressive." According to McWhorter, the "resistance to standard English"—which in many black communities has taken "a particularly pointed, hostile tenor"—represents "part of a general rejection of whites."[113]

Not even elected officials are immune from charges of "acting white." Washington, D.C. mayor Anthony Williams, an Ivy Leaguer who dons a bow tie, has been ridiculed by many black constituents for not being "black enough."[114] As black history professor Roger Wilkins puts it, "Williams is not a fellow who looks like he's spent a lot of time hanging out with a bunch of black guys. There's not the lingo. There's not the body language. He calls himself a nerd, and nerdishness is not a part of the black culture."[115]

Such comments, whether uttered by students or educators, are considered sociological contributions if spoken by blacks, but merely negative "stereotypes" if voiced by whites. This begs an important question: If many blacks themselves view studying and learning as "white" behaviors—and if they intentionally avoid such activities so as to "act black"—why should it be deemed racist for a white teacher like Arthur Katzman to perceive "no liking of learning" among black students?

Whites must indeed choose their words carefully when speaking about racial matters—a lesson that William Newill, editor of Willingboro, New Jersey's *Burlington County Times* (*BCT*), learned the hard way. In September 1993 Newill's publication printed an article about Priscilla Anderson, a local black assemblywoman and public high-school guidance counselor. The piece reported that Ms. Anderson—in an effort to devote more time to her legislative duties—had missed an astonishing fifty-nine working days from her counseling job in one school year. Several days after the article appeared, a *BCT* editorial criticized Anderson for "double-dipping at the taxpayers' expense."[116]

Many of Willingboro's black residents and civic leaders attributed the newspaper's negative portrayal of Ms. Anderson to racism. "They wouldn't print it if it was against a white man," said the Reverend Morris Baxter,[117] asserting that the newspaper's primary intent was "to scandalize the reputation of the only black woman in the Legislature."[118] Responding to these accusations, Editor Newill said, "The issue was never race or gender. It was accountability of a public official, and public officials are not exempted from accountability because of race or gender."[119] Newill explained that newspapers could not serve the public interest if editors were forced to suppress unfavorable revelations about black public officials simply to avoid being branded as "biased" or "racist."[120] Sandra Hardy, an executive in the *Burlington County Times'* parent company, rebuked Newill and demanded that he apologize to black groups "for any misunderstandings." Unwilling to bow to such pressure, Newill resigned.[121]

Even a purely innocent word can spark charges of racism if misunderstood by the supersensitive. In a January 1999 budget meeting, David Howard, a white aide to Washington mayor Anthony Williams, told two colleagues—Marshall Brown and John Fanning—that there would be a paucity of money available for the city's constituent services office. "I will have to be niggardly with this fund," said Howard, "because it's not going to be a lot of money."[122] At that point Fanning, a black man, angrily stormed out of the room—having mistaken the word "niggardly," which means stingy or miserly, for a racial slur.[123] Within a few days, a disconsolate Mr. Howard, whose apology to Fanning was rejected, resigned his post. While NAACP chairman Julian Bond opposed the resignation on grounds that no one should "have to censor [their] language to meet other people's lack of understanding,"[124] a number of prominent blacks deemed Howard's transgression rather serious. Alluding to eighteenth-century Scandinavian roots of the word "niggardly," former National Bar Association president Keith Watters asked suspiciously, "Do we really know where the Norwegians got that word?"[125] Jesse Jackson, who once used the anti-Jewish slur "Hymietown" when referring to New York City, asserted that the use of "niggardly" ought to be avoided in everyday speech because of its potential to offend. "You've got to be pretty heavy to get into the Scandinavian roots of a word from two centuries ago," he said.[126]

The David Howard controversy was not the first involving the word "niggardly." In 1998 a *Dallas Morning News* food reviewer caused a stir by reporting that a certain restaurant's food was bland because of the chef's "niggardly hand with seasonings." When it was later learned that the chef was black, the paper printed an immediate clarification.[127]

Clearly, the guardians of "honor" can find racism virtually anywhere. In February 1999, black community leaders were dismayed by what they termed a racially offensive drawing that adorned a take-home flyer from a Mount Vernon, New York elementary school. This yellow leaflet, which contained information about upcoming school events, featured a clip-art likeness of six children—five white and one black. Unfortunately, in the process of reprinting the clip art onto yellow paper, the black child's features, which were clear in the original illustration, had been unintentionally obscured. Thus, unlike the smiling white faces, the lone black face was completely darkened and had no discernible features other than a tongue sticking out of its mouth. When school officials nonetheless chose—without a trace of malice, but simply for the sake of convenience—to use those flyers rather than print up a whole new set, the president of the NAACP's New Rochelle chapter was outraged. "This is nothing unusual for institutional racism," he said. "It didn't surprise me or shock me at all." Schools Superintendent Linda Kelly quickly sent a letter of apology to all parents who had received the flyer.[128]

Apart from the darkened features, another point of contention was that only the black child was sticking his tongue out. Presumably we are to believe that this fact betrays not only the artist's subliminal racism, but also the bigotry of those employees whose "insensitivity" had blinded them to the drawing's potential to offend. Perhaps we are to conclude that in the future, only *white* children should be shown doing anything amusing or mischievous, lest the champions of "honor" again feel the pea of suspected prejudice through a thousand mattresses.

While seizing any opportunity to spotlight even the faintest hint of *white* racism, most "civil rights leaders" are conspicuously silent in the face of even the most blatant *black* racism. In the 1980s, for example, such activists uniformly denounced all American politicians, corporations, and universities with any ties to South Africa. Yet they said nothing when, within the past five years, both the NAACP and Congressional Black Caucus (CBC) made "sacred covenants" with Louis Farrakhan's Nation of Islam (NOI)—an organization notorious for its vulgar antiwhite rhetoric. Why, we must ask, did the black community herald those alliances with silence rather than criticism? Moreover, what do those alliances tell us about the racial attitudes of the NAACP and the CBC? One writer marvels at Americans' placid acceptance of the CBC's covenant with Farrakhan:

> Imagine two dozen white congressmen calling a press conference to announce their alliance with the Aryan Nation. The outrage would be tremendous. No one who is anyone would miss the opportunity to call their own news conference and call for the resignation of every congressman involved. Heads would roll and [Attorney General] Janet Reno would find a way to launch a federal investigation. The President would speak to the nation from the Oval Office, and Peter Jennings, Dan Rather, and Tom Brokaw would all do special reports on how such a catastrophe could have possibly happened

in such a progressive country. The House Ethics Committee would call for immediate hearings out of which a "law" would be passed. We would hear nothing else for months.[129]

Some black "leaders" find remarkably creative ways to justify the mainstream "civil rights" cartel's embrace of people like Farrakhan and his colleague Khalid Abdul Muhammad, whose principal doctrines are discussed in chapter 2. Harlem Democratic senator David Paterson—contending that blacks and Jews ascribe differing degrees of importance to spoken words—deems NOI rhetoric not only harmless, but at worst, "puerile."[130] Jews, he asserts, are simply more sensitive than blacks to verbal criticism and, consequently, are needlessly offended by statements made with innocuous intent:

> It does not take a scholar of rhetoric to understand that black conversations and meetings sometimes include rhetorical comments . . . that many white Americans find offensive. . . . [Jews are especially sensitive to] harsh language [because their historical experience indicates that] language can set horrible events in motion. [Blacks] may fail to appreciate this [sensitivity] because our historical experience has been so different. Black bondage was physical before it was verbal. We did not speak the language of the slave traders.[131]

The claim that blacks attach comparatively little importance to language is, of course, preposterous. Recall, for instance, Jesse Jackson's vexation when a public official referred to LIRR gunman Colin Ferguson as an "animal" (see chapter 4). And remember the outrage ignited by the words of Al Campanis, Jimmy "The Greek" Snyder, Dale Lick, Jeff Goldstein, Arthur Katzman, William Newill, and Francis Lawrence—to name just a few. As the late columnist Eric Breindel wrote, "The notion that blacks don't take language all that seriously invites an obvious query: If black rhetoric isn't to be taken at face value when it involves expressions of hostility toward Jews—and whites, in general—why should it be taken more seriously when it turns on allegations of [white] racism?"[132]

Mr. Paterson's assertions about black attitudes toward language seemed especially absurd in October 1994, when Jesse Jackson and Al Sharpton held a press conference in New York City to denounce talk-radio host Bob Grant for being a "racist." Said Jackson about Grant's occasionally harsh rhetoric, "It may be free speech, but it's wrong speech, . . . foul speech that's calculated to hurt, demean, and divide."[133] "We do not believe there should be a double standard to hate speech," added the Reverend Reginald Jackson.[134] To buttress their contention that Grant was a loathsome character, the ministers cited a series of instances where the broadcaster had been critical of black people. Curiously, however, these paragons of "sensitivity" neglected to mention that every quote they cited had been directed not at blacks as a whole, but at *specific* black individuals— usually criminals or politicians—whose behaviors or ideas Grant had found worthy of reproach. Neither did they mention that Grant had regularly denounced, in just as acerbic a manner, many more *white* individuals than black—his most frequent targets in recent years being Bill Clinton, Al Gore, Janet Reno, and Mario Cuomo—to name just a few. Nor did they bother to acknowledge that Grant had, for many years, consistently *lauded* many blacks whom he held in high esteem. In short, Grant neither praised nor condemned any racial group as a whole, but rather judged people on their *individual* merits—the very *antithesis* of racism.

It is also worth noting that while Grant's detractors were busy condemning hate, none of them saw fit to criticize the talk-radio personalities of WLIB, a black New York station notorious for airing antiwhite rhetoric and frequently used as a public forum by Al Sharpton and Jesse Jackson.[135] Nor did the critics say a word about another New York station, WRKS-FM, whose weekly Sunday-morning talk show features callers and guests alike attributing virtually every problem facing black America to the white man's allegedly intrinsic evil. During a 1998 guest appearance by Khalid Abdul Muhammad—the same Mr. Muhammad whose public speeches are consistently filled with vulgar diatribes against whites and Jews—a cavalcade of callers praised him for his courage and honesty.[136]

In the final analysis, the significant issue is not whether one believes that Bob Grant or any other radio personality is a racist, but whether our society will continue to tolerate the transparent double standard by which "civil rights leaders" select the targets they condemn. Sharpton in particular exposed his own hypocrisy when, on July 29, 1994, he appeared at Brooklyn's Friendship Baptist Church to take part in a ceremony honoring Khalid Abdul Muhammad.[137]

Could anyone professing to admire the likes of Mr. Muhammad have anything credible to say about the evils of racism?

The Media's "Racism"

The very same defenders of "honor" who so adroitly find and condemn white bigotry are remarkably blind to *anti*white bigotry. For instance, they took no notice of a potentially offensive advertisement in the November 1994 issue of the computer magazine *PC World*. Designed to promote a product that removes "trash" (i.e., the unwanted remnants of old programs) from computers, the ad featured a photograph of three white men and a white woman, along with their dog, seated in front of a trailer home. The woman was scantily clad and posed suggestively, while the men were garbed in various combinations of overalls, tank tops, and army fatigues. Adorned with tattoos and headbands, they were "white trash" personified.[138] Apparently, the watchdogs of "propriety"—ever alert for examples of racial disrespect by the media—saw nothing disagreeable about the ad.

Nor was there any outcry in March 1996 when the television sitcom *Boston Commons* aired an episode wherein a black character's reference to whites as "crackers" was followed by audience laughter.[139] If a white character, however, had flippantly made a derogatory slang reference to blacks, "civil rights leaders" across the country would have surely and swiftly denounced such "callousness."

Consider also what occurred just prior to the 1988 U.S. presidential election, when a George Bush campaign advertisement made it known that Massachusetts, where Democratic candidate Michael Dukakis was governor, had implemented a furlough program allowing weekend releases for incarcerated violent felons. The ad further revealed—*with no mention of race*—that a convicted murderer named Willie Horton, while out on furlough from a Massachusetts prison, had raped and tortured a woman in Maryland. Republicans used this story to support their contention that Dukakis, because he favored the furlough program, was too soft on crime.[140]

Before long, however, political action groups and journalists revealed that Horton was black and his rape victim was white, prompting the disciples of "fairness" to accuse Republicans of exploiting white America's fear of black criminals. Jesse Jackson and vice presidential candidate Lloyd Bentsen were among numerous Democrats to denounce the Horton ad as racist. Jackson called it "the kind of race-conscious political behavior that is rotting our society."[141] Along the same lines, Dukakis campaign manager Susan Estrich, a professor at Harvard Law School, explained that the Bush campaign's use of the Horton story was a transparent appeal to white racism.[142] It is unclear whether these critics would have objected to an ad featuring a *white* rapist and a *black* victim. Of course, given the virtual nonexistence of white-on-black rape in this country (see chapter 7 for statistics), it is unlikely that such a scenario ever even occurred under the Massachusetts furlough program. Moreover, we must wonder why it should be regarded as racist for an ad to focus on a case involving a black criminal and a white victim—a relatively common occurrence—especially if that ad never mentions the race of either party. Curiously, while critics were quick to condemn the Horton ad, no one asked whether Horton's rape itself may have been racially motivated.[143] For the "civil rights" cabal and the media, the raging river of racism flows only in one direction.

Frivolous charges of white racism have created entirely new myths that the American public largely believes to be true. For instance, black "leaders" have long grumbled about the supposedly negative stereotypes of blacks portrayed in television programs and motion pictures. In an NAACP report on media bias, author Serita Coffee states, "I would never say that all movies are racist. However, I have yet to find one that isn't."[144] One white writer concurs that the movie industry is rife with "incredibly deft" racism.[145]

These allegations, however, are convincingly refuted by hard evidence. Over and over, movie makers nowadays go to great lengths to portray blacks positively—even if this means casting black actors in roles originally intended for whites. For example, the heroic white sonar operator in Tom Clancy's novel *Hunt for Red October* is, in the movie version of the story, played by a black. Similarly, when Tom Wolfe's *Bonfire of the Vanities* was made into a screenplay, the role of a major, sympathetic white character was changed to that of a black—even though Wolfe had deliberately tried to portray his characters as racially realistic.[146]

The motion picture *Glory*, promoted as a historically accurate account of a black regiment fighting for the Union Army during the Civil War, depicts the black soldiers as escaped slaves who courageously go into battle against their former masters. But in reality, most of those soldiers were recruited in the North and had always been free. The movie also shows the regiment's members agitating for their civil rights, though in real life it was their white commander who insisted that they be paid as much as white Union soldiers. Several other elements of the film that demean whites and glorify blacks are nothing more than made-for-Hollywood fiction: a racist quartermaster refuses to provide the black soldiers with shoes, a black soldier is brutally flogged, and another black soldier quotes Emerson.[147]

In the 1995 movie *Copycat*, a white psychiatrist, played by actress Sigourney Weaver, addresses a large audience on the topic of serial killers. At one point during her speech, she asks all the males in attendance to rise. Once they are on their feet, she instructs those men of Asian and African descent to sit down again, leaving only white men standing. Then, directing those who are seated to look closely at the standing whites, the psychiatrist says, "Let me tell you something. Nine out of ten serial killers are white males aged twenty to thirty-five." Notably, this scene sparked absolutely no controversy in the media. Yet one can well imagine the venom with which the "civil rights" brigade would have attacked any similarly staged scene discussing the astonishing frequency with which young black males perpetrate most types of violent crimes, both *inter*racially and *intra*racially (see chapter 4 for statistics).

In the popular 1996 movie *A Time to Kill*, a young black southern girl is brutally raped by two white men. While contemplating what action he ought to take, the girl's distraught father laments another recent case in which four local whites who had gang-raped a black girl were acquitted in court. After much soul-searching, the father—secure in the belief that no southern white jury will convict his daughter's attackers—kills them himself. Notably, all the rapists in this movie are white and all their victims black (even though, as discussed in chapter 7, white-on-black rape is exceedingly rare in the United States). While Klansmen and their burning crosses play a prominent role throughout the film, there is no hint of black racism in the story. At one point, the young rape victim's father candidly tells his white attorney that white people have always been "the bad guys," a contention which the lawyer accepts with resignation. When the father is eventually tried for the murder of his daughter's attackers, the white jurors are fully prepared to render guilty verdicts—until, at the last moment, the defense attorney encourages them to imagine how they would view the same case if the defendant and his daughter were white.

The same type of racial manipulation is seen in television's supposedly reality-based docudramas, many of which deliberately exaggerate white characters' cruelty and black characters' virtue. One such film dealt with a 1984 case involving a vindictive white man who hired two blacks to slash and badly disfigure the face of Marla Hanson, an aspiring white model from New York. In the real-life trial, black defense attorney Alton Maddox subjected Miss Hanson to a brutal cross-examination, portraying her as a racist slut who was accusing his clients [the actual slashers] of the crime only because they were black. In the docudrama version, however, not only is the abusive defense attorney white, but a sympathetic white prosecutor who helped Miss Hanson endure her real-life ordeal is depicted as black. As Jared Taylor observes, "The changes are consistent: An unattractive character is changed to a white, and attractive characters become black."[148]

The Howard Beach killing (discussed in chapter 3) also inspired a docudrama that similarly distorts the facts of the case to discredit its white characters. In the film's depiction of the initial confrontation, the blacks do not flash a knife, spit at the whites, or shout racial slurs as they did in the real-life event. Instead, the whites attack them without provocation and shout, "Get out of the neighborhood, niggers!" And whereas one of the black victims in the actual altercation received a cut that took five stitches to close, in the TV version his injuries require sixty-seven stitches. The movie also portrays Howard Beach as a neighborhood that blacks can scarcely enter without great personal risk. In truth, however, a bowling alley *across the street* from the attack site has a black league that meets regularly.[149]

Few people realize just how grossly television programs exaggerate white criminality and minimize black criminality. Though blacks constitute some 12 to 13 percent of all the characters in TV dramas, virtually matching their representation in the American population, they commit only 10 percent of the violent crimes in such programs—a far cry from the real-life figure of 42 percent.[150] Perhaps most distorted is the TV world's depiction of murder. Of all homicides that occur in television dramas, black characters commit scarcely 3 percent, meaning that African Americans are about 18 times *less* likely to kill on television than in real life.[151] On the other hand, whites, who commit fewer than half of real-world murders, account for about 90 percent of the killings on the small screen.[152] As ABC's vice president for motion pictures and television explained in 1986, "Almost every villain you see [on TV] is a WASP. . . . In their desire to avoid stereotyping, I think broadcast standards and practices sometimes go to an absurd extreme."[153]

Amazingly, none of this information stops the incessant allegations that racism pervades the television industry. Jesse Jackson, for one, complains that TV programming stirs up "antiblack fervor" by depicting blacks as "less hardworking" and "more violent" than they really are.[154] Black novelist Ishmael Reed accuses television of portraying blacks "the way the Nazi press of pre-Holocaust Germany covered the Jews."[155] According to entertainer Bill Cosby, TV script writers who create black characters do little more than "drive by a black housing project and take a quick look. They see the pimp, the dealer, the strutting street kid. What they never see, because they never look for it, is the hardworking mother and father upstairs who are trying to move up and out."[156]

There are some critics, of course, who will be dissatisfied no matter how African Americans are portrayed. A black professor at Cornell University, for instance, actually finds fault with television series that show blacks in positive roles. Programs depicting blacks as successfully middle class, he explains, send the dangerous message that racism might not be such a scourge on the black race after all.[157]

Apart from the matter of whether black TV characters are admirable people, some "civil rights leaders" claim that African American actors are numerically underrepresented in weekly comedy and drama series. In July 1999, NAACP president Kweisi Mfume angrily threatened to boycott the major networks because "none of the twenty-six new shows for the [upcoming] fall season have a minority in a lead or starring role." Yet Mfume's allegation was utterly untrue. Contrary to his claim, one of the four main characters on ABC's forthcoming series *Snoops* was a black woman. On NBC's ensemble drama *Third Watch*, a black policeman and black doctor were major characters. On the Fox network's *Ryan Caulfield*, the title character's fellow rookie cop was a Hispanic woman, the desk sergeant a black woman, and the precinct captain a black man. And the CBS hospital drama *City of Angels*, scheduled to begin airing in January 2000, will feature an almost entirely black and Hispanic cast.[158]

Blacks were also well represented in the casts of programs returning from the previous year. The popular NBC police drama *Law and Order*, for instance, added a black main character to its troupe for 1999. On ABC, *The Hughleys* centered entirely around a black family living in a white suburb, *The Practice* featured several major black characters, and numerous other programs included secondary but regular black roles. CBS, meanwhile, had nine shows with black or other ethnic minority characters in lead roles.[159]

False Conclusions

In May 1998 Al Sharpton accused ten large American corporations of withholding advertising dollars from radio stations geared to black listeners. His charge was based on the contents of an internal document from Katz Radio Group, a company that helps local radio stations attract national and regional advertising. The document recommended that Katz sales representatives, when trying to promote clients with largely white audiences, remind prospective advertisers that white listeners as a whole are more affluent than their minority counterparts—and are thus likelier to spend money on the advertised products. Threatening to boycott the allegedly offending companies, Sharpton lamented that their purported preference to advertise on "white" rather than "ethnic" stations "minimizes the humanity of the people in our [black] community." He further vowed to pressure officials to withhold public funding from those companies.[160]

Eight months later the Civil Rights Forum, an advocacy group based in Washington, D.C., released a report showing that indeed advertisers often bypassed or paid less money to stations with mostly black audiences. "Those stations that serve minority communities are not getting their fair share of advertising dollars," said Federal Communications Commission chairman Bill Kennard.[161] "Our ability to serve our communities," added Pierre Sutton of the National Association of Black-Owned Broadcasters, "is severely hampered by advertisers who refuse to advertise on our stations."[162] Black columnist Dewayne Wickham asserted that the very existence of black-owned radio stations was being "threatened by a widespread practice of discrimination among advertisers who dwell in the bigotry underground."[163]

Presumably it never occurred to these critics that economics, and not racism, explained the alleged inequity. Because radio ads can be expensive, advertisers care first and foremost about getting good returns on their investments—regardless of whether blacks or whites own the stations airing the ads. It is logical for advertisers to evaluate audience demographics when selecting where to air their messages. All station owners understand this, as evidenced by the fact that they customarily furnish prospective advertisers with media kits detailing a host of audience characteristics—among which are income, age, education, gender, spending habits, and recreational activities. Since black Americans overall, and thus black listeners, have lower average incomes than whites, stations geared to black audiences may be less attractive to many advertisers. In addition, the median age of black Americans is twenty-eight, which is seven to twelve years younger than the median for most white ethnic groups.[164] Consequently, black listening audiences contain a significantly smaller proportion of twenty-five- to fifty-four-year-olds—the age bracket that advertisers most covet. Notwithstanding these compelling facts, however, the Clinton administration threatened federal scrutiny of any advertisers suspected of not reserving a "fair share" of their business for minority broadcasters.[165]

In 1994, New York mayor Rudolph Giuliani decided to eliminate some 15,000 public-sector city jobs—deeming it economically imperative to decrease the number of nonessential employees on the city payroll. The Department of Social Services was hit particularly hard by these cuts—losing some 3,600 workers, 64 percent of whom were black. Meanwhile, police and firefighters—among whom whites were represented in much higher proportions—were exempted from the budget ax.[166] Predictably, minority "leaders" charged that the mayor's budget was racist. In response, Giuliani budget director Abe Lackman testified that the mayor had not assessed how the planned cuts would affect minorities. There was no reason to have done so, he explained, since the goal was simply to eliminate waste and unnecessary bureaucracy, not to count bodies of various skin tones. "In all my discussions with my staff and with the agencies and with the mayor," said Lackman, "the question or the issue of the racial composition of the work force never came up a single time."[167] Another Giuliani spokesman added, "It seems to me if you emphasize police over something else, you're emphasizing public safety, not the color of cops."[168] But such rational explanations meant nothing to the mayor's critics.

New York governor George Pataki came under similar fire in February 1999, when Jesse Jackson condemned him for "spending more money on jails rather than schools."[169] But instead of characterizing his disagreement with Pataki as one of policy or philosophy, Jackson portrayed the governor as a racist. Likening Pataki to the former segregationist governors George Wallace and Orval Faubus, Jackson said, "America deserves leadership of hope and healing. And whether you're blocking school doors in Alabama or Arkansas, or simply locking kids out of closed school doors in New York, that is not the wave of the American future."[170]

"Civil rights" advocates often allege that white merchants in black ghettos are racists because they supposedly "overcharge" their customers, most of whom are poor. These crusaders contend that if a storekeeper in a blighted inner city charges patrons $1.05 for a soft drink that national chains sell elsewhere for 89 cents, his motivation is to exploit his black clientele. But such accusations are nothing more than moral posturing, as Thomas Sowell explains:

> The tragic fact is that it costs more money to do business in neighborhoods with high crime and vandalism, regardless of the color of the people in such neighborhoods. . . . You can bring in all the shrinks you want and hold all the sensitivity sessions you want — and it will still cost more to sell that can of soda in a store with higher rates of shoplifting, vandalism and such that add to the cost of doing business.[171]

Studies claiming to have discovered evidence of white racism usually receive bold newspaper headlines—as in April 1994 when *The New York Times* printed an article under the caption, "Poor and Black Patients Slighted, Study Says."[172] "Seriously ill Medicare patients who are black and poor," began the piece, "receive worse care than other equally sick Medicare patients in every type of hospital in America, a new study has found." Deep in the article, however, it was revealed not only that the overall long-term survival rates for black and white patients were exactly the same, but also that the short-term survival rate of black heart-attack patients was 18 percent *higher* than that of their white counterparts.[173] How can such information be reconciled with a dramatic headline suggesting that America's medical care system treats whites better than blacks?

A 1990 study by the National Center for Health Statistics

(NCHS) showed not only that black pregnant women in the United States received less prenatal care than their white counterparts, but also that black infant mortality rates were higher than those of whites. When these findings were first announced, the media were quickly flooded with charges that thousands of black infants—whose mothers presumably had no access to proper prenatal care—were dying because America was "neglecting" its minorities.[174] As author John Edgar Wideman asked rhetorically, "Do black newborns die at three times the rate of white babies because of some factor intrinsic to blackness, or because being black means they're treated by society as only one-third as valuable as white newborns?"[175]

Curiously, none of the critics seemed to notice that according to the very same NCHS study, Mexican Americans received even less prenatal care than blacks but had infant mortality rates equal to those of whites. Nor did anyone note that Americans of Philippine, Chinese, and Japanese ancestry received less prenatal care than whites and yet had substantially *lower* infant mortality rates than whites.[176] In other words, infant mortality rates had no consistent correlation with amounts of prenatal care, which in turn were largely dependent on expectant mothers' attitudes about such care. Some health-conscious pregnant women, for example, visit doctors infrequently and nevertheless experience few medical complications, either during pregnancy or afterward. Meanwhile, others drink, smoke, and abuse drugs during pregnancy—consequently delivering a disproportionate number of low-birth-weight or drug-addicted babies, often into father-absent circumstances. These heedless women also tend to receive little prenatal care—not because it is inaccessible to them, but because they are relatively indifferent to the health of their developing fetuses. Sadly, such destructive behaviors are especially common among young, unmarried black women, who are twice as likely as their Asian and Hispanic counterparts to give birth to drug-addicted babies.[177] Comparing only blacks with other blacks, those mothers who choose not to get prenatal care are twice as likely to smoke, and six times as likely to drink, as those who do. "The prenatal care is not what makes the difference [in the health of newborns]," explains Thomas Sowell. "It is just a symptom of a set of attitudes."[178]

The Family Research Council (FRC) reports that regardless of race, "teenage single-parent mothering is the single greatest contributor to low-birth-weight babies."[179] "Studies show," adds the FRC, "that the high rate of out-of-wedlock births to young mothers is the primary explanation for America's low international standing on measures of infant mortality."[180] These findings are particularly relevant to contemporary black newborns, 70 percent of whom begin their lives without fathers.[181] While the problems that afflict these unfortunate infants are tragic, they must be ascribed to parental irresponsibility, not racism.

In August 1994 another prominent, front-page headline in *The New York Times* announced, "Suburban Taxes Are Higher for Blacks, Analysis Shows." The accompanying article reported that in eighteen of thirty-one suburban areas whose tax rates had been analyzed, black homeowners paid slightly higher property taxes than whites paid on comparable homes. Queens College professor Andrew Beveridge, who conducted the research, said of his findings, "It means that if one of the routes in the U.S.A. to middle-class status has been to move to the suburbs and live a comfortable suburban lifestyle, trying to achieve that is going to cost more for blacks."[182] "We are talking about fundamental bread and butter racial issues," added Billy J. Tidwell, the National Urban League's director of research. "It appears we have a long way to go, perhaps longer than we had recognized."[183] In a similar vein, a black homeowner lamented, "In many, many situations in this country, racism is alive and well."[184] Indeed, the property tax gap seemed like a glaring example of discrimination in its truest form.

A careful analysis of the research, however, reveals a major limitation in its methodology. While the objective was to compare the tax assessments on properties of comparable worth, the study relied entirely on homeowners' assessments of their own houses' values, rather than on empirical data from actual home sales.[185] The validity of the results, then, was contingent upon the ability of homeowners to estimate the market values of their real estate. Yet even if we make the very large assumption that the homeowner appraisals were accurate, the apparent injustice uncovered by Professor Beveridge is easily explained by the interplay of two factors having nothing whatsoever to do with racism.

First is the fact that many municipalities nationwide raise property tax assessments on houses only when they are sold—a color-blind process that rewards long-term residents with smaller tax hikes than newcomers, regardless of their race.[186] A second consideration is the massive recent migration of black Americans to the suburbs. During the 1980s the proportion of all blacks living in suburban areas rose from one-fourth to one-third[187]—a growth rate nearly four times faster than that of whites.[188] Between 1970 and 1995, black suburbanites tripled in number, from 3.6 million to 10.6 million.[189] Thus, *if* blacks as a group now bear a slightly disproportionate property tax burden, it is only because so many of them have recently bought suburban homes—a fact that actually reflects increasing black prosperity. But the "civil rights" vision, seeing bias everywhere, perverts even statistics that give evidence of black progress into barometers of alleged discrimination.

It is worth noting that the recent black migration to suburbia has created a substantial decline in racially segregated residential patterns. Between 1970 and 1980 the level of racial segregation dropped in 208 of the 232 metropolitan areas recognized by the Census Bureau, and over the following decade dropped again in 195 metropolitan areas.[190] During the 1980s the proportion of blacks living in neighborhoods that were at least 90 percent black shrank from 52 percent to 44 percent, a substantial drop in a mere ten years.[191] As of 1994, fully 83 percent of blacks reported having at least *some* white neighbors, considerably more than the 70 percent figure of 1976, or the 66 percent figure of 1964.[192] While some observers may wish that residential segregation would decline still more rapidly, it has inarguably diminished over the past quarter-century.[193] In fact, this increased racial mixing is significantly more impressive than the numbers may at first glance suggest, given that roughly 80 percent of blacks polled report a preference for living in neighborhoods that are between one-half and three-fourths black. In addition, about one-fourth of those same respondents profess a preference for *all*-black neighborhoods.[194] Obviously, such attitudes limit the degree to which racial mixing can occur.[195] Whites too report a preference for living in neighborhoods that are at least 80 percent white,[196] but their concerns seem more related to class than to race. As scholars Stephan and Abigail Thernstrom explain, "white objections to living near at least moderate numbers of blacks of similar social status have declined to the vanishing point."[197]

In March 1999 another allegation of discriminatory property taxes made big news. "Property Taxes in Nassau Called Biased," read the *New York Times* headline.[198] At issue was a Justice Department charge that black and Hispanic homeowners in New York's Nassau

County were paying higher property taxes than whites on homes of similar value. "This is a scandal," a local black resident complained.[199] Zachary Carter, the U.S. attorney for the Eastern District of New York, warned that he would sue the county unless the tax structure was immediately changed.[200]

A review of the data showed that overall, Nassau minorities did in fact pay disproportionately higher taxes than whites in the same county. Yet this was not due to racism, but to a race-*neutral* procedure by which property values were assessed—a procedure that only *coincidentally* had a disparate impact on blacks and Hispanics. At the time of the controversy, Nassau homes were still being assessed based on 1938 construction costs, while the land they were built on was assessed according to 1964 property values. But home and property values had risen more quickly in wealthier, predominantly white areas than in poorer, mostly minority areas. Thus houses costing the same when they were built decades ago were still being assessed at equal rates in 1999, even though the white homes had appreciated considerably more by that time. Though this formula applied equally to all homeowners regardless of race, the chorus of "civil rights" champions echoed their familiar mantra. Among them was Leon Friedman of the New York Civil Liberties Union, who pronounced the county's tax system "unfair and discriminatory."[201]

The news media will go to extraordinary lengths to "prove" the prevalence of white racism. In July 1994, New York's nightly NBC television news aired a story titled "Rides or Racism?"—which focused on the alleged difficulty that blacks in New York City encounter when attempting to hail taxi cabs. To dramatize the point, NBC set up a scenario in which a black man stood alongside a busy city street and tried to flag down approaching cabs, while several yards beyond him was a white man hailing the same cabs. The TV audience was then treated to film footage of several instances in which cabbies drove past the black man and picked up the white. "It's kind of sad," lamented anchorwoman Sue Simmons.[202]

Unfortunately, television viewers were never told what percentage of the cabbies under surveillance actually bypassed the black man, or even what color those cabbies were. In fact, the reporters failed to mention that not only are white cab drivers in New York City relatively few in number, but that fully one-half of the city's cabbies are *black*. While it was therefore quite possible that some, or even all, of the cabbies who drove past the black man were black themselves, NBC reported the story as if it were axiomatic that each of the offending drivers was white. Moreover, no one at NBC deemed it relevant to mention that in similar past studies, black cabbies had been just as likely as their white counterparts to "discriminate" against black fares. For example, when Howard University researchers found in 1990 that blacks were more likely than similarly attired whites to be bypassed by taxis, *not even one* of the "prejudiced" drivers was white; all were either native-born blacks, African immigrants, or Middle Easterners.[203]

Is it not possible that a cabbie of any color, knowing the widespread nature of violent black crime, might bypass a black fare not because of racism but because of justifiable fear? Is it altogether unreasonable for taxi drivers to "stereotype" blacks as being more dangerous than whites? Might an instinct for self-preservation, rather than raw bigotry, have been responsible for the scenes that NBC filmed? Such analysis proved too deep for NBC's taste. The station preferred instead to offer its viewers a neatly wrapped package tied with a white racist bow.

Sadly, it can be argued that New York cabbies *are* justified in their fear of black riders, for blacks commit a shockingly disproportionate share of the city's robberies and violent crimes. Though they constitute only 25 percent of the city's population, blacks are charged with 56 percent of its murders, 62 percent of its robberies, and 55 percent of its assaults.[204] Even more to the point, black men aged sixteen to forty commit 85 percent of all felonies against New York cab drivers.[205] Coupled with these statistics is the fact that driving a cab is, according to the U.S. Labor Department, the most dangerous occupation in America. Cab drivers are murdered on the job at a higher rate than bartenders, gas station attendants, convenience store cashiers, and policemen.[206]

In December 1994 former New York City mayor David Dinkins made big news when he revealed that he too had been bypassed by a Manhattan cab driver. Calling it "a sad and unfortunate circumstance" that "has been going on for a long time," Mr. Dinkins expressed his hope that "one day, people will be judged by the content of their character and not the color of their skin. But, too often now, racism rears its ugly head."[207] While the ex-mayor's stated ideals are commendable, it is difficult to imagine how a cab driver might be able to judge the character of someone standing at least several yards from him on a street corner. Being "non-judgmental" could cost a cabbie his life.

Cab drivers clearly discriminate when they judge prospective black passengers as being more dangerous than white fares. Yet such discrimination—however unfortunate—is not necessarily sinister. Indeed everyone discriminates, all the time, everywhere. Imagine, for instance, that a lone woman is walking along a city street toward a train station. When choosing which route she will take, she must prudently discriminate between areas that appear safe and those that do not—considering such factors as whether a road is dark or well lit, deserted or peopled, clean or filthy. Like such pedestrians, cab drivers are more concerned with protecting their own safety than with rejecting racial stereotypes. Thus their hesitancy to pick up black fares is in most cases due to fear, not racism. As one Asian cabbie in New York explains, "Often you risk your life with young black men."[208] *Black* cabbies, it should be noted, feel the very same fear. "I don't want to get robbed," reasons one black driver. "Do you know what the black crime rate is in New York? Do you want me to risk a gun to my head? What's wrong with you?"[209] Similarly, a black cabbie in Washington, D.C. says, "I won't pick up three black men at one time. If I pick up two, I sit one up front. There are some places I simply won't go. Listen, I've had a gun pointed to the back of my head. I have to look after myself, because no one else will."[210] Another black driver candidly tells the *Washington Post* that he does not pick up young black males at all because "I'd rather be fined [for discrimination] than have my wife a widow."[211] Certainly these cabbies generally view black men as potential criminals—which is unfortunate, since most blacks are law-abiding people. But such stereotyping will not be overcome by pious platitudes about racial justice. It will only diminish or end when the violent crime rate of inner-city blacks decreases. The real problem, then, is black crime and the stereotypes that *it* engenders.

As the comments of the black cabbies in the preceding paragraph attest, fear of black crime is not an exclusively white phenomenon. Law-abiding *black* citizens—particularly those with families—have been fleeing our nation's crime-ridden inner cities for more than a decade. Between 1985 and 1990, some 157,000 African Americans moved out of Washington, D.C.—fully *one fifth* of the city's population.[212] During that same period another 200,000 blacks—weary of the constant danger of assault by members of their own race—left New York City.[213] Former New Yorker Lawrence Hamilton, for one, took his wife and two children to the suburbs for fear of "getting a phone call that one of my children was shot dead in school."[214] Another ex-Manhattanite, James Boykin, decided to leave the city when he realized that his children could "recognize the caliber and the type of gun that's being used outside."[215] Says yet another ex-New Yorker, "I couldn't live that life anymore. It's a life of fear."[216] These blacks, and thousands more like them, did not flee their urban neighborhoods because white racists were harassing them or burning crosses on their front lawns—but because of the likelihood that *black* criminals eventually would harm them and their families. Their exodus from New York, it should be noted, occurred before the mayoral administration of Rudolph Giuliani, under whose leadership the city's crime rates have plummeted significantly since 1993.

Many watchdogs of racism indignantly claim to have uncovered an insidious plot designed essentially to poison and exterminate black Americans. The concept of "environmental justice" entered the activist playbook in 1982, when protest groups tried to block a hazardous-waste landfill from coming to a mostly black North Carolina county. One of the protesters, a District of Columbia congressional representative, pressured the federal government's General Accounting Office (GAO) to investigate whether such noxious dumping grounds were disproportionately located in minority communities. Within a year the GAO reported that indeed they were, sparking further allegations of "environmental racism" all over the United States. For more than a decade, sensational references to "racial genocide" and "cancer alleys" abounded.[217] By 1992 there were at least ten minority-based environmental groups denouncing the "radioactive colonialism" and "garbage imperialism" that ostensibly threatened black lives everywhere.[218] Two years later the Clinton administration issued an executive order directing every federal agency to make "environmental justice" a top priority.[219]

Empirical evidence, however, now shows that the alarmists were utterly wrong about this purported national crisis. We now know that every early study claiming to have found evidence of "environmental racism" made critical methodological errors.[220] Thus, not only is it untrue that hazardous-waste landfills tend to be situated near minority neighborhoods, but *fully 78 percent are in areas with more white than nonwhite inhabitants.*[221] Moreover, health data show no evidence of minorities being poisoned in disproportionate numbers by toxic sites.[222]

Banks and "Racism"

Lending institutions are often accused of racism when they refuse to grant home mortgages in certain poor, inner-city, minority neighborhoods. "Civil rights leaders," naturally, assure us that such "redlining" is motivated by bankers' contempt for nonwhites—a message dutifully echoed by most in the mainstream media. For example, when a highly publicized 1989 review of ten million loan applications found that white applicants were denied mortgages 26 percent of the time while blacks were rejected 50 percent of the time, news headlines announced that blacks were twice as likely as whites to be rejected for mortgages. Scarcely mentioned, however, was the fact that this study did not account for such factors as each applicant's debt burden, credit history, value of collateral, or size of down payment. Without such information, of course, the findings were practically worthless.[223]

In 1993 Attorney General Janet Reno, along with Housing and Urban Development (HUD) Secretary Henry Cisneros, expressed dismay over yet another report that the nationwide rejection rate of black mortgage applicants was about twice as high as that of their white counterparts. In response to this report, Reno warned that "no bank" would be "immune" to an aggressive Justice Department campaign to punish discrimination.[224] In a similar vein, Comptroller of the Currency Eugene Ludwig told the Senate Banking Committee, "We have to use every means at our disposal to end discrimination and to end it as quickly as possible."[225] Assistant Attorney General Deval Patrick went still further, pledging to work for the elimination of all racial disparities in mortgage lending—*even where those disparities were not due to discrimination.*[226]

Curiously, much less publicity was given to an important 1993 Boston Federal Reserve study showing that black loan applicants not only had greater debt burdens and poorer credit histories than white applicants, but tended also to seek loans covering a higher percentage of the property values in question. The Boston study found that after correcting for standard credit criteria—income, net worth, age, education, probability of unemployment, and credit history—the loan-rejection gap between racial groups virtually disappeared.[227] According to Federal Reserve Governor Lawrence Lindsey, these variables accounted for nearly all group differences in rejection rates. Likewise, Federal Deposit Insurance Corporation economist David Horne finds no evidence of discriminatory patterns in mortgage lending.[228]

The heralds of "redlining" would do well to remember that money lenders are in business for one reason only: to make profitable loans that have a good likelihood of being repaid. In today's competitive marketplace, very few salesmen in any industry would foolishly pass up profitable transactions simply to indulge their own bigotry. Why should we assume that the mortgage lending business is uniquely peopled by racists? As analyst Robert Stowe England astutely observes, "The essentially irrational assumption underlying the notion that there is widespread discrimination in mortgage lending is that lenders are willing to give up good profits in order to feed their subtle but thorough-going racism."[229]

Above all else, banks are concerned with loan *default* rates, not rejection rates, because lower default rates mean higher profits for lenders. Obviously, then, banks take a big risk when making loans where default rates are high—as in many black ghettos. Adding to this risk are a number of borrower-protection laws that make it costly for banks to try to collect on delinquent accounts. Furthermore, regulations limiting the interest rates that lenders may charge often make the maximum allowable rate too low to adequately compensate banks for approving loans in high-risk neighborhoods. Economist Walter E. Williams explains, "Redlining need not be a result of bankers' racism. In many cases (perhaps almost all) it occurs not because bankers are unwilling to make home loans to inner-city blacks but because the inner-city is not perceived as a profitable market. . . . Interestingly, black-owned banks that do not find the ghetto an attractive place to make loans are not called racist."[230]

Census data show that whites and blacks, as groups, currently have similar overall default rates on home mortgage loans. If banks were discriminating against blacks by holding them to stricter standards than whites (in terms of debt level, expense level, income, and credit history), white borrowers undoubtedly would have a *higher* default rate than blacks.[231] The fact that the default rates of whites and blacks are so similar, then, is strong evidence that lenders are applying race-neutral standards in awarding loans. Thus it would be most imprudent to compel banks to lend money to high-risk applicants, as "civil rights" advocates recommend, simply to make *rejection* rates equal for all groups. Such a policy, which would require increased numbers of loans to underqualified black applicants, would inevitably lead to higher black default rates. Consequently, foreclosures in poor, inner-city communities would multiply, less capital would be available for creditworthy borrowers, and mortgage rates would rise for everyone in order to offset the losses from bad loans.[232]

Such prospects, however, do not trouble the crusaders for "fairness" and "equity," who continue to see shadows of racism on virtually every landscape. Jesse Jackson, for instance, asserted in 1991 that the racial disparity in mortgage rejection rates proved "what we have known for decades: Banks routinely and systematically discriminate against African Americans . . . in making mortgage loans."[233] Notably, Jackson did not mention that in that very same year, whites were *less* likely than Asians to be approved for mortgages. Indeed no one—least of all Jesse Jackson—suggested that bankers were favoring Asians over whites.[234] Neither has Jackson ever addressed the fact that black-owned banks actually invest more of their loan portfolios outside the communities in which they are located than do white-owned banks.[235] Nor has he acknowledged that as long ago as 1977 the Community Reinvestment Act required depository institutions "to make an affirmative effort to lend in low-income communities."[236] Neither has he commented on a recent finding that in Houston, white-owned banks as a whole were approving black loan applications 50 to 60 percent of the time, while the city's only black-owned bank was approving just 17 percent of black applicants.[237] These numbers reflect the fact that black-owned banks, insulated from charges of racism if they reject black applicants, are more likely than white-owned banks to turn down high-risk blacks.[238]

Today all mortgage lenders must publicly disclose their loan approval rates for applicants of every racial and ethnic background—leaving themselves vulnerable to discrimination charges if they report "too many" rejections of blacks and Hispanics. This disclosure requirement, along with the tough enforcement of fair-lending laws, has fueled a recent surge in loans to nonwhites. Because lenders try to demonstrate their "color-blindness" by aggressively seeking inner-city black and Hispanic borrowers, loan initiatives targeting low-income minorities are proliferating in almost every American city. From 1993 to 1994, home loan approvals for blacks increased by 38 percent—far greater than the 12 percent climb for whites.[239] Between 1993 and 1997, black home-buying rose by 60 percent, nearly four times the 16 percent rate for whites.[240] Loans to blacks nowadays are often at below-market terms, with lenders waiving or reducing closing costs, waiving or reducing down payments, and waiving or relaxing standards for borrower credit ratings. As Federal Reserve officials readily acknowledge, low-income minority borrowers in many cities can now find mortgage credit on better terms than affluent whites.[241] Unfortunately the lower standards for loans to nonwhites have begun to produce higher default rates among the beneficiaries of such preferences[242]—a fact with which "civil rights leaders" never burden the American public.

Politics and "Racism"

Because race remains our most widely exploited national dilemma, it is not surprising that unscrupulous political candidates are ever-eager to blast their opponents with charges of bigotry in blunderbuss fashion. Consider what occurred in 1993 when New York's incumbent black mayor, David Dinkins, was preparing to run for re-election against white challenger Rudolph Giuliani, whom he had defeated in the city's mayoral election four years earlier. With the two candidates locked in a close race as the 1993 election neared, Dinkins supporter Al Sharpton publicly exhorted white New Yorkers to vote for the "best" candidate, regardless of color. "It's time for people to rise above racism," said Sharpton. "Blacks have voted for many candidates out of their race, but whites don't."[243] Echoing Sharpton's thoughts was President Bill Clinton, who not only rebuked white voters for their "deep-seated reluctance . . . to reach out across [racial] lines," but also suggested that Dinkins would have been comfortably ahead in voter polls were it not for the fact that "too many of us are still too unwilling to vote for people who are different than we are."[244] Black columnist Earl Caldwell called the president's remarks "magnificent."[245]

But while these speakers portrayed race-conscious voting as an exclusively white trait, the facts told a very different story. Just days before the 1993 election, the Reverend Calvin Butts urged a large black congregation in Harlem to actively support Dinkins. Citing three major cities whose black mayors had recently been voted out of office, Butts boldly announced, "We [blacks] lost Los Angeles. We lost Philadelphia. We lost Chicago. We're not going to lose New York."[246] Dinkins himself showed no reluctance to inject race into the election, saying nothing to refute the claims of a black minister who charged that Giuliani's campaign was "dominated by fascists."[247] Neither did the mayor disagree with one of his own aides who said that Giuliani had surrounded himself with "racists."[248] Nor did Dinkins comment on Representative Charles Rangel's assertion that Giuliani's "best asset" was his white skin.[249] In fact Dinkins, who touted himself the mayor "of all the people,"[250] created additional controversy by telling a black radio audience, "I don't care what other folks are saying. When the brothers and sisters come out and encourage me, it makes everything all right."[251] One can only imagine the monumental indignation that would have erupted—rightfully—had a white mayor in a similar situation bluntly declared that only the opinions and support of other whites mattered to him. Such a person surely would have been spotlighted by "civil rights leaders" as a national symbol of racism. Yet when an African American makes a statement of this nature, these very same "leaders" applaud him. Jesse Jackson, for example, who once referred to Dinkins as Martin Luther King's "present" to New York City,[252] never wavered from characterizing the mayor as a "healer."[253]

While Sharpton, Clinton, Butts, Rangel, and Jackson apparently considered all Giuliani ballots to be tarnished by racism, even a cursory glance at Dinkins's mayoral record reveals a slew of items that easily could have disenchanted voters of any color. For instance, he had been ineffectual in quelling the Crown Heights and Washington Heights riots of 1991 and 1992. He had permitted an illegal, racially motivated boycott of two Korean markets in Brooklyn to destroy both businesses.[254] He had instituted numerous racial set-aside programs for the awarding of city contracts, despite the notoriously inefficient and wasteful nature of such schemes—to say nothing of their gross injustice. He had presided over New York during a period when its violent crime rate reached an all-time high, when its welfare roll grew to an astonishing one-seventh of the population,[255] and when prohibitive taxes forced many businesses to flee the city. In 1989, before Dinkins took office, New York was ranked 7th in the *Places Rated Almanac,* which rates cities for their overall livability. By 1993, as his term drew to a close, the city had slipped to 105th in the rankings.[256] A 1993 poll of New Yorkers found that 59 percent thought that life in the city had gotten worse on the mayor's watch, while just 8 percent thought it had improved.[257] Presumably, however, we are to believe that none of this was of any real import. According to our "civil rights" prophets, in the final analysis all voter decisions boiled down to race—except, of course, the decisions of black voters supporting Dinkins.

As the 1993 election approached, the Reverend John Brandon of Harlem was one of the few public figures courageous enough to criticize the black community's tendency to vote strictly along racial lines. Condemning "the use of fear and race in the campaign to force blacks into conformity," he warned that "we [blacks] are becoming the incarnations of the evils we pretend to despise." Unfortunately, because Mr. Brandon's political stance differed so markedly from that of his parishioners and mainstream black "leaders," he was eventually ousted from his pastor's position.[258]

Giuliani won the 1993 election despite the fact that black New Yorkers gave Dinkins 97 percent of their votes[259]—just as they had done in 1989, *when fully one-third of white voters had supported Dinkins.*[260] Yet Dinkins said nothing about his virtually unanimous black support, blaming his defeat largely on the fact that "only" one-fourth of whites had voted for him.[261] It was "silly to suggest," he said, that race had not affected the result.[262] "There is no question that race prevailed over reason," agreed Jesse Jackson.[263]

Most blacks interviewed by *The New York Times* felt that Dinkins would have won the election if he were white.[264] David Jones, executive director of the city's Community Service Society, said, "Anyone who denies there was a strong racial component [to the voting] is living in a dream world. We've got a problem here in the city, no doubt about it. There is a great deal of anger that there was a double standard here."[265] Brooklyn high-school principal Frank Mickens declared,

"This has been a referendum on race. . . . We don't have any power as African Americans."[266] Geoffrey Canada, executive director of the Rheedlen Centers for Children and Families, lamented, "People feel that we as black Democrats played by the rules, and the rules were changed. . . . It's clear we have not come as far as we would like to believe. A lot of us were fooling ourselves about race in this city. We had a taste of inclusion, many of us for the first time in our lives. We really felt part of this city and part of the politics of this city. For many of us, we feel that's over."[267]

Not surprisingly, the tendency of "civil rights leaders" and community activists to ascribe racism only to *white* voters extends far beyond the boundaries of New York. When Jesse Helms ran for a North Carolina Senate seat against black candidate Harvey Gantt in 1990, Helms received 65 percent of the white vote, while Gantt got 93 percent of the black vote—but it was whites who were widely accused of voting by race. Incidentally, this very same Harvey Gantt originally broke into politics in 1983 when he was elected mayor of Charlotte, North Carolina, a city whose population was three-quarters white.[268]

The myth that white voters are reluctant to support black political candidates permeates the media. Columnist Richard G. Carter, for one, contends that Jesse Jackson failed in his bid to win the Democratic party's presidential nomination in the 1980s largely because of white America's racism:

> Racism is like a sharp ax. It started swinging Jesse Jackson's way in November 1983, when he first announced his candidacy for the nation's top job. The whacks got more and more vicious in 1987 when he began running hard again. . . . Anyone who thinks Jesse failed to get the nonminority. . . votes he needed because of political inexperience or left-wing pronouncements is dreaming. White America just can't stand the thought of a black president. The White House will remain lily-white.[269]

In a similar vein, New York congressman Charles Rangel states, "Whites don't support black candidates to the same degree that blacks support white candidates. It's unfortunate but there is a dramatic fallout of white votes just because of race. I challenge anyone to dispute that."[270] Los Angeles congresswoman Maxine Waters concurs, "Black people elect [both] black and white people to

Congress. Whites, for the most part, elect only white people to Congress."[271] Dr. Keith Reeves of Harvard's JFK School of Government puts it bluntly: "Whites are not equal-opportunity voters."[272] Because Rangel, Waters, Reeves, and others of their ilk have rarely, if ever, been challenged to prove such assertions, they disdainfully ignore the undeniable truth that in recent decades whites have been far more willing than blacks to vote across racial lines.

For instance, Edward Brooke was a black senator in Massachusetts from 1967 to 1979—when only 3 percent of the state's population was black.[273] Similarly, a majority-white Georgia district elected black candidate Andrew Young to Congress as early as 1972.[274] A decade later, black congressman Alan Wheat received 65 percent of the white vote in mostly-white Kansas City, Missouri.[275] In 1989 Douglas Wilder was elected the first black governor of Virginia, a state whose electorate was only 15 percent black. He won the election with about 40 percent of the white vote and, of course, virtually all of the black vote.[276] In the 1994 congressional races, black candidates J.C. Watts of Oklahoma and Gary Franks of Connecticut were victorious in districts that were 93 percent and 95 percent white, respectively.[277] Two years later, nine black candidates nationwide were elected to Congress from majority-white districts, including several who received *very* strong white support.[278] Among the victors was Sanford Bishop, Jr., a Georgia Democrat whose district is nearly two-thirds white.[279] In 1997 Paul Harris won a legislative seat in mostly-white Virginia.[280] Even in the poorest rural district of the Deep South's poorest state, Mississippi, the majority-white population proved it was capable of electing a black candidate when it sent Mike Espy to Congress in 1987.[281]

Many mostly-white cities, large and small, have elected black mayors in recent years. In Los Angeles, where just 14 percent of the population is black, Tom Bradley was elected mayor five times between 1973 and 1989.[282] In fact, when he was first elected in 1973, he would have won even with no black support, but with white votes alone.[283] In 1989 Norm Rice became the mayor of Seattle, winning 58 percent of the vote in a city whose population was just 10 percent black.[284] Kansas City, Missouri elected a black mayor in 1991, though blacks comprised only 30 percent of the city's population.[285] That same year Denver elected a black mayor with a population that was 12 percent black.[286] Also in 1991, Willie Herenton was elected mayor of Memphis, which is 57 percent white, and within a year had a 60 percent approval rating among the city's white voters.[287] In 1993 Michael White won the mayoralty of Cleveland, which is less than half black,[288] and four years later he was re-elected. In 1995 Ron Kirk garnered nearly two-thirds of the white vote to win the mayoral race in Dallas, which is just 30 percent black.[289] A year later LaMetta Wynn easily defeated four white male rivals, including the incumbent, to win the mayoral race in Clinton, Iowa, a town that is more than 95 percent white.[290] In 1997 another black woman, Sharon Saylas Belton, was re-elected mayor of Minneapolis, where just 13 percent of all residents are black.[291] That same year, 31 percent of St. Louis's white voters supported black candidate Freeman Bosley, Jr., although three white opponents ran against him.[292] Preston Daniels, meanwhile, became the first black mayor of 93 percent-white Des Moines, Iowa,[293] and Lee Brown was elected mayor of Houston, where fewer than three in ten residents are black.[294] Also in 1997, Indianapolis Democrat Julia Carson took 53 percent of the white vote in her 69 percent white district.[295]

Even Stone Mountain, Georgia, the town where the twentieth-century Ku Klux Klan was born in 1915, elected a black mayor, Chuck Burris, in 1997. "There is a new Klan in Stone Mountain," said Burris, "only it's spelled with a C: c-l-a-n, citizens living as neighbors. And I guess I'm the black dragon." Burris noted that during the campaign he had felt no racial animosity from either of his two opponents, both of whom were white.[296]

Within the past decade, black mayors have headed our country's three largest cities—New York, Chicago, and Los Angeles—all of which have majority-white populations. Recent years have also seen black mayors elected in such minority-black cities as Roanoke, Rockford, Dayton, Tallahassee, Cincinnati, Grand Rapids, Pontiac, Boulder, Detroit, Little Rock, Philadelphia, and Hartford—to name just a few.[297] In 1968 the entire southern half of the United States had only three black mayors, but by 1996 there were nearly 300.[298] Between 1967 and 1993, black mayors were elected in eighty-seven American cities with populations exceeding 50,000—and in two-thirds of those cities blacks comprised a minority of eligible voters.[299] As of June 1995, thirty-four cities with populations greater than 50,000 had black mayors—and in thirteen of those cities whites were a majority.[300] As of 1996, sixty-seven cities with populations exceeding

25,000 had black mayors, 58 percent of whom were elected in places where whites outnumbered blacks.[301] And contrary to popular stereotypes, southern white voters have been just as willing as their northern counterparts to support black candidates. As of 1992, fully 62 of the South's 215 black mayors represented towns and cities with populations more than 50 percent white.[302]

Even for the most important elective office in the world, white Americans overall show no reluctance to support a black candidate. When General Colin Powell was considering running for president of the United States in 1996, he led incumbent Bill Clinton in virtually every reputable poll of American voters, the great majority of whom are white. In an October 1995 *Time*/CNN poll, for instance, Powell beat Clinton 51 percent to 34 percent.[303] On election day 1996, exit polls indicated that Powell would have won by at least 11 percentage points.[304] Consistent with these findings, a 1996 Gallup poll found that fully 93 percent of whites would be willing to vote for a black presidential candidate.[305]

Between 1970 and 1987, the number of black elected officials nationwide increased from 1,479 to 6,384. Today there are more than 8,000. This meteoric rise simply could not have occurred without white votes.[306] Critics, however, will point out that these 8,000 black representatives comprise only 1.6 percent of all elected officials nationwide, while blacks are 11.3 percent of the voting-age population. But the 1.6 percent figure is misleading for two reasons. First, it should be noted that more than half of all black Americans (and, therefore, potential black candidates) reside in the South, where the political system historically has had fewer elective offices than other regions of the United States.[307] Second, the vast majority of black candidates are Democrats—usually *liberal* Democrats—who are weak competitors for offices in Republican districts. Indeed, only about 60 of our country's 8,000 black elected officials are Republicans.[308] The real question then is: What proportion of those offices *held by Democrats* do blacks occupy?[309] As of 1992, blacks held 14.4 percent of the Democratic seats in the U.S. House of Representatives—a strong representation.[310] This figure rose to 18 percent after the 1994 congressional elections, and then dropped slightly in 1996 when white Democrats regained a few seats while the number of black Democrats remained constant.[311] Black politicians have also fared reasonably well at the state level, occupying about 10 percent of the seats in the lower state legislative chambers and roughly 8 percent of the seats in state senates.[312] These figures include many states wherein African Americans are but a small fraction of the electorate. In states with sizable numbers of black residents, the percentage of black Democratic state legislators is commensurate with the black presence in the overall population.[313]

The willingness of white voters to support black political candidates was put to a major test in 1996. After the Supreme Court had ruled, a year earlier, that racially gerrymandered congressional districts were unconstitutional, those districts were redrawn on geographic rather than racial lines. This meant that several mostly minority districts became mostly white—a development that agitated gerrymandering's advocates. Jesse Jackson predicted that the Court's ruling would cause a "kind of ethnic cleansing" in Congress.[314] A spokesman for the American Civil Liberties Union warned that we soon would see "the bleaching of America."[315] One NAACP leader, evoking images of lynchings, proclaimed that "the noose" was "tightening" around the proverbial neck of the black community's participation in American politics.[316] The NAACP's Theodore Shaw lamented that before long, the entire membership of the Congressional Black Caucus "will be able to meet in the back seat of a taxicab."[317] Elaine Jones, who directs the NAACP Legal Defense and Education Fund, said that gerrymandering's demise would "torch the fundamental rights of African Americans, Hispanics, and others to be included as participatory citizens in this democracy."[318] Deval Patrick, who was then the Assistant U.S. Attorney for Civil Rights, predicted "a return to the days of all-white government."[319] The clear consensus of the "civil rights" cabal was that the bigotry of white voters would surely preclude blacks from winning political offices in the newly redrawn districts. As usual, however, such dire warnings bore no resemblance to reality. In the 1996 congressional elections, all five black incumbents whose districts were newly majority-white—one in Florida and two each in Texas and Georgia—were re-elected.[320] Nationwide, thirty-four of the thirty-five black incumbents won re-election.[321]

These examples of white voters supporting black candidates contrast sharply with the remarkable black solidarity that fueled Marion Barry's recent political comeback. Thanks to his near-unanimous black support, Barry won Washington, D.C.'s 1994 mayoral election despite his revolting history of administrative corruption and cocaine abuse. Black columnist Carl Rowan candidly acknowledged that a contempt for whites was a major factor motivating blacks to vote for such a deeply flawed candidate. "For a lot of poor blacks in Washington," wrote Rowan, ". . . Barry's previous betrayals and disgraceful behavior are not as important as the fact that an overwhelming percentage of white voters are against him."[322] A black Washington official concurred. "I got to the polling station," he said, "and saw all these poor kids handing out flyers, and I felt energized. It was a 'f—— you, Whitey' kind of vote."[323] Race played a similarly key role in Carol Moseley-Braun's 1992 victory in the Illinois Senate race, after which the *Economist* observed that her supporters were "less enamored of her than of what she represent[ed]—a racial first."[324]

Indeed *blacks*, not whites, have demonstrated a refusal to vote across racial lines in elections with at least one black candidate on the ballot.[325] The unyielding nature of this refusal is staggering. As of 1992, *every* congressional district in America with a majority-black population had a black representative.[326] Of majority-black cities with populations over 200,000, every one except Richmond, Virginia had a black mayor.[327]

Even a proven fraud like Al Sharpton receives strong black support when running for elective office, though a dubious list of "accomplishments" like his would surely have crippled the candidacy of any white with a similar history. Notwithstanding his ignominious track record, the vocal activist garnered 70 percent of the black vote in a 1992 New York Senate primary.[328] Five years later Sharpton sought the Democratic party's nomination to run for mayor in New York City, and again black voters backed him in numbers large enough to bring him to within a hairsbreadth of forcing a runoff against Ruth Messinger, the heavy pre-primary favorite. During their campaigns, both Messinger and Sal Albanese, the third major Democratic hopeful, were careful not to criticize Sharpton for his long catalogue of abuses, fearful that doing so would cost them much-needed black support.

Black Church Fires—A "Cultural Conspiracy"?

In the early months of 1996, the national media teemed with stories about an apparent epidemic of racially motivated arsons targeting southern black churches. Between January 1, 1995 and

June 18, 1996, fires struck thirty-four of these houses of worship, inspiring extensive commentary by journalists, "civil rights leaders," and politicians.[329] A national database search in early July 1996 found that more than 2,200 news articles had been written about black church burnings—including three large layouts in *USA Today* on consecutive days.[330] "Arson at Black Churches Echoes Bigotry of Past," read one *USA Today* headline.[331]

Most analysts suggested that the fires were not accidents, but were deliberately set by white racists. Black *New York Times* columnist Bob Herbert wrote, "The fuel for these fires can be traced to a carefully crafted environment of bigotry and hatred that has developed over the past quarter-century."[332] "The fires speak of racial divisions out of the old South," reported another *Times* piece.[333] Along the same lines, *The Christian Science Monitor* spoke of "the apparent racist motives behind the burnings."[334] "Who's Burning the Black Churches?" asked a *Newsweek* cover caption.[335] In the corresponding article, the authors wrote that "the sheer number of black church arsons, which now equals the worst years of white racist terror in the 1950s and 60s, suggests a spreading virus of copycat malice."[336] "A nationwide climate of racial rancor," they added, was "inducing some people to act out their hostilities."[337] A guest writer for the same publication theorized that the black churches were being targeted because "they were the birthplace of the civil rights movement, and for some [whites] that's unforgivable. The flaming old churches are like signal fires from one disgruntled band of whites to another."[338] A *U.S. News & World Report* piece saw "little doubt that racism is the root cause of many of the recent Southern fires."[339] Headlines everywhere focused on the seeming crisis. "Black Churches—Who Is Setting the Fires?" asked *U.S. News*.[340] "Flames of Hate: Racism Blamed in Shock Waves of Church Burnings," read the New York *Daily News*.[341] "A Rush of Torchings at Black Churches Has Resurrected the Ugly Specter of Racism," added the *Toronto Star*.[342]

President Clinton went to South Carolina and knelt in prayer at a black church newly constructed on the site of one that had been burned down. "It is the cruelest of ironies," he said, "that an expression of bigotry in America that would sweep this country is one that involves trashing religious liberty."[343] In a national radio address, the president asserted that "racial hostility" was clearly "the driving force" behind the fires. Pledging his commitment to ending racially motivated arson,[344] he asked "every citizen in America to say . . . we are not slipping back to those dark [racist] days."[345] He then likened the motives underlying the torchings to the ethnic hostilities that had recently triggered violence in Rwanda and Bosnia.[346] Hillary Clinton saw similarities to the Nazi Holocaust.[347]

According to a number of "civil rights leaders," the church fires were the result of a national conspiracy rooted in racial intolerance.[348] "You're talking about a well-organized white-supremacist movement," said the Reverend Mac Charles Jones of the Center for Democratic Renewal.[349] Jesse Jackson warned that an odious "cultural conspiracy" was creating "a kind of antiblack mania, a kind of white riot."[350] Eleanor Holmes Norton saw the burnings as "something far more dangerous" than a mere conspiracy.[351] Congresswoman Maxine Waters declared, "Never in my wildest dreams did I expect to be refocused on such outright tyranny."[352] North Carolina governor James B. Hunt asserted that our country unfortunately had "a great history of black churches being attacked."[353] And in a gesture of extreme concern, the National Trust for Historic Preservation added black churches to its list of the "most endangered" historic places in America. "We are taking this unprecedented step," said National Trust president Richard Moe, "because of the urgency to mobilize support for some of the most significant community institutions in America."[354]

The FBI and the U.S. Bureau of Alcohol, Tobacco, and Firearms (ATF) assigned 200 field agents—jointly supervised by the Justice and Treasury Departments—to investigate the fires and search for evidence of a racist conspiracy.[355] Nevertheless, the foot soldiers of "justice" accused federal authorities of giving the church fires low priority.[356] Said the Reverend Joseph Lowery, "We have been sorely disappointed that until recently law enforcement in particular . . . [has] seemed only mildly interested in focusing on these acts of terrorism."[357]

It is notable that while black church burnings were so prominently in the news, few Americans were ever made aware that white congregations all over the country had taken up special collections to help rebuild those churches. Neither did many people hear about the white volunteers who traveled to southern communities from as far away as Canada to take part in the rebuilding efforts.[358] Nor did "civil rights leaders" inform Americans that there really had been no sudden spate of fires targeting black churches; that while black church burnings were indeed occurring at a slightly higher-than-usual rate, there had certainly been no *dramatic* rise in the incidence of such events. Arsons in black churches always had been, and still were, relatively uncommon occurrences. In fact, recent years had brought a significant *decline* in church burnings—black *and* white. In this country of 300,000 houses of worship, there were 520 fires to churches and related properties in 1994—far fewer than the 1,420 church arsons of 1980. Between 1990 and 1996, the yearly average was about 600. During that same six-year period, a grand total of about 80 black churches were burned—just a shade under 14 per year. While *any* church burning is certainly cause for public outrage, there would have to be some 80 black church arsons each year to be roughly proportional, per capita, to white church arsons.[359] In other words, for years media pundits and "civil rights leaders" ignored the fact that white churches were being disproportionately targeted by arsonists. Then, when the number of black church burnings increased slightly, these same individuals reacted as if a national crisis had suddenly struck.

Curiously, the alarmists who dutifully denounced the "racist" arsons never acknowledged the absence of proof that even a handful of those fires had indeed been set for racial reasons. As of July 1996, explained the State Fire Marshal of Alabama, ATF investigators had "not uncovered . . . a single piece of information to substantiate racially motivated fires."[360] By the end of 1998, only three of the more than seventy church fires investigated by the Justice Department could be tied to racial motives. The national Church Arson Task Force likewise discovered few racial links.[361]

Many church fires, in fact, are started by people of the same racial and religious backgrounds as the worshippers who attend those churches. One white Protestant man, for example, recently set thirty-two fires at Protestant churches;[362] another man raised as a Jew burned twelve synagogues;[363] and yet another white man was arrested in 1999 for having burned more than fifty white churches in eleven states.[364] But because there was no white-on-black angle to these disgraceful crimes, few Americans ever heard about them.

Nor are many people aware that a number of the arsonists responsible for the infamous southern black church fires were themselves African Americans. In South Carolina, where twenty-seven black churches were burned between January 1990 and June 1996, eight of the eighteen culprits apprehended thus far are black.[365] Once again, pyramids of myth built on the sweeping generalizations of the "civil rights" cabal crumble to dust when confronted with truth.

Chapter 14

Time to Lie No More

Once to every man and nation comes
the moment to decide,
In the strife of Truth with Falsehood,
for the good or evil side.
—J. R. Lowell[1]

Martin Luther King, Jr.'s dream—that every individual might be judged by the content of his character rather than the color of his skin—symbolized what was good in the civil rights goals of a generation ago. Sadly, his successors have forsaken that dream. King's noble words, which seared our nation's conscience and gave voice to a revolution in American thought, have been perverted—by those who claim to be continuing his work—into the very antithesis of his vision.

Starting in the mid- to late 1960s, civil rights activists who had marched with King began to abandon the color-blind ideal, in favor of a more militant approach that repudiated every American institution as fundamentally racist.[2] Malcolm X, for one, articulated the bitterness of millions of urban blacks. He was, in the words of one writer, "the original apostle of black rage"[3]—a rage that gradually became transfigured into a "posture of stylized rebellion against mainstream society."[4] Focusing on our country's historical injustices,[5] Malcolm insisted that blacks were not really Americans, but "victims of Americanism."[6] Instead of the American dream, he claimed, blacks could experience only the "American nightmare."[7] Asserting that whites were irredeemably racist "devils,"[8] he urged a "bloody," uncompromising revolution to overthrow the American system.[9] He steadfastly opposed integration, which he warned "would destroy our people."[10] His enmity toward whites was indeed profound. After a U.S. airliner carrying 120 white passengers crashed near Paris, he called it "a very beautiful thing" that God had gotten "rid of 120 of them at one whop."[11] It was not until near the end of his life that Malcolm began to acknowledge that "not all white people are racists."[12] But this break with his past was far from complete at the time of his death; to his last days, he continued to launch incendiary attacks on whites in general and Jews in particular.[13]

While Malcolm X promoted the "black is beautiful" model of racial pride, he also celebrated what has been described as a "bad negro" version of blackness.[14] Ostensibly in the name of pride, he equated underclass culture with "authentic" blackness.[15] "Genuine" blacks, in this view, respected underclass mores simply because they stood so visibly outside of the "evil" American mainstream. This perspective, which differed sharply from that of Dr. King, became increasingly popular by the end of the 1960s. As Professor Cornel West puts it, "King was near death politically and organizationally before he was murdered."[16]

As the 1960s progressed, other prominent black figures joined Malcolm X in rejecting the ideal of an integrated, color-blind society. In 1965, Congress of Racial Equality leader James Farmer wrote, "We have found the cult of color-blindness not only quaintly irrelevant but seriously flawed. America could only become color-blind when we gave up our color. We would have to give up our identities."[17]

The following year, the Black Panther Party came into existence and demanded that all black inmates be released from American prisons, regardless of their crimes.[18] Convinced that the U.S. government could be overthrown by armed revolution, party founder Bobby Seale actually marched with some friends into the California Assembly, armed with rifles and shotguns, to make their demands known.[19]

Also in 1966, King follower John Lewis was replaced as chairman of the Student Nonviolent Coordinating Committee (SNCC) by Stokely Carmichael, a West Indian activist who supported Black Power, which he described as "a movement that will smash everything Western civilization has created."[20] A year later an SNCC leaflet stated, "We [blacks] must fill ourselves with hate for all things white."[21]

In 1967 Carmichael collaborated with Charles Hamilton to write *Black Power*, which advocated the strengthening of black race-consciousness and bluntly repudiated integration. That same year the black theologian James Cone published *Black Theology and Black Power*, which encouraged blacks to "affirm the very characteristic which the oppressor ridicules—*blackness*. Black people must withdraw and form their own culture, their own way of life."[22]

Carmichael's successor as head of the SNCC was H. Rap Brown, who exhorted blacks to "wage guerrilla war on the honkie white man."[23] "If America don't come around," he said during the Detroit riot of 1967, "we going to burn it down, brother."[24] "Get you some guns," he urged his black listeners, because "the only thing a honkie respects is force."[25] In calculated contradiction to Dr. King's nonviolent ideal, Brown said, "Don't be trying to love the honkie to death. Shoot him to death. Shoot him to death, brother, 'cause that's what he's out to do to you."[26] In a similar vein, the activist Julius Lester published a 1968 manifesto that stated, "Psychologically blacks have always found an outlet for their revenge . . . every day when white folks die. It is clearly written that the victim must become the executioner."[27]

Rage was clearly the mood of ever-increasing numbers of radicals purporting to speak for the black community. Not surprisingly, then, their message took root in millions of American minds, even while vital civil rights advances were dramatically improving black life. On August 11, 1965—just five days after the Voting Rights Act became law—a horrific riot broke out in the Watts section of South-Central Los Angeles. Over the next three years, more than 100 additional riots would erupt in various cities nationwide. All told, an estimated 500,000 blacks participated in these disturbances, which resulted in some 50,000 arrests and 8,000 deaths and injuries.[28]

It should be noted that black rage expressed itself not only in group rioting, but also in the skyrocketing incidence of isolated violent crimes. The rate at which blacks—especially young males—were arrested for homicide tripled during the 1960s.[29] It was a curious phenomenon: At the very point in history that black Americans were finally granted the liberties they had long been denied, their collective outrage soared to unprecedented heights. This development can only be attributed to the omnipresent, inflammatory rhetoric of an increasingly militant crop of "civil rights" leaders who, to satisfy their own lust for power—and in many cases their own deeply felt racist impulses—kept black Americans feeling angry and abused.

The 1968 Kerner Commission report, issued by President Lyndon Johnson's National Advisory Committee on Civil Disorders, both reflected and legitimized the rage that was becoming increasingly identified with "authentic" blackness. Dominated by white liberals and the NAACP's Roy Wilkins, the Kerner Commission concluded that *society*, and not the rioters, was to blame "for the explosive mixture which has been accumulating in our cities."[30] Endorsing Malcolm X's view that America was, at its core, a racist nation, the Commission's report soon became the most authoritative and widely cited civil rights document of its time.[31]

Clearly, the civil rights movement was undergoing a monumental transformation, one which would undermine efforts to improve race relations for decades to come. As scholar Dinesh D'Souza writes, the movement's leadership "was moving from southern integrationists toward northern militants. Religious leaders were being displaced by lawyers, social workers, and full-time activists. . . . Nonviolence was no longer the operating philosophy."[32] In 1972 several thousand African Americans convened in Gary, Indiana for the National Black Political Convention. Among those in attendance were Jesse Jackson and Benjamin Chavis, who joined other delegates in rejecting integration and raising their fists in Black Power salutes.[33]

The heirs to this philosophical sea change are the "civil rights leaders" of our day, who teach, with near unanimity, that most whites are racists intent on consigning blacks to perpetual subservience. It is not surprising that in response to such instruction, many blacks surrender to hopelessness and apathy, convinced that even their best efforts to live the American dream are doomed to failure in this "racist" land. It can reasonably be argued that this self-defeating belief system is more damaging to contemporary black Americans than all the white racism that ever existed. Consider the example of a thirteen-year-old drug dealer in New York who complains, "If you [are] not white and your mom's got no money, what [are] you going to do? . . . I think everything is against the black man. You have to sell your soul to live with white people."[34] Though the youngster who spoke these words has an alcoholic, crack-addicted mother and no father, he nonetheless attributes his life of crime to the "fact" that white society has done him wrong. Never does it occur to him that factors other than racism—such as the irresponsible individuals who spawned him but were unwilling to parent him properly—might have contributed to his difficulties. He is, if nothing else, a creation of our "civil rights leaders," under whose hateful tutelage he has been molded into a cynical, angry racist himself.

The notion that white malevolence forces blacks into criminality is a cornerstone of the new "civil rights" creed. In *Why Blacks Kill Blacks*, psychiatrist Alvin Poussaint writes, "Reacting to the futility of his life, the individual derives an ultimate sense of power when he holds the fate of another human being in his hands. . . . Similarly, frustrated men may beat their wives and children in order to feel manly. . . . Violent acts and crime often become an outlet for a desperate man struggling against feelings of inferiority. Needless to say, black men often do not have access to legitimate means of making it in our society."[35]

Rejecting this deterministic view of moral depravity, Shelby Steele writes:

> [Such a contention] sees blacks only as victims, without any margin of choice. It . . . identifies only the forces which [pressure] blacks to do poorly. By overlooking the margin of choice open to them, this theory fails to recognize the degree to which they are responsible for their own poor showing. . . . [A] margin of choice is always open to blacks (even slaves had some choice). And . . . we relinquish that choice in the name of race. With the decline in racism the margin of black choice has greatly expanded. . . . But anything that prevents us from exploiting our new freedom to the fullest is now as serious a barrier to us as racism once was. . . . Choice lives in even the most blighted circumstances.[36]

Steele laments that so many black Americans have developed "a way of seeing that minimalizes opportunity to the point where it can be ignored." In black communities, he observes, "the most obvious entrepreneurial opportunities are routinely ignored. It is often outsiders or the latest wave of immigrants who own the shops, restaurants, cleaners, gas stations, and even the homes and apartments."[37]

Martin Luther King, Jr. articulated a comparable message more than three decades ago:

> We must not let the fact that we are the victims of injustice lull us into abrogating responsibility for our own lives. We must not use our oppression as an excuse for mediocrity and laziness. Our crime rate is far too high. Our level of cleanliness is frequently far too low. We are too often loud and boisterous, and spend far too much on drink. By improving our standards here and now, we will go a long way toward breaking down the arguments of the segregationist. . . . The Negro will only be free when he reaches down to the inner depths of his own being and signs with the pen and ink of assertive manhood his own emancipation proclamation.[38]

In a similar vein, black columnist William Raspberry exhorts African Americans to recognize that, notwithstanding whatever racism they may encounter from time to time, they are free to work at building better lives for themselves:

> I've just bought a Lotto ticket, and I'm driving to work with thoughts of liberation on my mind. If I'm as lucky as I deserve to be, I will shortly be able to stop worrying about money, pay off the mortgage, do some serious traveling, buy some clothes, do some good in the world, lose some weight and get in shape . . . .
>
> Lose some weight? How did that get on the list?
>
> The more I think about it, the more I think it got on the same way most of the other items got on. Lack of money can be such an important barrier to the things we want to do that we come to consider it the *only* barrier. It isn't.
>
> I certainly could use some more money; I've got three children in college and plenty of family and friends in need. But then I think of the things I really want to do—ought to do—and I'm surprised at how little they have to do with money. Aside from paying off the mortgage (which is up to date and no particular problem) and feeling more secure financially (as much a matter of attitude as income), money is not the reason for my inaction.
>
> I don't travel as much as I'd like because I'm too busy, or it's too hard to get family vacation times coordinated, or I've made commitments that get in the way. I don't buy clothes because (1) I hate shopping and (2) I refuse to invest in a wardrobe until I first lose weight and get in shape. And why don't I lose weight and get in shape? I don't know, but it has nothing to do with money.

Why am I going on about these things? Because they remind me of what I hear so many young African Americans going through.

For them, the culprit isn't lack of money but racial disadvantage, and the dreamt-of cure is not a lucky Lotto ticket but the defeat of racism.

If it weren't for racism, I'd have better grades and I'd be able to get into the graduate school of my choice—and also have the money to pay the tuition there. If it weren't for racism, I would have had my promotion by now. I wouldn't have been stopped for speeding, and if I had I certainly wouldn't have been given that big a ticket. You think that cop would have arrested me for what I said if I'd been white?

I hear the recitals—the excuses—and I find them as fanciful as my dreams of winning the lottery and getting in shape. Most of the things complained of would be considerably eased by some combination of exertion, self-discipline, and mouth control. Racism serves as a sort of generalized rationalization for not trying.

Sometimes it's subtle, as when students seek to write papers that are merely passable, convinced that their strivings for excellence will be ignored by a white professor. Sometimes it's overt. Just a couple of weeks ago, I heard a young man on Black Entertainment Television's "For Black Men Only" say words very close to these: "There's no point in trying, you know, because they are not going to let a black man succeed."

I hear versions of that thought with dismaying frequency—and not just from the despairing underclass. College students will tell you that all your exhortations to excellence and ethical hard work are worthless because "the black man doesn't stand a chance." Law enforcement officers, judges, test administrators and the media are all members of a giant conspiracy to keep black people down.

Point to those black people who have not been kept down, and they'll turn the tables on you. "Oh, they'll let a few get through, just to make the system look good. But it's always a carefully chosen few."

These chosen ones, it goes without saying, never include outspoken, tell-it-like-it-is folk like themselves—only those who are willing to "go along with The Man's program."

And what does going along with the program mean? Don't be surprised if it turns out to mean something as simple as *trying.*

My lottery-ticket musings don't obviate the fact that I could put a windfall of money to good use. There are things I could do, for my family and for others, if I only had the wherewithal. There are eminently worthwhile programs, courageous community workers, struggling advocates of the ill-housed, the ill-fed, the ill-educated and the ill-loved—all of whom I'd love to be able to help.

Similarly, my criticism of the "no hope" rhetoric of many young blacks does not disprove their sense of pervasive racism. It's *out* there, and it does, in fact, put unnecessary and unfair limits on them. They'd love to see an end to racism, believing that when that day finally comes, they'll shed their anger, spread their wings and soar.

But the truth is that most of the things I say I'd do if I had the money are things I could at least *begin* doing right now. And for many of them (like getting in shape) money is an utter irrelevancy.

And so it is with my young friends. Most of what they imagine they'd do but for racism they could at least begin to do now. And for much of it, racism might prove an irrelevancy. It's all right if I keep dreaming of Lotto and if they keep dreaming of some magical evaporation of racism—as long as we both accept the necessity of doing what we can right now.[39]

Imprisoned by the false and pitiable conviction that only the "civil rights" establishment can deliver them to a better life, the people of whom Mr. Raspberry writes are held captive by the notion that a "white power structure" is committed to their psychological and economic enslavement. As black columnist E.R. Shipp writes, many black Americans actually wonder "how it would feel to be free."[40] Sadly, this mindset of victimhood has harmed the black community more profoundly than leg irons ever could, creating an entirely new breed of slaves—those unable to understand that they are already free. It is inexpressibly tragic that in this era of unprecedented opportunity, black "leaders" jealously discourage the liberation of black minds.

The Great Progress Already Made

Cultivating hope for the future requires, as a first step, discarding present lies. Perhaps the most insidious lie of our day holds that blacks have made relatively little progress—socially or economically—over the past half-century. As black historian John Hope Franklin says, "Many young blacks are angry because they do not believe that we have come very far. And there are times when I have to agree with them."[41] Activist William Cavil concurs that "every group has managed to flourish and get ahead except African Americans."[42]

Notwithstanding the great popularity of such nonsense, black and white Americans alike must learn what the "civil rights" messiahs have never told them. For instance, between 1940 and 1997 our country's black college population rose from 45,000 to 1.4 million, a thirtyfold increase.[43] Whereas blacks in 1960 were just 41 percent as likely to attend college as whites, today they are 76 percent as likely— a remarkable figure when one considers that black students, as a group, leave high school with grades and standardized-test scores that put them years behind their white peers in terms of reading, writing, mathematics, and science.[44] Moreover, black young adults are now just as likely as their white counterparts to have completed high school—a significant change from 1960, when blacks were only 59 percent as likely as whites to have done so.[45]

In the business world, black progress has been just as impressive as in academia. Between 1983 and 1991, the number of blacks in managerial and professional specialty occupations grew by 700,000—a 50 percent increase.[46] Since 1970 the proportion of black families earning more than $50,000 per year (in today's dollars) has increased from 8 percent to 20 percent.[47] Between 1967 and 1997, the average income of two-parent black families rose (in constant 1997 dollars) from $30,314 to $51,279. This 69 percent rise was substantially higher than the 53 percent increase for similar white families.[48] Between 1990 and 1998, the annual buying power of black consumers grew by two-thirds, from $300 billion to $500 billion.[49] In January 1999 the black unemployment rate fell to an all-time low of 7.8 percent.[50] And while this figure is about twice the corresponding white rate, the existing racial gap is due principally to the black community's higher proportion of incarcerated and unmarried males. That is, prisoners do not have jobs, and single men of all races are less likely to work than married men. Correcting for these factors shrinks the racial gap virtually to the vanishing point.[51] Yet "civil rights leaders" do not publicize such information, preferring instead to give the false impression that black Americans are destined to be forever poor. This impression, in turn, provides the basis upon which our racial hucksters continue to proclaim their own relevance.

Most Americans would be surprised to learn that for nearly thirty years, young black married couples outside the South have had incomes virtually identical to those of their white counterparts.[52] In fact, young black working couples actually earned 4 percent *more* than comparable white couples as early as 1970.[53] Not only was that *before* affirmative action became widespread, but also *before* it became synonymous with preferences and quotas. As scholars Stephan and Abigail Thernstrom put it, "The growth of the black middle class long predates the adoption of race-conscious social policies. In some ways, indeed, the black middle class was expanding more rapidly before 1970 than after."[54] In fact, the pace of black economic progress in the 1940s and 1950s was perhaps faster than after 1964.[55] Moreover, the South today is no longer without its share of prosperous black households. Since 1981, black families with two college-educated, working spouses have earned slightly more than white families of the same description in every age group and in every region of the country.[56]

Thanks to contemporary "civil rights" rhetoric, the majority of Americans are unaware of what remarkable economic strides blacks have made during the past five decades. Whereas the 1959 median income of young black males just out of college was 30 percent below that of their equally educated nonblack peers, by 1969 it was 4 percent *higher* than that of their peers.[57] Similarly, while black male college graduates with more than six years of work experience earned 25 percent less than their white counterparts in 1967, they had closed this gap to 2 percent by 1978.[58] The current median income of black males as a whole, regardless of their education, is about 67 percent as high as the white male median. This rates significantly better than the 59 percent figure of 1970 and the 41 percent figure of 1940.[59] While some readers may consider the 67 percent figure disturbingly low, it is misleading in that it does not compare the earnings of whites and blacks of similar age and ability. Rather, it reflects the earnings of each group *as a whole*. But after controlling for age and I.Q., we find that the average black, full-time worker earns 1 percent *more* than his white counterpart.[60] Correcting further for marital status (since married men of all races earn about 30 percent more than single men of the same age) gives black men substantially higher earnings than white men.[61]

The gains of black women have been no less extraordinary. Whereas in 1946 their median income was only 36 percent that of white women, by 1974 this figure had risen to 98 percent.[62] As early as 1950, black female college graduates earned 91 percent as much as their white counterparts, and by 1960 they were earning 2 percent more than those counterparts.[63] The racial gap in women's incomes then widened considerably, in favor of blacks, during the ensuing decade. By 1970, black women with college degrees were earning fully 25 percent more than white women of the same description, while black female professionals earned 18 percent more than their white equivalents.[64] To this day, college-educated black women earn 10 percent more than similarly educated white women[65]—largely because the former, as a group, have been at their jobs somewhat longer than the latter.[66] Among *all* women of comparable credentials, including non-college graduates, black and white earnings are about the same.[67]

Between 1982 and 1987, the number of black-owned companies in the United States increased by over 30 percent and their business receipts more than doubled.[68] During the ensuing ten years, black-owned business enterprises nearly doubled in number. Between 1972 and 1991, the number of black accountants grew by 479 percent, black lawyers by 280 percent, and black computer-programmers by 343 percent.[69] Between 1950 and 1990, while the black population in America doubled, the number of blacks in white-collar jobs increased more than ninefold.[70] Today there are 18 times as many black lawyers as in 1950, 19 times as many black editors and reporters, and 33 times as many black engineers.[71] Whereas in 1966 fewer than 1 percent of corporate America's managers were black, by 1978 this figure had risen to 3.7 percent, and in 1990 it stood at 5.2 percent.[72] Also as of 1990, fully 32 percent of black men and 59 percent of black women were in white-collar, middle-class occupations—a far cry from the 1940 figures of 5 percent and 6 percent.[73] As of 1993, some 28 percent of all college-educated black men working full time held executive, administrative, or managerial jobs—virtually identical to the 30 percent figure for white men in those same categories.[74] Incidentally, the corresponding figure for Asian Americans aged twenty-five to forty-four was 63 percent.[75]

A 1994 study of family earnings in Queens, New York found that black households had median incomes higher than those of their white neighbors.[76] American-born black couples, for instance, earned about $50,000 per year, slightly more than the $49,900 median of their white counterparts.[77] The disparity was much greater among immigrant couples—with blacks earning about $48,800 annually, and whites $40,500.[78] Stunned by these findings, Dr. Joseph Salvo of the local Planning Department conducted his own analysis of some 200,000 native-born Queens couples and found an even greater gap than the first study—a $49,300 median for black couples, and a $47,500 median for white couples.[79] "Statisticians might argue that both figures really represent a range of several thousand dollars," said a surprised Dr. Salvo, "but it is amazing that they're even close."[80]

In truth, however, it is not amazing at all. At the time of Salvo's study, black household incomes already exceeded those of whites in at least 130 cities and counties across the United States.[81] In 1995 the median yearly income of black families nationwide rose by 3.6 percent, far more than the 2.2 percent gain of white families.[82] Between 1993 and 1996, black family incomes rose by 13.4 percent, while white earnings grew by just 5 percent.[83] In fact, blacks are the only racial or ethnic group whose current, inflation-adjusted income exceeds its 1989 level.[84] Today 41 percent of blacks view themselves as middle class.[85] This is consistent with the fact that about 49 percent of black families now have incomes equalling at least double the poverty line, a remarkable increase over the 1 percent figure of 1940.[86]

Most Americans, of course, are shocked to learn such information, from which they have been dutifully shielded by "civil rights leaders." In their never-ending quest to prove that the United States treats blacks poorly, these crusaders like to point out that the average income of black families nationally is 39 percent lower than the corresponding white average ($25,970 vs. $42,646).[87] Parading such figures before the American public as "evidence" of racism, these deceitful demagogues imply that blacks are paid just 61 percent as much as whites for doing the same work—a suggestion which, not surprisingly, leads us nowhere near the truth. As noted earlier, when we compare the incomes of equivalent black and white subgroups— categorized by such variables as occupation, education, age, I.Q., marital status, and geographic location—we find that blacks do just as well as their white counterparts. It is only when we make no distinctions between these subgroups—and we compare the *overall* incomes of blacks and whites, respectively—that earnings seem to shift heavily in favor of whites. But there are several very logical reasons for this shift, none of which has anything to do with racism.

First, overall black-white income differences are heavily affected by occupational choices. White males, for example, are far more likely than black males to go into such lucrative fields as engineering, science, medicine, dentistry, and law.[88] Obviously, if proportionately more whites than blacks elect, for whatever reasons, to work in high-paying fields, the average earnings of each race are affected by those choices. Racism, however, is not even part of the equation. In fact, as discussed in chapter 9, the recruitment of blacks is a top priority for America's professional schools.

Differences in areas of specialization also account for the fact that black university professors, as a group, earn less than their white colleagues. Yet when "civil rights leaders" cite this income gap as evidence of racism in academia, they fail to note the rather obvious fact that not all professors have commensurate backgrounds or qualifications. Indeed, when we compare the earnings of instructors with equivalent degrees in the same subject areas and from comparable institutions, the black-white income disparity completely disappears—in many fields actually reversing, with blacks earning more than their similarly credentialed white peers.[89] These reversals, it should be noted, are due in part to the fact that black professors are in high demand among schools striving to fulfill their affirmative action quotas.[90] As early as 1973, black professors were already earning about $2,000 more per year than their equally qualified white colleagues.[91]

The relative incomes of blacks and whites are further affected by the educational attainment of each race as a group. Whites, for instance, are nearly twice as likely as blacks to hold college degrees—and thus tend to have greater earning power.[92] Moreover, the extent to which parents of any race value education has a profound effect on their children's success later in life. As early as 1969, black men who had grown up in homes where there were magazines, books, and library cards had incomes identical to those of whites from similar homes and educational backgrounds.[93]

Contributing further to the 61 percent statistic is the fact that our country's black population has a median age of just over twenty-eight—about seven to twelve years younger than the corresponding median of many white ethnic groups.[94] Young people tend to have less work experience, lower incomes, and less accumulated wealth than their elders—regardless of race. For example, families headed by twenty-two-year-olds bring in approximately $5,000 less in annual income than families headed by thirty-year-olds.[95] Similarly, while blacks in their twenties are relatively unlikely to own a home, three-fourths of black married couples aged forty-five to fifty-four are homeowners, as are 81 percent of black couples aged fifty-five to sixty-four.[96] As of 1994, a mere 22 percent of black heads of households were fifty-five or older, as compared to fully 32 percent of their white counterparts.[97] "Civil rights leaders," however, generally do not bother to factor the effects of age into their analysis of American "racism."

Income statistics are further influenced by the fact that 56 percent of black Americans, versus just 34 percent of whites,[98] live in the South, where people of all races earn substantially less than those residing in any other region of the country—about 8 percent below the national average.[99] This does not necessarily mean, of course, that the South's standard of living is especially low, since the *cost* of living there is also comparatively low. As Professor Martin Gross puts it, "Arkansas is not Connecticut."[100] Consider that in 1993 the governor and lieutenant governor of Arkansas earned $33,000 and $29,000, respectively—adequate incomes for residents of that state, where a small family can live reasonably well on such money. By contrast, eastern or midwestern suburbanites and city-dwellers, who must deal with high taxes and a high cost of living, struggle even with incomes significantly higher than these.[101] A Connecticut resident earning $40,000, for example, may have more difficulty paying his bills than a person in Arkansas who makes $30,000, yet raw income statistics alone deceptively suggest that the former is wealthier. Average black incomes, then, are weighted downward by the black population's geographic distribution—as well as by the other variables discussed in this section. As Dr. Walter E. Williams explains, "Income differences can be the result of factors . . . having little or nothing to do with discrimination. Factors racially benign such as age, geography, educational attainment, family size, and personal occupational choice can account for the results we see."[102]

When comparing the incomes of various groups, it is also useful to evaluate the relative knowledge and skills of the people being compared. A recent study of male full-time workers aged twenty-six to thirty-three found that when their education was measured by years of school completed, blacks earned 19 percent less than comparably educated whites. But when the yardstick was how well they performed on tests of verbal and mathematical proficiency, black men earned 9 percent *more* than whites of similar abilities.[103]

A Family Affair

Of all the factors influencing any group's overall income average, none is as important as family stability. Consider that fewer than 46 percent of black American households with children have two parents—a stark contrast to the nearly 80 percent figure for whites.[104] While some 70 percent of black births today are to unwed mothers,[105] the corresponding figures for white, Japanese, and Chinese Americans are 24 percent, 10 percent, and 6.7 percent, respectively.[106] In 1987, for the first time in the history of any American racial or ethnic group, the birth rate for *unmarried* black women surpassed that for *married* black women, and that trend has continued ever since.[107] The black out-of-wedlock birth rates in some inner cities now exceed 80 percent.[108] In Washington, D.C., 97 percent of all babies born to black teens are out of wedlock.[109] Because unmarried teenage mothers—whatever their race—typically have no steady employment, 77 percent of them apply for welfare benefits within five years after giving birth to their first child.[110]

Not surprisingly, such father-absent families—black and white alike—generally occupy the bottom rung of our society's economic ladder.[111] Unwed mothers, regardless of their race, are four times more likely to live in poverty than the average American.[112] Female-headed black families earn only 36 percent as much as two-parent black families, and female-headed white families earn just 46 percent as much as two-parent white families.[113] Not only do unmarried mothers tend to earn relatively little, but their households are obviously limited to a single breadwinner—thus further widening the income gap between one-parent and two-parent families.[114] An astonishing 85 percent of all black children in poverty live in single-parent, mother-child homes.[115] The poverty rate for black children living in *two*-parent families is about 13 percent, scarcely one-fifth the rate of those without fathers.[116] Unfortunately, only one-third of black children now live with both parents.[117] No group can withstand such a calamitous breakdown of its family structure without experiencing devastating social consequences. The absence of marriage and family life is the single most reliable predictor of a self-perpetuating underclass.[118]

The dissolution of the black family has had a profound effect not only on the number of black female welfare recipients, but also on the incomes of black males. Divorced, separated, and single men of all races work 20 percent fewer hours and earn 30 percent less money than married men. The fact that there are proportionately twice as many unmarried black men as unmarried white men has enormous implications for the relative incomes of each race.[119] Yet when we compare the earnings of similarly educated men living in similar family structures, the racial income gap *not only disappears but actually shifts in favor of blacks.*[120]

Plainly, then, most of what "civil rights leaders" recklessly ascribe to racism is in fact a consequence of family breakdown. Consider, for instance, that while white household incomes nationwide rose by 0.8 percent in the 1970s, black household incomes *fell* by 11 percent overall.[121] Though the champions of "justice" impulsively depicted this as evidence of discrimination in the workplace, in reality the black drop-off was due to the unprecedented proliferation of fatherless black families. Greater numbers of unwed, unskilled, poorly educated, jobless black mothers meant more black welfare recipients. And with each new recipient, another low-income "household" was established. It was in *these* homes that virtually all of the decline in black incomes occurred.[122] Meanwhile, the earnings of intact, black husband-and-wife families actually rose four times more quickly than those of comparable white families in the 1970s. And in homes where both spouses worked, black family income increased *five* times more quickly than white family income.[123]

While the overall black poverty rate remains about three times higher than the white poverty rate (26 percent vs. 9 percent),[124] the "face" of black poverty has changed dramatically in recent decades. At one time, almost all black families were poor, regardless of whether one or both parents were present. Today, however, two-parent black families are rarely poor. Consider that in 1959, fully 61 percent of black children from intact families lived below the poverty level. By 1969 this figure had dropped to just 25 percent, and in 1995 it stood at 13 percent.[125] Also in 1995, black married-couple families as a whole earned about 13 percent less than similar white families ($41,307 vs. $47,539).[126] But even this relatively small disparity completely disappears when we take into account the factors discussed in the preceding section: occupational choices, educational attainment, age, geographic location, and comparative skills.[127] Among black families where both the husband and wife work full-time, the current poverty rate is a mere 2 percent.[128]

The clear lesson is that intact families are far more likely to be prosperous than fatherless families, regardless of their race. As social commentator George Gilder explains, "poverty stems mainly from the breakdown of family responsibilities among fathers."[129] "If work effort is the first principle of overcoming poverty," he adds, "marriage is the prime source of upwardly mobile work."[130] Gilder elaborates eloquently on this theme:

> It is love that changes the short horizons of youth and poverty into the long horizons of marriage and career. When marriages fail, the man often returns to the more primitive rhythms of singleness. On the average, his income drops by one-third and he shows a far higher propensity for drink, drugs, and crime. But when marriages in general hold firm and men in general love and support their children, lower-class style changes into middle-class futurity.
>
> The key to the intractable poverty of the hardcore American poor is the dominance of single and separated men in poor communities. Black "unrelated individuals" are not much more likely to be in poverty than white ones. The problem is neither race nor matriarchy in any meaningful sense. It is familial anarchy among the concentrated poor of the inner city, in which flamboyant and impulsive youths rather than responsible men provide the themes of aspiration. The result is that male sexual rhythms tend to prevail, and boys are brought up without authoritative fathers in the home to instill in them the values of responsible paternity: the discipline and love of children and the dependable performance of the provider role. . . . [A] condition of widespread illegitimacy and family breakdown can be a sufficient cause of persistent poverty, separating men from the extended horizons embodied in their children.[131]

National Urban League president Hugh Price concurs that black economic progress—like the economic advancement of any other group—is largely contingent on family solidarity. He observes, for instance, that "[b]lacks blessed with strong family and community support, solid education and social skills, personal drive and a dose of good luck have surged into the social and economic mainstream."[132] "There are three things black parents must persuade their teenagers to do," adds Price. "First, get their high-school diploma. Second, get married before having their first child. Third, hold off on having their first child until after they turn twenty themselves. Only about 8 percent of children raised in households that follow these rules experience poverty. By contrast, 80 percent of youngsters that ignore these rules end up poor."[133]

Articulating a similar theme many years ago, Martin Luther King, Jr. said, "Nothing is so much needed as a secure family life for a people to pull themselves out of poverty."[134] Indeed, without stable families to provide their children with emotional support, physical safety, and ethical codes by which to live, the poor are destined to remain poor—whatever their race. In the absence of families, whites and blacks alike tend to grow up economically and morally deprived. It is not white racism, but the cataclysmic breakdown of the black family, that has created what we call the black underclass—a growing entity whose constituents differ qualitatively from members of the also-growing black middle class.[135] Cleve Freeman, a middle-class black from Los Angeles, describes this cultural divide: "Even though I am black and [was] raised in a tough part of this city, there are two different cultures of black people. They [in the underclass] are operating in a different world. We don't know them."[136]

Children in single-parent households are raised not only with economic, but also social, disadvantages. They are four times as likely as children from intact families to be abused or neglected,[137] much likelier to have trouble academically,[138] and twice as prone to drop out of school.[139] Moreover, growing up without a father is a far better forecaster of a boy's future criminality than either race or poverty.[140] Regardless of race, 70 percent of all young people in state reform institutions were raised in fatherless homes,[141] as were 60 percent of rapists, 72 percent of adolescent murderers, and 70 percent of long-term prison inmates.[142] "Even if white people were to become morally rejuvenated tomorrow," writes Walter E. Williams, "it would do nothing for the problems plaguing a large segment of the black community. Illegitimacy, family breakdown, crime, and fraudulent education are devastating problems, but they are not civil rights problems."[143]

The messiahs of "justice," however, paint a very different picture. Playing their all-purpose trump card, they characterize such problems as nothing more than by-products of white racism. Unfortunately their view, through decades of constant repetition, has won the minds of many black Americans. "Instead of admitting that racism has declined," observes Shelby Steele, "we [blacks] argue all the harder that it is still alive and more insidious than ever. We hold race up to shield us from what we do not want to see in ourselves."[144]

Reverend Jesse Peterson of Los Angeles, who has counseled many black teenagers in youth detention centers, has witnessed firsthand the struggles faced by fatherless youngsters. "When I observed and spoke to those young men," says Peterson, "I could see that truly their need was not for affirmative action, not welfare, not programs, but the crucial need in the lives of those young men was the attention of a father. It was, finally, heartwarming to observe some of the boys . . . who stood and shared the need they felt for a close father figure."[145]

In September 1994 President Clinton, speaking at the National Baptist Convention in Washington, D.C., stated that America's out-of-wedlock birth rate was "a disaster."[146] "I know not everybody's going to be in a stable, traditional family like you see on one of those 1950s sitcoms," he said, "but we'd be better off if more people were. . . . It is wrong. And someone has to say again, it is simply not right. . . . You shouldn't have a baby when you're not married."[147] Notably, some prominent blacks felt insulted by the fact that Mr. Clinton had addressed his remarks to a black audience. "One would expect him to come here and speak of economic stimulus and jobs and economic development," complained Jesse Jackson. "Instead, we're getting moral lessons on how to live."[148] In a similar vein, columnist Carl Rowan was "bothered by a subtle demagogic racism that oozes from their [white politicians'] sermons."[149] "There is always the implication," Rowan said, "that young black women started the sexual looseness."[150] Remarkably, people such as Jackson and Rowan can detect racial insensitivity even in a call for the diminution of out-of-wedlock births. Even while seven of every ten black babies are born to unmarried mothers, these men are offended that any white person would dare call attention to the problem.

A Sense of Perspective

Clearly, the notion that blacks earn only 61 percent as much as comparable whites is one of the colossal myths of our time—simply because it does not compare like with like. That is, it does not consider how income is affected by occupational choice, education, skill, age, geography, and family structure. Nonetheless the statistic is hailed by "civil rights" messiahs as evidence of ongoing discrimination against black Americans. These same "leaders," however, carefully avoid acknowledging that Chinese and Japanese Americans, whose ancestors faced extreme discrimination in this country, have had median incomes significantly higher than those of *whites* for decades.[151] Never is it suggested that the Asian-white income gap reflects pro-Asian, antiwhite societal biases. Shelby Steele observes:

> Asians from various backgrounds—particularly recent immigrants from Southeast Asia—have certainly endured racial discrimination and hostility. Yet, as a group, they have by most measures thrived in America. One of the things this indicates is that, today, race is not the determining variable it once was. I think the difference between black and Asian success turns on the fact that Asians came to this country with values well suited to the challenges and opportunities of freedom. I make this comparison only to underscore the importance of these values, not to inflate Asians or condemn blacks. Nevertheless, our leadership, and black Americans in general, have woefully neglected the power and importance of these values.[152]

Without question, values have a greater effect on social adjustment and economic achievement than does skin color. Black West Indian immigrants, for instance, not only have crime rates dramatically lower than those of American-born blacks living in the very same ghettos, but lower also than those of white Americans.[153] *Second-generation* West Indians in the U.S. are more likely to have professional occupations than either whites or Anglo-Saxons.[154] Foreign-born blacks also possess a remarkable entrepreneurial spirit, as demonstrated by the fact that they own a disproportionately high percentage of the black businesses in their neighborhoods.[155] Not surprisingly, then, their incomes are substantially higher than those of native blacks. As long ago as 1969, when American-born blacks were earning 38 percent less than the average American, the incomes of first-generation West Indian immigrants were within 6 percentage points of the American average. *Second*-generation West Indians, meanwhile, earned 15 percent *more* than the national average.[156] As of 1990, immigrants from Jamaica, Barbados, and Tobago had median household incomes equal to or higher than that of Americans in general.[157]

What accounts for the impressive success of black immigrants in this country? Why are they relatively unaffected by the "societal racism" often cited as a "root cause" of black crime and poverty? Perhaps it is that those immigrants, unlike American-born blacks, have not been saddled with the enormous handicap of growing up in a culture where "civil rights leaders" spend every waking moment trying to convince their flock of society's contempt for blacks. Most Americans, accustomed as they are to hearing the babble of such individuals incessantly denouncing our "racist" nation, would be astonished to learn that *blacks in America have far outperformed blacks in any other society on earth with a substantially black population.*[158] As black Harvard sociologist Orlando Patterson puts it, "America, while still flawed in its race relations . . . is now the least racist white-majority society in the world; has a better record of legal protection of minorities than any other society, white or black; [and] offers more opportunities to a greater number of black persons than any other society, including all of Africa."[159] Even during the dark days of segregation, blacks in the U.S. lived better than their counterparts anywhere else in the world. Consider what Booker T. Washington wrote in 1901:

> [W]hen we rid ourselves of prejudice, or racial feeling, and look facts in the face, we must acknowledge that, notwithstanding the cruelty and moral wrong of slavery, the ten million Negroes inhabiting this country, who themselves or whose ancestors went through the school of American slavery, are in a stronger and more hopeful condition, materially, intellectually, morally, and religiously, than is true of an equal number of black people in any other portion of the globe.[160]

Racial justice in the United States has, of course, progressed far beyond what it was in Washington's day. But black Americans will be unable to realize their full potential until they take the bold step of turning away from those demagogues intent on resurrecting enemies that were vanquished long ago.

The "Legacy of Slavery"

"Civil rights leaders" commonly ascribe the black community's high rates of broken homes and teenage pregnancies to a phenomenon ominously called the "legacy of slavery,"[161] whose underlying assumption is that these pathologies were inflicted on the black race by the transatlantic slave trade. Black scholars Alvin Poussaint, Patricia Williams, and Molefi Asante, to name just a few, trace the currently high rate of out-of-wedlock black births back to slavery.[162] Presumably, the numberless black families torn asunder by slavers, coupled with the horrid degradation suffered by the race as a whole, somehow damaged black people's ability to form and preserve family units.[163] As Daniel Patrick Moynihan expressed it in 1965, "It was by destroying the Negro family that white America broke the will of the Negro people."[164] Three centuries of "injustice," he added, had caused a "tangle of pathology" that had left "deep-seated structural distortions in the life of the Negro American."[165] "In its lasting effects on individuals and their children," Moynihan explained, American slavery was "indescribably worse than any recorded servitude, ancient or modern."[166] Two years earlier, Moynihan and Professor Nathan Glazer had written, "The experience of slavery left as its most serious heritage a steady weakness in the Negro family."[167] "The most rudimentary type of family organization," asserted another writer of the period, "was not permitted to survive [under slavery], to say nothing of the extensions of the family. The mother-child family, with the father either unknown, absent, or, if present, incapable of wielding influence, was the only type of family that could survive."[168] Today, Orlando Patterson laments that "275 years of assault" by white slavers "on the key roles of father and husband . . . messed up the gender relations of African American men and women, and they're still very fragile."[169] The clear consensus, then, has been that enslavement caused the proliferation of the "fatherless matrifocal family."[170]

Though this plausible-sounding theory has gained wide public acceptance, it is utterly discredited by weighty evidence. Throughout the epoch of slavery and into the early decades of the twentieth century—when discrimination was much greater than it is today—most black children grew up in two-parent households. An unmarried teenage girl raising a child alone was rare among blacks.[171] Post-Civil War studies revealed that most black couples in their forties had been together for at least twenty years.[172] In southern urban areas around 1880, nearly three-fourths of black households were husband- or father-present; in southern rural settings, the figure approached 86 percent.[173] During the ensuing half-century, this norm remained essentially unchanged. In 1925 New York City, for example, about 85 percent of kin-related black households were headed by two parents; no more than 8 percent of black females aged twenty-five to forty headed father-absent households; and more than 80 percent of black children under the age of six lived with both parents.[174] In 1940, the black out-of-wedlock birth rate nationwide was 19 percent[175]—a far cry from the current figure of 70 percent. As late as 1950, black women nationwide were more likely to be married than white women, and only 9 percent of black families with children were headed by a single parent. Today that figure exceeds 54 percent.[176] In the 1950s, black children had a 52 percent chance of living with both their biological parents until age seventeen; by the 1980s those odds had dwindled to a mere 6 percent.[177] In 1959, only 2 percent of black children were reared in households in which the mother never married; today that figure approaches 60 percent.[178] Without question something has gone terribly wrong in recent years, but clearly it has nothing to do with slavery. During the nine decades between the Emancipation Proclamation and the 1950s, the black family remained a strong, stable institution. It is intellectually irresponsible to ascribe its current crisis to some residual influence of slavery.

Farewell to Dead Crusades

Today's "civil rights" activists have a paramount interest in convincing the black community that white malice is everywhere. To justify their own continued existence as "leaders," they portray black Americans as a people still suffering under white tyranny and still in need of shepherding along the path toward freedom. Like Jesse Jackson, who in January 1999 spoke to Wall Street business leaders about black Americans' ongoing "struggle" to advance economically,[179] most contemporary activists encourage blacks not only to view themselves as victims, but also to exploit the implied moral superiority conferred by such status. Shelby Steele explains:

The most obvious and inarguable source of black innocence is the victimization that blacks endured for centuries at the hands of a race that insisted on black inferiority. . . . Like all victims, what blacks lost in power they gained in innocence—innocence that, in turn, entitled them to pursue power. This was the innocence that fueled the civil rights movement of the sixties and that gave blacks their first real power in American life—victimization metamorphosed into power via innocence. But this formula carries a drawback that I believe is virtually as devastating to blacks today as victimization once was. It is a formula that binds the victim to his victimization by linking his power to his status as a victim. And this, I'm convinced, is the tragedy of black power in America today. It is primarily a victim's power, grounded too deeply in the entitlement derived from past injustice and in the innocence that Western/Christian tradition has always associated with poverty.[180]

In a similar vein, Steele criticizes "civil rights leadership's" continuing depiction of whites as "exploiters":

In the sixties, blacks and white liberals often engaged in something that might be called the harangue-flagellation ritual. Blacks felt anger, white liberals felt guilt, and when they came together blacks would vent their anger by haranguing the whites, who often allowed themselves to be scourged as a kind of penance. The "official" black purpose of this was to "educate" whites on the issue of race, and in the sixties this purpose may sometimes have been served. But [today], after a marked decline in racism and . . . decades of consciousness-raising, the rite had become both anachronistic and, I think, irresponsible.[181]

In the tradition of the 1960s, many contemporary Americans—black and white alike—gravitate toward activism in order to devote themselves to socially meaningful work. This impulse finds perhaps its most rewarding expression in activities geared toward helping those perceived to be needy. Fighting for the civil rights of the "oppressed" is such an activity, and contemporary crusaders for this cause commonly draw parallels between their own efforts and the epic struggles of those who marched for civil rights three decades ago. Bearing little resemblance to their predecessors, however, these new crusaders are principally concerned with perpetuating the illusion of engagement in a noble mission—refusing to acknowledge that the battle has largely been won. Consider, for example, the August 28, 1993 gathering of 75,000 people in our nation's capital to commemorate the thirtieth anniversary of the March on Washington where Martin Luther King, Jr. delivered his immortal "I Have a Dream" speech. Exhorting those in attendance to help "rekindle" Dr. King's dream,[182] the memorial's guest speakers lamented that blacks had made little enduring progress—either socially or economically—in the years since King's address. The listeners roared in agreement, resolving to carry the torch of social activism in hopes that one day they might at last be "free." In response, Emanuel McLittle wrote in *Destiny* magazine: "We [blacks] have gone beyond what we could not even imagine in 1963, and still we march . . . looking for that thrill again and again. . . . To be sure, we [should support] any effort that will improve the lot of any American. But getting special permits to block cars, trucks and trains which are busy with commerce, so that a large moving picnic with placards can reaffirm [its] usefulness is approaching the realm of absurdity."[183]

On Martin Luther King Day 1995, Dexter Scott King, son of the slain civil rights leader, expressed his own desire to share in the glory of his father's cause. "My father delivered political freedom," he told a church congregation in Atlanta. "I'm calling home all those freedom fighters who marched with my father. Dexter Scott King is going to be there with you this time, and we will make it to the promised land."[184] That same day, Jesse Jackson urged blacks to honor Dr. King's legacy through protests, boycotts, and marches. "Today the King dream is under threat," he warned parishioners in a Harlem church.[185]

People like Dexter King and Jesse Jackson seem not to have noticed that by the mid-1960s, many of the civil rights movement's legitimate objectives had been codified as law and accepted by most of society. Indeed, after the Voting Rights Act of 1965 was ratified, Martin Luther King, Jr. himself declared, "There is no more civil rights movement."[186] Other prominent blacks, unfortunately, were reluctant to let go of the once-honorable endeavor that had become the centerpiece of their lives. Instead they clung to it ever more tightly—and in the process crushed the moral foundation that had been its very source of power. As Thomas Sowell puts it, they decided that they "needed new missions—and they found them."[187] These "leaders," Sowell adds, are people "whose own employment and visibility depend upon maintaining an adequate flow of injustices. . . . They [continue] to call themselves 'civil rights' organizations and the media have largely repeated that designation. In reality, the crusade for civil rights ended years ago. The scramble for special privileges, for turf, and for image is what continues on today under that banner and with that rhetoric."[188]

Shelby Steele sees modern-day "civil rights leaders" in much the same light, observing that they indiscriminately "whine" and "complain" not because they seek redress "but because [they] seek the status of victim[s]."[189] "The barriers to black progress in America today," he adds, "are clearly as much psychological as they are social or economic. . . . But we haven't fully admitted this to ourselves."[190] He then sets forth what he believes black "leadership" should communicate to African Americans:

> There will be no end to despair and no lasting solution to any of our problems until we rely on individual effort within the American mainstream—rather than collective action against the mainstream—as our means of advancement. . . . [The] reality that I and many other blacks have discovered [is] that there is today, despite America's residual racism, an enormous range of opportunity open to blacks in this society.
>
> I believe black leadership must make this nexus its primary focus. They must preach it, tell it, sell it, and demand it. Our leadership has looked at government and white society very critically. Now they must help us look at ourselves. We need our real problems named and explained; otherwise, we have no chance to overcome them. Their impulse is to be "political," to keep the larger society on edge, to keep them feeling as though they have not done enough for blacks. . . . But the price they pay for this form of "politics" is to keep blacks focused on an illusion of deliverance by others, and no illusion weakens us more. Our leaders must take a risk. They must tell us the truth, tell us of the freedom and opportunity they have discovered in their own lives. They must tell us what they tell their own children when they go home at night: to study hard, pursue their dreams with discipline and effort, to be responsible for themselves, to have concern for others, to cherish their race and at the same time make their own lives as Americans. When our leaders put a spotlight on our victimization and seize upon our suffering to gain us ineffectual concessions, they inadvertently turn themselves into enemies of the truth, not to mention enemies of their own people.[191]

Critics of such viewpoints commonly accuse black conservatives like Steele of naively believing that white racism has been entirely eradicated. Dr. Walter E. Williams effectively responds to those detractors:

> Saying that the civil rights struggle is over and won is not the same as saying that all vestiges of discrimination are gone. It is to say that codified and rampant discrimination is a thing of the past. . . .
>
> Most of the social pathology that characterizes a large percentage of the black community is entirely new in our history. At a time when there was far greater racial discrimination, and far fewer prospects for upward mobility, blacks who graduated from high school had a higher achievement level, black neighborhoods were safer, there was greater family stability, and illegitimacy was a tiny fraction of what it is today. If, as so many "experts" claim, discrimination and a legacy of slavery explain what we see today, a natural question to ask [is], "How come those conditions were not worse at a time when racial discrimination was rampant and codified?"[192]

Like Williams and Steele, black talk-radio host Ken Hamblin denounces what he calls the "blame whitey"[193] mentality that is crippling the black community:

> We are teaching black kids that they are victims—the only victims—and that everything that goes wrong in life is part of some racist conspiracy. We are teaching them to be hostile, and it's leading to a kind of xenophobia. . . . I want to know why 60 percent [actually over 70 percent] of black babies are being born out of wedlock. Is that the fault of white people? I want to know why so many black kids can't speak proper English. I want to know why black people can't pass a civil service examination. The excuse is it's culturally biased. Well, I'd like to know what could possibly be culturally biased on a test for a firefighter.
>
> Let's get serious. White people don't have time to sit around trying to figure out ways to hurt black people. They're too busy trying to pay the bills, raise their families, straighten the kids' teeth— just like most black families.
>
> [W]e have focused on the failures, catered to them, rather than looked at the successes. And we've gotten so ridiculously hypersensitive about anything at all that might be construed as racist. We have no sense of humor anymore.[194]

Supreme Court Justice Clarence Thomas is another African American who rejects the "civil rights" establishment's contention that black skin is a shroud of oppression. Opposing racial preferences and extolling the virtue of hard work, he accepts no rationalizations that blame either society or economic hardship for any individual's moral depravity. "I had never heard any excuses made," he says. "Nor had I seen my role models take comfort in excuses."[195]

Such attitudes have won Thomas no friends among mainstream black pundits, many of whom dismiss him outright as an "inauthentic" black. Political scientist Manning Marable, for instance, asserts that "ethnically, Thomas has ceased to be an African American."[196] Movie director Spike Lee calls Thomas "a handkerchief-head, chicken-and-biscuit eating Uncle Tom,"[197] while author June Jordan characterizes him as a "virulent Oreo phenomenon," a "punk-ass," and an "Uncle Tom calamity."[198] Because these sentiments permeated the black community from the moment Thomas was nominated to the Supreme Court in 1991, his appointment was vigorously opposed by black liberals and "civil rights" organizations nationwide. The late Haywood Burns, who was dean of a New York law school and chairman emeritus of the National Conference of Black Lawyers, called Thomas a "counterfeit hero" whose ideals had "crushed or forever deferred" the dreams of millions of blacks.[199] Columnist Julianne Malveaux, meanwhile, told a television audience, "I hope [Thomas's] wife feeds him lots of eggs and butter and he dies early, like many black men do, of heart disease.... He is an absolutely reprehensible person."[200] From the podium of the NAACP's 1995 convention, Thomas was denounced as a "pimp" and a "traitor."[201] With comparable contempt, the Reverend Joseph Lowery of the Southern Christian Leadership Conference says, "I have told [Justice Thomas] I am ashamed of him, because he is becoming to the black community what Benedict Arnold was to the nation he deserted; and what Judas Iscariot was to Jesus: a *traitor*; and what Brutus was to Caesar: an *assassin*!"[202]

Missouri Democrat William Clay labels Thomas and other black conservatives "Negro wanderers" whose goal is to "maim and kill other blacks for the gratification and entertainment of ultraconservative white racists."[203] Similarly, Mr. Clay describes black conservative Gary Franks as a "Negro Dr. Kevorkian, a pariah" who exhibits a "foot-shuffling, head-scratching brand of Uncle Tomism."[204] Former NAACP executive director Benjamin Hooks denounces black conservatives as "a new breed of Uncle Tom ... some of the biggest liars the world ever saw."[205] Afrocentric historian John Henrik Clarke calls them "frustrated slaves crawling back to the plantation."[206] Khalid Abdul Muhammad puts it still more bluntly: "When white folks can't defeat you, they'll always find some Negro, some boot-licking, butt-licking, bamboozled, half-baked, half-fried, sissified, punkified, pasteurized, homogenized Nigger that they can trot out in front of you."[207]

Clearly, mainstream black "leadership" is utterly intolerant of African Americans with dissenting views. Consider, as another example, that the Congressional Black Caucus's thirty-nine liberal Democratic members voted in 1993 to ostracize Gary Franks, the group's lone conservative. A spokesman for Franks observed that CBC members "seem to have this misplaced notion that all blacks in America are liberal Democrats, which makes you wonder why that isn't seen as a racist or stereotyping view of blacks. . . . [Some people say] certain blacks are not authentic blacks, and they seem to think if you're not a liberal Democrat, you're not a true black."[208] In a similar vein, in July 1998 Clarence Thomas publicly responded to his critics when addressing the National Bar Association, our country's largest group of black lawyers.[209] "Long gone is a time," he observed, "when we [blacks] opposed the notion that we all looked alike and talked alike. Somehow we have come to exalt the new black stereotype above all and demand conformity to that norm. . . . I have come here today . . . to assert my right to think for myself, to refuse to have my ideas assigned to me as though I was an intellectual slave because I'm black."[210]

Conformity of thought—so compatible with the contemporary "civil rights" movement's socialistic ideals—is clearly "the spirit of unity" that former NAACP head Benjamin Chavis covets.[211] Indeed, it is hardly surprising that Chavis was once the titular head of the Communist Party USA's legal arm.[212] "People with different points of view," declares Jesse Jackson, "can still have unity on racial issues."[213] But such "unity," based only on skin color, is in fact the most divisive force in our nation today. It was this very "unity" that allowed a charlatan like Al Sharpton to win 70 percent of the black vote in a recent New York Senate primary.[214] Sharpton's fellow frauds, of course, see nothing wrong with this. Jesse Jackson and current NAACP president Kweisi Mfume, for instance, enthusiastically supported Sharpton during his 1997 run for New York City mayor.[215] Jackson went so far as to casually dismiss the role Sharpton had played in the Tawana Brawley charade a decade earlier (see chapter 7) as nothing more than a youthful "mistake." He not only praised Sharpton for his new "mature and non-divisive" political style,[216] but hailed his mayoral campaign as a "mission about life and hope and healing."[217]

The core message of today's "civil rights leadership" is that our "racist" country deserves the black community's contempt. Symptomatic of this view was Ben Chavis's 1994 attempt to bring into the NAACP's fold a number of prominent black militants. Among those recruited were Alton Maddox (the attorney best known for his role in the Tawana Brawley hoax), Al Sharpton (well known for his role in many hoaxes), Maulana Karenga (the head of a radical nationalist group), Angela Davis (the communist who participated in a 1970 hostage-taking in which four people were killed), the Reverend Calvin Butts (who "sees" white racism virtually everywhere), and Professor Cornel West (who has called the 1992 Los Angeles riots a "display of justified social rage" against a "racist patriarchal nation").[218] Conspicuously uninvited were people who do not trace all black problems to the doorstep of whites.

Chavis's pursuit of such individuals as Maddox, Sharpton, Karenga, Davis, Butts, and West clearly signals the NAACP leadership's profound philosophical shift of recent decades. But even more troubling is the moral rot that has set into this once-noble organization, whose leaders are now quite willing to favor big donors over honorable men and women. In earlier decades, the NAACP fought many difficult and vital battles to pass anti-lynching legislation, to ensure voting rights for southern blacks, to abolish racial discrimination from the criminal-justice system, to allow blacks equitable access to public education, to desegregate public facilities, and to guarantee equal employment opportunity for all, regardless of race.[219] But today this same organization embraces affirmative action, gerrymandering, and a host of other policies designed not to help create a color-*blind* society, but a color-*conscious* one. In 1993, with great fanfare, the NAACP entered into a "sacred covenant" with the Nation of Islam and granted the infamous racist Louis Farrakhan a lifetime membership. In July 1997 the notoriously corrupt boxing promoter Don King, who once stomped a man to death in a dispute over a gambling debt, received the NAACP's coveted President's Award.[220] Checkered though his past was, King's many large donations to black organizations apparently rendered his sins irrelevant to the "civil rights" crowd.

About eighteen months later, shortly after the 1998 elections, NAACP president Kweisi Mfume asked his organization's members to send him money for the express purpose of helping future Democratic candidates oust key Republicans from political office. "We [already] helped defeat anti-rights incumbent senators in New York and North Carolina," he boasted, "and helped pick up five Democratic seats in the House."[221] Clearly this was a trend Mfume hoped would continue. But by its own written policy, the NAACP is chartered to be a nonpartisan entity that—like other tax-exempt groups—neither endorses nor opposes particular political candidates.[222] Such details, however, did not concern Mfume at all.

In short, the NAACP is but a shell its former self, having degenerated into little more than a bastion of black racism. Thomas Sowell observes:

> Once the NAACP stood on the frontiers of the fight for human rights, on behalf of the most despised victims of intolerance. This took real courage, not rhetorical bravado, at a time when bombings and lynchings were the weapons of their enemies, and when many paid with their lives for standing up for what was right. But even monuments can become overgrown by weeds, splattered by bird-droppings and corroded by the elements. Even a great crusade can degenerate into a hustle.[223]

Along the same lines, black columnist Michael Meyers calls the NAACP "an organization with thousands of chapters, but no vision and no direction except that of racial primitivism."[224]

The Illusion of Pride

While "civil rights leaders" have effectively taught the black community that racial pride is a trait well worth cultivating, their version of pride is often rooted in a never-ending contempt for whites— ostensibly in retribution for past and present white sins. It has spawned such things as Afrocentric education and exclusively black political groups, social organizations, college dormitories, student unions, school graduation ceremonies, beauty pageants, and news programs. Protests, marches, and even riots have resulted from a million perceived affronts to that pride. Few modern-day activists understand that *genuine* pride is not so quick to take offense; that it is a quiet affair which neither blusters, brags, nor intimidates; that it does not spend every waking moment militantly searching for those who would cast aspersions upon it. Far removed from vainglory, true pride is founded on one's knowledge that he is not spiritually elevated in proportion to the number of grievances he can recite; that the sinfulness of others does not improve him; and that injustices committed against his ancestors do not make him just. Rather than racial "pride," then, a far worthier goal might be racial humility.

Conclusion

Without a doubt, white racism continues to exist and always will exist to some degree in America, for ours is a nation of people, not angels. We are reminded of this by such gruesome incidents as the 1998 killing of James Byrd, a black Texan who was chained to the back of a pickup truck and dragged to his death by three openly racist white men.[225] But contrary to the claims of the "civil rights" cabal, not only is such white-on-black violence remarkably rare in contemporary America, but it draws the harsh condemnation of virtually all whites when it does occur. Long gone are the days when whites were relatively untroubled by antiblack atrocities; when blacks, particularly in the South, had more to fear from an excursion into a white neighborhood than into a black one; and when most whites opposed equal rights for blacks.[226] It is time for Americans of all colors to awaken from the hypnotic trance induced by our nation's demagogues, and to acknowledge the profound attitudinal transformation that whites in this country have undergone during the past several decades. Without such an awakening, blacks will continue to view whites through a warped historical lens that distorts, rather than clarifies, reality. Contemplate the following facts, a number of which are also discussed in the first chapter:

• In the 1930s and 1940s, only 40 percent of white Americans favored integrated schools.[227] As of 1956 the figure was up to 49 percent,[228] by the early 1970s it stood at 84 percent,[229] and today it exceeds 90 percent.[230]

• Whereas half a century ago slightly fewer than 50 percent of whites favored integrated public transportation and accommodations, the corresponding proportion today is over 90 percent.[231]

• Five to six decades ago, about 58 percent of whites supported antiblack employment discrimination.[232] By 1963 that figure had shrunk to about 17 percent,[233] by 1972 it was 3 percent,[234] and today it is virtually zero.[235]

• Before the middle of the twentieth century, more than half of all whites believed that blacks were inherently less intelligent than whites.[236] By 1956 the proportion of those believing this had dwindled to just 23 percent,[237] by the early 1970s they were scarcely 20 percent,[238] and today they are in the neighborhood of 6 percent.[239]

• In 1958 only 4 percent of whites approved of interracial marriages,[240] whereas today about 61 percent accept such unions.[241]

• In 1939 just 19 percent of East coast whites thought that blacks "should be allowed to live wherever they want to live" without laws or social pressures to dissuade them. Among midwestern whites, the figure was 12 percent.[242] By 1956, however, about half of whites nationwide said they would have no objection to a black of the same social class moving into their block,[243] and by the early 1970s this figure was up to about 85 percent.[244] While whites remain strongly opposed to living in impoverished and deteriorating neighborhoods with significant black populations, white aversion to integration with blacks of the same social class has disappeared almost entirely.[245] In other words, the impulse to avoid integration is much more a matter of class than of race, as evidenced by the fact that middle-class blacks are just as unwilling as whites to live in dangerous black neighborhoods.[246]

• In 1957 fewer than four in ten whites said they would consider voting for a black presidential candidate[247]—a far cry from today's 93 percent figure.[248]

Contemporary America is a very different place than it was several decades ago. Unfortunately, the champions of "justice"—in their zeal to stay in business—have ignored these profound changes and have persisted in portraying our country as a racist snakepit. Consequently, many blacks continue to view white racism as their principal obstacle in life. In a 1989 ABC/*Washington Post* survey, 26 percent of blacks professed to believe that *most* whites shared the racist views of the Ku Klux Klan; another 25 percent of blacks felt that *at least one-fourth* of whites harbored those attitudes.[249] Between 1983 and 1994, the proportion of blacks who thought that "most white people" wanted to see them "get a better break" fell from 33 percent to 25 percent. Meanwhile, the fraction who believed that most whites either wanted to "keep blacks down" or did not care either way rose from one-half to two-thirds.[250] A 1992 Anti-Defamation League poll found that some 68 percent of blacks saw "about half" of white Americans as "basically prejudiced."[251] Clearly, there is a gaping gulf between contemporary white racial attitudes and black beliefs about those attitudes.

The harm that such misconceptions do to race relations is exacerbated by the many white elected officials who, for fear of being called racists, lack the courage to differentiate agents of truth from the intellectually bankrupt opportunists now dominating the "civil rights" establishment. Consider, for example, that Bill Clinton actually praised Al Sharpton's "character" during a 1997 political rally in New York.[252] Similarly, when Clinton selected Maxine Waters to be his administration's urban affairs advisor,[253] he tacitly endorsed Waters's widely recognized view that black Americans *ought* to be angry at white society.[254] The president conveyed the same message by appointing Benjamin Chavis to the 1993 transition team that helped the new White House staff commence its tenure in Washington.[255] Chavis, of course, would soon thereafter display his low regard for white people by announcing his "sacred covenant" with Louis Farrakhan.[256] Indeed, Chavis has consistently embraced those who hold the United States in contempt; those who openly celebrate their "black rage"; those who, like the gang members he recruited into the NAACP, have devastated countless American communities. How regrettable it is that our president's understanding of what constitutes black leadership led him to pander to individuals as unworthy as Sharpton, Waters, and Chavis.

To Mr. Clinton, interracial friction is largely the fault of whites—as evidenced by his 1997 appointments to the Advisory Board on Race and Reconciliation, a seven-member panel consisting solely of individuals who favored affirmative action and traced most black problems to white bigotry. Though the president's stated purpose for forming the panel was to stimulate a "national dialogue" on racial issues, the group in fact produced nothing more than a protracted ideological monologue. As panel chairman and retired Duke University professor John Hope Franklin candidly said, "The white side has been in control of virtually everything, so they're the ones who need educating on what justice and equality mean."[257] "This country," he added, "cut its eyeteeth on racism with black-white relations."[258] "I don't think a conversation on race can take place," Franklin elaborated, "without a discussion of the development and perfection of the doctrine of racial superiority that was more carefully and more successfully projected after slavery than during slavery. It was after slavery that you get some of the most barbaric manifestations of hate and of the sense of white superiority. I think in part [that happened] because whites are poor losers. This country has never confronted its own holocaust, its own violence."[259] When asked whether it would have been useful to include on the panel Ward Connerly, who had led the 1996 fight to end affirmative action in California, Franklin said, with annoyance, that Connerly had "nothing to contribute" to the mix.[260] In his 1993 book *The Color Line*, Franklin stated that opposition to affirmative action was a racist ploy.[261]

Another panel member, Angela Oh, was perhaps best known for her passionate defense of the 1992 Los Angeles rioters. "The people I saw running into the markets," she said at the time, "were stealing basics—diapers, food, dish racks. These were not luxury items that they were taking."[262] Alongside Oh on the panel was former Mississippi governor William Winter, who contends that black Americans are actually losing ground socially and economically. "The twin goals of achieving racial equality and the elimination of racial prejudice," he says, "continue to recede before all the advances we have made."[263]

Perhaps America's most audible ideological monologue flows from the garrulous tongue of Louis Farrakhan, the preeminent "civil rights leader" of our day, who devotes considerable energy to denouncing the United States as a nation that oppresses blacks. Oppression elsewhere in the world, however, seems not to trouble him. Indeed, early in 1996 Farrakhan went on a "World Friendship Tour" during which he exchanged pleasantries with government leaders in Iran, Iraq, Libya, Syria, and Sudan—five of the most politically oppressive nations on earth, and all of which are on the State Department's list of nations that support terrorism.[264] In 1997 he again visited these countries and embraced the tyrants ruling them. Whatever Farrakhan's highest ideals may be, they clearly have nothing to do with either justice or freedom. In this respect, he is no different from others in the mainstream "civil rights" establishment.

In his historic 1963 "I Have a Dream" speech, Martin Luther King, Jr. prophetically warned against the antiwhite rhetoric that has dominated the "civil rights" orthodoxy of the past quarter-century. Looking out at his vast audience, much of which was comprised of whites,[265] Dr. King said, "Let us not seek to satisfy our thirst for freedom by drinking from the cup of bitterness and hatred. The marvelous new militancy which has engulfed the Negro community must not lead us to a distrust of all white people, for many of our white brothers, as evidenced by their presence here today, have come to realize that their destiny is tied up with our destiny and that their freedom is inextricably bound to our freedom. We cannot walk alone."[266] It is only by embracing such wisdom, rather than the fashionable lies of our day, that *all* Americans can at long last bury the myths that now poison black-white relations in our country.

Notes

Chapter 1
The Myths That Divide Us

1. Samuel Johnson, from James Boswell's *The Life of Samuel Johnson*, April 3, 1776. See Bergen Evans, arr., *Dictionary of Quotations* (New York: Delacorte Press, 1968), p. 54.

2. Stephan Thernstrom and Abigail Thernstrom, *America in Black and White* (New York: Simon & Schuster, 1997), pp. 25, 31, 40, 41, 42, 43.

3. James P. Smith, "Poverty and the Family," in Gary Sandefur and Marta Tienda, eds., *Divided Opportunities: Minorities, Poverty, and Social Policy* (New York: Plenum Press, 1988), p. 142.

4. Gunnar Myrdal, *An American Dilemma* (New York: Harper & Row, 1944), p. 365.

5. Robert Higgs, "Black Progress and the Persistence of Racial Economic Inequalities, 1865-1940," in Steven Shulman and William Darity, Jr., eds., *The Question of Discrimination: Racial Inequality in the U.S. Labor Market* (Middletown, Conn.: Wesleyan University Press, 1989), p. 36.

6. Thernstrom, *America in Black and White*, p. 34.

7. *Ibid.*, p. 30.

8. Steven F. Lawson, *Black Ballots: Voting Rights in the South, 1944-1969* (New York: Columbia University Press, 1976), p. 15.

9. Thernstrom, *America in Black and White*, p. 152.

10. Dinesh D'Souza, *The End of Racism* (New York: The Free Press, 1995), p. 176.

11. *Ibid.*, p. 175.

12. Thernstrom, *America in Black and White*, pp. 47-48.

13. *Ibid.*, p. 47.

14. Gunnar Myrdal, *An American Dilemma*, p. 543. Charles S. Johnson, *Patterns of Negro Segregation* (New York: Harper & Brothers, 1943), pp. 18-19. Thernstrom, *America in Black and White*, pp. 47-48.

15. Thernstrom, *America in Black and White*, pp. 48-50.

16. *Ibid.*, p. 178.

17. Dinesh D'Souza, *The End of Racism*, p. 178.

18. *Ibid.*, pp. 170-172.

19. *Ibid.*, p. 179.

20. Eric Foner and John A. Garraty, eds., *The Reader's Companion to*

American History (Boston: Houghton Mifflin Company, 1991), p. 844.

21. Thernstrom, *America in Black and White*, p. 55.

22. *Ibid.*, p. 56. St. Clair Drake and Horace R. Cayton, *Black Metropolis: A Study of Negro Life in a Northern City* (New York: Harcourt Brace, 1945), pp. 99-100.

23. Thernstrom, *America in Black and White*, p. 178.

24. *Ibid.*, p. 56.

25. *Ibid.*, pp. 53, 178.

26. *Ibid.*, p. 56.

27. Gunnar Myrdal, *An American Dilemma*, pp. 529-530.

28. Thernstrom, *America in Black and White*, p. 61.

29. *Ibid.*, p. 62.

30. *Ibid.*, p. 54.

31. *Ibid.* U.S. Bureau of the Census, "Current Population Reports, Special Studies," P-23, *The Social and Economic Status of the Black Population in the United States: An Historical View, 1790-1978* (Washington, D.C.: U.S. Government Printing Office, 1979), p. 15.

32. Thernstrom, *America in Black and White*, p. 55.

33. U.S. Bureau of the Census, *Historical Statistics of the United States: Colonial Times to 1970* (Washington, D.C.: U.S. Government Printing Office, 1975), pp. 131, 1140.

34. Stanley Lebergott, *Manpower in Economic Growth: The United States Record Since 1800* (New York: McGraw-Hill, 1964), p. 512. Thernstrom, *America in Black and White*, p. 77.

35. Thernstrom, *America in Black and White*, pp. 65, 79.

36. *Ibid.*, p. 69.

37. *Ibid.*, p. 81.

38. U.S. Bureau of the Census, "Current Population Reports, Special Studies," P-23-80, *The Social and Economic Status of the Black Population in the United States: An Historical View, 1790-1978*, pp. 13-14.

39. Thernstrom, *America in Black and White*, pp. 69-70.

40. *Ibid.*, p. 77.

41. Lerone Bennett, Jr., *The Shaping of Black America* (New York: Penguin Books, 1993), p. 273. Hugh Davis Graham, *The Civil Rights Era: Origins and Development of National Policy* (New York: Oxford University Press, 1990), pp. 10-11.

42. Dinesh D'Souza, *The End of Racism*, p. 191.

43. James L. Sundquist, *Politics and Policy: The Eisenhower, Kennedy, and Johnson Years* (Washington, D.C.: Brookings Institution, 1968), pp. 515-518.

44. Michael Sovern, *Legal Restraints on Racial Discrimination in Employment* (New York: Columbia University Press, 1966), pp. 10-17. Hugh Davis Graham, *The Civil Rights Era: Origins and Development of National Policy*, pp. 9-14.

45. U.S. Bureau of the Census, *Historical Statistics of the United States: Colonial Times to 1970*, pp. 55-56, 303, 370. Dinesh D'Souza, *The End of Racism*, pp. 192, 614.

46. Thernstrom, *America in Black and White*, p. 79.

47. *Ibid.*, p. 81.

48. *Ibid.*, pp. 81-82.

49. Gerald David Jaynes and Robin M. Williams, Jr., eds., *A Common Destiny: Blacks and American Society* (Washington, D.C.: National Research Council, National Academy Press, 1989), p. 295.

50. James P. Smith and Finis R. Welch, "Black Economic Progress After Myrdal," *Journal of Economic Literature* 17 (June 1989), p. 544.

51. Gerald David Jaynes and Robin M. Williams, Jr., eds., *A Common Destiny: Blacks and American Society*, p. 295.

52. James P. Smith and Finis R. Welch, "Closing the Gap: Forty Years of Economic Progress for Blacks" (Santa Monica, Calif.: The Rand Corporation, 1986), p. 104.

53. Thernstrom, *America in Black and White*, p. 83.

54. *Ibid.*, pp. 82-83.

55. *Ibid.*, p. 82.

56. *Ibid.*, p. 70.

57. Dinesh D'Souza, *The End of Racism*, p. 191.

58. Robert W. Mullen, *Blacks in America's Wars* (New York: Monad Press, 1973), pp. 60-61.

59. Dinesh D'Souza, *The End of Racism*, p. 191.

60. William G. Mayer, *The Changing American Mind: How and Why American Public Opinion Changed Between 1960 and 1988* (Ann Arbor: University of Michigan Press, 1993), p. 366. Paul B. Sheatsley, "White Attitudes Toward the Negro," *Daedalus* (Winter 1966), pp. 219, 222.

61. *Ibid.*

62. *Ibid.*

63. Thernstrom, *America in Black and White*, p. 104.

64. William G. Mayer, *The Changing American Mind: How and Why American Public Opinion Changed Between 1960 and 1988*, p. 366. Paul B. Sheatsley, "White Attitudes Toward the Negro," *Daedalus* (Winter 1966), pp. 219, 222.

65. Thernstrom, *America in Black and White*, p. 150.

66. *Ibid.*, pp. 107-110.

67. Catherine A. Barnes, *Journey from Jim Crow: The Desegregation of Southern Transit* (New York: Columbia University Press, 1981), p. 242.

68. Martin Luther King, Jr., *Stride Toward Freedom: The Montgomery Story* (New York: Harper & Row, 1958), pp. 80-81.

69. Thernstrom, *America in Black and White*, p. 111.

70. Martin Luther King, Jr., *Stride Toward Freedom: The Montgomery Story*, p. 190.

71. Gerald N. Rosenberg, *The Hollow Hope: Can Courts Bring About Social Change?* (Chicago: University of Chicago Press, 1991), pp. 114-115.

72. Thernstrom, *America in Black and White*, p. 113.

73. David R. Goldfield, *Black, White, and Southern: Race Relations and*

Southern Culture, 1940 to the Present (Baton Rouge: Louisiana State University Press, 1990), p. 120. Gerald N. Rosenberg, *The Hollow Hope: Can Courts Bring About Social Change?*, p. 134.

74. Thernstrom, *America in Black and White*, p. 135.

75. James L. Sundquist, *Politics and Policy: The Eisenhower, Kennedy, and Johnson Years*, p. 260.

76. Taylor Branch, *Parting the Waters: America in the King Years, 1954-1963* (New York: Simon & Schuster, 1988), p. 825.

77. Thernstrom, *America in Black and White*, p. 136.

78. *Ibid.*, p. 114.

79. Dinesh D'Souza, *The End of Racism*, p. 253.

80. Steven A. Holmes, "A Rose-Colored View on Race," *The New York Times* (June 15, 1997).

81. Dinesh D'Souza, *The End of Racism*, p. 165.

82. Andrew Kull, *The Color-Blind Constitution* (Cambridge: Harvard University Press, 1992), p. 183.

83. William J. Bennett, *The De-Valuing of America* (New York: Summit Books, 1992), p. 191.

84. *Ibid.*

85. Charles Lawrence, "The Id, the Ego and Equal Protection: Reckoning with Unconscious Racism," *Stanford Law Review* 49 (1987), pp. 317, 326.

86. Patricia Williams, *The Alchemy of Race and Rights* (Cambridge: Harvard University Press, 1980), pp. 49, 101, 120.

87. Roy Brooks, *Rethinking the American Race Problem* (Berkeley: University of California Press, 1990), pp. 89, 165-166.

88. Bernard Boxill, *Blacks and Social Justice* (Lanham, Maryland: Rowman and Littlefield, 1992), p. 11.

89. William Allen, Drew Days, Benjamin Hooks, and William Bradford Reynolds, "Affirmative Action and the Constitution," seminar at American Enterprise Institute, Washington, D.C. (May 21, 1985), p. 3. Cited by Dinesh D'Souza, *The End of Racism*, p. 164.

90. Statement of Commissioners Blandina Ramirez and Mary Frances Berry, *Toward an Understanding of Stotts*, U.S. Commission on Civil Rights (January 1985). Cited by Dinesh D'Souza, *The End of Racism*, p. 165.

91. Dinesh D'Souza, *The End of Racism*, p. 167.

92. Jim Sleeper, "The Decline and Rise of Bigotry," *Cosmopolitan* (June 1994), p. 208.

93. Rochelle Stanfield, "The Split Society," *National Journal* (April 2, 1994), p. 764.

94. Michael Meyers, "A King Day Snubfest," *New York Post* (January 20, 1998), p. 29.

95. Plato, *The Republic*, translated by Francis MacDonald Cornford (New York and London: Oxford University Press, 1966), Chapter 9, section titled, "Cen-

sorship of Literature for School Use," pp. 69-70. This translation was originally published in England in 1941.

96. E.L. Thornbrough, ed., *Booker T. Washington* (Englewood Cliffs, NJ: Prentice Hall, 1969), p. 57.

Chapter 2
A Racist Nation

1. Thomas Paine, Introduction to *Common Sense* (1776).

2. Derrick Bell, *Faces at the Bottom of the Well* (New York: Basic Books, 1992), p. 3.

3. Dinesh D'Souza, *The End of Racism*, p. 17.

4. Derrick Bell, *Faces at the Bottom of the Well*, pp. 21, 12.

5. *Ibid.*, p. 4.

6. *Ibid.*, p. 12.

7. *Ibid.*, p. 113.

8. *Ibid.*, p. 12.

9. *Ibid.*, p. 152.

10. *Ibid.*, p. 155.

11. *Ibid.*, p. 10.

12. Lino Graglia, "Affirmative Discrimination," *National Review* (July 5, 1993), p. 30. This essay was adapted from a chapter in *The Imperiled Academy*, ed. Howard Dickman (New Jersey: Transaction Press, 1993).

13. Robert Boynton, "Professor Bell, Sage of Black Rage," *New York Observer* (October 10, 1994), p. 1.

14. Jacques Steinberg, "CUNY Professor Criticizes Jews," *The New York Times* (August 6, 1991), p. B3.

15. Alessandra Stanley, "City College Professor Assailed for Remarks on Jews," *The New York Times* (August 7, 1991), p. B4.

16. Jaques Steinberg, "CUNY Professor Criticizes Jews," *The New York Times* (August 6, 1991), p. B3.

17. Alessandra Stanley, "City College Professor Assailed for Remarks on Jews," *The New York Times* (August 7, 1991), p. B4.

18. "Anti-Defamation League: Tatum's a Force for Evil," *New York Post* (March 16, 1993), p. 8.

19. Steven Yates, *Civil Wrongs* (San Francisco: Institute for Contemporary Studies, 1994), p. 77.

20. Dennis Prager, audiotape titled "Multiculturalism and the War Against Western Values," (Culver City, California: *Ultimate Issues*, October 7, 1991).

21. Scott McConnell, "Bridge to Nowhere," *New York Post* (October 15, 1993), p. 21.

22. Carolyn A. Butts, "Black Community Says, 'You Can't Have Dr. Jeffries,' " *The Amsterdam News* (August 24, 1991), p. 9.

23. Ralph Wiley, *What Black People Should Do Now* (New York: Ballantine Books, 1993), p. 146.

24. *Ibid.*, p. 145.

25. *Ibid.*, p. 164.

26. *Ibid.*, p. 254.

27. Jared Taylor, *Paved with Good Intentions* (New York: Carroll & Graf, 1992), pp. 68-69.

28. Juan Williams, "D.C.: Divided We Fall," *Washington Post* (March 26, 1989), p. D1.

29. Ann Devroy, " 'Selective Enforcement' Issue Raised by NAACP," *Washington Post* (January 23, 1990), p. A8.

30. Ralph Wiley, *What Black People Should Do Now*, pp. 349-350.

31. Michael York and Elsa Walsh, "Barry Indicted on Cocaine, Perjury Charges; Mayor Calls Process a 'Political Lynching,' " *Washington Post* (February 16, 1990), p. A1. Mike McAlary, "Easy to Crack Jokes but Harder to Laugh," *Daily News* (New York) (June 10, 1990).

32. Dinesh D'Souza, *The End of Racism*, p. 489.

33. Ann Devroy, " 'Selective Enforcement' Issue Raised by NAACP," *Washington Post* (January 23, 1990), p. A8. "Barry's Free Ride," *The New Republic* (May 7, 1990), p. 8.

34. Jennifer Allen, "The Black Conspiracy Establishment," *7 Days* (January 17, 1990), p. 16.

35. Carl Rowan, "The Barry Verdict: A Victory for No One," *Washington Post* (August 15, 1990), p. A21.

36. "Barry's Free Ride," *The New Republic* (May 7, 1990), p. 7. Jared Taylor, *Paved with Good Intentions*, p. 70.

37. Jared Taylor, *Paved with Good Intentions*, p. 70.

38. Cornel West, *Race Matters* (New York: Vintage Books, 1993), p. 130.

39. Angela C. Allen and Andy Geller, "Harsh Words Justified by Harsh Times: Youths," *New York Post* (September 6, 1998), p. 2.

40. Cornel West, *Race Matters*, p. 7.

41. *Ibid.*, p. 20.

42. *Ibid.*, p. 27.

43. *Ibid.*, p. 28.

44. *Ibid.*, p. 106.

45. *Historic Documents of 1987* (Washington, D.C.: Congressional Quarterly, Inc., 1988), p. 43.

46. *Ibid.*, p. 47.

47. *Ibid.*, p. 50.

48. *Ibid.*, p. 58.

49. *Ibid.*

50. Earl Caldwell, "Money Can't Buy What Media Has Given to

Farrakhan," *Daily News* (New York) (February 4, 1994), p. 39.

51. Richard G. Carter, "Racism Wins, and America Is the Loser," *Daily News* (New York) (July 19, 1988), p. 31.

52. E.R. Shipp, "A 'New Era,' Yes, but Gov Also Faces a New Racist Tide," *Daily News* (New York) (January 4, 1995), p. 27.

53. E.R. Shipp, "Camille Cosby's Right—and Wrong," *Daily News* (New York) (July 21, 1998), p. 29.

54. E.R. Shipp, "Racial Profiling Is Old News to Us," *Daily News* (New York) (March 11, 1999).

55. Carl Rowan, "No Apology for Slavery, Mr. President," *New York Post* (June 18, 1997), p. 27.

56. Carl Rowan, "Tiger Woods Is Not the Answer," *New York Post* (April 16, 1997), p. 23.

57. Carl Rowan, *The Coming Race War in America: A Wake-Up Call* (Boston: Little, Brown, 1996), p. 4.

58. Carl Rowan, "No Lethal Injection Can Kill Racism," *New York Post* (March 1, 1999).

59. *Ibid.*

60. Deroy Murdock, "The Greatest Story Never Told: Everyday America's Racial Harmony," *The American Enterprise* (November/December 1998), p. 25.

61. William Murchison, "Enough Talk about 'Racism,' " *Conservative Chronicle* (September 7, 1994), p. 17.

62. Otto Kerner et al., *Report of the National Advisory Commission on Civil Disorders* (New York: Bantam Books, 1968), p. 203.

63. Don Feder, "Farrakhan Highlights Black Leadership's Failure," *Conservative Chronicle* (March 30, 1994), p. 28.

64. "Fighting Racism," *USA Today* (January 21, 1991), p. 9A.

65. Deroy Murdock, "The Greatest Story Never Told: Everyday America's Racial Harmony," *The American Enterprise* (November/December 1998), p. 25. Michael Meyers, "On Beyond Niggardly: Hypocrisy at the NAACP," *New York Post* (February 2, 1999).

66. Otto Strong and Rose Kim, "Farrakhan Rips Social Ills," *Newsday* (New York) (December 19, 1993), p. 3.

67. Chris Policano, "Farrakhan: Black Men Must Stop Black Crime," *New York Post* (January 25, 1994), p. 2. Angela C. Allen, " 'Black Men Only' Rally Runs Afoul of State Anti-Bias Law," *New York Post* (January 24, 1994), p. 5.

68. Jared Taylor, *Paved with Good Intentions*, p. 355.

69. "Their Church and State," *Destiny* (February 1994), p. 3.

70. David Jackson, "Ascent and Grandeur," *Chicago Tribune* (March 15, 1995).

71. Reuters, "More Venom for Jews and Asians," *New York Post* (October 14, 1995), p. 7.

72. Steven A. Holmes, "As Farrakhan Groups Land Jobs from Government, Debate Grows," *The New York Times* (March 4, 1994), p. A1. Richard Cohen,

"Deeply-Rooted Bigotry," *New York Post* (February 7, 1994), p. 21. Steven Yates, *Civil Wrongs* (San Francisco: Institute for Contemporary Studies, 1994), p. 31. "In Brief," *The Chronicle of Higher Education*, February 12, 1992).

73. Eric Breindel, "Once Again, a Tired Warning to Jews: 'Don't Overreact,' " *New York Post* (March 31, 1994), p. 23.

74. William Henry III, "Pride and Prejudice," *Time* (February 28, 1994), p. 26.

75. Dinesh D'Souza, *The End of Racism*, pp. 428-429.

76. William Henry III, "Pride and Prejudice," *Time* (February 28, 1994), p. 22.

77. *Ibid.* Arch Puddington, "Black Anti-Semitism and How It Grows," *Commentary* (April 1994), p. 21. Juan Williams, "A Paralysis of Leadership," *New York Post* (February 18, 1994), p. 31.

78. Ed Koch, "Hypocrisy on Same-Sex Marriage," *New York Post* (April 12, 1996), p. 35.

79. Michael Meyers, "Sucking Up to Sharpton," *New York Post* (January 19, 1999).

80. Dinesh D'Souza, *The End of Racism*, pp. 425-426.

81. Kenneth T. Jackson, *The Ku Klux Klan in the City* (Chicago: Ivan Dee Publishers, 1992), p. 247.

82. "Excerpts from Farrakhan Talk: 'Still 2 Nations, One Black, One White,' " *The New York Times* (October 17, 1995), p. A20.

83. Million Man March, televised on C-SPAN (October 16, 1995).

84. *Ibid.*

85. "Excerpts from Jackson's Address to Washington March," *The New York Times* (October 17, 1995), p. A20.

86. *Ibid.* Million Man March, televised on C-SPAN (October 16, 1995).

87. Million Man March, televised on C-SPAN (October 16, 1995).

88. "Excerpts from Jackson's Address to Washington March," *The New York Times* (October 17, 1995), p. A20.

89. Black African Holocaust Nationhood Conference, at Coolidge High School in Washington, D.C., televised on C-SPAN (October 15, 1995).

90. *Ibid.*

91. *Ibid.*

92. *Ibid.*

93. *Ibid.*

94. *Ibid.*

95. *Ibid.*

96. *Ibid.*

97. *Ibid.*

98. Khalid Abdul Muhammad, transcript of Kean College address (November 29, 1993).

99. *Ibid.*

100. *Ibid.*

101. *Ibid.*

102. *Ibid.*

103. A.M. Rosenthal, "On Black Anti-Semitism," *The New York Times* (January 11, 1994), p. A21.

104. *Ibid.*

105. "Confronting a Hate Speech," *The New York Times* (January 26, 1994), p. A20. Arch Puddington, "Black Anti-Semitism and How It Grows," *Commentary* (April 1994), p. 22.

106. Roger Wilkins, "A Loud Silence on Racism," *The New York Times* (January 8, 1994), p. 23.

107. Minoo Southgate, "Radio in Black and White," *National Review* (December 5, 1994), p. 25.

108. Eric Breindel, "Jesse Condemned Speech—But Why His Surprise?" *New York Post* (January 27, 1994), p. 23.

109. Alan Finder, "Muslim Gave Racist Speech, Jackson Says," *The New York Times* (January 23, 1994), p. 21.

110. Steven A. Holmes, "Farrakhan Repudiates Speech for Tone, Not Anti-Semitism," *The New York Times* (February 4, 1994), p. A1. Marilyn Rauber, "Black Reps Break off Pact with Farrakhan," *New York Post* (February 3, 1994), p. 14.

111. Jared Taylor, *Paved with Good Intentions*, p. 254.

112. Eric Breindel, "Jesse Condemned Speech—But Why His Surprise?" *New York Post* (January 27, 1994), p. 23.

113. *Ibid.*

114. Timothy Clifford, "He Criticizes Messenger, Not Message," *Daily News* (New York) (February 4, 1994), p. 5.

115. *Ibid.*

116. A.M. Rosenthal, "On Black Anti-Semitism," *The New York Times* (January 11, 1994), p. A21.

117. Gregg Birnbaum, Sandy Gonzalez, and William Neuman, "Farrakhan's Aide to Speak at 2nd School," *New York Post* (January 26, 1994), p. 14.

118. Jane Furse, "Ex-Farrakhan Aide Turns Down Volume," *Daily News* (New York) (February 16, 1994), p. 10.

119. Ed Koch, "You Can't Segregate Good from Bad in a Racist Demagogue," *New York Post* (March 2, 1994), p. 2.

120. *Ibid.*

121. William Neuman, "Khalid Salutes the LIRR Gunman," *New York Post* (April 21, 1994), p. 3.

122. Rocco Parascandola, "Khalid Spews More Venom at Catholics & Jews," *New York Post* (March 4, 1994), p. 2.

123. Neil Graves, "Khalid Calls Mandela Pawn of Supremacists," *New York Post* (May 13, 1994), p. 7.

124. Steven A. Holmes, "Howard University Is Stung by Portrayal As Anti-Semitic," *The New York Times* (April 21, 1994), p. D24.

125. Tom Topousis, "Rangel Relents & Welcomes Youth March," *New York Post* (September 1, 1998), p. 7.

126. Black African Holocaust Nationhood Conference, at Coolidge High School in Washington, D.C., televised on C-SPAN (October 15, 1995).

127. Ed Koch, "It's Not Just Anti-Semitism," *New York Post* (October 20, 1995), p. 23.

128. Michael Meyers, "How Ben Chavis Lynched Himself," *New York Post* (August 29, 1994), p. 21.

129. Cory Siemaszko, "Chavis' Spouse Irked Staff: Mag," *Daily News* (New York) (August 29, 1994), p. 3.

130. Marilyn Rauber, "Black Pols Turn Backs on Pact with Islam Leader," *New York Post* (January 25, 1994), p. 2. Minoo Southgate, "Black Power, Nineties Style," *National Review* (December 13, 1993), p. 46.

131. Robert Hanley, "Black Poet Says Faculty 'Nazis' Blocked Tenure," *The New York Times* (March 15, 1990), p. B3.

132. *Ibid.*

133. *Chicago Defender*, (February 26, 1994), p. 19.

134. Dudley Randall, ed., *The Black Poets* (New York: Bantam Books, 1971), pp. 226-7.

135. Ellis Cose, *The Rage of a Privileged Class* (New York: HarperCollins, 1993), pp. 1, 5.

136. John Leo, "When Cities Give up Their Streets," *U.S. News & World Report* (July 26, 1993), p. 20.

137. Roberta Hershenson, "Students Speak out on Racial Discord in Their Lives," *The New York Times* (March 7, 1993), Section 13, (Westchester Edition), p. 1.

138. John Leo, "Censorship by Theft," *U.S. News & World Report* (November 15, 1993), p. 24. Scott McConnell, "A Breathtaking Lack of Journalistic Backbone," *New York Post* (November 26, 1993), p. 27.

139. John Leo, "Censorship by Theft," *U.S. News & World Report* (November 15, 1993), p. 24.

140. John Leo, "The Spineless Award," *Daily News* (New York) (November 28, 1998), p. 25.

141. *Ibid.*

142. Roger Wilkins, "A Loud Silence on Racism," *The New York Times* (January 8, 1994), p. 23.

. 143. Evan Gahr, "Clinton Stacks Race Panel," *New York Post* (September 30, 1997), p. 25.

144. Dinesh D'Souza, *The End of Racism*, p. 70.

145. Andrea Peyser, "With Role Models Like These . . . ," *New York Post* (November 24, 1993), p. 18.

146. Bill Hoffman, "Urban Rebel Lived on the Violent Fringe," *New York Post* (September 14, 1996), p. 5.

147. Al Guart and Alex Monsky, "Rap Star Busted for Hotel Attack," *New York Post* (November 20, 1993), p. 5.

148. Al Guart, "Shakur's Lawyer Raps Cops," *New York Post* (November 30, 1993), p. 15.

149. Andrea Peyser, "With Role Models Like These . . . ," *New York Post* (November 24, 1993), p. 18.

150. *Ibid.*, pp. 2, 18. Bill Hoffman, "Urban Rebel Lived on the Violent Fringe," *New York Post* (September 14, 1996), p. 5.

151. Devlin Barrett and Andy Geller, "Rapper Takur Dead," *New York Post* (September 14, 1996), p. 5.

152. David Mills, "Sister Souljah's Call to Arms," *Washington Post* (May 13, 1992).

153. *Ibid.*

154. "Getting Real at the NAACP," *Newsweek* (June 14, 1993), p. 68.

155. Dinesh D'Souza, *The End of Racism*, p. 401.

156. Daniel Goleman, "Black Scientists Study the 'Pose' of the Inner City," *The New York Times* (April 21, 1992), p. C7.

157. *Ibid.*

158. *Ibid.*, p. C1.

159. *Ibid.*

160. Dean Chang, "Escape from New York," *Daily News* (New York) (March 20, 1994), p. 12.

161. "Seeing the Simpson Case in Black and White," *New York Post* (November 9, 1994), p. 15.

162. Playthell Benjamin, "Jesse Bravely Battles Cynicism but Too Few Are Listening," *Daily News* (New York) (May 17, 1994), p. 29.

163. Audrey Edwards and Craig K. Polite, *Children of the Dream: The Psychology of Black Success* (New York: Doubleday, 1992), p. 190.

164. *Informed Sources* television program (Public Broadcasting), New York, Channel 13 (February 17, 1996).

165. "Activist Malcolm X Lives on As Blacks Yearn for 'Clarity,' " *San Jose Mercury News* (April 19, 1992), p. 12A.

166. Henry Louis Gates, Jr., *Loose Canons: Notes on the Culture Wars* (New York: Oxford University Press, 1992), p. 50.

167. Richard Delgado, "Words That Wound: A Tort Action," in Mari J. Matsuda et al., *Words That Wound: Critical Race Theory, Assaultive Speech and the First Amendment* (Boulder: Westview Press, 1993), p. 90.

168. Jerry Gray, "Panel Says Courts Are 'Infested with Racism,' " *The New York Times* (June 5, 1991), p. B3.

169. Andrew Hacker, *Two Nations: Black and White, Separate, Hostile, Unequal* (New York: Ballantine Books, 1992), p. 24. Lynne Duke, "The White Stuff: A Theory of Race, *Washington Post* (April 14, 1992), pp. B1, B3. Dinesh D'Souza, *The End of Racism*, pp. 17-18.

170. Toni Morrison, *Playing in the Dark: Whiteness and the Literary Imagination* (Cambridge: Harvard University Press, 1982), p. 63.

171. Kenneth T. Jackson, *The Ku Klux Klan in the City*, p. 255.

172. Elaine Jones, "In Peril: Black Lawmakers," *The New York Times* (September 11, 1994).

173. "Sonny Carson for the Defense," *New York Post* (September 10, 1994), p. 10.

174. "NAACP's Rev. Emmett Burns Confronts White Picketers at National Headquarters," *Jet* (January 22, 1990), p. 14.

175. Robert D. McFadden, "Taunts and Rage Greet Protest March in Canarsie," *The New York Times* (August 11, 1991), p. 34.

176. Brendan Bourne, "Mrs. Cos Says America Taught Her Son's Killer to Hate Blacks," *New York Post* (July 9, 1998), p. 10.

177. *Ibid.*

178. Jared Taylor, *Paved with Good Intentions*, p. 103.

179. Jason DeParle, "For Some Blacks, Social Ills Seem to Follow White Plans," *The New York Times* (August 11, 1991), Section 4, p. 5.

180. *Ibid.*

181. *Ibid.*

182. *Ibid.*

183. Jennifer L. Hochschild, *Facing Up to the American Dream: Race, Class, and the Soul of the Nation* (Princeton: Princeton University Press, 1995), p. 106, Table 5.1. Thernstrom, *America in Black and White*, pp. 515-516.

184. *Ibid.*

185. "Bill Cosby's AIDS Conspiracy," *New York Post* (December 4, 1991), p. 29.

186. David France, "Challenging the Conventional Stance on AIDS," *The New York Times* (December 22, 1998).

187. David Silverman, "Blacks, Jews Working to Heal Rift," *Chicago Tribune* (July 22, 1988), Section 2, p. 6.

188. David France, "Challenging the Conventional Stance on AIDS," *The New York Times* (December 22, 1998).

189. *The World Almanac: 1998* (Mahwah, New Jersey: World Almanac Books, 1997), p. 975.

190. "Duke Election Symptomatic of U.S. Racism: Jackson," *Jet* (March 6, 1989), p. 7.

191. "What's Ahead for Blacks and Whites?" *Ebony* (November 1990), p. 76.

192. Jesse Jackson et al., "The Continuing American Dilemma," *New Perspectives Quarterly* (Summer 1991) p. 10.

193. *Ibid.*, p. 14.

194. Thernstrom, *America in Black and White*, p. 506.

195. *Ibid.*

196. *Ibid.*

Chapter 3
Deaths Remembered and Lives Forgotten

1. Benjamin Franklin, *Poor Richard's Almanac*, 1758. See Bruce Bohle, arr., *The Home Book of American Quotations* (New York: Dodd, Mead, & Company, 1967), p. 420.

2. Terry E. Johnson et al., "Mean Streets in Howard Beach," *Newsweek* (January 5, 1987), pp. 24-25.

3. "Manslaughter, Not Murder," *Time* (January 4, 1988), p. 38. Jared Taylor, *Paved with Good Intentions*, p. 231.

4. Terry E. Johnson et al., "Mean Streets in Howard Beach," *Newsweek* (January 5, 1987), p. 25.

5. Joseph Sobran, "The Use and Abuse of Race: Howard Beach," *National Review* (March 27, 1987), p. 28.

6. *Ibid.*

7. *Ibid.*, pp. 28-29.

8. *Ibid.*, p. 28.

9. *Ibid.*

10. Terry E. Johnson et al., "Mean Streets in Howard Beach," *Newsweek* (January 5, 1987), p. 24.

11. *Ibid.*

12. *Ibid.*

13. *Ibid.*

14. *Ibid.*, p. 25.

15. Terry E. Johnson with Peter McKillop, "Howard Beach: An Angry Tide," *Newsweek* (January 12, 1987), p. 25.

16. Robert D. McFadden, "Black Man Dies after Beating by Whites in Queens," *The New York Times* (December 21, 1986), p. 44.

17. Terry E. Johnson with Peter McKillop, "Howard Beach: An Angry Tide," *Newsweek* (January 12, 1987), p. 25.

18. Terry E. Johnson et al., "Mean Streets in Howard Beach," *Newsweek* (January 5, 1987), p. 24.

19. Joseph Sobran, "The Use and Abuse of Race: Howard Beach," *National Review* (March 27, 1987), p. 29.

20. Robert D. McFadden, "Black Man Dies after Beating by Whites in Queens," *The New York Times* (December 21, 1986), Section 1, p. 1.

21. Joseph Sobran, "The Use and Abuse of Race: Howard Beach," *National Review* (March 27, 1987), p. 28.

22. Robert D. McFadden, "3 Youths Are Held on Murder Counts in Queens Attack," *The New York Times* (December 23, 1986), p. B4.

23. Ronald Smothers, "Black Leaders Say Queens Attack Is Evidence of 'Pervasive Problem,' " *The New York Times* (December 23, 1986), p. A1.

24. *Ibid.*

25. *Ibid.*

26. *Ibid.*, p. B4.

27. *Ibid.*

28. Robert D. McFadden, "3 Youths Are Held on Murder Counts in Queens Attack," *The New York Times* (December 23, 1986), p. B4.

29. Mark A. Uhlig, "Strife Assailed at Queens Attack Victim's Funeral," *The New York Times* (December 27, 1986), p. 26.

30. *Ibid.*

31. *Ibid.*, p. 26.

32. Ronald Smothers, "1,200 Protesters of Racial Attack March in Queens," *The New York Times* (December 28, 1986), Section 1, p. 1.

33. *Ibid.*, Section 1, p. 26.

34. *Ibid.*

35. *Ibid.*

36. "Racial Attack Victim Arrested in Stabbing," *The New York Times* (December 28, 1986), Section 1, p. 26.

37. Ray Kerrison, "Only Roy Can Rip Dave on Race Issues," *New York Post* (June 16, 1993), p. 11. Anne E. Murray and Mel Juffe, "Cop Busts Howard Beach Victim Again," *New York Post* (July 5, 1988), p. 7.

38. Ari L. Goldman, "In a Black Church, Painful Memories," *The New York Times* (December 29, 1986), p. B3.

39. Joseph Sobran, "The Use and Abuse of Race: Howard Beach," *National Review* (March 27, 1987), p. 28.

40. "Cuomo to Appoint Panel on Bias-Related Violence," *The New York Times* (January 8, 1987), p. B2.

41. *Ibid.*

42. Lydia Chavez, "Teachers Bristle at Plan for Course on Racism," *The New York Times* (January 10, 1987), p. 31.

43. Nick Ravo, "Black Friends Deny Suspects in Attack Are Racist," *The New York Times* (December 24, 1986), p. B4.

44. Associated Press, "Second Man Arrested in Beating in Queens," *The New York Times* (December 28, 1986), Section 1, p. 27.

45. "A Mixed Verdict on Howard Beach," *Newsweek* (January 4, 1988), p. 25.

46. *Ibid.*

47. Robert D. McFadden, "3 Youths Are Held on Murder Counts in Queens Attack," *The New York Times* (December 23, 1986), p. B4.

48. Associated Press, "Teen-Ager Is Held in Fatal Stabbing," *The New York Times* (December 27, 1986), p. 27.

49. David L. Lewis, "Frank's Killer Gets Maximum," *Reporter Dispatch* (Gannett Suburban Newspapers) (November 26, 1992).

50. Mike Hurewitz, "Court Told of Teens' Slaying in HS Hallway," *New York Post* (June 24, 1993), p. 8.

51. Julio Laboy, "Teen Slain in Schoolyard," *New York Newsday* (April 7, 1993), p. 5. Lynda Richardson, "On a Child's Playground, Death Intrudes in a Game," *The New York Times* (April 12, 1993), p. B3.

52. Peter Moses, "2 Harlem Supers Slain in One Hour," *New York Post* (June 28, 1993), p. 8.

53. George James, "Arrest Made in Slayings in Brooklyn," *The New York Times* (August 25, 1993), p. B4.

54. Al Guart, "Thieves Shoot Bronx Dad Dead," *New York Post* (October 21, 1993), p. 12.

55. Douglas Kennedy, "Good Kid Shot Dead—over a Stare," *New York Post* (April 5, 1994), p. 5.

56. Murray Weiss, Jenny Havilah, and Jason Gonzalez, "Neighbors of Slain Widow, 88, Chase Suspect Straight to Cops," *New York Post* (April 15, 1994), p. 4.

57. Kieran Crowley, "Triple Slayer Taunts Victims As Judge Throws Away the Key," *New York Post* (January 29, 1999), p. 24.

58. Jodi Wilgoren, "5 Teen-Agers Arrested After Slaying That Followed Ball Game," *The New York Times* (January 30, 1999), p. B1.

59. *Ibid.*

60. *Ibid.*

61. "A Mixed Verdict on Howard Beach," *Newsweek* (January 4, 1988), p. 25.

62. Patrick J. Buchanan, "Brawley Just What N.Y. Liberals Wanted," *Reporter Dispatch* (Gannett Suburban Newspapers) (October 3, 1988).

63. "Brooklyn Man Held in Shooting of Friend," *The New York Times* (July 12, 1993), p. B2.

64. Joseph Perkins, "Selective Outrage," *New York Post* (April 29, 1993), p. 27.

65. *Ibid.*

66. *Ibid.*

67. *Ibid.*

68. *Ibid.* (Perkins wrote in 1993 that young blacks committed 19 percent of the nation's murders, but this statistic has since been updated to 30 percent. See Stephan Thernstrom and Abigail Thernstrom, *America in Black and White* (New York: Simon & Schuster, 1997), p. 266.

69. Joseph Perkins, "Selective Outrage," *New York Post* (April 29, 1993), p. 27.

70. Dennis Hevesi, "Koch Angered by Response to Burnings," *The New York Times* (August 29, 1987), p. 30.

71. *Ibid.*

Chapter 4
The Double Standard of Bloodshed

1. Thomas Jefferson, *Writings*, Vol. II, p. 43. See Burton Stevenson, arr., *The Home Book of Quotations, Classical and Modern* (New York: Dodd, Mead, and Company, 1967), p. 151.

2. Robert D. McFadden, " 'Day of Outrage' March Ends in Violence," *The New York Times* (September 1, 1989), p. B1.

3. *Ibid.*, p. B4. M.A. Farber, "Black-Korean Who-Pushed-Whom Festers," *The New York Times* (May 7, 1990), pp. B1, B10.

4. Robert D. McFadden, " 'Day of Outrage' March Ends in Violence," *The New York Times* (September 1, 1989), p. B1. Associated Press, "Arrest in Murder of Huey Newton," *The New York Times* (August 26, 1989), p. 7.

5. Robert D. McFadden, " 'Day of Outrage' March Ends in Violence," *The New York Times* (September 1, 1989), p. B4.

6. *Ibid.*

7. *Ibid.*

8. James C. McKinley Jr., "Protesters and Police Trade Blame for Violence," *The New York Times* (September 2, 1989), p. 28.

9. Dennis Hevesi, "Protests Worth Risk, Supporters Say," *The New York Times* (September 2, 1989), p. 28.

10. *Ibid.*

11. *Ibid.*

12. *Ibid.*

13. *Ibid.*

14. *Ibid.*

15. Herbert Daughtry, "Who Really Killed Yusef Hawkins?" *The New York Times* (August 29, 1989), p. A19.

16. *Ibid.*

17. *Ibid.*

18. *Ibid.*

19. Celestine Bohlen, "Racial Link in Brooklyn Killing Divides the Mayoral Candidates," *The New York Times* (August 29, 1989), p. B4.

20. Constance L. Hays, "Jackson Tells Bensonhurst School to Reaffirm Rights Effort," *The New York Times* (September 20, 1989), p. B1

21. *Ibid.*

22. Celestine Bohlen, "Racial Link in Brooklyn Killing Divides the Mayoral Candidates," *The New York Times* (August 29, 1989), p. B4.

23. "10,000 Attend Rap Concert to Call Attention to Racism," *The New York Times* (September 18, 1989), p. B5.

24. Felicia R. Lee, "Intolerance Will Be Topic for Students," *The New York Times* (September 18, 1989), p. B5.

25. *Ibid.*, p. B1.

26. Devin S. Standard, "A Young Black Man Asks: Will I Be Next?" *The New York Times* (September 2, 1989), p. 23.

27. *Ibid.*

28. *Ibid.*

29. *Ibid.*

30. John Tierney, "Free Speech Lives in a Brooklyn Plaza," *The New York Times* (May 16, 1990), p. B1.

31. *Ibid.*, p. B2.

32. Miguel Garcilazo et al., "The Battle of Brooklyn Bridge," *New York Post* (September 1, 1989), p. 4.

33. Bob Drury, "Waylaid by Whites 'out for a Fight,' " *Newsday* (New York) (August 25, 1989), p. 5.

34. Jared Taylor, *Paved with Good Intentions*, p. 86.

35. *Ibid.* William Glaberson, "A Black from Bensonhurst Tells of Carrying Bats to White Friends," *The New York Times* (April 25, 1990), p. B1.

36. Jared Taylor, *Paved with Good Intentions*, p. 87.

37. *Ibid.*

38. Eric Breindel, "Double Standard on Racism," *New York Post* (September 28, 1989), p. 33.

39. Ted Joy, "Danny Gilmore, RIP," *The Quill* (May 1989), pp. 21-27.

40. James Barron, "Tourist-Slaying Suspects Are Tied to a Gang of Ritualistic Muggers," *The New York Times* (September 5, 1990), p. A1. Jack Curry, "Tourist Slain in a Subway in Manhattan," *The New York Times* (September 4, 1990), p. B1.

41. James Barron, "Tourist-Slaying Suspects Are Tied to a Gang of Ritualistic Muggers," *The New York Times* (September 5, 1990), p. A1.

42. Jared Taylor, *Paved with Good Intentions*, p. 89. Mike Barnacle, "A Double Standard for Race Crimes?" *Asbury Park Press* (March 7, 1991), p. A21.

43. Knight-Ridder News, "AWOL Marine in Indiana Admits Seven Racial Killings, Sources Say," *Miami Herald* (February 2, 1991). Jared Taylor, *Paved with Good Intentions*, p. 89.

44. "The Killing Class," *Miami Herald* (February 24, 1991), p. 5J.

45. *Ibid.*

46. Donna Gehrke, " 'I Felt Power' While Slaying 6 People, Former Yahweh 'Death Angel' Testifies," *Miami Herald* (January 30, 1992), p. 1A.

47. Jared Taylor, *Paved with Good Intentions*, p. 91.

48. *Ibid.*

49. Jennifer Havilah, "Mockery of Justice," *New York Post* (May 9, 1995), p. 9.

50. Peter Applebome, "Tourist Killing Casts Pall over Miami," *The New York Times* (April 6, 1993), p. A16.

51. Stephen McFarland, "2 Charged in Miami Tourist Slay," *Daily News* (New York) (April 9, 1993), p. 8.

52. Alice McQuillan, "Traffic Stop Nets Cab-Slay Suspects," *New York Post* (April 29, 1993), p. 6.

53. "Fla. Teen Gets 20 Years for Shooting of Tourist," *Daily News* (New York) (May 15, 1993), p. 13.

54. Larry Celona and Bill Hoffman, "Cops Nab Teen Punks in Slaying at Prospect Pk.," *New York Post* (June 5, 1993), p. 5. Lynette Holloway, "4 Youths Arrested in Killing of Bicyclist in Park," *The New York Times* (June 5, 1993), p. 23. Larry Celona and Bill Hoffman, "Neighbors Can't Believe 4 Kids Would Kill," *New York Post* (June 5, 1993), p. 5.

55. Michael Cooper, "Youth Is Accused of Killing to Get $2 for Junk

Food," *The New York Times* (February 12, 1998).

56. "3 Blacks Sentenced in '90 Racial Attack," *Chicago Tribune* (May 20, 1992), p. 3.

57. *Ibid.*

58. Jared Taylor, *Paved with Good Intentions*, p. 89.

59. Rex Henderson, "Beating Death of White Raises Social Tensions," *Tampa Tribune* (May 20, 1990), p. B1.

60. Jared Taylor, *Paved with Good Intentions*, p. 90.

61. Suzanne Sataline and Charles M. Sennott, "Jury Convicts Drifters in Tampa Racial Attack," *Daily News* (New York) (September 8, 1993), p. 5.

62. Larry Rohter, "Tourist Is Killed in Florida Despite Taking Precautions," *The New York Times* (September 9, 1993), p. A16.

63. "3 Charged in Black Woman's Beating Death," *The New York Times* (September 9, 1993), p. A19.

64. *Ibid.*

65. "Gang Is Suspected in Woman's Death by Arson," *The New York Times* (September 25, 1990), p. B2.

66. John Rogers and Philip Messing, "Youths Say They Torched Man for Fun: Cops," *New York Post* (August 4, 1995), p. 16.

67. Dirk Johnson, "Friend Says Two Officers Stranded Man before Killing," *The New York Times* (November 5, 1995), Section 1, p. 18.

68. *Ibid.*

69. Laura Italiano, "Civil-Rights Widows Bid Farewell to 'Sister' Betty," *New York Post* (June 20, 1997), p. 13.

70. Bruce Weber, "Black Children Beaten in Bias Attack, Police Say," *The New York Times* (January 7, 1992), p. B3. Maria Newman, "Victim of Bias Attack, 14, Wrestles with Anger," *The New York Times* (January 9, 1992), p. B3.

71. Jared Taylor, *Paved with Good Intentions*, p. 271.

72. Bruce Weber, "Black Children Beaten in Bias Attack, Police Say," *The New York Times* (January 7, 1992), p. B3.

73. *Ibid.*

74. Maria Newman, "Officials Pledge Drive to Counter Bias Attack," *The New York Times* (January 8, 1992), p. B3.

75. Jared Taylor, *Paved with Good Intentions*, p. 271.

76. Maria Newman, "Officials Pledge Drive to Counter Bias Attack," *The New York Times* (January 8, 1992), p. B3.

77. *Ibid.*

78. Maria Newman, "Avoiding Confrontations in Wake of Racial Attack," *The New York Times* (January 13, 1992), p. B3.

79. Maria Newman, "Victim of Bias Attack, 14, Wrestles with His Anger," *The New York Times* (January 9, 1992), p. A1.

80. Mitch Gelman, "State Urges Bias Crime Crackdown," *Newsday* (New York) (January 14, 1992).

81. Maria Newman, "Avoiding Confrontations in Wake of Racial Attack,"

The New York Times (January 13, 1992), p. B3.

82. Maria Newman, "Officials Pledge Drive to Counter Bias Attack," *The New York Times* (January 8, 1992), p. B3.

83. Maria Newman, "Avoiding Confrontations in Wake of Racial Attack," *The New York Times* (January 13, 1992), p. B3.

84. Maria Newman, "Victim of Bias Attack, 14, Wrestles with His Anger," *The New York Times* (January 9, 1992), p. A1.

85. *Ibid.*

86. *Ibid.*

87. *Ibid.*

88. *Ibid.*

89. *Ibid.*, p. B3.

90. Maria Newman, "Avoiding Confrontations in Wake of Racial Attack," *The New York Times* (January 13, 1992), p. B3.

91. Jared Taylor, *Paved with Good Intentions*, p. 271.

92. Maria Newman, "Victim of Bias Attack, 14, Wrestles with His Anger," *The New York Times* (January 9, 1992), p. B3.

93. Jared Taylor, *Paved with Good Intentions*, p. 272.

94. *Ibid.*, pp. 271-272.

95. *Ibid.*, p. 272. Michele Parente, "Bias Rape in Brooklyn," *Newsday* (New York) (January 15, 1992), p. 3.

96. Ian Fisher, "2 Girls Are Target of Bias Attack, the Police Say," *The New York Times* (January 11, 1992), p. 23.

97. *Ibid.*

98. Scott McConnell, "When the Crime Is White on Black . . . ," *New York Post* (January 11, 1992).

99. *Ibid.*

100. *Ibid.*

101. Jared Taylor, *Paved with Good Intentions*, p. 271.

102. "City Hall's Curious Silence," *New York Post* (February 26, 1992). Scott McConnell, "Double Standard," *New York Post* (February 29, 1992).

103. "Bias Attack Is Reported in Crown Heights," *The New York Times* (April 1, 1992), p. B3.

104. Shawn G. Kennedy, "Agencies Respond to Possible Bias Attack in Bronx," *The New York Times* (October 25, 1993), p. B4.

105. Scott McConnell, "Bridge to Nowhere," *New York Post* (October 15, 1993), p. 21.

106. Richard Perez-Pena, "Men Charged with Killing of an Artist," *The New York Times* (August 13, 1993), p. B3.

107. "New Trial in Killing of Student," *The New York Times* (February 14, 1993), p. 49.

108. Chris Oliver, "British Tourist Murdered in Fla.," *New York Post* (September 15, 1993), p. 8.

109. Larry Rohter, "British Tourist Is Slain in Florida; State Orders Patrols

at Rest Areas," *The New York Times* (September 15, 1993), p. A1. Chris Oliver, "British Tourist Murdered in Fla.," *New York Post* (September 15, 1993), p. 8.

110. Larry Rohter, "Miami Unnerved by a Tourist's Killing," *The New York Times* (September 12, 1993), p. 26.

111. Kieran Crowley et al., "LIRR Massacre," *New York Post* (December 8, 1993), p. 5.

112. Robert D. McFadden, "A Long Slide from Privilege Ends in Slaughter on a Train," *The New York Times* (December 12, 1993), p. 1. [A sixth shooting victim died on December 12, 1993, as noted by Suzanne Sataline, "6th LIRR Death," *Daily News* (New York) (December 13, 1993), p. 4.]

113. Seth Faison, "A Gunman Fires at Commuters in One Car," *The New York Times* (December 8, 1993), p. 1.

114. *Ibid.*, pp. 1, 2. Kieran Crowley et al., "LIRR Massacre," *New York Post* (December 8, 1993), p. 5. Jere Hester, "He Wouldn't Stop Shooting," *Daily News* (New York) (December 8, 1993), p. 2. Bruce Frankel and Sandra Sanchez, "Gunman Shoots up N.Y. Commuter Train," *USA Today* (December 8, 1993), p. 1. Bruce Frankel and Steve Marshall, "On the Train, Nowhere to Run," *USA Today* (December 8, 1993), p. 3A.

115. "Gunshots and Screams," *Daily News* (New York) (December 8, 1993), p. 5.

116. James Lyons, "RR Shooter Used a 9-mm Pistol," *Daily News* (New York) (December 8, 1993), p. 8.

117. *Ibid.*

118. Kieran Crowley et al., "Gunman's Heart Was Full of Hate," *New York Post* (December 9, 1993), p. 4.

119. Luc Sante, "The Lunatic Blur," *The New York Times* (December 9, 1993), p. A31.

120. Les Payne, "Madness Rocked LIRR, Not Race," *Newsday* (New York) (December 19, 1993), p. 38. Dean Chang, "No Place Is Totally Safe," *Daily News* (New York) (December 8, 1993), p. 8.

121. Luc Sante, "The Lunatic Blur," *The New York Times* (December 9, 1993), p. A31.

122. Minoo Southgate, "LIRR Case: Diversion and Denial," *New York Post* (December 22, 1993), p. 27.

123. Kieran Crowley et al., "Gunman's Heart Was Full of Hate," *New York Post* (December 9, 1993), p. 4.

124. Robert Gearty, "Jesse Again Hits L.I. Exec.," *Daily News* (New York) (December 13, 1993), p. 4. (George Wallace and Orval Faubus were southern segregationists during the 1950s and 1960s.)

125. *Ibid.*

126. Kieran Crowley, "Rifkin's Mom: Cops Nixed Call to Lawyer," *New York Post* (December 14, 1993), p. 18.

127. Alice McQuillan et al., "Beaten by Gang," *Daily News* (New York) (October 3, 1994), p. 5.

128. Bob Grant, WOR radio, first two weeks of May 1997; also June 9, 1997.

129. "Jesse & Gulotta Speak out on the LIRR Horror," *Daily News* (New York) (December 15, 1993), p. 39.

130. Neil Graves and Sandy Gonzalez, "Revs. Jesse & Al in Peace Preach," *New York Post* (December 13, 1993), p. 4.

131. *Britannica Book of the Year*, 1969 (Chicago: William Benton, 1969), p. 643.

132. Stephanie Gutmann, "Don't Link Slayings to Racism, Jackson Tells Students," *New York Post* (December 15, 1993), p. 16.

133. "Jesse & Gulotta Speak out on the LIRR Horror," *Daily News* (New York) (December 15, 1993), p. 39.

134. Stephanie Gutmann, "Don't Link Slayings to Racism, Jackson Tells Students," *New York Post* (December 15, 1993), p. 16.

135. Robert Davis, "S.C. Sheriff Wins Praise at Tough Time," *USA Today* (November 8, 1994), p. A5.

136. Don Terry, "False Accusation in South Carolina Hurts Blacks, *The New York Times* (November 6, 1994), p. 22.

137. *Ibid.*

138. Eric Breindel, "The LIRR Killer: Racist Hater or Simply Society's Victim?" *New York Post* (December 16, 1993), p. 33.

139. Esther Iverem, "Racial Remarks Force Recall of State Manual," *The New York Times* (May 4, 1987), p. B3. "Manual: All Whites Racist," *Omaha World-Herald* (May 4, 1987). Ze'ev Chafets, "The Tragedy of Detroit," *The New York Times Magazine* (July 29, 1990), p. 50. Spike Lee, "The Playboy Interview," *Playboy* (July 1991), p. 52. *Rolling Stone* (July 11-25, 1991). Dinesh D'Souza, *The End of Racism*, pp. 405-406.

140. Whitney Young, *Beyond Racism* (New York: McGraw-Hill, 1969), p. 85.

141. Coramae Richey Mann, "The Reality of a Racist Criminal Justice System," *Criminal Justice Research Bulletin* 3, No. 5 (1987), p. 2.

142. Dinesh D'Souza, *The End of Racism*, p. 392.

143. *Ibid.*

144. *World Book Encyclopedia* (Chicago: World Book, Inc., 1994), Volume 11, p. 390. *The Encyclopedia Americana* (Danbury, Connecticut: Grolier Inc., 1990), Volume 4, p. 36. Dinesh D'Souza, *The End of Racism*, p. 392.

145. Dinesh D'Souza, "Black Racism and Its Role in the Harlem Massacre," *New York Post* (December 28, 1995), p. 23.

146. Thomas Sowell, *Conquests and Cultures* (New York: Basic Books, 1998), p. 368.

147. Eric Breindel, "The LIRR Killer: Racist Hater or Simply Society's Victim?" *New York Post* (December 16, 1993), p. 33.

148. Jim Sleeper, "Kuntsler Really Is a Fan of Black Rage," *Daily News* (New York) (April 5, 1994), p. 33.

149. William Neuman, "Khalid Salutes the LIRR Gunman," *New York Post* (April 21, 1994), p. 3.

150. Dinesh D'Souza, *The End of Racism*, p. 5.

151. Robert D. McFadden, "A Long Slide from Privilege Ends in Slaughter on a Train," *The New York Times* (December 12, 1993), pp. 1, 56.

152. "Sociologist: Immigrant Experience Probably Traumatic for Ferguson," *Reporter Dispatch* (Gannett Suburban Newspapers) (December 10, 1993), p. 18A.

153. Minoo Southgate, "Balkanization in the Air," *National Review* (February 21, 1994), p. 28.

154. Jeff Greenfield, "LIRR Explanation? Nothing but Insanity," *New York Post* (December 13, 1993), p. 23.

155. Deroy Murdock, "Fighting the Hoods n' the Hood," *New York Post* (January 24, 1994), p. 15.

156. Minoo Southgate, "Balkanization in the Air," *National Review* (February 21, 1994), p. 28.

157. *Ibid.*

158. *Ibid.*

159. *Ibid.*

160. *Ibid.*

161. Lawrence Potter, "Colin Ferguson, Son of Black Rage," *Destiny* (February 1994), p. 16.

162. "Attack Victim: A Kid That Everybody Liked," *The New York Times* (June 7, 1991), p. B4. Craig Wolf, "3 Arrested in Beating of a Black," *The New York Times* (June 6, 1991), p. B1.

163. Sarah Lyall, "Atlantic Beach Struggles to Explain Assault on Black Youth," *The New York Times* (June 7, 1991), p. B1.

164. Sarah Lyall, "Dissenting Voices before Sharpton Protest," *The New York Times* (June 8, 1991), p. 27.

165. George James, "Tourist Raped in Central Park, Police Say," *The New York Times* (September 27, 1994), p. B8.

166. "4 Charged in Beating of Lone Black Family," *The New York Times* (September 27, 1994), p. A20.

167. Don Terry, "Chicago Neighborhood Reveals an Ugly Side," *The New York Times* (March 27, 1997), p. A18. Associated Press, "Jackson Urges Clinton to Do More Against Racism," *Chicago Tribune* (March 31, 1997).

168. Associated Press, "Jackson Urges Clinton to Do More Against Racism," *Chicago Tribune* (March 31, 1997).

169. Miguel Garcilazo, "Grief & Shock in Victim's Nabe," *Daily News* (New York) (January 5, 1994), p. 3. Robert Hanley, "3 Lives Converge in a Killing," *The New York Times* (January 5, 1994), p. B6.

170. Robert Hanley, "Home from College and Charged with Murder," *The New York Times* (January 9, 1994), p. 26.

171. Dennis Hevesi, "Residents in a Project Stood up to a Gang," *The New York Times* (March 27, 1994), p. 26.

172. Mike McAlary, "Gang Wasn't Color-Blind," *Daily News* (New York) (March 28, 1994), p. 5.

173. "Hate Crime Hypocrites: Silent Again," *New York Post* (May 19, 1997).

174. Michael Stone, "What Really Happened in Central Park," *New York* (August 14, 1989), p. 30ff. Jared Taylor, *Paved with Good Intentions*, pp. 98-99. Howard Kurtz, " 'Wilding' Attack Left Jogger Battered and Dying, Court Is Told," *Washington Post* (June 26, 1990), p. A4.

175. Jared Taylor, *Paved with Good Intentions*, pp. 98-100.

176. William Glaberson, "In Jogger Case, Once Viewed Starkly, Some Skeptics Side with Defendants," *The New York Times* (August 8, 1990), p. B3.

177. Jared Taylor, *Paved with Good Intentions*, pp. 99-100.

178. William Raspberry, "Our Missing Anger," *Washington Post* (May 1, 1989), p. A9.

179. Karl Zinsmeister, "When Black and White Turn Gray," *The American Enterprise* (November/December 1998), p. 7.

180. Paul Johnson, *Modern Times* (New York: Harper Perennial, 1992), p. 118.

181. Shelby Steele, *The Content of Our Character* (New York: HarperCollins Publishers, 1990), pp. 15-16.

182. Robert D. McFadden, "300 Demonstrators Are Met with Silence in Bensonhurst," *The New York Times* (September 10, 1989), p. 34.

183. *Sourcebook of Criminal Justice Statistics: 1996* (Washington, D.C.: U.S. Department of Justice, 1997), p. 384, Table 4.10.

184. Ed Koch, "Death-Penalty Foes Use Tortured Logic in Race-Bias Argument," *New York Post* (April 29, 1994), p. 4. Joseph Perkins, "Selective Outrage," *New York Post* (April 29, 1993), p. 27. William Bennett, John Dilulio, Jr., and John Waters, *Body Count: Moral Poverty . . . and How to Win America's War Against Crime and Drugs*, (New York: Simon & Schuster, 1996), p. 22.

185. *Sourcebook of Criminal Justice Statistics: 1995* (Washington, D.C.: U.S. Department of Justice, 1996), p. 562, Table 6.26. Thernstrom, *America in Black and White*, p. 264.

186. Patrick J. Buchanan, "Liberals Give License to the Criminals," *Reporter Dispatch* (Gannett Suburban Newspapers) (May 6, 1989), p. A8.

187. Jason DeParle, "42 % of Young Black Males Go through Capital's Courts," *The New York Times* (April 18, 1992), p. A1. Michael Tonry, *Malign Neglect: Race, Crime, and Punishment in America* (New York: Oxford University Press, 1995), pp. 29-30.

188. Marilyn Rauber, "Third of Young Black Men Tangle with the Law: Study," *New York Post* (October 5, 1995), p. 22.

189. Richard Miniter, "Strangely Fragile?" *The American Enterprise* (November/December 1998), p. 29.

190. Scott McConnell, "Exit the Hillary Cult," *New York Post* (March 11, 1994), p. 17.

191. Felicia R. Lee, "Facing Down His Color As a Path to Privilege," *The New York Times* (May 5, 1999).

192. Ralph Wiley, *Why Black People Tend to Shout* (New York: Birch Lane Press, 1991), p. 81.

193. Gerald David Jaynes and Robin M. Williams, Jr., eds., *A Common Destiny: Blacks and American Society*, pp. 23, 464. See also Christopher Jencks, *Rethinking Social Policy: Race, Poverty, and the Underclass* (Cambridge: Harvard University Press, 1992), p. 182.

194. Thernstrom, *America in Black and White*, p. 263.

195. *Ibid. Sourcebook of Criminal Justice Statistics: 1994* (Washington, D.C.: U.S. Department of Justice, 1995), p. 340.

196. Dinesh D'Souza, *The End of Racism*, p. 7.

197. Thernstrom, *America in Black and White*, p. 263.

198. U.S. Department of Justice, Federal Bureau of Investigation, *Crime in the United States 1995: Uniform Crime Reports* (Washington, D.C.: U.S. Government Printing Office, 1996), p. 16.

199. "Uncivil Wars," *Economist* (October 7, 1989), p. 38.

200. "Who Will Help the Black Man?" *New York Times Magazine* (December 4, 1994), p. 74.

201. John McCormick and Pat Wingert, "A Crime As American As a Colt .45," *Newsweek* (August 15, 1994), p. 23. See also Thernstrom, *America in Black and White*, p. 263, which puts the figure at 93 percent.)

202. Thernstrom, *America in Black and White*, p. 272.

203. Isabel Wilkerson, "Facing Grim Data on Young Black Males, Blacks Grope for Ways to End Blight," *The New York Times* (July 17, 1990), p. A14.

204. George James, "East New York Homicide Breaks a Deadly Record," *The New York Times* (December 20, 1993), p. B3.

205. Emily M. Bernstein, "Shots into Crowd Kill Youth in Harlem," *The New York Times* (July 19, 1993), p. B3.

206. Associated Press, "Study Details Crime Fears," *The New York Times* (June 20, 1994), p. A14.

207. Katherine McFate and David A. Bositis, *Joint Center for Political and Economic Studies 1996 National Opinion Poll: Social Attitudes* (Washington, D.C.: Joint Center for Political and Economic Studies, 1996), Table A2.

208. Thomas Sowell, "Black 'Leadership' Losing Valuable Support," *Conservative Chronicle* (September 28, 1994), p. 15.

209. Playthell Benjamin, "Black-on-Black Crime Is Killing Our Community," *Daily News* (New York) (December 11, 1995), p. 23.

210. *Ibid.*

211. Derrick Bell, *Faces at the Bottom of the Well*, p. 196.

212. Associated Press, "Farrakhan Links Race to Transplants," *The New York Times* (May 2, 1994), p. A18.

213. Scott McConnell, "Crime: Some Radical Solutions," *New York Post* (January 14, 1994), p. 21.

214. Richard Cohen, "Common Ground on Crime," *New York Post* (December 24, 1993), p. 17. Lynne Duke, "Confronting Violence," *Washington Post* (January 8, 1994), p. A10. "A New Civil Rights Frontier," *U.S. News and World Report* (January 17, 1994).

215. Wayne Edwards, "Three Strikes?," *Destiny* (February 1994), p. 16.

216. Gertrude Ezorsky, *Racism and Justice: The Case for Affirmative Action* (Ithaca and London: Cornell University Press, 1991), p. 12.

217. E.R. Shipp, "Ending Apartheid Here and in S. Africa," *Daily News* (New York) (May 18, 1994), p. 31.

218. Cornel West, *Race Matters*, p. 110.

219. Felicia R. Lee, "Black Men: Are They Imperiled?" *The New York Times* (June 26, 1990), p. B3.

220. Daniel Goleman, "Black Scientists Study the 'Pose' of the Inner City," *The New York Times* (April 21, 1992), pp. C1, C7.

221. *Ibid.*

222. *Ibid.*

223. *Ibid.*

224. Felicia R. Lee, "Black Men: Are They Imperiled?" *The New York Times* (June 26, 1990), p. B3.

225. Dinesh D'Souza, *The End of Racism*, p. 5.

226. *Crime and the Black Community* (Albany: The Governor's Advisory Committee for Black Affairs, December 1987), pp. 14, 18.

227. *Ibid.*, p. 26.

228. *Ibid.*, p. 28.

229. *Ibid.*, p. 29.

230. Ishmael Reed, "The Sermons Clinton Should Give," *The New York Times* (January 15, 1994), p. 21.

231. Amy Pagnozzi, "Many Shades of Hate," *Daily News* (New York) (September 21, 1994), p. 15.

232. Ralph Wiley, *What Black People Should Do Now*, pp. 153, 146.

233. *Ibid.*

234. *Crime and the Black Community* (December 1987), p. 20.

235. William Wilbanks, "Is Violent Crime Intraracial?," *Crime and Delinquency* (Vol. 31, No. 1, January 1985), p. 117.

236. William Wilbanks, *The Myth of a Racist Criminal Justice System* (Monterey, California: Brooks/Cole Publishing Company, 1987), p. 4. (Italics were added in text for emphasis.)

237. Thernstrom, *America in Black and White*, p. 272.

238. *The World Almanac: 1998*, p. 376.

239. William Wilbanks, "Is Violent Crime Intraracial?," *Crime and Delinquency* (Vol. 31, No. 1, January 1985), pp. 120-121.

240. Thernstrom, *America in Black and White*, pp. 272, 281.

241. William Wilbanks, "Is Violent Crime Intraracial?," *Crime and Delinquency* (Vol. 31, No. 1, January 1985), pp. 120-121.

242. John Dilulio, Jr., "My Black Crime Problem, and Ours," *City Journal* (Spring 1996), p. 25.

243. Jared Taylor, "Suppressed Rage," *Destiny* (April 1995), pp. 18-19.

244. Karl Zinsmeister, "Indicators," *The American Enterprise* (November/December 1998), p. 19.

245. Jared Taylor, *Paved with Good Intentions*, pp. 92-93.

246. Jared Taylor, "Suppressed Rage," *Destiny* (April 1995), pp. 18-19.

247. Dinesh D'Souza, *The End of Racism*, p. 404.

248. *Statistical Abstract of the United States: 1998* (Washington, D.C.: U.S. Bureau of the Census, 1998), p. 215, Table 314.

249. Thernstrom, *America in Black and White*, p. 272.

250. Thomas Sowell, *The Economics and Politics of Race* (New York: Quill, 1983), p. 128.

251. *Crime in the United States, 1996* (Washington, D.C.: U.S. Department of Justice, 1997), pp. 112-156. In 1996 there were 709 murders in Los Angeles, 196 in Atlanta, 328 in Baltimore, 983 in New York, 397 in the District of Columbia, 789 in Chicago, 428 in Detroit, and 414 in Philadelphia. Many of these, of course, were black-on-black.

252. Chrisena Coleman, "Oprah Adds Final Verse for NAACP," *Daily News* (New York) (July 15, 1994), p. 26.

253. Felicia R. Lee, "Black Men: Are They Imperiled?" *The New York Times* (June 26, 1990), p. B3.

254. Maria Newman, "Victim of Bias Attack, 14, Wrestles with His Anger," *The New York Times* (January 9, 1992), p. A1.

255. *Ibid.*

256. Virginia Breen, "O'Connor Asks City to Confront Racism," *Daily News* (New York) (February 15, 1999), p. 7.

257. Paul M. Sniderman and Thomas Piazza, *The Scar of Race* (Cambridge: Harvard University Press, 1993), p. 45.

258. Katherine McFate and David A. Bositis, *Joint Center for Political and Economic Studies 1996 National Opinion Poll: Social Attitudes*, Table A2.

259. William Wilbanks, *The Myth of a Racist Criminal Justice System*, p. 1. Benjamin A. Holden et al., "Color Blinded? Race Seems to Play an Increasing Role in Many Jury Verdicts," *The Wall Street Journal* (October 4, 1995), p. A1.

260. William Wilbanks, *The Myth of a Racist Criminal Justice System*, p. 33. John Dilulio, Jr. "My Black Crime Problem, and Ours," *City Journal* (Spring 1996), p. 23.

261. "Race and Crime," *Investor's Business Daily* (February 21, 1996).

262. William Wilbanks, *The Myth of a Racist Criminal Justice System*, p. 2.

263. "Beyond Rodney King: Police Conduct and Community Relations," a report prepared by the Criminal Justice Institute, Harvard Law School, and the William Monroe Trotter Institute, University of Massachusetts at Boston for the NAACP, March 1993, unpublished draft copy, pp. 10, 11, 15, 20, 21. (Cited by Thernstrom, *America in Black and White*, p. 269.)

264. Sam Roberts, "For Some Blacks, Justice Is Not Blind to Color," *The New York Times* (September 9, 1990), p. 5.

265. Scott McConnell, "The Farrakhan Dilemma," *New York Post* (October 18, 1995), p. 19. Jesse Jackson's address at the Million Man March (October 16, 1995).

266. Elaine Rivera, "Many Officials See One Cause: Racism," *Newsday* (New York) (October 4, 1990), p. 8.

267. Minoo Southgate, "Black Power, Nineties Style," *National Review* (December 13, 1993), p. 48.

268. Angela C. Allen, "Black Group Vows to Root out 'Rogue Cops,' " *New York Post* (February 22, 1994), p. 9.

269. Cornel West, *Race Matters*, pp. 8-9.

270. Andrew Hacker, *Two Nations* (New York: Charles Scribner's Sons, 1992), p. 188. [The figure cited by Hacker needs updating, in light of the fact that one-third of all black men in their twenties are currently in prison, on probation, or on parole. See Marilyn Rauber, "Third of Young Black Men Tangle with the Law: Study," *New York Post* (October 5, 1995), p. 22.]

271. E.R. Shipp, "Turning Cons Loose Is No Answer," *Daily News* (New York) (November 9, 1994), p. 29.

272. Herbert Daughtry, "Who Really Killed Yusef Hawkins?" *The New York Times* (August 29, 1989), p. A19.

273. Jerry Gray, "Panel Says Courts Are 'Infested with Racism,' " *The New York Times* (June 5, 1991), p. B1.

274. *Ibid.*

275. *Ibid.*, p. B3.

276. Tracy Thompson, "Blacks Sent to Jail More Than Whites for Same Crimes," *Atlanta Journal and Constitution* (April 30, 1989), p. 1A. Jared Taylor, *Paved with Good Intentions*, p. 41.

277. Fox Butterfield, "Inmates Serving More Time, Justice Department Reports," *The New York Times* (January 11, 1999).

278. David Tuller, "Prison Term Study Finds No Race Link," *San Francisco Chronicle* (February 16, 1990), p. 2. Jared Taylor, *Paved with Good Intentions*, p. 40.

279. Walter Olson, "Is It Really an *In*justice System?" *New York Post* (September 30, 1996), p. 21. William Wilbanks, *The Myth of a Racist Criminal Justice System*, p. 6. Dinesh D'Souza, *The End of Racism*, p. 283.

280. Thernstrom, *America in Black and White*, pp. 272-273.

281. William Wilbanks, *The Myth of a Racist Criminal Justice System*, p. 6.

282. *Ibid.*, p. 50.

283. Bob Grant, on his New York radio program on station WABC (October 6, 1995).

284. Thomas McCardle, "Justice's Scales: Race -Weighted? Yes, but Not in the Way That's Often Claimed," *Investor's Business Daily* (November 29, 1996).

285. *Ibid.*

286. Mike McAlary, "Minority Jurors in B'klyn As Blind As White Ones in Calif.," *New York Post* (October 30, 1992), p. 3. Benjamin A. Holden et al., "Color Blinded? Race Seems to Play an Increasing Role in Many Jury Verdicts," *The Wall Street Journal* (October 4, 1995), p. A1. Daniel Levine, "Race over Reason in the Jury Box," *The Reader's Digest* (June 1996), pp. 127-128.

287. Thernstrom, *America in Black and White*, p. 517.

288. Mike McAlary, "Minority Jurors in B'klyn As Blind As White Ones

in Calif.," *New York Post* (October 30, 1992), p. 3. Benjamin A. Holden et al., "Color Blinded? Race Seems to Play an Increasing Role in Many Jury Verdicts," *The Wall Street Journal* (October 4, 1995), p. A1. Daniel Levine, "Race over Reason in the Jury Box," *The Reader's Digest* (June 1996), pp. 127-128.

289. *Ibid.*

290. Daniel Levine, "Race over Reason in the Jury Box," *The Reader's Digest* (June 1996), pp. 123-124.

291. Thernstrom, *America in Black and White*, p. 517.

292. Paul Duggan and Cindy Loose, "Mistrial Declared in Hill Killing," *Washington Post* (April 27, 1994), p. A1. Paul Duggan, "D.C. Man Convicted, in Second Trial, of Slaying Senate Aide," *Washington Post* (September 7, 1994), p. D1.

293. Daniel Levine, "Race over Reason in the Jury Box," *The Reader's Digest* (June 1996), p. 126.

294. Thernstrom, *America in Black and White*, p. 517.

295. William Wilbanks, *The Myth of a Racist Criminal Justice System*, pp. 6, 89.

296. Jared Taylor, *Paved with Good Intentions*, p. 39. William Wilbanks, *The Myth of a Racist Criminal Justice System*, pp. 145-146.

297. Bob Herbert, "A Brewing Storm," *The New York Times* (February 11, 1999), p. A33.

298. Dan Barry and Marjorie Connelly, "Poll in New York Finds Many Think Police Are Biased," *The New York Times* (March 16, 1999), p. B8.

299. *Ibid.*, p. A1.

300. Thernstrom, *America in Black and White*, p. 271.

301. William Wilbanks, *The Myth of a Racist Criminal Justice System*, pp. 64-65.

302. *Ibid.*, p. 65.

303. Thernstrom, *America in Black and White*, p. 272.

304. William Wilbanks, *The Myth of a Racist Criminal Justice System*, p. 67.

305. *Ibid.*

306. *Ibid.*, p. 68.

307. *Ibid.*, pp. 69-70.

308. *Ibid.*, p. 70.

309. *Ibid.*, p. 67. John DiIulio, Jr., "My Black Crime Problem, and Ours," *City Journal* (Spring 1996), pp. 18-19.

310. William Wilbanks, *The Myth of a Racist Criminal Justice System*, p. 73.

311. *Ibid.*

312. *Ibid.*, p. 79.

313. Daniel Georges-Abeyie, "The Criminal Justice System and Minorities," *The Criminal Justice System and Blacks*, ed. Daniel Georges-Abeyie (New York: C. Boardman Co., 1984), pp. 125-150. Jared Taylor, *Paved with Good Intentions*, pp. 35-36.

314. Jared Taylor, *Paved with Good Intentions*, p. 36.

315. William Wilbanks, *The Myth of a Racist Criminal Justice System*, p. 15. Thernstrom, *America in Black and White*, p. 276.

316. William Wilbanks, *The Myth of a Racist Criminal Justice System*, p. 78. Jared Taylor, *Paved with Good Intentions*, p. 37.

317. William Wilbanks, *The Myth of a Racist Criminal Justice System*, p. 2.

318. Sean Piccoli, "Malcolm X, the Legacy: Does Black Racism Exist?" *The Washington Times* (November 18, 1992), pp. E1, E2.

319. William Wilbanks, *The Myth of a Racist Criminal Justice System*, p. 3.

320. William Wilbanks, "Color Blind," *National Review* (April 26, 1993), pp. 52-53.

321. *Ibid.*

322. John DiIulio, Jr., "My Black Crime Problem, and Ours," *City Journal* (Spring 1996), p. 19.

323. *Ibid.*

324. William Wilbanks, "Color Blind," *National Review* (April 26, 1993), pp. 52-53.

325. Charles H. Logan and John J. DiIulio, Jr., "Ten Deadly Myths About Crime and Punishment in the U.S." See Robert James Bidinotto, ed., *Criminal Justice* (Irvington-on-Hudson, New York: Foundation for Economic Education, 1994), p. 165.

326. Thernstrom, *America in Black and White*, p. 273.

327. Walter Olson, "Is It Really an *Injustice* System?" *New York Post* (September 30, 1996), p. 21.

328. William Wilbanks, *The Myth of a Racist Criminal Justice System*, p. 98.

329. *Ibid.*, p. 120.

330. John DiIulio, Jr., "My Black Crime Problem, and Ours," *City Journal* (Spring 1996), p. 19. Charles H. Logan and John J. Dilulio, Jr., "Ten Deadly Myths About Crime and Punishment in the U.S." See Robert James Bidinotto, ed., *Criminal Justice*, p. 165.

331. John DiIulio, Jr., "My Black Crime Problem, and Ours," *City Journal* (Spring 1996), pp. 18-19.

332. *Ibid.*, p. 19.

333. *Ibid.*, p. 20.

334. *Ibid.*, p. 19.

335. Iver Peterson, "Whitman Says Troopers Used Racial Profiling," *The New York Times* (April 21, 1999), p. B8.

336. Kevin Flynn, "Two Polar Views of Police and Race at U.S. Hearing," *The New York Times* (May 27, 1999).

337. Steven A. Holmes, "Clinton Orders Investigation on Possible Racial Profiling," *The New York Times* (June 10, 1999).

338. Jackson Toby, " 'Racial Profiling' Doesn't Prove Cops Are Racist," *The Wall Street Journal* (March 11, 1999).

339. *Ibid.*

340. Iver Peterson, "Whitman Says Troopers Used Racial Profiling," *The*

New York Times (April 21, 1999), p. B8.

341. Jeffrey Goldberg, "The Color of Suspicion," *The New York Times Magazine* (June 20, 1999), p. 56.

342. *Ibid.*, pp. 54-55.

343. *Ibid.*, p. 53.

344. *Ibid.*, pp. 53-54.

345. John DiIulio, Jr., "My Black Crime Problem, and Ours," *City Journal* (Spring 1996), pp. 19-20.

346. *Ibid.*, p. 19.

347. *Ibid.*, pp. 19-20.

348. Richard Cohen, "Class, Not Race," *New York Post* (November 15, 1995), p. 25.

349. John DiIulio, Jr., "My Black Crime Problem, and Ours," *City Journal* (Spring 1996), pp. 19-20.

350. Randall Kennedy, "Blacks and Crime," *The Wall Street Journal* (April 8, 1994), p. A 16. Thernstrom, *America in Black and White*, p. 278.

351. Thernstrom, *America in Black and White*, p. 264.

352. *Ibid.*, pp. 278-279.

353. *Ibid.*, p. 275.

354. William Wilbanks, *The Myth of a Racist Criminal Justice System*, p. 17.

355. *Ibid.*, p. 18.

356. *Ibid.*

357. J. Daryl Charles, "Justice by Quota," *National Review* (September 12, 1994), p. 76.

358. Ed Koch, "Death-Penalty Foes Use Tortured Logic in Race-Bias Argument," *New York Post* (April 29, 1994), p. 4.

359. *Sourcebook of Criminal Justice Statistics: 1994*, p. 587. Thernstrom, *America in Black and White*, p. 274.

360. Ed Koch, "Many Flaws in Racial Argument Against Executions," *New York Post* (July 22, 1994), pp. 4, 20.

361. William Wilbanks, *The Myth of a Racist Criminal Justice System*, p. 17. Jared Taylor, *Paved with Good Intentions*, p. 40.

362. Samuel Francis, " 'Racial Justice Act': More Racial Than Just," *Conservative Chronicle* (August 3, 1994), p. 3.

363. *Ibid.* Alfred B. Heilburn, Jr. et al., "The Death Sentence in Georgia, 1974-1987: Criminal Justice or Racial Injustice?", *Criminal Justice and Behavior* (June 1989), pp. 139-154. Darryl Charles, "Justice by Quota," *National Review* (September 12, 1994), p. 76.

364. Darryl Charles, "Justice by Quota," *National Review* (September 12, 1994), p. 76.

365. Samuel Francis, " 'Racial Justice Act': More Racial Than Just," *Conservative Chronicle* (August 3, 1994), p. 3. Thernstrom, *America in Black and White*, p. 276.

366. Darryl Charles, "Justice by Quota," *National Review* (September 12, 1994), p. 76.

367. Thernstrom, *America in Black and White*, pp. 276-277.

368. Samuel Francis, " 'Racial Justice Act': More Racial Than Just," *Conservative Chronicle* (August 3, 1994), p. 3. Thernstrom, *America in Black and White*, pp. 275-276.

369. Thernstrom, *America in Black and White*, p. 275.

370. John DiIulio, Jr., "My Black Crime Problem, and Ours," *City Journal* (Spring 1996), p. 21.

371. *Ibid.*

372. William F. Buckley, Jr., "The Myth of Mass Illegitimacy," *New York Post* (August 12, 1996), p. 21.

373. Elaine Kamarck, "Fatherless Homes: A Violent Link," *Los Angeles Times* (May 7, 1992), p. B7.

374. Mona Charen, "Liberal Tinkering Has Put Our Civilization at Risk," *Conservative Chronicle* (August 24, 1994), p. 21.

375. Andrew Hacker, "The Myths of Racial Division," *The New Republic* (March 23, 1992), p. 22.

376. Jared Taylor, *Paved with Good Intentions*, p. 37. Thernstrom, *America in Black and White*, p. 264.

377. Sandy Gonzalez and Bill Hoffmann, "Jury Has No Mercy for Subway Vigilante," *New York Post* (April 24, 1996), pp. 2-3.

378. Ray Kerrison, "Goetz's Loss Proves Trial by Jury Has Become a Joke," *New York Post* (April 25, 1996), p. 4.

Chapter 5
Rage

1. Morris Kline, *Mathematics for the Non-Mathematician* (New York: Dover Publications, 1967), p. 462.

2. Stacey Koon, *Presumed Guilty* (Washington, D.C.: Regnery Gateway, 1992), p. 31. David Whitman, "The Untold Story of the L.A. Riot," *U.S. News & World Report* (May 31, 1993), p. 35.

3. *Ibid.*

4. Jared Taylor, *Paved with Good Intentions*, p. 225.

5. David Whitman, "The Untold Story of the L.A. Riot," *U.S. News & World Report* (May 31, 1993), p. 35.

6. *Ibid.*, p. 36.

7. Linda Deutsch, "Jury Believed Police Had Right to Use Plenty of Force," *Orange County* (Calif.) *Register* (April 30, 1992), p. A4. Sheryl Stolberg, "Jurors Tell of Angry, Bitter Deliberations," *Los Angeles Times* (May 8, 1992), p. A3.

8. *Ibid.* Jared Taylor, *Paved with Good Intentions*, p. 225. Stacey Koon, *Presumed Guilty*, pp. 38-39.

9. Greg Meyer, "We Must Have a Way to Safely Take a Suspect Down," *San Jose Mercury News* (May 3, 1992), p. 1.

10. David Whitman, "The Untold Story of the L.A. Riot," *U.S. News & World Report* (May 31, 1993), p. 39.

11. Stacey Koon, *Presumed Guilty*, p. 93.

12. *Ibid.*

13. *Ibid.*

14. Rush Limbaugh, *The Way Things Ought to Be* (New York: Pocket Books, 1992), p. 217.

15. *Ibid.*

16. In 1989, Rodney King used a two-foot-long tire iron as a weapon when robbing a Korean storekeeper. Earlier that same year, he was arrested for soliciting sex from an undercover policewoman. Two years before that, in 1987, he was sentenced to probation after pleading no contest to battery charges filed by his wife. In June 1983, he was convicted of reckless driving after attempting to run over his future wife following an argument. That same year, he was convicted on a trespassing charge that had been reduced from a theft charge. For further details about King's criminal past, see Stacey Koon, *Presumed Guilty*, p. 31.

17. Jared Taylor, *Paved with Good Intentions*, p. 226.

18. *Ibid.* Stacey Koon, *Presumed Guilty*, p. 257.

19. Jared Taylor, *Paved with Good Intentions*, p. 226.

20. *Ibid.*

21. *Ibid.*, pp. 226-227.

22. Paul Lieberman, "Jurors Tell of Their Fear and Disbelief," *San Francisco Chronicle* (May 1, 1992), p. 1.

23. Rush Limbaugh, *The Way Things Ought to Be*, p. 218.

24. Stacey Koon, *Presumed Guilty*, p. 51.

25. Jared Taylor, *Paved with Good Intentions*, p. 226.

26. Richard Serrano, "Cops in Beating Acquitted on 10 of 11 Counts," *San Francisco Chronicle* (April 30, 1992), p. A1. Sheryl Stolberg, "Jurors Tell of Angry, Bitter Deliberations," *Los Angeles Times* (May 8, 1992), p. A3. Jared Taylor, *Paved with Good Intentions*, pp. 226-227. Rush Limbaugh, *The Way Things Ought to Be*, p. 218.

27. Fred Barnes, "Stunned," *The New Republic* (May 5, 1992), p. 14.

28. Thernstrom, *America in Black and White*, p. 269.

29. David Whitman, "The Untold Story of the L.A. Riot," *U.S. News & World Report* (May 31, 1993), pp. 38, 44.

30. *Ibid.*, pp. 46-47.

31. *Ibid.*, p. 47.

32. *Ibid.*, p. 57.

33. Jane Gross, "Body and Dreams Trampled, a Riot Victim Fights On," *The New York Times* (October 22, 1993), p. A18.

34. David Whitman, "The Untold Story of the L.A. Riot," *U.S. News & World Report* (May 31, 1993), p. 57.

35. Jane Gross, "Body and Dreams Trampled, a Riot Victim Fights On," *The New York Times* (October 22, 1993), p. A18.

36. David Whitman, "The Untold Story of the L.A. Riot," *U.S. News &*

World Report (May 31, 1993), p. 57.

37. Jane Gross, "Body and Dreams Trampled, a Riot Victim Fights On," *The New York Times* (October 22, 1993), p. A18.

38. David Whitman, "The Untold Story of the L.A. Riot," *U.S. News & World Report* (May 31, 1993), p. 47.

39. *Ibid.*

40. *Ibid.*, p. 50.

41. "We're on Your Side, Victim Told Attackers," *San Jose Mercury News* (May 4, 1992), p. 9A.

42. David Whitman, "The Untold Story of the L.A. Riot," *U.S. News & World Report* (May 31, 1993), pp. 50, 52. Jared Taylor, *Paved with Good Intentions*, p. 227.

43. David Whitman, "The Untold Story of the L.A. Riot," *U.S. News & World Report* (May 31, 1993), p. 52.

44. *Ibid.*, p. 47.

45. *Ibid.*, p. 36. "The Toll," *Los Angeles Times* (May 7, 1992), p. A6.

46. Steven Chin, "Innocence Lost: L.A.'s Koreans Fight to Be Heard," *San Francisco Examiner* (May 9, 1992), p. 1.

47. Jared Taylor, *Paved with Good Intentions*, p. 228.

48. Rush Limbaugh, "My Conversation with Star Parker," *Limbaugh Letter* (March 1994), p. 7.

49. *Los Angeles Times* (May 5, 1992).

50. David Mills, "Sister Souljah's Call to Arms," *Washington Post* (May 13, 1992).

51. Deroy Murdock, "Fighting the Hoods n' the Hood," *New York Post* (January 24, 1994), p. 15.

52. Minoo Southgate, "Black Power, Nineties Style," *National Review* (December 13, 1993), p. 46.

53. Dennis Prager, "Liberalism and the Los Angeles Riots," (audiocassette of address given May 26, 1992). Prager quotes this phrase from the May 5, 1992 *Los Angeles Times*. For more information about audiocassette, contact *Ultimate Issues* in Culver City, California.

54. Cornel West, *Race Matters*, p. 3.

55. *Ibid.*, p. 11.

56. "Understanding the Riots," (Part 4), *Los Angeles Times* (May 14, 1992). Articles by: David Shaw (Section T, p. 7); Janny Scott (Section T, p. 1); David Lamb (Section T, p. 2); Walter Mosley (Section T, p. 6); Otis O'Solomon (Section T, p. 3).

57. Minoo Southgate, "Black Power, Nineties Style," *National Review* (December 13, 1993), p. 47.

58. *Ibid.*

59. Aldore Collier, "Maxine Waters: Telling It Like It Is in L.A.," *Ebony* (October 1992), p. 38.

60. Edwin S. Rubenstein, *The Right Data* (New York: *National Review*, 1994), p. 350.

61. *Ibid.*

62. *Ibid.*, p. 351.

63. Rush Limbaugh, " 'Neglected' Cities: The Big Lie," *Limbaugh Letter* (June 1993), p. 11.

64. *Ibid.*

65. *Ibid.*

66. Aldore Collier, "Maxine Waters: Telling It Like It Is in L.A.," *Ebony* (October 1992), p. 35.

67. "Maxine Waters: Straight Talk from South Central," *Ladies' Home Journal* (August 1992), p. 112.

68. Aldore Collier, "Maxine Waters: Telling It Like It Is in L.A.," *Ebony* (October 1992), p. 38.

69. Minoo Southgate, "Black Power, Nineties Style," *National Review* (December 13, 1993), p. 47.

70. David Whitman, "The Untold Story of the L.A. Riot," *U.S. News & World Report* (May 31, 1993), p. 37.

71. *Ibid.*, p. 47.

72. Dennis Prager, "Liberalism and Conservatism: A Moral Comparison," (audiocassette of address given June 8, 1994). For more information about audio-cassette, contact *Ultimate Issues* in Culver City, California.

73. David Whitman, "The Untold Story of the L.A. Riot," *U.S. News & World Report* (May 31, 1993), p. 47.

74. *Ibid.*, p. 58.

75. *Ibid.*, p. 39.

76. *Ibid.*

77. Credit for this idea goes to Dennis Prager, *Ultimate Issues*.

78. "Postgame Riots Leave Two Dead," *New York Post* (June 22, 1993), p. 75.

79. *Ibid.*

80. *Ibid.*

81. *Ibid.*

82. "Gang Members 'Reach Agreements' at Summit," *Reporter Dispatch* (Gannett Suburban Newspapers) (May 2, 1993), p. 14A.

83. *Ibid.*

. 84. Minoo Southgate, "Black Power, Nineties Style," *National Review* (December 13, 1993), p. 47.

85. Wayne Edwards, "Three Strikes?", *Destiny* (February 1994), p. 16. Don Terry, "Chicago Gangs, Extending Turf, Turn to Politics," *The New York Times* (October 25, 1993), p. A12. Walter E. Williams, "Struggle for Civil Rights Is Over," *Conservative Chronicle* (April 27, 1994), p. 26. Paul Leavitt, "Street Gangs Hailed As a 'New Frontier'," *USA Today* (October 25, 1993), p. A3.

86. Minoo Southgate, "Black Power, Nineties Style," *National Review* (December 13, 1993), p. 46.

87. Don Terry, "Chicago Gangs, Extending Turf, Turn to Politics," *The New York Times* (October 25, 1993), p. A12.

88. Bill Carpenter, "No 'Poetic Justice' in the Killing of Qa'id Teal," *Destiny* (February 1994), p. 18.

89. Joseph Perkins, "Selective Outrage," *New York Post* (April 29, 1993), p. 27.

90. Jodi Wilgoren, "Yale Students Hit King Case Verdict," *Boston Globe* (May 3, 1992), p. 42. Peter Canellos, "Mass. Students Protest King Verdict, Racism," *Boston Globe* (May 5, 1992), p. 23.

91. Chris Dufresne, "Davis, Strawberry Welcome Fan Who Can't Avoid Media," *Los Angeles Times* (April 14, 1993), p. C4.

92. Charles M. Sennott, "Plea for Calm As L.A. Trial Rests," *Daily News* (New York) (April 7, 1993), p. 20.

93. Lynette Holloway, "As Los Angeles Case Goes to Jury, New York City Calls for Calm," *The New York Times* (April 11, 1993), p. 25.

94. Minoo Southgate, "Black Power, Nineties Style," *National Review* (December 13, 1993), p. 46.

95. Patrick J. Buchanan, "Rewarding L.A.'s Rioters," *New York Post* (August 7, 1993), p. 11.

96. *Ibid.*

97. *Ibid.*

98. *Ibid.*

99. *Ibid.*

100. Associated Press, "Rodney King Arrested on Drunken Driving Charge," *Reporter Dispatch* (Gannett Suburban Newspapers) (August 22, 1993), p. 5A. John L. Mitchell, "King Ordered into Alcohol Treatment Program," *Los Angeles Times* (August 25, 1993), p. B1. "Police Arrest Rodney King," *The New York Times* (May 23, 1995), p. A12. Susan Moffat, "Alhambra Police Arrest Rodney King in Assault Incident," *Los Angeles Times* (July 15, 1995), p. B1.

101. "Vivid Testimony by Rodney King in His Civil Suit," *The New York Times* (March 29, 1994), p. A21.

102. Seth Mydans, "Civil Suit over Police Beating Goes to Jurors in Los Angeles," *The New York Times* (April 14, 1994), p. A18.

103. *Ibid.*

104. Andy Soltis, "Angry King: $3.8M Isn't Good Enough," *New York Post* (April 21, 1994), p. 18.

105. "Paying Rodney King," *Destiny* (June 1994), p. 3.

106. Murray Weiss, "A Victim's Dad: NYPD Reckless, Not Racist," *New York Post* (February 21, 1999).

107. Larry Rohter, "Miami to Pay Millions for Police Abuse That Left Victim in Coma," *The New York Times* (July 1, 1993), p. A10.

108. Kevin McLaughlin, "Berserk Cop Kills 3 R.I. Teens," *New York Post* (April 15, 1993), p. 9.

109. Kieran Crowley and Neil Graves, "Four Guards Charged in Beating Death of Inmate," *New York Post* (May 27, 1999), p. 18.

110. Kenneth B. Noble, "Videotape of Beating by Authorities Jolts Los Angeles," *The New York Times* (April 3, 1996), p. A10. Andy Soltis, "FBI Probes 'Rodney King II' Incident," *New York Post* (April 3, 1996), p. 4. Richard Sisk and Jere Hester, "FBI Probes Calif. Beating," *Daily News* (New York) (April 3, 1996).

111. *Ibid.*

112. Ian Fisher, "Filmed Beating of Inmate Leads to Dismissal of 2 Prison Guards," *The New York Times* (January 5, 1994), p. B1.

113. "Arresting Behavior," *Daily News* (New York) (December 20, 1993), p. 8.

114. "New Tape of a Police Beating in California," *The New York Times* (August 14, 1994), p. A14.

115. Jennifer Havilah, "Too Shocking for Jury to See: Raging Rapist's Video Rampage," *New York Post* (September 9, 1995), p. 7.

116. Scott McConnell, "Newspapers out of Touch with Readers?," *New York Post* (November 12, 1993), p. 21.

117. George James, "Youth Shot in Struggle with Police on a Flatbush Street, Inciting New Protest," *The New York Times* (August 27, 1991), p. B3.

118. "Officer Is Cleared in Shooting," *The New York Times* (October 18, 1989), p. B2.

119. *Ibid.*

120. Charles Strum, "Gunman Kills a Detective in Courthouse," *The New York Times* (June 4, 1993), p. B1. Bryna Taubman, "Clerk Smuggled Gun into Court," *New York Post* (June 5, 1993), p. 7.

121. *Ibid.*

122. Larry Celona et al., "Cop Shot Dead in Brooklyn Robbery," *New York Post* (December 3, 1994), p. 4.

123. Dennis Hevesi, "Police Officer Is Fatally Shot in Drug Search," *The New York Times* (April 28, 1988), p. B1.

124. Joseph P. Fried, "Officer Guarding Drug Witness Is Slain," *The New York Times* (February 27, 1988), pp. 1, 34.

125. George James, "Drug Witness Is Resolute at Meeting," *The New York Times* (March 16, 1988), p. B3.

126. James C. McKinley Jr., "Struggle on Manhattan Roof Ends in Officer's Fatal Fall," *The New York Times* (October 18, 1989), p. B3.

127. Michael Meyers, "Shatiek Johnson's Wacko Bid at the Race Game," *New York Post* (August 4, 1998), p. 28.

128. Adam Nossiter, "Youth Says Officer Pushed Him out Window," *The New York Times* (August 6, 1995), p. 35.

129. "Youth Drops Accusation on Police, Relatives Say," *The New York Times* (August 7, 1995), p. B3.

130. Philip Messing, "Cops Didn't Push Me out Window, Wash. Hts. Teen Admits," *New York Post* (August 7, 1995), p. 4.

131. *Ibid.*

132. Associated Press, "Ky. Blacks Rampage after White Cop Slays Teen-Ager," *New York Post* (October 26, 1994), p. 14. Associated Press, "Black Unrest in Lexington, Ky." *The New York Times* (October 26, 1994), p. A18.

133. Wolfgang Saxon, "Officer Wounded in Central Park," *The New York Times* (July 13, 1986), pp. 1, 18.

134. Wolfgang Saxon, "3 Youths Held in Shooting of Officer, Now Paralyzed," *The New York Times* (July 14, 1986), p. B3.

135. Jane Gross, "One Youth Who Eluded the System's Grasp," *The New York Times* (July 15, 1986), pp. A1, B3.

136. Kirk Johnson, "Youth Indicted As a Minor in Shooting," *The New York Times* (July 19, 1986), p. 29.

137. *Ibid.*

138. Sandy Gonzalez and Cathy Burke, "Snafu Let Paralyzed Cop's Shooter out Early," *New York Post* (March 11, 1994), p. 5.

139. Douglas Kennedy, "Taste of Freedom Will 'Mess with His Mind,' " *New York Post* (March 11, 1994), p. 5.

140. *Ibid.*

141. *Ibid.*

142. William Tucker, "Anatomy of a Riot," *Reader's Digest* (July 1993), pp. 48-49.

143. *Ibid.*

144. James Dao, "Police Report on a Slaying Is Challenged," *The New York Times* (July 6, 1992), p. B3.

145. William Tucker, "Anatomy of a Riot," *Reader's Digest* (July 1993), p. 51.

146. Dennis Hevesi, "Upper Manhattan Block Erupts after a Man Is Killed in Struggle with a Policeman," *The New York Times* (July 5, 1992), Section 1, p. 20.

147. *Ibid.*, p. 20.

148. James Dao, "Amid Dinkins's Appeal for Calm, Protesters Skirmish with Police," *The New York Times* (July 8, 1992), p. B2.

149. James Dao, "Police Report on a Slaying Is Challenged," *The New York Times* (July 6, 1992), p. B3.

150. *Ibid.* William Tucker, "Anatomy of a Riot," *Reader's Digest* (July 1993), p. 50.

151. William Tucker, "Anatomy of a Riot," *Reader's Digest* (July 1993), p. 51.

152. James Dao, "Amid Dinkins's Appeal for Calm, Protesters Skirmish with Police," *The New York Times* (July 8, 1992), p. B2.

153. David Gonzalez, "Events Don't Surprise Dominican Residents," *The New York Times* (July 8, 1992), p. B2.

154. James Bennet, "A Neighborhood Bonded by Turmoil," *The New York Times* (July 7, 1992), p. B4. James Dao, "Angered by Police Killing, a Neighborhood Erupts," *The New York Times* (July 7, 1992), pp. A1, B4.

155. Dennis Hevesi, "Upper Manhattan Block Erupts after a Man Is Killed in Struggle with a Policeman," *The New York Times* (July 5, 1992), Section 1, p. 20.

156. James Dao, "Angered by Police Killing, a Neighborhood Erupts," *The New York Times* (July 7, 1992), p. A1. James Dao, "Amid Dinkins's Appeal for Calm, Protesters Skirmish with Police," *The New York Times* (July 8, 1992), p. B2.

157. James Dao, "Amid Dinkins's Appeal for Calm, Protesters Skirmish with Police," *The New York Times* (July 8, 1992), p. B2.

158. William Tucker, "Anatomy of a Riot," *Reader's Digest* (July 1993), p. 52.

159. David Gonzalez, "Events Don't Surprise Dominican Residents," *The New York Times* (July 8, 1992), p. B2.

160. Italics, not in original source, were added for emphasis.

161. James Dao, "Amid Dinkins's Appeal for Calm, Protesters Skirmish with Police," *The New York Times* (July 8, 1992), p. B2.

162. *Ibid.*, p. A1.

163. James Dao, "Angered by Police Killing, a Neighborhood Erupts," *The New York Times* (July 7, 1992), p. B4.

164. William Tucker, Anatomy of a Riot," *Reader's Digest* (July 1993), p. 51.

165. James Dao, "Angered by Police Killing, a Neighborhood Erupts," *The New York Times* (July 7, 1992), p. B4.

166. *Ibid.*

167. Robert D. McFadden, "In Police Shooting, a Preponderance of Evidence," *The New York Times* (September 12, 1992), p. 23.

168. *Ibid.*

169. *Ibid.*, pp. 23, 25.

170. *Ibid.*, p. 23.

171. William Tucker, "Anatomy of a Riot," *Reader's Digest* (July 1993), pp. 53-54.

172. *Ibid.*, p. 53.

173. Robert D. McFadden, "In Police Shooting, a Preponderance of Evidence," *The New York Times* (September 12, 1992), p. 25.

174. "The Lessons of Washington Heights," *The New York Times* (September 13, 1992), Section 4, p. 20. "District Attorney's Findings Regarding the Police Killing of Jose Garcia," *The New York Times* (September 11, 1992), p. B2.

175. "District Attorney's Findings Regarding the Police Killing of Jose Garcia," *The New York Times* (September 11, 1992), p. B2.

176. William Tucker, "Anatomy of a Riot," *Reader's Digest* (July 1993), p. 53.

177. "The Lessons of Washington Heights," *The New York Times* (September 13, 1992), Section 4, p. 20.

178. "Officer Fatally Shoots Knife-Wielding Man," *The New York Times* (July 5, 1992), Section 1, p. 23.

179. Peter Moses and Don Broderick, "Man Admits Killing Girl, 7, Over $40 & Drugs," *New York Post* (November 25, 1992).

180. Jorge Fitz-Gibbon, "Regaining Her Stolen Life," *Daily News* (New York) (March 28, 1994), p. 8.

181. Clifford J. Levy, "Officials Move to Quell Washington Hts. Unrest," *The New York Times* (July 11, 1993), p. 29.

182. *Ibid.*

183. *Ibid.*

184. Larry Olmstead, "Fears and Death on Eastern Parkway," *The New York Times* (May 2, 1993), p. 52.

185. Linda Massarella and Douglas Kennedy, "Cops Collar Deadly B'klyn Robbery Gang," *New York Post* (February 3, 1994), p. 9.

186. Minoo Southgate, "Radio in Black and White," *National Review* (December 5, 1994), p. 25.

187. Herbert Daughtry, "Who Really Killed Yusef Hawkins?" *The New York Times* (August 29, 1989), p. A19.

188. Neil Graves and Larry Celona, "Tears, Tribute for Cop Killed by Bucket," *New York Post* (October 11, 1993), p. 2. Raymond Hernandez, "Telling of Hurled Bucket, Man Reflects on Tragedy," *The New York Times* (November 3, 1993), p. B10.

189. Richard Perez-Pena, "Man Charged over Melee at a Mosque," *The New York Times* (January 20, 1994), p. B1.

190. *Ibid.*

191. Alison Mitchell, "With Defense of Police at Mosque, Giuliani Moves to Isolate 2 Critics," *The New York Times* (January 15, 1994), p. 24.

192. Fred Siegel, "A Single Standard Please, Rudy," *New York Post* (January 21, 1994), p. 23. Alice McQuillan, "Muslims Want Cops' Apology," *Daily News* (New York) (January 12, 1994), p. 15.

193. Andrew Rae, "Jesse Makes Splash in Call to Scour 'Dirty 30,' " *New York Post* (October 3, 1994), p. 16. Also see photo in *The New York Times* (October 3, 1994), p. B1.

194. George James, "Youths Take Officer's Gun and Beat Him in Bay Ridge," *The New York Times* (October 3, 1994), p. B8. Alice McQuillan et al., "Beaten by Gang," *Daily News* (New York) (October 3, 1994), p. 5. "5 Quizzed in Beating of B'klyn Transit Cop," *New York Post* (October 3, 1994), p. 5.

195. Thomas Sowell, *The Economics and Politics of Race*, pp. 171-172.

196. Stuart Marques, "5-Year 'Slap on Wrist' for Davis in Shootout," *Daily News* (New York) (December 16, 1988), p. 3.

197. Larry Rohter, "Miami Police Officer Is Acquitted in Racially Charged Slaying Case," *The New York Times* (May 29, 1993), pp. 1, 5.

198. *Ibid.*, p. 5.

199. "Sharpton to Lead March on Fifth Against Cops," *Daily News* (New York) (December 9, 1994), p. 31.

200. Douglas Montero and Cathy Burke, "Tears for Slain Teen, Jeers for Cops at Wake," *New York Post* (April 15, 1997).

201. Minoo Southgate, "Radio in Black and White," *National Review* (December 5, 1994), p. 25.

202. *Information Please Almanac: 1998* (Wilmington, Mass.: Houghton Mifflin Company, 1997), p. 855. These figures for police killings and injuries are calculated based on the yearly averages from 1987-1994.

203. E.R. Shipp, "Refuting Hate a Matter of Life and Death," *Daily News* (New York) (October 5, 1994), p. 35.

204. Chris Olert et al., "Dinkins and Brown Huddle over Police Killing," *New York Post* (March 3, 1990), p. 5. Jared Taylor, *Paved with Good Intentions*, p. 84.

205. "Why Did Violence Break Out? What They Said at the March," *New York Post* (September 9, 1998), p. 29.

206. *Ibid.*

207. *Ibid.*

208. Tom Topousis and Larry Celona, "Cops to Arrest Khalid—When They Find Him," *New York Post* (September 8, 1998), p. 6.

209. *Ibid.*

210. Michael Meyers, "A Double Standard on Hate Speech," *New York Post* (September 15, 1998), p. 31.

211. Karen Jenkins Holt, "Children Follow Adults' Lead, Blame Police in Ossining Fatal Shooting," *The Journal News* (Gannett Suburban Newspapers) (July 25, 1998), p. 12A.

212. *Ibid.*

213. *Ibid.*

214. Eric Breindel, " 'Trigger-Happy' Cops? The Facts Say Otherwise," *New York Post* (April 30, 1997), p. 25.

215. Robert L. McManus, "Conyers' Cop Con," *New York Post* (November 19, 1997), p. 33.

216. Eric Breindel, " 'Trigger-Happy' Cops? The Facts Say Otherwise," *New York Post* (April 30, 1997), p. 25.

217. *Ibid.*

218. Allen Salkin et al., "Cops Set to Talk: Lawyer," *New York Post* (February 7, 1999), p. 5. John Leo, "Rudy's Wakeup Call," *Daily News* (New York) (March 27, 1999), p. 19.

219. Michael Cooper, "Officers in Bronx Fire 41 Shots, and an Unarmed Man Is Killed," *The New York Times* (February 5, 1999), p. A1. Cathy Burke, "Cops Gun Down Unarmed Man," *New York Post* (February 5, 1999), p. 5. Douglas Montero, "Why Were So Many Bullets Fired?" *New York Post* (February 7, 1999), p. 5.

220. Angela Mosconi et al., "More Diallo-Slay Rage," *New York Post* (March 4, 1999). Frankie Edozien et al., "Thousands on the March," *New York Post* (April 16, 1999).

221. Cathy Burke, "Cops Gun Down Unarmed Man," *New York Post* (February 5, 1999), p. 5.

222. Austin Fenner and Frank Lombardi, "Jesse, Pols Blast Rudy's Police Policy," *Daily News* (New York) (February 20, 1999).

223. Angela C. Allen et al., "Angry Cries for Justice at Cop-Victim Memorial," *New York Post* (February 13, 1999), p. 5. "The Arsonists Hijack a Funeral," *New York Post* (February 13, 1999).

224. Michael Meyers, "Rudy's Self-Made Albatross," *New York Post* (February 16, 1999), p. 29.

225. Tracy Connor, "Hot Tempers, Cold Shoulder for Mayor," *New York Post* (February 13, 1999), p. 2.

226. *Ibid.*

227. Al Guart et al., "8 Nabbed at Diallo Protest," *New York Post* (February 23, 1999), p. 7.

228. *Ibid.*

229. Michael Meyers, "Rudy's Self-Made Albatross," *New York Post* (February 16, 1999), p. 29.

230. John Leo, "Rudy's Wakeup Call," *Daily News* (New York) (March 27, 1999), p. 19.

231. Reported by Bill O'Reilly, *The O'Reilly Factor*, Fox News Channel (August 4, 1999).

232. Jack Newfield, "GOP Councilmen Bid to Start a Race War," *New York Post* (February 26, 1999). Marvin Scott, *11 News Closeup* (February 27, 1999 broadcast on WPIX television in New York).

233. "The Crime Drop: A Boon to Minorities," *New York Post* (February 17, 1999).

234. Bill Gang, "Officer Cleared in Fatal Shooting," *Las Vegas Review-Journal* (May 7, 1999). Glenn Puit, "Jury Finds Deadly Shooting Justified," *Las Vegas Review-Journal* (May 8, 1999). Glenn Puit, "Kin of Man Killed by Police Call for Action," *Las Vegas Review-Journal* (April 17, 1999).

235. Associated Press, "Hundreds Protest Killing of California Woman by Police," *The New York Times* (May 11, 1999).

236. Michael Cooper, "Safir Calls Shooting an Accident but Says Youth Was Out Too Late," *The New York Times* (May 28, 1999), p. B1.

237. Al Guart et al., "5 Cops Charged in Louima Attack Will Be Indicted Today," *New York Post* (February 26, 1998), p. 2. Murray Weiss, "Grand Jury Set to Indict Louima 'Torture' Cops," *New York Post* (February 19, 1998), p. 2.

238. Jack Newfield, "A Look into the Eyes of a Sadist," *New York Post* (May 25, 1999). "Throw the Book at Justin Volpe," *New York Post* (May 25, 1999).

239. Associated Press, "Police Abuse Rare, Study Says," *The New York Times* (November 23, 1997), p. 29.

240. Robert L. McManus, "Conyers' Cop Con," *New York Post* (November 19, 1997), p. 33.

241. Linda Stasi, "Hot Ice T," *Daily News* (New York) (February 16, 1994), p. 17.

242. Kieran Crowley, "B'klyn Hero Cops Rescue Kid from Apartment Fire," *New York Post* (December 3, 1993), p. 22.

243. Richard Perez-Pena, "4 Officers Save 6-Year-Old from Burning Apartment," *The New York Times* (December 3, 1993), p. B3.

Chapter 6
Mythology Run Amuck—and Tragedy

1. Eric Hoffer, *The True Believer: Thoughts on the Nature of Mass Movements*, (New York: HarperCollins, 1989), p. 107.

2. John Kifner, "A Boy's Death Ignites Clashes in Crown Heights," *The New York Times* (August 21, 1991), p. B4. Evelyn Nieves, "The Accident That Started It All: The Focus of Protesters and a Grand Jury," *The New York Times* (August 23, 1991), p. B2.

3. Evelyn Nieves, "The Accident That Started It All: The Focus of

Protesters and a Grand Jury," *The New York Times* (August 23, 1991), p. B2. John Kifner, "Youth Indicted in Fatal Stabbing in Crown Heights Racial Rampage," *The New York Times* (August 27, 1991), p. A1. (The driver's name was originally reported as Yoseph Lisef. Within a few days after the accident, it was corrected to Yoseph Lifsh.)

4. Evelyn Nieves, "The Accident That Started It All: The Focus of Protesters and a Grand Jury," *The New York Times* (August 23, 1991), p. B2.

5. John Kifner, "A Boy's Death Ignites Clashes in Crown Heights," *The New York Times* (August 21, 1991), p. B1.

6. Evelyn Nieves, "The Accident That Started It All: The Focus of Protesters and a Grand Jury," *The New York Times* (August 23, 1991), p. B2.

7. *Ibid.*

8. *Ibid.*

9. John Kifner, "A Boy's Death Ignites Clashes in Crown Heights," *The New York Times* (August 21, 1991), p. B4.

10. Evelyn Nieves, "The Accident That Started It All: The Focus of Protesters and a Grand Jury," *The New York Times* (August 23, 1991), p. B2. John Kifner, "A Boy's Death Ignites Clashes in Crown Heights," *The New York Times* (August 21, 1991), p. B4.

11. Jared Taylor, *Paved with Good Intentions*, p. 97.

12. Vinette K. Pryce, "Many Blacks, No Jews Arrested in Crown Heights," *The Amsterdam News* (August 24, 1991), p. 1.

13. "Two Deaths Ignite Racial Clash in Tense Brooklyn Neighborhood," *The New York Times* (August 21, 1991), p. A1. Vinette K. Pryce, "Many Blacks, No Jews Arrested in Crown Heights," *The Amsterdam News* (August 24, 1991), p. 8.

14. Felicia R. Lee, "Bitterness Pervades Funeral for Crown Heights Boy, 7," *The New York Times* (August 27, 1991), p. B3.

15. Andrea Peyser, "With 'Peacemakers' Like the Rev. Al, Who Needs Rabble-Rousers?," *New York Post* (June 24, 1993), p. 4.

16. *Ibid.*

17. "Two Deaths Ignite Racial Clash in Tense Brooklyn Neighborhood," *The New York Times* (August 21, 1991), p. A1. James Barron, "Brooklyn Victims: Wrong Place and Time," *The New York Times* (August 21, 1991), pp. B1, B4.

· 18. *Ibid.*

19. John Kifner, "A Boy's Death Ignites Clashes in Crown Heights," *The New York Times* (August 21, 1991), p. B1.

20. Mike McAlary, "Hate Lines Both Sides of Eastern Parkway Gantlet," *New York Post* (August 21, 1991), p. 19.

21. John Kifner, "A Boy's Death Ignites Clashes in Crown Heights," *The New York Times* (August 21, 1991), p. B4.

22. James Barron, "Brooklyn Victims: Wrong Place and Time," *The New York Times* (August 21, 1991), p. B4.

23. *Ibid.*

24. Robert D. McFadden, "Teen-Ager Acquitted in Slaying During '91

Crown Heights Melee," *The New York Times* (October 30, 1992), p. A1. Ray Kerrison, "Last Chance at Justice for Yankel Begins Today," *New York Post* (August 28, 1995), p. 12.

25. *Ibid.*

26. Robert D. McFadden, "Teen-Ager Acquitted in Slaying During '91 Crown Heights Melee," *The New York Times* (October 30, 1992), p. B2.

27. Sean Piccoli, "Malcolm X, the Legacy: Does Black Racism Exist?" *The Washington Times* (November 18, 1992), pp. E1, E2.

28. John Kifner, "Clashes Persist in Crown Heights for 3d Night in Row," *The New York Times* (August 22, 1991), p. B2.

29. John Kifner, "Youth Indicted in Fatal Stabbing in Crown Heights Racial Rampage," *The New York Times* (August 27, 1991), pp. B3, A1.

30. John Kifner, "Clashes Persist in Crown Heights for 3d Night in Row," *The New York Times* (August 22, 1991), p. B2.

31. John Kifner, "A Boy's Death Ignites Clashes in Crown Heights," *The New York Times* (August 21, 1991), p. B4.

32. John Kifner, "Dinkins Vows Tough Tactics in Race Strife," *The New York Times* (August 23, 1991), p. B2.

33. *Ibid.*

34. *Ibid.*

35. *Ibid.*

36. John Kifner, "Clashes Persist in Crown Heights for 3d Night in Row," *The New York Times* (August 22, 1991), p. B1. John Kifner, "Dinkins Vows Tough Tactics in Race Strife," *The New York Times* (August 23, 1991), p. B1.

37. Felicia R. Lee, "For Many Young Blacks, Alienation and a Growing Despair Turn into Rage," *The New York Times* (August 25, 1991), Section 1, p. 36.

38. *Ibid.*

39. Eric Breindel, "Ruth & the Jewish Question," *New York Post* (October 9, 1997), p. 31.

40. John Kifner, "Youth Indicted in Fatal Stabbing in Crown Heights Racial Rampage," *The New York Times* (August 27, 1991), p. B3.

41. "An Apology to the Mayor?" *New York Post* (February 1, 1993), p. 20.

42. John Kifner, "Dinkins Vows Tough Tactics in Race Strife," *The New York Times* (August 23, 1991), p. B1. "Crown Heights: Time for an Apology," *New York Post* (February 2, 1998), p. 26.

43. *Accident Facts, 1993* (Itasca, Illinois: National Safety Council, 1994), p. 54.

44. Michael Meyers, "Sucking Up to Sharpton," *New York Post* (January 19, 1999).

45. John Kifner, "Youth Indicted in Fatal Stabbing in Crown Heights Racial Rampage," *The New York Times* (August 27, 1991), p. B3.

46. Todd S. Purdum, "A Frustrated Dinkins Appeals for Peace," *The New York Times* (August 23, 1991), p. B3.

47. John Kifner, "Youth Indicted in Fatal Stabbing in Crown Heights

Racial Rampage," *The New York Times* (August 27, 1991), p. B3. John Kifner, "Dinkins Vows Tough Tactics in Race Strife," *The New York Times* (August 23, 1991), p. B2.

48. Felicia R. Lee with Ari L. Goldman, "The Bitterness Flows in 2 Directions," *The New York Times* (August 23, 1991), p. B1. James Barron, "Fear, Loss, and Rage Tear Area," *The New York Times* (August 22, 1991), p. B3.

49. Felicia R. Lee with Ari L. Goldman, "The Bitterness Flows in 2 Directions," *The New York Times* (August 23, 1991), p. B3.

50. James Barron, "Fear, Loss, and Rage Tear Area," *The New York Times* (August 22, 1991), p. B3.

51. Felicia R. Lee with Ari L. Goldman, "The Bitterness Flows in 2 Directions," *The New York Times* (August 23, 1991), p. B3.

52. Alison Mitchell, "Anger, on Both Sides of Eastern Parkway," *The New York Times* (October 31, 1992), p. 24.

53. Vinette K. Pryce, "Many Blacks, No Jews Arrested in Crown Heights," *The Amsterdam News* (August 24, 1991), p. 1.

54. James Barron, "Fear, Loss, and Rage Tear Area," *The New York Times* (August 22, 1991), p. B3.

55. Todd S. Purdum, "Dinkins, Seeking Peace, Finds Menacing Crowd," *The New York Times* (August 22, 1991), p. B2.

56. Robert D. McFadden, "Teen-Ager Acquitted in Slaying During '91 Crown Heights Melee," *The New York Times* (October 30, 1992), p. B2.

57. *Ibid.*, p. A1.

58. *Ibid.*, p. B2.

59. Minoo Southgate, "Hate Radio and Crown Heights," *New York Post* (July 27, 1993), p. 19.

60. Robert D. McFadden, "Teen-Ager Acquitted in Slaying During '91 Crown Heights Melee," *The New York Times* (October 30, 1992), p. B2.

61. Eric Breindel, "Behind the Crown Hts. Verdict," *New York Post* (November 5, 1992), p. 33.

62. *Ibid.*

63. Robert D. McFadden, "Teen-Ager Acquitted in Slaying During '91 Crown Heights Melee," *The New York Times* (October 30, 1992), p. B2.

64. Eric Breindel, "Behind the Crown Hts. Verdict," *New York Post* (November 5, 1992), p. 33.

65. Robert D. McFadden, "Teen-Ager Acquitted in Slaying During '91 Crown Heights Melee," *The New York Times* (October 30, 1992), p. B2.

66. *Ibid.*

67. "The Crown Heights Pogrom: Case Closed," *New York Post* (January 19, 1993), p. 20.

68. Eric Breindel, "Behind the Crown Hts. Verdict," *New York Post* (November 5, 1992), p. 33.

69. Ray Kerrison, "A Vicious Slaying the City Forgot," *New York Post* (April 26, 1989).

70. *Ibid.*

71. James C. McKinley Jr., "Man Held in Killing of 3 at a Bodega in Brooklyn," *The New York Times* (June 8, 1991), p. 27.

72. Robert D. McFadden, "As Children Play, a Flash of Gunfire Takes a Life," *The New York Times* (June 7, 1991), p. B1.

73. Bill Farrell and Joanne Wasserman, "Guilty of Murder in Crown Heights," *Daily News* (New York) (November 25, 1992), p. 4. Ari L. Goldman, "Angry Protests Follow Killing in Brooklyn," *The New York Times* (February 7, 1992), p. B1.

74. William Recktenwald, "Drunk Driver Gets Prison in Student's Death," *Chicago Tribune* (July 6, 1988), Section 2, p. 3.

75. Ian Fisher, "Cyclist Hit Twice and Dragged by Drunken Driver, Police Say," *The New York Times* (June 1, 1993), p. B2.

76. "Party Ends in Tragedy With 3 Kin Struck Dead," *Daily News* (New York) (May 3, 1994), p. 3. Sandy Gonzalez et al., "Death Driver's Thirty-Year Rap Sheet," *New York Post* (May 3, 1994), p. 4.

77. *Ibid.*

78. Joe Sexton, "Suspended Driver Is at Wheel of Car That Kills Professor," *The New York Times* (May 19, 1994), pp. A1, B6. Douglas Kennedy and Cathy Burke, "Death Driver Had 5 License Suspensions," *New York Post* (May 19, 1994), p. 8.

79. Al Guart and Jonathan Karl, "Cops: DWI Driver Kills EMS Hero," *New York Post* (June 18, 1994), p. 10.

80. "Man Nabbed in Hit-Run Death of Heroic Hubby," *New York Post* (July 27, 1993), p. 13.

81. Miguel Garcilazo et al., "The Riot That Didn't Happen," *Daily News* (New York) (September 8, 1993), p. 25.

82. John Marzulli, " 'We Told Her Not to Go'—Woman Slain at Caribbean Day Fest," *Daily News* (New York) (September 8, 1993), p. 25.

83. George James, "Girl, 5, Is Killed by a Hit-and-Run Livery-Cab Driver," *The New York Times* (July 14, 1993), p. B3.

84. Sandy Gonzalez and Colin Miner, "Unlicensed Driver Mows Down 3 Kids in Bronx," *New York Post* (June 20, 1994), p. 8.

85. John T. McQuiston, "Runaway Stolen Car Kills Boy, 4, and 2 Brooklyn Men Are Seized," *The New York Times* (July 12, 1990), p. B3.

86. Lynette Holloway, "Car Careens over Curb, Killing Boy, 4," *The New York Times* (May 2, 1993), p. 45.

87. Larry Celona et al., "Black Driver Runs Down Jewish Boy, 8, in Crown Hts." *New York Post* (September 15, 1993), p. 4.

88. Kevin McLaughlin, "Hope Is Fading for Hit-Run Coma Kid," *New York Post* (April 22, 1993), p. 9.

89. Mike Koleniak, "Cops: Tot Killed for Dancing in Front of TV," *New York Post* (October 24, 1990), p. 19. "Man Is Held in Fatal Beating of Companion's Daughter, 2," *The New York Times* (October 24, 1990), p. B3.

90. Garry Pierre-Pierre, "Fewer Killings Tallied in '93 in New York," *The New York Times* (January 2, 1994), Section 1, p. 19.

91. Kimberly J. McLarin, "6 Weeks after Prison, an Arrest," *The New York Times* (May 8, 1993), p. 26. Mike Koleniak, "Slain Girl's Mom: Kill Him!" *New York Post* (May 8, 1993), p. 3. Blanca M. Quintanilla, "Sex-Slay Suspect in Midst Angers N.J. Residents," *Daily News* (New York) (May 8, 1993), p. 4.

92. "Convict Held in Sex Assault and Murder of Girl, 6," *The New York Times* (July 21, 1993), p. B8. Joseph F. Sullivan, "When Crime Invades a Backyard, a Neighborhood Is Shocked," *The New York Times* (July 22, 1993), p. B7.

93. Clifford J. Levy, "Youths Held in the Killing of a Child, 4," *The New York Times* (March 24, 1994), p. B6.

Chapter 7
America: "Rapist of Blacks"?

1. R.G. Ingersoll, *The Great Infidels*. See Burton Stevenson, arr., *The Home Book of Quotations* (1952), p. 577.

2. Shelby Steele, *The Content of Our Character*, pp. 174-175.

3. Michael Meyers, "March of the Wooden Soldiers," *New York Post* (December 22, 1994), p. 35. Dinesh D'Souza, *The End of Racism*, p. 253. Thernstrom, *America in Black and White*, p. 500.

4. "Brawley Case: Stubborn Puzzle, Silent Victim," *The New York Times* (February 29, 1988), pp. A1, B5.

5. Esther Iverem, "Attack Puts Quiet Hudson Area in Civil Rights Fight," *The New York Times* (January 28, 1988), p. B1.

6. Richard T. Pienciak, "Key Findings in the Report," *Daily News* (New York) (October 7, 1988), p. 42.

7. Esther Iverem, "Attack Puts Quiet Hudson Area in Civil Rights Fight," *The New York Times* (January 28, 1988), p. B2.

8. *Ibid.*, p. B1.

9. James Barron, "Abrams Office to Investigate Attack on Black Teen-Ager," *The New York Times* (January 27, 1988), p. B3.

10. *Ibid.*

11. *Ibid.*

12. Esther Iverem, "Attack Puts Quiet Hudson Area in Civil Rights Fight," *The New York Times* (January 28, 1988), p. B1.

13. "U.S. Studying Dutchess Assault," *The New York Times* (February 5, 1988), p. B3.

14. James Barron, "Federal Inquiry Sought on Attack," *The New York Times* (February 4, 1988), p. B3.

15. Philip S. Gutis, "Racial Case Is Detailed by Maddox," *The New York Times* (February 10, 1988), p. B1.

16. *Ibid.*, p. B4.

17. *Ibid.*

18. James Barron, "Girl's Lawyers Agree to Assist Attack Inquiry," *The New York Times* (February 12, 1988), p. B3.

19. *Ibid.*

20. *Ibid.*, p. B1.

21. *Ibid.*, p. B3.

22. *Ibid,*, p. B1.

23. Michel Marriott, "Talks Collapse in a Racial Attack Case," *The New York Times* (February 18, 1988), p. B3.

24. Robert D. McFadden, "Girl's Lawyers Sought Limits on Inquiry," *The New York Times* (February 19, 1988), p. B2.

25. E.R. Shipp, "Actions of Brawley Lawyers Raise Troubling Questions," *The New York Times* (February 23, 1988), p. B1.

26. *Ibid.*

27. *Ibid.* Craig Wolff, "Grand Jury Selected in Brawley Case," *The New York Times* (March 1, 1988), p. B2.

28. James Barron, "Cuomo Presses for Testimony in Racial Case," *The New York Times* (February 25, 1988), p. B24.

29. James Barron, "Cuomo Won't Remove Abrams in Brawley Case," *The New York Times* (February 23, 1988), p. B3.

30. *Ibid.*

31. Michel Marriott, "Talks Collapse in a Racial Attack Case," *The New York Times* (February 18, 1988), p. B3.

32. Eric Breindel, "Explanation for Farrakhan's 'Rhetoric' Takes a New Form," *New York Post* (March 24, 1994), p. 25. Mark Kriegel, "Alton Maddox Knows Chutzpah," *Daily News* (New York) (November 21, 1997), p. 8.

33. Sam Roberts, "What's Behind the Resistance in Brawley Case?" *The New York Times* (March 3, 1988), p. B1.

34. Jeffrey Schmalz, "Racial Puzzle for Cuomo," *The New York Times* (March 9, 1988), p. B4.

35. E.R. Shipp, "Actions of Brawley Lawyers Raise Troubling Questions," *The New York Times* (February 23, 1988), p. B3.

36. Sam Roberts, "What's Behind the Resistance in Brawley Case?" *The New York Times* (March 3, 1988), p. B1.

37. E.R. Shipp, "Actions of Brawley Lawyers Raise Troubling Questions," *The New York Times* (February 23, 1988), p. B3.

38. James Barron, "Cuomo Presses for Testimony in Racial Case," *The New York Times* (February 25, 1988), p. A1.

39. *Ibid.*, p. B24.

40. *Ibid.*

41. Craig Wolff, "Grand Jury Selected in Brawley Case," *The New York Times* (March 1, 1988), p. B2.

42. Esther Iverem, "Attack Puts Quiet Hudson Area in Civil Rights Fight," *The New York Times* (January 28, 1988), p. B1.

43. Robert D. McFadden, "A Dutchess Prosecutor Vows Brawley Case

Slander Suit," *The New York Times* (March 14, 1988), p. B3.

44. *Ibid.*

45. *Ibid.*

46. Richard T. Pienciak, "6 Interviews That Shook Tawana Team," *Daily News* (New York) (June 16, 1988), p. 4.

47. *Ibid.*

48. Richard T. Pienciak, "Sharpton Ex-Aide: It's a 'Pack of Lies,' " *Daily News* (New York) (June 15, 1988), p. 3.

49. *Ibid.*

50. *Ibid.*

51. Bob Herbert, "A Search for Truth Rocks Brawley Case," *Daily News* (New York) (June 16, 1988), p. 4.

52. Lyle V. Harris, " 'Donahue' Goes to Church," *Daily News* (New York) (June 16, 1988), p. 5.

53. Ann V. Bollinger and Phil Messing, "Mason: Medics Wanted Tawana to Die," *New York Post* (July 1, 1988).

54. Ralph Blumenthal, "Brawleys Pay Surprise Visit to Lawmaker," *The New York Times* (August 30, 1988), p. B4.

55. *Ibid.*

56. Richard T. Pienciak, "Tawana Lied," *Daily News* (New York) (October 7, 1988), p. 3.

57. *Ibid.*

58. Richard T. Pienciak, "Key Findings in the Report," *Daily News* (New York) (October 7, 1988), p. 42.

59. *Ibid.*

60. *Ibid.*

61. *Ibid.* "From Fiber and Smudges, Questions in Brawley Case," *The New York Times* (March 10, 1988), p. B4.

62. "From Fiber and Smudges, Questions in Brawley Case," *The New York Times* (March 10, 1988), p. B4.

63. Pete Hamill, "Black Media Should Tell the Truth," *New York Post* (September 29, 1988), p. 5.

64. "Evidence Points to Deceit by Brawley," *The New York Times* (September 27, 1988), p. B4.

65. Ruth Landa, "Protests Voiced," *Daily News* (New York) (October 7, 1988), p. 3.

66. *Ibid.*

67. Thomas Morgan, "Sharpton Arrested in Protests," *The New York Times* (September 30, 1988), p. B3.

68. Earl Caldwell, "Maddox in the Legal Fight of His Life," *Daily News* (New York) (May 30, 1993), p. 29.

69. Ruth Landa, "Protests Voiced," *Daily News* (New York) (October 7, 1988), p. 3.

70. Jeffrey Rosen, "The Bloods and the Crits," *The New Republic* (December 9, 1996), p. 32.

71. Dinesh D'Souza, *The End of Racism*, p. 491.

72. Jim Sleeper, "New York Stories," *The New Republic* (September 10, 1990), p. 21.

73. Jim Sleeper, "Kuntsler Really Is a Fan of Black Rage," *Daily News* (New York) (April 5, 1994), p. 33.

74. Philip Messing and Esther Pessin, "Suspended Maddox Vows Havoc," *New York Post* (May 22, 1990).

75. Niles Lathem, "Pagones' Mouth Watering As Rev. Al Gets Grilled Today," *New York Post* (February 9, 1998), p. 18. Jack Newfield, "10-Year-Old Interview Comes Back to Haunt Him," *New York Post* (February 10, 1998), p. 6.

76. Niles Lathem, "Rev. Al Admits He Never Heard Rape Tale from Tawana," *New York Post* (February 10, 1998), p. 6. Niles Lathem, "Damaging Videos a Blast from the Past to Rev. Al," *New York Post* (February 11, 1998), p. 18.

77. Bob Herbert, "A Long-Running Betrayal," *The New York Times* (July 16, 1998).

78. Alan Sverdlik, "Pagones and Wife Split," *New York Post* (February 16, 1999), p. 7.

79. Niles Lathem, "Rev. Al in Dissing Match," *New York Post* (July 30, 1997), p. 5.

80. Earl Caldwell, " 'Boston Story' Is Not an Isolated One," *Daily News* (New York) (January 10, 1990).

81. Salvatore Arena, "State Court Disbars a Brawley Attorney," *Daily News* (New York) (January 27, 1995), p. 5. Steve Dunleavey, "Mason: King of the Shysters," *New York Post* (July 9, 1998).

82. Joanna Molloy, "Subway-Push Victim Vows to Face Attacker," *Daily News* (New York) (April 28, 1993), p. 3. Joanna, Molloy, "Woman's a Prisoner Too after Pressing Rape Case," *Daily News* (New York) (April 29, 1993), p. 24.

83. Joanna Molloy, "Subway-Push Victim Vows to Face Attacker," *Daily News* (New York) (April 28, 1993), p. 3.

84. Dennis Hevesi, "Girl Is Raped in Bias Case, Police Report," *The New York Times* (January 15, 1992), p. B1.

85. Craig Wolff, "5 Youths Arrested in Rape of Coney Island Jogger," *The New York Times* (April 14, 1994), pp. B1, B3. Larry Celona et al., "Cops Say 14-Yr.-Old Held Gun in Rape," *New York Post* (April 14, 1994), pp. 4, 5. Chris Oliver et al., "Teens Turned in by Local Girls in Boardwalk Rape," *Daily News* (New York) (April 14, 1994), p. 7.

86. Scott McConnell, "A Tale of Two Gang Rapes," *New York Post* (April 15, 1994), p. 19.

87. Julia Limb, "3 Teen Carjackers Charged in 'Lovers Lane' Rape," *New York Post* (October 14, 1994), p. 3. Lynette Holloway, "3 Teen-Agers Are Charged in Rape on a Brooklyn Pier," *The New York Times* (October 14, 1994), p. B3.

88. Wayne Edwards, "Three Strikes?", *Destiny* (February 1994), p. 16.

89. E.R. Shipp, "Sex Assault Cases: St. John's Verdict Touches Off Debate," *The New York Times* (July 25, 1991), p. B6.

90. *Ibid.*

91. *Ibid.*, p. B1.

92. *Ibid.*, p. B6.

93. *Ibid.*, p. B1.

94. William Wilbanks, "Frequency and Nature of Interracial Crimes," submitted for publication to *Justice Professional* (November 7, 1990). Data derived from Department of Justice, *Criminal Victimization in the United States, 1987*, p. 53. Cited by Jared Taylor, *Paved with Good Intentions*, p. 93.

95. Dinesh D'Souza, *The End of Racism*, p. 408.

96. Jared Taylor, *Paved with Good Intentions*, p. 93.

97. *Ibid.* Gary D. LaFree, "Male Power and Female Victimization: Toward a Theory of Interracial Rape," *American Journal of Sociology*, Vol. 88, No. 2 (September 1982).

98. *Ibid.*

99. William Wilbanks, "Is Violent Crime Intraracial?," *Crime and Delinquency* (Vol. 31, No. 1, January 1985), pp. 120-121.

100. Michael Meyers, "The Brawley Bunch: Still Ready for Slime Time," *New York Post* (December 9, 1997), p. 29. (Note: The italics in text were added for emphasis.)

Chapter 8
"Bloodsuckers" and "Interlopers"

1. Francis Bacon, Aphorisms. See *Dictionary of Quotations* (1968), p. 54.

2. M.A. Farber, "Black-Korean Who-Pushed-Whom Festers," *The New York Times* (May 7, 1990), p. B10.

3. *Ibid.*

4. *Ibid.*

5. Dinesh D'Souza, *The End of Racism*, p. 415.

6. Eric Breindel, "Flatbush Racism: An Untold Story," *New York Post* (April 26, 1990).

7. M.A. Farber, "Black-Korean Who-Pushed-Whom Festers," *The New York Times* (May 7, 1990), p. B10.

8. *Ibid.*

9. Eric Breindel, "Flatbush Racism: An Untold Story," *New York Post* (April 26, 1990).

10. *Ibid.* Jared Taylor, *Paved with Good Intentions*, p. 115.

11. Calvin Sims, "Shoppers Complain of Hostile Treatment, but Choices Are Few," *The New York Times* (May 17, 1990), p. B1. James Barron, "Tension, and Attention, Outside Brooklyn Court," *The New York Times* (May 10, 1990), p. B3.

12. James Barron, "Tension, and Attention, Outside Brooklyn Court," *The New York Times* (May 10, 1990), p. B3.

13. Todd S. Purdum, "Dinkins Asks for Racial Unity and Offers to

Mediate Boycott," *The New York Times* (May 12, 1990), p. 27.

14. Calvin Sims, "Shoppers Complain of Hostile Treatment, but Choices Are Few," *The New York Times* (May 17, 1990), p. B1.

15. *Ibid.*, p. B4.

16. Mireya Navarro, "For a Store Owner, Boycott Raises Fears of Misunderstandings," *The New York Times* (May 17, 1990), p. B4.

17. Don Terry, "Dinkins Responds to 2d Boycott of a Korean Store," *The New York Times* (August 28, 1990), p. B1.

18. Don Terry, "Diplomacy Fails to End Store Boycott in Flatbush," *The New York Times* (July 16, 1990), p. B5.

19. M.A. Farber, "Black-Korean Who-Pushed-Whom Festers," *The New York Times* (May 7, 1990), p. B10.

20. *Ibid.*

21. *Ibid.* Dinesh D'Souza, *The End of Racism*, p. 415.

22. James Barron, "Tension, and Attention, Outside Brooklyn Court," *The New York Times* (May 10, 1990), p. B3.

23. Todd S. Purdum, "Judge Critical of Dinkins over Boycott," *The New York Times* (May 11, 1990), p. B1.

24. Todd S. Purdum, "Angry Dinkins Defends Role in Race Case," *The New York Times* (May 9, 1990), p. B4. Todd S. Purdum, "Judge Critical of Dinkins over Boycott," *The New York Times* (May 11, 1990), p. B1.

25. Todd S. Purdum, "Angry Dinkins Defends Role in Race Case," *The New York Times* (May 9, 1990), p. B4.

26. Jared Taylor, *Paved with Good Intentions*, p. 116.

27. Todd S. Purdum, "Angry Dinkins Defends Role in Race Case," *The New York Times* (May 9, 1990), p. B1.

28. *Ibid.*

29. Todd S. Purdum, "Judge Critical of Dinkins over Boycott," *The New York Times* (May 11, 1990), p. B2.

30. Todd S. Purdum, "Dinkins Asks for Racial Unity and Offers to Mediate Boycott," *The New York Times* (May 12, 1990), p. 1.

31. " 'This City Is Sick of Violence': Dinkins's Address," *The New York Times* (May 12, 1990), p. 27.

32. Todd S. Purdum, "Dinkins Asks for Racial Unity and Offers to Mediate Boycott," *The New York Times* (May 12, 1990), p. 27.

33. *Ibid.*

34. " 'This City Is Sick of Violence': Dinkins's Address," *The New York Times* (May 12, 1990), p. 27.

35. Ray Kerrison, "Pat Proves It's Not Poverty—It's the Family, Stupid," *New York Post* (January 12, 1994). Thernstrom, *America in Black and White*, p. 255. Walter E. Williams, "Blacks and Crime," *More Liberty Means Less Government* (Stanford: Hoover Institution Press, 1999), p. 21.

36. Jared Taylor, *Paved with Good Intentions*, p. 111.

37. Max I. Dimont, *Jews, God, and History* (New York: Penguin USA,

1994), pp. 373-374. This book was originally published in 1962.

38. Robert D. McFadden, "Blacks Attack 3 Vietnamese; One Hurt Badly," *The New York Times* (May 14, 1990), pp. A1, B5.

39. *Ibid.*

40. Arnold H. Lubasch, "Protesters Lose Their Attorney in Store Boycott," *The New York Times* (May 17, 1990), p. B4. Ari L. Goldman, "Racial Unity and Dissent in Brooklyn," *The New York Times* (May 29, 1990), p. B3.

41. Don Terry, "Diplomacy Fails to End Store Boycott in Flatbush," *The New York Times* (July 16, 1990), p. B1.

42. Arnold H. Lubasch, "Protesters Lose Their Attorney in Store Boycott," *The New York Times* (May 17, 1990), p. B4.

43. Arnold H. Lubasch, "Korean Stores Win Restrictions in Boycott," *The New York Times* (September 18, 1990), p. B1. David Gonzalez, "Bombs Found on Store Roof in Brooklyn," *The New York Times* (September 24, 1990), p. B1. Jared Taylor, *Paved with Good Intentions*, pp. 116, 118.

44. Todd S. Purdum, "Dinkins Supports Shunned Grocers," *The New York Times* (September 22, 1990), p. 1.

45. David Gonzalez, "8 Arrested in Boycott of Brooklyn Store," *The New York Times* (September 25, 1990), p. 34.

46. Todd S. Purdum, "Dinkins Supports Shunned Grocers," *The New York Times* (September 22, 1990), p. 1.

47. *Ibid.*

48. David Gonzalez, "8 Arrested in Boycott of Brooklyn Store," *The New York Times* (September 25, 1990), p. 34.

49. James Barron, "Boycotted Market to Hire a Black," *The New York Times* (September 26, 1990), p. B3. David Gonzalez, "Boycotted Store Hires a Black," *The New York Times* (September 27, 1990), p. B2.

50. "Defeat for Anti-Korean Bigotry," *New York Post* (February 4, 1991). Jared Taylor, *Paved with Good Intentions*, p. 118.

51. Paul Schwartzman, "Korean Deli Owner Gives Up," *New York Post* (May 28, 1991).

52. Sam Howe Verhovek, "Strolling, Cuomo Talks about Slavery to Asians," *The New York Times* (June 2, 1990), p. 31.

53. *Ibid.*

54. Zachary Margulis, "3 Teens Held in Rob-Slay," *Daily News* (New York) (December 2, 1993), p. 22. George James, "3 Youths Seized in Slaying of Woman in Holdup," *The New York Times* (December 2, 1993), p. B1.

55. Mike Pearl and Bill Hoffman, "Smirking Subway Pusher: I Killed Her," *New York Post* (March 29, 1996), p. 14.

56. Cathy Burke, "Madman Had Rap Sheet," *New York Post* (December 11, 1995), p. 5.

57. Cathy Burke, "Sharpton and Protester Caught in Tale of the Tape," *New York Post* (December 13, 1995), p. 7. "A Challenge to Al Sharpton," *New York Post* (December 16, 1995), p. 12.

58. *Ibid.*

59. Cathy Burke, "Sharpton and Protester Caught in Tale of the Tape," *New York Post* (December 13, 1995), p. 7.

60. "Racial Terror in Harlem," *New York Post* (December 12, 1995), p. 28.

61. Minoo Southgate, "Racist Rhetoric Fueled Harlem Inferno," *Daily News* (New York) (December 18, 1995), p. 25.

62. Cathy Burke, "Sharpton and Protester Caught in Tale of the Tape," *New York Post* (December 13, 1995), p. 7.

63. *Ibid.*

64. "A Challenge to Al Sharpton," *New York Post* (December 16, 1995), p. 12.

65. "Racial Terror in Harlem," *New York Post* (December 12, 1995), p. 28.

66. Michael Meyers, "Where Were Harlem's 'Responsible' Leaders?" *New York Post* (December 18, 1995), p. 23.

67. *Ibid.*

68. *Ibid.* Robert D. McFadden, "Giuliani and Bratton See Racism in Harlem Fire," *The New York Times* (December 10, 1995), p. A1. Robert D. McFadden, "In Nightmare of Anger, Store Becomes Flaming Madhouse," *The New York Times* (December 9, 1995), p. A1.

69. Michael Meyers, "Where Were Harlem's 'Responsible' Leaders?" *New York Post* (December 18, 1995), p. 23.

Chapter 9
In the Name of Diversity

1. C.S. Lewis, cited by *Limbaugh Letter* (January 1998), p. 11.

2. Patricia Mangan, "Today's Lesson: Ending Violence," *Daily News* (New York) (November 22, 1993), p. 23.

3. Thomas Sowell, *Race and Culture* (New York: Basic Books, 1994), p. 177.

4. Stephen Yates, *Civil Wrongs*, p. 50.

5. Lino A. Graglia, "Affirmative Discrimination," *National Review* (July 5, 1993), p. 29. Courtney Leatherman, "2 of 6 Regional Accrediting Agencies Take Steps to Prod Colleges on Racial, Ethnic Diversity," *Chronicle of Higher Education* (August 15, 1990), p. 1.

6. Stephen Yates, *Civil Wrongs*, p. 49.

7. *Ibid.*, p. 50.

8. *Ibid.* Scott Jaschik and Robert R. Schmidt, Jr., "College Accreditors Spur Use of Quotas, Federal Officials Say," *Chronicle of Higher Education* (December 4, 1991), pp. A37, A43.

9. Thomas Sowell, *Is Reality Optional?*, (Stanford, California: Hoover Institution Press, 1993), p. 157.

10. *The World Almanac: 1997* (Mahwah, New Jersey: World Almanac Books, 1996), p. 379.

11. Thomas Sowell, *Is Reality Optional?*, p. 157.

12. Abigail Thernstrom, "On the Scarcity of Black Professors," *Commentary* (July 1990), p. 22.

13. "Yale Trying to Recruit Minority Faculty," *Omaha World-Herald* (February 11, 1990).

14. Dinesh D'Souza, "Illiberal Education," *Atlantic* (March 1991), p. 62. Dinesh D'Souza, *Illiberal Education*, (New York: The Free Press, 1991), p. 158.

15. Abigail Thernstrom, "Permaffirm Action." *The New Republic* (July 31, 1989), p. 17.

16. Jared Taylor, *Paved with Good Intentions*, p. 165.

17. "Racism, Cynicism, and Musical Chairs," *Economist* (June 25, 1988), p. 30.

18. Jared Taylor, *Paved with Good Intentions*, p. 167.

19. *Ibid.*

20. *Summary Report 1992: Doctorate Recipients from United States Universities* (Washington, D.C.: National Academy Press, 1993), Appendix A, pp. 44-47.

21. John Bunzel, "Minority Faculty Hiring," *The American Scholar* (Winter 1990), p. 46.

22. Abigail Thernstrom, "On the Scarcity of Black Professors," *Commentary* (July 1990), p. 23.

23. George Gilder, *Wealth and Poverty* (San Francisco, California: Institute for Contemporary Studies, 1993), p. 77.

24. Gerald N. Rosenberg, *The Hollow Hope: Can Courts Bring About Social Change?* (Chicago: University of Chicago Press, 1991), p. 50.

25. Thernstrom, *America in Black and White*, p. 141.

26. *Ibid.*

27. *Ibid.*

28. *Ibid.*

29. *Ibid.*, p. 150.

30. Lino Graglia, "Affirmative Discrimination," *National Review* (July 5, 1993), p. 26.

31. Herman Belz, *Equality Transformed* (New Brunswick and London: Social Philosophy and Policy Center, 1991), p. 14.

32. Thernstrom, *America in Black and White*, p. 118.

33. Thomas Sowell, *Civil Rights: Rhetoric or Reality?*, (New York: William Morrow and Company, 1984), p. 37.

34. *Ibid.*, p. 39.

35. *Ibid.*, p. 40.

36. *Ibid.*

37. *Ibid.*

38. Hugh Davis Graham, *The Civil Rights Era: Origins and Development of National Policy* (New York: Oxford University Press, 1990), p. 33.

39. Herman Belz, *Equality Transformed*, p. 20.

40. Hugh Davis Graham, *The Civil Rights Era: Origins and Development of National Policy*, pp. 111-113.

41. Dinesh D'Souza, *The End of Racism*, p. 224.

42. Jared Taylor, *Paved with Good Intentions*, p. 126.

43. Lino Graglia, "Affirmative Discrimination," *National Review* (July 5, 1993), p. 26. (The italics in the quotation do not appear in the original source, but have been added for emphasis.) Also see Thernstrom, *America in Black and White*, p. 172.

44. Thernstrom, *America in Black and White*, pp. 172-173.

45. Dinesh D'Souza, *The End of Racism*, p. 218.

46. *Ibid.*, pp. 220-221.

47. *Ibid.*, p. 218.

48. *Ibid.*, pp. 218-219.

49. Thernstrom, *America in Black and White*, p. 173.

50. *Ibid.*

51. Dinesh D'Souza, *The End of Racism*, p. 221. Thernstrom, *America in Black and White*, p. 428.

52. Thomas Sowell, *Civil Rights: Rhetoric or Reality?*, p. 41.

53. *Ibid.*

54. Dinesh D'Souza, *The End of Racism*, p. 221.

55. Thomas Sowell, *Civil Rights: Rhetoric or Reality?*, p. 41.

56. Nathan Glazer, *Affirmative Discrimination: Ethnic Inequality and Public Policy* (New York: Basic Books, Inc., Publishers, 1975), p. 60.

57. *Ibid.*

58. *Ibid.*

59. Lino Graglia, "Affirmative Discrimination," *National Review* (July 5, 1993), p. 26.

60. *Ibid.*

61. Dinesh D'Souza, *The End of Racism*, p. 225.

62. Lino Graglia, "Affirmative Discrimination," *National Review* (July 5, 1993), p. 26.

63. *Ibid.*, p. 28.

64. Stephen Yates, *Civil Wrongs*, p. 4.

65. Lino Graglia, "Affirmative Discrimination," *National Review* (July 5, 1993), p. 28.

66. Thernstrom, *America in Black and White*, p. 425.

67. Thomas Sowell, *Civil Rights: Rhetoric or Reality?*, pp. 41-42.

68. *Ibid.*, p. 41. Jared Taylor, *Paved with Good Intentions*, pp. 128-129.

69. Dinesh D'Souza, *The End of Racism*, p. 319.

70. Herman Belz, *Equality Transformed*, pp. 83-84.

71. Lino Graglia, "Affirmative Discrimination," *National Review* (July 5, 1993), pp. 28, 30. Frederick R. Lynch, *Invisible Victims* (New York: Prager Publishers, 1991), p. 13.

72. Thernstrom, *America in Black and White*, pp. 437-438.

73. *Ibid.*, p. 439. Ed Koch, "The Quota Fight Gets Crazier," *New York Post* (December 5, 1997), p. 35.

74. Sam Howe Verhovek, "In Battle Over Preferences, Race and Gender Are at Odds," *The New York Times* (October 20, 1998), p. A20.

75. John Beirne, "Social Work Program May Get Reprieve," *Reporter's Impact* (March 1, 1993). This source is the Mercy College student newspaper.

76. "How Affirmative Action Really Works," *The Wall Street Journal* (May 15, 1991), p. A14.

77. *Affirmative Action Register* (February 1993), p. 19.

78. *Ibid.*, p. 16.

79. *Ibid.*, p. 13.

80. *Ibid.*, p. 4.

81. *Ibid.*

82. *Ibid.*

83. *Affirmative Action Register* (January 1993), pp. 7, 9.

84. *Ibid.* p. 29.

85. *Ibid.*, p. 28.

86. *Ibid.*

87. *Ibid.*, p. 15.

88. *Ibid.*, p. 9.

89. *Ibid.*, p. 6.

90. *Chronicle of Higher Education* (August 17, 1994), p. B10.

91. *Ibid.*, p. B11.

92. *Ibid.*, p. B16.

93. *Ibid.*, p. B12.

94. *Affirmative Action Register* (January 1993), p. 26.

95. Carl Cohen, "Race, Lies, and 'Hopwood,' " *Commentary* (June 1996), p. 41.

96. Frederick Lynch, *Invisible Victims*, p. 206.

97. *Ibid.*, p. 211.

98. *Ibid.*

99. *Ibid.*, p. 213.

100. Nathan Glazer, *Affirmative Discrimination: Ethnic Inequality and Public Policy*, p. 61.

101. Alan H. Goldman, *Justice and Reverse Discrimination* (Princeton, New Jersey: Princeton University Press, 1979), p. 213.

102. *Ibid.*

103. Nathan Glazer, *Affirmative Discrimination: Ethnic Inequality and Public Policy*, p. 61.

104. *Ibid.*

105. John H. Bunzel, "Exclusive Opportunities," *The American Enterprise* (March/April 1990), pp. 3-5.

106. *Ibid.*

107 *Ibid.*

108. *Ibid.*

109. *Ibid.*

110. Jared Taylor, *Paved with Good Intentions*, p. 167.

111. Frederick Lynch, *Invisible Victims*, p. 39.

112. Nathan Glazer, *Affirmative Discrimination: Ethnic Inequality and Public Policy*, p. 60.

113. William Hawkins, "Letter from the Volunteer State," *Chronicles* (November 1988), p. 46.

114. Johnnetta B. Cole, *Conversations: Straight Talk with America's Sister President* (New York: Anchor Books, 1993), p. 56.

115. Fox Butterfield, "Harvard Law School Torn by Race Issue," *The New York Times* (April 26, 1990), p. A20. Jared Taylor, *Paved with Good Intentions*, p. 199.

116. *Ibid.* Fox Butterfield, "Harvard Law Professor Quits Until Black Woman Is Named," *The New York Times* (April 24, 1990), p. A1.

117. Fox Butterfield, "Harvard Law School Torn by Race Issue," *The New York Times* (April 26, 1990), p. A20.

118. *Ibid.*

119. Carl Rowan, " 'Merit' Is a White Code Word for Maintaining Privilege," *New York Post* (May 24, 1990), p. 29.

120. "A Class Sends Message to Harvard Law School," *The New York Times* (November 21, 1990).

121. Dinesh D'Souza, *Illiberal Education*, pp. 136-139.

122. Robert Mitchell, *The Multicultural Student's Guide to Colleges* (New York: Farrar, Straus, and Giroux, 1996).

123. Jonathan Rabinovitz, "For SUNY at Old Westbury, Charges of a Faith Not Kept," *The New York Times* (March 22, 1993), p. B1.

124. Eric L. Hirsch, "Columbia University: Individual and Institutional Racism," *The Racial Crisis in American Higher Education*, Philip G. Altbach and Kofi Lomotey, eds. (Albany: State University of New York Press, 1991), p. 208.

125. Samuel Weiss, "Baruch College Is Reaccredited; Pledges Reforms," *The New York Times* (June 28, 1990), p. B2. Felicia Lee, "Minorities at Baruch College Charge Neglect Despite Ethnic Mix," *The New York Times* (April 21, 1990), p. 1.

126. "Lamar Alexander and the Diversity Police," *New York Post* (December 2, 1991).

127. Samuel Weiss, "Baruch College Is Reaccredited; Pledges Reforms," *The New York Times* (June 28, 1990), p. B2.

128. Frances Marcus, "After 19 Years, Louisiana Still Seeks a Way to Mix Races at Its Colleges," *The New York Times* (December 27, 1988), p. A11. Jim Sleeper, "The Policemen of Diversity," *Washington Post* (June 30, 1991), p. C1. Jared Taylor, *Paved with Good Intentions*, pp. 178, 210.

129. Nick Anderson, "Minority Enrollment Edges up at Stanford," *San Jose Mercury News* (June 23, 1990), p. 2B.

130. John Leo, "The Luring of Black Students," *U.S. News & World*

Report (March 15, 1993), p. 20. Fox Butterfield, "Colleges Luring Black Students with Incentives," *The New York Times* (February 28, 1993), p. 30.

131. *Ibid.*

132. Stephen Yates, *Civil Wrongs*, p. 34.

133. *Ibid.*, p. 46.

134. Lino Graglia, "Affirmative Discrimination," *National Review* (July 5, 1993), p. 28.

135. Jared Taylor, *Paved with Good Intentions*, p. 170.

136. Donald Stewart, "Thinking the Unthinkable," *Vital Speeches of the Day* (May 1, 1989), p. 447. Thomas Sowell, *Inside American Education* (New York: The Free Press, 1993), p. 128. Dinesh D'Souza, *The End of Racism*, p. 310.

137. Dinesh D'Souza, *Illiberal Education*, p. 41. Dinesh D'Souza, *The End of Racism*, p. 303.

138. Elizabeth Greene, "SAT Scores Fail to Help Admissions Officers Make Better Decisions, Analysts Contend," *Chronicle of Higher Education* (July 27, 1988), p. A20.

139. James Fallows, "The Tests and the Brightest," *The Atlantic* (February 1980), p. 38.

140. Thernstrom, *America in Black and White*, pp. 401-402.

141. Richard Seymour, "Why Plaintiffs' Counsel Challenge Tests, and How They Can Successfully Challenge the Theory of Validity Generalization," *Journal of Vocational Behavior* 33 (1988), pp. 331-364.

142. Lino Graglia, "Affirmative Discrimination," *National Review* (July 5, 1993), p. 28. Thomas Sowell, *Inside American Education*, p. 128. Dinesh D'Souza, *The End of Racism*, pp. 312-313.

143. Jacqueline Fleming, "Standardized Test Scores and the Black College Environment," *Going to School*, Kofi Lomotey, ed. (Albany: State University of New York Press, 1990), pp. 143-152.

144. John Leo, "Stop Blaming the Tests," *U.S. News & World Report* (March 20, 1989), p. 80. Dinesh D'Souza, *The End of Racism*, pp. 312-313.

145. John Leo, "Stop Blaming the Tests," *U.S. News & World Report* (March 20, 1989), p. 80. Jared Taylor, *Paved with Good Intentions*, p. 170.

146. Lino Graglia, "Affirmative Discrimination," *National Review* (July 5, 1993), p. 28.

147. Jared Taylor, *Paved with Good Intentions*, p. 170.

148. John H. Bunzel, "The University's Pseudo-Egalitarianism," *The Wall Street Journal* (July 12, 1991), p. A10.

149. Arch Puddington, "Speaking of Race," *Commentary* (December 1995), p. 23.

150. Theodore Cross, "What if There Was No Affirmative Action in College Admissions? A Further Refinement of Our Earlier Calculations," *Journal of Blacks in Higher Education* 5 (Autumn 1994), p. 55.

151. Dinesh D'Souza, *The End of Racism*, p. 303. Data supplied by the College Board, Princeton, New Jersey.

152. Larry Dublin, "Class Divisions," *The Journal News* (Gannett Suburban Newspapers) (February 2, 1999), p. 4A.

153. Dinesh D'Souza, *Illiberal Education*, p. 265.

154. Andrew Hacker, *Two Nations*, p. 143. Jared Taylor, *Paved with Good Intentions*, p. 170.

155. Thomas Sowell, *The Economics and Politics of Race*, p. 140.

156. John H. Bunzel and Jeffrey Au, "Diversity or Discrimination: Asian Americans in College," *The Public Interest* (Spring 1987), p. 55.

157. National Center for Education Statistics, *Digest of Educational Statistics: 1995*, p. 138. Cited by Thernstrom, *America in Black and White*, p. 383.

158. Thernstrom, *America in Black and White*, pp. 382-383.

159. Pam Belluck, "Reason Is Sought for Lag by Blacks in School Effort," *The New York Times* (July 4, 1999), p. 15.

160. *Ibid.*

161. The Family Research Council, "Illegitimacy's Disastrous Effects," *In Focus* (April 1995).

162. National Center for Education Statistics, *Disparities in Public School District Spending, 1989-1990*, NCES 95-300 (Washington, D.C.: U.S. Government Printing Office, 1995), p. 15.

163. John H. Bunzel, "Affirmative Action Admissions: How It 'Works' at Berkeley," *The Public Interest* (Fall 1988), pp. 124, 125.

164. Sally C. Pipes, "Quashing Quotas," *Investor's Business Daily* (March 1, 1995).

165. Dinesh D'Souza, *Illiberal Education*, p. 39. Alvin P. Sanoff et al., "Race on Campus," *U.S. News & World Report* (April 19, 1993), p. 55.

166. Thernstrom, *America in Black and White*, p. 193.

167. *Ibid.*, p. 382.

168. Thomas Sowell, *Preferential Policies*, (New York: William Morrow & Company, 1990) pp. 98-100.

169. Dinesh D'Souza, *Illiberal Education*, p. 39.

170. Thernstrom, *America in Black and White*, pp. 406-407.

171. *Ibid.*, p. 410.

172. *Ibid.*, p. 411.

173. Thomas Sowell, *Inside American Education*, p. 141.

174. Thernstrom, *America in Black and White*, p. 399. John Leo, "The Luring of Black Students," *U.S. News & World Report* (March 15, 1993), p. 20.

175. College Entrance Examination Board, *1995 National Ethnic/Sex Data* (New York: College Board, 1995).

176. *Ibid.*

177. *Ibid.*

178. *Ibid.*

179. Thomas Sowell, *Inside American Education*, p. 142.

180. Dinesh D'Souza, *Illiberal Education*, p. 41.

181. Dinesh D'Souza, *The End of Racism*, p. 303.

182. Walter E. Williams, "Race, Scholarship, and Affirmative Action: Campus Racism," *National Review* (May 5, 1989), p. 36.

183. Joseph P. Shapiro, "How Much Is Enough?" *U.S. News & World Report* (February 13, 1995), p. 38.

184. Thernstrom, *America in Black and White*, p. 399.

185. Thomas Sowell, "The New Racism on Campus," *Fortune* (February 13, 1989), p. 115 ff.

186. Thernstrom, *America in Black and White*, p. 400.

187. Thomas Sowell, "The New Racism on Campus," *Fortune* (February 13, 1989), p. 115 ff.

188. Walter E. Williams, "Race, Scholarship, and Affirmative Action: Campus Racism," *National Review* (May 5, 1989), p. 38.

189. *Ibid.*

190. Lino Graglia, "Affirmative Discrimination," *National Review* (July 5, 1993), p. 28.

191. John Leo, "The Luring of Black Students," *U.S. News & World Report* (March 15, 1993), p. 20.

192. *Ibid.*

193. *Ibid.*

194. *Ibid.*

195. Lino Graglia, "Affirmative Discrimination," *National Review* (July 5, 1993), p. 31.

196. Fox Butterfield, "Colleges Luring Black Students with Incentives," *The New York Times* (February 28, 1993), p. 1.

197. *Ibid.*

198. Brian McGrory, "Affirmative Action: An American Dilemma," *Boston Globe* (May 23, 1995), p. 1.

199. Fox Butterfield, "Colleges Luring Black Students with Incentives," *The New York Times* (February 28, 1993), p. 30.

200. *Ibid.*

201. *Ibid.* John Leo, "The Luring of Black Students," *U.S. News & World Report* (March 15, 1993), p. 20.

202. Lino Graglia, "Affirmative Discrimination," *National Review* (July 5, 1993), p. 31.

203. Claudia H. Deutsch, "Diversity Bedevils M.B.A. Programs," *The New York Times* (April 4, 1993), Section 4A, p. 22.

204. *Ibid.*

205. *Ibid.*

206. *Ibid.*

207. Michael Levin, *Feminism and Freedom* (New Brunswick, N.J.: Transaction Books, 1987), p. 119. Charles Murray, "The Coming of Custodial Democracy," *Commentary* (September 1988), p. 24. Ethan Bonner, "Colleges Look for Answer to Racial Gaps in Testing," *The New York Times* (November 8, 1997), p. A12.

208. Robert Zelnick, *Backfire* (Washington, D.C.: Regnery Publishing, Inc., 1996), p. 151.

209. Thomas Sowell, "An Early Quota 'Victory' Turns out the Contrary," *New York Post* (August 28, 1997), p. 31.

210. Stephan Thernstrom, "The Scandal of the Law Schools," *Commentary* (December 1997), p. 31.

211. Clifford Alexander, "What Affirmative Action Really Means," *The New York Times* (December 16, 1991).

212. Jimmie Briggs, "Hope of Our Past," *Emerge* (March 1994), p. 23.

213. Allan P. Sindler, *Bakke, DeFunis, and Minority Admissions: The Quest for Equal Opportunity* (New York: Longman, 1978), pp. 63-67. Thernstrom, *America in Black and White*, p. 413.

214. Thernstrom, *America in Black and White*, pp. 413-414.

215. Hilton Kramer, "Exhibit A for Quotas—Not," *New York Post* (September 2, 1997). Thomas Sowell, "An Early Quota 'Victory' Turns out the Contrary," *New York Post* (August 28, 1997), p. 31.

216. Thomas Sowell, "An Early Quota 'Victory' Turns out the Contrary," *New York Post* (August 28, 1997), p. 31.

217. Hilton Kramer, "Exhibit A for Quotas—Not," *New York Post* (September 2, 1997).

218. Thomas Sowell, "An Early Quota 'Victory' Turns out the Contrary," *New York Post* (August 28, 1997), p. 31.

219. Hilton Kramer, "Exhibit A for Quotas—Not," *New York Post* (September 2, 1997).

220. Jared Taylor, *Paved with Good Intentions*, pp. 181-182.

221. Stephan Thernstrom, "The Scandal of the Law Schools," *Commentary* (December 1997), p. 28.

222. Stephen Chapman, "A Law School Uproar Raises Unpleasant Facts About Race," *Chicago Tribune* (April 21, 1991).

223. Robert Zelnick, *Backfire*, p. 197.

224. Stephan Thernstrom, "The Scandal of the Law Schools," *Commentary* (December 1997), p. 30.

225. Tamar Lewin, "Minorities Achieve High Success Rate in Bar Exams, Study Says," *The New York Times* (May 20, 1998), p. B9.

226. Stephan Thernstrom, "The Scandal of the Law Schools," *Commentary* (December 1997), p. 30.

227. Thomas Sowell, *Inside American Education*, pp. 138-139.

228. *Ibid.*, p. 139.

229. Robert Klitgaard, *Choosing Elites* (New York: Basic Books, Inc., 1985), p. 175. Thomas Sowell, *Inside American Education*, p. 140.

230. Robert Klitgaard, *Choosing Elites*, p. 162.

231. Jeffrey Rosen, "Damage Control," *The New Yorker* (February 23 and March 2, 1998), p. 60.

232. Thomas Sowell, *Inside American Education*, pp. 123-124.

233. "Fitzsimmons Answers Questions on Admissions and Financial Aid," *Harvard Alumni Gazette* (February 1990), p. 5. Cited by Thomas Sowell, *Inside American Education*, p. 123.

234. Robert Klitgaard, *Choosing Elites*, p. 31.

235. Lawrence Feinberg, "Harvard: The Best, Not the Brightest?" *Washington Post Book World* (November 19, 1989), p. R13.

236. Thomas Sowell, *Inside American Education*, p. 123.

237. *Ibid.*

238. *Ibid.*, p. 124.

239. *Ibid.*, pp. 125-126.

240. *Ibid.*, p. 124.

241. Carl Cohen, "Race, Lies, and 'Hopwood,' " *Commentary* (June 1996), p. 41.

242. *Ibid.*

243. William G. Bowen and Derek Bok, *The Shape of the River* (Princeton: Princeton University Press, 1998), p. 26.

244. Robyn Blumner, "An Unwelcome Visitor," *New York Post* (February 7, 1999), p. 55.

245. Carl Cohen, "Race, Lies, and 'Hopwood,' " *Commentary* (June 1996), p. 41.

246. Steven A. Holmes, "A New Turn in Defense of Affirmative Action," *The New York Times* (May 11, 1999).

247. Anthony Lewis, "Turn of the Tide?" *The New York Times* (May 18, 1998), p. A19.

248. Bill Kauffman, "Out of the Box," *The American Enterprise* (November/December 1998), p. 39.

249. Walter E. Williams, "Race, Scholarship, and Affirmative Action: Campus Racism," *National Review* (May 5, 1989), pp. 37-38.

250. *Ibid.*

251. Dinesh D'Souza, *Illiberal Education*, pp. 29, 36.

252. Thomas Sowell, "Balkanizing the Schools of America," *New York Post* (April 30, 1993), p. 27.

253. June Kronholz, "Scholarship Program for Whites Becomes a Test for Preferences," *The Wall Street Journal* (December 23, 1997), pp. A1, A6.

254. Walter E. Williams, "Race, Scholarship, and Affirmative Action: Campus Racism," *National Review* (May 5, 1989), p. 38.

255. Richard Bernstein, "Racial Discrimination or Righting Past Wrongs?" *The New York Times* (July 13, 1994), p. B8.

256. Richard Bernstein, "Law School Calls Bias Ruling a Victory," *The New York Times* (August 21, 1994), p. 26. Richard Bernstein, "Racial Discrimination or Righting Past Wrongs?" *The New York Times* (July 13, 1994), p. B8.

257. Richard Bernstein, "Law School Calls Bias Ruling a Victory," *The New York Times* (August 21, 1994), p. 26.

258. George F. Will, "The Diversity Cult," *New York Post* (March 28, 1996), p. 31. Sam Howe Verhovek, "For Four Whites Who Sued University, Race Is the Common Thread," *The New York Times* (March 23, 1996), p. A6.

259. Peter Applebome, "Texas Is Told to Keep Affirmative Action in Univer-

sities or Risk Losing Federal Aid," *The New York Times* (March 26, 1997), p. B11.

260. *Ibid.* Peter Applebome, "In Shift, U.S. Tells Texas It Can't Ignore Court Ruling Barring Bias in College Admissions," *The New York Times* (April 15, 1997), p. A20.

261. John Parker, book review, *Destiny* (February 1994), p. 29. Jared Taylor, *Paved with Good Intentions*, p. 181.

262. Jared Taylor, *Paved with Good Intentions*, p. 181.

263. Lino Graglia, "Affirmative Discrimination," *National Review* (July 5, 1993), p. 29.

264. *Ibid.*

265. Sam Howe Verhovek, "Texas Law Professor Prompts a Furor over Race Comments," *The New York Times* (September 16, 1997), p. A28.

266. *Ibid.*

267. *Ibid.*

268. *Ibid.*

269. *Ibid.*

270. *Ibid.*

271. Dinesh D'Souza, *Illiberal Education*, pp. 28-29, 36.

272. *Ibid.*, p. 37.

273. *Ibid.*, p. 38.

274. *Ibid.*, p. 37.

275. Robyn Blumner, "An Unwelcome Visitor," *New York Post* (February 7, 1999), p. 55.

276. Dinesh D'Souza, *Illiberal Education*, pp. 35-36.

277. Jared Taylor, *Paved with Good Intentions*, p. 172. Dinesh D'Souza, *Illiberal Education*, p. 36.

278. *Ibid.*

279. Thernstrom, *America in Black and White*, p. 401.

280. Robert Berman, "Grade Inflation Not Just for the Rich," *New York Post* (March 1, 1998), p. 49.

281. John Leo, "The Luring of Black Students," *U.S. News & World Report* (March 15, 1993), p. 20.

282. Robert Berman, "Grade Inflation Not Just for the Rich," *New York Post* (March 1, 1998), p. 49.

283. Thernstrom, *America in Black and White*, p. 386.

284. Matthew Robinson, "Why Universities Do Not Teach," *Investor's Business Daily* (March 21, 1996). Diane Ravitch, "Do It Right the First Time," *Forbes* (February 10, 1997), p. 80.

285. Thomas Sowell, "Thoughts on the Passing Scene," *New York Post* (March 27, 1997), p. 25.

286. Todd Ackerman, "Texas A&M Study Calls for Boost in Minority Recruiting," *Houston Chronicle* (May 16, 1992).

287. Thomas Sowell, "Thoughts on the Passing Scene," *New York Post* (March 27, 1997), p. 25.

288. Thomas DeLoughry, "At Penn State, Polarization of Campus Persists Amid Struggles to Ease Tensions," *The Chronicle of Higher Education* (April 26, 1989).

289. Lino Graglia, "Affirmative Discrimination," *National Review* (July 5, 1993), p. 29.

290. Walter E. Williams, "Race, Scholarship, and Affirmative Action: Campus Racism," *National Review* (May 5, 1989), p. 37.

291. *Ibid.*

292. *Ibid.*

293. *Ibid.*

294. *Ibid.*

295. U.S. Department of Education, *Higher Education Opportunities for Minorities and Women—Annotated Selections* (Washington, D.C.: U.S. Department of Education, 1989), p. 7.

296. *Ibid.*, pp. 22, 23, 57, 78.

297. U.S. Department of Education, *Higher Education Opportunities for Minorities and Women—Annotated Selections* (1989).

298. *The Minority Student's Complete Scholarship Book* (Naperville, Illinois: Sourcebooks, 1997).

299. *The Black Student's Guide to Scholarships* (Lanham, Maryland: Madison Books, 1996).

300. Andres Tobar, *The Hispanic Scholarship Directory* (Carlsbad, California: WPR Publishing, 1997).

301. Doris Young and William Young, *The Higher Education Moneybook for Women and Minorities* (Washington, D.C.: Young Enterprises Intl., 1996).

302. *Directory of Financial Aid for Minorities* (San Carlos, California: Reference Service Press, 1997).

303. *National Directory of Minority Organizations* (Chicago: Ferguson Publishing Co., 1997).

304. Willis L. Johnson, ed., *The Big Book of Minority Opportunities* (Garrett Park, Maryland: Garrett Park Press, 1995).

305. *Barron's Complete College Financing Guide* (Hauppauge, N.Y.: Barron, 1997), pp. 190-191.

306. J. Robert Dumouchel, *Government Assistance Almanac, 1991-92* (Detroit and Washington, D.C.: co-published by Omnigraphics, Inc. and Foggy Bottom Publications, 1991), pp. 333-334.

307. *Ibid.*, pp. 353-354.

308. Linda Greenhouse, "Supreme Court to Review Record on Bias in Mississippi Colleges," *The New York Times* (April 16, 1991), p. A19. Jared Taylor, *Paved with Good Intentions*, p. 251.

309. Associated Press, "Minorities Deserving of Financial Aid, Study Says," *Gazette Telegraph* (Colorado Springs) (June 22, 1991). Jared Taylor, *Paved with Good Intentions*, p. 251.

310. Fox Butterfield, "Colleges Luring Black Students with Incentives,"

The New York Times (February 28, 1993), p. 30.

311. Jared Taylor, *Paved with Good Intentions*, p. 174.

312. Fox Butterfield, "Colleges Luring Black Students with Incentives," *The New York Times* (February 28, 1993), p. 30.

313. "Tuition at Campus Is Free for All Black Freshmen," *The New York Times* (March 9, 1990), p. A12.

314. Jared Taylor, *Paved with Good Intentions*, pp. 173-174.

315. Don Wycliffe, "Science Careers Are Attracting Few Blacks," *The New York Times* (June 8, 1990), p. 1.

316. "Yale Trying to Recruit Minority Faculty," *Omaha World-Herald* (February 11, 1990).

317. "Minority Update," *The Chronicle of Higher Education* (June 27, 1990), p. A32.

318. Colette Connolly, "Speech Program Receives Grant for Minority Students," *Reporter's Impact* (November 24, 1993), p. 3.

319. *Ibid.*

320. "Free Graduate School for Minority Students," *The New York Times* (March 21, 1990), p. B5.

321. Kathleen Teltsch, "Grant Seeks to Attract Minorities to Teaching," *The New York Times* (September 23, 1990).

322. U.S. Department of Education, *Higher Education Opportunities for Minorities and Women—Annotated Selections* (1989), p. 39.

323. Jared Taylor, *Paved with Good Intentions*, p. 175.

324. U.S. Department of Education, *Higher Education Opportunities for Minorities and Women—Annotated Selections* (1989), pp. 76, 81.

325. *Ibid.*, p. 26.

326. "Black History Month," *Reference Service Press* (February 1996).

327. *Ibid.*

328. U.S. Department of Education, *Higher Education Opportunities for Minorities and Women—Annotated Selections* (1989), p. 46.

329. *Ibid.*, p. 71.

330. *Ibid.*, p. 56.

331. *Ibid.*, p. 62.

332. *Ibid.*, p. 52.

333. *Ibid.*, p. 70.

334. *Ibid.*, p. 67.

335. *Ibid.*, p. 64

336. *Ibid.*, pp. 63-64.

337. *Ibid.*, p. 49.

338. *Ibid.*, pp. 52-53.

339. *Ibid.*, p. 49

340. *Ibid.*, p. 18.

341. Tamara Henry, "Race-Based Scholarships Now 'Proper,' " *USA Today* (March 18, 1993), p. 1. Sabra Chartrand, "Administration Backs Race-Based

Scholarships," *The New York Times* (October 27, 1993), p. B8.

342. Sabra Chartrand, "Administration Backs Race-Based Scholarships," *The New York Times* (October 27, 1993), p. B8.

343. *Ibid.*

344. "Court Bars Racially Restricted Scholarships," *Reporter Dispatch* (Gannett Suburban Newspapers) (October 28, 1994), p. 6B.

345. Stephen A. Holmes, "Minority Scholarship Plans Are Dealt Setback by Court," *The New York Times* (May 23, 1995), p. B9.

346. Jared Taylor, *Paved with Good Intentions*, pp. 169-170.

347. Kenneth Pins, "Black Hoop Coaches Make Voices Heard," *Reporter Dispatch* (Gannett Suburban Newspapers) (October 20, 1993), p. 3D. Jared Taylor, *Paved with Good Intentions*, p. 170.

348. Catherine S. Manegold, "Fewer Men Earn Doctorates, Particularly Among Blacks," *The New York Times* (January 18, 1994), p. A14.

349. *Ibid.*

350. Alvin P. Sanoff et al., "Race on Campus," *U.S. News & World Report* (April 19, 1993), p. 61.

351. "Future of Blacks in U.S. Draws 400 to Harvard," *The New York Times* (February 8, 1989), p. B11.

352. *Ibid.*

353. *Ibid.*

354. Kenneth J. Cooper, "Seeking Better Teachers," *Washington Post Education Review* (November 18, 1990), pp. 20-21.

355. National Research Council, *A Common Destiny: Blacks and American Society* (Washington, D.C.: National Academy Press, 1989), p. 363.

356. Dinesh D'Souza, *The End of Racism*, p. 306. William Raspberry, "An Old Debate Is Changing," *Chicago Tribune* (January 21, 1985), p. 11.

357. National Center for Education Statistics, *Digest of Educational Statistics: 1995*, NCES 95-029 (Washington, D.C.: U.S. Department of Education, 1995), p. 150.

358. Rogers Elliott, "Tests, Abilities, Race, and Conflict," *Intelligence* 12 (1988), p. 343.

359. Faustine Jones-Wilson, "The State of African-American Education," in Kofi Lomotey, ed., *Going to School: The African-American Experience* (Albany: State University of New York Press, 1990), p. 47.

360. Thernstrom, *America in Black and White*, p. 374.

361. Joseph Berger, "Pessimism in Air As Schools Try Affirmative Action," *The New York Times* (February 27, 1990), p. B1. Abigail Thernstrom, "Beyond the Pale," *The New Republic* (December 16, 1991), p. 22.

362. Thernstrom, *America in Black and White*, p. 374.

363. Joseph Berger, "Pessimism in Air As Schools Try Affirmative Action," *The New York Times* (February 27, 1990), p. B1. Abigail Thernstrom, "Beyond the Pale," *The New Republic* (December 16, 1991), p. 22. Jared Taylor, *Paved with Good Intentions*, p. 209.

Notes　541

364. Ronald G. Ehrenberg, Daniel D. Goldhaber, and Dominic J. Brewer, "Do Teachers' Race, Gender, and Ethnicity Matter?" *Journal of Economic Literature Classification* (March 1, 1994).

365. Thomas Sowell, "Buzzwords Mask Real Ills of Society," *Daily News* (New York) (July 27, 1990), p. 33.

366. Thernstrom, *America in Black and White*, pp. 373-374.

367. Joseph Berger, "Plan for Schools on Minority Hiring," *The New York Times* (February 16, 1990), p. A1. Joseph Berger, "Pessimism in Air As Schools Try Affirmative Action," *The New York Times* (February 27, 1990), p. B1. Jared Taylor, *Paved with Good Intentions*, p. 135.

368. Robert Detlefsen, *Civil Rights Under Reagan* (San Francisco: Institute for Contemporary Studies, 1991), p. 74.

369. Frederick Lynch, *Invisible Victims*, p. 39.

370. Chancellor Williams, *The Destruction of Black Civilization: Great Issues of a Race from 4500 B.C. to 2000 A.D.* (Chicago: Third World Press, 1987), p. 131.

371. Dinesh D'Souza, *The End of Racism*, p. 369.

372. *Ibid.*

373. Ivan Van Sertima, "Future Directions for African and African-American Content in the School Curriculum," in Asa Hilliard, ed., *Infusion of African and African-American Content in the School Curriculum* (Morristown, New Jersey: Aaron Press, 1989), pp. 87-88, 95. Ivan Van Sertima, "African Science Before the Birth of the New World" *The Black Collegian* (January-February 1992), p. 69.

374. Na'im Akbar, *Visions for Black Men* (Nashville: Winston-Derek, 1991), p. 48.

375. John G. Jackson, *Introduction to African Civilization* (New York: Carol Publishing, 1970), p. 23.

376. Dinesh D'Souza, *The End of Racism*, p. 370.

377. *Ibid.* Wade Nobles, *African Psychology: Toward Its Reclamation, Reascension & Revitalization* (Oakland: Black Family Institute, 1986), p. 24.

378. Na'im Akbar, *Visions for Black Men*, p. 28.

379. Chancellor Williams, *The Destruction of Black Civilization*, p. 135. Dinesh D'Souza, *The End of Racism*, p. 372.

380. *Ibid.*

381. Dinesh D'Souza, *The End of Racism*, p. 373.

382. Ivan Van Sertima, "African Science Before the Birth of the New World" *The Black Collegian* (January-February 1992), pp. 69-70.

383. *Ibid.*

384. Na'im Akbar, *Visions for Black Men*, p. 57.

385. Chancellor Williams, *The Destruction of Black Civilization*, pp. 164-165.

386. John Leo, "Truth Doesn't Seem to Matter Much Anymore," *Daily News* (New York) (December 10, 1996), p. 37.

387. Dinesh D'Souza, *The End of Racism*, p. 381.

388. Thernstrom, *America in Black and White*, p. 369.

389. "Quotas in School Discipline," *National Review* (February 7, 1994), p. 22.

390. Thernstrom, *America in Black and White*, pp. 315-316.

391. *Ibid.*, p. 316.

392. Alan Goldman, *Justice and Reverse Discrimination*, pp. 211, 212.

393. Lino Graglia, "Affirmative Discrimination," *National Review* (July 5, 1993), p. 30.

394. *Ibid.*

395. William O. Douglas, *The Court Years: 1939-1975* (New York: Random House, 1980), p. 149.

396. Karl Zinsmeister, "When Black and White Turn Gray," *The American Enterprise* (November-December 1998), p. 7.

397. Gertrude Ezorsky, *Racism and Justice: The Case for Affirmative Action*, p. 42.

398. Cokie Roberts and Steven V. Roberts, "Diversity Is Still Vital," *Daily News* (New York) (August 30, 1997), p. 21.

399. *Ibid.*

400. *Ibid.*

401. Patrick J. Buchanan, "Chelsea, for Example," *New York Post* (August 23, 1997), p. 15.

402. Ethan Bronner, "Fewer Minorities Entering U. of California," *The New York Times* (May 21, 1998), p. A28.

403. *Ibid.*

404. *Ibid.*

405. Associated Press, "Calif. Affirmative-Action Ban Now Law," *New York Post* (August 29, 1997).

406. George F. Will, "Jesse's Double Standard on Democracy and Race," *New York Post* (September 10, 1997).

407. Cokie Roberts and Steven V. Roberts, "Diversity Is Still Vital," *Daily News* (New York) (August 30, 1997), p. 21.

408. *Ibid.*

409. *Ibid.*

410. *Ibid.*

411. Ethan Bronner, "Fewer Minorities Entering U. of California," *The New York Times* (May 21, 1998), p. A28.

412. *Ibid.*

413. Frank Bruni, "Blacks at Berkeley Are Offering No Welcome Mat," *The New York Times* (May 2, 1998), p. A1.

414. *Ibid.*, p. A8.

415. Ethan Bronner, "Black and Hispanic Admissions Off Sharply at U. of California," *The New York Times* (April 1, 1998), p. B11.

416. *Ibid.*

417. Patrick J. Buchanan, "Chelsea, for Example," *New York Post* (August 23, 1997), p. 15.

418. Thomas Sowell, "Affirmative Action Fog and Lies," *New York Post* (September 30, 1997), p. 27. Rush Limbaugh, "My Conversation with Ward Connerly," *Limbaugh Letter* (August 1997), p. 9. Thomas Sowell, "Affirmative Action's Other Side," *New York Post* (June 8, 1999).

419. Thomas Sowell, "Affirmative Action Fog and Lies," *New York Post* (September 30, 1997), p. 27.

420. Steven A. Holmes, "Victorious Preference Foes Look for New Battle-fields," *The New York Times* (November 10, 1998).

421. Tamar Lewin, "Affirmative Action Voided at Public School," *The New York Times* (November 20, 1998).

422. *Ibid.*

423. Booker T. Washington, *Up from Slavery* (New York: Dell Publishing Company, 1965), p. 37.

424. *Ibid.*, p. 40.

425. William Raspberry, "Confidence Spurs Competence in Minority Students," *Daily News* (New York) (July 19, 1994), p. 31.

426. *Ibid.*

427. Thomas Sowell, "Let's Stop Understanding Black Failures," *New York Post* (June 28, 1997), p. 15.

428. Civia Tamarkin and Marva Collins, *Marva Collins' Way* (Los Angeles: J.P. Tarcher, Inc., 1982), pp. 216-223.

429. Thomas Sowell, "Minority Schools and the Politics of Education," *Imprimis* (January 1999), p. 2.

430. Ronald Smothers, "To Raise the Performance of Minorities, a College Increased Its Standards," *The New York Times* (June 29, 1994), p. A21.

431. *Ibid.*

432. William Raspberry, "Confidence Spurs Competence in Minority Students," *Daily News* (New York) (July 19, 1994), p. 31.

433. *Ibid.*

434. Shelby Steele, *The Content of Our Character*, pp. 87-89, 118-122.

Chapter 10
The Disaster of Preferential Policies

1. Charles V. Roman, "What the Negro May Reasonably Expect of the White Man," *American Civilization and the Negro* (1916). Cited by Dorothy Winbush, ed., *My Soul Looks Back 'Less I Forget: A Collection of Quotations by People of Color* (New York: HarperCollins, 1993), p. 31.

2. James Bennet, "Union Plans Bias Lawsuit over Agency Promotions," *The New York Times* (March 15, 1993), p. B3.

3. *Ibid.*

4. "Color Them Black," *Time* (October 31, 1988), p. 19. Frederick Lynch, *Invisible Victims*, p. 28.

5. Jared Taylor, *Paved with Good Intentions*, pp. 129-130.

6. *Ibid.*, p. 130

7. *Ibid.*, p. 158.

8. Robert G. Holland, "Dirty Secrets," *Chronicles* (February 1992), p. 44.

9. Jared Taylor, *Paved with Good Intentions*, p. 131.

10. Frederick Lynch, *Invisible Victims*, p. 27.

11. Sonia Nazario, "Many Minorities Feel Torn by Experience of Affirmative Action," *The Wall Street Journal* (June 27, 1989), p. A1.

12. Dinesh D'Souza, *The End of Racism*, p. 294.

13. Jared Taylor, "Suppressed Rage," *Destiny* (April 1995), p. 22.

14. Associated Press, "Non-White Firefighter Applicants Get Boost," *New York Post* (February 1, 1991).

15. Clint Bolick, *Changing Course* (New Brunswick, N.J.: Transaction Books, 1988), p. 69.

16. Jodi Wilgoren and Michael Cooper, "Police Trailing Other Cities in Diversity," *The New York Times* (March 8, 1999).

17. Jonathan P. Hicks, "Minority Groups Call for Changes in Police Recruiting Methods," *The New York Times* (November 1, 1992), Section 1, p. 51.

18. Timothy Callahan and Charles Bahme, *Fire Service and the Law* (Quincy, Mass.: National Fire Protection Association, 1987), p. 56.

19. Michael D. Levin-Epstein, *Primer of Equal Employment Opportunity* (Washington, D.C.: Bureau of National Affairs, 1987), pp. 90-91, 93.

20. Dinesh D'Souza, *The End of Racism*, p. 298.

21. Michael D. Levin-Epstein, *Primer of Equal Employment Opportunity*, p. 89.

22. *Ibid.*, p. 92.

23. Robert Detlefsen, *Civil Rights Under Reagan*, pp. 34, 37. Dinesh D'Souza, *The End of Racism*, p. 222.

24. Dinesh D'Souza, *The End of Racism*, p. 320.

25. *How to Eliminate Discriminatory Practices: A Guide to EEO Compliance* (New York: AMACOM, 1975), p. 70.

26. Nathan Glazer, *Affirmative Discrimination: Ethnic Inequality and Public Policy*, p. 59.

27. *Ibid.*

28. Alfred Blumrosen, *Modern Law: The Law Transmission System and Equal Employment Opportunity* (Madison: University of Wisconsin Press, 1993), p. 230

29. Walter E. Williams, "OSHA Looking out for You," *Conservative Chronicle* (January 25, 1995), p. 1.

30. Louis Freedberg, "The Enforcer," *San Francisco Chronicle* (June 4, 1995), p. 1. Thernstrom, *America in Black and White*, p. 423.

31. *Ibid.*

32. Jared Taylor, *Paved with Good Intentions*, p. 149.

33. Dinesh D'Souza, *The End of Racism*, p. 320. Rush Limbaugh, "Affir-

mative Action: End It," *Limbaugh Letter* (April 1995), p. 4. Robert Zelnick, *Backfire*, p. 10.

34. Rush Limbaugh, "Affirmative Action: End It," *Limbaugh Letter* (April 1995), p. 4. Dinesh D'Souza, *The End of Racism*, p. 320.

35. Jared Taylor, *Paved with Good Intentions*, p. 149.

36. Harish C. Jain and Peter J. Sloan, *Equal Employment Issues: Race and Sex Discrimination in the U.S., Canada, and Britain* (New York: Praeger, 1981), p. 101.

37. Dinesh D'Souza, *The End of Racism*, p. 320.

38. Rush Limbaugh, "Affirmative Action: End It," *Limbaugh Letter* (April 1995), p. 4. Dinesh D'Souza, *The End of Racism*, p. 320.

39. Jared Taylor, *Paved with Good Intentions*, p. 149.

40. Michael D. Levin-Epstein, *Primer of Equal Employment Opportunity*, p. 151. Dinesh D'Souza, *The End of Racism*, p. 320.

41. Robert Zelnick, *Backfire*, p. 42.

42. Michael D. Levin-Epstein, *Primer of Equal Employment Opportunity*, p. 320.

43. Dinesh D'Souza, *The End of Racism*, p. 320.

44. Robert Zelnick, *Backfire*, p. 43.

45. Robert Bork, *Slouching Towards Gomorrah* (New York: HarperCollins, 1996), pp. 234, 236.

46. Rush Limbaugh, "Affirmative Action: End It," *Limbaugh Letter* (April 1995), p. 4. Dinesh D'Souza, *The End of Racism*, p. 335.

47. Sally C. Pipes, "Quashing Quotas," *Investor's Business Daily* (March 1, 1995).

48. Linda Greenhouse, "Court Bars Plan Set up to Provide Jobs to Minorities," *The New York Times* (January 24, 1989), p. 1. Stephen Yates, *Civil Wrongs*, p. 5.

49. Stephen Yates, *Civil Wrongs*, pp. 6-8, 9.

50. *Ibid.*, p. 44.

51. Michael deCourcy Hinds, "Minority Business Set Back Sharply by Courts' Rulings," *The New York Times* (December 23, 1991), p. A1. "Affirmative Action," *Economist* (April 15, 1995), p. 21.

52. Ralph Vartabedian, "U.S. Program to Help Minority Firms Plagued by Failures," *Los Angeles Times* (July 7, 1991), p. D1.

53. Thernstrom, *America in Black and White*, p. 440.

54. *Ibid.* Greg Foster, "Tax Breaks for Being Black," *The Wall Street Journal* (November 8, 1995), p. A20.

55. Paul M. Barrett, "Successful, Affluent, but Still 'Disadvantaged,' " *The Wall Street Journal* (June 13, 1995), p. B1.

56. Dinesh D'Souza, *The End of Racism*, p. 236.

57. Ralph Vartabedian, "U.S. Program to Help Minority Firms Plagued by Failures," *Los Angeles Times* (July 7, 1991), p. D1.

58. Michael D. Levin-Epstein, *Primer of Equal Employment Opportunity*, p. 96.

59. Felicia R. Lee, "Council Passes Civil Rights Bill for New York," *The New*

York Times (June 6, 1991), p. B4. Jared Taylor, *Paved with Good Intentions*, p. 146.

60. Jared Taylor, *Paved with Good Intentions*, p. 147.

61. Timothy Noah and Albert Karr, "What New Civil Rights Law Will Mean," *The Wall Street Journal* (November 4, 1991), p. B1.

62. Jared Taylor, *Paved with Good Intentions*, pp. 159-160.

63. Michael Taylor, "AC Transit Aide Suspended for Biased Remarks," *San Francisco Chronicle* (May 12, 1990), p. A7.

64. "Civil Rights Exemption," *The Wall Street Journal* (July 25, 1990), p. A12.

65. Eric Felten, *The Ruling Class* (Washington, D.C.: Regnery Gateway, 1993), p. 7.

66. Mona Charen, "Sweetness and Light for Ginsburg," *New York Post* (July 26, 1993), p. 17.

67. *Ibid.*

68. Jared Taylor, *Paved with Good Intentions*, pp. 149-150.

69. Frederick Lynch, *Invisible Victims*, p. 145.

70. *Ibid.*

71. "Airline Creates Affirmative Action Program to Settle Job Bias Suit," *The New York Times* (May 12, 1991).

72. Frederick Lynch, *Invisible Victims*, p. 145.

73. Thernstrom, *America in Black and White*, p. 503.

74. *Ibid.*, p. 504.

75. *Ibid.*

76. *Ibid.*, pp. 503-504. Demetrius Patterson, "Texaco Plaintiffs Celebrate," *Reporter Dispatch* (Gannett Suburban Newspapers) (March 13, 1997).

77. Al Guart, "Texaco Execs Not Guilty," *New York Post* (May 13, 1998), p. 7.

78. Jared Taylor, *Paved with Good Intentions*, p. 146.

79. Steven A. Holmes, "Some Employees Lose Right to Sue for Bias at Work," *The New York Times* (March 18, 1994), pp. A1, B6.

80. *Ibid.*

81. Thomas Sowell, *Preferential Policies*, pp. 44-45.

82. *The Official NBA Basketball Encyclopedia* (New York: Villard Books, 1994).

83. Thomas Sowell, *Civil Rights: Rhetoric or Reality?*, p. 19. *The Baseball Encyclopedia* (New York: MacMillan Publishing Co., Inc., 1985).

84. "A Tenuous Bond From 9 to 5," *Newsweek* (March 7, 1988), p. 25.

85. Lawrence Otis Graham, *The Best Companies for Minorities* (New York: Plume, 1993), pp. 53, 63, 108, 203.

86. *Ibid.*, pp. 266, 312-313.

87. Howard Gleckman et al., "Race in the Workplace," *Business Week* (July 8, 1991), p. 52.

88. Lawrence Otis Graham, *The Best Companies for Minorities*, pp. 186, 68.

89. *Ibid.*, p. 24.

90. Jonathan Tilove, "Many Major Corporations Committed to Affirmative Action," *Grand Rapids Press* (August 4, 1991), p. D7.

91. Lawrence Otis Graham, *The Best Companies for Minorities*, p. 408.

92. *Ibid.*, p. 191.

93. Lawrence Otis Graham, *The Best Companies for Minorities*.

94. *Ibid.*, pp. 122, 368.

95. *Ibid.*, p. 5.

96. *Ibid.*

97. *Ibid.*, p. 119.

98. *Ibid.*, p. 408.

99. *Ibid.*, p. 24.

100. *Ibid.*, p. 188.

101. David J. Fox, "Disney Sets up Minority Program," *Los Angeles Times* (September 27, 1990).

102. Lawrence Otis Graham, *The Best Companies for Minorities*, pp. 59, 71, 84.

103. *Ibid.*, p. 323.

104. *Ibid.*, p. 386.

105. *Ibid.*, p. 260.

106. Alan Farnham, "Holding Firm on Affirmative Action," *Fortune* (March 13, 1989), p. 88.

107. *Ibid.*

108. *Ibid.*

109. Lawrence Otis Graham, *The Best Companies for Minorities*, p. 64.

110. *Ibid.*, p. 44.

111. *Ibid.*, p. 123.

112. *Ibid.*, p. 188.

113. *Ibid.*, pp. 236, 270, 382. Jared Taylor, *Paved with Good Intentions*, p. 155. Mark Land, "Where Diversity Survives Hard Times," *USA Today* (January 8, 1992), p. 8B.

114. Jonathan Tilove, "Recruiting Minorities by the Numbers Nothing New," *Grand Rapids Press* (June 9, 1991), p. F1. Claudia Deutsch, "Listening to Women and Blacks," *The New York Times* (December 1, 1991), p. 25. Lawrence Otis Graham, *The Best Companies for Minorities*, p. 64,

115. Lawrence Otis Graham, *The Best Companies for Minorities*, p. 156.

116. *Ibid.*, pp. 93-94.

117. *Ibid.*, p. 279.

118. Joan Rigdon, "PepsiCo's KFC Scouts for Blacks and Women for Its Top Echelons," *The Wall Street Journal* (November 13, 1991), p. 1.

119. Lawrence Otis Graham, *The Best Companies for Minorities*, p. 297.

120. *Ibid.*, p. 32.

121. *Ibid.*, p. 239.

122. Joan Rigdon, "PepsiCo's KFC Scouts for Blacks and Women for Its Top Echelons," *The Wall Street Journal* (November 13, 1991), p. 1.

123. Lawrence Otis Graham, *The Best Companies for Minorities*, p. 342.

124. *Ibid.*, p. 398.

125. *Ibid.*, p. 129.

126. *Ibid.*, p. 309.

127. *Ibid.*, p. 300.

128. *Ibid.*, p. 172.

129. *Ibid.*, p. 320.

130. *Ibid.*, p. 227.

131. *Ibid.*, p. 387.

132. *Ibid.*, pp. 347-348.

133. John Wagner, "Black Papers Are Fighting for Survival," *The Wall Street Journal* (October 4, 1990), p. B1.

134. Lawrence Otis Graham, *The Best Companies for Minorities*, p. 165.

135. *Ibid.*, p. 210.

136. *Ibid.*, p. 56.

137. *Ibid.*, p. 152.

138. *Ibid.*, p. 222.

139. *Ibid.*, p. 129.

140. *Ibid.*, p. 105.

141. *Ibid.*, p. 286.

142. *Ibid.*, pp. 247, 226.

143. *Ibid.*, p. 342.

144. Robert Brustein, "As the Globe Turns," *The New Republic* (February 18, 1991), p. 53.

145. *Ibid.*

146. "$20 Million Is Given in Effort to Increase Minority Instructors," *The New York Times* (October 8, 1993), p. A25.

147. Lawrence Otis Graham, *The Best Companies for Minorities*, p. 24.

148. *Ibid.*, p. 256.

149. *Ibid.*, p. 46.

150. *Ibid.*, p. 309.

151. *Ibid.*, p. 345.

152. *Ibid.*, p. 71.

153. *Ibid.*, p. 115.

154. *Ibid.*, p. 335.

155. *Ibid.*, pp. 96, 197-198.

156. *Ibid.*, p. 165.

157. *Ibid.*, p. 149.

158. Udayan Gupta, "Affirmative Buying," *The Wall Street Journal* (April 3, 1992), p. R12.

159. Lawrence Otis Graham, *The Best Companies for Minorities*.

160. Elizabeth Fowler, "Univex Chief Expands Role on Minorities," *The New York Times* (August 8, 1988), p. 25.

161. Christopher Williams, "Big Business Reaches out to Minority Sup-

pliers," *The New York Times* (November 12, 1989).

162. Jared Taylor, *Paved with Good Intentions*, p. 162.

163. *Moneyline* (television program on CNN), hosted by Lou Dobbs (March 11, 1997).

164. *Ibid.*

165. *Ibid.*

166. *Ibid.*

167. Derrick Bell, *Faces at the Bottom of the Well*, p. 5.

168. *Ibid.*, p. 15.

169. Carl Rowan, "Message to Black Youth: Learning Liberates," *New York Post* (May 2, 1995), p. 21.

170. Gertrude Ezorsky, *Racism and Justice*, p. 18.

171. Linda Chavez, "Demystifying Multiculturalism," *National Review* (February 21, 1994), p. 26. Frederick Lynch, "Workforce Diversity: PC's Final Frontier?" *National Review* (February 21, 1994), p. 34.

172. Thomas Sowell, *Is Reality Optional?*, p. 160. Lawrence Otis Graham, *The Best Companies for Minorities*, p. 241.

173. "Seeing Through Black Eyes," *Newsweek* (March 7, 1988), p. 26. Jared Taylor, *Paved with Good Intentions*, p. 33.

174. Dinesh D'Souza, *Illiberal Education*, p. 217.

175. *Ibid.*, pp. 215-220.

176. *Ibid.*, p. 219.

177. "White, Male, and Worried," *Business Week* (January 31, 1994), p. 51.

178. Bill Gifford, "The Unbearable Whiteness of Being," *Washington City Paper* (November 12, 1993), p. 30.

179. Robert Bork, *Slouching Towards Gomorrah*, p. 246.

180. Thomas Sowell, *Is Reality Optional?*, p. 160.

181. Frederick Lynch, "Workforce Diversity: PC's Final Frontier?" *National Review* (February 21, 1994), p. 34.

182. Associated Press, "Male Employees Accuse F.A.A. of Sex Harassment at Workshops," *The New York Times* (September 8, 1994), p. A22.

183. *Ibid.*

184. Dinesh D'Souza, *The End of Racism*, p. 327.

185. Lawrence Otis Graham, *The Best Companies for Minorities*.

186. Heather MacDonald, "The Diversity Industry," *The New Republic* (July 5, 1993), p. 23. Frederick Lynch, "Workforce Diversity: PC's Final Frontier?" *National Review* (February 21, 1994), p. 34.

187. Linda Chavez, "Demystifying Multiculturalism," *National Review* (February 21, 1994), p. 26.

188. Phyllis A. Wallace, ed., *Equal Employment Opportunity and the AT&T Case* (Cambridge, Mass. and London, England: The MIT Press, 1976), p. 269.

189. Gertrude Ezorsky, *Racism and Justice*, p. 41.

190. Phyllis A. Wallace, ed., *Equal Employment Opportunity and the AT&T Case*, p. 288.

191. Jared Taylor, *Paved with Good Intentions*, p. 158.

192. Frederick R. Lynch, *Invisible Victims*, p. 44.

193. Robert Zelnick, *Backfire*, pp. 73-74.

194. *Ibid.*, p. 74.

195. *Ibid.*

196. *Ibid.*, pp. 74-75.

197. *Ibid.*, p. 75.

198. Dinesh D'Souza, *The End of Racism*, p. 222.

199. Robert Zelnick, *Backfire*, p. 75.

200. *Ibid.*

201. *Ibid.*, p. 76.

202. *Ibid.*, p. 77.

203. *Ibid.*, p. 92.

204. *Ibid.*

205. *Ibid.*

206. Jared Taylor, *Paved with Good Intentions*, p. 132.

207. Robert Zelnick, *Backfire*, p. 92.

208. *Ibid.*, pp. 95-96.

209. Minoo Southgate, "Black Power, Nineties Style," *National Review* (December 13, 1993), p. 46.

210. Don Feder, "Farrakhan Highlights Black Leadership's Failure," *Conservative Chronicle* (March 30, 1994), p. 28.

211. Minoo Southgate, "Black Power, Nineties Style," *National Review* (December 13, 1993), p. 46.

212. *Ibid.*

213. *Ibid.*, p. 47.

214. Chrisena Coleman, "AT&T Called to Task: Sharpton to Protest Cartoon," *Daily News* (New York) (September 29, 1993), p. 30.

215. *Ibid.*

216. Tom Lowry, "AT&T Called to Task: SCLC Has Heat on in Atlanta," *Daily News* (New York) (September 29, 1993), p. 30. Gary Stern, "AT&T Takes Action Over Drawing," *Reporter Dispatch* (Gannett Suburban Newspapers) (October 2, 1993), p. 3B.

217. Minoo Southgate, "Black Power, Nineties Style," *National Review* (December 13, 1993), p. 47.

218. Frederick Lynch, *Invisible Victims*, p. 45.

219. *Ibid.*

220. Hilton Kramer, "The Triumph of Cynicism," *New York Post* (April 15, 1997).

221. Associated Press, "Black Caucus Flexes Its Muscles," *The Washington Times* (September 15, 1989).

222. Paul Craig Roberts, "Quotas Here, Quotas There, Quotas Everywhere," *Conservative Chronicle* (March 2, 1994), p. 18.

223. Dinesh D'Souza, *The End of Racism*, p. 292.

224. James Workman, "Gender Norming," *The New Republic* (July 1, 1991), p. 16.

225. Dinesh D'Souza, *The End of Racism*, p. 292.

226. Shanon LaFraniere, "Agents Say FBI Has Adopted Hiring, Promotion Quotas," *The Washington Post* (June 17, 1991), p. A1.

227. Paul Craig Roberts, "Quotas Here, Quotas There, Quotas Everywhere," *Conservative Chronicle* (March 2, 1994), p. 18. Dinesh D'Souza, *The End of Racism*, p. 292.

228. Paul Craig Roberts, "Quotas Here, Quotas There, Quotas Everywhere," *Conservative Chronicle* (March 2, 1994), p. 18.

229. "Quotas in the Marine Corps," *New York Post* (September 27, 1998), p. 58.

230. Deroy Murdock, "Moving to Split Racial Hairs," *New York Post* (July 7, 1994), p. 25.

231. Iver Peterson, "Justice Dept. Switches Sides in Racial Case," *The New York Times* (August 14, 1994), pp. 37, 46.

232. James K. Glassman, "New Affirmative-Action Defense: Gagging Critics," *New York Post* (November 28, 1997), p. 35. Angela C. Allen and Andy Geller, "Blacks Ante up to Keep Bias Suit out of Court," *New York Post* (November 22, 1997), p. 5. Barry Bearark, "Rights Groups Ducked a Fight, Opponents Say," *The New York Times* (November 22, 1997), pp. A1, B5. Linda Greenhouse, "Tactical Retreat: New Jersey School Move Leaves Affirmative Action in Limbo," *The New York Times* (November 22, 1997), pp. A1, B4.

233. "Affirmative-Action Cowardice," *New York Post* (February 7, 1999), p. 54.

234. Stephen Labaton, "Affirmative Action Case Embroils Clinton," *The New York Times* (April 25, 1995), p. A15.

235. "Black Judgeships Offered," *Houston Chronicle* (February 20, 1991).

236. Catherine Ryan, "Council Favors Woman or Minority for Judgeship," *Reporter Dispatch* (Gannett Suburban Newspapers) (March 26, 1993).

237. Deborah Orin, "Clinton Says Affirmative Action's Still a Good Thing," *New York Post* (July 20, 1995), p. 8.

238. Todd S. Purdum, "President Shows Fervent Support for Goals of Affirmative Action," *The New York Times* (July 20, 1995), p. B10.

239. Roberto Suro, "In Redistricting, New Rules and New Prizes," *The New York Times* (May 5, 1990). Charles Lane, "Ghetto Chic," *The New Republic* (August 12, 1991), p. 14. Jared Taylor, *Paved with Good Intentions*, pp. 191-192.

240. *Ibid.*

241. Charles Krauthammer, "The Voters Proved Hollowness of Race Gerrymandering," *Daily News* (New York) (November 18, 1996), p. 27.

242. Deroy Murdock, "Moving to Split Racial Hairs," *New York Post* (July 7, 1994), p. 25.

243. Thernstrom, *America in Black and White*, p. 294.

244. "Remapping Rulings Favor Minorities," *San Francisco Chronicle*

(January 8, 1991), p. A2. Jared Taylor, *Paved with Good Intentions*, pp. 191-192.

245. Linda Greenhouse, "Justices, in 5-4 Vote, Reject Districts Drawn with Race the 'Predominant Factor,'" *The New York Times* (June 30, 1995), p. A1.

246. Deroy Murdock, "Moving to Split Racial Hairs," *New York Post* (July 7, 1994), p. 25.

247. Jared Taylor, *Paved with Good Intentions*, p. 185.

248. *Ibid.*

249. Steven A. Holmes, "F.C.C. to Ease Rules on Stations' Hiring of Women and Minorities," *The New York Times* (November 19, 1998), p. A23.

250. Jared Taylor, *Paved with Good Intentions*, pp. 185-186.

251. *Ibid.*, p. 185.

252. Steven A. Holmes, "F.C.C. to Ease Rules on Stations' Hiring of Women and Minorities," *The New York Times* (November 19, 1998), p. A23.

253. Eric Felten, "Pay Up or Else," *Insight* (May 20, 1991), p. 13.

254. Reuters, "A New Blow to Viacom Deal," *The New York Times* (March 29, 1995), p. D2. Jared Taylor, *Paved with Good Intentions*, p. 186.

255. "Invidious Distinction," *The New Republic* (February 5, 1990), p. 4. "Making It Clear," *Economist* (January 28, 1989), p. 21.

256. Greg Foster, "Tax Breaks for Being Black," *The Wall Street Journal* (November 8, 1995), p. A20.

257. *Ibid.*

258. Dinesh D'Souza, *The End of Racism*, p. 237.

259. Ruth Shalit, "Race in the Newsroom," *The New Republic* (October 2, 1995), p. 20.

260. Hilton Kramer, "Hard Questions for the *Times*," *New York Post* (November 30, 1993), p. 17.

261. Ruth Shalit, "Race in the Newsroom," *The New Republic* (October 2, 1995), p. 20.

262. Cal Thomas, "Diversity and the Fall of Journalism's Empire," *Journal News* (Gannett Suburban Newspapers) (November 20, 1998), p. 11B.

263. *Ibid.*

264. *Ibid.*

265. John Leo, "The Demonizing of White Men," *U.S. News & World Report* (April 26, 1993), p. 24.

266. Alicia Shepard, "High Anxiety: The Call for Diversity in the Newsroom Has White Men Running Scared," *American Journalism Review* (November 1993), pp. 19-21.

267. Ruth Shalit, "Race in the Newsroom," *The New Republic* (October 2, 1995), p. 20.

268. *Ibid.*, p. 23.

269. *Ibid.*, p. 26.

270. *Ibid.*, p. 20.

271. "Race in the Workplace: Is Affirmative Action Working?" *Business Week* (July 8, 1991), p. 56.

272. Ray Kerrison, "NYNEX Rings in New Year Ominously," *New York Post* (January 2, 1991), p. 4.

273. Frederick Lynch, *Invisible Victims*, pp. 5-6.

274. Dan Janison, "City Has Ethnic-Hiring Numbers—Now What?" *New York Post* (June 12, 1993), p. 16.

275. *Ibid.*

276. Hilary Stout, "Education Agency Set to Crack Down on Loan Defaults," *The Wall Street Journal* (May 3, 1991), p. A7A.

277. "False Note," *The New Republic* (March 27, 1989), p. 9. Jared Taylor, *Paved with Good Intentions*, p. 194.

278. "False Note," *The New Republic* (March 27, 1989), p. 9.

279. James Popkin, "Propagandists or Saviors?" *U.S. News & World Report* (September 12, 1994), pp. 40-43. Marshall J. Breger, "Discrimination in Favor of Farrakhan," *The Wall Street Journal* (July 24, 1995), p. A12.

280. Jared Taylor, *Paved with Good Intentions*, p. 196.

281. *Los Angeles Times* (July 12, 1981). Cited by Frederick Lynch, *Invisible Victims*, p. 26.

282. Thomas Sowell, *Preferential Policies*, p. 15.

283. *Ibid.*, p. 52.

284. *Ibid.*, pp. 52, 53, 54-57.

285. *Ibid.*, pp. 57-59.

286. *Ibid.*, pp. 60-63.

287. Edward W. Desmond, "Fatal Fires of Protest," *Time* (October 15, 1990), p. 63. Thomas Sowell, *Preferential Policies*, p. 53.

288. Thomas Sowell, *Preferential Policies*, p. 98.

289. *Ibid.*, pp. 100-101.

290. *Ibid.*, p. 100.

291. *Ibid.*

292. Edward W. Desmond, "Fatal Fires of Protest," *Time* (October 15, 1990), p. 63.

293. "Affirmative Action Fights, Indian Style," *Newsweek* (September 17, 1990), p. 44.

294. Lee Adair Lawrence, "Christians and the Caste Controversy," *Christian Century* (November 7, 1990), p. 1,014.

295. *Ibid.*

296. Jonah Blank, "Quotas that Are Cast in Stone," *U.S. News & World Report* (March 27, 1995), p. 38.

297. "Affirmative Action, Indian Style," *Fortune* (December 3, 1990), p. 190.

298. *Ibid.*

299. *The World Almanac: 1997*, p. 820.

300. Thomas Sowell, *Preferential Policies,* pp. 77, 81.

301. *Ibid.*, pp. 78-79.

302. *Ibid.*, pp. 76-77.

303. S.J. Tambiah, *Sri Lanka: Ethnic Fratricide and the Dismantling of*

Democracy (Delhi: Oxford University Press, 1986), pp. 71-72. Thomas Sowell, *Preferential Policies,* pp. 81-82.

304. Thomas Sowell, *Preferential Policies,* p. 85. Thomas Sowell, *Compassion Versus Guilt* (New York: Quill, 1987), p. 196.

305. Thomas Sowell, *Compassion Versus Guilt,* p. 196.

306. Thomas Sowell, *Preferential Policies,* p. 85.

307. Associated Press, "32 Killed in Sri Lanka As Bombs Destroy Bus," *The New York Times* (March 6, 1998), p. A6.

308. Thomas Sowell, *Preferential Policies,* p. 83.

309. *Ibid.*, pp. 69-72.

310. *Ibid.*, pp. 73-74.

311. *Ibid.*, pp. 75-76.

312. *Ibid.*, pp. 46-47.

313. *Ibid.*, p. 46.

314. *Ibid.*, p. 47.

315. Thomas Sowell, *The Economics and Politics of Race,* p. 54.

316. Carl Wittke, *We Who Built America* (Case Western Reserve University Press, 1939), p. 84. Thomas Sowell, *The Economics and Politics of Race,* p. 56.

317. Thomas Sowell, *The Economics and Politics of Race,* p. 56.

318. *Ibid.*, p. 57.

319. *Ibid.*

320. *Ibid.*, p. 58.

321. George Potter, *To the Golden Door: The Story of the Irish in Ireland and America* (Greenwood Press, 1960), p. 94.

322. Marie and Connor Cruise O'Brien, *A Concise History of Ireland* (New York: Beckman House, 1972), p. 25. Nathan Glazer and Daniel Patrick Moynihan, *Beyond the Melting Pot* (Cambridge, Mass.: MIT Press, 1966), p. 232.

323. Thomas Sowell, *The Economics and Politics of Race,* p. 63.

324. Andrew M. Greeley, *That Most Distressed Nation* (New York: Quadrangle Books, 1972), p. 129.

325. *Ibid.*, p. 134.

326. Thomas Sowell, *The Economics and Politics of Race,* p. 64.

327. *Ibid.*, p. 68.

328. *Ibid.*, p. 66.

329. Frederick Engels, *The Condition of the Working Class in England in 1844* (London: George Allen and Unwin, Ltd., 1952), p. 91.

330. Thomas Sowell, *The Economics and Politics of Race,* p. 69.

331. Dinesh D'Souza, *The End of Racism,* p. 137.

332. *Ibid.*

333. Barry Schwartz, ed., *White Racism* (New York: Laurel Leaf Books, 1978), p. 58.

334. Thomas Sowell, *The Economics and Politics of Race,* p. 62.

335. W.E.B. Du Bois, *The Philadelphia Negro* (Schocken Books, 1967), p. 387.

336. William McFeely, *Frederick Douglass* (New York: W.W. Norton, 1991), p. 126.

337. Andrew M. Greeley, *That Most Distressed Nation*, pp. 34-35.

338. Thomas Sowell, *The Economics and Politics of Race*, p. 68.

339. *Ibid.*, p. 71.

340. *Ibid.*, p. 70.

341. Leonard Covello, *The Social Background of the Italo-American School Child* (Totowa, New Jersey: Rowman and Littlefield, 1972), p. 25.

342. Thomas Sowell, *The Economics and Politics of Race*, p. 74.

343. Robert F. Foerster, *The Italian Emigration of Our Times* (Arno Press, 1969), p. 257.

344. Thomas Sowell, *The Economics and Politics of Race*, p. 77.

345. *Ibid.*, p. 76.

346. *Ibid.*, p. 77.

347. *Ibid.*, p. 78.

348. U.S. Bureau of the Census, *Current Population Reports*, Series P-20, No. 221 (Washington: Government Printing Office, 1971), p. 19.

349. Richard Gambino, *Blood of My Blood* (Cutchogue, New York: Buccaneer Books, 1991), p. 87. Thomas Sowell, *The Economics and Politics of Race*, p. 79.

350. Thomas Sowell, *Civil Rights: Rhetoric or Reality?*, pp. 19-21.

351. William Petersen, "Chinese-Americans and Japanese-Americans," in Thomas Sowell, ed., *Essays and Data on American Ethnic Groups* (Washington, D.C.: The Urban Institute, 1978), p. 84. Jared Taylor, *Paved with Good Intentions*, p. 113.

352. Thomas Sowell, *Ethnic America* (New York: Basic Books, 1981), pp. 175, 177.

353. Thernstrom, *America in Black and White*, p. 536.

354. Thomas Sowell, *Civil Rights: Rhetoric or Reality?*, pp. 43-45, 48. *Statistical Abstract of the United States: 1996*, p. 74, Table 91.

355. Thomas Sowell, *Migrations and Cultures* (New York: Basic Books, 1996), pp. 118-119.

356. *Ibid.*, p. 139.

357. Max I. Dimont, *Jews, God, and History*, p. 241. Thomas Sowell, *The Economics and Politics of Race*, p. 82.

358. Thomas Sowell, *The Economics and Politics of Race*, p. 84.

359. Louis Wirth, *The Ghetto* (Chicago: University of Chicago Press, 1956), p. 32.

360. *Ibid.*

361. Philip Ziegler, *The Black Death* (Wolfeboro Falls, New Hampshire: Alan Sutton Publishing Inc., 1991), pp. 74, 75, 77, 78.

362. Thomas Sowell, *The Economics and Politics of Race*, pp. 82-83.

363. *Ibid.*, pp. 85-86.

364. *Ibid.*, p. 86.

365. Thomas Sowell, *The Economics and Politics of Race*, p. 89.

366. Max L. Margolis and Alexander Marx, *A History of the Jewish People* (New York: Harper & Row, 1927), p. 556. Max I. Dimont, *Jews, God, and History*, pp. 245-246.

367. Max I. Dimont, *Jews, God, and History*, pp. 245-246.

368. Thomas Sowell, *The Economics and Politics of Race*, p. 90.

369. *Ibid.*, p. 88.

370. *Ibid.*, p. 91.

371. *Ibid.*, pp. 91-92.

372. *Ibid.*, p. 92.

373. *Ibid.*

374. Judith Laikin Elkin, *Jews of the Latin American Republics* (Chapel Hill, North Carolina: University of North Carolina Press, 1980), pp. 214-237.

375. Thomas Sowell, *The Economics and Politics of Race*, p. 139.

376. Thomas Sowell, *Civil Rights: Rhetoric or Reality?*, p. 20.

377. David Boaz, "Yellow Peril Reinfects America," *The Wall Street Journal* (April 7, 1989).

378. Jared Taylor, *Paved with Good Intentions*, p. 111.

379. *Ibid.*, pp. 110-111.

380. *Ibid.*, p. 110.

381. Thomas Sowell, *The Economics and Politics of Race*, p. 47.

382. Jared Taylor, *Paved with Good Intentions*, p. 111.

383. *Ibid.*

384. *Ibid.*

385. *Ibid.*

386. Thomas Sowell, *The Economics and Politics of Race*, p. 47.

387. *Ibid.*, p. 48.

388. *Ibid.*, p. 49.

389. *Ibid.*

390. *Ibid.*

391. Thernstrom, *America in Black and White*, pp. 535-536.

392. *Harvard Encyclopedia of American Ethnic Groups* (Cambridge, Mass.: Harvard University Press, 1980), p. 1,021.

393. *Ibid.*, p. 1,022.

394. *Ibid.*, p. 1,026.

395. Francesco Cordasco, ed., *Dictionary of American Immigration* (Metuchen, New Jersey and London: The Scarecrow Press, 1990), p. 753.

396. Thomas Sowell, *Civil Rights: Rhetoric or Reality?*, p. 77.

397. *Ibid.*, p. 78.

398. *Harvard Encyclopedia of American Ethnic Groups*, p. 1,022. Thomas Sowell, *The Economics and Politics of Race*, p. 78.

399. Dinesh D'Souza, *The End of Racism*, p. 137.

400. *Harvard Encyclopedia of American Ethnic Groups*, p. 1,022.

401. *Ibid.*

402. *Ibid.*, p. 1,023.

403. *Ibid.*

404. *Ibid.*, p. 1,022.

405. *Ibid.*, p. 1,025.

406. Jonathan Kaufman, "Help Unwanted," *The Wall Street Journal* (June 6, 1995), p. A8.

407. Thomas Sowell, *Preferential Policies*, p. 88.

408. Thernstrom, *America in Black and White*, p. 535.

409. Dinesh D'Souza, *Illiberal Education*, pp. 29, 36.

410. Thomas Sowell, *Preferential Policies*, p. 88.

411. *Ibid.*, p. 149.

412. *Ibid.*, p. 89.

413. Joseph Kahn, "Jackson Challenges 'Capital of Capital,' " *The New York Times* (January 16, 1999), p. C3.

414. Richard Benedetto, "Jackson 'Keeps Door Open' for a Run at White House," *USA Today* (June 19, 1995), p. 6A.

415. George Gilder, *Wealth and Poverty*, p. 76.

416. *Ibid.*, pp. 79-80.

417. Booker T. Washington, *Up From Slavery*, p. 158.

418. George Gilder, *Wealth and Poverty*, pp. 77-78.

419. Dirk Johnson, "In Denver, the Surprising New Face of Right-Wing Talk Radio," *The New York Times* (January 2, 1994), Section 4, p. 7.

420. Jay Diamond program, WABC radio in New York (1993).

421. Thomas Sowell, *Preferential Policies*, chapter 6.

422. *Ibid.*, pp. 148-149.

423. Thomas Sowell, *The Economics and Politics of Race*, pp. 247-248.

424. Kevin Sack, "Atlanta Leaders See Racial Goals As Olympic Ideal," *The New York Times* (June 10, 1996), p. A1.

425. Thomas Sowell, *Civil Rights: Rhetoric or Reality?*, pp. 50-51.

426. Jared Taylor, *Paved with Good Intentions*, p. 211.

427. Dinesh D'Souza, *The End of Racism*, p. 320.

428. Stephen Carter, *Reflections of an Affirmative Action Baby* (New York: Basic Books, 1991), p. 71.

429. Arch Puddington, "What to Do about Affirmative Action," *Commentary* (June 1995), p. 23. Thomas Sowell, *Civil Rights: Rhetoric or Reality?*, pp. 49-50. Thernstrom, *America in Black and White*, pp. 187-188, 234.

430. Thomas Sowell, *The Economics and Politics of Race*, pp. 190-191.

431. Robert Bork, *Slouching Towards Gomorrah*, p. 238.

432. *Ibid.*

433. Joseph Perkins, "Why Blacks Lag," *New York Post* (June 3, 1995). Perkins writes that 195,000 blacks are in correctional institutions, but that figure includes only jail inmates and does not include inmates at federal or state prisons. See *Sourcebook of Criminal Justice Statistics, 1996*, p. 510, Table 6.12.

434. Joseph Perkins, "Why Blacks Lag," *New York Post* (June 3, 1995).

435. Dinesh D'Souza, *The End of Racism*, p. 14.

436. *Ibid.*, pp. 253-254.

437. Linda Chavez, "Defining Multiculturalism," *National Review* (February 21, 1994), p. 26. Dinesh D'Souza, *The End of Racism*, p. 253.

438. Thomas Sowell, *Preferential Policies*, pp. 22-23.

439. *Ibid.*, pp. 20-22. Thomas Sowell, "Govt.'s the Problem," *New York Post* (August 4, 1995), p. 25.

440. Thomas Sowell, "Govt.'s the Problem," *New York Post* (August 4, 1995), p. 25.

441. Jared Taylor, *Paved with Good Intentions*, p. 163.

442. Thomas Sowell, "Govt.'s the Problem," *New York Post* (August 4, 1995), p. 25.

443. Dinesh D'Souza, *The End of Racism*, pp. 276-277.

444. Thernstrom, *America in Black and White*, p. 448.

445. *Ibid.*, p. 449.

446. Steven A. Holmes, "U.S. Issues New, Strict Tests for Affirmative Action Plans," *The New York Times* (June 29, 1995), p. A1.

447. "High Court Crushes Quotas," *New York Post* (June 13, 1995), p. 4. Linda Greenhouse, "By 5-4, Justices Cast Doubts on U.S. Programs That Give Preferences Based on Race," *The New York Times* (June 13, 1995), pp. A1, D25.

448. Linda Greenhouse, "In Step on Racial Policy," *The New York Times* (June 14, 1995), p. A17.

449. B. Drummond Ayres, Jr., "Efforts to End Job Preferences Are Faltering," *The New York Times* (November 20, 1995), pp. A1, B10.

450. George F. Will, "The Advisory Board That Time Forgot," *New York Post* (September 27, 1998), p. 57.

451. Ben Wattenberg, "Spokesman for the Colorblind Point of View," *New York Post* (February 21, 1997), p. 27.

452. Richard Cohen, "The Overlooked Costs of Affirmative Action," *New York Post* (July 23, 1997), p. 29.

453. Associated Press, "Study: Fewer Minorities Enter U.S. Medical Schools," *Reporter Dispatch* (Gannett Suburban Newspapers) (November 2, 1997).

454. *Ibid.*

455. Paul M. Sniderman and Thomas Piazza, *The Scar of Race*, p. 131.

456. Dinesh D'Souza, *The End of Racism*, p. 14.

457. *Ibid.*

458. *Ibid.*

459. Patricia Williams, *The Alchemy of Race and Rights* (Cambridge, Mass.: Harvard University Press, 1991), p. 103.

460. Adam Nagourney, "At NAACP Dinner, Gore Praises Affirmative Action and Declares War on Prejudice," *The New York Times* (April 26, 1999).

461. Thomas Sowell, "Random Thoughts on the Passing Scene," *New York Post* (December 28, 1998), p. 25.

462. "Affirmative Reaction," *Investor's Business Daily* (December 26, 1996).

463. "Atlanta's Mayor Defies Threat to Affirmative Action," *The New York Times* (July 16, 1999).

464. "Final Cut: Spike Lee and Henry Louis Gates, Jr. Rap on Race, Politics and Black Cinema," *Transition*, Issue 52, (1991), p. 185.

465. Eric Breindel, "Black Conservatives: Fair Game for All?" *New York Post* (March 5, 1997), p. 23.

466. *Ibid.*

467. Ben Wattenberg, "Spokesman for the Colorblind Point of View," *New York Post* (February 21, 1997), p. 27.

468. Maggie Gallagher, "A Supreme Court Ruling Is Final (Unless It's Not)," *New York Post* (July 4, 1995), p. 13.

469. Jack Newfield, "Black Clergymen Hope Justice Thomas Repents," *New York Post* (July 28, 1995), p. 12.

470. Eric Breindel, "Black Conservatives: Fair Game for All?" *New York Post* (March 5, 1997), p. 23.

471. L. Gordon Crovitz, *Confronting the Future* (Washington, D.C.: Regnery Gateway, 1992), p. 14.

472. "Clarence Thomas, Black Independent Supreme, in the Lion's Den," *The American Enterprise* (November/December 1998), p. 44.

473. *Ibid.*

474. Marilyn Rauber, "Top Court 'Earthquake' KOs Racial Vote Districts," *New York Post* (June 30, 1995), p. 2.

475. *Ibid.*

Chapter 11
The Beloved Homeland

1. Thomas Sowell, "Minority Schools and the Politics of Education," *Imprimis* (January 1999), p. 1.

2. Lynda Richardson, "A Massacre Remembered in a Fest," *The New York Times* (June 16, 1993), p. B3.

3. "A Movement Reborn?," *Newsweek* (December 10, 1984), p. 40. "Protests Against S. Africa Spreading to Major Cities; 19 Black Leaders Arrested," *Jet* (December 17, 1984), p. 6.

4. "Protests Against S. Africa Spreading to Major Cities; 19 Black Leaders Arrested," *Jet* (December 17, 1984), p. 6.

5. *Ibid.* "Amy Carter Arrested in S. African Embassy Protests," *Jet* (April 29, 1985), p. 12. "Leaders Jailed in Protest Against S. Africa at Its Embassy in Washington," *Jet* (December 10, 1984), p. 6. "King Family Arrested and Jailed for Embassy Protest," *Jet* (July 15, 1985), p. 5.

6. "Amy Carter Arrested in S. African Embassy Protests," *Jet* (April 29, 1985), p. 12.

7. Jeannye Thornton and Michael Doan, "As Heat on South Africa Builds Across the U.S.—," *U.S. News & World Report* (December 17, 1984), p. 34. Monroe W. Karmin, "As U.S. Boycott of Apartheid Picks up Steam," *U.S. News & World Report* (September 9, 1985), p. 34.

8. Monroe W. Karmin, "As U.S. Boycott of Apartheid Picks up Steam," *U.S. News & World Report* (September 9, 1985), p. 34.

9. Joseph Contreras, "Caught in the Crossfire," *Newsweek* (January 20, 1992), p. 59.

10. D. Michael Cheers, "Jesse Jackson: Rebuilding Bridges to Africa," *Ebony* (December 1986), p. 138. "King Family Arrested and Jailed for Embassy Protest," *Jet* (July 15, 1985), p. 5.

11. Elizabeth Weiner, "Protesters Try a Boycott in the U.S.," *Business Week* (January 20, 1986), p. 42. Monroe W. Karmin, "As U.S. Boycott of Apartheid Picks up Steam," *U.S. News & World Report* (September 9, 1985), p. 34.

12. Monroe W. Karmin, "As U.S. Boycott of Apartheid Picks up Steam," *U.S. News & World Report* (September 9, 1985), p. 34.

13. Frederic Dicker and Chris McKenna, "Apartheid Flap: Gov Pulls $1M from Bank," *New York Post* (July 17, 1990).

14. Monroe W. Karmin, "As U.S. Boycott of Apartheid Picks up Steam," *U.S. News & World Report* (September 9, 1985), p. 34.

15. Jeannye Thornton and Michael Doan, "As Heat on South Africa Builds Across the U.S.—," *U.S. News & World Report* (December 17, 1984), p. 33.

16. Monroe W. Karmin, "As U.S. Boycott of Apartheid Picks up Steam," *U.S. News & World Report* (September 9, 1985), p. 34.

17. *Ibid.*

18. "NAACP's Annual Confab Displays Future Plans," *Jet* (July 15, 1985), p. 18.

19. John Darnton, "Crisis-Torn Africa Becomes Continent of Refugees," *The New York Times* (May 23, 1994), p. A3.

20. George B.N. Ayittey, *Africa Betrayed* (New York: St. Martin's Press, 1992), pp. xix and xx.

21. *Ibid.*

22. *Ibid.*, pp. 119-120, 211, 219.

23. *Ibid.*, p. xix.

24. *Ibid.*, p. 120.

25. *Ibid.*, pp. 211, 219.

26. *Ibid.*, pp. 217, 223.

27. *Ibid.*, p. 217.

28. *Ibid.*

29. *Ibid.*, p. 211.

30. *Ibid.*

31. *Ibid.*, p. 117.

32. *Ibid.*

33. George B.N. Ayittey, "The African Power Equation," *The Washington Times* (April 20, 1998), p. A17.

34. *Ibid.*

35. *Ibid.*

36. George B.N. Ayittey, *Africa Betrayed*, p. 117.

37. *Ibid.*, p. 8.

38. George B.N. Ayittey, *Africa in Chaos* (New York: St. Martin's Press, 1998), pp. 5-6.

39. George B.N. Ayittey, *Africa Betrayed*, p. 8.

40. George B.N. Ayittey, "African Thugs Keep Their Continent Poor," *The Wall Street Journal* (January 2, 1998).

41. *Ibid.*

42. George B.N. Ayittey, *Africa Betrayed*, p. 236.

43. *Ibid.*, p. 120.

44. Bill Keller, "Africa Allows Its Tragedies to Take Their Own Course," *The New York Times* (August 7, 1994), Section 4, p. 6. George B.N. Ayittey, *Africa Betrayed*, p. 120.

45. George B.N. Ayittey, *Africa Betrayed*, p. 120.

46. Keith B. Richburg, *Out of America* (New York: Basic Books, 1997), pp. 24-25.

47. George B.N. Ayittey, "African Thugs Keep Their Continent Poor," *The Wall Street Journal* (January 2, 1998).

48. *The World Almanac: 1998*, p. 793. George Thomas Kurian, ed., *Encyclopedia of the Third World*, 4th Edition (New York and Oxford: Facts on File, 1992), p. 1,123. *Information Please Almanac: 1997* (Boston and New York: Houghton Mifflin Co., 1997), p. 223.

49. George Thomas Kurian, ed., *Encyclopedia of the Third World*, 4th Edition, p. 1,123.

50. Reuters, "Liberia Troops Accused of Massacre in Church," *The New York Times* (July 31, 1990), p. A1.

51. Associated Press, "Orgy of Killing in Liberia," *New York Post* (June 7, 1993), p. 8. "300 Liberians Are Reported Slain," *The New York Times* (June 7, 1993), p. A6.

52. Associated Press, "Orgy of Killing in Liberia," *New York Post* (June 7, 1993), p. 8.

53. *Ibid.*

54. Pierre Etienne Dostert, *Africa 1996* (Harper's Ferry, West Virginia: Stryker-Post Publications, 1996), p. 57. Associated Press, "Troops Take Food As Liberia Starves," *New York Post* (November 1, 1990).

55. Pierre Etienne Dostert, *Africa 1993* (Harper's Ferry, West Virginia: Stryker-Post Publications, 1993), p. 57.

56. " 'No Calm, No Peace' in Liberia," *USA Today* (May 6, 1990), p. 5A.

57. Pierre Etienne Dostert, *Africa 1993*, p. 57.

58. *Ibid.*

59. *Ibid.*

60. Post Wire Services, "Liberia Prez Doe Killed in Shootout," *New York Post* (September 11, 1990).

61. Pierre Etienne Dostert, *Africa 1993*, p. 58.

62. *The World Almanac: 1998*, p. 805.

63. Carol L. Thompson et al., eds., *The Current History Encyclopedia of Developing Nations* (New York: McGraw-Hill, 1982), p. 79.

64. Thomas Sowell, *Preferential Policies*, pp. 74-75. Pierre Etienne Dostert, *Africa 1993*, p. 75.

65. *The World Almanac: 1998*, p. 805.

66. Howard W. French, "Nigerians Fear New Strife Could Blow the Country Apart," *The New York Times* (August 14, 1994), p. 16.

67. Pierre Etienne Dostert, *Africa 1993*, p. 75.

68. *Ibid.*

69. *Ibid.*

70. Linus U.J. Thomas-Ogboji, *African Weekly News* (May 26, 1995), p. 6. Cited by George B.N. Ayittey, *Africa in Chaos*, p. 1.

71. Pierre Etienne Dostert, *Africa 1993*, p. 78.

72. George B.N. Ayittey, "An African Tradition Holds the Key," *Los Angeles Times* (June, 14, 1998).

73. Pierre Etienne Dostert, *Africa 1996*, p. 74. *Information Please Almanac: 1997*, p. 242.

74. George B.N. Ayittey, "An African Tradition Holds the Key," *Los Angeles Times* (June, 14, 1998).

75. George B.N. Ayittey, "African Thugs Keep Their Continent Poor," *The Wall Street Journal* (January 2, 1998).

76. George B.N. Ayittey, "An African Tradition Holds the Key," *Los Angeles Times* (June, 14, 1998).

77. Howard W. French, "West Africa Trembles with Nigeria," *The New York Times* (June 14, 1998).

78. *Ibid.* George B.N. Ayittey, "An African Tradition Holds the Key," *Los Angeles Times* (June, 14, 1998).

79. *The World Almanac: 1998*, p. 739.

80. John Darnton, "Civil War of Nearly Two Decades Exhausts Resource-Rich Angola," *The New York Times* (May 9, 1994), pp. A1, A6. Jane Standley, "Angola's Forgotten Conflict," *British Broadcasting Corporation Online Network* (January 28, 1999).

81. John Darnton, "Civil War of Nearly Two Decades Exhausts Resource-Rich Angola," *The New York Times* (May 9, 1994), p. A6.

82. Jane Standley, "Angola's Forgotten Conflict," *British Broadcasting Corporation Online Network* (January 28, 1999). Antony Goldman, "Angola: The Roots of Conflict," *British Broadcasting Corporation Online Network* (January 28, 1999).

83. John Darnton, "Civil War of Nearly Two Decades Exhausts Resource-Rich Angola," *The New York Times* (May 9, 1994), p. A6.

84. Justin Pearce, "Landmines: War's Deadly Legacy," *British Broadcasting Corporation Online Network* (January 29, 1999).

85. John Darnton, "Civil War of Nearly Two Decades Exhausts Resource-Rich Angola," *The New York Times* (May 9, 1994), p. A6.

86. Pierre Etienne Dostert, *Africa 1993*, p. 86. Carol L. Thompson et al., eds., *The Current History Encyclopedia of Developing Nations*, p. 13. *The World Almanac: 1997*, p. 748.

87. George Thomas Kurian, ed., *Encyclopedia of the Third World*, p. 277.

88. Carol L. Thompson et al., eds., *The Current History Encyclopedia of Developing Nations*, p. 13.

89. *Ibid.*, p. 11.

90. Pierre Etienne Dostert, *Africa 1993*, p. 87.

91. *Ibid.*

92. Carol L. Thompson et al., eds., *The Current History Encyclopedia of Developing Nations*, p. 13. George Thomas Kurian, ed., *Encyclopedia of the Third World*, p. 275.

93. George Thomas Kurian, ed., *Encyclopedia of the Third World*, p. 275.

94. Jared Taylor, *Paved with Good Intentions*, p. 275.

95. Reuters, "Tribal Warfare Kills Thousands in Burundi," *The New York Times* (October 28, 1993), p. A20.

96. *Ibid.*

97. Donatella Lorch, "Burundi after Mutiny: Horror Stories Everywhere," *The New York Times* (November 21, 1993), p. A3.

98. *Ibid.* Reuters, "2 Burundi Tribes Battle in Capital," *The New York Times* (March 24, 1994), p. A6.

99. Donatella Lorch, "Burundi after Mutiny: Horror Stories Everywhere," *The New York Times* (November 21, 1993), p. A3. Reuters, "Huge Death Toll Feared in Burundi," *The New York Times* (November 28, 1993), Sec. 1, p. 7.

100. Reuters, "Huge Death Toll Feared in Burundi," *The New York Times* (November 28, 1993), Sec. 1, p. 7.

101. Reuters, "2 Burundi Tribes Battle in Capital," *The New York Times* (March 24, 1994), p. A6.

102. "Burundi Sanctions Lifted," *British Broadcasting Corporation Online Network* (January 23, 1999).

103. Pierre Etienne Dostert, *Africa 1993*, pp. 92-93.

104. *The World Almanac: 1997*, p. 813. Pierre Etienne Dostert, *Africa 1993*, p. 93.

105. Carol L. Thompson et al., eds., *The Current History Encyclopedia of Developing Nations*, p. 85.

106. Pierre Etienne Dostert, *Africa 1996*, p. 86.

107. *The World Almanac: 1997*, p. 813.

108. George Thomas Kurian, ed., *Encyclopedia of the Third World*, p. 1,614.

109. Post Wire Services, "Rocket Attack on Plane Kills 2 African Bigs," *New York Post* (April 7, 1994), p. 15. News Wire Services, "Plane Attack Kills African Presidents," *Daily News* (New York) (April 7, 1994), p. 12.

110. Donatella Lorch, "Anarchy Rules Rwanda's Capital and Drunken Soldiers Roam City," *The New York Times* (April 14, 1994), p. A1.

111. Associated Press, "Death Toll Hits 10,000 in Rwanda Capital," *New

York Post (April 11, 1994), p. 8. Gregory Beals, "Witness to Carnage," *Daily News* (New York) (April 21, 1994), p. 15. Associated Press, "A Rwandan Villager Tells of Killing Kids," *Daily News* (New York) (May 16, 1994), p. 13.

112. Associated Press, "Death Toll Hits 10,000 in Rwanda Capital," *New York Post* (April 11, 1994), p. 8.

113. *Ibid.*

114. Donatella Lorch, "Anarchy Rules Rwanda's Capital and Drunken Soldiers Roam City," *The New York Times* (April 14, 1994), p. A1.

115. Donatella Lorch, "Children's Drawings Tell Horror of Rwanda in Colors of Crayons," *The New York Times* (September 16, 1994), p. A1.

116. Robert D. McFadden, "Western Troops Arrive in Rwanda to Aid Foreigners," *The New York Times* (April 10, 1994), pp. A1, A6.

117. Associated Press, "Lull in Rwanda Fighting Allows Aid Deliveries," *The New York Times* (May 13, 1994), p. A5.

118. Walter Goodman, "Genocide in Africa, Quibbles in the West," *The New York Times* (January 26, 1999).

119. Donatella Lorch, "Thousands of Fleeing Rwandans Mass in Remote Tanzanian Area," *The New York Times* (May 19, 1994), p. A1.

120. Raymond Bonner, "In a Panic, Rwandans Die in Stampede," *The New York Times* (July 18, 1994), p. A 7. Michael O. Allen, "1 Dies Every Minute," *Daily News* (New York) (July 26, 1994), p. 5.

121. Walter Goodman, "Genocide in Africa, Quibbles in the West," *The New York Times* (January 26, 1999).

122. *The Wall Street Journal*, (August 25, 1994), p. A1.

123. Jonathan Karl, "Ferrer Demands Boss Boot Buddy over 'Race' Remark," *New York Post* (July 19, 1994), p. 4. Joe Sexton, "Yankees Offer an Apology for Comments," *The New York Times* (July 19, 1994), p. B1.

124. E.R. Shipp, "Muslim Message That Should Be Heeded," *Daily News* (New York) (August 17, 1994), p. 25.

125. Raymond Bonner, "Rwandans Who Massacred Now Terrorize Camps," *The New York Times* (October 31, 1994), pp. A1, A10.

126. *Ibid.*

127. *Ibid.*

128. *Ibid.*, p. A10.

129. Curtis Bunn, "Harsh Glimpse of Reality," *Daily News* (New York) (August 26, 1994), p. 82.

130. *Ibid.*

131. *Ibid.*

132. Curtis Bunn, "Journey Has Long Way to Go," *Daily News* (New York) (August 29, 1994), p. 46.

133. *The World Almanac: 1998*, p. 755. Pierre Etienne Dostert, *Africa 1993*, p. 94.

134. Pierre Etienne Dostert, *Africa 1993*, p. 96.

135. *Ibid.*, p. 96.

136. George B.N. Ayittey, *Africa Betrayed*, p. 254.

137. Pierre Etienne Dostert, *Africa 1996*, p. 97.

138. George B.N. Ayittey, *Africa Betrayed*, p. 254.

139. Pierre Etienne Dostert, *Africa 1993*, p. 98.

140. *Ibid.*

141. *Ibid.*

142. George B.N. Ayittey, *Africa Betrayed*, pp. 8-9.

143. "Refugees: Babies Tossed in Pits, Civilians Burned Alive," *The Journal News* (Gannett Suburban Newspapers) (January 15, 1999), p. 15A.

144. "The Talk of the Town," *The New Yorker* (October 26 and November 2, 1998), p. 51.

145. Angus Deming et al., "Idi Amin's Rule of Blood," *Newsweek* (March 7, 1977), p. 35.

146. *Ibid.*

147. *Ibid.* George Thomas Kurian, ed., *Encyclopedia of the Third World*, p. 2,005.

148. Angus Deming et al., "Idi Amin's Rule of Blood," *Newsweek* (March 7, 1977), p. 29.

149. Angus Deming et al., "Amin's Purge," *Newsweek* (March 14, 1977), p. 26.

150. Angus Deming et al., "Idi Amin's Rule of Blood," *Newsweek* (March 7, 1977), p. 30.

151. *Ibid.*

152. *Ibid.*, p. 32.

153. *Ibid.*, p. 30.

154. *Ibid.*

155. *Ibid.*, pp. 30, 32.

156. *Ibid.*, p. 30.

157. *Ibid.*

158. *Ibid.*, p. 32.

159. George Thomas Kurian, ed., *Encyclopedia of the Third World*, p. 2,005.

160. Dennis Prager, "When Anger Overwhelms Love," *Ultimate Issues* (Issue #4, 1992), p. 3.

161. Pierre Etienne Dostert, *Africa 1993*, p. 181.

162. Dennis Prager, "When Anger Overwhelms Love," *Ultimate Issues* (Issue #4, 1992), p. 3.

163. Susan Minot, "A Mother's Christmas Quest," *The New York Times* (December 26, 1998).

164. *Ibid.*

165. *Ibid.*

166. George Thomas Kurian, ed., *Encyclopedia of the Third World*, p. 156.

167. Donatella Lorch, "Thousands Flee Kenya Ethnic Strife," *The New York Times* (September 7, 1993), p. A3.

168. *Ibid.*

169. James C. McKinley, Jr., "Ethnic Strife in Kenya Derails Talks on Reform," *The New York Times* (August 21, 1997).

170. James C. McKinley, Jr., "Ethnic Violence Flares Anew After Election in Kenya," *The New York Times* (January 31, 1998).

171. George Thomas Kurian, ed., *Encyclopedia of the Third World*, p. 730.

172. *Ibid.*

173. Pierre Etienne Dostert, *Africa 1993*, p. 50.

174. *Ibid.* George Thomas Kurian, ed., *Encyclopedia of the Third World*, p. 732.

175. Pierre Etienne Dostert, *Africa 1993*, p. 50.

176. George Thomas Kurian, ed., *Encyclopedia of the Third World*, p. 732.

177. George B.N. Ayittey, *Africa Betrayed*, p. 121.

178. *Ibid.*

179. The *World Almanac: 1998*, p. 837. Pierre Etienne Dostert, *Africa 1993*, pp. 151, 154.

180. Pierre Etienne Dostert, *Africa 1993*, p. 154.

181. *Ibid.*, p. 151.

182. Pierre Etienne Dostert, *Africa 1996*, p. 159.

183. George B.N. Ayittey, *Africa Betrayed*, p. 173.

184. *Ibid.*, p. 174.

185. *The World Almanac: 1998*, p. 751.

186. Carol L. Thompson et al., eds., *The Current History Encyclopedia of Developing Nations*, pp. 18-20.

187. *Ibid.*, p. 20.

188. *Ibid.*

189. *Ibid.*

190. *Ibid.*, p. 30.

191. *Ibid.*, pp. 31-32. George Thomas Kurian, ed., *Encyclopedia of the Third World*, p. 616.

192. Carol L. Thompson et al., eds., *The Current History Encyclopedia of Developing Nations*, p. 32.

193. George B.N. Ayittey, *Africa Betrayed*, pp. 145-146.

194. Pierre Etienne Dostert, *Africa 1993*, p. 163.

195. *Ibid.*, p. 164.

196. *Ibid.*

197. *Ibid.*

198. *The World Almanac: 1998*, p. 818.

199. George Thomas Kurian, ed., *Encyclopedia of the Third World*, p. 1,762. *Information Please Almanac: 1996*, p. 264. *Whitaker's Almanac* (London: J. Whitaker and Sons, 1993), p. 1,012.

200. *Ibid.*

201. *Information Please Almanac: 1996*, p. 264.

202. George Thomas Kurian, ed., *Encyclopedia of the Third World*, p. 1,762. *Information Please Almanac: 1996*, p. 264. *Whitaker's Almanac*, p. 1,012.

203. George Thomas Kurian, ed., *Encyclopedia of the Third World*, p. 1,764.

204. Associated Press, "Police Open Fire in Somali Stadium," *The New York Times* (July 11, 1990). George Thomas Kurian, ed., *Encyclopedia of the Third World*, p. 1,764.

205. *Information Please Almanac: 1996*, p. 264.

206. *Ibid.*

207. Pierre Etienne Dostert, *Africa 1993*, p. 174.

208. *Ibid.*

209. Donatella Lorch, "Drought and Fighting Imperil 2 Million in Sudan," *The New York Times* (February 10, 1994), p. A3.

210. Pierre Etienne Dostert, *Africa 1993*, p. 174.

211. *The World Almanac: 1998*, p. 821.

212. Carol L. Thompson et al., eds., *The Current History Encyclopedia of Developing Nations*, p. 98.

213. Paul H. Lieben, "The Horrors of Sudan," *Destiny* (December 1994), p. 40.

214. Agence France-Presse, "Sudan Peace Talks Try to End 14-Year War," *The New York Times* (October 30, 1997), p. A17. Mary Ann Glendon, "Sudan's Unpunished Atrocities," *The New York Times* (December 8, 1998).

215. Mary Ann Glendon, "Sudan's Unpunished Atrocities," *The New York Times* (December 8, 1998).

216. George Thomas Kurian, ed., *Encyclopedia of the Third World*, p. 1,802.

217. Pierre Etienne Dostert, *Africa 1993*, p. 196.

218. George Thomas Kurian, ed., *Encyclopedia of the Third World*, p. 1,802.

219. Donatella Lorch, "Drought and Fighting Imperil 2 Million in Sudan," *The New York Times* (February 10, 1994), p. A3. Pierre Etienne Dostert, *Africa 1993*, p. 197.

220. Hilary Mackenzie, "Enmeshed in Conflict and Drought, Southern Sudan Starves," *The New York Times* (July 22, 1998).

221. *Ibid.*

222. Mark Doyle, "Freetown Struggles to Recover," *British Broadcasting Corporation Online Network* (January 22, 1999).

223. Caroline Hawley, "A Country Torn by Conflict," *British Broadcasting Corporation Online Network* (January 12, 1999).

224. Norimitsu Onishi, "A Brutal War's Machetes Maim Sierra Leone," *The New York Times* (January 26, 1999), p. A1. Elizabeth Rubin, "Saving Sierra Leone, at a Price," *The New York Times* (February 4, 1999).

225. Barbara Crossette, "In West Africa, a Grisly Extension of Rebel Terror," *The New York Times* (July 30, 1998), p. A6.

226. *Ibid.*

227. Norimitsu Onishi, "A Brutal War's Machetes Maim Sierra Leone," *The New York Times* (January 26, 1999), p. A6.

228. Tony Martin, speaker at Black Holocaust Conference at Coolidge High School in Washington, D.C., televised on C-SPAN (October 15, 1995).

229. Thomas Sowell, *Civil Rights: Rhetoric or Reality?*, p. 22.

230. Tom Masland et al., "Slavery," *Newsweek* (May 4, 1992), p. 30.

231. *Ibid.*

232. Thomas Sowell, *Barbarians Inside the Gates* (Stanford: Hoover Institution Press, 1999), p. 165. George B.N. Ayittey, *Africa Betrayed*, p. 124. Tom Masland et al., "Slavery," *Newsweek* (May 4, 1992), p. 32. Charles Jacobs and Mohamed Athie, "Bought and Sold," *The New York Times* (July 13, 1994), p. A19. "The African Slave Trade," *The City Sun* (February 1, 1995).

233. Charles Jacobs and Mohamed Athie, "Bought and Sold," *The New York Times* (July 13, 1994), p. A19. Tom Masland et al., "Slavery," *Newsweek* (May 4, 1992), p. 30.

234. Tom Masland et al., "Slavery," *Newsweek* (May 4, 1992), p. 30.

235. Charles Jacobs and Mohamed Athie, "Bought and Sold," *The New York Times* (July 13, 1994), p. A19. "The African Slave Trade," *The City Sun* (February 1, 1995).

236. George B.N. Ayittey, *Africa Betrayed*, p. 125. Charles Jacobs and Mohamed Athie, "Bought and Sold," *The New York Times* (July 13, 1994), p. A19. Minoo Southgate, "Slavery Ignored," *National Review* (October 23, 1995), p. 26.

237. Mary Ann Glendon, "Sudan's Unpunished Atrocities," *The New York Times* (December 8, 1998), p. A27.

238. Charles Jacobs and Mohamed Athie, "Bought and Sold," *The New York Times* (July 13, 1994), p. A19.

239. Robert Hughes, *Culture of Complaint* (New York and Oxford: The New York Public Library and Oxford University Press, 1993), p. 145.

240. Howard W. French, "Africa's Culture War: Old Customs, New Values," *The New York Times* (February 2, 1997).

241. Robert Hughes, *Culture of Complaint*, p. 145.

242. Charles Jacobs and Mohamed Athie, "Bought and Sold," *The New York Times* (July 13, 1994), p. A19.

243. "Slavery: Yes—in Africa," *The New York Times* (July 18, 1994), p. 20.

244. Minoo Southgate, "America's Black Leaders Ignore Arab Slave Trade," *New York Post* (June 14, 1995), p. 21. Minoo Southgate, "Slavery Ignored," *National Review* (October 23, 1995), p. 26.

245. George B.N. Ayittey, "African Thugs Keep Their Continent Poor," *The Wall Street Journal* (January 2, 1998).

246. "A Movement Reborn?," *Newsweek* (December 10, 1984), p. 40.

247. "Leaders Jailed in Protest Against S. Africa at Its Embassy in Washington," *Jet* (December 10, 1984), p. 7.

248. Michael D. Cheers, "Jesse Jackson and Heads of African Nations Map Plans to Seek Shift in U.S. Policy," *Jet* (October 6, 1986), pp. 4, 8.

249. George B.N. Ayittey, *Africa Betrayed*, p. 286.

250. *Ibid.*, p. 285.

251. Walter E. Williams, on Rush Limbaugh radio program, WABC New York, (December 27, 1993).

252. Thomas Sowell, *Compassion Versus Guilt*, p. 80. Keith B. Richburg,

Out of America, pp. 207-208. Associated Press, "Six More Killed As Blacks Fight Blacks in South Africa," *New York Post* (April 28, 1990), p. 15.

253. Keith B. Richburg, *Out of America*, p. 207.

254. Thomas Sowell, *Compassion Versus Guilt* (New York: Quill, 1987), p. 61.

255. Walter E. Williams, *The State Against Blacks* (New York: New Press, 1982), p. 3.

256. *Ibid.*

257. *Ibid.*

258. George B.N. Ayittey, *Africa Betrayed*, p. 129.

259. *Ibid.*, p. 3.

260. British Broadcasting Corporation Online Network, "Light Weapons Trade 'Fuels African Wars,' " (July 15, 1999).

261. Thomas Sowell, *The Economics and Politics of Race*, p. 16.

262. "Blacks Less Free Under Blacks: Tutu," *The Washington Times* (March 27, 1990).

263. Thomas Sowell, *The Economics and Politics of Race*, p. 153.

264. George B.N. Ayittey, *Africa Betrayed*, p. 131.

265. *Ibid.*, p. 132.

266. *Ibid.*

267. *Ibid.*, p. 319.

268. Keith B. Richburg, *Out of America*, pp. xii-xiv.

Chapter 12
The Chains of Slavery

1. Michel de Montaigne, *Essays*, I.xxxi. See *Dictionary of Quotations* (1968), p. 54.

2. *The New Encyclopaedia Britannica, Micropaedia* (Chicago: Encyclopaedia Britannica, Inc., 1992), Volume 10, p. 874.

3. *The Encyclopedia Americana* (1990) (Danbury, Conn.: Grolier, Inc., 1990), Volume 25, p. 21.

4. *Ibid.*

5. Peter Kolchin, *American Slavery: 1619-1877* (New York: Hill and Wang, 1993), pp. 11-12.

6. *Grolier Encyclopedia* (Danbury, Connecticut), "Slavery."

7. Thomas Sowell, *The Economics and Politics of Race*, p. 122. *The Encyclopedia Americana* (1990), Volume 25, p. 21.

8. *The Encyclopedia Americana* (1990), Volume 25, p. 21. Thomas Sowell, *Conquests and Cultures*, p. 111.

9. Thomas Sowell, *Conquests and Cultures*, p. 154.

10. *The Encyclopedia Americana* (1990), Volume 25, p. 21.

11. Thomas Sowell, *The Economics and Politics of Race*, p. 121.

12. Thomas Sowell, *Race and Culture*, p. 186. Thomas Sowell, *Conquests and Cultures*, p. 109.

13. Milton Meltzer, *Slavery: A World History*, Part 1, pp. 9-12.

14. *The Encyclopedia Americana* (1990), Volume 25, p. 19. *The New Encyclopaedia Britannica* (1992), Volume 27, p. 286.

15. *The New Encyclopaedia Britannica* (1992), Volume 27, p. 286.

16. Milton Meltzer, *Slavery: A World History* (New York: Da Capo Press, 1993), Part 1, p. 18.

17. Thomas Sowell, *Race and Culture*, p. 186.

18. Lionel Casson et al., *Ancient Egypt* (New York: Time-Life Books, 1965), p. 102.

19. Hilton Kramer, "*Times* Won't Tell the Truth about Sharpton," *New York Post* (January 2, 1995), p. 17.

20. Thomas Sowell, *Race and Culture*, p. 194.

21. William L. Westermann, *The Slave Systems of Greek and Roman Antiquity* (Philadelphia: The American Philosophical Society, 1955), p. 23. David Brian Davis, *Slavery and Human Progress*, (New York: Oxford University Press, 1984), p. 33. Robert Hughes, *Culture of Complaint*, p. 142.

22. Milton Meltzer, *Slavery: A World History*, Part 1, p. 82. Robert Hughes, *Culture of Complaint*, p. 142.

23. *The Encyclopedia Americana* (1990), Volume 25, p. 19. Will Durant, *The Life of Greece*, (New York: Simon and Schuster, 1966), pp. 278-279.

24. Will Durant, *The Life of Greece*, p. 279.

25. *Ibid.*

26. Milton Meltzer, *Slavery: A World History*, Part 1, p. 72.

27. *The Encyclopedia Americana* (1990), Volume 25, p. 19.

28. *Grolier's Encyclopedia*, "Slavery."

29. Will Durant, *The Life of Greece*, p. 74.

30. *The Encyclopedia Americana* (1990), Volume 25, p. 19.

31. *Ibid.*

32. *Ibid.*

33. Will Durant, *The Life of Greece*, p. 280.

34. *Grolier's Encyclopedia*, "Slavery."

35. *The Encyclopedia Americana* (1990), Volume 25, p. 19.

36. Paul Louis, *Ancient Rome at Work* (New York: Barnes & Noble, Inc., 1965), pp. 131-132. (First printing 1927)

37. William L. Westermann, *The Slave Systems of Greek and Roman Antiquity*, pp. 85, 63.

38. *The Encyclopedia Americana* (1990), Volume 25, p. 20.

39. *The Encyclopaedia Britannica* (1990) (Chicago: Encyclopaedia Britannica, 1990), Volume 27, p. 287.

40. *Ibid.*

41. Bernard Lewis, *The Muslim Discovery of Europe* (New York: W.N. Norton, 1982), pp. 191-192.

42. Thomas Sowell, *Race and Culture*, p. 194.

43. *Ibid.*, p. 195.

44. *The Encyclopedia Americana* (1990), Volume 25, p. 20.

45. *Ibid.*

46. Richard Hellie, *Slavery in Russia: 1450-1725* (Chicago: University of Chicago Press, 1982), pp. 21-22. Thomas Sowell, *Conquests and Cultures*, p. 190.

47. Lord Kinross, *The Ottoman Centuries: The Rise and Fall of the Turkish Empire* (New York: William Morrow, 1977), p. 221.

48. *Ibid.*, p. 223.

49. Thomas Sowell, *Race and Culture*, p. 187.

50. *Ibid.*

51. Thomas Sowell, *Conquests and Cultures*, pp. 190-191.

52. Thomas Sowell, *Race and Culture*, p. 186.

53. *The New Encyclopaedia Britannica, Micropaedia* (1992), Volume 10, p. 874.

54. Ellen Irene Diggs, *Black Chronology From 4000 B.C. to the Abolition of the Slave Trade* (Boston: G.K. Hall & Co., 1983), p. 21.

55. R.W. Beachey, *The Slave Trade of Eastern Africa* (New York: Harper & Row, 1976), p. 162. R.W. Beachey, *The Slave Trade of Eastern Africa: A Collection of Documents* (London: Rex Collings Ltd., 1976), p. 77. Robert Hughes, *Culture of Complaint*, p. 142.

56. Milton Meltzer, *Slavery: A World History* (New York: De Capo Press, 1993), Part 2, p. 62.

57. Thomas Sowell, *Conquests and Cultures*, p. 267.

58. *Ibid.*

59. Milton Meltzer, *Slavery: A World History*, Part 2, p. 62. Thomas Sowell, *The Economics and Politics of Race*, p. 227. *Concise Columbia Electronic Encyclopedia* (New York: Columbia University Press, 1994).

60. Richard F. Townsend, *The Aztecs* (London: Thames and Hudson, 1992), pp. 90-91, 101.

61. Thomas Sowell, *Conquests and Cultures*, p. 276.

62. Hugh Thomas, *Conquest: Montezuma, Cortes, and the Fall of Old Mexico* (New York: Simon and Schuster, 1993), pp. 25-26.

63. Thomas Sowell, *The Economics and Politics of Race*, pp. 227-228.

64. Thomas Sowell, *Conquests and Cultures*, p. 281.

65. Thomas Sowell, *Conquests and Cultures*, pp. 289-290. Dinesh D'Souza, *The End of Racism*, p. 350.

66. Milton Meltzer, *Slavery: A World History*, Part 2, pp. 66, 68. Orlando Patterson, *Freedom in the Making of Western Culture* (New York: Basic Books, 1991), p. 12. Dinesh D'Souza, *The End of Racism*, p. 73.

67. Milton Meltzer, *Slavery: A World History*, Part 2, p. 64.

68. Orlando Patterson, *Slavery and Social Death: A Comparative Study* (Cambridge: Harvard University Press, 1982), p. 84. Milton Meltzer, *Slavery: A World History*, Part 2, pp. 64-65.

69. Milton Meltzer, *Slavery: A World History*, Part 2, pp. 69-73.

70. *Ibid.*, Part 2, pp. 71-73.

71. Dinesh D'Souza, *The End of Racism*, pp. 75-76.

72. *Ibid.*, p. 75.

73. *Ibid.*, p. 76.

74. Thomas Sowell, *Race and Culture*, pp. 187-188.

75. *Ibid.*, p. 187.

76. *The New Encyclopaedia Britannica* (1992), Volume 27, p. 286.

77. *Ibid.*

78. *Ibid.*

79. Frederick Cooper, *Plantation Slavery on the East Coast of Africa* (New Haven and London: Yale University Press, 1977), p. 12.

80. Thomas Sowell, "Phony Black History," *New York Post* (April 8, 1995), p. 11. *The Encyclopaedia Britannica* (1990), Volume 27, p. 287. Thomas Sowell, *Conquests and Cultures*, p. 111.

81. Ehud R. Toledano, *The Ottoman Slave Trade and Its Suppression: 1840-1890* (Princeton: Princeton University Press, 1982), pp. 51-52.

82. *Ibid.*, pp. 51-53.

83. Reginald Coupland, *East Africa and Its Invaders* (Oxford: The Clarendon Press, 1961), p. 143.

84. R.W. Beachey, *The Slave Trade of Eastern Africa*, pp. 189-191.

85. *Ibid.*, pp. 190-191.

86. *Ibid.*, p. 191.

87. Thomas Sowell, *Conquests and Cultures*, p. 154.

88. E.W. Bovill, *The Golden Trade of the Moors* (London: Oxford University Press, 1968), pp. 245-246.

89. Thomas Sowell, *Conquests and Cultures*, p. 153.

90. Robert Hughes, *Culture of Complaint*, p. 142.

91. Dinesh D'Souza, *The End of Racism*, p. 73.

92. Robert Hughes, *Culture of Complaint*, pp. 142-143.

93. John Reader, *Africa* (New York: Alfred A. Knopf, Inc., 1997), p. 291.

94. R.W. Beachey, *The Slave Trade of Eastern Africa*, p. 182.

95. John Thornton, *Africa and Africans in the Making of the Atlantic World, 1400-1680* (Cambridge: Cambridge University Press, 1992), pp. 74-76, 95.

96. Kevin Beary, "African Roots," *National Review* (March 10, 1997), p. 46.

97. Thomas Sowell, *Race and Culture*, p. 188.

98. Robert Hughes, *Culture of Complaint*, p. 143.

99. Thomas Sowell, "Black 'Leaders' Ignoring a Lot of Black History," *New York Post* (February 15, 1997), p. 15.

100. Thomas Sowell, *The Economics and Politics of Race*, p. 94. Thomas Sowell, *Race and Culture*, p. 188.

101. Basil Davidson, *The African Slave Trade* (Boston: Little, Brown, and Co., 1980), pp. 42, 105-106, 208.

102. Thomas Sowell, *The Economics and Politics of Race*, p. 228.

103. John Reader, *Africa*, p. 342.

104. *Ibid.*

105. *Ibid.*, p. 393.

106. Orlando Patterson, *Slavery and Social Death: A Comparative Study*, pp. 121-122.

107. E. Franklin Frazier, *Race and Culture Contacts in the Modern World* (Boston: Beacon Press, 1957), p. 67.

108. Zora Neale Hurston, *Dust Tracks on a Road* (New York: Harper Perennial, 1991), p. 145. Cited by Dinesh D'Souza, *The End of Racism*, p. 74.

109. Thomas Sowell, *Race and Culture*, p. 189.

110. Orlando Patterson, *Slavery and Social Death: A Comparative Study*, pp. 27-28.

111. Thomas Sowell, *The Economics and Politics of Race*, p. 228.

112. Thomas Sowell, *Race and Culture*, p. 195.

113. *Ibid.*, pp. 190-191.

114. *Ibid.*

115. Thomas Sowell, *Conquests and Cultures*, p. 109.

116. Suzanne Miers and Igor Kopytoff, "African 'Slavery' As an Institution of Marginality," *Slavery in Africa*, Suzanne Miers and Igor Kopytoff, eds., (Madison, Wisconsin: The University of Wisconsin Press, 1977), p. 24.

117. Frederick Cooper, *Plantation Slavery on the East Coast of Africa*, pp. 17, 19.

118. Carol P. MacCormack, "Wono: Institutionalized Dependency in Sherbro Descent Groups," *Slavery in Africa*, Suzanne Miers and Igor Kopytoff, eds., p. 200.

119. Suzanne Miers and Igor Kopytoff, "African 'Slavery' As an Institution of Marginality," *Slavery in Africa*, Suzanne Miers and Igor Kopytoff, eds., p. 52.

120. *Ibid.*

121. Robert Hughes, *Culture of Complaint*, p. 144.

122. Roberta Ann Dunbar, "Slavery and the Evolution of Nineteenth-Century Damagaram," *Slavery in Africa*, Suzanne Miers and Igor Kopytoff, eds., p. 163.

123. Ralph A. Austen, "Slavery Among Coastal Middlemen: The Duala of Cameroon," *Slavery in Africa*, Suzanne Miers and Igor Kopytoff, eds., p. 315.

124. Victor C. Uehendu, "Slaves and Slavery in Igboland, Nigeria," *Slavery in Africa*, Suzanne Miers and Igor Kopytoff, eds., p. 129.

125. K. Nwachukwu-Ogedengbe, "Slavery in Nineteenth-Century Aboh," *Slavery in Africa*, Suzanne Miers and Igor Kopytoff, eds., p. 145.

126. John Reader, *Africa*, p. 403.

127. Ralph A. Austen, "Slavery Among Coastal Middlemen: The Duala of Cameroon," *Slavery in Africa*, Suzanne Miers and Igor Kopytoff, eds., p. 329.

128. *Ibid.*

129. K. Nwachukwu-Ogedengbe, "Slavery in Nineteenth-Century Aboh," *Slavery in Africa*, Suzanne Miers and Igor Kopytoff, eds., pp. 144-145.

130. *Ibid.*, p. 145.

131. *Ibid.*

132. Victor C. Uchendu, "Slaves and Slavery in Igboland, Nigeria," *Slavery in Africa*, Suzanne Miers and Igor Kopytoff, eds., p. 131.

133. Ralph A. Austen, "Slavery Among Coastal Middlemen: The Duala of Cameroon," *Slavery in Africa*, Suzanne Miers and Igor Kopytoff, eds., p. 315.

134. *Ibid.*

135. *Ibid.*

136. Suzanne Miers and Igor Kopytoff, "African 'Slavery' As an Institution of Marginality," *Slavery in Africa*, Suzanne Miers and Igor Kopytoff, eds., p. 13.

137. R.W. Beachey, *The Slave Trade of Eastern Africa*, pp. 196-197.

138. Suzanne Miers and Igor Kopytoff, "African 'Slavery' As an Institution of Marginality," *Slavery in Africa*, Suzanne Miers and Igor Kopytoff, eds., p. 12.

139. *Ibid.*

140. *Ibid.*, p. 13.

141. *Ibid.*, p. 12.

142. *Ibid.*, p. 13.

143. *Ibid.*

144. John Reader, *Africa*, p. 409.

145. *Ibid.*, p. 410.

146. Suzanne Miers and Igor Kopytoff, "African 'Slavery' As an Institution of Marginality," *Slavery in Africa*, Suzanne Miers and Igor Kopytoff, eds., pp. 13-14. Kevin Beary, "African Roots," *National Review* (March 10, 1997), p. 46.

147. R.W. Beachey, *The Slave Trade of Eastern Africa*, p. 182.

148. Suzanne Miers and Igor Kopytoff, "African 'Slavery' As an Institution of Marginality," *Slavery in Africa*, Suzanne Miers and Igor Kopytoff, eds., p. 13.

149. *Ibid.*

150. Frederick Cooper, *Plantation Slavery on the East Coast of Africa*, p. 16.

151. Roberta Ann Dunbar, "Slavery and the Evolution of Nineteenth-Century Damagaram," *Slavery in Africa*, Suzanne Miers and Igor Kopytoff, eds., p. 160.

152. *Ibid.*

153. R.W. Beachey, *The Slave Trade of Eastern Africa*, p. 182.

154. *Ibid.*, p. 192.

155. *Ibid.*

156. *Ibid.*

157. *Ibid.*, pp. 192-193.

158. *Ibid.*, p. 193.

159. *Ibid.*

160. *Ibid.*

161. *Ibid.*

162. Suzanne Miers and Igor Kopytoff, "African 'Slavery' As an Institu-

tion of Marginality," *Slavery in Africa*, Suzanne Miers and Igor Kopytoff, eds., p. 14.

163. Thomas Sowell, *The Economics and Politics of Race*, p. 226.

164. *Ibid.*, p. 227.

165. L.H. Gann and Peter Duignan, *Burden of Empire* (New York, Washington, and London: Frederick A. Praeger, 1967), p. 155. Roger Summers, *Inyanga: Prehistoric Settlements in Southern Rhodesia* (Cambridge, England, 1958), p. 225.

166. L.H. Gann and Peter Duignan, *Burden of Empire*, p. 155.

167. Thomas Sowell, *The Economics and Politics of Race*, p. 227.

168. L.H. Gann and Peter Duignan, *Burden of Empire*, p. 160.

169. *The Encyclopaedia Britannica* (1926) (New York: The Encyclopaedia Britannica, Inc., 1926), Volume 28, p. 1,052.

170. Thomas Sowell, *Conquests and Cultures*, p. 121.

171. L.H. Gann and Peter Duignan, *Burden of Empire*, p. 141.

172. *Ibid.*, p. 140.

173. *Ibid.*, pp. 134, 138-139.

174. *Ibid.*, p. 138.

175. *Ibid.*, p. 139.

176. *Ibid.*, p. 141.

177. Dinesh D'Souza, *The End of Racism*, p. 52. L.H. Gann and Peter Duignan, *Burden of Empire*, p. 142.

178. L.H. Gann and Peter Duignan, *Burden of Empire*, pp. 142, 149.

179. Thomas Sowell, *The Economics and Politics of Race*, p. 16.

180. Dinesh D'Souza, *The End of Racism*, p. 53.

181. *Ibid.*

182. L.H. Gann and Peter Duignan, *Burden of Empire*, p. 144. Dinesh D'Souza, *The End of Racism*, pp. 54, 375.

183. L.H. Gann and Peter Duignan, *Burden of Empire*, pp. 146-147. Dinesh D'Souza, *The End of Racism*, p. 52.

184. L.H. Gann and Peter Duignan, *Burden of Empire*, p. 147.

185. *Ibid.*

186. *Ibid.*, p. 148.

187. *Ibid.*, pp. 153, 155.

188. John Reader, *Africa*, p. 295.

189. L.H. Gann and Peter Duignan, *Burden of Empire*, pp. 145, 153.

190. *Ibid.*, p. 145.

191. Thomas Sowell, *The Economics and Politics of Race*, p. 122.

192. Thomas Sowell, "Paying for Slavery," *Economist* (August 13, 1994), pp. 28-29.

193. Thomas Sowell, "Phony Black History," *New York Post* (April 8, 1995), p. 11.

194. Dinesh D'Souza, *The End of Racism*, p. 77.

195. *Ibid.*, pp. 77-79.

196. *Ibid.*, p. 91.

197. Lerone Bennett, *The Shaping of Black America* (Chicago: Johnson Publishing Co., 1975), p. 147.

198. Peter J. Parish, *Slavery: History and Historians* (New York: Harper & Row, 1989), pp. 73, 86.

199. W. E. B. Du Bois, *Black Reconstruction* (New York: S.A. Russell, 1935), p. 9.

200. Robert W. Fogel and Stanley L. Engerman, *Time on the Cross* (Boston: Little, Brown, and Co., 1974), Chapter 4.

201. W. E. B. Du Bois, *Black Reconstruction*, p. 39.

202. Robert W. Fogel and Stanley L. Engerman, *Time on the Cross*, Chapter 4.

203. Dinesh D'Souza, *The End of Racism*, p. 89.

204. Gwendolyn Midlo Hall, *Social Control in Slave Plantation Societies* (Baltimore: Johns Hopkins University Press, 1971), Chapter 2. Thomas Sowell, *The Economics and Politics of Race*, p. 96.

205. *The Encyclopedia Americana* (1990), Volume 25, pp. 22-23.

206. *Ibid.*

207. *Ibid.*

208. *The New Encyclopaedia Britannica, Micropaedia* (1992), Volume 10, p. 874.

209. Frank Wesley Pitman, "Slavery on British West India Plantations in the Eighteenth Century," *Journal of Negro History* (October 1926), pp. 630, 637. Thomas Sowell, *The Economics and Politics of Race*, p. 104. Thomas Sowell, *Race and Culture*, p. 200.

210. Thomas Sowell, *The Economics and Politics of Race*, p. 96.

211. Dinesh D'Souza, *The End of Racism*, p. 91.

212. Thomas Sowell, *Race and Culture*, pp. 210-211.

213. *Ibid.*, p. 211.

214. L.H. Gann and Peter Duignan, *Burden of Empire*, p. 158.

215. *The Encyclopaedia Britannica* (1990), Volume 27, p. 290.

216. L.H. Gann and Peter Duignan, *Burden of Empire*, p. 158.

217. Dinesh D'Souza, *The End of Racism*, p. 105.

218. L.H. Gann and Peter Duignan, *Burden of Empire*, p. 158.

219. Thomas Sowell, *Race and Culture*, pp. 211-213.

220. L.H. Gann and Peter Duignan, *Burden of Empire*, p. 156.

221. *Ibid.*

222. *Ibid.*

223. *Ibid.*

224. Basil Davidson, *The African Slave Trade*, p. 255. L.H. Gann and Peter Duignan, *Africa South of the Sahara* (Stanford: Hoover Institution Press, 1981), p. 4.

225. Dinesh D'Souza, *The End of Racism*, pp. 105-106.

226. Robert Hughes, *Culture of Complaint*, p. 144.

227. Thomas Sowell, *Race and Culture*, pp. 212-213.

228. Patrick Manning, *Slavery and African Life* (New York: Cambridge University Press, 1990), p. 140. John Reader, *Africa*, pp. 430-431.

229. Patrick Manning, *Slavery and African Life*, pp. 140, 142.

230. John Reader, *Africa*, p. 430.

231. Patrick Manning, *Slavery and African Life*, p. 142.

232. John Reader, *Africa*, p. 431.

233. Patrick Manning, *Slavery and African Life*, p. 140.

234. *Ibid.*, p. 143.

235. John Reader, *Africa*, p. 432.

236. *Ibid.*

237. *Ibid.*, p. 431.

238. *Ibid.*

239. *Ibid.*, pp. 431-432.

240. Jenifer Warren, "Demanding Repayment for Slavery," *Los Angeles Times* (July 6, 1994), pp. A1, A5. Lena Williams, "Group of Blacks Presses the Case for Reparations for Slavery," *The New York Times* (July 21, 1994), p. B10.

241. Eloise Salholz and Frank Washington, "Paying for Sins of the Past," *Newsweek* (May 22, 1989), p. 44.

242. Thomas Sowell, "Paying for Slavery," *Economist* (August 13, 1994), pp. 28-29. Dinesh D'Souza, *The End of Racism*, p. 68.

243. Robert Hughes, *Culture of Complaint*, p. 145.

244. Thomas Sowell, *Race and Culture*, p. 215. Susanne Everett, *History of Slavery* (Edison, New Jersey: Chartwell Books, 1996), pp. 68-69.

245. Thomas Sowell, *Race and Culture*, p. 215.

246. *Ibid.*

247. *Ibid.*

248. Thomas Sowell, *Conquests and Cultures*, p. 167.

249. *Ibid.*, pp. 167-168.

250. *Ibid.*, p. 168.

251. *Ibid.*

252. Thomas Sowell, *Race and Culture*, p. 219.

253. *Ibid.*

254. Thomas Sowell, *The Vision of the Anointed* (New York: Basic Books, 1995), p. 200.

255. Booker T. Washington, *Selected Speeches*, edited by E. Davidson Washington (New York: Doubleday, 1932), p. 37. Booker T. Washington, *Up From Slavery* (New York: Penguin Books, 1986), p. 16.

256. Zora Neale Hurston, "How It Feels to Be Colored Me," excerpted in Henry Louis Gates, ed., *Bearing Witness* (New York: Pantheon Books, 1991), pp. 34-35.

Chapter 13
Finding Racism Everywhere

1. Bertrand Russell, *Sceptical Essays* (New York: Norton, 1928), p. 28.

2. Rush Limbaugh, "America Is Not a Racist Country," *Limbaugh Letter* (November 1995), p. 5.

3. *Ibid.*

4. *Ibid.*

5. *Ibid.*

6. E.R. Shipp, "Referendum on Blacks?" *Daily News* (New York) (November 9, 1994), p. 19.

7. Deborah Orin, "Rangel Draws Ire by Calling 'Tax Cuts' a Code for Racism," *New York Post* (November 3, 1994), p. 26.

8. Daniel Goleman, "Anger over Racism Is Seen As a Cause of Blacks' High Blood Pressure," *The New York Times* (April 24, 1990), p. C3.

9. Thernstrom, *America in Black and White*, p. 19.

10. Daniel Goleman, "Anger over Racism Is Seen As a Cause of Blacks' High Blood Pressure," *The New York Times* (April 24, 1990), p. C3.

11. Warren E. Leary, "Study Hints of Reason for Blacks' High Rate of Heart Disease," *The New York Times* (June 26, 1994), p. 15.

12. Alan L. Otten, "Unnatural Causes Claim Lives of More Children," *The Wall Street Journal* (February 13, 1989), p. B1. *Health: United States, 1993* (Hyattsville, Maryland: U.S. Dept. of Health and Human Services, 1994), pp. 93-94.

13. Associated Press, "White Women Show Rise in Smoking Among Young," *The New York Times* (November 6, 1994), p. 43.

14. *Ibid.*

15. Daniel Goleman, "Second Assault on Crime Victims: Long-Term Mental Troubles," *The New York Times* (May 3, 1990), p. B14.

16. *Ibid.*

17. Cecil Harris, "Boeheim Calls Foul," *New York Post* (January 21, 1994), p. 73.

18. "Thompson Boycotting to Protest Rule," *Chicago Tribune* (January 14, 1989), Section 2, p. 2. "Thompson Plans to Boycott Game in NCAA Protest," *Los Angeles Times* (January 14, 1989), Section III, p. 1. M.F. Heller, "Thompson's Next Move Uncertain," *The Washington Times* (January 20, 1989), p. C1. Dave Sell, "Thompson Comes Back for 'Lucky' Victory," *Washington Post* (January 22, 1989), p. C4.

19. Joe Drape, "Athletic Eligibility: Key N.C.A.A. Rule Is Voided As Biased," *The New York Times* (March 9, 1999), pp. A1, D10.

20. *Ibid.*, p. A1.

21. Phil Mushnick, "Aw-ful Truth: Thompson a Fraud," *New York Post* (January 26, 1994), p. 54.

22. Associated Press, "Black Coaches May Boycott," *New York Post* (January 12, 1994), p. 51.

23. Phil Mushnick, "Aw-ful Truth: Thompson a Fraud," *New York Post* (January 26, 1994), p. 54.

24. *Ibid.*

25. Phil Mushnick, "Hoop-O-Crites," *New York Post* (January 14, 1994), p. 83.

26. Stephen Chapman, "Race, the Heisman Trophy, and Susan Smith," *Conservative Chronicle* (December 7, 1994), p. 9.

27. *Ibid.*

28. Richard G. Carter, "He Puts the Knock on Knicks Trade," *Daily News* (New York) (March 9, 1989), p. 47.

29. Wallace Matthews, "Sammy Victimized by New Color Line," *New York Post* (September 15, 1998), pp. 94-95.

30. *Ibid.*

31. *Ibid.*

32. Associated Press, "Slammin' Sosa Is Mr. Baseball to the People of Dominican," *New York Post* (October 24, 1998), p. 76.

33. *Ibid.*

34. *Ibid.*

35. Associated Press, "Jackson Leads Protest Outside Camden Yards," *New York Post* (July 14, 1993), p. 63.

36. Peter Richmond, "Joe Morgan's Cool Anger," *GQ* (October 1998), p. 106.

37. Thad Mumford, "Affirmative Action Is KO'd in the Sports Section, Too," *The New York Times* (February 2, 1997).

38. Michael Meyers, "Jesse and the Oscars," *New York Post* (April 1, 1996), p. 19.

39. Phil Mushnick, "Boss' Lapels up for Sale," *New York Post* (May 5, 1997), p. 65. Phil Mushnick, "A Real 'Con' Job," *New York Post* (December 7, 1997), p. 105.

40. Mark A. Uhlig, "Racial Remarks Cause Furor," *The New York Times* (January 16, 1988), pp. 47, 50.

41. "Racial Remark Stalls Job Seeker," *The New York Times* (July 22, 1993), p. A18.

42. *Ibid.* "Remark Ends a Job Candidacy," *The New York Times* (July 29, 1993), p. A21.

43. Wendell Jamieson and Helen Kennedy, "Legendary Miler Runs into Race Row," *Daily News* (New York) (September 14, 1995), p. 12.

44. Harvey Araton, "All Is Never Quiet on Barkley Front," *The New York Times* (November 5, 1992), p. B27.

45. Ian O'Connor, "When Saying Their Success Is Strictly Physical, Whites Shortchange Black Athletes with . . . White Man's Diss - Ease," *Daily News* (New York) (September 15, 1995), p. 89.

46. *Ibid.*

47. Ralph Wiley, *Why Black People Tend to Shout* (New York: Penguin Books, 1992), p. 184.

48. "The Black Dominance," *Time* (May 9, 1977), pp. 57-60.

49. Tom Friend, "Where Hurley Stands Is 5-11 and in the NBA," *The New York Times* (November 14, 1993), Section 8, p. 5.

50. Anthony L. Gargano, "Worm's Threats Pure Bull," *New York Post* (October 24, 1997), p. 100.

51. "Some Answers No One Expected," *The New York Times* (April 8, 1987), p. B10.

52. Phil Mushnick, "Kraft Quotes Were Monkeyed Around," *New York Post* (July 27, 1994), p. 60. David L. Lewis, "But Official Denies He Bad-Mouthed Neighbors," *Daily News* (New York) (July 19, 1994), p. 5. Joe Sexton, "Yankees Offer an Apology for Comments," *The New York Times* (July 19, 1994), p. B1. David L. Lewis, "But Official Denies He Bad-Mouthed Neighbors," *Daily News* (New York) (July 19, 1994), p. 5.

53. Phil Mushnick, "Kraft Quotes Were Monkeyed Around," *New York Post* (July 27, 1994), p. 60.

54. Jonathan Karl, "Ferrer Demands Boss Boot Buddy over 'Race' Remark," *New York Post* (July 19, 1994), p. 4.

55. "White Sez Kraft Got the Shaft," *Daily News* (New York) (August 1, 1994), p. 37.

56. Frank Isola, "Barkley 'Hates' to Avoid Controversy," *Daily News* (New York) (February 13, 1995), p. 42.

57. Wallace Matthews, "Call Him Sir Chump," *New York Post* (February 23, 1998).

58. Phil Mushnick, "Monkey Business: The 'Frank' Truth," *New York Post* (March 6, 1996), p. 59.

59. Phil Mushnick, "Double Standard on Race," *New York Post* (March 1, 1998), p. 91.

60. *Ibid.*

61. Gregory Clay, "The Sound and Fury," *Daily News* (New York) (December 5, 1998), p. 65.

62. Phil Mushnick, "Trump Cox's Race Card," *New York Post* (December 4, 1998), p. 104.

63. Peter Botte, "Isles Tune Out Racism Claims," *New York Post* (December 4, 1996), p. 60.

64. Phil Mushnick, "Macho Mucho Moron," *New York Post* (July 18, 1997), p. 112.

65. Ronald Sullivan, "Judge Finds Bias in Terminal Search," *The New York Times* (April 25, 1990), p. B3. Ronald Sullivan, "Police Say Drug-Program Files Are Not Biased," *The New York Times* (April 26, 1990), p. B3.

66. Ronald Sullivan, "Police Say Drug-Program Files Are Not Biased," *The New York Times* (April 26, 1990), p. B3.

67. Ronald Sullivan, "Judge Finds Bias in Terminal Search," *The New York Times* (April 25, 1990), p. B3.

68. Rita Kramer, "Adoption in Black and White," *The Wall Street Journal* (October 24, 1994), p. A14.

69. Robert Zelnick, *Backfire*, p. 14.

70. *Ibid.* Rita Kramer, "Adoption in Black and White," *The Wall Street Journal* (October 24, 1994), p. A14.

71. Deroy Murdock, "Everyday America's Racial Harmony," *The American Enterprise* (November/December 1998), p. 26.

72. "Look It Up," *Daily News* (New York) (March 19, 1998).

73. *Ibid.*

74. Associated Press, "NAACP May Join Suits Against Gun Makers," *The Journal News* (Gannett Suburban Newspapers) (February 21, 1999), p. 4A. Bill Varner, "NAACP May Sue TV Networks and Gun Makers," *The Journal News* (Gannett Suburban Newspapers) (July 13, 1999).

75. Michael A. Fletcher, "Voting Rights for Felons Win Support," *Washington Post* (February 22, 1999), p. A1.

76. Brett Pulley, "Living off the Daily Dream of Winning a Lottery Prize," *The New York Times* (May 22, 1999), p. B6.

77. *Ibid.*

78. Bill Dentzer, "Westchester Fights Award in Race Bias," *Reporter Dispatch* (Gannett Suburban Newspapers) (January 13, 1998), p. 7A.

79. "Michael Jackson, What Have You Done?," *Destiny* (February 1994), p. 4.

80. Carl Rowan, "NAACP Must Oust Gibson and Chavis Now," *New York Post* (August 3, 1994), p. 21.

81. Stephen A. Holmes, "Court Rejects Bid by Chavis to Regain Job," *The New York Times* (August 25, 1994), p. A13. Kyle Smith, "Chavis: Jews & Blacks Conspired Against Me," *New York Post* (August 26, 1994), p. 2.

82. Chrisena Coleman, "NAACP Chief Sez He's Not Quitting, Urges Black Unity," *Daily News* (New York) (August 17, 1994), p. 10.

83. E.R. Shipp, "Muslim Message That Should Be Heeded," *Daily News* (New York) (August 17, 1994), p. 25.

84. Ishmael Reed, *Airing Dirty Laundry* (Reading, Mass.: Addison-Wesley, 1993), pp. xiv, 68.

85. Lena Williams, "Growing Black Debate: Racism or an Excuse?" *The New York Times* (April 5, 1992).

86. Tony Snow, "Blacks Should Not Abandon King's Dream," *Conservative Chronicle* (September 7, 1994), p. 28.

87. *Ibid.*

88. *Ibid.*

89. William Murchison, "Enough Talk about 'Racism,' " *Conservative Chronicle* (September 7, 1994), p. 17.

90. *Ibid.*

91. Patricia Mangan and Dick Sheridan, "Black and Hispanic Youths Are 90 Percent of Truant Roundup," *Daily News* (New York) (May 19, 1994), p. 12.

92. Cara Bonnett, "Regent: Bias Plays Role in Special Ed," *The Journal News* (Gannett Suburban Newspapers) (February 6, 1999), pp. 1A, 2A.

93. Family Research Council, "Illegitimacy's Disastrous Effects," *In Focus* (April 1995).

94. *Ibid.*

95. Michael Meyers, " 'Nappy Hair': A Rotten Lie," *New York Post* (December 8, 1998), p. 35. Clyde Haberman, "Cry Racism, and Watch Knees Jerk," *The New York Times* (December 4, 1998). Susan Edelman, "Book-Flap Teacher: I'm Gone," *New York Post* (December 1, 1998), p. 7.

96. Cleave Townsend, "White Male Rage," *Destiny* (April 1995), pp. 14-16.

97. *Ibid.*, pp. 16-17.

98. Dinesh D'Souza, *The End of Racism*, p. 233.

99. Charles Gasparino and Joseph N. Boyce, "Jackson, Wall Street Have Their Big Day, But Will It Fuel Minority Opportunities?" *The Wall Street Journal* (January 16, 1998), p. C1. Charles Gasparino and Joseph N. Boyce, "Jesse Jackson Lobbies Wall Street for Greater Diversity," *The Wall Street Journal* (December 23, 1997), p. C1.

100. Doreen Carvajal, "Protest Against President Halts Basketball Game at Rutgers," *The New York Times* (February 8, 1995), p. B1.

101. Jim Nolan et al., "Race-Charge Teacher May Face Dismissal," *New York Post* (October 5, 1989), p. 29.

102. Rita Delfiner, "Pol in 'Racist' Furor Draws More Heat," *New York Post* (January 19, 1990).

103. Seth Mydans, "Black Identity vs. Success and Seeming 'White,' " *The New York Times* (April 25, 1990), p. B9.

104. *Ibid.*

105. *Ibid.*

106. *Ibid.*

107. Nwamaegwu Jeremi Duru, "You're Just Trying to Act White," *Washington Post* (May 19, 1991).

108. Lise Funderburg, *Black, White, Other: Biracial Americans Talk About Race and Identity* (New York: William Morrow, 1994), pp. 115-116.

109. "The Hidden Hurdle," *Time* (March 16, 1992), p. 44.

110. Ron Susskind, "In Rough City School, Top Students Struggle to Learn—and Escape," *The Wall Street Journal* (May 26, 1994), pp. A1, A8.

111. Pam Belluck, "Reason Is Sought for Lag by Blacks in School Effort," *The New York Times* (July 14, 1999), p. 15.

112. John McWhorter, "Shrinking from Success," *The American Enterprise* (November/December 1998), p. 30.

113. *Ibid.*, p. 31.

114. Maureen Dowd, "Niggardly City," *The New York Times* (January 31, 1999).

115. *Ibid.*

116. Jon Nordheimer, "Touching Nerves in Newsrooms," *The New York Times* (November 22, 1993), pp. B1, B6.

117. *Ibid.*, p. B6.

118. *Ibid.*

119. *Ibid.*

120. *Ibid.*

121. *Ibid.*

122. Linton Weeks, "An Official's Vocabulary Lesson," *Washington Post* (January 28, 1999).

123. Donna Britt, "Two Tastes of the Power of Words," *Washington Post* (January 29, 1999), p. B1. Maureen Dowd, "Niggardly City," *The New York Times* (January 31, 1999).

124. "About 'Niggardly,' " *Washington Post* (January 29, 1999), p. A24.

125. Melinda Hennenberger, "Race Mix-up Raises Havoc for Capital," *The New York Times* (January 29, 1999), p. A10.

126. Maureen Dowd, "Niggardly City," *The New York Times* (January 31, 1999).

127. Linton Weeks, "An Official's Vocabulary Lesson," *Washington Post* (January 28, 1999).

128. Caren Halbfinger, "Drawing of Black Child Draws Outcries," *The Journal News* (Gannett Suburban Newspapers) (February 4, 1999), pp. 1A, 2A.

129. "Their Church and State," *Destiny* (February 1994), p. 3.

130. Eric Breindel, "Explanation for Farrakhan's 'Rhetoric' Takes a New Form," *New York Post* (March 24, 1994), p. 25.

131. *Ibid.*

132. *Ibid.*

133. Barbara Ross, "Boycott Grant's Tune—Jesse," *Daily News* (New York) (October 28, 1994), p. 8.

134. Gersh Kuntzman, "Jesse Leads Ad Boycott of Radio's Bob Grant," *New York Post* (October 26, 1994), p. 17.

135. Michael Meyers, "Bob Grant's Critics Are Showing Their Hypocrisy," *New York Post* (October 31, 1994), p. 23.

136. Paul Budline, "Hate-FM, Thanks to AmEx," *New York Post* (June 30, 1998), p. 29.

137. Curtis Sliwa, broadcast on Curtis Sliwa radio program on WABC radio in New York (October 28, 1994).

138. *PC World* (November 1994), p. 159.

139. *Boston Common*, NBC television program (March 28, 1996).

140. Dinesh D'Souza, *Illiberal Education*, pp. 96-97.

141. "The Continuing American Dilemma," *New Perspectives Quarterly* (Summer 1991), p. 11.

142. Dinesh D'Souza, *Illiberal Education*, pp. 96, 97.

143. *Ibid.*, p. 97.

144. "Imagine That," *The Washington Times* (April 1, 1992), p. A6.

145. Robert Cauthorn, "Cinema Apartheid," *Arizona Daily Star* (July 15, 1990), p. D1.

146. Jared Taylor, *Paved with Good Intentions*, p. 230.

147. *Ibid.*

148. *Ibid.*, pp. 230-231.

149. *Ibid.*, p. 231.

150. *Ibid.*, p. 232. Jared Taylor puts the figure for black representation among TV characters at 10 to 12 percent. A more recent survey places the figure between 12 and 13 percent, as reported on the July 13, 1999 Fox News Channel telecast of *Hannity and Colmes*.

151. Dinesh D'Souza, *The End of Racism*, p. 263.

152. Jared Taylor, *Paved with Good Intentions*, p. 233.

153. Stephen Farber, "Minority Villains Are Touchy Network Topic," *The New York Times* (March 1, 1986), p. 50.

154. Clifford May, "Jackson Urges Voters' Support for Dinkins Bid," *The New York Times* (September 4, 1989), p. 30.

155. Ishmael Reed, *Airing Dirty Laundry*, pp. 7, 70. Ishmael Reed, "Stats, Lies, & Videotape," *Emerge* (April 1994).

156. "Bill Cosby Sees Red over TV Stereotypes," *New York Post* (November 29, 1993), p. 8.

157. Henry Gates, "TV's Black World Turns—But Stays Unreal," *The New York Times* (November 12, 1989), p. H1.

158. Eric Mink, "NAACP Stirs Nets' Response," *Daily News* (New York) (July 14, 1999), p. 73. Lawrie Mifflin, "N.A.A.C.P. Plans to Press for More Diverse TV Shows," *The New York Times* (July 13, 1999). *Hannity & Colmes* television broadcast, Fox News Channel (July 13,1999).

159. *Ibid.*

160. Terry Pristin, "Ad Agency Urges Avoiding Black and Hispanic Radio," *The New York Times* (May 13, 1998), p. B7.

161. Associated Press, "Report: Minority-Owned Stations Often Passed up by Advertisers," *The Journal News* (Gannett Suburban Newspapers) (January 15, 1999), p. 3D.

162. *Ibid.*

163. Dewayne Wickham, "Black-Owned Radio Falls to Discrimination," *The Journal News* (Gannett Suburban Newspapers) (January 20, 1999).

164. Dinesh D'Souza, *The End of Racism*, p. 301.

165. Stuart Elliott, "White House Presses to Insure Minority-Owned Agencies and Media Get a Fair Share of Business," *The New York Times* (February 23, 1999), p. C8.

166. David Seifman, "Race Not an Issue As Rudy's Team Draws up Hit List," *New York Post* (March 2, 1994), p. 10.

167. *Ibid.*

168. *Ibid.*

169. Yancey Roy, "Pataki Policies Wallace-Like, Jackson Rails," *The Journal News* (Gannett Suburban Newspapers) (February 10, 1999), p. 3A.

170. Fredric U. Dicker, "Jesse Compares Pataki to Racist Govs," *New York Post* (February 10, 1999), p. 6.

171. Thomas Sowell, "Letter from the Ghetto," *New York Post* (January 21, 1994), p. 23.

172. Sandra Blakeslee, "Poor and Black Patients Slighted, Study Says," *The New York Times* (April 20, 1994), p. B9.

173. *Ibid.*

174. Thomas Sowell, *The Vision of the Anointed*, pp. 32-33.

175. John Edgar Wideman, *Fatheralong: A Meditation on Fathers and Sons, Race and Society* (New York: Pantheon Books, 1994), p. xvii.

176. Thomas Sowell, *The Vision of the Anointed*, pp. 32-33. Thomas Sowell, "Attitude's to Blame, Not Racism," *New York Post* (March 18, 1994), p. 19. Robert Pear, "Infant Mortality Rate Drops but Racial Disparity Grows," *The New York Times* (July 10, 1995), p. B9.

177. Thomas Sowell, *The Vision of the Anointed*, pp. 32-33, 54-55. Joel Kitkin, "A City Torn Apart," *Los Angeles Times* (May 3, 1992), Page M1.

178. Thomas Sowell, "Squeamish Words and Dying Babies," *Barbarians Inside the Gates*, p. 183.

179. Family Research Council, "Illegitimacy's Disastrous Effects," *In Focus* (April 1995).

180. *Ibid.*

181. William F. Buckley, Jr., "The Myth of Mass Illegitimacy," *New York Post* (August 12, 1996), p. 21.

182. Diana Jean Schemo, "Suburban Taxes Are Higher for Blacks, Analysis Shows," *The New York Times* (August 17, 1994), pp. A1, A6.

183. *Ibid.*, p. A6.

184. *Ibid.*

185. *Ibid.*, pp. A1, A6.

186. *Ibid.*, p. A6.

187. *Ibid.*

188. Thernstrom, *America in Black and White*, p. 212.

189. *Ibid.*, p. 211.

190. Thernstrom, *America in Black and White*, p. 215.

191. *Ibid.*, p. 217.

192. *Ibid.*, p. 218.

193. *Ibid.*, p. 219.

194. *Ibid.*, p. 226.

195. *Ibid.*, p. 229.

196. *Ibid.*

197. *Ibid.*, p. 230.

198. John T. McQuiston, "Property Taxes in Nassau Called Biased," *The New York Times* (March 9, 1999), p. B1.

199. *Ibid.*

200. *Ibid.*

201. *Ibid.*, pp. B1, B5.

202. NBC TV, 11:00 News in New York, anchored by Chuck Scarborough and Sue Simmons (July 19, 1994).

203. Jared Taylor, *Paved with Good Intentions*, p. 58.

204. Ed Koch, "What Are the Numbers on Interracial Crime?" *New York Post* (July 14, 1995), p. 21. Jared Taylor, *Paved with Good Intentions*, p. 58.

205. Jared Taylor, *Paved with Good Intentions*, p. 58.

206. Dinesh D'Souza, "The Racist Cabbie: Is He a Myth?", *New York Post* (October 16, 1995), p. 23.

207. Jonathan Karl and John Rogers, "Dinkins Livid about Cabbie's 'Racist' Snub," *New York Post* (December 3, 1994), p. 8.

208. *Ibid.*

209. Dinesh D'Souza, *The End of Racism*, p. 251.

210. *Ibid.*

211. *Ibid.*, p. 252.

212. Walter E. Williams, "Will We Ever Learn?" *More Liberty Means Less Government*, p. 47.

213. Dean Chang, "Escape from New York," *Daily News* (New York) (March 20, 1994), p. 12.

214. *Ibid.*

215. *Ibid.*

216. Dean Chang, "Woman Left Fear Behind in Brooklyn," *Daily News* (New York) (March 20, 1994), p. 13.

217. David Friedman, "The 'Environmental Racism' Hoax," *The American Enterprise* (November/December 1998), p. 75.

218. Jared Taylor, *Paved with Good Intentions*, p. 60.

219. David Friedman, "The 'Environmental Racism' Hoax," *The American Enterprise* (November/December 1998), p. 76.

220. *Ibid.*, p. 75.

221. Jared Taylor, *Paved with Good Intentions*, p. 61.

222. David Friedman, "The 'Environmental Racism' Hoax," *The American Enterprise* (November/December 1998), p. 75.

223. Jared Taylor, *Paved with Good Intentions*, p. 57.

224. Robert Stowe England, "Assault on the Mortgage Lenders," *National Review* (December 27, 1993), p. 52. Dinesh D'Souza, *The End of Racism*, p. 279.

225. Carl Horowitz, "Affirmative Action for Banks?" *Investor's Business Daily* (March 31, 1995).

226. *Ibid.*

227. Thomas Sowell, *The Vision of the Anointed*, p. 41. Dinesh D'Souza, *The End of Racism*, p. 280.

228. Robert Stowe England, "Assault on the Mortgage Lenders," *National Review* (December 27, 1993), p. 52.

229. *Ibid.*

230. Walter E. Williams, *The State Against Blacks*, pp. 29-30.

231. Robert Stowe England, "Assault on the Mortgage Lenders," *National Review* (December 27, 1993), p. 52. Robert Bork, *Slouching Towards Gomorrah*, p. 237.

232. Robert Stowe England, "Assault on the Mortgage Lenders," *National Review* (December 27, 1993), p. 54.

233. Jesse Jackson, "Racism Is the Bottom Line in Home Loans," *Los Angeles Times* (October 28, 1991).

234. "Unloved by Banks," *Economist* (October 26, 1991), p. 29.

235. Walter E. Williams, *The State Against Blacks*, p. 30.

236. "Affirmative Action for Banks?" *Investor's Business Daily* (March 31, 1995).

237. Jared Taylor, *Paved with Good Intentions*, p. 57.

238. *Ibid.*, pp. 57-58.

239. John B. Wilke, "Giving Credit: Mortgage Lending to Minorities Shows a Sharp 1994 Increase," *The Wall Street Journal* (February 13, 1996), pp. A1, A8.

240. Bill Dedman, "For Black Home Buyers, a Boomerang," *The New York Times* (February 13, 1999).

241. John B. Wilke, "Giving Credit: Mortgage Lending to Minorities Shows a Sharp 1994 Increase," *The Wall Street Journal* (February 13, 1996), pp. A1, A8.

242. *Ibid.*

243. Chrisena Coleman and Denene Millner, "Revs. Rail Against Bias," *Daily News* (New York) (September 29, 1993), p. 26.

244. Todd S. Purdum, "Supporting Dinkins, Clinton Worries about Role of Race," *The New York Times* (September 27, 1993), p. A1.

245. Earl Caldwell, "Powerful Force of Change Is in the Air," *Daily News* (New York) (September 29, 1993), p. 35.

246. Dan Janison, "Rev. on Dave: Blacks Won't Lose N.Y.", *New York Post* (October 25, 1993), p. 2.

247. Eric Breindel, "Playing the Race Card: Guinier's Blinkered View," *New York Post* (October 21, 1993), p. 23.

248. *Ibid.*

249. Minoo Southgate, "Black Power, Nineties Style," *National Review* (December 13, 1993), p. 48.

250. Michael H. Cottman, "Perilous Politics on Next Journey," *Newsday* (New York) (October 28, 1991). Sam Roberts, "Dinkins Defeats Giuliani in Close Race," *The New York Times* (November 8, 1989), p. A1.

251. Steven Lee Myers, "Dinkins's Radio Message Draws Civil-Rights Fire," *The New York Times* (July 25, 1993), p. 32.

252. Simon Anakwe, "Dinkins Is Dr. King's Present, Says Jesse," *The Amsterdam News* (January 21, 1989), p. 8.

253. Howard Kurtz, "In Pursuit of the Crucial Constituency: New York's Mayoral Candidates, Racing Hard to the Finish," *Washington Post* (November 1, 1989), p. D1.

254. See chapters 5, 6, and 8 for details on these events.

255. Christopher Ruddy, "Welfare Crisis," *New York Post* (January 4, 1994), p. 5.

256. David Savageau and Richard Doyer, *Places Rated Almanac* (New

York: Simon and Schuster, 1993), p. 406.

257. A.M. Rosenthal, "On Civil Disrespect," *The New York Times* (October 26, 1993), p. A21. Thernstrom, *America in Black and White*, p. 307.

258. David Seifman, "Rev. Forced Out of Church Joins Rudy's Team," *New York Post* (March 8, 1994), p. 18. Jim Sleeper, "Blacks, Rudy, and the American Way," *Daily News* (New York) (December 7, 1993), p. 41.

259. William F. Buckley Jr., "Is Mr. Clinton Culturally Integrated?" *National Review* (February 7, 1994), p. 78.

260. D.D. Guttenplan, "Whites Join Blacks for Dinkins," *Newsday* (New York) (September 13, 1989), p. 3. "Sources of Support," *Newsday* (New York) (November 8, 1989), p. 5.

261. Thernstrom, *America in Black and White*, p. 307.

262. "Dave Fights Mayoral 'Race' to the Bitter End," *New York Post* (December 27, 1993), p. 4.

263. Thomas B. Edsall, "Conflicting Trends Seen in Whites' Willingness to Vote for Blacks," *Washington Post* (December 19, 1993), p. A27.

264. Felicia R. Lee, "For Blacks, Loss by Dinkins Undermines Hopes of Change," *The New York Times* (November 4, 1993), p. B4.

265. *Ibid.*, p. A1.

266. *Ibid.*, p. B4.

267. *Ibid.*

268. Marilyn Millow and Myron Waldman, "White Vote Backed Helms," *Newsday* (New York) (November 8, 1990). Michael Kinsley, "What's Really Fair," *Time* (November 19, 1990), p. 124. Donald Baer, "The Race in Black and White," *U.S. News & World Report* (July 23, 1990), p. 29.

269. Richard G. Carter, "Racism Wins, and America Is the Loser," *Daily News* (New York) (July 19, 1988), p. 31.

270. Rush Limbaugh television program (November 4, 1993).

271. "Maxine Waters: Straight Talk from South Central," *Ladies' Home Journal* (August 1992), p. 113.

272. Michael Meyers, "An Ivy League Exercise in the Rhetoric of Race," *New York Post* (April 29, 1996), p. 21.

273. Jared Taylor, *Paved with Good Intentions*, p. 267. Andrew Hacker, *Two Nations*, p. 208.

274. Larry Tye, "In South, Ballot Box Inequality Lingers On," *Boston Globe* (July 23, 1990), p. 1.

275. Juan Williams, "Alex Williams and the Crossover Strategy," *Washington Post Magazine* (February 12, 1989), p. 21.

276. Michael Oreskes, "Black Virginian Close to a Historic Triumph," *The New York Times* (November 8, 1989), p. A1.

277. Thernstrom, *America in Black and White*, p. 301.

278. Kevin Sack, "In the Rural South, Seeds of a Biracial Politics," *The New York Times* (December 30, 1998).

279. *Ibid.*

280. Associated Press, "Black Republican Wins Virginia Seat," *Christian Science Monitor* (November 5, 1997), p. 2.

281. Robin Toner, "Real-Life Politics in Deep South," *The New York Times* (March 30, 1989), p. A10. Jared Taylor, *Paved with Good Intentions*, p. 267.

282. M. Barone, "The Inward Turn of Black Americans," *U.S. News & World Report* (May 8, 1989), p. 33. *Statistical Abstract of the United States: 1997*, p. 46, Table 46.

283. Thernstrom, *America in Black and White*, p. 287.

284. David Shribman and James Perry, "Black Moderates Win at Polls by Targeting Once-Elusive Whites," *The Wall Street Journal* (November 9, 1989), p. A1.

285. William Robbins, "Old Outpost of Slavery Joins Era of Black Mayor," *The New York Times* (March 28, 1991), p. A20. *Statistical Abstract of the United States: 1997*, p. 46, Table 46.

286. Jared Taylor, *Paved with Good Intentions*, p. 267.

287. *State and Metropolitan Area Data Book: 1997-98* (Washington, D.C.: U.S. Bureau of the Census, 1998). Greg Freeman, "A Modern Tale of Two Cities," *St. Louis Post-Dispatch* (September 22, 1992), p. 1C.

288. For a racial breakdown of Cleveland's population, see *Statistical Abstract of the United States: 1997*, p. 45, Table 46.

289. Alan Bernstein, "Dallas Sets Pace for the Notion of a Black Houston Mayor," *Houston Chronicle* (May 14, 1995), p. 30.

290. Ann Scott Tyson, "First Female Black Mayor Brings Mother's Touch to Iowa Politics," *Christian Science Monitor* (September 12, 1996), p. 3.

291. *Christian Science Monitor* (November 6, 1997), p. 18. *Statistical Abstract of the United States: 1997*, p. 46, Table 46.

292. Joe Holleman, "Mayoral Vote reflects Divisions," *St. Louis Post-Dispatch* (April 8, 1993), p. 1A.

293. *Christian Science Monitor* (November 6, 1997), p. 18.

294. For a racial breakdown of Houston's population, see *Statistical Abstract of the United States: 1997*, p. 45, Table 46.

295. Deroy Murdock, "Everyday America's Racial Harmony," *The American Enterprise* (November/December 1998), p. 26.

296. Kevin Sack, "Birthplace of Klan Chooses a Black Mayor," *The New York Times* (November 22, 1997).

297. Jared Taylor, *Paved with Good Intentions*, p. 267. Thernstrom, *America in Black and White*, pp. 286-287.

298. Thernstrom, *America in Black and White*, p. 287.

299. *Ibid.*, p. 286.

300. Robert Zelnick, *Backfire*, p. 242.

301. Thernstrom, *America in Black and White*, p. 295.

302. Jared Taylor, *Paved with Good Intentions*, p. 266.

303. Richard Stengel, "Riding the Backlash," *Time* (October 16, 1995), p. 70.

304. Ben Wattenberg, "In the Realm of Race, the Trend Is to Blend," *Baltimore Sun* (November 29, 1996), p. 27A. Thernstrom, *America in Black and White*, p. 297.

305. Steven A. Holmes, "A Rose-Colored View of Race," *The New York Times* (June 15, 1997).

306. Robert Zelnick, *Backfire*, p. 241. Jared Taylor, *Paved with Good Intentions*, p. 266.

307. Thernstrom, *America in Black and White*, p. 290.

308. *Ibid.*, p. 302.

309. *Ibid.*, pp. 288-289.

310. *Ibid.*, p. 289.

311. *Ibid.*

312. *Ibid.*, p. 290.

313. *Ibid.*

314. Charles Krauthammer, "The Voters Proved Hollowness of Race Gerrymandering," *Daily News* (New York) (November 18, 1996), p. 27.

315. George Will, "Blinded on Race," *New York Post* (November 29, 1996), p. 41.

316. *Ibid.*

317. Deroy Murdock, "Everyday America's Racial Harmony," *The American Enterprise* (November/December 1998), p. 26.

318. Charles Krauthammer, "The Voters Proved Hollowness of Race Gerrymandering," *Daily News* (New York) (November 18, 1996), p. 27.

319. Deroy Murdock, "Everyday America's Racial Harmony," *The American Enterprise* (November/December 1998), p. 26.

320. George Will, "Blinded on Race," *New York Post* (November 29, 1996), p. 41.

321. Deroy Murdock, "Everyday America's Racial Harmony," *The American Enterprise* (November/December 1998), p. 26.

322. Carl Rowan, "Why Marion Barry May Win in D.C.," *New York Post* (September 7, 1994), p. 21.

323. Hanna Rosin, "The Party's Over," *GQ* (June 1998), p. 178.

324. "Fears and Expectations," *Economist* (October 24, 1992), p. 25.

325. Dinesh D'Souza, *The End of Racism*, p. 407. Thernstrom, *America in Black and White*, p. 294.

326. Jared Taylor, *Paved with Good Intentions*, p. 267.

327. *Ibid.*

328. Francis X. Clines, "One Stop at a Time, Sharpton Broadens Political Following," *The New York Times* (September 3, 1994), p. 22.

329. Michael Fletcher, "Fire Destroys Black Church in N. Carolina," *Washington Post* (June 18, 1996), p. A3.

330. Michael Fumento, "A Church Arson Epidemic? It's Smoke and Mirrors," *The Wall Street Journal* (July 8, 1996), p. A8.

331. Michael Fumento, "Politics and Church Burnings," *Commentary* (October 1996), p. 57.

332. *Ibid.*, pp. 57-58.

333. Fox Butterfield, "Old Fears and New Hope," *The New York Times* (July 21, 1996), p. 12.

334. Elizabeth Levitan Spaid, "Churches Rebuild After Burnings," *Christian Science Monitor* (June 17, 1996), p. 18.

335. *Newsweek* (June 24, 1996), front cover.

336. Martha Brant et al., "Fires in the Night," *Newsweek* (June 24, 1996), p. 30.

337. *Ibid.*

338. Melissa Fay Greene, "The Fire Last Time," *Newsweek* (June 24, 1996), p. 34.

339. Gordon Witkin, "Who Is Torching the Churches?" *U.S. News & World Report* (June 24, 1996), p. 32.

340. *U.S. News & World Report* (June 24, 1996), front cover.

341. Michael Fumento, "Politics and Church Burnings," *Commentary* (October 1996), p. 57.

342. *Ibid.*

343. "Hiding Behind the Smoke," *Washington Post* (June 18, 1996), p. A13.

344. Martha Brant et al., "Fires in the Night," *Newsweek* (June 24, 1996), p. 32.

345. Michael Fumento, "A Church Arson Epidemic? It's Smoke and Mirrors," *The Wall Street Journal* (July 8, 1996), p. A8.

346. Michael Fumento, "Politics and Church Burnings," *Commentary* (October 1996), p. 57.

347. *Ibid.*

348. Gordon Witkin, "Who Is Torching the Churches?" *U.S. News & World Report* (June 24, 1996), p. 32.

349. Michael Fumento, "A Church Arson Epidemic? It's Smoke and Mirrors," *The Wall Street Journal* (July 8, 1996), p. A8.

350. Michael Fumento, "Politics and Church Burnings," *Commentary* (October 1996), p. 57.

351. *Ibid.*

352. *Ibid.*

353. Todd S. Purdum, "Clinton and Southern Governors Confer on Efforts to Deter Burning of Black Churches," *The New York Times* (June 20, 1996), p. A18.

354. Stephen C. Fehr, "U.S. Historic Trust Puts Black Churches on Endangered List," *Washington Post* (June 18, 1996), p. A3.

355. Martha Brant et al., "Fires in the Night," *Newsweek* (June 24, 1996), p. 30.

356. Michael Fletcher, "Fire Destroys Black Church in N. Carolina," *Washington Post* (June 18, 1996), p. A3.

357. Gordon Witkin, "Who Is Torching the Churches?" *U.S. News & World Report* (June 24, 1996), p. 32.

358. Elizabeth Levitan Spaid, "Churches Rebuild after Burnings," *Christian Science Monitor* (June 17, 1996), pp. 1, 5.

359. "Hiding Behind the Smoke," *Washington Post* (June 18, 1996), p. A13.

360. Michael Fumento, "A Church Arson Epidemic? It's Smoke and Mirrors," *The Wall Street Journal* (July 8, 1996), p. A8.

361. Deroy Murdock, "Everyday America's Racial Harmony," *The American Enterprise* (November/December 1998), p. 25.

362. "Hiding Behind the Smoke," *Washington Post* (June 18, 1996), p. A13.

363. *Ibid.*

364. "Indiana Man Admits to 50 Church Arsons," *The New York Times* (February 24, 1999), p. A18.

365. Michael Fumento, "A Church Arson Epidemic? It's Smoke and Mirrors," *The Wall Street Journal* (July 8, 1996), p. A8.

Chapter 14
Time to Lie No More

1. J.R. Lowell, *The Present Crisis*. See Burton Stevenson, arr., *The Home Book of Quotations* (1952), p. 2,060.

2. Dinesh D'Souza, *The End of Racism*, pp. 207-208.

3. *Ibid.*, p. 208.

4. *Ibid.*

5. *Ibid.*

6. *Ibid.*, p. 209.

7. *Ibid.*

8. Thernstrom, *America in Black and White*, p. 168.

9. Malcolm X, *Malcolm X Speaks: Selected Speeches and Statements* (New York: Pathfinder Books, 1965), p. 9.

10. Malcolm X, *By Any Means Necessary* (New York: Pathfinder Books, 1970), p. 120. Malcolm X, *The Autobiography of Malcolm X* (New York: Grove Press, 1965), p. 245.

11. Thernstrom, *America in Black and White*, p. 168.

12. Malcolm X, *The Autobiography of Malcolm X*, p. 301.

13. Thernstrom, *America in Black and White*, p. 168.

14. Dinesh D'Souza, *The End of Racism*, p. 210.

15. *Ibid.*

16. Cornel West, *Keeping Faith: Philosophy and Race in America* (New York: Routledge, 1993), pp. 280-281.

17. James Farmer, *Freedom: When?* (New York: Random House, 1965), p. 87.

18. Philip S. Foner, ed., *The Black Panthers Speak* (Philadelphia: J.B. Lippincott, 1970), pp. 1, 3. See Dinesh D'Souza, *The End of Racism*, p. 210.

19. Thernstrom, *America in Black and White*, pp. 166-167.

20. C. Vann Woodward, *The Strange Career of Jim Crow* (New York: Oxford University Press, 1974), pp. 197-198.

21. Thernstrom, *America in Black and White*, p. 167.

22. Stokely Carmichael and Charles V. Hamilton, *Black Power: The Politics of Liberation in America* (New York: Vintage Books, 1967), pp. xi, 5, 41, 44, 54.

James Cone, *Black Theology and Black Power* (New York: Seabury Press, 1969), p. 18. See Dinesh D'Souza, *The End of Racism*, pp. 210-211.

23. Thernstrom, *America in Black and White*, p. 167.

24. *Ibid.*

25. *Ibid.*

26. *Ibid.*

27. Julius Lester, *Look Out, Whitey! Black Power's Gon' Get Your Mama* (New York: Dial Press, 1968), p. 137.

28. Harvard Sitkoff, *The Struggle for Black Equality, 1954-1992* (New York: Hill & Wang, 1993), pp. 185-189. Manning Marable, *Race, Reform, and Rebellion: The Second Reconstruction in Black America* (Jackson: University Press of Mississippi, 1989), pp. 102-103.

29. Thernstrom, *America in Black and White*, p. 173.

30. Dinesh D'Souza, *The End of Racism*, pp. 213-214.

31. *Ibid.*

32. *Ibid.*, p. 214.

33. Henry Hampton and Steve Fayer, Voices of Freedom: *An Oral History of the Civil Rights Movement from the 1950s Through the 1980s* (New York: Bantam Books, 1991), pp. 571-572, 576.

34. Felicia R. Lee, "On a Harlem Block, Hope Is Swallowed by Decay," *The New York Times* (September 8, 1994), p. B8.

35. Alvin Poussaint, *Why Blacks Kill Blacks* (New York: Emerson Hall Publishers, 1972), pp. 52, 72.

36. Shelby Steele, *The Content of Our Character*, pp. 27-28.

37. *Ibid.*, p. 50.

38. Dinesh D'Souza, *The End of Racism*, p. 198.

39. William Raspberry, "Wishing Won't Make It So" *Washington Post* (January 13, 1993), p. A21.

40. E.R. Shipp, "Ending Apartheid, Here & in S. Africa," *Daily News* (New York) (May 18, 1994), p. 31.

41. Dinesh D'Souza, *The End of Racism*, p. 8.

42. Peter Collier and David Horowitz, eds., *Second Thoughts About Race in America* (Lanham, Maryland: Madison Books, 1991), p. 137.

43. Thernstrom, *America in Black and White*, p. 18.

44. *Ibid.*, pp. 192-193.

45. *Ibid.*, p. 191.

46. Black Expo USA, (Reported on Rush Limbaugh television program (October 27, 1993).

47. Irwin M. Seltzer, "The American Dream Is Very Much Alive," *New York Post* (March 14, 1996), p. 25.

48. Karl Zinsmeister, "Indicators," *The American Enterprise* (November/December 1998), p. 18.

49. Richard Miniter, "Strangely Fragile?" *The American Enterprise* (November/December 1998), p. 29.

50. John M. Berry, "Minorities Make Gains in Job Market," *The Journal News* (Gannett Suburban Newspapers) (February 6, 1999), p. 1D.

51. Thernstrom, *America in Black and White*, pp. 250-255.

52. Jared Taylor, *Paved with Good Intentions*, p. 25.

53. Thomas Sowell, *The Economics and Politics of Race*, pp. 190-191.

54. Thernstrom, *America in Black and White*, pp. 184, 187.

55. *Ibid.*, p. 234

56. Tony Snow, "Blacks Should Not Abandon King's Dream," *Conservative Chronicle* (September 7, 1994), p. 28. Walter E. Williams, "White People Are Divine," *More Liberty Means Less Government*, p. 6.

57. Richard B. Freeman, *Black Elite* (New York: McGraw-Hill, 1976), p. 31.

58. Finis Welch, "Affirmative Action and Its Enforcement," *The American Economic Review* (May 1981), p. 132.

59. Thernstrom, *America in Black and White*, p. 195.

60. George Gilder, "The Roots of Black Poverty," *The Wall Street Journal* (October 30, 1995).

61. *Ibid.*

62. Richard B. Freeman, *Black Elite*, p. 21.

63. Walter E. Williams, *The State Against Blacks*, p. 56. Jared Taylor, *Paved with Good Intentions*, p. 24.

64. Walter E. Williams, *The State Against Blacks*, p. 56.

65. Irwin M. Seltzer, "The American Dream Is Very Much Alive," *New York Post* (March 14, 1996), p. 25. *The Economic Status of Black Women: An Exploratory Investigation* (Washington, D.C.: U.S. Commission on Civil Rights, 1990), p. 12. Christopher Jencks, *Rethinking Social Policy: Race, Poverty, and the Underclass* (Cambridge, Mass: Harvard University Press, 1992), p. 40.

66. Thomas Sowell, *Civil Rights: Rhetoric or Reality?*, pp. 101-102.

67. Dinesh D'Souza, *The End of Racism*, p. 301.

68. "The Minorities Decade," *The Wall Street Journal* (August 13, 1991), p. A16.

69. Dorothy Gaiter, "Diversity of Leaders Reflects the Changes in Black Communities," *The Wall Street Journal* (May 6, 1992), p. 1.

70. Thomas Edsall and Mary Edsall, "Race," *Atlantic* (May 1991), p. 55.

71. Thernstrom, *America in Black and White*, p. 183.

72. Joan Rigdon, "For Black Men, Success Resolves Few Problems," *The Wall Street Journal* (May 8, 1992), p. B1.

73. Thernstrom, *America in Black and White*, p. 185.

74. Steven A. Holmes, "Income Gap Persists for Blacks and Whites," *The New York Times* (February 23, 1995), p. A21.

75. Thernstrom, *America in Black and White*, p. 535.

76. Sam Roberts, "Black Household Income Leads Whites' in Queens," *The New York Times* (June 6, 1994), p. A1.

77. *Ibid.*

78. *Ibid.*

79. *Ibid.*, p. B7.

80. *Ibid.*

81. *Ibid.*, p. A1.

82. Stephen A. Holmes, "Quality of Life Is up for Many Blacks, Data Say," *The New York Times* (November 18, 1996), p. A1.

83. Richard W. Stevenson, "Black-White Economic Gap Is Narrowing, White House Says," *The New York Times* (February 10, 1998).

84. Steven A. Holmes, "Quality of Life Is up for Many Blacks, Data Say," *The New York Times* (November 18, 1996), p. A1.

85. Thernstrom, *America in Black and White*, p. 200.

86. *Ibid.*, p. 196.

87. *Ibid.*, pp. 196-197.

88. Walter E. Williams, *The State Against Blacks*, p. 60. *Statistical Abstract of the United States: 1995*, pp. 411-413, Table 649.

89. Thomas Sowell, *Civil Rights: Rhetoric or Reality?*, p. 77. Thomas Sowell, *The Economics and Politics of Race*, p. 197. Thomas Sowell, "Affirmative Action: A Worldwide Disaster," *Commentary* (December 1989), p. 26.

90. Chapter 9 details many examples of schools taking extraordinary measures to boost minority hiring.

91. Richard B. Freeman, *Black Elite*, p. 39. George Gilder, *Wealth and Poverty*, p. 77.

92. Thernstrom, *America in Black and White*, p. 197.

93. Walter E. Williams, "White People Are Divine," *More Liberty Means Less Government*, p. 6.

94. Dinesh D'Souza, *The End of Racism*, p. 301.

95. George Gilder, *Wealth and Poverty*, p. 145.

96. Thernstrom, *America in Black and White*, p. 199.

97. *Ibid.*, pp. 197-198.

98. *Ibid.*, p. 197.

99. George Gilder, *Wealth and Poverty*, p. 145. Thernstrom, *America in Black and White*, p. 197.

100. Martin L. Gross, *A Call for Revolution* (New York: Ballantine Books, 1993), p. 102.

101. *Ibid.*, pp. 102-103.

102. Walter E. Williams, *The State Against Blacks*, p. 61.

103. George Farkas and Keven Vicknair, "Appropriate Tests of Racial Wage Discrimination Require Controls for Cognitive Skills," *American Sociological Review* 61 (August 1996), pp. 557-560.

104. Tamar Lewin, "Black Children Living With One Parent Put at 55%," *The New York Times* (July 15, 1990), p. 17.

105. William F. Buckley, Jr., "The Myth of Mass Illegitimacy," *New York Post* (August 12, 1996), p. 21.

106. Matthew Robinson, "Can the U.S. Afford Illegitimacy?" *Investor's Business Daily* (October 16, 1995). *Statistical Abstract of the United States: 1996*, p. 74, Table 91.

107. Thernstrom, *America in Black and White*, p. 240.

108. Matthew Robinson, "Can the U.S. Afford Illegitimacy?" *Investor's Business Daily* (October 16, 1995).

109. William F. Buckley, Jr., "Care for the Illegitimate, or Reduce Illegitimacy?" *New York Post* (February 12, 1997), p. 27.

110. William F. Buckley, Jr., "The Myth of Mass Illegitimacy," *New York Post* (August 12, 1996), p. 21. Carl Horowitz, "The Human Cost of Illegitimacy," *Investor's Business Daily* (March 8, 1995).

111. Thomas Sowell, *Civil Rights: Rhetoric or Reality?*, p. 48.

112. Associated Press, "Single Women and Poverty Strongly Linked," *The New York Times* (February 20, 1994), p. 35. "The Roots of Inequality," *Investor's Business Daily* (April 8, 1996), p. 2.

113. Thernstrom, *America in Black and White*, p. 197, Table 8.

114. "The Roots of Inequality," *Investors Business Daily* (April 8, 1996), p. 2.

115. Thernstrom, *America in Black and White*, p. 237.

116. *Ibid.*, pp. 236-237.

117. *Ibid.*, p. 238, Table 4.

118. Jared Taylor, *Paved with Good Intentions*, pp. 296-299.

119. George Gilder, *Wealth and Poverty*, p. 146. In 1995 Gilder updated the statistic, to 30 percent, for the income disparity between married and single men. See George Gilder, "The Roots of Black Poverty," *The Wall Street Journal* (October 30, 1995).

120. *Ibid.*

121. Jared Taylor, *Paved with Good Intentions*, p. 27.

122. *Ibid.*

123. Gordon Green and Edward Welniak, "Measuring the Effects of Changing Family Composition During the 1970s in Black-White Differences in Income," (Washington, D.C.: Bureau of the Census, Department of Commerce, 1982). Cited by Michael Levin, *Feminism and Freedom*, p. 279. Warren T. Brookes, "Why Income Gap Between White and Black Has Widened," *San Francisco Chronicle* (December 25, 1990), p. C3.

124. Thernstrom, *America in Black and White*, p. 233, Table 1.

125. *Ibid.*, p. 236, Table 2.

126. *Ibid.*, p. 197, Table 8.

127. *Ibid.*, p. 197. Dinesh D'Souza, *The End of Racism*, pp. 300-302.

128. Thomas Sowell, "Squeamish Words and Dying Babies," *Barbarians Inside the Gates*, p. 183.

129. George Gilder, *Wealth and Poverty*, p. 81.

130. *Ibid.*

131. *Ibid.*

132. Hugh B. Price, "Hard-Fought Battle for Civil Rights Is Hardly Over," *Daily News* (New York) (August 29, 1994), p. 23.

133. Bob Herbert, "Don't Flunk the Future," *The New York Times* (August 13, 1998).

134. Charles J. Sykes, *A Nation of Victims* (New York: Saint Martin's Press, 1992), p. 69.

135. Felicia R. Lee, "On a Harlem Block, Hope Is Swallowed by Decay," *The New York Times* (September 8, 1994), p. A1.

136. Robert Reinhold, "An Edgy Los Angeles Awaits a Jury's Verdict," *The New York Times* (April 11, 1993), Section 1, p. 14.

137. Bryce Christensen, *Chronicles* (May 1989), p. 9.

138. Family Research Council, "Illegitimacy's Disastrous Effects," *In Focus* (April 1995).

139. Jared Taylor, *Paved with Good Intentions*, p. 297.

140. Elaine Kamarck, "Fatherless Families: A Violent Link," *Los Angeles Times* (May 7, 1992), p. B7.

141. Mona Charen, "Liberal Tinkering Has Put Our Civilization at Risk," *Conservative Chronicle* (August 24, 1994), p. 21.

142. *Ibid.*

143. Walter E. Williams, "Struggle for Civil Rights Is Over," *Conservative Chronicle* (April 27, 1994), p. 26.

144. Shelby Steele, *The Content of Our Character*, p. 24.

145. Jesse Peterson, "Longing for Fathers," *Issues and Views* (Spring 1996), p. 8.

146. Deborah Orin, "President Laments 'Disaster' of Unwed Moms," *New York Post* (September 10, 1994), p. 8.

147. *Ibid.*

148. *Ibid.*

149. Carl Rowan, "Where Do Family Values Begin?," *New York Post* (September 14, 1994), p. 25.

150. *Ibid.*

151. Thomas Sowell, *The Economics and Politics of Race*, p. 187. Jared Taylor, *Paved with Good Intentions*, pp. 111, 113.

152. Shelby Steele, *The Content of Our Character*, p. 69.

153. Thomas Sowell, *The Economics and Politics of Race*, p. 192.

154. Thomas Sowell, *Civil Rights: Rhetoric or Reality?*, pp. 78-79.

155. Jared Taylor, *Paved with Good Intentions*, p. 25.

156. Thomas Sowell, "Three Black Histories," *Essays and Data on American Ethnic Groups*, ed. Thomas Sowell, pp. 42, 44. Thomas Sowell, *The Economics and Politics of Race*, p. 107.

157. Thomas Sowell, *Conquests and Cultures*, p. 170.

158. George Gilder, "The Roots of Black Poverty," *The Wall Street Journal* (October 30, 1995).

159. Orlando Patterson, "Race, Gender and Liberal Fallacies," *The New York Times* (October 20, 1991). Larry Elder, "The Market Is Racism's Enemy," *The American Enterprise* (November/December 1998), p. 65.

160. Booker T. Washington, *Up from Slavery*, p. 24.

161. Thomas Sowell, *Civil Rights: Rhetoric or Reality?*, p. 75.

162. Dinesh D'Souza, *The End of Racism*, pp. 67-68.

163. Thomas Sowell, *Civil Rights: Rhetoric or Reality?*, p. 75.

164. Herbert G. Gutman, *The Black Family in Slavery and Freedom* (New

York: Vintage Books, 1976), p. xvii.

165. *Ibid.*

166. *Ibid.*, p. 462.

167. *Ibid.*, p. xix.

168. *Ibid.*, p. xvii.

169. Jonathan Alter, "The Long Shadow of Slavery," *Newsweek* (December 8, 1997), p. 63.

170. Herbert G. Gutman, *The Black Family in Slavery and Freedom*, p. xviii.

171. Thomas Sowell, *Civil Rights: Rhetoric or Reality?*, p. 75.

172. Thomas Sowell, *The Economics and Politics of Race*, p. 125.

173. Herbert G. Gutman, *The Black Family in Slavery and Freedom*, p. 444.

174. *Ibid.*, p. xix.

175. Walter E. Williams, "Race Hustlers," *More Liberty Means Less Government*, p. 23.

176. Tamar Lewin, "Black Children Living With One Parent Put at 55%," *The New York Times* (July 15, 1990), p. 17. Bill McAllister, "To Be Young, Male, and Black," *Washington Post* (December 28, 1989), p. A1. Jared Taylor, *Paved with Good Intentions*, p. 297.

177. Mortimer Zuckerman, "Mentioning the Unmentionable," *U.S. News & World Report* (June 4, 1990), p. 82.

178. Robert Woodson, "We Need to Examine Some Side Effects of the Civil Rights Movement," *Issues & Views* (Fall 1991), p. 4. Jared Taylor, *Paved with Good Intentions*, p. 295.

179. Joseph Kahn, "Jackson Challenges 'Capital of Capital,' " *The New York Times* (January 16, 1999).

180. Shelby Steele, *The Content of Our Character*, p. 14.

181. *Ibid.*, p. 31.

182. Deneen L. Brown, "Rekindling the Dream," *Reporter Dispatch* (Gannett Suburban Newspapers) (August 29, 1993), pp. 1A, 8A.

183. "The Thrill Is Gone," *Destiny* (September 1993), p. 3.

184. Ronald Smothers, "In Atlanta, Holiday of Dreams, Memories, and a Tug of War," *The New York Times* (January 17, 1995), p. B4.

185. Janny Scott, "Preachers and Plain Folk Gather to Honor Dr. King," *The New York Times* (January 17, 1995), p. B4.

186. Dennis Chong, *Collective Action and the Civil Rights Movement* (Chicago: University of Chicago Press, 1991), p. 194.

187. Thomas Sowell, *Civil Rights: Rhetoric or Reality?*, pp. 108, 117.

188. *Ibid.*, p. 117.

189. Shelby Steele, *The Content of Our Character*, p. 33.

190. *Ibid.*, p. 34.

191. *Ibid.*, pp. 173, 174.

192. Walter E. Williams, "Race and Sex," *More Liberty Means Less Government*, p. 2.

193. Dirk Johnson, "In Denver, the Surprising New Face of Talk Radio," *The New York Times* (January 2, 1994), Section 4, p. 7.

194. *Ibid.*

195. Richard Sennett, "A Role Model unto Himself," *The New York Times* (August 12, 1991), p. A15.

196. Manning Marable, "Clarence Thomas and the Crisis of Black Political Culture," in Toni Morrison, ed., *Race-ing Justice, En-gendering Power* (New York: Pantheon Books, 1992), p. 82.

197. "On the Record," *National Review* (August 12, 1991).

198. June Jordan, *Technical Difficulties: African American Notes on the State of the Union* (New York: Vintage Books, 1994), pp. 206, 217.

199. Haywood Burns, "Clarence Thomas, a Counterfeit Hero," *The New York Times* (July 9, 1991), p. A19.

200. Julianne Malveaux, on PBS television program *To the Contrary* (November 4, 1994). Cited by *Human Events* (November 7, 1997), p. 6.

201. Eric Breindel, "Black Conservatives: Fair Game for Slander?" *New York Post* (March 5, 1997), p. 23.

202. *Ibid.*

203. *Ibid.*

204. *Ibid.*

205. "Civil Rights and Wrongs," *The Wall Street Journal* (July 19, 1990), p. A10.

206. John Henrik Clarke, "Black Pseudo-Scholars Are in with White America, but They Deserve to Be Outed," *City Sun* (New York) (August 26-September 2, 1992).

207. Juan Williams, "A Paralysis of Leadership," *New York Post* (February 18, 1994), p. 31.

208. Deborah Orin, "Black Caucus Shows Door to Its Lone GOPer," *New York Post* (July 30, 1993), p. 8.

209. Neil A. Lewis, "Justice Thomas Suggests Critics' Views Are Racist," *The New York Times* (July 30, 1998), p. A1.

210. "Justice Thomas Answers His Critics," *New York Post* (July 31, 1998), p. 25.

211. Minoo Southgate, "Black Power, Nineties Style," *National Review* (December 13, 1993), p. 46.

212. *Ibid.*

213. *Ibid.*

214. Francis X. Clines, "One Stop at a Time, Sharpton Broadens Political Following," *The New York Times* (September 3, 1994), p. 22.

215. "Jesse Endorses Sharpton for Mayor," *New York Post* (August 13, 1997), p. 20.

216. Eric Breindel, "Ruth Flunks the Sharpton Test," *New York Post* (September 19, 1997), p. 33.

217. Michael Meyers, "Dem Mayoral Runoff: A Boon to Extremists," *New York Post* (September 16, 1997), p. 29.

218. Stephen A. Holmes, "Rights Chief Upsets Board of NAACP," *The*

New York Times (April 10, 1994), p. L19.

219. Dinesh D'Souza, *The End of Racism*, p. 190.

220. Richard Cohen, "NAACP Tank Job," *New York Post* (July 18, 1997), p. 27.

221. Michael Meyers, "On Beyond 'Niggardly': Hypocrisy at the NAACP," *New York Post* (February 2, 1999).

222. *Ibid*. Michael Meyers, "The Shame of the NAACP," *New York Post* (July 7, 1998), p. 27.

223. Thomas Sowell, "The NAACP Hustle," *New York Post* (June 17, 1994), p. 23.

224. Michael Meyers, "Rhetorical Bombs Are Bursting in Air," *New York Post* (May 10, 1996), p. 23.

225. Associated Press, " 'KKK' Trio Held in Horror Slay," *New York Post* (June 10, 1998), p. 7. Tracy Connor, "Leaders Seek Hope in Texas Funeral," *New York Post* (June 14, 1998), p. 3.

226. Thernstrom, *America in Black and White*, p. 76.

227. Dinesh D'Souza, *The End of Racism*, p. 253.

228. Thernstrom, *America in Black and White*, p. 102.

229. *Ibid.*, p. 500.

230. Dinesh D'Souza, *The End of Racism*, p. 253.

231. *Ibid.*

232. Thernstrom, *America in Black and White*, p. 141.

233. *Ibid.*

234. *Ibid.*, p. 500.

235. *Ibid.* Dinesh D'Souza, *The End of Racism*, p. 253.

236. Dinesh D'Souza, *The End of Racism*, p. 253.

237. Thernstrom, *America in Black and White*, p. 104.

238. *Ibid.*, p. 500.

239. Paul M. Sniderman and Thomas Piazza, *The Scar of Race*, p. 40.

240. Thernstrom, *America in Black and White*, p. 101.

241. "A Rose-Colored View of Race," *The New York Times* (June 15, 1997).

242. Thernstrom, *America in Black and White*, p. 60.

243. *Ibid.*, p. 18.

244. *Ibid.*, p. 500.

245. *Ibid.*, p. 223.

246. *Ibid.*

247. *Ibid.*, p. 297.

248. "A Rose-Colored View of Race," *The New York Times* (June 15, 1997).

249. Thernstrom, *America in Black and White*, p. 506.

250. *Ibid.*

251. *Ibid.*

252. Deborah Orin, "Prez Mum on Rev. Al Snapshot," *New York Post* (November 19, 1997), p. 33.

253. Minoo Southgate, "Black Power, Nineties Style," *National Review* (December 13, 1993), p. 47.

254. Aldore Collier, "Maxine Waters: Telling It Like It Is in L.A.," *Ebony* (October 1992), pp. 35-38.

255. "Chavis to Head NAACP," *Christian Century*," (April 28, 1993), p. 447.

256. Michael Meyers, "How Ben Chavis Lynched Himself," *New York Post* (August 29, 1994), p. 21.

257. Evan Gahr, "Clinton Stacks Race Panel," *New York Post* (September 30, 1997), p. 25.

258. *Ibid.*

259. "John Hopeless Franklin," *New York Post* (December 3, 1997), p. 34.

260. Abigail Thernstrom, "Who's Afraid to Debate Affirmative Action?" *The New York Times* (November 22, 1997).

261. Evan Gahr, "Bulworthless," *The American Enterprise* (November/December 1998), p. 62.

262. *Ibid.*, p. 63. Evan Gahr, "Clinton Stacks Race Panel," *New York Post* (September 30, 1997), p. 25.

263. Evan Gahr, "Clinton Stacks Race Panel," *New York Post* (September 30, 1997), p. 25.

264. Richard Sisk, "Farrakhan Slap on Wrist?" *Daily News* (New York) (March 21, 1996), p. 32.

265. Ed Koch, on his radio program on station WABC in New York (October 11, 1995).

266. Tony Snow, "Blacks Should Not Abandon King's Dream," *Conservative Chronicle* (September 7, 1994), p. 28.